ANCIENT CIVILIZATIONS

ANCIENT CIVILIZATIONS

THE ILLUSTRATED GUIDE TO BELIEF, MYTHOLOGY, AND ART

GENERAL EDITOR: PROFESSOR GREG WOOLF

THUNDER BAY
P·R·E·S·S

San Diego, California

CONTENTS

Thunder Bay Press
An imprint of the Advantage Publishers Group
5880 Oberlin Drive, San Diego, CA 92121-4794
www.thunderbaybooks.com

Created, edited, and designed by
Duncan Baird Publishers
Sixth Floor
Castle House
75–76 Wells Street
London W1T 3QH

ISBN: 1-59223-489-5

Library of Congress Cataloging-in-Publication Data
available upon request.

Typeset in AGaramond
Color reproduction by Colourscan
Printed in Thailand by Imago

1 2 3 4 5 09 08 07 06 05

DUNCAN BAIRD PUBLISHERS
Editor: James Hodgson
Designer: Gail Jones
Managing Editor: Christopher Westhorp
Managing Designer: Manisha Patel
Picture research: Susannah Stone, Cecilia Weston Baker,
Julia Ruxton, and Julia Brown

For a complete list of contributing consultants, writers,
and artists, see page 687.

Title page: *A first-century* CE *limestone panel depicting the Buddha's footprints, from the Great Stupa at Amaravati, India.*

FOREWORD

Civilization is always a matter of perspective, of inclusion and exclusion, of us and them. For the Romans, civilization was marked out by laws, customs, morality. Those of their enemies who dressed strangely, drank beer instead of wine, sacrificed people rather than animals, were ruled by women rather than men, or fought naked with ferocious but short-lived courage, instead of in disciplined military formations, were deemed barbarians. The idea of civilization is unthinkable without its opposite, barbarism: Egyptian pharaohs ruled a land surrounded by nomads and other outsiders; Chinese emperors distinguished the inhabitants of their realm from those beyond the Great Wall; and Aztec rulers differentiated the civilized peoples with whom they traded and warred, from more savage neighbours. For Roman writers, civilized peoples inhabited cities and practiced agriculture; they were well-ordered individuals and societies; they had a past—history—and a future; they were, the Romans believed, "people like us."

Such ideas concerning the nature of civilization have appeared repeatedly throughout history. Sometimes the ideas were borrowed, as Romans appropriated from the Greeks, and Europeans of the eighteenth and nineteenth centuries adopted different concepts of civilization from Roman writings. But often they were independently conceived—the great Arab historian Ibn Khaldun, for example, elaborated his own theories of civilization and history in the fourteenth century. As far as we know, the idea of "civilization" arrived with agriculture and has only really been important in societies based on it. The use of the terms "wild" and "cultivated", "savage" and "tame", recalls the domestications of crops and animals. Civilized peoples have often maligned their neighbors on the grounds of taste and behavior, with the result that they considered them less than fully human.

Civilization, for the civilized, is the essential expression of what it means to be human. Writing first appeared (as it did several times) only within societies that depended on agriculture; indeed, only among those agrarian societies that also built cities and created the political institutions that we associate with states. By and large, monumental temples, palaces, and rich tombs, metallurgy, works of art and drama, and complex cuisines are also confined to such "civilized" peoples. And the reason for this is simple. Humans who forage for their food nearly always need to be on the move. They live at low population densities. Like rolling stones, they gather little of the moss from which history is made. Healthier than farmers, with more leisure, and ruled over by no kings, priests or emperors, hunter–gatherers have nevertheless almost all vanished. It is startling to think that until 12,000 years ago this was the way we all lived, and that until 6,000 years ago most people remained "uncivilized." Farmers have existed for less than one percent of the half-million-year lifetime of *Homo sapiens*.

All the societies whose art and monuments and cultures are described in *Ancient Civilizations* belong to this tiny fraction of human history. Even so, the list is not exhaustive. We survey the several cradles of civilization: Egypt and the Fertile Crescent, India, China and Mesoamerica. It was here that the first domestications took place; here, too, that the first cities and kingdoms were founded. These societies are quite alike. Their agriculture often depended on water management in arid zones, their rulers frequently claimed divine sanction, they invented—independently—temples, sacrifice and war. It was in these civilizations that hierarchies and class relations appeared, with warriors having superiority over peasants, and craftspeople, merchants, scribes, and religious specialists appearing for the first time.

Civilization expanded restlessly into the uncultivated margins, taking new forms as it did so. Tropical southern China, woodland Europe, and the high plains of Tibet and the Andes were not insuperable obstacles. Selecting distinctive civilizations from around the Middle Ages is more fraught with difficulty. The great medieval civilizations of Islam, Byzantium, and the Christian West might justly have claimed a place in this book. So too might the African kingdoms of Kush and Dahomey and that of the enigmatic builders of Great Zimbabwe, and the island civilizations of Japan and Polynesia. However, Viking and so-called Celtic cultures remain fascinating because they were more civilized than often portrayed by their enemies. Aztec civilization, for all it was a bronze age empire, was contemporary with early modern Europe—fatally so as it turned out.

At that point, around five hundred years ago, the globe began suddenly to shrink with the great trading voyages of Arabs and Chinese in the Indian Ocean, of Austronesians in the Pacific, and of Europeans across the Atlantic and then around the globe. During the fourteenth century Marco Polo traveled from Venice to the eastern and southern limits of the Mongol empire, and Ibn Battuta traveled the Muslim world from Morocco to the Gold Coast, Zanzibar, India, and the Far East. Columbus, Cabot, Vasco da Gama, as well as the great treasure fleets that China sent across the Indian Ocean to east Africa, all sailed in the fifteenth century. These recent interconnections have given civilization and barbarism entirely new meanings. The moral ground has shifted under our feet. But as the modern world develops new understandings of how to be cultivated and cultivators, it is both instructive and inspiring to look back at the spectacular experiments in civility created all around the world—experiments in which many of today's values and cultural treasures were forged.

Professor Greg Woolf
University of St. Andrews, Scotland

CHAPTER ONE

EGYPT

The civilization of ancient Egypt was largely the product of its geography,

particularly its river, the Nile. The Greek historian Herodotus called Egypt

"the gift of the Nile" because the country depended on the river for its very existence.

Egyptians themselves called their country Kemet, "Black Land," which refers to the

strip of fertile riverbank, bounded by Deshret, "Red Land," the vast, sterile desert.

The dominant colors of the Egyptian world—blue skies, golden sun, red desert, green

river margins, the black, silt-laden Nile—are the chief hues of Egyptian art, which

also reflects the layers of sky, desert, field, and river. This world existed in a state of

equilibrium, of finely balanced opposites: Kemet and Deshret, day and night, life

and death, order and chaos.

THE SOUL OF EGYPT

Ancient Egyptian civilization was centered around its highly complex religion. Understanding the essence of this religion is the key to a vast and sometimes bewildering legacy of myth and ritual, through which the wisdom of ancient Egypt reveals itself.

The Egyptians believed that the balance of order and chaos in the universe could only be maintained by the gods and goddesses and their representative on Earth, the king, or pharaoh. Originally, these deities simply symbolized aspects of the natural world—the sun, the sky, the land, and the river. For example, the annual inundation of the Nile was personified by the androgynous god Hapy. Each god gradually developed a more complex personality and history as every area of the country embellished the stories and myths surrounding its own local deity. Eventually, many divinities came to share titles and attributes, and thus emerged the highly sophisticated pattern of religious belief that was so characteristic of ancient Egypt.

The divine forces required constant replenishment through worship and devotion if they were to guarantee

the continuity of the cosmic equilibrium. They were therefore honored in numerous portrayals that adorn everything from monumental temples to delicate works of art. But it was above all in the performance of daily rites in the temples that the Egyptians venerated their deities. The temples were "storehouses" for divine power, which was maintained and directed by the priesthood for the good of the whole country. The high priest—always delegating for the king, the child of the gods—acted as intermediary between the mortal and divine worlds. He and his fellow priests and priestesses honored the deities with a constant stream of offerings, music, and dance, which was believed to encourage the divine spirit to reside within the temple—essential if the cosmic order was to be upheld.

The one constant in Egyptian history is the Nile. Without the great river there would simply be desert—its proximity to places of human settlement is a constant reminder to the Egyptians of their reliance upon it. Before the building of modern dams, the Nile flooded every year, depositing rich black silt that produced an abundance of crops. The strip of greenery bordering the river—in sharp contrast to the sand and rock beyond—would have been familiar to the ancient Egyptians and is echoed in the horizontal layering often found in Egyptian art.

THE STORY OF EGYPT

Egypt's ancient historical period lasted for more than 3,000 years—from about 3100BCE to 392CE. During this time the country experienced both chaos and order as power shifted between separate kingdoms and central government, interspersed with invasions from abroad and empire building.

From the prehistoric cultures of the Nile valley two opposing kingdoms emerged, one in the north (Lower Egypt) and one in the south (Upper Egypt). They were unified around 3100BCE by King Narmer at the start of the "Archaic Period." This period lasted several centuries until the early phase of Egyptian civilization known as the "Old Kingdom" (2675–2350BCE). Narmer's successors established their base at Memphis (near modern Cairo), and organized the country through a highly efficient bureaucracy. These early rulers created enough wealth to fund ambitious building schemes, culminating in the great pyramid complexes of Khufu, Khafre (Fourth dynasty), and other kings. But centuries of pyramid construction drained the economy and central authority broke down in about 2130BCE. The Old Kingdom was followed by the "First Intermediate Period," in which the absence of a powerful political center is reflected in a lack of artistic standardization and idiosyncratic provincial art styles.

Egypt was reunited in approximately 2000BCE by princes of Thebes in the south, who inaugurated the "Middle Kingdom." Under the kings of the Eleventh and Twelfth dynasties (ca. 2081–1759BCE), Thebes and its god, Amun, gained in importance, royal power was centralized, and Egypt's frontiers were expanded. In terms of art, language, and literature, the Middle Kingdom is regarded as ancient Egypt's "Classical Age."

Princes of Asiatic (Palestinian) origin known as the Hyksos ("Rulers of Foreign Lands") took control of the north in about 1640BCE and for a century (the "Second Intermediate Period") Egypt was split, with native Thebans ruling in the south. The country was reunited around 1530BCE under another Theban dynasty, marking the start of the "New Kingdom." A succession of warrior-pharaohs created a great empire, stretching from Nubia to the Euphrates, and Egypt became the richest and most powerful country in the ancient world. As in earlier ages, much of Egypt's wealth was channeled into great building projects to enhance the prestige of deities and kings. New Kingdom pharaohs embellished the temple of Amun at Karnak, and built temples and tombs for themselves across the river.

Artistic and architectural achievement reached a peak under Amenhotep III (ca. 1390–1353BCE), but his son Akhenaten (ca. 1353–1335BCE) destabilized the country during the so-called "Amarna period" (see page 27). Akhenaten's short-lived successors—including his son Tutankhamun—gave way to a former general, Horemheb (ca. 1319–1292BCE), who began to restore Egypt's fortunes. Horemheb was followed by the "Ramesside" kings of the Nineteenth and Twentieth dynasties (ca. 1292– 1075BCE)—eleven of whom bore the famous name of Ramesses. Egypt kept its powerful position in the face of invasions by Mediterranean migrants and Libyans. But Libyan settlers seized the north in approximately 1075BCE and the New Kingdom finally collapsed. Only after several centuries of fragmentation (the "Third Intermediate Period") was the country reunited (ca. 750BCE) by Nubian kings, who were succeeded by a final era of native rule (ca. 664–525BCE).

From then on, Egypt was governed almost without interruption by successive foreign invaders. Persians (525–409BCE and 343–332BCE) and Greeks (332–30BCE) ruled in the traditional pharaonic way and the country's ancient culture remained largely intact. The Romans who followed (from 30BCE) were absentee rulers, but they continued to endorse the old culture and religion. This period of toleration came to an end in 392CE, when the empire officially adopted Christianity and ordered all the Egyptian temples to close. It is at this point that ancient Egyptian civilization ends, having withstood everything but the loss of its gods.

THE EGYPTIAN WORLD

Mediterranean Sea

Damietta (Damyut)

Rosetta (el-Rashid)

Alexandria

Busiris

LOWER EGYPT

Bubastis

Heliopolis

Giza • Cairo
Abusir
Sakkara • Memphis
Dahshur

Lake Moeris **UPPER EGYPT**

Meidum

FAIYUM

Medinet el-Faiyum

Herakleopolis Magna

Nile River

Key

● Ancient site

○ Other town or city

1 – Malkata (palace of Amenhotep III)
2 – Temple of Ramesses III
3 – Temple of Amenhotep III
4 – Temple of Ay/Horemheb
5 – Temple of Thutmose IV
6 – Temple of Ramesses II
7 – Temple of Thutmose III
8 – Temple of Nebhepetre Mentuhotep
9 – Temple of Hatshepsut (Deir el-Bahari)
10 – Temple of Ramesses IV
11 – Temple of Sety I

Beni Hassan
Hermopolis • Deir el-Bersheh
Magna • el-Amarna

Asyut

Red Sea

THEBES

Valley of the Kings
THEBAN PEAK ▲ 9
8
Valley of the Queens 10 11
7
4 5 6
1 2 3 Royal mortuary temples

Karnak

WESTERN THEBES

EASTERN THEBES

Nile River

Luxor

0 — 2 km
0 — 1 mile

Abydos • Dendera

Thebes (Luxor)

Hierakonpolis • Nekheb (el-Kab)
Edfu

0 — 100 km
SCALE
0 — 50 miles

Kom Ombo

Aswan
Philae

N

ART AND WRITING

Although ancient Egyptian art is often breathtakingly beautiful, its aesthetic appeal is secondary to its function, which was originally either religious or funerary, or both. It is also inextricably linked to the script which often accompanied it and which illuminated the meaning of the imagery.

Ancient Egyptian art was mainly inspired by familiar images taken from nature. The distinctive style seen in paintings, relief, sculpture, and jewelry was formalized at the very beginning of the historic period and remained largely unchanged for 3,000 years.

Most art was created to adorn dark temple interiors, away from public view, or else to be buried with the dead in their tombs in order to protect and sustain them in the afterlife. This explains why two-dimensional scenes, with their apparently simplistic form and lack of perspective, can initially look almost childish to modern eyes. But this is to misunderstand their function. It was believed that the correct ritual formulae could literally bring such representations to life. In order to be able to see, hear, smell, and speak normally, the image of a deity or of a deceased person had to be portrayed with every relevant physical feature depicted as clearly as possible. In art in two dimensions the face is therefore shown in profile to give maximum definition to the eyes and mouth, while the eye is represented whole, as if seen from the front.

Inanimate objects would be rendered with similar clarity: items were shown piled up in layers, even to the point of appearing to float in air. The same was the case with the contents of a closed box—which would have been hidden from view and thus effectively "lost" if illustrated realistically. The real food and drink put in a temple or a tomb to sustain a deity or a dead person would also be depicted and described on the walls, and accompanying scenes and models of food production would ensure an eternal supply of sustenance.

Even portrayals of physical activities, such as dancing, were created for a specific purpose, despite the fact that nowadays they are often popularly regarded as little more than pleasant decoration. However, the depiction of dance and the playing of lively music was believed to assist in awakening the god in its temple shrine or in reviving the senses of the deceased in his or her tomb.

WORDS OF THE GODS

Ancient Egyptian art is inseparable from the script that accompanies it. These "picture words," known as

---

• THE MEANING OF COLOR •

The functional, coded nature of Egyptian art was enhanced by the careful choice of material and color. The land of Egypt, represented politically by the White Crown of Upper Egypt and the Red Crown of Lower Egypt, was also divided into the "Black Land" (Kemet), where vegetation flourished, and the hostile red desert wastes (Deshret). Thus black and green were used in representations of Osiris, the god of fertility and eternal life, while red was used in depictions of his evil brother Seth, the god of chaos. The calm, ethereal blue of the sky, as reflected in the Nile, was echoed in the choice of blue to represent divinity, and the golden yellow of the sun was a protective hue. Men and women were conventionally depicted with different skin tones—ruddy for males and paler for females.

hieroglyphs, from the Greek for "sacred carved writing," first developed in about 3100BCE and were initially employed by a small literate bureaucracy to keep records. The script later came to be used for the monumental stone inscriptions covering tombs, temples, obelisks, and sculpture, as well as for ritual texts on papyrus and religious objects.

Because they mostly appeared in a religious context, hieroglyphs were known in Egyptian as *medou netjer*, "words of the gods." They were said to have been invented by Thoth, the god of writing. The cursive "shorthand" form of hieroglyphs, referred to as "hieratic" ("sacred script"), was employed for day-to-day transactions, and this was superseded in the Late Period (664–332BCE) by a form called "demotic" ("popular script").

From this time, use was increasingly made of Greek letters to write the Egyptian language, and in the Roman era a Greek-based alphabet—called "Coptic" from *Aiguptos*, the Greek for "Egyptian"—became popular among a growing Christian population. Hieroglyphs remained in use by the priests of the old religion, but the Roman ban on non-Christian worship in 392CE spelled the end of the ancient writing system. The last firmly dated hieroglyphic inscription was made at Philae on 24 August, 394CE. Knowledge of hieroglyphs died with the last priests of the old faith, and their meaning was lost for 1,400 years.

Fabulously crafted in gold, lapis lazuli, carnelian, and feldspar, this rearing uraeus *(cobra) was made for King Senwosret II; it represents Wadjet, the snake goddess of Lower Egypt. The king set the image on his brow so that fire could be spat into the eyes of his enemies.*

DECODING HIEROGLYPHS

For centuries, people wrongly assumed that these strange ancient signs were entirely symbolic, and many wildly inaccurate attempts at translation were made. However, in 1799 an ancient inscription was discovered by French soldiers at el-Rashid (Rosetta) on the Mediterranean coast. It was a royal decree issued during the reign of King Ptolemy V (205–180BCE), and it was written twice in Egyptian (in hieroglyphs and demotic) and once in Greek. By enabling linguists to compare the same text in Egyptian and a living tongue, Greek, the "Rosetta Stone" proved to be the key that would unlock the language—and through it, the civilization—of ancient Egypt for the modern world.

The Englishman Thomas Young (1773–1829) was the first to recognize that hieroglyphs could be phonetic, with signs representing individual sounds and not just whole words or concepts. But he did not appreciate the full implications of this discovery, and it was a Frenchman, Jean-François Champollion (1790–1832), who first revealed the great complexity of the Egyptian writing system. From his study of the Rosetta Stone, Champollion deduced that hieroglyphs consisted of three basic types: "phonograms" (representing sounds), "ideograms" and "logograms" (representing words), and "determinatives" (which simply emphasize meaning). The phonograms in turn fall into three categories.There is a basic "alphabet" of twenty-four hieroglyphs, each of which represents a single consonant (for example, 𓃀 = b, 𓅓 = m, 𓂋 = r). Other phonograms—several hundred in total—are

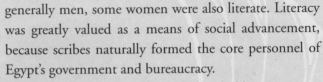

categorized as representing either two sounds or three sounds (for example, ⚍ = ms, 🕯 = nfr).

For most of Egyptian history, vowels were not written and where a vowel is not known, Egyptologists conventionally insert an "e" so that a word can be pronounced. Hieroglyphs can be written vertically (from top to bottom) or horizontally (from left to right or right to left). There is no punctuation.

The use of hieroglyphs was largely restricted to a literate élite who made up approximately one percent of the population, and although professional scribes were generally men, some women were also literate. Literacy was greatly valued as a means of social advancement, because scribes naturally formed the core personnel of Egypt's government and bureaucracy.

The written word was believed to hold great power, comparable to that contained within artistic images, which explains the fact that some hieroglyphic symbols in religious inscriptions were occasionally mutilated when they were carved to "neutralize" potential dangers. Royal names were written within an oval ring, or "cartouche" (▭) to protect them, with line upon line of cartouches making up the "King Lists" which record the royal lineage. These lists were often highly selective—those monarchs who were regarded as less than perfect by later pharaohs were deleted from the official records. If a royal name was removed in this way, or scraped or chiseled from his own monuments, it was as if the individual concerned had ceased to exist. This fate befell several pharaohs in the course of Egyptian history, including the "heretic" Akhenaten. Conversely, simply to speak the name of a deceased person was believed to make him or her live again, which explains why the name of the deceased is repeated so frequently in tomb inscriptions.

Because of their potency, names were carefully chosen, and often included the name of a god or king—for example, Amenhotep ("Amun is Content"), Tutankhamun ("Living Image of Amun"), and Pepiankh ("Pepi Lives"). Simpler names included Nefer ("Beautiful," as in Nefertiti and Nefertari), Seneb ("Healthy"), and Sheshen ("Lotus"), which became—via Hebrew—the name Susannah or Susan.

The black basalt slab known as the Rosetta Stone bears the same inscription in three scripts: hieroglyphic (top), demotic (middle), and Greek (bottom). By comparing the Egyptian to the Greek, 19th-century linguists were able to decipher the ancient Egyptian language. The stone dates from 196BCE—the ninth year of the reign of Ptolemy V—and records the honors given to the king by the priests of Memphis.

◆ GLYPH AND SYMBOL ◆

Their complex meaning yet simple aesthetic appeal explains the use of hieroglyphs as both functional and decorative devices. They appeared in diverse aspects of Egyptian life, from great stone edifices to small items of personal jewelry. The *djed* symbol, for example, representing the backbone of Osiris, meant stability and strength. The "key of life" sign, or *ankh*, was another frequently used symbol, alongside the signs for beauty, joy, and protection, among others, and the potent names of gods and kings. Royal names were written in an oval ring, or cartouche, and if they contained the name of a god, this was always placed first. Thus Tutankhamun ("Living Image of Amun") was written "Amun-Tut-Ankh" (see below).

Nowhere is the effect of the hieroglyphic script felt more powerfully than in the monumental inscriptions that cover the Egyptians' vast religious and funerary buildings. The ever-changing play of sunlight and shadow creates a constantly shifting image throughout the course of the day, but the lines of pictorial script and accompanying artistic scenes convey an overall feeling of balance. This can be seen particularly at Karnak (see pages 28–29), from the sublime raised reliefs of its Middle Kingdom chapels to the sunken relief of the repetitious cartouches of the Ramesside pharaohs of the New Kingdom. The Ramesside kings carved their royal names and titles deeply into the stone, in the hope that they would last for eternity. Should the name be erased, as happened with "anomalous" rulers such as Akhenaten and Hatshepsut in the Eighteenth dynasty, the individual would be consigned to oblivion—which for the Egyptians was the most terrible fate imaginable.

KH
W   F   W
KH-W-F-W = KHUFU, "CHEOPS"

A   MN   T   W   T   "ANKH"
       N
A-MN-N-T-W-T-ANKH = TUTANKHAMUN

BOUNTIES OF
THE BLACK LAND

The dual world of ancient Egypt—river and desert, fertile strip and barren wastes—was held in balance by the gods through their intermediary, the king. He was supported by the priesthood, the nobility, and the civil service, who in turn depended on the producers of Egypt's economic wealth.

The Egyptians imagined a universe created and regulated by the gods, a place of balance, truth, and harmony—characteristics personified by the goddess Ma'at. They conceived of the afterlife simply as a parallel Egypt, complete with its dominating river, where there was neither illness nor famine, a place where crops grew to a great height, free of drought or insect damage, and where harvesting was an easy task to be performed in one's finery.

In reality, however, the rich bounty provided by the Nile did not come without hard work on the part of the farmers who grew the country's staple crops of barley and wheat. They broadcast seed by hand in the fall, following the Nile's annual summer flood, which watered the fields and replenished them with deposits of rich black silt. To take full advantage of the inundation, and to increase the amount of farmland available, farmers also undertook widespread irrigation schemes.

Although the majority of the population of ancient Egypt was involved in agriculture and aspects of food production, many people were also potters, weavers, carpenters, metalworkers, and stonemasons—the essential craftspeople responsible for the buildings and artifacts so greatly admired today. But the most privileged occupation of all was that of the scribe, a position exempt from taxation and carrying considerable prestige and authority, to the extent that officials often chose to be portrayed as a scribe, cross-legged with a papyrus

scroll unrolled on their lap, reed pen in hand, and perhaps an ink palette slung over one shoulder.

Scribes were trained in schools attached to temples, and mastering the complexities of hieroglyphic writing was a long and arduous task. In the ancient text *The Satire of the Trades*, a father encourages his son in his studies to become a scribe, "the greatest of all callings." After ridiculing the hardships of other professions—"each more wretched than the other"—the father concludes that "there's no profession without a boss, except for the scribe; he is the boss. Hence if you know writing it will be better for you than any other profession."

This statue dates from about 2500BCE and was discovered in a tomb at Sakkara. It depicts the deceased as a scribe seated in the classic pose of his profession, with a papyrus scroll open on his lap and his pen poised. His somewhat pendulous breasts and incipient paunch are also typical of scribal portraits and indicate a well-fed—and therefore prosperous—individual.

• ART AND NATURE •

Ancient Egyptian craftsmen were inspired by the natural world around them. Working within strict artistic conventions, they succeeded in capturing the vitality of familiar plants, animals, and birds. The images chosen repeatedly emphasize the concept of regeneration and were believed to have the ability to transmit the very life-force that they represented—from the scarab beetle and tilapia fish, which were believed capable of self-generation, to the animals and plants offered as food to the souls of the dead. The life-giving properties of the Nile were represented by the lotus flower and papyrus reed, the heraldic plants respectively of Upper and Lower Egypt. Other regional emblems included the sedge plant and the bee, and the white and red crowns.

Geese were often depicted, notably in a famous painted frieze from the *mastaba* tomb of Neferma'at and Atet at Meidum. They were symbols of the earth god Geb and of Amun, as well as serving as messengers to the gods. Geese were also used to represent the souls of the pharaohs. At the accession of a new king, four geese were sent as heralds to the cardinal points.

THE MANY FROM THE ONE

The peoples of the various regions of ancient Egypt had different theories of how the world was created, but all agreed that life originated following an eruption of earth, which rose out of the waters of chaos. It is believed that the pyramids were built to represent this primeval mound.

Egyptian religion was highly complex and involved the worship of the many gods and goddesses whose painted, incised, and sculpted images can still be seen adorning tombs and temples and a range of everyday artifacts. It was, above all, except during the Amarna period (see page 27), a tolerant, all-encompassing belief system, which was able to embrace apparently contradictory myths and legends. Every story about the gods had its local variations, but each was regarded as no less valid than the next. Even such a fundamental myth as the story of the creation of the world came in three strikingly different—but equally accepted—versions.

The Egyptians believed that life first emerged from the dark and formless void of Nun, the waters of chaos. At the beginning of time, a mound of earth rose out of Nun—an event that was graphically reenacted every year when the land began to appear above the receding floodwaters of the Nile—and it was on this mound that the gods created life.

The important Egyptian temples of Heliopolis, Memphis, and Hermopolis each claimed to mark the site of the primeval mound. At Heliopolis, the supreme creator was considered to be the sun god Atum, who emerged as the first sunrise from a lotus flower that sprouted on the mound. Atum contained within himself the life-force of the universe, from which he created the twin gods Shu, the god of air, and Tefnut, the goddess of moisture. Atum did this either by ejaculating or, according to another version of the myth, by "sneezing out Shu and spitting out Tefnut."

Shu and Tefnut coupled to produce the earth god Geb and the sky goddess Nut, who had intercourse together. Shu separated them, but not before they had produced four children: Osiris, Isis, Seth, and Nephthys. Thereafter, Shu supported the arched body of Nut, which formed the sky and held back the forces of chaos. With Atum, these nine gods are known as the Ennead (from Greek *ennea*, "nine").

The Memphis account of creation was based on the creative word of the god Ptah, who personified the

This scene from the Ptolemaic-period temple of the goddess Hathor at Dendera portrays the arched body of the sky goddess Nut. She is shown swallowing the sun as it begins its nighttime journey through her body; she then gives birth to it each dawn so that it can illuminate the land—here shown in stylized form with, in the center, an image bearing the face of Hathor that represents Dendera temple.

OPPOSITE *Carved on the ceiling of the temple at Dendera, the so-called "Dendera Zodiac" depicts the deities and celestial beings believed to inhabit the Egyptian heavens (see pages 54–55). The original ceiling is now displayed in the Musée du Louvre in Paris, France.*

primeval mound. According to this version, Ptah thought the world into being and made all things a reality simply by speaking their names. One theory holds that the name of a shrine to Ptah at Memphis, Hwt-ka-Ptah, became *Aiguptos*, the Greek word that is the origin of "Egypt."

According to the priests of Hermopolis, the first life was formed by the eight deities of the Ogdoad (Greek *okto*, "eight"), who existed in the primeval waters. Nun and his female counterpart, Naunet, represented the forces of the waters themselves; Heh and Hauhet represented infinity; Kek and Kauket represented darkness; and Amun and Amaunet represented the hidden force of life. From the combined energy of the Ogdoad, life

sprang into being and the primeval mound was created, from which the sun burst forth.

THE PYRAMIDS: SEATS OF THE SUN GOD

The primeval mound of creation, upon which the sun god came into being (see page 22), was said to be repre-

---

The Hermopolis account of creation is depicted in this scene from the Book of the Dead of the priest Khensumose (from about 1000 BCE). On the first day of creation, the sun rises in three stages over the primeval mound, which is surrounded by waters poured out by two female deities associated with the north (right) and the south (left). On the mound are eight figures representing the Ogdoad creator deities, who are depicted tilling the soil of the first land.

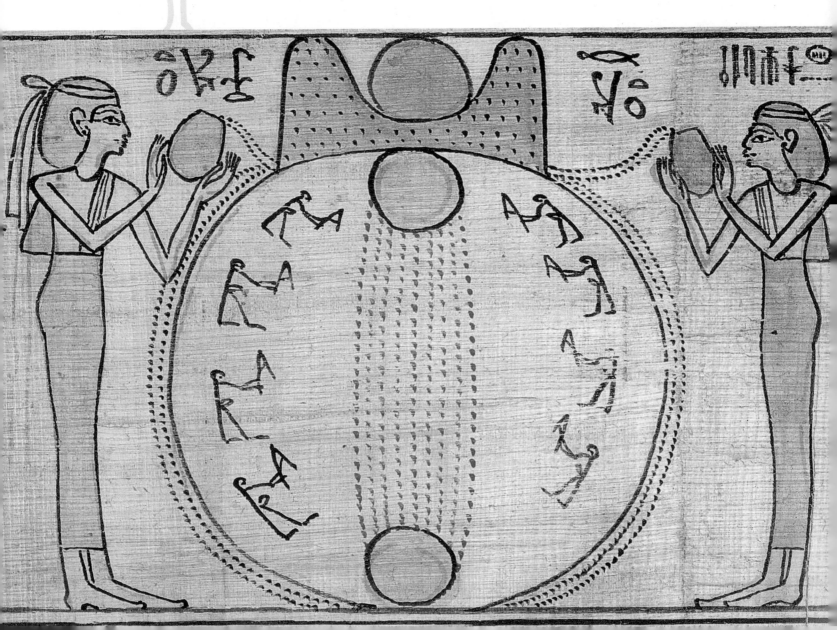

sented by the structures that are without doubt ancient Egypt's most familiar monuments: the pyramids. The three great pyramids at Giza are the most famous examples, but more than eighty pyramids of varying size were built between the Third and Twelfth dynasties, the best surviving ones dating from the Old Kingdom (Third to Fifth dynasties, 2675–2350BCE)—all of them sited within a 12-mile (20-km) radius of the ancient capital, Memphis. The earliest pyramid is the Third-dynasty "step pyramid" of Sakkara, so called because of its step-like structure, which evolved from the earlier rectangular tomb known, from its appearance, as a *mastaba* (Arabic, "bench").

Constructed by the architect Imhotep as a tomb for his king, Djoser, or Zoser (ca. 2650BCE), the step pyramid began as a *mastaba* before being raised to a height of 200 feet (60m) by adding four further, and successively smaller, *mastaba*s to produce its stepped profile.

The transition from the step pyramid to the true pyramid is attributed to King Snofru (ca. 2625–2585BCE), the first ruler of the Fourth dynasty. The partial collapse of Snofru's pyramid at Meidum reveals how its original stepped sides were filled in to create a smooth outline. Snofru's "Bent Pyramid" at Dahshur was probably the first monument planned from the outset as a true pyramid, but his architects changed the gradient of its sides part of the way up, probably because the original angle was found to be too unstable. In the end, the first true pyramid was to be Snofru's "Red Pyramid," again at Dahshur. Every pyramid was topped with a small capstone, or pyramidion, that was often inscribed and gilded to reflect the sun's dawn rays.

Once the building technique had been perfected, it was duplicated at Giza by Snofru's son Khufu (Cheops), who created the "Great Pyramid," the largest of all. Nearby lies the pyramid of his son, Khafre (Chephren), which with its associated temple structures—including the Sphinx (see box, right)—form the most complete of all such funerary complexes. A smaller pyramid of Khafre's son, Menkaure, completes the Giza monuments.

The Fifth-dynasty pyramids at Abusir and Sakkara are much smaller and, rather than being made of solid stone, consist of stone facings on a core of rubble. The pyramid of Unas (ca. 2371–2350BCE) was the first to include any form of inscription. The interior walls of his pyramid, like those of his Sixth-dynasty successors, are inscribed with funerary writings known as the "Pyramid Texts."

Following the decline of the Old Kingdoms, pyramid-building ceased. It began again at Dahshur, Lahun, and Hawara as the Middle Kingdom pharaohs reestablished their power. These pyramids had mudbrick cores and, when their outer stone casings were later stripped away, they eroded to formless stumps.

• THE GUARDIAN IN THE SAND •

As the earliest monumental sculpture from dynastic Egypt, the Great Sphinx of Giza is the most famous of the country's numerous sphinxes. It reclines at the necropolis on the Giza plateau before the pyramid of Khafre (ca. 2555–2532BCE), whose face it bears atop its leonine body. The Great Sphinx faces the rising sun—a silent witness to more than 1,660,000 sunrises during the course of the past four and a half millennia. By the New Kingdom, however, this magnificent monument had fallen into disrepair. It was restored by Thutmose IV (ca. 1400–1390BCE) while he was still a prince. According to a stela that Thutmose erected between its paws after he ascended to the throne of Egypt, the Sphinx had appeared to the prince in a dream when he fell asleep in its shadow while out hunting. The monument, almost engulfed with sand at the time, had promised him the throne if he restored it to its former glory. Thutmose ordered that the task should be undertaken and some years later he did indeed become king.

LORD OF THE HORIZON

The sun has always been the dominant factor in Egyptian life. As both creator and destroyer, it is responsible for the rich harvests of the floodplain and the barren wastes of the desert. In ancient Egypt, the sun was the supreme divinity, although the sun and the sun god came in many guises.

As the universal source of energy, the sun's light brought order to the chaos of darkness, and when the first dawn broke over the primeval mound (see page 22), so life began. The cult center of the sun was Iunu, better known by its Greek name of Heliopolis ("City of the Sun"), where the myth of the Ennead taught that the creative power of the sun, in the form of the god Atum ("the All"), made all things. By contrast, in other versions of the creation myth, the sun itself was created along with everything else in the universe.

The sun god generally took the form of the god Re, or Ra, whose name simply means "the Sun." Re is depicted as a falcon, a ram, or a human with a falcon's or ram's head. The god's form changed with the sun's daily passage through the sky. At dawn, the sun was Khepri ("the Evolving One"), represented by the scarab. Khepri was imagined propelling the sun through the sky in much the same manner as the beetle pushed along its ball of dung. The sun rising in the east was associated, too, with the falcon god Horus ("the Far One"), also known as Harakhty ("Horus of the Horizon"). The two were often combined as a single solar deity, Re-Harakhty.

Similarly, Re was again associated with Atum, in the form of Re-Atum, to represent the sun at the end of the day. As the sun set in the west, to be swallowed by the sky goddess Nut, it sank down into the underworld (Duat). On his nocturnal journey through the underworld, Re confronted the forces of darkness and chaos, led by his eternal enemy Apep, or Apophis, the giant serpent of chaos. Apep nightly threatened to swallow the sun and so destroy all life. Each dawn, after Apep had been subdued, Re emerged victorious from the underworld, reborn in the east as the child of Nut, amid the redness of her birth blood (see page 22).

Although the sun remained the supreme deity throughout Egyptian history, the Theban pharaohs of the early New Kingdom elevated their local god, Amun, to the status of national deity, linking him with the sun god to create Amun-Re (see page 29). With the accession of Thutmose IV (ca. 1400–1390BCE), whose claim to the throne was supported by the rival priests of the sun god in Heliopolis, political power began to shift

On this painted wooden funerary stela, the lady Taperet (ca. 900BCE) is shown praying to the falcon-headed sun god Re-Harakhty before a table laden with offerings of bread, wine, and lotus flowers. In return, the god, who is equipped with symbols representing power, radiates his beneficial solar rays toward her.

The scarab, or dung beetle, represented Khepri, the sun god at dawn, whose name means "the Evolving One"—the Egyptians believed the scarab to be self-generating, because its young emerged as if from nowhere out of the ball of dung in which they had incubated. Just as the parent beetle was often seen rolling a dung ball from its burrow, so too Khepri was depicted pushing up the sun from the underworld (right). The young scarab crawled from its ball and took flight—an act believed to represent the sun god rising up into the heavens. A potent symbol of rebirth, the scarab features prominently in funerary art, such as the exquisite pectoral jewelry that adorned royal mummies.

away from Amun. The sun god was increasingly worshipped in the form of the Aten, the sun disk. Thutmose's son Amenhotep III (ca. 1390–1353 BCE), developed this policy further and restored the sun-centered kingship that had characterized the Pyramid Age a thousand years earlier.

Amenhotep III aligned himself with the sun god by taking the titles "Chosen one of Re," "Image of Re," and the "Dazzling Aten." The Aten name was also used for a royal barge, a battalion of soldiers, and a new royal palace on the west bank of the Nile at Thebes—deliberately distancing the king from the clergy of Amun, who were based at Karnak on the east bank.

The reign of Amenhotep's son Amenhotep IV, or Akhenaten (ca. 1353–1336 BCE), is usually described as a time of a sudden change in Egyptian religion, art, and literature. These changes—the prominence given to the Aten, innovation in architecture, and the development

of more naturalistic art styles—can actually be traced back to Amenhotep III. But they were taken further by Akhenaten. His zealous promotion of the Aten—or rather, of his father united with the sun in the form of the Aten—at the expense of Amun and the other gods and goddesses, created widespread unrest and political and economic instability. Traditional temples were closed down and the capital was moved to a new city, Akhetaten (el-Amarna), which Akhenaten ordered to be constructed in an isolated area of central Egypt.

In the confused aftermath of Akhenaten's reign, his ephemeral successors (who included his son Tutankhamun) restored order by returning to Thebes and reverting to the worship of the traditional gods led by Amun. The Aten—and Akhenaten himself, who was known from that time as "the Heretic of Amarna"—was simply obliterated from all official records.

THE UNKNOWABLE LORD

As one of the eight creator deities of the Ogdoad, Amun ("the Hidden One") appears in Egyptian creation mythology alongside his female equivalent, Amaunet, to represent the hidden life-force of the universe. The temple built in his honor at Karnak was to become the largest in Egypt.

Amun was first mentioned in the Fifth-dynasty pyramid texts at Sakkara, in the north of the country, but it was in the south that he rose to prominence. He was worshipped as the local deity of the Theban region from at least as early as the Eleventh dynasty (ca. 2081–1938BCE), and his fortunes rose with those of the Middle Kingdom pharaohs who came from this area. Amun soon became known as "the King of the Gods."

The centre of the worship of Amun lay at Karnak, on the Nile at Thebes. The temple complex there was embellished by successive pharaohs until it became Egypt's largest. As pharaohs offered increasing amounts of tribute to Karnak, Amun's priests began to accumulate wealth and power to rival that of the monarchy itself.

At Karnak, Amun was associated with the Theban goddess Mut, who was revered as one of the symbolic divine mothers of the pharaoh. She supplanted Amaunet as the consort of Amun. With their child, the moon god Khonsu, they made up the "Divine Triad." All three had temples at the Karnak complex.

Amun is generally depicted in human form wearing a double-plumed crown, but he can also be represented by a ram, a goose, or even a snake. As Amun-Kematef ("He Who Has Completed His Moment"), he was envisioned as a snake shedding its skin in a constant cycle of renewal. Amun's creative power was reinforced when he was linked with the fertility god, Min, to create the virile Amun-Kamutef ("Bull of His Mother").

During the New Kingdom, Amun's status was further enhanced by linking him with the sun god, Egypt's supreme deity, to create Amun-Re, the ruler of the gods and—except during the Amarna period (see page 27)—the state deity. Ultimately, all Egypt's gods came to be seen as aspects of Amun, who was believed to be the supreme mystery, the divine creative force of the universe. As such, he was referred to as "the Unknowable."

THE DOMAIN OF AMUN

The origins of the great temple of Amun at Karnak date back to around 2000BCE, when local rulers set up a shrine to the god. From that time on, almost all the pharaohs sought to display their piety by adding to the temple, attempting in the process to outdo their predecessor in the size and splendor of the columns, pylons (ceremonial gateways), and statues erected in Amun's honor.

The temple itself was built along traditional Egyptian lines. It was constructed around a "holy of holies"—the innermost sanctuary in which Amun's cult statue resided, originally within a cedarwood shrine. This statue was thought capable of receiving the divine spirit of the god. The main temple axis runs westward from the sanctuary toward the Nile, with a second axis running south toward the separate temple of Amun's consort Mut. Set along each axis are hypostyle (columned) chambers, adorned with relief scenes of the pharaoh before the Divine Triad of Amun, Mut, and their child Khonsu. The famous Hypostyle Hall built by Sety I (ca. 1290–1279BCE) contains 134 huge columns, each carved in the form of a papyrus plant to create a magnificent stylized papyrus grove.

Before each of Karnak's columned halls stands a huge pylon that originally marked the front of the temple. The pylon was adorned with royal statuary, obelisks, and tall flagpoles that stood in the long vertical niches that can still be seen on the façade. Successive pharaohs simply built their own halls and pylons in front of the existing ones, so the latest structures are furthest away from the central shrine—which was itself renewed by Philip Arrhidaeus (323–317BCE). The pylon nearest the river is known as the First Pylon, but it dates from the late Thirtieth dynasty and was therefore actually the last of Karnak's fourteen ceremonial gateways to be built.

In front of the First Pylon is a processional avenue of ram-headed sphinxes, which once led to a small harbor linked to the Nile. This was the mooring place for the barque in which the cult statue of Amun was ferried either across the river to "visit" the royal funerary temples on the west bank, or upriver to the temple of Luxor just under two miles (3km) to the south. The god could also make the journey to Luxor overland, along another grand avenue of sphinxes.

OPPOSITE *The now roofless Hypostyle Hall of Karnak temple covers an area of almost 6,000 square yards (5,000 sq m). Its 134 monumental columns set in sixteen rows are inscribed with the repeated cartouches of Ramesses II. However, the building work was undertaken by his father, Sety I, using plans drawn up by his own father Ramesses I.*

THE MIGHTY GODDESSES

Every aspect of ancient Egyptian life combined elements that were both male and female, active and passive, aggressive and benign. In some lands, "female" might imply passive and gentle, but this was not the case in Egypt, as can clearly be seen in the way Egyptians perceived their deities.

In contrast to many ancient cultures, some of the most fearsome Egyptian divinities were female—although a number of goddesses had two distinct sides to their character and could also be protective and benign if sufficiently placated.

The task of protecting the pharaoh himself was undertaken by the twin goddesses Nekhbet and Wadjet, known as "the Mighty Ones." Nekhbet, the vulture goddess of Upper Egypt, shielded the king with her outstretched wings; her northern counterpart was Wadjet, the cobra goddess of Lower Egypt, who could spit fire into the eyes of the king's enemies (see illustration, page 17). The pharaoh wore images of both goddesses on his brow and his relationship with them was emphasized in the royal title "He of the Two Ladies."

The king was also guarded by the lioness goddess Sekhmet, "the Powerful One," who directed the forces of aggression and destruction. She was the daughter of the sun god, and in her vengeful aspect she was called "the Eye of Re," the one who slaughters Re's enemies with her fiery breath. Her association with the blood of battle is reflected in her title "Lady of Red Linen." Sekhmet could cause pestilence and disease, and her priests were trained in medicine in order to counteract her powerful effects.

Originally regarded as an aspect of Sekhmet, the goddess Bastet was eventually tamed into the form of the much-loved domestic cat. She was worshipped predominantly at Bubastis in the Delta, and recent examination of the huge numbers of cat mummies buried here and at Sakkara has revealed that many had been bred especially to be offered back to the goddess.

Another female deity associated with warfare was the ancient northern goddess Neith, "Mistress of the Bow, Ruler of Arrows," who was represented by a shield with crossed arrows. She was a goddess whose astute judgment was sought by the other gods. Some late texts say that Neith spat out the evil underworld serpent Apep, the enemy of Re, although elsewhere she is imagined as the sun god's mother and protector.

The scorpion goddess Selket was another maternal guardian of the king. The hippopotamus goddess Taweret ("the Great One") protected women in childbirth, and despite her ferocious appearance—to frighten away malevolent spirits—she was regarded as benign.

The nurturing aspect of the cow was adopted for one of Egypt's most popular goddesses, Hathor, who was portrayed either in bovine form or as a human figure with a horned crown with sun disk to represent her role

---

• DENDERA: HOUSE OF HATHOR •

From the time of the Old Kingdom, the temple of Dendera in Upper Egypt was the center of the cult of the multifaceted goddess Hathor. The existing complex of buildings there dates mainly from the Greco-Roman period and is one of the best-preserved in all of Egypt—complete with hypostyle hall, zodiac ceiling (see page 23), crypt, and sanatorium.

The rear exterior wall of the temple carries a huge relief scene of the queen Cleopatra VII (51–30BCE) and Caesarion, her son by the Roman leader Julius Caesar. Carved soon after Caesar's assassination in 44BCE, the scene has recently been interpreted as expressing Cleopatra's desire to be seen as the goddess Isis, who was left to raise her child Horus alone following the murder of her husband Osiris (see page 33). By the time of Cleopatra, Isis and Hathor had merged to become a single, benign goddess of motherhood and fertility.

The face of the goddess Hathor adorns a column capital in the hypostyle hall of the temple erected in her honour at Dendera, the center of the cult dedicated to Hathor. Note the copious hair being held back by cow ears, which symbolize the goddess's bovine aspect.

as daughter of the sun god, the benign aspect of the fierce lioness Sekhmet. Such blending of goddesses can also be seen in the way in which Hathor's cult was gradually absorbed into that of Isis—both, for example, were regarded as the mother of the king and often shared regalia and symbolism. Hathor herself is generally referred to as the goddess of love and beauty, and also as "the Mistress of Drunkenness" who oversaw music, dancing, and all forms of revelry. As "the Lady of the West," this much-loved and joyful goddess received the souls of the dead into the afterlife.

ISIS: THE DIVINE MOTHER

Ultimately the greatest of all the goddesses, Isis came to be regarded as the most powerful figure in the Egyptian pantheon, and as the Egyptian deity par excellence. By Roman times her cult had become international, with temples of the goddess on three continents. Isis was even worshipped in the imperial outpost of Britain—courtesy of her devotees in the Roman army.

Isis was a goddess of enormous magical powers and was said to be "more powerful than a thousand soldiers," and "more clever than a million gods." In the story of Isis and Osiris (see page 33), it is Isis who takes

Isis nurses the infant Horus in this Late Period faience figurine. The form of the sculpture resembles the Egyptian hieroglyph for "throne"—the meaning of the name Isis. As her cult spread throughout the Roman world, such depictions of the goddess and her infant son became widespread and served as the models for Christian representations of the Virgin and Child.

the lead in resurrecting the dead Osiris by means of her magic. Isis was "the Mistress of the Gods, who knows Re by his own name"—using her guile, she was said to have tricked the sun god, Re, into revealing his secret name, knowledge of which brought limitless power.

Isis employed her great might to protect her young son Horus (see box, opposite), with whom she is often depicted to emphasize her role as devoted mother. Isis was also regarded as the symbolic mother of the king, "the living Horus" on Earth. This royal connection is reflected in Isis's name, which means "the Throne." The hieroglyph for "throne" (⌐) forms the goddess's crown, although she is also portrayed wearing the horned crown of Hathor, with whom Isis was closely connected and whose cult—like those of many other goddesses—she eventually absorbed.

Isis appears in her maternal capacity with her sister Nephthys on sarcophaguses, protecting the mummy within, and the two are joined by Neith and Selket as the protectors of the embalmed viscera of the deceased.

Isis was worshipped throughout Egypt, with important shrines at Giza, Thebes, Abydos, and Dendera, but the center of her cult was in the far south on the island of Philae in the Nile, a place once believed to be the source of the river itself. The present temple buildings of Philae are relatively late, dating from the Twenty-fifth dynasty (760–656BCE) to Roman times.

Because of its remote southerly location, Philae was able to function well into the Christian era, and indeed it was the last pagan temple in Egypt. The Roman empire ordered the closure of all non-Christian places of worship in 392CE, but the cult of Isis at Philae was fully replaced by Christian worship only in 551CE, at which time many images of the old gods and goddesses were defaced. Philae is also the site of the last datable hieroglyphs, roughly carved on 24 August, 394CE. There are also graffiti at Philae in demotic, the popular written form of ancient Egyptian, dating from 452CE—long after most Egyptians had converted to Christianity and were using the Greek-based Coptic script.

◆ THE BATTLES OF HORUS ◆

The falcon god Horus—"Lord of the Sky" and the god of the east—was sometimes in need of the assistance of some of the great goddesses. His eyes were the sun and moon, and as Harakhty ("Horus of the Horizon"), he was linked with the sun god in the form Re-Harakhty. Usually depicted as the bird of prey itself or as a falcon-headed man, Horus was the son of Isis and Osiris. His parents had ruled Egypt together until Osiris was murdered by his jealous brother Seth, the lord of chaos, who usurped the throne. The grieving Isis restored her husband's dismembered body by magic, and conceived their son Horus. She then raised the infant (known to the Greeks as Harpocrates, or "Horus the Child") in secret. The adult Horus (Haroeris, or "Horus the Elder") set out to avenge his father and reclaim the throne as his rightful inheritance.

In the story of the battles of Horus and Seth, Horus first took his case to the gods, all of whom supported his claim—except for the sun god Re, who believed Seth, as the fiercer and stronger of the two rivals, should keep the throne. Unable to come to a unanimous decision, the gods appealed to the great goddess Neith, who decided in favor of Horus. The gods duly awarded him the throne, but Seth disputed their decision and challenged his nephew to physical combat. The result was a series of ferocious battles, depicted in reliefs at the temple of Horus at Edfu.

During their titanic struggles, Horus appealed to Neith once again, while Osiris spoke to Re from the underworld and threatened to unleash the spirits of retribution if justice was not done. And so the gods finally restored Horus to his throne. Seth accepted the decision and henceforth used his formidable energies to assist Re in the fight against the forces of darkness.

As Horus ruled Egypt, the land of the living, so Osiris became the ruler of the underworld, the land of the afterlife. Every pharaoh was revered as "the Living Horus," the incarnation of Horus on Earth. The king continued his royal role after death when he descended to the underworld to become united with Osiris.

In one of their battles Seth is said to have gouged out Horus's left eye; in another version of the story, Seth rips out both eyes and buries them in the desert, where they grow into lotus flowers. In both versions, the goddess Hathor restores Horus's sight using a potion. The motif known as the Eye of Horus (above) therefore came to represent the power of healing or making something perfect again, and its name, *wedjat*, means "sound," or "whole." The form of the *wedjat* resembles the markings of a falcon's eye, with an extended line of the sort applied by Egyptians with eye-paint. The *wedjat* was a potent force and a powerful amulet, which was often worn as protective jewelry.

KINGS OF THE TWO LANDS

At the heart of the Egyptian world stood the king, or pharaoh. As an absolute monarch his—or, rarely, her—command was law, and it was at his behest and in his name that taxes were gathered, justice was administered, and wars were waged. However, the pharaoh was more than simply a head of state, he was essential to the maintenance of cosmic order (ma'at).

The pharaoh—a word derived from the Egyptian *per-aa*, which originally meant "great house," or "palace"—was the central figure in Egyptian life, the counterpoise between the mortal and divine worlds and the upholder of order. It was believed that Egypt would descend into chaos in the absence of its king. The pharaoh was the mediator between humans and the celestial realm of the gods and goddesses, whose divinity he shared and from whom he derived his power. Descended from the sun god Re, the king was identified in life with Horus and in death with Osiris, ruler of the underworld.

The Egyptians believed that in the beginning they were ruled by the gods themselves. In one myth, the sun god Re was the first king, ruling over a golden age of plenty. But when he grew old, his human subjects began to question his right to rule and to plot against him, so he sent his daughter—the avenging Eye of Re—to destroy the traitors. He abandoned the world for a celestial realm, and humans fell from grace and began to fight among themselves at the loss of the sun. Seeing the chaos below, Re sent Thoth, god of wisdom, to restore order, before appointing a succession of gods to rule as king in his place: Shu, Geb, and then Osiris.

In the myth of the Ennead (see page 22), Osiris was the first king of Egypt, inheriting the right to the throne as the firstborn of the four offspring of Geb and Nut. Osiris and Isis, his sister and queen, presided over an era of peace and prosperity in which they brought wisdom to humankind. Osiris was murdered by his jealous brother Seth, who usurped the throne until Horus, Osiris's son, finally took back the crown.

Horus was the last god to rule Egypt. He was succeeded by human rulers known as "the Followers of Horus," but by the time of Narmer—the legendary king who was said to have united the two lands of Upper and Lower Egypt (see page 14)—all Egyptian kings were identified with the god as "the Living Horus."

The story of Osiris and Horus underpinned the Egyptian ideal that succession should be from father to son. Thus every king showed great filial piety toward the ruler he had succeeded, whether the previous pharaoh was his real father or not: the new king was the chief officiant at his predecessor's funeral and regarded it as his duty to complete his monuments.

An important element of Egyptian kingship was the concept that the king was of divine birth, the result of a liaison between the queen mother and the god Amun-Re. This conferred on him the divine right to rule, which he repeatedly confirmed through the performance of temple rituals (in his capacity as the country's high priest) and the celebration of special royal religious festivals.

OPPOSITE *A painted wall scene from the tomb of Horemheb (ca. 1319–1292BCE) in the Valley of the Kings that depicts the 18th-dynasty pharaoh wearing the* nemes *headcloth (center). Horemheb is flanked by the goddess Isis (wearing the regalia of Hathor) and her son Horus (wearing the dual Red and White Crown of Upper and Lower Egypt).*

• SMITING THE FOE •

As intermediary between the human and divine worlds, it was the role of the pharaoh to enable order to triumph over chaos, and the king's earthly duty to overcome Egypt's enemies. The pharaoh is always portrayed as victorious against his adversaries and the standard pose of royal invincibility is known as "Smiting the Foe," a composition in which the monarch is depicted poised to strike the fallen enemy, whom he is shown holding by the hair. The scene is depicted here (left) on the slate palette of King Narmer (from about 3100BCE) and it was executed in more or less the same form from that time right through to the Roman period—capturing the most dramatic and suspenseful moment, with the king raising his mace before striking the death blow. One of the best-known examples of it is the relief on the northern exterior wall of the Great Hypostyle Hall of the temple of Amun at Karnak, showing Sety I, of the Nineteenth dynasty, smiting Libyan captives before the god Amun.

UNITY AND DIVISION

After the reigns of Egypt's predynastic rulers (the "Followers of Horus"), Upper and Lower Egypt were united for the first time in about 3100BCE when King Narmer of Upper Egypt defeated the chief of Lower Egypt and became the ruler of a single kingdom.

The unification of Egypt marks the beginning of the Old Kingdom and the country's written history: hieroglyphic script first appeared in this period. The new writing was employed to organize and run the state from the capital city of Memphis, which Narmer's successors established at the apex of the Delta.

Although the kings of the late predynastic and early dynastic periods were buried at Abydos, reflecting their southern origins, Third-dynasty rulers chose to be buried near their capital in the Memphite necropolis of Sakkara. Here, the step pyramid complex of Djoser—the first of Egypt's many pyramids—encapsulates the power of the monarchy in stone (see page 25). Increasingly ambitious building schemes were undertaken. King Snofru (ca. 2625–2585BCE), the founder of the Fourth dynasty, which marked the beginning of the Old Kingdom, built three pyramids, including the first true pyramid, the so-called "Red Pyramid," at Dahshur.

Subsequent rulers of the Old Kingdom went on to construct massive pyramid complexes at Giza. The first and largest of these—the Great Pyramid—was built by Snofru's son Khufu (Cheops), about whom very little is known: his only likeness is a tiny ivory figurine and the extant accounts of his life are largely fictional. Close to the Great Pyramid lies the pyramid of Khufu's son Khafre (Chephren), where a stunning life-size figure was found representing Khafre held in the protective wings of the god Horus, with whom all kings identified. At this point, royal devotion to the sun god—so clearly demonstrated by the pyramid monuments—is also expressed in the adoption of the royal title *sa-re*, "Son of Re."

The smallest of the three Giza pyramids was built by Khafre's son Menkaure (Mycerinus). Additions made to the complex during the Fifth and Sixth dynasties indicate that Menkaure's cult flourished for hundreds of years after his death.

A decline in royal power occurred during the Sixth dynasty. By the death of Pepy II (ca. 2288–2194BCE), who, at the end of his extremely long reign, had come to be seen as an ageing, weakened old man rather than as an omnipotent god on Earth, royal power was severely undermined. Provincial officials began to create their own petty kingdoms and the country gradually fragmented until central authority broke down into the anarchy of the First Intermediate Period.

THEBES

Following a century of division and civil war during the First Intermediate Period, Egypt was reunited under the southern warrior princes of Thebes (modern Luxor). Nebhepetre Mentuhotep II (ca. 2008–1957BCE) finally defeated his northern rivals, who had made Herakleopolis their capital. Under the Eleventh-dynasty kings, the previously provincial town of Thebes became the most important city in the land, and the status of the local god, Amun of Karnak, was significantly enhanced. Mentuhotep embarked upon ambitious building schemes, including the construction of an imposing terraced funerary temple below the cliffs at Deir el-Bahari on the Theban west bank, behind which he and the royal women were buried.

Although subsequent pharaohs of the Middle Kingdom moved back north to the traditional capital of Memphis, they continued to add to Mentuhotep's achievements and, under the capable rule of kings such as Senwosret III and Amenemhet III, the country thrived. Their successful military campaigns consolidated and expanded Egypt's borders, which the army defended from a series of fortresses. Successive regimes also strengthened and centralized the bureaucracy to reduce the power of regional governors (nomarchs).

In terms of art and literature, this prosperous time is

The sun bursts through the clouds above the pyramids of Khufu, Khafre, and Menkaure at Giza. These massive monumental structures were intended to serve as lasting reminders of the greatness of the pharaohs who built them.

regarded as the "classical" period of Egyptian culture. Large-scale projects, such as land reclamation and the erection of impressive pyramids, heralded the monarch's return to absolute power. Royal portraiture depicted mighty rulers with stern, careworn faces reflecting the burdens of kingship.

The first seven kings of the Twelfth dynasty (four named Amenemhet and three named Senwosret) enjoyed a continuous father-son succession until Amenemhet IV died without an heir. He was succeeded by the second of Egypt's female pharaohs, his sister Sobekneferu. The instability caused by the long series of ephemeral monarchs under the following dynasties—around seventy kings in 150 years—led to continuous infiltration by Asiatic settlers. Absorbed into Egyptian

society and ultimately also the government, Asiatics eventually took the throne in approximately 1640BCE and were known to the native Egyptians as "Hyksos" ("Rulers of Foreign Lands"). They reigned in the north while Thebes remained independent in the south, and thus Egypt entered its Second Intermediate Period. The Theban princes struggled against the Hyksos until Egypt was finally reunited under the Thebans by Ahmose (ca. 1539–1514BCE).

THE AGE OF EMPIRE

The start of the Eighteenth dynasty under King Ahmose (ca. 1539–1514BCE) marks the beginning of the New Kingdom—the golden age of ancient Egypt. After the expulsion of the Hyksos, a series of unrelenting warrior-pharaohs campaigned vigorously and created the greatest empire yet seen.

Ahmose was succeeded by his son Amenhotep I, who followed in his father's military footsteps to pacify Nubia. He also founded the village of Deir el-Medina for the workers who built the royal tombs in the Valley of the Kings, burial site of the New Kingdom rulers. The following three monarchs, all called Thutmose, were the sons of non-royal women, and strengthened their claims to the throne by marrying into the female royal line. On the sudden death of Thutmose II (ca. 1482–1479BCE), his heir was still too young to rule, and so the widowed queen, Hatshepsut, reigned as regent for around twenty prosperous years until Thutmose III, her stepson and nephew, was of age. The adult Thutmose III was the so-called "Napoleon of Ancient Egypt," who expanded the Egyptian empire into Asia as far north as the Euphrates. His son Amenhotep II consolidated Egypt's control over the vassal states of the Levant.

Egypt had become the most powerful country in the ancient world, its victories cemented by diplomatic alliances. At the center of this mighty empire stood Thebes. The city's local god, Amun, was elevated to the status of a national deity, and as a result Amun's clergy at Karnak grew in wealth and power (see pages 28–29).

Upon the accession of one of Amenhotep II's younger sons as Thutmose IV, the power of the Karnak priests began to be curtailed. Thutmose IV's son,

• THE FACE OF POWER •

Egyptian royal portraiture often displays the emblems of pharaonic power, such as the regalia of crook and flail, scepter and mace, and the many forms of regal costume. Kings were usually depicted wearing one of a large range of crowns, most of which bore the *uraeus* (sacred serpent) over the brow. Upper and Lower Egypt were symbolized by the White Crown (*Hedjet*) and Red Crown (*Deshret*) respectively, while the Red and White Crown combined (*Pschent*) represented the "Two Lands" of the united Egypt. The plumed *Atef* Crown was worn on certain ritual occasions and was associated with the god Osiris. The blue-and-yellow striped headcloth (*Nemes*) was popular with rulers throughout the pharaonic period. The Blue Crown (*Khepresh*), which was linked with the sun god, was frequently worn by Eighteenth-dynasty pharaohs.

White Crown   Red and White Crown

Amenhotep III (ca. 1390–1353BCE), further distanced the crown from the temple of Amun, favoring instead the cult of the sun in the form of the Aten disk. This process was continued by Amenhotep IV, later Akhenaten (ca. 1353–1336BCE), whose extreme measures in promoting the Aten threatened the fabric of Egyptian culture (see page 27). In closing down the traditional temples and relocating his capital, Akhenaten created political and economic instability that brought the country close to chaos.

Akhenaten's son and successor Tutankhamun restored order by returning to Thebes and reestablishing the worship of the traditional gods. The last king of the Eighteenth dynasty, Horemheb (ca. 1319–1292BCE), set about restoring Egypt's neglected empire through reconquest—an imperialistic policy that was continued by the following dynasty, typified by Sety I and his famous son, the celebrated Ramesses II (ca. 1279–1213BCE).

FAITH AND GLORY

The temple of Luxor was built by Amenhotep III as a place to celebrate the annual Opet festival in which the king united with his divine *ka* (spirit) to strengthen his ability to rule. During the festival, the cult statue of the god Amun was carried to Luxor from the much larger temple of Amun at Karnak to the north (see page 29) along a processional way lined with sphinxes.

Amenhotep's graceful columns and interior buildings, partly decorated by his grandson Tutankhamun, were then later extended by Ramesses II in an attempt to emulate his illustrious predecessor. Alexander the Great also restored and made additions to some of the interior buildings almost a thousand years later.

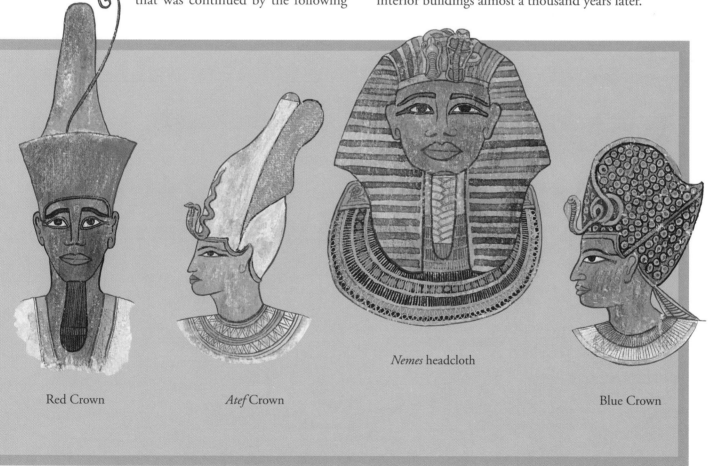

Red Crown

Atef Crown

Nemes headcloth

Blue Crown

THE ROLE OF WOMEN

In the early days of Egyptology, European gentlemen-scholars were startled to discover images of women in prominent or even dominating roles. They dismissed much of what they found as "fictional" or "ritualistic," but ancient Egyptian women were influential.

It is clear from artistic, literary, and archaeological evidence that Egyptian women were regarded as the equals of their male counterparts. They were legally independent citizens and exercised varying degrees of self-determination unusual in the male-dominated ancient world. Their freedom certainly shocked the Greeks: the historian Herodotus (fifth century BCE) wrote that women "go to market and take part in trading, whereas men sit at home and do the weaving." The Egyptians, he concluded, "seem to have reversed the normal practices of mankind."

Generally, women married and had children, but were nevertheless visible throughout Egyptian society,

laboring in the fields and conscripted alongside men for public works. Both male and female servants are portrayed cleaning houses, making beds, brewing, and baking—laundry, however, was done by professional washermen. As for their wealthy employers, the men usually worked outside the home whereas women, although shown in outdoor scenes, spent considerably

Female servants wait on the wealthy in this banquet scene from the 18th-dynasty tomb of Rekhmire in Thebes. As the central servant girl—unusually shown from the back rather than the side—pours out perfume for the seated lady on her right, she says: "For your ka (soul)."

This famous head of Nefertiti, wife of Akhenaten (1353–1336BCE), shows the queen with her trademark tall blue crown, which she is depicted wearing when undertaking the symbolic royal duties normally reserved for the sovereign himself.

more of their time indoors—as reflected in the artistic convention that gives them paler skin. But both men and women attended social occasions together.

Women were paid for the work they did, and could own, buy, and sell their own property, make wills, and choose which of their children would inherit. Many women held religious posts and females are also known to have acted as overseer of doctors, steward, judge, governor, and even vizier—the highest administrative rank below the king. The monarch was normally male, but women were known to occupy the throne in their own right.

Although it is often stated that there is no evidence of female scribes, some women must have been able to consult written records in the course of their official duties. By Greco-Roman times women's literacy is well proven: the famous Cleopatra VII wrote and spoke at least seven languages, including Egyptian—she was the first of the Ptolemaic dynasty to learn the language of her subjects.

The tendency to avoid sexual stereotyping applied also to deities. Gods and goddesses might be either passive or active, and many of Egypt's most fearsome deities were female (see pages 30–33). The potential for female aggression is reflected in texts and in depictions of women stabbing soldiers, firing arrows, and physically overpowering men—images supported by the weapons found with female burials.

ROYAL WOMEN

Royal mothers and wives, such as Ramesses II's principal wife, Nefertari, enjoyed great influence and prestige. A small number of royal women even took the throne as

• FASHION AND FINERY •

With their fine clothing, elaborately styled coiffures, colorful jewelry, and striking cosmetics, the Egyptians were an image-conscious people. Appearances were of paramount importance and their style of dress developed from a sense of practicality combined with a love of beauty. Clothing was designed to counteract the effects of the climate. Most garments were made out of plain linen, with the basic Egyptian wardrobe consisting of a kilt (often with tunic and cloak) for men and a dress for women, together with a loincloth and sandals for both sexes. This relatively simple clothing was generally offset by collars, necklaces, bracelets, anklets, belts, and earrings. The effect was completed—by both men and women—with the addition of a wig or false braids, eyepaint, and a generous amount of perfume.

Sobekneferu (ca. 1763–1759BCE), who ruled with full royal titles at the end of the Twelfth dynasty. As a dutiful heir, she completed the building projects begun by her father, Amenemhet III, and was represented wearing the royal *nemes* headcloth and kilt over female dress.

Three centuries later, following the early death of her husband Thutmose II in about 1479BCE, Hatshepsut, the daughter of Thutmose I, assumed traditional kingly regalia. After initially ruling as regent, she went on to command complete power, reestablishing long-distance trading networks, mounting several military campaigns, and constructing an impressive funerary temple (see page 38 and box, opposite).

Another famous Egyptian queen, Nefertiti, was actively involved in the reforms that replaced the traditional religious framework with the cult of the Aten. She appears twice as often as her husband, Akhenaten, in certain reliefs at Karnak and some scholars believe that Nerfertiti also ruled independently as king after Akhenaten's death in around 1336BCE.

The most famous of all the formidable Ptolemaic women who ruled Egypt was Cleopatra VII, whose twenty-one-year reign (51–30BCE) briefly restored the country's greatness in the face of Roman aggression. Her suicide marked the end of Egypt's self-government and is often taken as the notional end of ancient Egypt.

The position of pharaoh was more commonly held by a man, so the most influential women at the Egyptian court were usually his mother, sisters, wives, daughters, and female relatives. The titles accorded to the queen—who was either the king's "Great Wife" (principal wife) or his mother—generally refer to her in relation to her husband, her son, or her children: ("Wife of the King Whom he Loves"; "Consort of Horus";

kings in their own right: female rulers are known from a very early period and there is evidence that women occupied the throne on at least five occasions. In the Second dynasty, there was said to be a law which permitted women to reign, although they usually acted as regents for underage sons who later became pharaohs.

Egypt's first recorded female king was the Sixth-dynasty monarch Neith-ikret (ca. 2148–2144BCE), who was long remembered as "the bravest and most beautiful woman of her time." Neith-ikret seems to have reigned on her own behalf rather than for a son, as did

"Mother of the King"; "Mother of the King's Children"). Some queens were also known as "Mistress of the Two Lands," "Great One of the Scepter," or the somewhat less imposing "Beautiful of Appearance upon Gazing." Like the king, the queen was regarded as semi-divine and given honors befitting a goddess: queens of the Old Kingdom were buried in pyramid tombs and provided with the ceremonial boats necessary to sail the heavens with the gods. The tomb of Menkaure's daughter, Khentkawes, has been referred to as the "fourth pyramid" of Giza, because it stands before the remaining three we see today (see page 25).

The royal women associated with the Eleventh-dynasty king Mentuhotep II (ca. 2008–1957BCE) were all buried close to him within his imposing funerary complex at Deir el-Bahari. The mothers, wives, and daughters of later Middle Kingdom pharaohs were also buried in pyramids, and wooden caskets filled with gorgeous jewelry have been discovered in several of their tombs.

Some royal women were admired for their military prowess. The Eighteenth-dynasty queen Ahhotep rallied Egyptian troops against the Hyksos (see page 37) after both her husband and eldest son had fallen in battle; in the words of her surviving son, Ahmose, "she cared for her soldiers, she brought back her fugitives and gathered up her deserters, she has pacified the south and expelled her rebels." In her rich burial, weapons and golden military decorations lay beside her mirror, fan, and jewelry. The power of Queen Nefertiti is displayed in scenes in which—wearing the monarch's Blue Crown and wielding a scimitar—she is shown executing foreign prisoners.

Queen Tiy, the "Great Royal Wife" of Amenhotep III (ca. 1390–1353BCE), achieved a level of prominence never before seen for a royal consort. While the king was worshipped as the earthly manifestation of the sun god, Tiy was regarded as Hathor, and in the goddess's guise as the fierce lioness, Sekhmet, Tiy was able to bestow everything from peace and love to divine retribution.

◆ THE TEMPLE OF THE GODDESS KING ◆

Inspired by the earlier funerary temple of Mentuhotep II, which is situated at Deir el-Bahari below the Theban cliffs, "King" Hatshepsut (ruled ca. 1479–1458BCE) chose to have her funerary temple built along similar lines. Her graceful temple was set in a series of terraces adorned with an array of delicately carved relief scenes and huge statues of the "king" in the guise of Osiris. The temple's central axis extends across a great forecourt, where it originally formed an avenue flanked with trees and statues of the illustrious female monarch in full pharaonic regalia. Hatshepsut's body was buried in a tomb on the other side of the cliffs in the Valley of the Kings.

Two of the daughters of Amenhotep and Tiy were also made "Great Royal Wives," to reflect Hathor's triple role as mother, wife, and daughter of the sun god. Such marriages helped keep power within the ruling house and reinforced the king's divine status.

Minor royal wives also wielded a certain amount of power, because they sometimes had the opportunity to influence the succession. Like the queen, they were honored with the title "Mother of the King" if their son was chosen as heir to the throne. This sometimes led to intrigue and plotting—the so-called "Harim Conspiracy," for example, resulted in the assassination attempt on the life of Ramesses III, when one of his minor wives conspired to have her son made pharaoh.

Many of the king's wives were foreign, sent to the Egyptian court in order to seal diplomatic relations. In a dispatch to one of his Asiatic vassals, Amenhotep III wrote, "Send very beautiful women—but none with shrill voices!"

WORDS OF POWER

From the Memphite creation myth, in which the universe was created by the power of intellect alone, it is clear that the ancient Egyptians realized the infinite possibilities and vast potential of the human mind. They were also adept practitioners of magic, both in the temple and at home.

The Egyptian god of knowledge was Djehuty, or Thoth, who was represented as an ibis (or ibis-headed man) or as a baboon with a crown combining the crescent moon and full moon. He was generally regarded as a child of the sun god Re, who appointed him as his deputy to keep earthly affairs in order. Re allowed Thoth to give humans the knowledge of hieroglyphs, which contained all wisdom and could be used to organize and administer the country.

Since the written word was regarded as highly potent, Egypt's literate minority—educated in temple colleges called "houses of life"—were considered to have special powers. The "lector-priest" (*hery-heb*), who read out the ritual texts during temple ceremonies, was often seen as a magician, since it was he who spoke the magical "words of power." All texts used in sacred temple rituals were regarded as "books of Thoth" and were stored in temple libraries, such as those at Edfu and at Thoth's cult center, Hermopolis. By the late Roman period, it was said that the entire knowledge of the ancient Egyptians—including mathematics, medicine, geography, astrology, and law—was contained in forty-two such books, which had been written by Thoth himself. The Greeks identified Thoth with their own god Hermes, and so began the legend of Hermes Trismegistos ("Thrice-Great Hermes/Thoth"), and his book of magic, *Hermetica*.

Repeated references to this mysterious book by ancient Greek and Latin authors intrigued scholars in Renaissance Europe, and Egypt gained a reputation as the fount of all wisdom. Since hieroglyphs could not at that time be translated, Egypt remained a land of mystery, and the strange rites depicted on temple walls and elsewhere gave rise to much speculation.

Now that the accompanying hieroglyphic inscriptions can be read, we know that most ancient Egyptian rituals had a very specific and practical religious purpose, often far removed from the highly esoteric significance that later ages commonly ascribed to them. The "wisdom of Egypt" certainly existed, but it was a far more practical body of knowledge than has often been supposed.

Dating to the Middle Kingdom, this blue-glazed faience fertility figurine depicts a naked woman covered in tattoo marks and wearing a bead-and-shell hip belt. Such figures have been found in tombs and may have been aids to the regeneration of the dead.

MAGIC AND MYSTERIES

It is often difficult for modern observers of ancient Egypt to disentangle religion from magic. This is not surprising, because for the Egyptians themselves, the distinction hardly existed. They believed that it was possible to alter the world around them by directing the unseen forces of gods and spirits, and the magician's role often differed very little from that of the priest or physician. State-organized temple religion employed magical rites on a daily basis. Texts containing spells had names such as "The Book to Appease Sekhmet," "Formulae for Repelling the Evil Eye," and "The Book of the Capture of the Enemy." While these mysterious texts were being recited, the magician would often destroy wax or clay images of a person or other being perceived to threaten the divine order—such as enemies of the state or the adversaries of the sun god. The combination of the spoken word and the performance of a

• CHARMS AND AMULETS •

Magical charms and amulets were worn by both the living and the dead to repel harmful forces and bestow beneficial effects. They were produced in various materials and colors and generally took the form of popular gods, ritual objects, animals, plants, body parts, or the names of kings. The amulet shown here, from about 1295BCE, takes the form of a temple pylon and features the goddesses Isis (left) and Nephthys and numerous auspicious emblems: the Eye of Horus; the spine or pillar of Osiris (*djed*, 𓊽); the scarab; and the knot of Isis (*tyet*, 𓎬). Other symbols commonly incorporated into amulets include the *ankh* (𓋹, "life"), the fish (*nekhaw*, which was worn by children to prevent drowning), *sa* (𓍢, "protection"), and the sign for "joy" (𓏲).

ritual act was believed to ensure the security of the kingdom and to restore balance to the universe.

Such rites could also be practiced on a small scale for an individual's benefit, and magic was often used in a domestic context by the many ordinary Egyptians who did not have access to the temple interior. People honored both the gods and ancestral spirits at household shrines, and specific spells were employed at particular times of life. It was thought especially important that childbirth be accompanied by the correct magical procedures. A pregnant woman could appeal to deities of magic, such as Bes, Taweret, and Hathor, to protect her and her child from evil spirits and ease her labor—one spell for hastening birth implored Hathor to "send the sweet north wind." The popular dwarf god, Bes, is often shown dancing and playing instruments in his role as the protector of women in childbirth—music and noisy revelry were believed to drive away malevolent spirits.

The role of the divine mother, Isis, in protecting her son, Horus, was alluded to in spells designed to protect Egyptian children from snake and scorpion bites, burns, and other afflictions. Practical medical treatments were often prescribed alongside incantations and amulets that were believed to guard against illness.

Divination was another aspect of Egyptian magic. One ritual to invoke the god Anubis, for example, involved covering a bowl of water with a film of oil, in which images would appear to the medium. Egyptians also believed that the dead could be contacted through letters placed at their tombs requesting the help of the deceased and asking them to act as intermediaries between their living relatives and the gods.

THE TEMPLE

The focus of every ancient Egyptian settlement was the temple, a great center of activity which, in addition to its religious function, served as a combination of town hall, college, library, and medical clinic. However, only a priest was permitted access to the sacred inner part of the temple, which was regarded as a kind of storehouse of divine power.

The representative of the gods on Earth was the king, who was thus the supreme priest of every temple. But, given that there was at least one temple in every town, he delegated his priestly duties to the high priest of each temple. Below the high priest were various ranks of clergy, from the "lector-priest"—a very senior cleric versed in the temple's secret scriptures—to those who tended the temple's sacred cattle. Many priests worked part-time for one month in every three. Regardless of rank, the role of all priests was to direct divine power to beneficial ends by performing rituals and to serve the gods.

Priests lived in their own small community attached to the temple. At Karnak, they lived beside the temple's sacred lake, an artificial pool where all priests were required to bathe twice each day and twice each night, because those involved in holy rites had to be completely pure (*waab*). For the same reason, priests also had to shave all their body hair every other day and wear only pure linen robes.

Following precise procedures and rituals, the priests honored deities daily with a constant stream of food offerings, wine, perfumes, incense, and flowers. The gods would also be entertained by temple musicians and dancers: one text records rites associated with "the Golden Goddess, Hathor," in which singers chanted invocations and dancers moved to the rhythmic accompaniment of the *sistrum*, a sacred rattle. Such devotions were believed to encourage the spirit of the deity to reside within the sacred statue that was kept in a shrine in the dark innermost sanctuary of the temple, to which the king and the high priest alone had access. Only by maintaining the divine presence within each temple could the cosmic order be upheld over the disorder and chaos depicted on the temple exterior.

Each morning, the purified high priest entered the dark shrine, dimly lit by flickering oil lamps. He carefully opened the sealed wooden doors of the shrine and approached the divine statue, greeting it and making offerings of perfume. With the little finger of his right hand, he anointed the deity's brow with sacred oils of cedar and myrrh. The statue would then be adorned with cosmetics and ceremonial clothing before being presented with food, drink, and huge floral bouquets—their fragrance was believed to be that of the gods themselves. Incense, used to welcome and sustain the gods and to repel malevolent spirits, was of great importance. It was made in bulk by priests in temple "perfume laboratories," where lists of aromatic ingredients were recorded on the walls.

In addition to such intimate temple rituals, to which only a few had access, more than fifty public festivals were celebrated regularly throughout the year. The Egyptians were the first to observe a 365-day calendar, which consisted of 360 days plus five great holy days to mark the birthdays of Osiris, Isis, Horus, Seth, and Nephthys. Other important feast days included the Festival of Hathor, at which the goddess's statue was taken from her shrine at Dendera and presented to the people amid joyful music and dancing in celebration of a good harvest. Similar events accompanied the wedding-like Feast of the Beautiful Meeting, when Hathor's statue traveled south from Dendera to spend two weeks with her "husband" Horus at Edfu.

Accompanied by a great retinue of priests, priestesses, musicians, and dancers, the entire local population would turn out during these public holidays to take part in the revelry and enjoy great quantities of food and drink—drunkenness was actively encouraged as a means of honoring the gods.

The annual feast of Opet at Thebes was one of an important number of festivals designed to enhance and replenish the king's strength. During the festival, the sacred image of Amun, Egypt's national deity, was borne upriver amid scenes of jubilation from the attendant crowds from Karnak to Luxor temple, where the king took part in a secret rite in the inner shrine. This was followed by his public appearance, reinvigorated and god-like, before his subjects who, according to scenes represented on the walls of the temple, would dance ecstatically in celebration.

PALACE OF THE HAWK GOD

The temple of Horus at Edfu is the best-preserved of all ancient Egyptian temples. The present buildings stand on the site of the original New Kingdom structure, which was constructed along the standard east–west axis. However, most of the surviving edifices are relatively late—they were begun by Ptolemy III in 237BCE.

A detail of a 4th-dynasty funeral relief showing Princess Nefertiabet seated before an offering table ladened with bread and meat. It was important to honor the gods through such acts of generous consumption.

The inner parts of the temple were finished by 212BCE by Ptolemy IV, and Ptolemy VIII had completed their decoration by 142BCE. Ptolemy IX made further additions and the external decoration was completed by Ptolemy XII in 57BCE.

The Edfu temple has a *mammisi*—a structure associated with rituals surrounding the birth of the god Horus—carved with scenes featuring the figures of the pharaoh, Ptolemy VIII (170–164BCE, 145–116BCE), and his mother, wife, and child, accompanied by the god Bes, who was associated with childbirth. There are also scenes relating to the divine union between the god Horus and the goddess Hathor, an occasion celebrated at Edfu during the Feast of the Beautiful Meeting.

The temple is fronted by a massive pylon, decorated with huge figures of the king smiting his enemies, and flanked by large statues of Horus. Beyond the pylon, in the first court, various scenes depict rituals in which the monarch is purified and crowned, as well as festival processions and scenes of dancing and celebration associated with the meeting of Horus and Hathor.

In the ambulatory around the walls of the court, sunken relief scenes portray the "Triumph of Horus." In this ritual play, which was performed each year, Horus—personified by the king—defeated the forces of evil embodied in the figure of the god Seth (portrayed as a hippopotamus, which is depicted on a miniature scale in order to reduce the magical potency of the image).

On the far side of the court from the pylon is the entrance to the temple proper, flanked by two further statues of Horus. Inside, the first hypostyle (columned) hall is embellished with scenes showing the foundation ceremony of the temple complex. The hall also has its own library, which once contained texts used in sacred rituals, and a robing room, in which the priests' vestments were kept.

The second, and smaller, hypostyle hall beyond also houses storerooms for both solid and liquid offerings, as well as a wonderfully preserved perfume laboratory, the walls of which are inscribed with lengthy recipes for the preparation of the perfumes and incense that were made here for use during the daily rituals.

The temple's inner sanctuary contains the shrines in which the sacred cult statue of Horus originally resided. The statue was joined annually by the statue of Hathor, brought from the temple at Dendera for the Feast of the Beautiful Meeting.

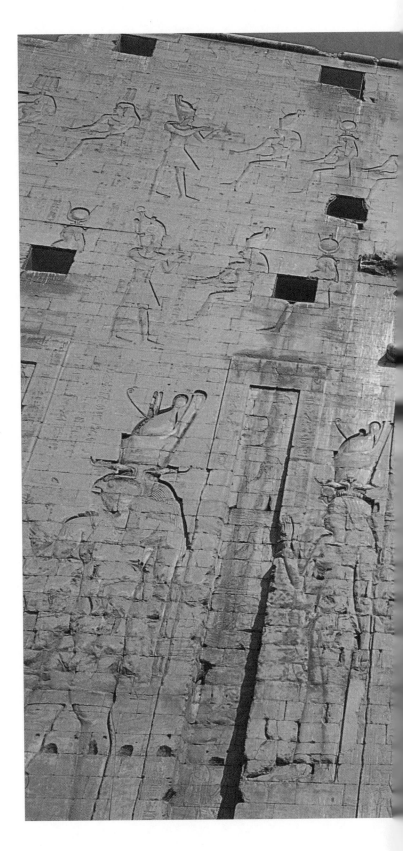

The entrance to Edfu temple is marked by this great pylon, which is carved with huge figures representing Horus among the gods. The vertical grooves in which the temple's enormous flagpoles were once inserted are still clearly visible. Above the gateway is a solar disk flanked by a pair of uraei *(sacred serpents).*

A BLESSED ETERNITY

The most familiar images of ancient Egypt—from mummies to pyramids—are all associated with death and burial, and the Egyptians have consequently long been thought of as a morbid people, obsessed with mortality. Yet nothing could be further from the truth.

Egyptians loved life so passionately that they wanted it to last forever, and did everything in their power to prolong it indefinitely. They preserved and wrapped the body, placed it in a secure tomb, and surrounded it with all the items essential for its eternal well-being in the blissful and prosperous realm of Osiris, lord of the underworld paradise.

The story of Isis and Osiris, in which Osiris is resurrected from the dead, helps to explain the Egyptians'

understanding of death as simply a continuation of life. At the beginning of the saga, Osiris and Isis, his sister and wife, ruled over Egypt during a golden age of peace and prosperity. But their jealous brother, Seth—the lord of chaos—envied their happiness and success, and plotted to murder Osiris and seize the throne for himself.

Seth invited Osiris to a banquet, at which he tricked his unsuspecting brother into trying out a fine coffin

that he had commissioned. As soon as Osiris was inside, Seth sealed the coffin and flung it into the Nile—Osiris drowned and death was created.

Following the murder, the distraught Isis managed to retrieve her husband's body, only to have it snatched away from her by Seth, who savagely dismembered it and scattered the pieces far and wide across Egypt. Not to be deterred, Isis adopted the form of a kite and took to the skies with her sister, Nephthys, and together they managed to retrieve each part. The god's head, for example, was found at Abydos and his heart at Athribis. Every site at which one of Osiris's body parts was found later became a place of pilgrimage associated with his worship. Isis then put Osiris's body back together with the help of Anubis, the god of embalming, and so produced the first mummy. All subsequent mummies were believed to be protected by the god who had preceded them.

This scene is from the Book of the Dead produced in about 1285BCE for a royal scribe, Hunefer. It depicts the passage of the deceased (shown, far left and center, wearing white robes) through "the Hall of Two Truths," the final stage before entering the afterlife. Anubis weighs the heart of the deceased to determine whether he is worthy of passing into the afterlife. Thoth records the verdict and Horus leads the successful candidate to the throne of Osiris. (See also pages 53–54.)

Using her immense magical powers, Isis then restored Osiris back to life and reinvigorated him temporarily so that she could conceive their son, Horus. Isis quite literally created new life from death—a miraculous act captured in a number of relief scenes and sculpture. She raised Horus in secret, and he grew up to reclaim the throne from his usurping uncle, Seth (see box, page 33).

While Horus became the king on Earth, his resurrected father, Osiris, became lord of the underworld. The embodiment of justice and righteousness, Osiris guaranteed salvation to all those who died and were judged worthy of everlasting life in the underworld paradise. For the ancient Egyptians, he gave eternal hope to the living.

PREPARING FOR THE AFTERLIFE

In ancient Egyptian belief, the preservation of the corpse—mummification—was fundamental to the continuation of life after death. In the earliest period of the country's history, bodies were simply placed into hollows in the sand, where they were dessicated and preserved naturally by the hot, dry conditions. As burial practices among the élite became increasingly sophisticated, purpose-built, rectangular tombs (mastabas) replaced burial in the sand (see page 25), and natural preservation gave way to artificial preservation techniques. The word "mummy" itself comes from moumia, the Persian word for "bitumen"—the substance that the Egyptians were once, wrongly, believed to have used in the preservation of bodies.

As the mummification process became more refined and elaborate, all internal organs, except for the heart and kidneys, were removed and preserved separately inside what are known as "canopic jars." Meanwhile, the eviscerated body was dried out beneath a layer of natron salts. The corpse was then washed and purified,

---

In this illustration, from the Book of the Dead buried with the scribe Ani (ca. 1290BCE), the deceased is shown plowing, reaping, and threshing; sailing across the Lake of Offerings; and worshipping a range of gods including Re, the seven Hathor cows, and the Heron of Plenty.

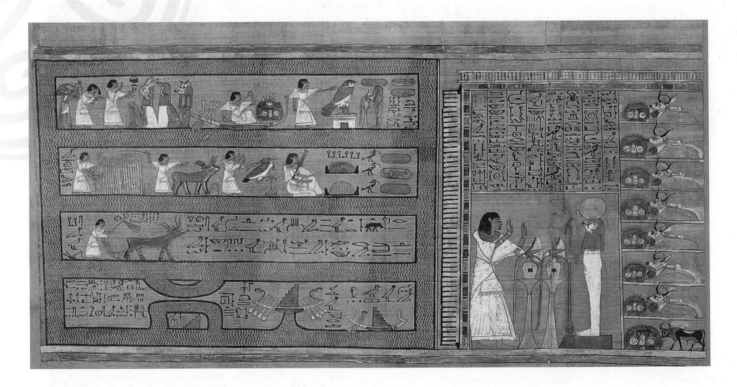

the incision sewn up, and the skin anointed with a variety of oils, spices, and resins. Finally, the body was wrapped in fine linen bandages. Instructions in the "Book of the Dead"—the Egyptian "handbook" for ensuring the deceased's proper burial and safe passage into paradise—state that the dead had to be "pure, clean, clothed in fresh linen, and anointed with the finest myrrh oil," in order to enter the afterlife.

As the embalmers wrapped the body, protective amulets were placed among the bandages while priests recited the incantations needed to activate them. Following the standard seventy-day embalming process, the prepared corpse—complete with its funerary mask depicting the deceased as living and youthful—was placed in its coffin. It was then ready for the ritual funeral procession, accompanied by priests, *muu* dancers, mourners, and servants carrying all the necessary funerary equipment.

Before the tomb, and amid clouds of purifying incense, the priests performed the "Opening of the Mouth" ceremony, essential for reanimating the *ka* (soul) and senses of the deceased. The noise and movement of music and dancing were believed to reactivate hearing and sight; incense and flowers brought back the sense of smell; and offerings of choice cuts of meat and wine enabled the deceased to eat and drink in the afterlife. The standard offering formulae recited during this ceremony request for the deceased "a thousand of every good and pure thing for your *ka* and all kinds of offerings on which the gods live."

The reanimated mummy was then laid to rest in its tomb and surrounded by funerary objects ranging from items used in daily life to those designed specifically for burial, such as the Book of the Dead and other instructive funerary texts, and *shabti*s (magical figurines that were believed to come to life and act as servants for their owner). With the funeral complete, the deceased set out from the tomb on a hazardous journey through the underworld—which culminated in his or her judgment before the throne of Osiris, the lord of the dead.

• THE VALLEY OF THE KINGS •

As the sun sank into the Theban Hills on the western horizon, dead souls sank down into the eternal embrace of Hathor, goddess of the West, who was regularly shown emerging from the hillside at her sacred site of Deir el-Bahari. Here, the Eleventh-dynasty king Nebhepetre Mentuhotep II (ca. 2008–1957BCE) was laid to rest in his tomb below his funerary temple, surrounded by six priestesses of the goddess, who would protect his spirit.

The later New Kingdom pharaohs, from Amenhotep I to Ramesses XI, also associated Deir el-Bahari with Hathor, but amended the earlier arrangement by constructing a separate temple and tomb; their funerary temples, which face the river, remain highly visible, whereas their tombs were hidden in the valleys on the other side of the hills. The main valley—named after the kings buried within its depths—is marked by the natural pyramid shape of the Theban Peak, a rock known to the Egyptians by the apt name of Meretseger, or "She who Loves Silence." The superbly decorated rock-cut tombs include the huge funerary chambers of Thutmose III, Amenhotep II, Horemheb, Sety II, and the later Ramesside kings. Favorite courtiers, such as Yuya and Thuya, were also occasionally buried here as a mark of honor.

IN THE HALL OF OSIRIS

The judgment before Osiris (see illustration, pages 50–51) was the key stage in the transformation of the deceased into an *akh*—a spirit that could help its living relatives. In a chamber of the underworld called "the Hall of Two Truths," the deceased was led by Anubis before Osiris, god of the underworld and ultimate judge of the dead, and forty-two gods making the assessment. The deceased was presented with a long list of sins and had to deny each in turn. Anubis tested the veracity of their denials by weighing their heart—the seat of thought and consciousness—against a feather representing *ma'at* (truth). If heart and feather were of equal weight, the deceased was declared "true of voice" and "justified." Thoth recorded the judgment and Horus led the deceased to the throne of Osiris—and from there they passed into the blessed afterlife. But if the heart was heavy with sin and tipped the scales, it was thrown to Ammut, a hybrid monster that annihilated evildoers by devouring their hearts.

VISIONS OF PARADISE

The Egyptians' ultimate aim was to live forever in their beloved homeland; they envisaged eternal paradise as simply a continuation of their lives on Earth, albeit with a few refinements. In the idealized afterlife, the *shabti* figures (see page 53) would perform all manual work—detailed models placed in tombs often represented the kind of activities they would perform. Harvests would be enormous, and drought and illness nonexistent. The deceased and their families would enjoy banquets and boating trips, or relax in their flower gardens. An inscription on Tutankhamun's drinking cup expresses the ultimate Egyptian wish: "May your soul live, may you spend millions of years, O lover of Thebes, with your face to the north wind and your eyes beholding happiness."

To help the deceased reach blessed eternity, funerary texts acted as a kind of guidebook to the afterlife. The earliest surviving maps from Egypt are those depicting the route to the afterlife in texts known as "The Book of Two Ways," which were painted on the inside of Middle Kingdom coffins. Later incantations in the New Kingdom Book of the Dead are entitled "Spell for Not Dying a Second Time," "Spell Not to Rot and Not to Do Work in the Land of the Dead," and "Spell for Not Having your Magic Taken Away"—as well as "Spells of Transformation," which would change the deceased's form to facilitate his or her passage through the underworld. One magic formula for transforming the dead person into a lotus states: "I am this pure lotus flower that has ascended by the sunlight and is at the nose of the sun god, Re. I am the pure lotus that ascends upward." The lotus opening its petals at dawn symbolized the morning sun emerging from the darkness of night, and, similarly, life arising from the darkness of death.

Funerary texts present several conceptions of paradise. Thus the deceased may inhabit the underworld with Osiris; or rise up to the heavens to become one of the "Imperishable Stars" (see below); or join the sun god, Re, in his "Barque of the Millions" in its journey across the sky. Later myths incorporate the Re and Osiris stories, as the two gods meet each night in the underworld on the sun's voyage through the darkness. As with the various creation myths (see pages 22–24), the acceptance of a range of ultimate destinations for the deceased is typical of the Egyptians' tolerant and multifaceted belief system.

THE HEAVENLY REALM

The Egyptians studied the movements of the moon and stars from observatories situated on their temple roofs, and a section of the priesthood was trained in astronomy to ensure that the necessary rituals were performed at the correct hour. Stellar motifs were often used to embellish the ceilings of both temples and tombs. Many of these decorations depict the sky goddess Nut as a star-covered woman stretching out above the surface of the Earth—she is often shown performing a similar act of protection over the deceased on the inside of their coffins lids. The coffin lid depicting Nut, opposite, dates to the latest period of ancient Egyptian history, but references to the sky goddess have been found in sources as early as the Old Kingdom Pyramid Texts (see page 25).

The dead themselves were also thought to rise up to join the ranks of the "Imperishable Stars," a term used of the stars around the Pole Star, which were visible in the night sky at all times of the year. This belief is first referred to in the Pyramid Texts. By the Middle Kingdom, sarcophagus lids were decorated with

The interior of the painted wooden coffin lid of Soter, dating to the 2nd century CE, was found on the Theban west bank. It shows the Egyptian sky goddess Nut stretching out over the deceased in her traditional pose. The figures are all represented in a more Hellenized form—even the goddess's hairstyle reflects the late date of the piece. Nut's position in the heavens among the stars is also bordered by the newly introduced Babylonian-Greek zodiac, which uses the 12 horoscope symbols still familiar to us today.

calendars illustrated with images of stars, especially Sothis (Sirius, the Dog Star), whose ascension on 19 July coincided with the beginning of the Nile inundation and marked the Egyptian New Year.

By the Middle Kingdom, the Egyptians had also identified five of the planets, and pictured them, like the Sun, in the guise of various gods sailing in their barques across the heavens: Mars was "Horus of the Horizon," or "Horus the Red"; Jupiter was "Horus who Limits the Two Lands" (or "the Glittering Star"); Saturn was "Horus, Bull of the Sky." Mercury was identified with Seth, and Venus was "the God of the Morning." The Egyptians recognized many of the constellations that we know today, although they perceived them to represent different images. Orion—one of the most important constellations in Egyptian astronomy—was seen as a man holding a staff and was identified with the god Osiris. There is a theory that the three Giza pyramids were built to align with Orion's Belt.

The Egyptian calendar was divided into "lucky" and "unlucky" days, in accordance with the annual cycle of religious festivals and mythical events. However, astrology did not reach Egypt until the Ptolemaic era, inspired by a combination of Babylonian and Greek beliefs. The famous Dendera Zodiac (see page 22) and a number of Roman coffins portray Nut surrounded by the signs of the zodiac. Magical papyri from this late period also feature auspicious star signs, and there are a variety of late astrological works attributed to Thoth in his Greco-Roman guise of Hermes Trismegistos.

CHAPTER TWO

MESOPOTAMIA AND PERSIA

The rediscovery of Mesopotamia may be archaeology's greatest triumph. Apart from a few unflattering references in the Bible and the Greek historian Herodotus, the land between the rivers Tigris and Euphrates in what is now Iraq had almost been forgotten by the West. But from the early nineteenth century on, a series of pioneering excavations cast new light on this ancient world. Babylon, reviled in the Old Testament, turned out to have been a great cultural center. More surprisingly still, traces were discovered of an earlier civilization predating Babylon by more than a millennium. This was Sumer, 'the birthplace of urban culture', writing, and wheeled transport. Even before the ancient Egyptians, the Sumerians had led the way into the historical era. The Persians were eastern neighbors of the Mesopotamians. They were never forgotten as the Sumerians had been, if only because of the wars that the kings of their Achaemenid dynasty fought against the Greeks. Civilization was slower to develop on the high Iranian plateau than in the adjoining river valley. Yet in the long run, Achaemenid Persia would triumph over Babylon and its northern neighbor Assyria, even while it assimilated much of their culture.

THE FERTILE CRESCENT

It was in Mesopotamia that the first cities grew, the wheel was invented, and the arts and sciences flourished. New concepts of kingship and statehood evolved, and the world's earliest codes of law were promulgated. Above all, writing was pioneered and humankind began to create a record of the past by setting down king-lists and chronicles. And all these developments owed an eternal debt to farming.

The giant steps that were taken towards the growth of urban civilization five or six thousand years ago on the plains of southern Iraq were only possible because of the benefits derived from the development of farming some four or five thousand years prior to that. Before agriculture, humans had wandered the Earth in nomadic bands, supporting themselves by hunting game and gathering wild foods—fruit, berries, seeds, and roots. The demands of the hunting lifestyle required them to travel in extended-family groups, typically of about thirty people. Larger gatherings were only possible when the vagaries of the food supply could be

The plains of northern Mesopotamia—even those seen here at the foot of the inhospitable peaks of the Zagros Mountains—have supported crop cultivation since around 6500BCE and continue to do so today.

overcome—such as when the migrations of animal herds provided hunters with a plentiful supply of meat.

The agricultural revolution changed all that. The trigger was the ending of the last Ice Age, which not only released more land as the glaciers receded but also contributed to a population explosion. The hunter-gathering lifestyle had always ensured that the globe was thinly populated, for each band needed a vast swathe of territory to support its needs—about 250 square miles (650 sq km), to judge from modern-day hunting peoples. As a result, current estimates suggest that there may only have been 10 million humans, at most, inhabiting the globe at the start of the eighth millennium BCE. Even so, the pressures on the land were considerable, and people had good reasons for seeking a way to guarantee and expand their food supply.

The cultivation of crops was the revolution that enabled this expansion to take place. It happened in the Fertile Crescent, a stretch of productive land arcing northward around the Arabian desert and in close proximity to the Euphrates and Tigris rivers (see map, page 61). Mesopotamia formed the eastern part of the arc, yet in the early days its flat valleys lagged behind other parts of the region. The first farmers actually inhabited the hillier regions of Palestine, Syria, and eastern Anatolia, as well as the foothills of the Zagros Mountains on what is now the Iraq–Iran border. There they found a combination of plentiful game—for they continued to rely on hunting for much of their protein—and reliable rainfall, encouraging the growth of vegetation such as emmer wheat and barley, which in time became the first crops.

The process that turned strands of wild wheat and barley into cultivable crops was a slow one. The plants were hard to harvest because they shattered when ripe, scattering their seeds to the winds. Eventually, however, mutant strains that did not shatter developed. Over time, these domesticated crops became wholly dependent on humans to gather their seeds and replant them. In return, they provided a reliable food source that allowed the former nomads to settle down permanently to tend their crops.

The new lifestyle spread only gradually along the Fertile Crescent, not least because farming was harder work than hunter-gathering; with only primitive tools of stone and wood to help them, the early cultivators must have found the tasks of plowing, planting, and weeding back-breaking. But the payoff was obvious: if it took a large area of land to feed a band of thirty hunter–gatherers, a mere 5 square miles (15 sq km) of good soil could support a farming village of 150 people.

Farming reached northern Mesopotamia as early as 6500BCE. Over the next 1,500 years it spread throughout the region. The epicenter of the early cultures remained in the north, where an intricate form of painted pottery, Halaf ware, was circulating along trade routes by about 5700BCE. At this time much of southern Mesopotamia was a thinly inhabited marshy wasteland. Between 5000 and 3000 BCE, however, the situation was to change radically; the backwater would emerge as the testing-ground of a whole new way of life.

When the Mesopotamian hunter-gatherer tribes settled and formed villages, they began to make implements, such as this Halaf ware vase, that would not have been suited to their former nomadic lifestyle.

THE LAND BETWEEN
THE RIVERS

*In Egypt, Africa's first cities grew up along the banks of the Nile, while in what is now Pakistan the
Indus played host to another breakthrough culture. Farming may have got under way in the foothills
of the Fertile Crescent, but it was in the river valleys that urban civilization was created.*

Mesopotamia, meaning "the land between the rivers," owed its name to the Greeks. The rivers in question here were the Euphrates and the Tigris, the two greatest inland waterways between the Nile and the Indus. Both had their sources in the highlands at the top of the Fertile Crescent, the Tigris rising south of Lake Van in modern Turkey and the Euphrates close to Mount Ararat, where Noah found refuge from the biblical Flood.

The cultural area associated with Mesopotamia in fact extended well beyond the rivers themselves, forming a broad triangle with its base along the foothills of the northern mountains and its apex at the head of the Gulf. To the east it was bounded by the Zagros mountain chain, while on the west the fertile land quickly gave way to the desert that separated the Crescent's two arms. The hardy Zagros hill peoples and the nomadic desert tribes were both to play an important part in Mesopotamian history, taking advantage of any signs of political weakness to attack the rich cities of the plain.

Although it was well watered, Mesopotamia was at first sight an unlikely place for civilization to bloom. The southern plains had plenty of rich agricultural land but very little else. Fields of barley and wheat flourished there on a thick blanket of alluvial mud. Otherwise the region had few resources to offer. There were no large rocks in the soil and little in the way of trees beyond date palms and shrubs; both stone and timber had to be imported. The only real mineral resource was bitumen, which was put to many uses: it served as a mortar for building, and was used to caulk the hulls of boats and to provide a waterproof lining for drains. Metal ores were entirely absent, and had to be brought in from the mountains to the north and east.

To compound the region's problems, the climate ran to extremes. Temperatures rose as high as 120°F (50°C) in summer, while the winters were cold and bleak. The flat lands were frequently swept by scorching winds and dust storms, and were also liable to disastrous floods. There were few natural defensive barriers other than the rivers themselves, so the plains were always vulnerable to foreign invasion and citizens had to shelter behind high walls. Large areas of coastal land at the head of the Persian Gulf were waterlogged; the local people lived in reed huts built over the waters and moved around in reed boats, much as the Marsh Arabs do to this day.

Yet there were compensating advantages. The fecundity of the soil was almost unmatched: the silt carried down by the rivers and distributed by the annual floods acted as a natural fertiliser, refreshing land that would otherwise quickly have become exhausted by overcultivation. There were plenty of fish in the rivers and the sea, and dates and other fruits flourished in irrigated gardens. The open landscape that made the region easy to invade also encouraged peaceful contact, and from an early time Mesopotamia was a highway for trade, connecting the Gulf coast and the Indus Valley to Anatolia and the eastern Mediterranean lands. Overland routes from the east served as conduits to the high plateau of central Persia. Within Mesopotamia itself, the two great rivers provided natural channels of communication.

Over the centuries, these natural advantages were to prove more than a match for the liabilities. The bounty of the region's fields supported an expanding population that soon outgrew the early farming villages. Instead people gathered in small towns that eventually developed into great cities. From the mud laid down by the rivers a whole new way of life was born.

THE MESOPOTAMIAN AND PERSIAN WORLDS

Black Sea

LYDIA

ANATOLIA

Lake Sevan

TAURUS MOUNTAINS

• Sardis

Lake Van

Lake Urmia

Caspian Sea

Tigris River

Euphrates River

• Nineveh
• Nimrud

ASSYRIA

Assur •   • Arba-Ilu

MEDIA

ELBURZ MOUNTAINS

• Tehran

ZAGROS MOUNTAINS

Mediterranean Sea

Mari •

AKKAD

Ecbatana •

ELAM

• Baghdad

Babylon •
Nippur •

SUMER

EGYPT

Uruk •
Larsa •

Ur •

Lagash •

• Susa

Nile River

• Eridu

Anshan
•   • Pasargadae

• Persepolis

ARABIAN DESERT

PARSA

*Persian
Gulf*

Red Sea

N

• Dilmun

SCALE

0	500	1,000 km

0	250	500 miles

WATERS OF LIFE

For the peoples of Mesopotamia all life originated with water. In the beginning, the myths stated, there was a watery chaos in which salt and freshwater were mixed together, just as they were in reality at the mouths of the Tigris and Euphrates rivers.

Apsu and Tiamat were the gods of fresh water and salt water, respectively, and the great creation poem the *Enuma Elish* told how, at a time "when sweet and bitter/mingled together, no reed was plaited, no rushes/muddied the water,/the gods were nameless, natureless, futureless," the two came together and "from Apsu and Tiamat/in the waters gods were created, in the waters/silt precipitated ... ."

The myth aptly characterized the origins of the civilization that grew up where the great rivers met the sea. Mesopotamia was, in effect, a desert brought to life by their waters, and it would never have amounted to more than two thin bands of greenery along their banks had it not been for their propensity to flood. Their headwaters in the northern mountains were turned into rushing torrents each spring by a combination of snowmelt and

seasonal rains. In the southern Mesopotamian plains where the current slowed, silt carried down from the hills was deposited on the rivers' beds and banks, forming levees that eventually raised the water level above that of the surrounding land. Each year these natural embankments were breached when the seasonal rains swelled the rivers beyond the normal high-water mark.

In most years, such floods were entirely beneficial, bringing life to land that would otherwise have been baked dry. But they were never entirely predictable—less so, for example, than those of the Nile, whose waters filtered through great lakes on their way to Egypt. There were no such natural reservoirs to moderate the flow of the Tigris or Euphrates, which in years of heavy rainfall could swamp entire regions of southern Mesopotamia, wiping out livestock and drowning villages. Memories of terrible deluges fed through into legend, eventually influencing the biblical tale of Noah (see page 73).

Usually, though, drought presented the greater risk. Even areas that were regularly flooded soon dried out unless the life-giving water could somehow be preserved. By around 4000BCE local farmers had devised a way to trap the floodwater in reservoirs and to channel it via ditches and canals to areas that it otherwise would not have reached. Over the centuries the schemes became ever more complex, requiring large labor forces first to dig the watercourses and then to keep them clear of silt. At the same time, a considerable amount of social cooperation was necessary to settle questions of land rights and boundaries affecting the newly reclaimed land.

The Tigris and the Euphrates are calm for most of the year, as suggested by this view of the Euphrates. However, in spring the rivers become raging torrents when they are fed by snow-melt from the mountains.

• THE LAND OF DILMUN •

Water played a crucial part in Mesopotamian legends of an earthly paradise called Dilmun where, according to an early poem, "the raven croaks not/The lion does not kill/nor the wolf slaughter the lamb ... ." Yet this blessed spot lacked fresh water until the god Enki caused moisture to rise from the earth, turning Dilmun into a land of plenty. Trading records from Mesopotamia show that a place called Dilmun actually existed in early times, and modern scholars have identified it with the island of Bahrain in the Persian Gulf, which is where this drinking cup was found. Consistently with the legend, Bahrain is famed for its fertility, and is in fact largely watered through a subterranean aquifer feeding up through numerous artesian wells.

It is no exaggeration to say that irrigation created the southern Mesopotamian civilization, which is to say the world's first urban culture. The amount of organization and collaboration that it involved forced the inhabitants of different villages to work together, which led to the birth of towns. At the same time, the stunning success of the projects in increasing the area and the productivity of the cultivated land supplied the food surpluses essential for city life to develop. Thanks to irrigation and the natural fertilizer in the river waters, lands that would otherwise have been barren blossomed: according to the estimates of scholars who have studied ancient harvest records, their wheat yield could compare with that achieved by a major grain-producing land like Canada today.

THE LOST WORLD OF SUMER

History now records that urban civilization was born in Sumer, the name given to the great alluvial plain that makes up the southern half of Mesopotamia. Yet just 150 years ago the very name of Sumer, and of the Sumerian people who inhabited it, had been forgotten.

Readers of the Old Testament were familiar with cultural centers such as Babylon and Assyria, and classical sources made reference to Mesopotamia, but neither source went back further than about 1000BCE, by which time Mesopotamian civilization was already two and a half millennia old.

The rediscovery of the earlier chapters of the region's history and, in particular, the rehabilitation of Sumer as a great creator culture, is an extraordinary scholarly detective story. Archaeology and linguistics came together in a fruitful partnership to fill the gap.

The process got under way with the decipherment of Akkadian, the language spoken in Babylon and Assyria. The key was a trilingual inscription carved 300 feet (100m) up on a sheer cliff face at Behistun in western Iran. Carved to commemorate the feats of Persia's King Darius I, it carried its message not just in Akkadian but also in Old Persian, which had already been translated, as well as in a third language eventually identified as Elamite. The man who cracked the tongue was Henry Rawlinson, an English soldier and diplomat. First he risked his life to transcribe the inscriptions, perched on a ladder balanced on a narrow ledge; then he spent years puzzling out the vocabulary and grammar of the Akkadian text, finally publishing his findings in 1851.

Knowledge of the language was quickly put to good use when a series of excavations in the mid-nineteenth century turned up thousands of inscribed clay tablets. The greatest find was Henry Layard's discovery of the library of Assyria's King Ashurbanipal at Nineveh, where more than 24,000 tablets were unearthed.

As the translators started to work their way through this rich vein of material, they soon began to notice oddities. The cuneiform (wedge-shaped) script in which the texts were written did not seem naturally adapted to Akkadian, a Semitic tongue whose variable vowel sounds could not be expressed in cuneiform. These discrepancies led an Irish scholar named Edward Hincks to suggest in 1850 that the Akkadians had adopted the script from some earlier, non-Semitic people.

The first person to attach the name "Sumerian" to the script's inventors was a French linguist, Jules Oppert. He took his cue from the phrase "King of Sumer and Akkad" that appeared in some Akkadian inscriptions. Archaeology soon provided irrefutable evidence of Sumer's existence. In 1854, J.E. Taylor, an English consul in the city of Basra, made finds that enabled scholars to identify a mound in the southern desert with the city of Ur, mentioned in the Bible as the home of the patriarch Abraham. Then, from 1877, the French diplomat Ernest de Sarzec—also a consul at Basra—began excavations at a site called Telloh. This turned out to cover the remains of the Sumerian city of Girsu, which in time yielded a treasure trove of cuneiform tablets, cylinder seals, and magnificent statues that left no doubt as to the reality of Mesopotamia's earliest civilization.

Subsequent excavations at such sites as Uruk, Eridu, Lagash, and Nippur confirmed the extraordinary richness of the world's first urban culture. Sumer, it turned out, was a world of rival city-states, each with its own patron god and a supporting network of neighboring fields and villages. An extraordinary truth gradually emerged: that the desert landscape that makes up much of today's southern Iraq had once produced bumper crops, and that the mounds that rose forlornly from its wastes sheltered the remains of the world's oldest cities.

This Akkadian cuneiform tablet, with its distinctive wedge-shaped script, dates to the 14th century BCE and is a letter written by Burnaburrias, a king of the Cassite dynasty of Babylon, to the Egyptian king Amenhotep IV.

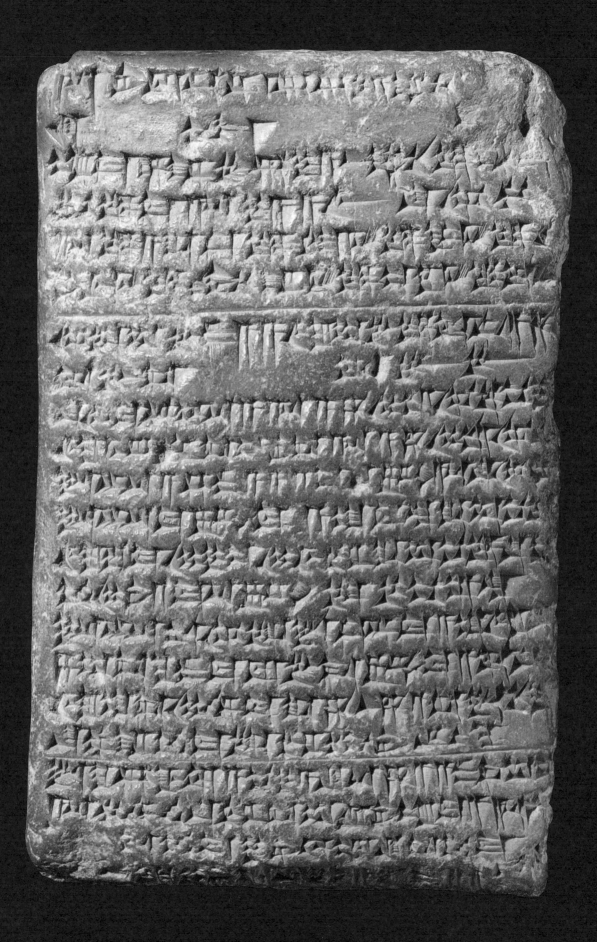

THE FIRST CITIES

The Mesopotamians themselves had a clear idea of where city living began. A clay tablet dating to about 2000BCE records that: "No reed had yet come forth; no tree had been created; no house had been built and no city existed. All the lands were sea. Then Eridu was made."

Eridu lay on the plain of Sumer about 13 miles (20km) southwest of Ur. Archaeologists who have explored the site have traced its history back through many layers of occupation to the start of Sumer's earliest culture, known as Ubaid from a site 4 miles (6km) from Ur where its artifacts were first discovered in 1919.

Historians today tend not to accord city status to anything built in the Ubaid period, which lasted from about 5900 to 4000 BCE. Villagers lived at the time in fragile reed huts rather like those built by the Marsh Arabs of southern Iraq into modern times. Lacking

metal and stone, they made most of their tools and utensils from fired clay. The evidence of graves suggests that they lived in an egalitarian society, with little distinction of class or rank. They fashioned bizarre terracotta statuettes of female figures with the heads of snakes or reptiles—no doubt representations of some local goddess.

Most significantly of all, the Ubaid people built temples. At Eridu the remains of no fewer than twelve separate structures have been identified, each one built on top of its predecessor once the mudbrick walls started to

crumble. The later examples were imposing structures with strong walls decorated with ornamental buttresses designed to relieve the monotony of the brickwork. Offerings of dried fish found even in the lower levels suggest that from early on the god worshipped there was Enki, a leading Sumerian deity who succeeded Apsu as the patron of fresh water. Significantly, Enki presided over irrigation, on which the whole civilization of Sumer was to be built.

To modern eyes, Eridu looks more like a town than a city, for all its undoubted significance in Sumer's early history. It extended over an area of only about 100 acres (40 hectares), and its population probably numbered in the thousands rather than tens of thousands. By the time that the Ubaid period came to an end it had been largely abandoned.

Most authorities agree that the first real city was Uruk, 50 miles (80km) to the north. Its remains were first identified in 1850 by the English archaeologist W.K. Loftus, although the site was not scientifically explored until the 1920s, when it was thoroughly investigated by a German team.

Like Babylon (Babel) and Sumer (Shinar), Uruk won a mention in the Old Testament under the name of Erech; it features with Babel and Akkad as one of the cities ruled by Nimrod, the "mighty hunter before the Lord." It may also have been the place referred to in the story of the Tower of Babel, as recounted in the Book of Genesis: "And as men migrated from the east, they found a plain in the land of Shinar and settled there. And they said to one another, 'Come, let us make bricks, and burn them thoroughly.' And they had bricks for stone, and bitumen for mortar. Then they said, 'Come, let us build ourselves a city, and a tower with

Uruk is commonly considered to be the first substantial Sumerian city and archaeologists have used its name to denote one of the earliest periods of Sumerian civilization (running from 4000 to 3200 BCE). Despite their age, these walls are remarkably well preserved.

its top in the heavens ... .'" Uruk was also the home of the legendary hero Gilgamesh (see pages 72–73), and a real-life ruler of that name appears on the king-list for the city.

Uruk's claim to pre-eminence rests partly on its size. Its outer wall, built early in the third millennium BCE, stretched for almost 6 miles (10km), enclosing an area of more than 1,200 acres (500 hectares). By that time the city may have had as many as 50,000 inhabitants. It had grown partly at the expense of the surrounding villages; archaeologists have estimated that there were at least 146 separate settlements in its vicinity in 4000BCE, but that six centuries later the figure had fallen to just twenty-four.

The newcomers were no doubt attracted by the extra economic opportunities that the city provided. While most villagers earned their living off the land, Uruk offered career openings for craftspeople—carpenters, sculptors, potters, metalsmiths, leatherworkers, weavers —as well as for tradespeople and merchants, administrators and priests. Prosperous citizens lived in two-story mudbrick houses, with wooden balconies on the upper floors. Even single-story buildings sometimes had several rooms, organized around a central courtyard.

Whatever their status, visitors to the city must have been awe-struck by its monumental buildings, which were unlike anything the world had ever seen before. As always in Sumer, the principal structures were temples. One was dedicated to Inana, goddess of love and sexuality; another, the White Temple, stood on an artificial mound 40 feet (12m) high. Yet it was the city wall itself that most impressed a Babylonian poet who, around the year 2000BCE, extolled Uruk in one of the many surviving versions of the *Epic of Gilgamesh* (see pages 72–73). "Look at it as it is today," he wrote. "The outer wall, where the cornice runs, shines with the brilliance of copper, and the inner wall has no equal. Touch the gateway —it is ancient. Climb on the walls of Uruk; walk along them, I say. Regard the foundation terrace and examine its construction—is it not burned brick and good?"

PATTERNS OF URBAN LIFE

Mesopotamia was an intensely urban culture. Cities pressed closely upon one another. Major centers such as Ur, Larsa, and Uruk were even in sight of each other, partly because the habit of building upon the rubble of earlier structures caused them to rise on mounds above the flat Sumerian plain.

Almost all the cities were ringed by monumental walls. These fortifications figured prominently in their civic self-image: conquerors would demolish them to break their enemies' pride as well as their defences. Beyond them stretched a patchwork of settlements and farms that served as suburbs. In Sumer there was no sharp divide between town and country. Many urban dwellers owned or worked plots in the surrounding fields, and Sumerian literature gives no hint of antagonism between urbanites and country dwellers; suspicions are reserved for the foreigners who lived beyond the pale of civilization in the mountains, forests, or deserts.

Within the walls all was noise and bustle. The residential quarters clustered higgledy-piggledy around a jumble of unplanned and unmade streets, cut at intervals by larger avenues. Amid the confusion, three focal points typically stood out. There would be the main temple compound, set within a walled enclosure. Smaller at first, but growing in size and importance as the centuries passed, was the palace complex where the city's ruler lived. Then, as most Sumerian cities were built either on the Euphrates itself or on a canal connected to the river, there would also be a harbor where river traffic docked. The port area was usually the main commercial district, for the wealthy traders and merchants had their offices nearby, and the surrounding streets resounded to the loading and unloading of cargo.

Even in the early days of city living there were good and bad neighborhoods. The quarters where the bulk of the population lived were crowded and evil-smelling,

This terracotta model of a flat-roofed house was found in western Syria and is believed to date to the 3rd millennium BCE. It may have been used as a votive offering.

for there was no organized refuse collection and household waste was simply dumped for stray animals to scavenge. Yet behind the blank, whitewashed walls that the houses presented to the street, each dwelling had its own small courtyard around which low-doored, windowless rooms clustered. This open area was the main stage on which daily life was played out: the cooking was done there over an open hearth, and families sheltered in its shade to relax and play. The surrounding rooms were topped by a flat roof made of palm planks topped by reeds covered in a layer of beaten earth. Families would sleep out on the roofs in the heat of summer, retreating indoors in winter.

Houses in the wealthier areas were similarly constructed, but sometimes rose two stories high, with a wooden balcony giving onto the courtyard. Inside the rooms, reed mats or terracotta tiles covered the beaten-earth floors. Furniture was sparse, for even well-to-do citizens often chose to sleep on reed mats rather than the table-like beds with built-in wooden bolsters that were the only available alternative. Wooden stools and chests made up most of the other furnishings, although there were also comfortable reed-backed chairs. There were no windows and only one small entrance-door giving onto the street, although some of the rooms had small vents near the ceiling, blocked by terracotta grids to keep out rats.

Social stratification was a natural consequence of the complexity of city life, which provided opportunities for many different occupations and stations. At the top of the social pyramid was the ruling élite of palace officials and chief priests, and at the bottom a subclass of slaves, many of them prisoners of war; others, however, were forced into slavery by debt, putting themselves and their families voluntarily into bondage in return for shelter and food. In between was a growing middle class, ranging from wealthy merchants and traders to a host of specialized craftspeople: potters, weavers, basketmakers, leatherworkers, jewellers, engineers.

What united these disparate citizens was a pride in their birthplace and a devotion to the god who watched over it from a sanctuary perched on top of the temple mound—the highest place in the city. They rejoiced, too, in the sophistication and opportunities for betterment provided by life in the city where, to quote the *Epic of Gilgamesh*, "the people are dressed in gorgeous robes, every day is a holiday, and the young men and girls are wonderful to see. How sweet they smell!"

Glass is one of the earliest artificial materials made by humankind. This fluted bottle (ca. 1300–1200BCE) was discovered in a grave at Ur by the English archaeologist Leonard Woolley (see pages 93–94).

THE VALUE OF WRITING

Writing—the Sumerians' most important legacy—was born out of administrative need. The more organized society became, the greater was its need for record-keeping. The first written documents were book-keepers' accounts, recording transactions or listing commodities.

From as early as 8000BCE, soon after the birth of agriculture, farmers in the Middle East used clay tokens to keep inventories. A cone shape, for example, might stand for barley; the size of the token, bigger or smaller, served to indicate the amount involved. In later times merchants adopted the tokens to serve as bills of lading accompanying goods that they were transporting or selling. The tokens were placed in balls of clay known as *bullae*, which were then sealed. The trader would scratch a numerical sign on the outside of the *bulla* to show how many tokens it contained.

Writing first developed as an extension of the *bulla* system. Instead of scratching marks on clay balls, temple scribes started making inscriptions on square or rectangular tablets of clay, each one about the size of a hand. At first the signs used were purely pictographic: an image of a hut meant "house," several heads of oxen represented "cattle." The tablets served to register the contributions paid by farmers as a tax to the temple granaries. Soon merchants were also using the tablets to take stock of their commodities, and administrators to record payments in kind to workers and craftspeople.

Even for record-keeping, however, the limitations of the pictograms soon became apparent. Abstract concepts could not easily be depicted pictorially, and neither could verbs, adjectives, or conjunctions.

• CYLINDER SEALS •

From about 4000BCE, at roughly the same time that writing was developing, Sumerians started using seals as marks of ownership. At first they chose simple stamps, but soon switched to cylinder seals—hollow tubes of stone or terracotta inscribed with markings that were particular to each individual. The example, right, was found in the royal cemetery at Ur and dates to ca. 2600BCE. Usually less than 2 inches (5cm) long, the seals were worn on a string or chain around their owner's throat, and were as essential a part of daily equipment as credit cards are today.

When rolled in wet clay, the seals left a unique impression that identified their owner. They could be used to sign clay tablets, but were also impressed on stoppers set over jars of food or drink to prevent tampering. Some householders even placed a clay seal stamped with their mark on the doors of their houses when they went out; they could then check to see if they had had unexpected visitors on their return.

The seals themselves were often exquisitely carved with images from everyday life —animals and plants were popular motifs. Some show religious rituals or mythological scenes, providing a valuable visual record of life in the first cities 5,000 years ago.

Pictographic script was also inefficient in that it needed a huge number of symbols; at least 2,000 separate characters were in use in Uruk in the early days.

The result was a gradual transition to a more phonetic form of writing, in which each mark on the tablet represented a sound rather than a physical object. Words were now represented not by a single picture but rather by a combination of marks. One effect was to substantially reduce the alphabet, to a total of about 600 symbols.

The form of writing also changed. To prepare a tablet, a scribe took a handful of clean, well-washed clay and shaped it into a smooth cushion. In the early days the scribe would then have used a cut reed to draw images on the wet clay, working in vertical columns from right to left. But drawing on clay was never easy, and people quickly learned that they could create a neater script by pressing marks into the surface than by drawing the stylus through it. The widest range of impressions was obtained by cutting the reed stem in a V shape that left wedges in the clay, leading the script to be known in later days as cuneiform ("wedge-shaped"). Scribes also in time abandoned the vertical columns, which smudged easily, in favour of horizontal lines written from left to right, like Western scripts today.

For the first centuries writing was a purely utilitarian skill, although one that required lengthy schooling for those who practiced it. From about 2500BCE on, though, it was used to record hymns and stories as well as business dealings, and literature was born. Cuneiform script also proved adaptable to other languages, and was adopted across large areas of the Middle East. In Mesopotamia itself it was still in use in the first century CE, more than three millennia after it first developed.

THE *EPIC OF GILGAMESH*

More than a thousand years before the Iliad *and the* Odyssey, *Mesopotamia had its own great work of literature. Like the Homeric poems, the* Epic of Gilgamesh *was not the creation of any one person. Instead it drew together a number of separate Sumerian poems, some of them dating back well into the third millennium* BCE.

The different sources for the *Epic of Gilgamesh* were woven together into a single work some time between 2000 and 1500 BCE, not in their original Sumerian tongue but in Akkadian, the language of Sumer's Semitic conquerors. Akkadian went on to become the main language of Mesopotamia, thereby ensuring the epic's survival through the centuries.

Gilgamesh's Sumerian roots are not in doubt. He was a real-life king of the city-state of Uruk. As the *Epic of Gilgamesh* tells the story, he was something of a tyrant, and no virgin in the city was safe from his insatiable sexual appetites. The citizens complained to the gods, who decided that he should meet his match. So they created a being of equal power, Enkidu, a wild man who lived in a state of nature beyond the reach of civilization. To tame him, a prostitute was sent from the city. She seduced him, and through the sexual act Enkidu lost the innocence that had previously allowed him to commune with animals. Instead he adopted the ways of civilization and headed for Uruk.

In the city he challenged Gilgamesh to a wrestling bout, and the two champions fought to a draw. Seized by mutual respect, they became firm friends, closer than brothers. To cement the bond, they set off on a perilous quest, back to the wilderness from which Enkidu had so recently emerged. They headed for the dangerous hill country to take on Huwawa, the Guardian of the Forest. With divine assistance they overcame this formidable giant and killed him, despite his pleas for mercy.

The two returned to Uruk in triumph. The love goddess Ishtar herself now offered her favors to Gilgamesh, who rashly spurned her advances. Incensed, she persuaded her father Anu to send a fearsome beast, the Bull of Heaven, to devastate Uruk. But the two heroes killed that monster too.

By their acts the heroes had stirred the wrath of the gods, who punished them for their presumption by

---

The slaying of Huwawa by Gilgamesh and Enkidu is one of the most celebrated episodes in the Epic of Gilgamesh. *Huwawa, the Guardian of the Forest, was often portrayed in Mesopotamian art, as in this face mask of the monster, found at Susa.*

causing the death of Enkidu. Grief-stricken for his friend, Gilgamesh determined to set off on a fresh quest. This time his goal was philosophical: he wanted to learn why people die and to find the secret of eternal life.

The search took him to the edge of the world, where he encountered Utnapishtim, the only man ever to have been granted immortality by the gods. Utnapishtim recounted his story—the tale of the Flood (see box, below). He also told Gilgamesh that death is the lot of all humankind. Gilgamesh refused to accept the fact, however, so Utnapishtim set him two challenges. First, he defied him to stay awake for seven nights. When Gilgamesh failed to do so, Utnapishtim next told him of a plant growing on the ocean's bed that could restore lost youth. Gilgamesh succeeded in obtaining the plant, only to have it snatched away by a serpent while he was bathing. After this second failure he finally came to accept that he too would have to die, for "wherever my foot rests, there I find death." He returned to Uruk a sadder and wiser man, aware that the best he could hope for was to leave as his monument the great deeds he had accomplished.

The *Epic of Gilgamesh* is the enduring masterpiece of Mesopotamian literature, evoking great themes that still resonate today. In its own era it was regarded as a classic across much of the Middle East, and the story was told and retold in slightly different versions for more than two thousand years.

• THE STORY OF THE FLOOD •

In 1872 George Smith, a young Assyriologist working at the British Museum, created a sensation by declaring that he had found a fragment of text that appeared to be from a Mesopotamian version of the biblical Flood story. The sentence read: "On Mount Nisir, the ship landed; Mount Nisir held the ship fast, allowing no motion." The following year the *Daily Telegraph* in London, England, sponsored an archaeological expedition to find the remaining fragments of the story, which Smith unearthed on the fifth day of excavation. Further research showed that his findings formed part of the *Epic of Gilgamesh*, which at the time had still to be fully translated.

The Babylonian Noah was a king named Utnapishtim who, like his Old Testament counterpart, received divine warning of a world-destroying flood and built an ark to save his family and various animals. The stories coincided down to such details as the release of three birds (in the Babylonian version, a dove, a swallow, and a raven) to find dry land when the waters stopped rising.

THE BIRTH OF LAW

As Mesopotamian society became more complex with the growth of cities, the need for established rules of conduct grew. Kings met the demand by issuing collections of laws, each based on precedent and intended to establish a uniform jurisdiction for all citizens.

The earliest surviving set of laws was promulgated by Ur-Nammu, founder of the Third dynasty of Ur, in about 2100BCE. His laws, written in the Sumerian language, are known from two damaged tablets, found respectively at Ur and Nippur. Only seventeen of the ordinances are legible, but they have surprised historians by their humanity and egalitarianism: in place of "an eye for an eye," the world's earliest known laws embraced the principle of monetary compensation for harm done. The preamble spelled out the king's intention to protect the poor and the weak, so that "the orphan is not given over to the rich man, the widow to the powerful man, nor the man of one *shekel* to the man of one *mina*." (One *mina* in Sumerian currency was worth sixty *shekel*s, and is thought to have had the value of an 18 ounce [500g] bar of silver.) The fine imposed for severing a bone with a weapon was one *mina*, while cutting a man's nose off cost the offender two-thirds of a *mina*.

Sumerian justice was officially dispensed by the king, although in practice he often delegated the job to a panel of justices. There were no juries. Typical court procedure involved requiring the plaintiff and the accused to swear to the truth of their claims before the gods. If both stuck to conflicting stories, the judges in extreme cases looked for direct divine guidance via trial by ordeal. The accused was thrown into a river to sink or swim; survival was taken as proof of innocence. Court verdicts could be appealed to the king.

The most complete set of laws to have survived from early times is the Code of Hammurabi, named after the king of Babylon from about 1800BCE. Hammurabi was the sixth in line of the Amorite dynasty that built up the Old Babylonian Empire, and his laws reflect the harsher traditions of the Semitic desert tribes. The death penalty was prescribed for robbery or false or unproven accusations of murder, while a woman who had her husband killed for love of another man faced impalement. There were also alarming sanctions for professional incompetence: if a house fell down killing the occupants, the builder faced death; a surgeon whose malpractice caused a patient's death could have his hand amputated.

Sexual misconduct was severely punished. A man found guilty of having intimate relations with his own daughter could be sentenced to exile; sleeping with a

---

• SUMERIAN PROVERBS •

Wisdom literature is one of the most ancient literary genres, well exemplified by the biblical Book of Proverbs. Yet this form of writing predates the Bible by many centuries, shown by the discovery of Mesopotamian collections dating to the early second millennium BCE. The Sumerian sayings have a wry worldly-wisdom all of their own, as the following examples suggest:

For his pleasure, marriage.
On his thinking it over: divorce.

Friendship lasts a day.
Kinship endures forever.

The man with much silver may be happy;
The man with much grain may be glad;
But the man who has nothing can sleep.

You may have a lord, you may have a king,
But the man to fear is the tax collector.

---

daughter-in-law brought the risk of death by drowning; and a mother and son who committed incest could be burned alive. Couples caught in adultery might be bound together and drowned unless the woman's husband agreed to forego the punishment.

Even so, Hammurabi's laws took mitigating circumstances into account. Infidelity in a woman was normally harshly punished, but a prisoner's wife who slept with another man "because there was no food in her house" incurred no penalty. The code allowed the husband of a woman with an incurable disease to marry again, but insisted that he should continue to support the sick woman. Children were protected against being undeservedly disinherited.

Such humanitarian impulses have no echo in a set of laws found in the ruins of Assur and dating from five or six centuries later. The attitude they adopted toward women was brutal, reflecting the values of an entirely male-dominated society. Wives in the Assyrian code were treated simply as chattels of their husbands. If the husband did wrong, his wife could be punished in his place; for example, a husband who raped a virgin might be sentenced to have his own wife raped and taken away from him. If a man struck another's wife, causing her to miscarry, his own pregnant wife might be treated in the same way. Even when a wife had committed no statutory offence, the law stipulated that her husband had the right to flog her, pull out her hair, or split her ears without incurring any legal liability. By an odd reversal of normal ideas of social progress, legislation in Mesopotamia seems to have moved backward from the relatively humane criteria of Sumerian times to an altogether more savage interpretation in the militaristic society of Assyria.

The 282 laws of the Code of Hammurabi are inscribed on this black basalt stela, which can be seen in the Louvre museum in Paris. At the top of the monolith is an engraving of Hammurabi (left) receiving the laws from Shamash, the god of justice.

WARS OF THE REGIONAL RIVAL STATES

When Sumer emerged into history, it consisted of about a dozen separate city-states. Like their counterparts in Renaissance Italy 4,500 years later, each city-state controlled an agricultural periphery of estates and farming villages and was engaged in a fierce rivalry with the others.

Sumer's abiding political weakness was that it never found a way of surmounting the divisions between its city-states. The result was a chronic state of warfare. Boundary disputes sparked many conflicts, as did wrangles over water rights, while the lack of natural defences on the Sumerian plain was a further issue. Throughout their history Sumer and its people were open to attack by both the Semitic nomads of the western desert and the mountain peoples of the Zagros foothills to the east.

In the constant jockeying for power, one city-state after another gained ascendancy. The first to claim overlordship seems to have been Kish, followed by Uruk and then Ur. From about 2500BCE two neighbors, Lagash and Umma, fought for supremacy. At first King Eanatum of Lagash managed to impose his will. Before long, however, a new ruler of Umma, Lugalzagesi, succeeded in turning the tables on the conquerors.

Lugalzagesi in his turn was defeated soon after, in his case to the first great empire-builder known to history. This was Sargon of Akkad, a region to the north of Sumer near to where modern Baghdad is now situated. The Akkadian people had infiltrated Mesopotamia from

◆ THE STANDARD OF UR ◆

Discovered by Leonard Woolley (see pages 93–94) in the 1920s, the Standard of Ur provides a vivid glimpse of the power structure in Sumer in the third millennium BCE. Its exact function remains uncertain, although Woolley himself believed that it was designed to be carried in royal processions. Its two faces depict Sumerian society at peace and war. The military side (right) shows the outcome of a successful campaign waged by an unknown ruler of Ur in about the year 2500BCE. The king appears at top center, surveying prisoners of war. The middle band shows caped infantrymen escorting captives; the soldiers are clutching spears and marching in step. At the bottom two-man chariots drawn by asses surge forward over dead enemy fighters.

the arid lands to the west over a period of centuries, and had come to share the culture of the Sumerians, but for one crucial difference: they spoke the Semitic Akkadian tongue, unrelated to the non-Semitic Sumerian language.

Under Sargon's rule, the focus of Sumerian civilization moved north. In a fifty-five-year reign he fought campaigns to all points of the compass, creating an empire that eventually stretched from the Persian Gulf to the Mediterranean Sea. Trade expanded, and ships journeyed regularly from the Mesopotamian river-ports to Dilmun (modern Bahrain) and to a country referred to in the texts as Meluhha, thought to have been the great Indus Valley civilization of what is now Pakistan.

Sargon's empire flourished briefly after his death, but within a century it had fallen apart. A period of anarchy ensued in which the Gutians, a hill people from the Zagros, seized much of northern Mesopotamia. This was a time of brief, little-remembered reigns, summed up laconically in the Sumerian king-list by the dismissive phrase: "Who was king? Who was not king?"

Order was finally restored by Ur-Nammu, founder of the Third dynasty of Ur. Under his rule and that of his successors Sumerian culture enjoyed a golden age in which literature and the arts flourished, as did bureaucracy; most of the Sumerian administrative records that have survived date from this time. Ur-Nammu was also a builder, and the ziggurat (stepped temple) he constructed for the moon-god Nanna at Ur was the largest yet seen, rising more than 65 feet (20m) high (see illustration, page 80).

Ur's renaissance also turned out to be Sumer's swan-song. In the course of the twenty-first century BCE, Amorite raiders from the western desert cut off the city's trading links to the north, severing essential lines of supply. Famine and unrest swept the southern plains. The *coup de grâce* was delivered by the Elamites of southwestern Iran, who in 2006 sacked Ur itself. Mesopotamian civilization as a whole recovered from the blow, but thereafter the Sumerian plain would be something of a backwater. Instead, the action moved north to the new powers of Babylon and Assyria.

THE PATH TO KINGSHIP

The wars between Sumer's city-states created a need for military leaders. Although the sources are vague about their structure of government in the early days, there is some evidence suggesting that decisions were taken by a

Known for his law code (see pages 74–75), Hammurabi, king of Babylon (ruled 1792–1750BCE), also built an empire that marked the end of Sumer as a separate political entity. This bronze and gold figure is believed to be of Hammurabi, praying to the god Amurru.

council of elders. In times of crisis, such a body would no doubt have felt obliged to appoint a single commander to coordinate the war effort. Over time, as periods of emergency grew more frequent, the war leaders would have held power for longer, gradually extending their authority beyond purely military matters.

By the first half of the third millennium BCE power had passed into the hands of individuals called *ensi*s. These officials had started to take on religious duties that had earlier fallen to the *en*, or high priest. The most important was the New Year's Day festival, when the *ensi* ascended to the shrine set on top of the city's main ziggurat or stepped temple (see pages 80–81). There he was symbolically joined in marriage to a priestess representing Inana, the goddess of fertility. In at least some cities the union went beyond mere symbolism and involved a sexual act. (In cities where a male god was worshipped, the priestess took the place of the *ensi*.) This ritual was thought to ensure the fecundity of the fields and the livestock, which was essential for the citizens' survival.

Although ultimate power now rested with the *ensi*, he was still expected to seek the counsel of his fellow citizens before settling on a course of action. A poetic fragment describing a dispute between two city-states some time early in the third millennium BCE spells out the procedure. Its hero is Gilgamesh—the same one celebrated in the great Sumerian epic (see pages 72–73). In this shorter, more realistic work, Gilgamesh appears in his real-life role as *ensi* of Uruk, confronted with an ultimatum from the lord of Kish, who apparently claimed rights of overlordship over Uruk. Gilgamesh has to decide whether to submit to his demand or to fight it. First he consults the elders of the city, who counsel submission. Their response displeases Gilgamesh, who then turns to a second body, that of "the fighting men of the city"—presumably a general assembly of all those of military age. They opt for armed confrontation. Gilgamesh, we learn, was delighted with their decision: "His heart rejoiced, his spirit brightened."

The question of overlordship grew increasingly important as the third millennium drew on. The Sumerians had a separate word for a ruler who claimed authority over more than one city-state: *lugal*, meaning literally "great man." The names of many of the *lugal*s

have been preserved in the Sumerian king-list, a document dating from the early second millennium but drawing on earlier material. This text divides Sumer's history into eras before and after the Flood, which, in Mesopotamian legend as in the Bible, almost destroyed humankind; the king-list dates it to sometime around 3000BCE. The antidiluvian rulers it enumerates belong firmly to the realm of myth, and are ascribed obviously improbable lifespans: eight of them are said to have ruled in Eridu for a total of 241,200 years.

The kings listed after the Flood are more historical, and the later ones have realistic reign lengths, measured in decades rather than centuries. Gilgamesh figures among them, as do Eanatum and Sargon of Akkad. Although the king-list presents a picture of one city-state dynasty succeeding another to the overlordship in orderly succession, other surviving documents reveal that the picture was actually more complicated. Many of the dynasties overlapped, and there must have been continual friction as they vied for supremacy.

All Mesopotamian rulers, whether *ensis* or *lugals*, were thought of as the earthly representatives of the patron god of the city they served, and so needed the support of the priesthood if they were to fulfill their functions satisfactorily. As the cities grew, so too did the bureaucracies that ran them. By the time of Sargon of Akkad the ruler could count in addition on the backing of a standing army, to judge from a text indicating that "5,400 soldiers ate in [Sargon's] presence daily".

Yet even the greatest rulers, Sargon among them, failed to found lasting dynasties. No enduring royal line like that of the pharaohs of Egypt ever developed in Mesopotamia; the forces of local separatism were too strong and the external threat was always too great. In the resigned words of a Sumerian proverb, "You go and carry off the enemy's land; the enemy comes and carries off your land." Even in the royal palaces, insecurity was the only lasting certainty.

This copper frieze (ca. 2600BCE) comes from the Temple of Ninhursag at Tell al-'Ubaid near Ur. Ninhursag was one of the great creator deities (see page 88) and she was also the tutelary goddess of the Sumerian kings, who styled themselves as her children.

TEMPLES AND ZIGGURATS

From early times the most prominent building in any Mesopotamian city was its central temple. This edifice was nothing less than the earthly home of the city's patron god, whose divine presence was represented by a cult statue, often magnificently adorned with gold and precious stones, that was kept in the principal shrine.

The earliest Mesopotamian temples that archaeologists have found were simple, single-roomed affairs, normally square or rectangular in shape and made of mud-brick like the houses that surrounded them. Some features that were to survive into later eras were already present in their layout—notably a niche opposite the main entrance that housed the cult statue, with a table placed in front of it to receive offerings. At first the exteriors were unadorned, but people soon started to pattern them with alternating buttresses and recesses, possibly in imitation of the patterned facades of reed houses in the Euphrates Delta region. This custom too survived, and decorative brick buttresses that created hard-edged shadows in the bright Mesopotamian sun would become a distinctive feature of the architecture of the region.

Mudbrick buildings had a limited lifespan when exposed to wind, rain, and dust-storms, and from time to time the temples had to be rebuilt; at Eridu,

the remains of twelve successive structures have been unearthed, each one built on the ruins of the one before. As a result the temples stood at a higher level than the rest of the city. This development may have led to the creation of ziggurats—stepped structures with three or more platforms of decreasing size that were to become the best-known landmarks of the Mesopotamian cities.

Ziggurats were built from about 2200 until 550 BCE, when Mesopotamia finally fell to the Persians. Solid inside except for drainage channels, their main external features were the huge staircases that led up the facade to the top level, where shrines to the gods were housed. The visual impact of these man-made mountains, rearing as much as 500 feet (150m) above ground level, was increased by the flatness of the surrounding plains; they dominated not just the cities spread out around them but also the whole horizon for many miles around.

The ziggurats were the central feature of extensive temple compounds—walled enclosures that also housed treasuries, grain stores, workshops, and living quarters for priests and other temple employees. There were many of these, for the temples were the centers of thriving mini-economies. Each one owned sizeable tracts of land outside the city walls. Some of the fields were farmed by the temple's own dependents, while another section, known as "the Lord's land," was worked by the community as a whole. The rest was parcelled out to sharecroppers, who handed over about one-seventh of the harvest to the religious authorities in lieu of rent.

The food that stocked the temple granaries supported not just the priests themselves but also a host of other retainers. There were administrators who oversaw the management of the estates, builders and other workers who maintained the edifice, craftsmen who produced furnishings and artworks to beautify it, and an

ancillary staff of cooks, cleaners, and guards. A tablet found in the ruins of the temple of the goddess Ninurta at Nippur lists scribes and accountants alongside more specialized employees such as a barber, a courtyard-sweeper, and a snake-charmer, all of whom had to be fed. By the start of the third millennium BCE, the main temple of Lagash was already providing daily rations of bread and beer for some 1,200 people.

The focus of all their efforts was the glorification of the deity whose image graced the principal shrine. Except on special occasions, few people were privileged to cast eyes on the sacred statue, for Mesopotamian religion was not participatory, at least in the sense that there were no regular services at which congregations gathered for worship. Instead, a small corps of priests catered to the gods' needs, bringing daily food offerings to lay before the cult statue, regularly bathing it and dressing it in finery, and occasionally even taking it on social visits to the temples of other deities. Most people only got a chance to glimpse their god at festival time, when the sacred image was taken in procession around the streets and the populace as a whole came out to give thanks for the divine protection it offered them.

• THE TOWER OF BABEL •

The biblical story of the Tower of Babel almost certainly reflects travelers' tales of the ziggurats of Mesopotamia, and more specifically the great stepped Etemenanki temple of Babylon, which rose 300 feet (90m) above the city. To the early Israelites the great, cosmopolitan city of Babylon, where many different languages were spoken, might well have seemed an image of confusion, leading Hebrew scribes to link the city's Akkadian name, Bab-ilu, with the Hebrew world *balal*, meaning "to mingle" or "to confound".

THE IMPORTANCE
OF EDUCATION

One of the functions of the early Mesopotamian temples was to provide an education for future priests and scribes. Lessons were offered in the edubba—*literally, "tablet house." At first these institutions were located within the temple compound; later, secular schools outside the walls also became common, for scribes were needed in many walks of life besides the religious sphere.*

A simple, medium-sized room lined with ranks of mudbrick benches to seat one, two, or four pupils is typical of the schools excavated in various parts of Mesopotamia. Such schools date back to the earliest days of writing in Uruk, where word-lists used by pupils have been found among the earliest written records. The Sumerian language was not an easy one to master, so education was a lengthy process, limited largely to children whose parents were wealthy enough to pay for it. Scholars who have examined lists of scribes complete with their fathers' occupations have found that most came from affluent homes: they were the children of city governors, high-ranking priests, top administrators, landowners—and, of course, other scribes.

The schools were run by headteachers known as *ummia*s or "experts," assisted by senior personnel called "fathers"; the pupils were officially described as "sons." Much of the day-to-day instruction was carried out by senior students or recent graduates referred to as "big brothers"; one of their principal duties was inscribing model sentences at the top of writing-tablets for the pupils to copy. There were also specialist teachers who concentrated on a single subject: the "scribe of counting" taught mathematics, while the so-called "scribe of the field" instructed pupils in geometry and land measurement, both vital skills for future surveyors. The more sinister-sounding "whip-keeper" was the person in charge of discipline. The student body would normally have been all male, although female scribes were not unknown.

Schoolchildren used clay tablets, such as this one (ca. 1900–1700BCE) to gain proficiency in the complex Sumerian language. A teacher would write some text on one side of the tablet (in this case, a proverb) and the pupil would try to reproduce it on the other side.

A contemporary description of an average schoolday has been found among the many thousands of school exercise tablets that have survived from ancient Mesopotamia. Much of the routine it describes has a familiar ring to anyone brought up by traditional teaching methods to this day. Asked by his father how he spends his days at school, the pupil replies that he gets up early in the mornings and asks his mother for his lunch-box. He then sets out for the tablet-house, where he recites the tablet he has written to his teacher, then prepares a new tablet and copies a fresh text. He is given oral work—maybe some sort of dictation—and then, after lunch, he receives another written assignment, probably fresh sentences to parse and copy. Naturally, students were given instruction in the grammatical principles underlying sentence construction as well as in the mechanics of cuneiform writing (see page 64).

The text then goes on to recount the experience of a bad day at school, once more with recognizable modern parallels. The pupil arrives late and is reprimanded by the monitor, after which he approaches the teacher "nervously, with a pounding heart," and offers a respectful curtsy. Things go from bad to worse: he is beaten respectively for talking in class, for indiscipline, and for unsatisfactory work. At home that evening he decides that things cannot go on in the same vein, so he has a word with his father and the two devise a strategy. Soon after, the schoolmaster is invited round to the family home, where he is sumptuously wined and dined and given presents: "a new garment, a gift, a ring for his finger." Warmed by the hospitality, the teacher delivers a glowing account of his student's progress: "You have performed your school activities well, you have become a man of learning." The moral of the tale seems clear: 4,000 years ago, just as today, effort and application were important, but personal relations and bringing influence to bear also had parts to play.

PAWNS OF THE GODS

Mesopotamia's peoples lived in a world thronged with gods. They recognized thousands of different divinities, each associated with a different aspect of the universe, from the sky and the sea to humble implements such as the plow and the hoe—there was even a god of brick-moulds.

Mesopotamian intellectuals tried, over time, to make sense of the multiplicity of gods in their religious tradition by assimilating lesser gods, and those with only local significance, to the greater deities, thereby presenting them as specialized aspects of their divinity. This tendency might eventually have led to a monotheistic vision of one god with many different facets, but that step was never finally taken in the 3,000 or more years for which the belief system flourished.

There are some indications that in the earliest times the gods were worshipped in animal form. Sumerian myths told of primeval forces in the shape of a sea-dragon and a monstrous bird (see illustration, below) that may have sheltered ancestral memories of old divinities overcome by the gods of the historical era. By the time written records began, however, the gods were thought of in human shape, sharing the same needs and emotions as the Sumerian people themselves. Like the Greek Olympians two millennia later, Sumer's gods ate, drank, lusted, quarreled, and intervened in earthly affairs. What separated them from humankind was their supernatual force and their immortality, although under special circumstances that could be forfeited—the myths had several stories of dead or dying gods.

The relationship of humans to gods was that of servant to master. A myth told how humankind had been fashioned out of mud to serve the gods, who were exhausted from digging out channels for the Tigris and Euphrates rivers and creating the irrigation infrastructure on which Mesopotamia depended. The making of people provided a workforce to take over these tiresome tasks, leaving the gods free to enjoy the life of a celestial landed nobility. Yet humans had other duties to keep the gods happy. In the words of one inscription, they had to "build temples to rejoice the hearts of the gods," and pay them regular tribute in the form of praise, worship, and offerings.

Mesopotamian religion was not for the most part an optimistic or consoling one. At best, people could hope not to offend the gods. At worst, they risked bringing down divine wrath in the form of drought, pestilence, floods, or foreign invasion. The story of the Great Flood revealed how the entire human race had once almost been destroyed as a consequence of divine irritation. Nor was there any hope of compensation after death, for all souls were bound for the underworld, a dismal realm ruled by the forbidding goddess of the dead, Ereshkigal.

Faced with such grim prospects, people took refuge in the worship of personal gods—lesser divinities resembling guardian angels who, if properly propitiated, could help them negotiate life's many pitfalls. These beings were patrons and protectors, willing to put in a good word for their clients in the divine audience chambers. As such, they acted as intermediaries between the individual and the greater gods, and it was to them that people offered up their daily prayers and supplications. A proverb succinctly summed up their crucial importance: "Without his personal god, a man does not eat."

• THE RIGHTEOUS SUFFERER •

The long-suffering attitude that humans were expected to take before the gods is the subject of a poem known as "The Righteous Sufferer." In the manner of the biblical Book of Job, the work recounts the misfortunes of a god-fearing individual who had apparently done nothing to deserve the divine wrath. In spite of his piety, however, he was heavily afflicted; his companions made false accusations against him, and supposed friends lied to him. "On the day when shares were allotted to all," he concludes, "my share was suffering." Confronted by such injustice, the man does not abandon his beliefs but instead turns to his personal god, lavishing praise and supplication on him. And, in the end, his prayers are answered. "The man—his god harkened to his bitter tears and weeping/... He turned his suffering into joy/Set by him kindly spirits as watchmen and guardians."

LORDS OF THE ELEMENTS

The gods of Mesopotamia were not equal in power or influence. Some were singled out for special reverence. Reasonably enough, these supergods were the ones associated with the great elemental forces of nature—it seemed only natural to the Sumerian mind that the god responsible for the heavens should be more powerful than one charged only with carpentry or the bread-oven.

At first the mightiest of all the deities were those associated with the four levels of creation. In the contemporary worldview, these were the firmament, the air, the earth, and the *apsu* or sweetwater ocean that the Sumerians believed to lie under the earth as the source of the fresh water on which life depended. Each realm had its presiding divinity, one of whom—Ninhursag, the earth mother—was a goddess (see page 88). Like all the major Sumerian gods, the four were later adopted by the Akkadians, who gave them names in their own Semitic tongue (which was the language of Babylon and Assyria; see page 64). As a result most leading divinities have two names, one Sumerian and one Akkadian (the latter being the version appended in brackets in the text below).

An (Anu), the god of the firmament, was the patron-god of Uruk, the first city, where his cult was based. In early times he seems to have been regarded as the head of the pantheon. His name meant "heavens" and his symbol was a star. For the most part, though, he remained a shadowy figure, and he soon passed on his position of supremacy.

By the middle of the third millennium BCE, primacy had passed to Enlil (Ellil), god of the air and of the winds. Although Enlil was regarded as An's son, he was nonetheless generally referred to as "father of the gods" and "king of heaven and earth." Enlil was considered primarily to be a beneficent force, but his wrath could be frightful. As a wind god, he could spread devastation, and it was his anger that had brought the Great Flood on humankind. His cult was centered at Nippur, which held religious primacy among the Sumerian city-states even though it was never the most influential city in political terms. His great temple there, the Ekur, was the most sacred shrine in the whole of Sumer; the rulers of other cities liked to boast that they had received their mandate to rule from Enlil. Like An before him, Enlil also lost influence in Babylonian times, when many of his functions were taken over by Marduk, the patron god of Babylon.

The deity who saved humankind from the Flood was Enki (Ea), who ruled over the *apsu* and fresh water. Revered as a fertility god who had brought agriculture to Sumer, he was generally regarded as benevolent, the source of all wisdom and creativity. It was to Enki that both gods and humans turned as a problem-solver in times of trouble. Yet his advice was not always good: it

◆ THE ENUMA ELISH ◆

Although elements of a creation story can be found in early Sumerian myth, the first surviving attempt at a comprehensive account dates from Old Babylonian times (ca. 1900–1600BCE). It takes the form of a lengthy liturgical poem, known from its opening words as the *Enuma Elish*: "When on high ... ." The hero of the story, which was ceremonially read out at the New Year's Festival in Babylon each year, was Marduk, the god of the city. The story describes the generation of the gods out of a watery chaos in which sweet and salt waters mixed. When strife breaks out between the first progenitors of the gods and their offspring, Marduk is chosen to confront Tiamat, goddess of the salt waters. He kills her, splitting her body open "like a dried fish," so that one half forms the heavens and the other the earth.

was he who had instructed Adapa, the Sumerian equivalent of Adam, not to eat the bread of life when it was offered by An. In another myth, he consumed eight forbidden plants in the paradise garden of Dilmun that caused him to sicken almost to death; some scholars see echoes of the biblical story of Adam and Eve in this tale.

Other elemental gods whose importance grew over the years were Nanna (Sin), the moon god; Nanna's son Utu (Shamash), the solar deity; and Iskur, a relatively minor Sumerian divinity who rose to prominence in later times as the storm god Adad. In Mesopotamian latitudes the crescent moon rises above the horizon at night with its two horns pointing upward; seeing the sight, parents would tell their children that it was Nanna's boat starting its journey across the night sky. Utu, in contrast, was thought to ride across the heavens in a chariot drawn by asses; because he looked down on the world and saw everything that happened in it, he became the god of justice and the divine lawgiver. Adad's home was on the mountaintops—distant and alien to the Sumerians of the southern Mesopotamian plain, these were close at hand for the Assyrians of the north, and so this god's influence waxed as power moved northward.

The source of Enki's great wisdom and influence was the Tablet of Destiny, on which all the fates were written. On one occasion, Enki prepares to bathe by undressing and putting down the tablet. The lion-headed eagle Imdugud (Anzu) seizes this opportunity to steal the tablet, but he is thwarted by the hero-god Ningirsu, who brings the captured Imdugud before Enki, a scene that is believed to be shown on this cylinder seal, with Imdugud depicted as a bird-man (second from left).

THE SUPREME GODDESSES

Among Mesopotamia's many goddesses, three stood out. One was Ninhursag, goddess of the earth and one of the quartet of great creator deities. Inana, better known under her Akkadian name of Ishtar, was a complex divinity, one of whose aspects was to preside over love and desire. The third, Inana's sister Ereshkigal, was a sinister figure who ruled as queen of the underworld (see pages 92–93).

Oddly for a mother goddess, Ninhursag was associated not with fields and pastures but with the hostile terrain of the desert and mountains. The original consort of the sky god An, she was thought of as the mother of the gods, and hence of all living things: one of her titles was Nintu ("she who gives birth"). The name could also mean "lady of the rib" in Sumerian, a pun that may have influenced the biblical story that Eve was made out of Adam's rib.

Ninhursag was intimately linked to the creation of the human race, which she and her son Enki were said to have fashioned out of clay. According to one version of the myth, they killed a lesser god—one of a group that had risen in revolt against the divine hierarchy—and mixed his blood with the clay. As a result, something of the divine essence entered humankind, in the form of a soul that could survive death; but as it came from a rebel god, it was inherently flawed.

Inana, or Ishtar, was worshipped from early times in Uruk, where her symbol was a reed column of a type still to be seen in houses in the Iraqi marshes. Her cult remained strong to Mesopotamia's last days. Over the centuries so many lesser goddesses became assimilated to her that by the first millennium BCE her name had become virtually synonymous with "goddess."

One reason for Inana's popularity was the wide-ranging nature of her cult, which had three main aspects. The most important was her role as goddess of sexual desire. In myth she was a lascivious figure who took many of the male gods as her lovers and who also lusted after human heroes like Gilgamesh. In this role she was the protectress of prostitutes, and memories of her cult no doubt fuelled bitter Israelite references to the Whore of Babylon. The Greek historian Herodotus reported after a visit to Babylon that every Babylonian woman had once in her life to go to the temple of Ishtar and prostitute herself with a stranger for money, although no Mesopotamian sources confirm this story. Yet, like the Roman Venus, she had a second, entirely different function as a war goddess: battlefields were described as her playground, and as Ishtar of Arbil she was a leading patron of the Assyrian war machine. Her third manifestation was astronomical: she was identified with the planet Venus, the morning and evening star.

The most enduring of all Sumerian myths described how Inana once ventured down to the underworld, intent on wresting power from her sister Ereshkigal. She, however, gave instructions that Inana should be stripped of a garment at each of the realm's seven gates, so that Inana eventually appeared before her naked. Ereshkigal then used her power to take her sister's life, leaving her body hanging like a piece of raw meat from a hook.

Under pressure from the other gods, Ereshkigal eventually agreed to restore Inana, but only if she sent someone to take her place. Inana returned to the upper world only to find her husband, the shepherd god Dumuzi, feasting rather than mourning as she had expected. In a fit of pique she nominated him as her stand-in. His fate subsequently inspired a lament that was one of the best-known works of Mesopotamian literature. One tradition held that Dumuzi's loyal sister Gestinana agreed to share his fate, spending six months of each year in the underworld in his place. This story seems to have inspired the Greek myth of Persephone, who was similarly condemned to spend half of each year in Hades (hell).

This large plaque, made of baked straw-tempered clay and dating to 1800–1750BCE, is known as the "Queen of the Night." The female figure is believed to be an aspect of Inana or her sister Ereshkigal.

A DEMON-PLAGUED UNIVERSE

In Mesopotamian religion, many spirits occupied the space separating the gods from humankind. Some had semi-divine status in their own right, while others were simply servants or emissaries of the higher divinities, sent to the human world to do their bidding. They took many forms—some hideous, others alluring—and wielded their considerable influence in a variety of ways.

People actively sought the protection of those spirit beings they thought to be benevolent, doing so through prayers and offerings. However, many beings were fearsome—some owing to their natural malevolence and others because their mission was to punish erring humans for the sins that they had committed.

Most fearful of all was the dreaded Lamashtu, a demoness who specialized in killing babies in or out of the womb. In a culture with high infant mortality, it was natural enough that miscarriages, stillbirths, and cot deaths should be blamed on a malevolent spirit. Lamashtu was truly frightful in aspect: she had the head of a lion, asses' teeth, naked breasts, a hairy body, blood-stained hands with claw-like fingernails, and talons in place of feet. Besides snatching infants, which she did by slipping into the houses of pregnant women and touching them seven times on the belly, she was also a bringer of disease. People wore amulets for protection from her wiles; some also sought to buy her off with offerings, particularly of centipedes.

The surest safeguard against Lamashtu, however, was to call on the help of her male equivalent, the equally terrifying Pazuzu. Like her he was talon-footed, although his body was scaly and his penis tipped with a serpent's head. A spirit of the desert winds, Pazuzu bore wings. He alone was thought to have the power to drive Lamashtu back to the underworld, so plaques showing his doglike face

The blood-curdling figure of Lamashtu appears on this early 9th-century BCE amulet designed to ward off evil. She is shown in her customary pose, standing on her sacred animal, the donkey, while suckling a piglet and a whelp and holding a snake in each hand.

and bulging eyes occupied space in many homes, placed there by the householder to curry favor.

Other nightmare beings haunted the Mesopotamian imagination. There was Namtaru, the plague demon; Rabisu, "the Croucher," a bogeyman who lurked in doorways and dark alleys; the *utukku*, which frequented deserts and wild places; and Lilitu, the original of the Hebrew Lilith, a female succubus who seduced men in their sleep. Particularly terrible were the spirits jokingly known as *galla*s or "constables." These were emissaries of the dread queen Ereshkigal, who sent them to the upper world to drag transgressors down to her dark realm. One of the best-known Mesopotamian poems told how *galla*s were sent to track down Dumuzi, husband of the love goddess Inana. after his wife had made an ill-advised visit to Erishkigal's domain. Its lines described how the *galla*s clustered around Inana on her return, hungry as the Greek Furies to find their prey:

> *Devils are fastened*
> *To her thighs, devils walk beside her,*
> *Meagre as reeds, thin as pikestaffs.*

> *There goes in front of her a thing*
> *With a scepter, but it is no minister.*
> *One walks beside her wearing a weapon*
> *On its hip, but it is not a warrior ...*

Faced with such terrors, householders went to considerable lengths to protect their homes from evil influences. Archaeologists in Ur and elsewhere have found small clay figurines buried under the floors of dwellings whose function was magically to drive away demons. Some were dragonlike creatures with a dog's head on a serpent's body; others were fish-men, wearing cloaks covered in scales. There were even magical guard-dogs, their names inscribed on their backs: "Loud Barker," "Don't Stop to Think! Bite!"

Such humble defenders had their grand counterparts in the magnificent winged bulls and lions that stood on guard at the gateways of Assyrian palaces. These hybrid creatures were similarly thought of as protective spirits, charged with the responsibilities of keeping out malevolent *djinn*s (spirits) and protecting the royal occupants from spiritual harm.

◆ GHOSTS ◆

Sumerians were firm believers in ghosts—"those whose towns are the ruins," as one text called them. They thought that dead people's spirits roamed restlessly if their bodies were left unburied, or if they had no kin to provide them with food and drink through regular funerary offerings. Those who had died violent deaths or who had offended the gods by breaking taboos were particularly at risk.

Malevolent ghosts could harm the living by "seizing" their minds or bodies, which they entered through the ear. Their victims would then be stricken down by disease. The only cure in such cases was to employ the services of an exorcist, who would perform elaborate rituals involving incantations and clay images. Sometimes an animal was used to tempt out the evil spirit, in the hope that it might choose to possess the beast in place of the afflicted man or woman. Memories of this practice survive in the biblical story of the Gadarene swine, which recounts how Jesus cured a man possessed by evil spirits, which then entered a herd of pigs, causing them to bolt into the sea and drown.

DEATH AND BURIAL

The Sumerians had a story to explain why all people had to die. They blamed an individual named Adapa—the name simply means "man," and he served as their primeval Adam. Adapa earned the enmity of the gods by cursing the south wind when it overturned his boat while he was out fishing. He was summoned to explain his misdeed to An, the father of the gods.

Adapa's expounding of his sin won him the favor of the great deity An, who offered Adapa the bread and water of eternal life. But—misadvised by Enki, the cunning god of water—Adapa rejected the offer. Instead, he chose two other gifts that were presented to him: oil and a robe. It was a fatal error—the oil was the type used to dress corpses, while the robe was a shroud. Through Adapa's choice, all humankind was condemned to mortality.

There was no Sumerian heaven, but there was a hell. The underworld, also referred to as "the Land of No Return," was the domain of the Ereshkigal, dark sister of the love goddess Inana. Traditions about its exact nature varied. At first it was known as Kur, "the mountain," that being the concept for all that was most foreign to the Mesopotamian plain-dwellers. Usually, however, it was located underground. In some legends it was approached across water—the "man-devouring river"—with the aid of a boatman, the Mesopotamian equivalent of the Greek Charon. In others it resembled a city, with seven walls and seven gates.

Yet all the stories agreed that it was an undesirable place. The spirits of the dead lived a ghostly half-life there, flitting like bats in the darkness. One legend told how the lord Gilgamesh once summoned his best friend Enkidu back from the underworld to describe the fate of the dead. Enkidu had no good news to report. Those with no grave were fated to wander eternally without rest; the childless wept continually; while people who died by fire were denied any existence at all, their souls being incinerated along with their bodies. The only consolation was for stillborn children who, having been denied life on Earth, played in Ereshkigal's realm "at a table of gold and silver, laden with butter."

For the most part, though, the spirits of the dead were tormented by hunger and thirst. For their suste-

---

This clay coffin was excavated at Uruk by the English archaeologist W.K. Loftus in 1850 (see page 67). It dates from the 1st century CE, when Mesopotamia was ruled by the Parthians. The coffin was built by joining slabs of clay to form a slipper-like shape.

nance they were dependent on the good will of their surviving relatives, who were expected to cater for them by making libations at their graves. Kinsfolk would gather at the tomb of a loved one to leave food and to pour water into the earth with the aid of a clay tube.

Funerary customs varied just as views of the afterlife did. Sumerians generally were not long-lived: average life expectancy at the time was less than forty years. Nearly all were then buried rather than cremated. Some were laid to rest in vaults under their own homes and as many as ten or more corpses have been found in these family mausoleums. This tradition proved long-lasting, and stretched to the highest social levels. In 1989 Iraqi archaeologists made stunning discoveries in a previously unsuspected network of tombs located beneath the harem quarters of the palace of the Assyrian kings in Nimrud. Two of the burial chambers, built for queens and princesses of the ninth and eighth centuries BCE, contained between them more than 82 pounds (37kg) of magnificent gold ornaments.

Most Mesopotamians, however, were buried in cemeteries. The dead were laid on their backs in individual, brick-lined graves that were sometimes reopened to admit a second family member. Some tombs also contained the remains of dogs. Pets were provided for after death just as their owners were—meat bones were laid near their mouths to sustain them in the afterlife.

In general, poorer citizens were laid to rest wrapped in reed matting, while the wealthy were equipped with wood or clay coffins. To judge from the edict of one reforming ruler of Lagash, the priests who conducted the funerals sometimes overcharged for their services— where they had previously demanded payment of seven measures of beer and 420 loaves of bread, the king (who reigned in the twenty-fourth century BCE) limited them in future to just three measures and eighty loaves.

THE ROYAL TOMBS OF UR

The grave goods placed in Mesopotamian tombs were normally modest and personal: jewelry, perhaps, or simple household utensils. A few members of the ruling élite, however, went to the grave in magnificent style. A series of extraordinary discoveries made at Ur would dramatically reveal just how spectacular some of the early interments must have been.

In 1922 the British Museum and the University of Pennsylvania jointly agreed to sponsor an expedition to the site of Ur, to be supervised by the Briton Leonard

The Royal Tombs of Ur contained numerous stunning artifacts, including this silver spouted jug (ca. 2600–2400BCE), which was found on the floor of the pit in the grave of Queen Puabi, near to three clusters of silver tumblers. The jug may have been used for serving wine.

Woolley. In all, Woolley was to spend twelve successive seasons unearthing the Sumerian city. What he found was to revolutionize people's views of early history.

Although Woolley learned much about the layout of Ur and its near neighbor al Ubaid, the most exciting finds came from a cemetery that had been located just outside the city walls, adjoining the main temple area. The site had apparently been used as a rubbish dump for several centuries before the first burials were made there in about 2500BCE.

In six years of digging, Woolley's team eventually uncovered 1,850 separate graves, spanning a period of about 500 years. The vast majority were simple affairs, in which a lone individual was found wrapped in reed matting in a plain rectangular pit, with at most a clay

pot or two containing food and drink to provide sustenance in the afterlife. A few tombs enclosed more elaborate grave goods, including vessels made of imported alabaster and soapstone, mirrors and razors of copper, and personal adornments in gold, silver and lapis lazuli.

These riches were as nothing in comparison with the treasures found in a group of sixteen more elaborate plots, tightly clustered at the heart of the cemetery. Woolley dubbed these the Royal Tombs. Unlike the simpler burials around them, they contained underground chambers built of brick or stone that were roofed with vaults or domes—the earliest known to architectural history. The builders of these small tomb-chambers constructed them at the bottom of deep pits, approached down earth ramps. The pits were filled in after the burial ceremonies, and funerary chapels may have been built above them.

Objects found in the royal tombs identified some of their occupants: two kings (Meskalamdug and Akalamdug) and a queen (Puabi). None of the names appears on the Sumerian king-list, leading historians to conclude that they must have been rulers of a local dynasty preceding the so-called First dynasty of Ur—actually the first of that city to qualify for inclusion by claiming overlordship over all of Sumer.

If the dead were city-state governors exercising suzerainty over no more than Ur itself, the wealth of the grave goods becomes all the more startling. A high proportion of Sumer's best-known artworks comes from the tombs. The Standard of Ur was found there (see page 76), as was the helmet of Meskalamdug, a wonderful work fashioned, complete with simulated ears and hair, from electrum (an alloy of gold and silver). No ancient civilization has produced artifacts of greater elegance

---

Ostriches were commonly found in the ancient Near East, and their eggs were often used as cups, bowls, and jars. It is unusual to find an ostrich-egg artifact that has survived intact, like this jar, which was discovered in the Royal Cemetery at Ur.

than Queen Puabi's golden headdress (see detail above) or the statuette representing a goat or ram caught in a thicket. Other luxury items range from a beautifully inlaid gaming board constructed of shell, bone, and lapis lazuli to harps ornamented in gold, one featuring a comic decorative panel showing an animal orchestra.

Yet the graves also contained more sinister evidence of the deceased's power and prestige. Some of the tombs were filled with the bones of other corpses besides those of their royal occupants. Two adjoining tombs contained the bodies of Queen Puabi and an unidentified man who was presumably her husband; between them they enclosed an additional 137 corpses, laid out in serried ranks outside the tomb-chambers. The bullock carts that had carried the grave goods to the funeral were there, together with the animals that pulled them along with their drivers and grooms and a ceremonial guard of six soldiers. Most of the bodies, though, were female—women dressed in court finery, suggesting that they were ladies in waiting to the royal couple rather than household slaves. Most of the victims seem to have died

This wreath of gold beech leaves forms part of the headdress worn by Queen Puabi in her tomb. Her body was also adorned with gold and lapis amulets and beads of gold, silver, carnelian, and lapis, and she was equipped with make-up, tweezers, and a tiny earwax spoon.

by their own hands—the cups found by the bodies as in most Sumerian burials in their case probably contained poison. In one tomb, however, the soldiers of the guard and a row of nine court women had been dispatched by blows to the head.

Nothing remotely on the scale of the death pits of Ur has been found anywhere else in Mesopotamia, and there are no literary references to such practices apart from an ambiguous passage in one version of the Gilgamesh story that speaks of the hero going to the grave accompanied by retainers. Scholarly opinion now holds that such large-scale killing was an aberration, practiced only for a short period in the early phases of Sumerian civilization.

BABYLON THE MIGHTY

In antiquity the glory of Babylon easily outshone that of any other Mesopotamian city, and its fame continues to resound today, although, ironically, it is now chiefly reflected through the distorting vision of the city's enemies. "The rivers of Babylon" have become an international symbol of exile, while the "whore of Babylon" epitomizes the corruption of big-city living.

Visitors to Babylon during its time of grandeur were complimentary: the fifth-century BCE Greek historian, Herodotus, called it the world's most splendid city—and its hanging gardens were, of course, one of the seven wonders of antiquity. Yet Babylon was a relative latecomer among the cities of Sumer and Akkad, and was not even mentioned until the twenty-third century BCE. It remained a small provincial town until it was raised to prominence by an immigrant dynasty that took power four centuries later. Uniquely, it enjoyed two distinct periods of empire separated by more than a millennium. In between its two eras of dominance it continued to be a great commercial and cultural hub, but mostly fell under foreign rule.

Babylon's first golden age started in the troubled period at the start of the second millennium BCE following the collapse of the Third dynasty of Ur. Incursions of Semitic Amorites from the western desert were blamed for Sumer's troubles at the time, and it was from one of the Amorite tribes that the line of kings that created the Old Babylonian empire sprang. Its founder was Hammurabi, sixth in succession and a calculating, hard-working monarch now best remembered for his celebrated law code (see pages 74–75).

When Hammurabi came to the throne, Babylon was a city-state on the Euphrates whose borders stretched no more than 55 miles (90km) from the city walls. At his death forty-two years later it was the dominant power in Mesopotamia, controlling all of Sumer and much of Assyria to the north. His empire was short-lived, however—its last vestiges were swept away in 1595BCE, when a Hittite army from Anatolia sacked the city.

Babylon recovered from the disaster under the sway of another foreign dynasty, this one implanted by the Cassites, a people from the Zagros Mountains. Cassite Babylon was not an imperial capital as Hammurabi's city had been, yet it remained the cultural hub of the region and was probably the wealthiest metropolis of its day.

This happy state of affairs was challenged from the thirteenth century BCE on by the rise of Assyrian power. For the next six centuries Babylon and Assur would vie for dominance in the region, with the balance of power mostly tipping in the Assyrians' favour; indeed for almost three centuries from about 900BCE on, Assyrians provided most of the city's rulers. Babylon's patron god, Marduk, was replaced at the head of the Mesopotamian pantheon by Ashur; in other respects, though, the new rulers mostly respected the city's cultural pre-eminence and treated its citizens generously.

The challenge to Assyrian overlordship came eventually from yet another immigrant group within Babylon: the Khuldu or Chaldeans, originating from the south-western territory of Elam. In 612BCE the Chaldean Nabopolassar allied with the Medes from east of the Zagros Mountains to capture the Assyrian capital, Nineveh, and put an end to 600 years of Assyrian power. In the wake of this victory, Nabopolassar's son Nebuchadnezzar was able to create the Neo-Babylonian Empire in the power vacuum created by Assyria's collapse. In the course of a reign lasting forty-three years Nebuchadnezzar stretched his dominion around the Fertile Crescent to the borders of Egypt. In 568 BCE he even invaded Egypt itself, although the campaign was ultimately unsuccessful.

Nebuchadnezzar is probably best remembered for sacking Jerusalem in 587 BCE and deporting thousands of Jews to Mesopotamia, thereby starting the Babylonian Captivity. In fact he had already obtained Judah's submission seventeen years earlier, only to see the Judean ruler defect three years later when the

The Zagros Mountains, original home of the Cassites who moved to rebuild Babylon following its sacking by the Hittites in 1595BCE. Many of Babylon's ruling dynasties had originated outside the city.

Babylonians suffered a temporary reversal at the hands of the Egyptian army. The forced exile of many of the kingdom's leading citizens was an act of retaliation.

Nebuchadnezzar was a great builder as well as a warrior. It was he who created the hanging gardens, supposedly to please his Median wife who missed the mountains of her own country. He also refurbished Babylon's principal temples, constructed massive new city walls, dug canals and a giant moat, and paved the city's processional way with limestone.

Brilliantly though it shone, Nebuchadnezzar's empire turned out to be Babylon's swansong. Just seventy-three years after Assyria's defeat, Babylon in its turn fell to the forces of Cyrus the Persian (see page 115). Although the city flourished under Achaemenid rule, and later under Alexander the Great who considered making it the capital of his empire, its fate had passed out of the hands of Mesopotamians and its days of glory were over. It finally lost its commercial primacy when Alexander's successor, Seleucus, founded a new, rival capital, Seleucia, only 40 miles (60km) away, while its cultural supremacy was undermined by the gradual abandonment of its Akkadian language in favour of Greek and Aramaic. By the start of the Christian era, Akkadian was a dead tongue, the temples of the ancient gods had fallen into disuse, and Babylonian culture was no more.

THE ARTS OF MESOPOTAMIA

Mesopotamia played a key role in the development of Western art, yet its contribution is not widely recognized, perhaps because relatively few works survive. Most of the remaining masterpieces of the culture are in a handful of institutions: the British Museum, the Louvre, the Berlin Museum, the Oriental Institute in Chicago, the University of Pennsylvania Museum, and the Baghdad Museum.

People seeking to appreciate Mesopotamian art today have to cross a yawning culture gap. To a modern viewer used to artistic self-expression for its own sake, it is important to understand that the conventions governing the monumental sculpture and statuary of ancient times left little room for such individualism. During this period art was firmly in the service of religion: it sought to glorify either the gods themselves or else the kings who were their earthly representatives. Artists were commissioned to present idealized images of power, and their style was necessarily stiff and formal. There was no place for personal idiosyncracies. The sculptors worked anonymously—none of their names are known today—and probably shared the status of other skilled craftspeople, admired for their remarkable technical skills.

As it happens, no major statues of gods or goddesses have survived. Literary texts reveal that they were often encrusted with jewels and precious metals, so most were

This gold cup was one of the treasures found in the Royal Tombs of Ur. It was recovered from the grave of Queen Puabi and dates to around 2600–2400 BCE. The gold from which it was made would probably have been imported from Iran or Anatolia.

probably broken up in antiquity by conquerors eager to despoil enemy booty as well as to trample down alien gods. The best-known kingly statues are those of Gudea, ruler of Lagash at the time of the Gutian overlordship in about 2150BCE. They show a stocky individual with his hands clasped in an attitude of prayer. The pose is significant, as the statues were designed to rest in temples, particularly that of the city-god Ningirsu. There they served as Gudea's locums, mutely offering thanks to the god in perpetuity, while leaving the king himself free to go about the business of governing.

Another characteristic artform of the time was the monumental relief, designed to commemorate a military victory; the Stela of the Vultures, which celebrated the victory of Lagash over Umma, was an early example. Naram-Sin, grandson of Sargon of Akkad, celebrated a triumph over the mountain-dwelling Lullubi with two such works, one of them carved on a cliff-face high in the Kurdish hill country. The rulers of Assyria (see pages 106–111) were to carry this tradition to new lengths, filling their artworks with gruesome details of impalements and beheadings.

The decorative arts of pottery and metalwork showed a lighter touch, being produced purely for pleasure rather than for purposes of aggrandisement or propaganda. For the modern world, the revelation here came with the unearthing of the Royal Tombs of Ur (see pages 93–95). The grave goods found in the tombs all fell into the category of luxury items, their value enhanced for their original owners by the fact that the metals used to make them had to be imported into Sumer, which had no sources of its own. Many displayed startlingly fine artistry, exhibiting a taste and elegance that would be hard to match on Fifth Avenue or Bond Street today.

A similar spirit of creativity inspired the carvers of humble cylinder seals (see pages 70–71), which often featured inventive and well-executed designs, particularly in early times. Some of these motifs went on to play a larger part in later cultures. The crescent moon, originally a symbol of the moon god Nanna, became a regular part of the iconography of Islamic art, while the Maltese cross and the *menorah* or seven-branched candlestick were respectively adopted by eastern Christian and Jewish traditions. The Ionian column that became a feature of classical Greek architecture also had a Mesopotamian prototype, based on the bundles of tall reeds, their tops turned over, that feature to this day in the construction of huts in the marshes of southern Iraq.

• CLAY CONES •

A distinctive feature of early Sumerian architecture was the use of nail-shaped clay cones to decorate the outsides of buildings. Where other cultures used pebble-like *tesserae* to create mosaics, the Sumerians, lacking stone, were forced back instead on their native mud. The pegs were baked hard, brightly colored at one end, and driven into the mud-brick facade of temples and palaces to form decorative abstract patterns. The cones went out of fashion in Babylonian–Assyrian times, but in earlier centuries the bold zigzags, chevrons and diamond shapes they formed did much to enliven the façades of Sumer's cities.

COSMOLOGY AND NUMBERS

One aspect of Mesopotamian culture that continued to resonate long after the civilization itself collapsed was its knowledge of the heavens. The Greeks in particular were fascinated by the Babylonian star-gazers. But cosmology was not the only field of learning in which the Babylonians excelled—their legacy in mathematics was similarly rich and influential.

There was a long astronomical tradition in Mesopotamia, stretching back at least to the Old Babylonian period. The earliest surviving record, a virtually complete list of the heliacal risings and settings of the planet Venus over a period of twenty-one years, dates back to the mid-seventeenth century BCE. The sightings were accurate enough to have become the basis for dating Old Babylonian history.

Other early astronomical documents include astrolabes—clay tablets inscribed with three concentric circles, each one divided up by twelve radii. Each of the thirty-six equally-sized divisions contained the names of constellations. The astrolabes apparently served as star maps, dividing up the visible stars between different sections of the heavens. The Assyrians similarly cut the eastern horizon into three vertical bands, referred to as the "ways" of the creator gods Anu, Enlil, and Ea.

Whatever the motives of the first astronomers, the study of the heavens soon became associated with omens. Mesopotamians saw the night sky as a blackboard on which the gods left cryptic messages. Celestial phenomena were linked to earthly events in the *Enuma Anu Enlil*, a collection of some 7,000 portents dating back to around 1500 to 1000 BCE. Such collections contained much valuable first-hand observation, combining it with predictions of what effect each event might have on earthly affairs: for example, if the moon was eclipsed in a given month under specified meteorological conditions, then that might mean there would be rebellion in Ur led by one of the king's sons who would die in the attempt and be succeeded by his brother. Such portents always concerned affairs of state: the gods only used the sky to communicate great matters.

Astronomical observation on an organized basis got under way in Babylon around the eighth century BCE; the Greek scientist Ptolemy would later claim to have access to comprehensive Babylonian records of eclipses running back to 747BCE. The achievements of the city's astronomers in Neo-Babylonian times, and later under the Persians and Greeks, were considerable. From 568BCE on records were kept of the five known planets (Mercury, Venus, Mars, Jupiter, and Saturn), listing their positions in relation to the fixed stars. Astronomers were able to predict eclipses of the sun and moon, recognizing that a cycle of eclipses recurs regularly after eighteen years. Halley's comet was observed in 164 and again in 87BCE. Around 375BCE the greatest of all Babylonian astronomers, a priest called Kidinnu, worked out the duration of the solar year to within four minutes

◆ THE BIRTH OF ASTROLOGY ◆

Mesopotamian astrologers sought omens in the heavens from early on, but astrology proper—the idea that the positions of the stars and planets can influence the fate of individual humans—was a late development. A significant step was taken with the organization of the stars, originally arranged in eighteen groups, into twelve constellations, each associated with a specific deity: the zodiac. The earliest surviving personal horoscope was drawn up for a child born on 29 April, 410BCE. It lists the position of the sun, moon, and planets in relation to the constellations at the time of his birth, then goes on to predict that "he will be short of cash ... and will not have enough food to satisfy his hunger ... His days will be long."

and thirty-three seconds—better than Western astronomy achieved until the late nineteenth century.

Mesopotamian astronomy had a practical side to it that coexisted with the desire to understand the messages of the gods. Its pragmatic aspect was driven largely by the need to record time. The Mesopotamians started their year with the appearance of the first new moon following the spring equinox. Thereafter they recognized twelve lunar months of twenty-nine or thirty days. Because this arrangement lagged behind the solar year by approximately eleven days, the Mesopotamian calendar was constantly falling out of time with the seasons. At first they dealt with the problem haphazardly; whenever the gap became glaringly obvious, a king would order the insertion of an intercalary month to bring the two together again. From the eighth century BCE onward, however, astronomers solved the problem by noting that 235 lunar months made up exactly nineteen solar years. On their advice King Nabunasir of Babylon decreed that seven extra lunar months should be intercalated every nineteen lunar years to close the gap. The Nabunasir calendar eventually became standard throughout Mesopotamia.

MASTERS OF MATHEMATICS

Mesopotamian mathematicians, like astronomers, were always more interested in the practical applications of knowledge than in abstract thought for its own sake. The ability to handle numbers was a vital tool for commerce, administration, and land management. A knowledge of mathematics was needed for such practical applications as land division and handing out rations. Scribes had to be able to work with figures if they were to account for administrative receipts and disbursements, to calculate the amount of interest due on loans, or to carry out basic surveying jobs such as estimating the number of mudbricks needed to build a house.

Mesopotamian mathematics was based on a sexagesimal system, which is to say that the number 60 played the pivotal role that 100 occupies in the decimal system.

The figure had much to recommend it in that it could be divided into many smaller numbers: 2, 3, 4, 5, 6, 10, 12, 15, 20, and 30 are all factors of 60. Of these, the number 12, along with 60 itself, assumed a special significance that both have retained to this day. It is thanks to the Mesopotamians that we still divide circles into 360 degrees and split hours into 60 minutes. Similarly, our division of the year into twelve months and the day into two twelve-hour cycles reflects Babylonian practice in separating each day into twelve "double hours." Confusingly, Mesopotamian mathematicians were also familiar with the decimal system and sometimes made use of it in conjunction with the more popular sexagesimal one; by a long-established tradition, it was the normal method used for reckoning amounts of grain.

Uniquely for the ancient world, the Mesopotamians employed a positional system of numbers, with the value of a given numeral varying according to its position in the written number. In this respect their method equated to our own, by which the numeral 3 in "333" can mean three hundred, thirty or three depending on its position in the sequence. By contrast, other early systems were juxtapositional, employing separate symbols for different values; in Roman numerals, for example, the letter V always stands for 5 and never for 50 or 500.

Scholars who have studied the Mesopotamian mathematical tablets have been impressed by the degree of sophistication that they reveal; one has compared the level of attainment reached by Babylon's mathematicians to that of European scholars in the early Renaissance period almost two millennia later. Mesopotamian mathematicians were hampered by not having a symbol for zero, at least until after the Greek conquest; in earlier centuries they sometimes left a blank space to indicate the presence of a nought in a line of figures, but the usage was not consistent. Even so, they managed to calculate the value of pi (the ratio of the circumference of a circle to its diameter) to within a margin of error of just 0.6 per cent, and worked out the square root of 2 correctly to 5 decimal places.

DREAMS AND DIVINATION

*It is no exaggeration to say that the Mesopotamians were obsessed with divination. They considered
themselves to be at the gods' mercy, reliant on divine goodwill for success in any goal or enterprise.
To avoid giving unintended offence to the gods, they employed specially trained diviners
to seek out omens and portents on Earth as well as by scanning the heavens (see page 100).*

No one took the task of placating the gods more seriously than the region's rulers, who bore a special burden of responsibility in their decision-making. The art of divination was even given a royal pedigree, being traced back to Ednmeduranki, one of the legendary rulers of Sumer in the days before the Flood. Direct evidence of royal concern with portents goes back as far as the eighteenth century BCE in the form of tablets sent to Zimrilim, king of Mari, warning him of prophetic dreams and visions reported in his lands.

The Assyrian kings were particularly exercised by divination, and kept sizeable staffs of soothsayers to take the auspices before any major political or military decision was made. They put particular reliance on reading the livers of sacrificial animals. Accurate models of livers marked up in sections (see illustration, opposite) have been found dating back to Old Babylonian times; they were probably used as training aids by the priests who specialized in the art.

Above all, Assyria's rulers feared solar or lunar eclipses, which were generally taken to portend a time when the king's life was at risk. If the signs were particularly bad, it was not unknown for a king to stand down temporarily, passing power to a surrogate ruler. At the end of the danger-time the stand-in was executed, thereby fulfilling the diviners' prophecy of a royal death, and the original king was free to mount the throne once more unscathed.

Many other forms of divination were practiced across Mesopotamia. There was a tradition of ecstatic prophecy dating back to the seventeenth century BCE or earlier. There were specialists who examined the movement of smoke from incense burners and of drops of oil on water; others studied the flight of birds or the behavior of animals. Another avenue to the gods was through dreams, and a caste of trained priests specialized in their interpretation. Dream books have survived listing the meaning assigned to specific nocturnal visions. There is evidence too that incubation—a technique involving sleeping in a temple in the hope that the god inhabiting it would send a message—was practiced in Mesopotamia. A further sign of the importance

◆ BELSHAZZAR'S FEAST ◆

The biblical story of Belshazzar's feast casts an interesting sidelight on the Babylonian concern for omens and the high regard in which they held those who could read them. It recounts how Belshazzar—historically, Belsharusur, governor of Babylon under his father Nabonidus, the last Neo-Babylonian ruler of Mesopotamia—saw a ghostly hand writing a message on a wall during a state banquet and sent for the Hebrew prophet Daniel to interpret it, offering to elevate him to third rank in the kingdom in return for his expertise. The words, transcribed in modern editions of the Bible as Mene, Mene, Tekel, and Parsin, are actually Babylonian weights; there were sixty *tekel*s (*shekel*s) and two *parsin* in one *mina*. Daniel interpreted this mysterious message as a sign of diminishing value; the later rulers of the empire, measured against its founder Nebuchadnezzar (see pages 96–97), had been "weighed in the balance and found wanting," and their realm would be divided and given to the Persians. The prophecy was duly fulfilled when Cyrus of Persia conquered Babylon in 539BCE; Belshazzar himself was killed in battle, and Nabonidus was taken prisoner.

attached to dreams is the crucial role that they play in literature: the *Epic of Gilgamesh* (see pages 72–73) alone contains half a dozen premonitory dreams, used to signal major developments in the plot.

Portents were studied particularly closely, and detailed collections of past omens and the events that ensued were assembled in the belief that, if they truly were signs from the gods, similar patterns might repeat themselves in the future. Amazingly, such collections made up more than a quarter of all the works found in the great library of Ashurbanipal, excavated at Nineveh in the mid-nineteenth century. The predictions they contain range from the portentous to the banal: "If an ass gives birth to a foal with two heads, there will be a change in the throne"; "If a fox runs into the public square, that city will be devastated"; "If a snake appears in a place where a man and wife are standing talking, the couple will divorce one another"; "If a white dog urinates on a man, hard times will ensue, but if a red dog does so, that man will find happiness." Occasionally alternative readings are offered: "When a halo surrounds the moon and Scorpio stands within it, it means either that priestesses will have intercourse with men or that lions will ravage and block the roads of the land."

One of the most common divination methods was to interpret the liver of a sacrificed animal. This model of a sheep's liver would have served as a guide to the priest who conducted the analysis: each box lays out the implications of a blemish appearing at the position in question.

MEDICINE AND MAGIC

Medicine and magic were inextricably linked in Mesopotamia, and both were also closely tied to divination. Sickness was generally thought of as punishment for some transgression, witting or unwitting, against the gods; alternatively, it could result from the actions of malicious demons like Lamashtu (see pages 90–91) or through black magic.

The first step in treating sickness was to work out what might have brought on the condition – a task for the *baru*-priest, or diviner. The various types of malady were associated with different supernatural forces, so a typical diagnosis might be "the hand of Ishtar," "the hand of Shamash," or "the hand of a ghost." Whoever had caused it was said to have "seized" the patient.

Another type of priest, the *ashipu*, or exorcist, then had the task of driving out the evil spirit responsible for the complaint. Lists of incantations prepared for student *ashipu*s have survived, and the headings into which they are divided give a clear idea of a typical caseload: "Headaches"; "Toothaches"; "Eye pain"; "To cure snakebite"; "To cure scorpion stings"; "To remove a curse"; "Magical rites for town, house, field, orchard, river."

The *ashipu*'s job started on the way to the patient's house, when he would keep a close eye out for prognostic omens. Again, some examples have been preserved: "If he sees a black pig, the patient will die. ... If he sees a white pig, the patient will be cured. ... If he sees a red pig, the patient will die on the third month or the third day." At the house he would dress up in clothing appropriate for the ritual: one required the *ashipu* to dress in red and wear a red

---

A belief in the power of evil spirits to cause illness persisted in Mesopotamia long after the decline of Babylon. This 6th-century CE bowl would have been used in a ritual of protection against demons.

Alongside the witchdoctor-like rituals of the *ashipu*s, a more pragmatic form of medicine was practiced by physicians known as *asu*s. While never questioning the supernatural causation of disease, the *asu*s limited themselves to treating the symptoms with practical remedies. One clay tablet from the late third millennium BCE lists fifteen different medications, sadly without specifying the conditions for which they were prescribed. They include infusions and decoctions to be taken internally and salves and embrocations for external use; enemas and suppositories were also employed. The ingredients include medicinal substances such as cassia, asafoetida, myrtle, and willow, as well as natural ingredients such as salt (prized for its antiseptic qualities) and saltpetre (an astringent). Herbal draughts were often mixed with milk or beer to make them palatable.

*Asu*s were respected professionals whose services were sought by the highest ranks of society; letters from palace archives tell of court physicians being sent like royal envoys from one city-state to another. Some of the correspondence in these collections also suggests an altogether more realistic approach to basic questions of health and hygiene than the priestly rituals of the *ashipu*s would ever have suggested.

One of the most remarkable examples is a letter sent by Zimrilim, king of Mari in the eighteenth century BCE, to his wife, advising her to take steps to prevent the spread of a contagious disease. "I have heard that the lady Nanname has been taken ill," the ruler writes. "She has many contacts with the people of the palace. Many ladies visit her house. Give strict orders: no one should drink from the cup she uses; no one should sit in her seat; no one should lie on her bed. She must no longer entertain guests. This disease is catching."

mask, holding a raven in his right hand and a falcon in his left. He then recited the required incantations while carrying out symbolic actions with the aid of everyday objects such as onions and dates. A spell to remove a curse read: "By the conjuration of Ea/Let the curse be peeled off like the skin of this onion/Let it be wrenched apart like this date/Let it be untwined like this wick."

One practice that *ashipu*s occasionally resorted to involved transferring the evil spirit responsible for a malady from the patient to an animal surrogate. A tablet from Assyria recounts how a sick man would be encouraged to sleep next to a goat kid. At dawn the demon would move from the patient to the kid, and the exorcist would then slit its throat, putting an end to the disease. The deception even stretched to dressing the kid in the sick man's clothes, sandals, and skullcap.

THE LORDS OF ASSUR

Apart from Babylon's brief resurgence under Nebuchadnezzar, the focus of Mesopotamian history in its later centuries moved northward to Assyria. The kingdom lay on the middle reaches of the Tigris River, about 100 miles (160km) beyond Babylon. Its core territory was small, being confined to the triangle of land between the cities of Assur, its capital, Nineveh, and Arba-Ilu (modern Erbil).

The Assyrians spoke Akkadian, the Semitic tongue used throughout Mesopotamia, and shared the culture of the rest of the region with one significant difference. For them the chief figure in the pantheon was not Marduk, the god of Babylon, or Enlil, revered in Sumer, but the deity from whom their capital took its name. (By convention, the god's name is usually transliterated as Ashur rather than Assur, to avoid confusion with the city.) The Assyrians were mostly hardy peasants who grew crops of barley and wheat and tended herds of cattle, sheep, and goats. Unlike southern Mesopotamia, the Assyrian lands received adequate rainfall, precluding the need for the large-scale irrigation that did so much to shape Sumerian society.

In the third millennium BCE Assyria was something of a backwater, recognizing the overlordship first of Akkad and then of the Third dynasty of Ur. The region first came to prominence around the year 1800BCE under a powerful ruler Shamshi Adad I, who annexed the neighboring kingdom of Mari to take control of much of northern Mesopotamia. The palace archives of Mari reveal Shamshi Adad as an intelligent, worldly-wise king with a talent for government. Yet the realm he created was short-lived, falling to Hammurabi of Babylon in the 1750s BCE.

Assyrian power was eclipsed for the next 400 years, as the nation fell under the sway first of Babylon and then of Mitanni, a powerful kingdom created by the Hurrian people between the Tigris and Euphrates rivers. The situation changed under Ashuruballit I (reigned 1365–1330BCE), who took advantage of civil war in Mitanni to crush the rival kingdom and extend Assyrian power as far as the Euphrates, inaugurating the Middle Assyrian period, so called to distinguish it from the Old Assyrian times of Shamshi-Adad and his successors.

Assyria took advantage of the troubled times at the end of the second millennium to become a major regional power. Under a succession of expansionist kings—Shalmaneser I, Tikulti-Ninurta I, Tiglath-Pileser I—its armies set out on campaigns almost every summer, striking in three directions: east to suppress the Zagros peoples, west into the lands between the two great rivers of Mesopotamia, and south to confront Babylon. At times there were breakthroughs: Tikulti-Ninurta defeated the Cassite king of Babylon to take Assyrian power temporarily to the Persian Gulf, while Tiglath-Pileser overcame the Aramaean peoples of the western desert to drive through to the Mediterranean.

These victories were achieved at a terrible cost for the losers. War in Mesopotamia, as elsewhere throughout history, had always been bloody and fierce, but the Assyrian rulers practiced cruelty on a scale that went beyond the norms to which the region was accustomed. The inscriptions that their rulers raised to commemorate victories positively gloried in bloodshed. For example, one king boasted, "I caused great slaughter. I destroyed, I demolished, I burned. I took their warriors prisoner and impaled them on stakes before their cities."

As well as bloody violence against captured enemy soldiers, later Assyrian kings also used mass deportation of civilians as a major instrument of policy. To lessen the risk of revolt in the lands they conquered, they shifted substantial sections of the population to serve as forced labor elsewhere in the empire. By one account, as many as four million people may have been forcibly displaced from their homes in the last three centuries of Assyrian rule.

For all their ruthlessness, Assyria's rulers encountered a setback at the turn of the first millennium, when

In keeping with the nation's aggressive ideology, Assyrian kings were expected to demonstrate their courage and fighting ability by killing large numbers of wild animals. Palace reliefs, such as the one shown here, celebrated their skill in shooting game with arrows from a chariot or taking on lions face to face with a spear. One inscription from Tiglath-Pileser I's reign boasted that the king had brought down six wild oxen, ten elephants, and no fewer than 920 lions, which were common in the Middle East at the time. He was able to achieve such mass slaughter only by having the animals trapped in the wild and then released into a game park for despatch.

resurgent Aramaean pressure cut off the vital trade route to the Mediterranean. It was restored early in the ninth century by Ashurnasirpal II, and thereafter the nation remained the dominant Mesopotamian power for three centuries—the era of the Neo-Assyrian Empire. A succession of mighty warrior-kings carried its dominion to new frontiers. Tiglath-Pileser III crushed the Aramaeans, stretching the empire's boundaries around the entire Fertile Crescent from the Persian Gulf to the borders of Egypt. Sennacherib sacked Babylon, destroying its temples and razing much of the city. Esarhaddon invaded Egypt itself, capturing the capital Memphis. His successor Ashurbanipal extended Assyrian power as far as Thebes in southern Egypt, taking the empire to its maximum extent.

When Ashurbanipal died in 626BCE, Assyria was the world's greatest power. Yet just fourteen years later the entire edifice collapsed under the assault of a resurgent Babylon in alliance with the Medes, a new power in Persia. For all its reach, the Neo-Assyrian Empire was always brittle, based on military coercion rather than cultural assimilation—a single crushing defeat was enough to sweep it away.

THE ASSYRIAN WAR MACHINE

War became a way of life for the Assyrians to a greater extent than for any other Mesopotamian people. In a way, their story resembled that of the Aztecs in Mesoamerica two millennia later (see pages 498–567): both were small nations in a world of rival city-states

who rose to pre-eminence not through any technological or economic advantage but by a single-minded dedication to the art and ideology of war.

Two factors predisposed the Assyrians for their military vocation. One was their relatively privileged location in well-watered lands lying on major trade routes: that leading up the Tigris Valley from Sumer to the northern reaches of the Fertile Crescent, and a second heading from Iran through the Zagros Mountains and on to the Mediterranean. The other factor was their territory's lack of natural defences other than those provided by the Tigris River and its tributaries. The Assyrians had a land worth defending, but their only means of doing so was through their own military muscle.

Assyria was particularly vulnerable to raids from the wild tribesmen of the neighboring Zagros Mountains,

so from an early time the rulers of Assur developed a pattern of punitive expeditions. Each summer, once the harvest, which took place in May and June, was safely in, they would summon the peasant farmers who made up the bulk of the population to leave the land and take up arms. The levies would march into the hills to confront whichever of their enemies had been most active lately, and would then return home in time for plowing and sowing, which in Assyria took place in the autumn. The pattern became so regular that one Assyrian monarch could speak of the month of Dumuzi (approximately our July) as "the month which the lord of wisdom, Ninshiku, has prescribed in a tablet of former times for mustering the army."

The tradition of summer campaigning became entrenched in the Assyrian lifestyle, surviving into the

Neo-Assyrian era. By that time, however, the nation's armies were traveling much further than the Zagros range. They were using the excellent roads built by their military engineers, mostly with the help of forced labor, to march to Syria, Palestine and even Egypt, and to penetrate deep into Asia Minor and the lands south of the Black Sea.

The nature of the army had also changed. In the later centuries the Assyrians themselves were a privileged minority within the empire who mostly managed to buy their way out of fighting duties, sending slaves or mercenaries to fight in their stead. The bulk of the force was by that time made up of foreigners. The commanders, however, remained Assyrian, as did the discipline that they imposed on their troops.

The Assyrian forces had four main arms: the light infantry, heavy infantry, chariots, and cavalry. The light infantry consisted of archers and slingers who wore short tunics and had no defensive weapons. The army's heart was the heavy infantry, protected by coats of mail and carrying shields that were sometimes taller than they were; they fought with bronze swords and lances. Chariots were pulled by at least two horses and carried three or four men: a driver, a bowman, and one or two shield-bearers. Over the centuries they were gradually replaced by the more mobile cavalry. The riders had neither saddles nor stirrups, and fought mostly with bows, although some also carried spears. At first they dismounted to unleash their arrows, but over the course of time they learned to shoot from horseback.

The king was the commander-in-chief of the army, drawing up plans of campaign and often personally conducting operations in the field. He relied on a skilled corps of engineers to get his troops to the battlefront and to conduct sieges, an essential part of warfare in the settled lands of the Fertile Crescent. Assyrian troops became experienced at tunneling, setting up earthworks, and filling in moats, as well as at launching assaults through breaches or up scaling ladders.

Yet the aspect of Assyrian warfare that left the most enduring mark on history was the deliberate use of terror as an instrument of policy. Their public proclamations were often blood-curdling. "I cut their throats like sheep," one inscription read; "my prancing steeds plunged into their welling blood as into a river; the wheels of my battle-chariot were spattered with blood and filth." The reality was quite as awful as the words: Shalmaneser I once blinded 14,000 prisoners to make them submissive.

The Assyrian penchant for cruelty and plunder ensured that their rule was rarely welcomed by subject peoples. In seeking to rule by fear they ultimately weakened the foundations of their empire and laid the groundwork for its final collapse.

THE MONUMENTAL HERITAGE

In the summer of 1847CE observers watching from the banks of the Tigris River could have seen an extraordinary sight. A massive raft supported by 600 inflated goatskins and crowded with spear-wielding Arabs floated downstream. The guards were protecting a massive winged bull that stood more than 14 feet (4m) high and weighed 30 tons.

The sculpture—one of many spectacular finds made by French diplomat Paul Emile Botta in a momentous dig at Khorsabad in Iraq—was on its way to a new home in Paris's Louvre Museum.

What Botta had discovered were the remains of Dur Sharrukin, built from 717BCE on by Sargon II as Assyria's new capital. Sargon intended the city to be a monument to his own grandeur, but he died before it was finished. The project expired with him, and the uncompleted metropolis was quickly abandoned. Yet its rediscovery in the nineteenth century CE revolutionized views of the ancient Near East and inspired the ensuing great age of Mesopotamian archaeology.

The work of Botta and his successors—notably Austen Henry Layard, who excavated Nimrud and Nineveh—revealed the splendor of Assyria in its late imperial age. The nation had inherited the artistic traditions of Sumer and Babylon, but added something new: a taste for monumental grandeur not dedicated to the gods, as in the great public buildings of Mesopotamia's past, but to the glorification of individual kings.

In the Assyrian cities, the most prominent complex of buildings was no longer the temple but the palace. Successive monarchs strove to outdo one another in the size and splendor of their monuments. Shalmaneser II's palace at Nimrud, excavated by Layard, already covered almost 12 acres (5 hectares), but Sargon's Khorsabad residence raised the stakes, extending to around 23 acres (10 hectares). Elevated on a platform of mudbricks above the level of the surrounding streets, it had walls 20 feet (6m) thick that were penetrated by seven monumental gateways, flanked by massive towers.

The architects and builders who put up the palaces had access to materials that their counterparts in Sumer had been denied. There was timber aplenty in the Assyrian hills, which they used for columns and roofing. More importantly still, they had stone. A soft gypsum limestone, quarried locally, served for cladding and facings, although the basic building material continued to be fired brick.

The limestone also proved an excellent material for the Assyrians' greatest contribution to the arts: orthostats, or upright stone slabs whose faces were carved in low relief. Rooms and corridors in the royal palaces were lined with the blocks to form a continuous narrative frieze. The subject matter was usually either warfare or hunting and the hero was always the king. Yet even if the form was predictable, the sculptors still found ways to bring the works to life. Some of the vitality of the best works comes from the sense of movement they convey; more is down to close observation, particularly of animals. Works like the lion hunt frieze carved for Ashurbanipal's palace at Nineveh around 640BCE and now in the British Museum, attain the timeless quality of great art.

Nothing else that has survived from Assyria matches the orthostats for vigor of conception and skill of execution. Traces of mural paintings have been found at several sites, but sadly not enough has survived for any judgment of their aesthetic quality to be made. The decorative arts also flourished in Neo-Assyrian times, although it is questionable how much, if any, of the work was done in Assyria itself. The miniature ivories that have delighted excavators at many sites were most likely carved in Syria or Palestine and brought to the imperial homeland as tribute or booty.

In many respects, the most surprising thing about Assyrian art is the small part it assigns to the gods. Ashur, the national deity, frequently appears, but only as a small figure contained within a winged disc, his symbol. In contrast, images of the kings are everywhere: killing game, conducting military operations, receiving the tribute of conquered nations. Assyria's ideology glorified power in the shape of the ruling monarch, and art's role was to celebrate his triumphs. Ashurnasirpal II set the tone in an inscription found in the residence he built for himself at Nimrud: "I founded therein a palace of cedar, cypress, juniper, boxwood, mulberry, pistachio wood, and tamarisk for my royal dwelling and for my lordly pleasure for all time. I fashioned beasts of the mountains and of the seas in white limestone and alabaster and set them up within its gates. ... I placed therein great quantities of silver, gold, lead, copper, and iron, the spoil of my hand from the lands which I have brought under my sway."

Unlike the Sumerians further south, the Assyrians were blessed with deposits of limestone, which they sculpted into imposing reliefs and monuments, such as this colossal guardian figure from the palace of Ashurnasirpal II at Nimrud.

PARSA AND ITS NEIGHBORS

For much of Mesopotamia's history, the region to the east of the Euphrates–Tigris valley was overshadowed by the brilliant civilization of the plains. The lands that were to become Persia for the most part seemed unwelcoming and barren to the residents of the Mesopotamian city-states.

The Zagros Mountains along Mesopotamia's eastern border were home to tribal peoples, some of whom, like the Gutians and Cassites, played a significant role in Sumerian and Babylonian history. They also sheltered precious resources of metal ores and timber that the valley dwellers coveted. Yet they never developed urban cultures of their own—the centers of population were too small and too isolated to encourage the development of a centralized state.

However, one region, lying between the southern end of the Zagros range and the Persian Gulf, did have the advantages of flat, cultivable land and a major river—the Karun, the most important waterway between the Tigris and the Indus in what is now Pakistan—and here an important civilization developed. This was Elam, Sumer's rival from early times. Villages appeared in the region as early as 7000BCE. Archaeologists have traced the origins of the region's capital, Susa, back to 4500BCE, and over the ensuing millennia it grew into a great city that became rich by trading the timber and minerals of the mountains to the lands to the west. Elam's citizens had their own Proto-Elamite language, not related to any other known tongue, and a patron deity, Napirisha, whose name meant "the Great God." They remained a force in Near Eastern politics until the 640s, when they were finally crushed by Ashurbanipal's army, only a few decades before Assyria itself fell to outside attackers.

Beyond the mountains and Elam's coastal plain stretched the huge Iranian plateau, a stony upland for the most part at least 1,650 feet (500m) above sea level. At its center lay salt deserts that were and still are some of the least welcoming regions on Earth. Yet the plains surrounding the dead heart provided good grazing land for pastoralists, and there was agricultural land too in the valleys descending from the hills, watered by rushing torrents. From time immemorial, some of this water was channeled down to the plains in ancient irrigation tunnels known as *qanats*, substantially increasing the area open to cultivation. Here too were valuable mineral deposits, ranging from gold, silver, and iron to marble, alabaster, and lapis lazuli.

This broad hinterland was slow to enter history. It first made its mark with the arrival of a new wave of settlers in the middle of the second millennium BCE. The newcomers were Aryans, part of the same great migration of peoples that settled India at about the same time, bringing with them the *Rig Veda* (see page 150) and other essential

This moulded clay figure, possibly representing a fertility goddess, from the Elamite capital of Susa dates to around 1300BCE. Two hundred basically identical figures were found, making this an early example of masss production.

elements of the Hindu religion. One group took up residence in what is now northwestern Iran—a name that itself means "land of the Aryan"—and made their capital at Ecbatana, modern Hamadan. These were the Medes. Another group traveled further south to the barren plains south-east of Elam. They called their kingdom Parsa and took for themselves the name of Persians.

The Medes were the first to make their mark on the wider world. Specializing in mounted warfare, they won a reputation as fierce warriors, and from the ninth century BCE on their name featured regularly in Assyrian annals. Sometimes the Assyrians employed them as mercenaries but more often they regarded them as potential enemies, particularly after the various Median tribes formed an alliance sometime around 670BCE. Their fears proved only too justified when the Median army joined up with Babylon to smash Assyrian power once and for all in 614BCE.

In the wake of Assyria's collapse, the Median leader Cyaxares went on to seize the northern part of the Assyrian dominions, while his ally Nebuchadnezzar of Babylon took the southern lands. Now the Medes ruled an empire that stretched all the way from eastern Turkey to northern Afghanistan. Cyaxares himself ruled in splendor; according to Herodotus, he lived in a palace surrounded by seven concentric walls, each one painted a different color. Only members of the royal household were admitted to see him, and "no one was allowed to laugh or spit in the royal presence."

Yet the power of the Medes was to be short-lived. A new leader arose among their southern cousins, the Persians of Parsa. This man was Cyrus, and in a thirty-year reign he not only overwhelmed the Medes but went on to create an empire the likes of which the world had never previously seen.

• LURISTAN BRONZES •

Luristan is a region of high valleys in the southern Zagros Mountains that gave Elam some of its early rulers. Today, however, it is best known as the source of thousands of bronze objects traded on the world's art markets that were excavated from the late 1920s on, at first largely by unauthorized diggers. The people who produced them were evidently warriors and horsemen, for weapons and equestrian items, such as the horse-bit below, figure prominently among their artifacts, along with personal adornments and votive objects. Not much else is known about them, except that they seem to have entered the region from about 1400BCE on, when the first bronzes were made, and were probably related to the Medes and Persians who arrived in neighboring areas at about the same time.

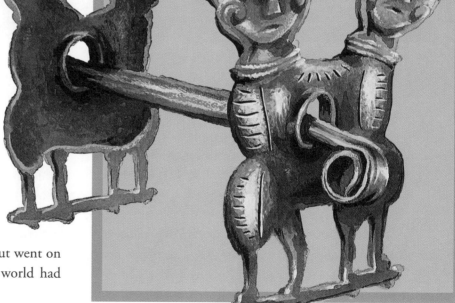

CYRUS THE CONQUEROR

The man who raised Persia to greatness was born between 590 and 580 BCE in the southern region of Parsa. Cyrus was the son of a local ruler holding power under the overlordship of the Medes. As the Greek historian Herodotus told the story, his grandfather was the Median emperor Astyages himself, who had married off a daughter to Cyrus's father, his vassal.

When Cyrus was born, Astyages had a prophetic dream that the newborn child would eventually dethrone him. He accordingly gave orders for the baby to be killed, but the officer charged with the mission disobeyed the emperor and gave him to shepherds to rear. When Astyages learned of this act of disobedience, he had the officer's own son murdered, serving his head to his father at a state banquet.

Whatever the truth of the stories, Cyrus became ruler of the kingdom of Anshan in 559 BCE, thereby inheriting half the realm created by a king named Achaemenes, the founder of the Achaemenid dynasty, sometime in the previous century. Cyrus's first task was to reunite the Achaemenid lands, a feat he soon achieved.

His next challenge came in 550, when Astyages led the Median army against the southern upstart. Before the two sides could join in battle, a pro-Persian faction in the Medes' ranks rebelled, seizing Astyages and handing him over in fetters. Cyrus was then able to take the Median capital of Ecbatana without a battle. Starting a pattern that he was to follow throughout his life, he spared Astyages's life and treated his new subjects with respect, keeping many Medes in high office, although now under the auspices of Persian overseers.

The empire that Cyrus inherited from the Medes was bordered to the west by Lydia, an Anatolian kingdom ruled by King Croesus (see box, below). Fearing domination by the expanding Persian realm, Croesus took pre-emptive action by invading Cyrus's lands. After two bloody but inconclusive battles, Cyrus's forces succeeded in trapping the Lydian ruler in his capital city, Sardis, which finally fell in 546BCE. There are conflicting accounts of Croesus's fate: according to one version, he perished by his own choice in the flames of his palace, but another recounts that he survived and was allowed an honorable retirement by his Persian conqueror.

The Greek cities on the Aegean's eastern coast, which had formerly done homage to Croesus, now came under Cyrus's sway. He spent some years consolidating his hold over Anatolia and the Iranian plateau. Then he turned his attention to the Median empire's eastern front in far-off Central Asia, building forts along the Syr Darya River to protect the border.

By 540 he was ready for the next great step. Babylon had carved an empire from the defeat of Assyria, but its current ruler Nabonidus had made himself unpopular by prolonged absences from the capital. Cyrus exploited his weakness, defeating the Babylonian army in battle and then entering the capital itself almost unopposed. Once again he proved magnanimous in victory, paying ostentatious respect to Babylon's patron deity Marduk, whose cult Nabonidus had neglected; in addition, many Babylonian office-holders were allowed to remain in their posts. He earned the gratitude of the Jews whom Nebuchadnezzar had exiled in Babylon (see pages 96–97) by allowing them to return to their homeland, winning praise in the Bible as "the Lord's anointed."

Cyrus was contemplating an invasion of Egypt, the Near East's last great independent power, when he was killed in 530BCE in a battle against nomads on the eastern frontier. By that time he had built an empire stretching from the Hellespont to the Aral Sea and from Sinai to the borders of India. In centuries to come he would be regarded as a model ruler even by his enemies; the Greek historian Xenophon would write a largely fictional account of *The Education of Cyrus*, intended as a blueprint for the upbringing of future leaders. He was an empire-builder on a scale not previously seen, and he could justifiably afford the boast made in an inscription found by archaeologists in Babylon in 1879: "I am Cyrus, king of the world, great king, legitimate king, king of Babylon, king of Sumer and Akkad, king of the four quarters of the Earth."

• THE RICHES OF CROESUS •

Croesus, the last king of Lydia, has entered legend as the paradigm of the wealthy man; the phrase "as rich as Croesus" can still be heard today. He owed his affluence mainly to the mineral resources of his Anatolian realm, based around the city of Sardis in what is now western Turkey, and particularly to its gold. Trade with the Greek cities on the Aegean coast also added to the general prosperity, as did a Lydian invention: the first coinage. Croesus himself introduced the use of coins of pure gold and silver—an innovation later borrowed by his Persian conquerors.

THE GREAT KINGS

The Persian Empire continued to expand under Cyrus's two successors. His heir, Cambyses, conquered Egypt, but died on his return to Persia. After a brief period of turmoil, the next king Darius I took the empire to its greatest extent, stretching its frontiers to the Indus Valley in modern Pakistan.

The first task of the newly acceded Darius was to strengthen his hold on the throne, for although he was of Achaemenid royal blood he was not a direct descendant of Cyrus. Having killed the usurper whose claims had drawn Cambyses back from Egypt, Darius then had to put down a series of uprisings across the empire. Having secured power, he then proceeded to put it to good use by setting the realm on an efficient administrative footing. He divided his dominions into twenty provinces, each ruled by an official known as a satrap. These plenipotentiaries were mostly chosen from the ranks of the Persian nobility, and they ruled over their local areas as quasi kings. To ensure their loyalty Darius took care to place secretaries and treasurers answerable directly to himself at each court; he also appointed roving officials known as "the king's eyes and ears" to seek out evidence of inefficiency or corruption.

The army also served as a counterweight to the satraps' power. At its heart was an élite force known as the 10,000 Immortals, so called because their number was immediately made up if anyone in their ranks was killed or injured. Darius had led the Immortals in Egypt and could count on their allegiance.

Good communications were essential for both military and administrative purposes, and Darius took pains to provide them. He equipped the empire's central artery, the 1,600-mile (2,500km) Royal Road running from Susa to Sardis in western Anatolia, with a chain of 111 inns, located on average 18 miles (30km) apart, a day's walk for foot travelers. He also established a mounted courier service of legendary efficiency.

Elsewhere in his realm Darius improved the desert routes from Ecbatana to Bactria and India and from Susa to Palestine and Egypt. Most remarkably of all, he linked the Mediterranean and Red seas by building a 125-mile (200km) waterway across the desert that predated the Suez Canal by more than 2,350 years.

The whole empire benefited from improved transport, as it did from the boost to commerce provided by the imperial peace. Standardized weights and measures were introduced, and Aramaic emerged as a *lingua franca* of business and diplomacy alongside the Old Persian spoken at court; its twenty-two-letter alphabet proved easier to write than the time-honored cuneiform script of Mesopotamia, which slowly fell into disuse. The king took advantage of his subjects' prosperity by ordering a general census of his lands, taking on average twenty per cent of each region's produce in the form of tribute (although his fellow Persians were tax-exempt).

Justice was also administered firmly and impartially. The biblical Book of Daniel speaks admiringly of "the

---

• THE ROCK TOMBS OF NAQSH-I RUSTAM •

The chief necropolis of the Achaemenid kings lay at Naqsh-i Rustam, a mountainous spur just 4 miles (6km) from Persepolis. In all, four rulers—Darius himself, plus his son Xerxes, grandson Artaxerxes I, and great-grandson Darius II—were buried there; between them, they ruled the Persian empire for more than a century, from 521 to 404 BCE. The four were laid to rest in rock-cut chambers located at the center of ornamented, cross-shaped recesses chiseled out of the sheer face of the cliffs; each facade was more than 75 feet (20m) high and 60 feet (15m) wide. The tombs themselves were empty when archaeologists investigated them in the 1930s.

law of the Medes and Persians which cannot be revoked," even by the king himself. Cambyses is reported to have had a judge caught taking a bribe flayed alive; he then had the skin used to upholster the judgment seat as a constant reminder to the dead man's successors not to commit the same fault.

Life under the early Achaemenids was no paradise; the kings ruled as absolute dictators, there was no freedom of speech, and punishments for those who offended their majesties were savage, ranging from mutilation to impalement. Even so, for law-abiding subjects Persian rule guaranteed peace and a chance of prosperity,

During his 35-year reign, Darius I (shown here in a relief found at Persepolis) not only extended the empire founded by Cyrus but also set up a sophisticated administrative system to make it governable.

along with the right to follow local customs and worship their own gods. In a time of almost constant strife, it is a credit to the administrative system created by Darius that it survived his death by 150 years, until Achaemenid rule finally collapsed under the onslaught of a new empire-builder, Alexander the Great.

PLACES OF POWER

The Persian Empire had no single capital. Power centered on the ruler, and its focus lay wherever he happened to be as he traveled around his widespread domains. However, the cities of Pasargadae and Persepolis stood out, having been built from nothing by Cyrus and Darius I respectively.

From Darius's time the main administrative headquarters of the empire was the old Elamite capital of Susa, but when the heat of summer became unbearable the royal retinue moved on to Ecbatana in the Median heartland, perched higher up on the Iranian plateau. Babylon remained important as an intellectual and cultural center, while the former Lydian capital of Sardis served as the imperial headquarters in the western lands.

PERSEPOLIS AND PASARGADAE

Two sites, however, were especially associated with the Achaemenid monarchy, having been founded and embellished by its greatest kings. Pasargadae was Cyrus's city, built in his home territory of Parsa supposedly on the site of the crucial victory over Astyages that set him on the path to empire. Less than forty years later Darius started work on the site now known as Persepolis, although the Persians themselves called it simply Parsa, after the land where it lay. The two cities were less than 45 miles (75km) apart on the dry plains of southern Iran, far from other centers of civilization. Both were created

as monuments to Achaemenid magnificence, and neither proved viable as a city after the dynasty collapsed.

Cyrus made Pasargadae a garden in the desert, providing it with elaborate waterworks to make its lawns and flowerbeds bloom. Although it lay 6,200 feet (1,900m) up in a region of hot summers and cold winters, its founder positively relished the asperities of the climate: "Soft lands breed soft men," he used to say.

Today, little remains of his creation. Archaeologists who investigated the site from 1928 on found the remains of a palace that had once covered an area of more than 7,000 square feet (650sq m), its central throne hall surrounded by porticoed colonnades. Fittingly, the chief surviving monument is Cyrus's own tomb, built of white limestone blocks on a stepped plinth, which still rises more than 35 feet (10m) high to the top of its sloping roof. The city itself seems to have been largely abandoned after Cyrus's death, although as an act of homage later Achaemenid rulers continued to travel to Pasargadae to be crowned.

Persepolis was the creation of Darius, who started construction in about 509BCE. Scholars still argue over its exact purpose, but it seems to have been intended primarily as a ceremonial center and treasury, secured by its very remoteness from the risk of plunder.

Both of the complex's principal functions came together in the New Year's Festival, a central point of Persian as well as of Mesopotamian public life, when ambassadors bearing tribute from all parts of the empire

ABOVE LEFT *The site of Persepolis was excavated in the 1930s by the Oriental Institute of Chicago.* OPPOSITE *The largest building on the terrace was the* apadana *or reception hall. The lion-and-bull motif on the west stairway to the* apadana, *shown here, occurs throughout the ancient Near East and may have an astronomical connotation.*

LEFT *Unlike Pasargadae, which effectively died with its creator, Cyrus, Persepolis continued to be used and developed by Darius's successors. His son Xerxes I built an enormous palace and a gate, part of which is shown here, and Darius's grandson Artaxerxes I completed the city.*

others bringing a parade of treasures including gold and ivory along with exquisite artifacts and animals, among them a lioness and cubs from Susa, horses from Scythia, and camels from the Central Asian deserts. The riches were stashed in storerooms that covered an area of more than 90,000 square feet (8,000sq m). Greek sources reported that, when Alexander the Great sacked the complex in 330BCE, his total haul was valued at 180,000 talents (about 5,500 tonnes) of silver. Sadly, the Macedonian conqueror did not content himself with looting Persepolis; he also gave instructions for the palace to be burned, and the royal buildings went up in smoke, leaving only ruins to survive his passage.

THE PALACE OF SUSA

As well as Persepolis and Pasargadae, the Achaemenid rulers created a third royal complex in the ancient Elamite capital of Susa, which under Darius became the administrative heart of the empire. As part of his renovation of the city, the emperor ordered in about 515BCE the construction of a magnificent palace, importing materials and craftsmen from all over his realm to embellish the building. The state rooms were decorated with exquisite friezes of glazed brick (see illustration, opposite), some of which can now be seen reconstructed in Paris's Louvre museum. Their subtle coloring and fine workmanship fully justify Darius's own assessment, preserved on a clay tablet found on the site: "A splendid work was ordered, and very splendidly it turned out."

gathered to do homage to the great king. The processions of gift-bearers can still be seen depicted on Persepolis's greatest surviving glory, the ceremonial staircases, their facades decorated in low relief, that led up to the *apadana* or main audience chamber. One of the two sets of stairs had already been exposed for centuries when archaeologists began to investigate the site in 1931, and was badly eroded. The following year, however, excavators exploring the hall's eastern façade discovered an identical set that had long been covered under soil and rubble, and which proved on excavation to be in almost pristine condition. Its carvings show Medes, Assyrians, Babylonians, Lydians, Indians, and

OPPOSITE *The palace at Susa was decorated with beautiful glazed-brick friezes believed to have been fashioned by Babylonian craftsmen. They include this one of archers belonging to the king's bodyguard.*

FORCES OF LIGHT AND DARKNESS

The religion of early Persia remains something of a mystery. There are no written records before the reign of Darius and few even then, so everything that is known about it has had to be recreated from later sources, along with a few enigmatic archaeological finds. Although the general outlines of the Persians' traditional faith can be discerned in this way, the details remain misty.

The Aryans who settled the Iranian plateau shared a similar cultural background with their cousins who moved to northern India in the course of the second millennium BCE, taking with them the *Rig Veda* scriptures (see page 150). Both Aryan branches worshipped many gods in the context of an unsystematic polytheism that associated its deities not just with the great natural forces—water, winds, the sun, the stars—but also with moral qualities such as loyalty and truth. The early Iranians apparently made a distinction between two types of divinity: *ahura*s, literally meaning "lords," applied to great gods concerned with the ordering of the universe, and *daeva*s (equivalent to the Indian *deva*), a word that originally meant "shining

one" and specifically applied to sky-gods. The two terms were to acquire very different connotations in later, Zoroastrian times.

The two faiths, Indian and Persian, also shared a similar structure of worship revolving around animal sacrifice and the consumption of a sacred liquor, known as *soma* in India and *haoma* in Iran. The active ingredient of *haoma* is thought to have been a medicinal herb of the family Ephedra, best known today as the source of the drug ephedrine, used in the treatment of hay fever and asthma. Whatever the substance was, it produced an intoxicating effect when mixed with milk or water and consumed by worshippers in the course of rituals. Leaves of the plant were also scattered over the sacrificial animal—in Iran most often a bull. After it had been killed, it was cooked and eaten by the participants.

A third element assumed a great importance in Iran just as it had in India. This was fire worship. Excavators in the Median lands of northwestern Iran have found the remains of a temple with a fire altar dating back to the eighth century BCE, 200 years before Cyrus's day. A respect for fire, regarded as a sacred, purifying force, would be one of the hallmarks of Persia's later Zoroastrian religion.

A final connection between Indian and Iranian practice was the existence of a semi-hereditary priesthood: in India the Brahmins and in Persia the Magi. According to the Greek writer Herodotus, who visited the country, the Magi were drawn from the ranks of a particular Median tribe whose special customs included interpreting dreams and exposing their dead to the elements—a tradition maintained to this day by the Parsees of Bombay, the last inheritors of the Zoroastrian faith. In later years the Magi acquired a reputation for exercising occult

One of the requirements of fire worship was to keep a sacred flame burning constantly in a temple. The Zoroastrian fire temple shown here was built at Spadan (modern-day Isfahan) during the Sassanian period (224 to ca. 642 CE), but the practice predated Zarathustra.

powers—the word "magic" harks back to them—but also for wisdom; in Christian tradition, the wise men from the east who brought gifts of gold, frankincense, and myrrh to Jesus' nativity were Magi. In Iran the Magi seem to have been ritual specialists whose presence was required to validate sacrificial rites and other ceremonies.

The religion of Iran when the Achaemenid dynasty came to power was, then, probably one of formalized rituals and multiple gods that lacked intellectual coherence and that was ripe for reform. All that was needed was a leader who could pull the various strings of belief together and give the Persians' traditional beliefs a new force and focus. Such a man was to be born in the late seventh century BCE, and his name was Zarathustra.

◆ MITHRAISM ◆

The Aryans of India and Iran shared a god named Mitra or Mithra—a minor solar deity in Hinduism but a central figure in Persian religion. Mithra, as he was known in Persia, was a fire god who also represented light and truth. According to the *Avesta*, the Persian scriptures, he had 10,000 eyes and ears and rode in a chariot drawn by white horses. A legend told how he fought a wild bull at the dawn of creation, subduing it and confining it in a cave; when it subsequently escaped, he slit its throat, and the Earth's vegetation grew from its life-giving blood.

In later times, under Greek and Roman influence, Mithra became more obviously a sun god. Under the Roman Empire, a cult of Mithras, as the god was now known, spread widely, carried by the legions as a soldier's faith that emphasized loyalty and honesty. The central act of worship in Mithraism was a bull sacrifice, carried out in underground chapels that recalled the cavern where the primeval animal had been confined.

THE FAITH OF ZARATHUSTRA

According to tradition, Zarathustra—known to the Greeks as Zoroaster, which explains the name of Zoroastrianism usually given to his faith—was born in 628BCE in a village that is now a suburb of the Iranian capital, Tehran. Little is known of his life, although he may have begun his career as a Magian priest dedicated to the cult of Mazda, one of the ahuras *(lords).*

Zarathustra had a religious vision in which he received the basic tenets of his creed. He then set out to preach the word, but was forced to flee his homeland because of his unorthodox views. He made his most important convert in 588BCE in the person of King Vishtaspa, ruler of a minor kingdom in eastern Iran. Thereafter he was able to count on state support in spreading his message. He is said to have died at the age of seventy-seven in 551BCE.

Most of what is known of Zarathustra's beliefs comes from the *Avesta*, the Zoroastrians' holy book. The sacred texts, however, were not written down until the time of the Sassanian Empire, the better part of a millennium after the prophet's death, and only one section of the work, the *Gathas* ("hymns"), is generally attributed to Zarathustra himself.

Working within the context of existing Persian beliefs, Zarathustra promoted a complete religious revolution. Where there had previously been many gods, he introduced monotheism. Although he continued to acknowledge the existence of lesser spirits, these now answered to a single controlling deity, Ahura Mazda ("Wise Lord"), who alone was worthy of worship. The master of creation, driving force of nature, originator of the moral order and supreme judge, Ahura Mazda was in effect omnipotent, although he could count for help in exercising his power on a Holy Spirit (Spenta Mainyu) aided by six beneficent entities known as the Amesha Spentas ("Bounteous Immortals"). These seven beings are thought by some religious authorities to have inspired the seven archangels before God's throne in the biblical Book of Revelations.

The universe that Ahura Mazda created was one of free choice, a fact that introduced a fundamental dualism into the world. Opposing the forces of truth that he represented was a figure of evil, Ahriman. He too had his band of supporters, the *daevas*, who in the Zoroastrian schema were fallen gods who had chosen wickedness and become demons. Although created by Ahura Mazda, Ahriman had deliberately selected the path of evil over good. Humans too had to make a choice: to follow the path of righteousness, which led to an eternal life of happiness and light, or to embrace falsehood and deceit and so condemn themselves, when their souls came before Ahura Mazda for judgment after death, to eternal darkness and horror.

If Ahriman was a precursor of the Judeo-Christian concept of Satan, Zarathustra's ideas similarly heralded later notions of the Last Judgment. In his vision there was to be an endtime, "the last turn of creation," in which Ahriman and all his works would be finally destroyed and the forces of light would triumph in a transfigured world. One conduit by which such ideas influenced Jewish tradition may have been the Old Testament prophet Daniel, who served as a high official at the Persian court under Darius and Xerxes.

In matters of ritual, Zarathustra retained the bull sacrifice of pre-Zoroastrian times while modifying the method of killing to reduce the animal's suffering. He also moderated the use of *haoma*, the sacred liquor, in religious rites to discourage abuses. However, he re-emphasized the importance of the fire ceremony, which became the central act of worship in his reformed faith. The sacred flame that burned in Zoroastrian fire temples was a symbol of purity, and to defile it was death; priests wore mouth masks to avoid contaminating it with their breath.

It remains unclear how widely Zarathustra's ideas spread in Achaemenid times. There is no mention of his name in contemporary inscriptions, nor of the Amesha

Spentas, who were central to his beliefs. Yet reliefs from Darius's day show the ruler worshipping at a fire altar with a winged disc representing Ahura Mazda floating over his head. The remains of a fire tower can also still be seen in front of Darius's tomb at Naqsh-i Rustam.

Under the later Achaemenids the strict monotheism of Zarathustra's vision seems to have been compromised, perhaps under the influence of the Magian priesthood. An inscription from Artaxerxes II's reign mentions two other gods besides Ahura Mazda: Mithra and Anahita, a fertility goddess linked with Ishtar. Under Greek rule (see pages 126–127) Zoroastrianism went out of favor, but it re-emerged as Persia's state religion under the Sassanian dynasty, which ruled the nation from 224CE. The triumph of Islam in the mid-seventh century largely supplanted it, and its followers became a persecuted sect. Even so, pockets of Zoroastrianism survive in Iran to this day, and the Parsi ("Persian") community in India continues to keep the faith alive.

This relief at Naqsh-i Rustam, the Achaemenid necropolis (see page 116), shows Ahura Mazda investing the first Sassanian king Ardashir I by handing him a diadem.

A CLASH OF EAST AND WEST

Under Cyrus and Darius, the Persian Empire provided peace and good governance for its subjects so long as they accepted Achaemenid rule. In the 150 years that followed Darius's death, however, its despotic nature became more marked and the prosperity that it initially brought gradually vanished.

Xerxes, Darius's successor, provoked the first signs of trouble for the Persian Empire when he tried to extend Achaemenid power into Europe by invading Greece. The disunited Greek city-states came together in face of the common threat and inflicted a stunning defeat on the huge Persian force, destroying its navy at the Battle of Salamis and its army at Plataea. Xerxes was forced to withdraw, and the Persians' formidable reputation was shattered; although their army would win later battles, there were no more attempts at territorial expansion. By that time the nature of the army had in any case changed dramatically—where once its backbone had been Persian footsoldiers with a direct allegiance to their king, it was now composed largely of mercenaries brought in from all parts of the empire to fight for pay.

There were problems too at the imperial court, where palace intrigue and rival claims to the throne combined to weaken the prestige of the kings. The situation was exacerbated by the rulers' own isolation. The penalty for entering the royal presence uninvited was death, and even when they were summoned, commoners had to abase themselves on the ground until told to stand. Trapped in their lonely eminence, the monarchs had little chance to assess public opinion or view the effects of their measures on the population at large.

In such an atmosphere the risk of palace coups was always great, and it was increased by the sheer number of individuals with royal blood who could put forward a claim to the throne. The kings kept a well-stocked harem of wives, and one reportedly sired 115 sons.

Matters came to a head in 424BCE on the death of Artaxerxes I, when three of the dead ruler's sons claimed the throne one after the other; the first was murdered by the second, and he in turn was killed by the third, who eventually took power as Darius II. A similar situation arose in 338BCE when Artaxerxes III was poisoned, along with most of his family, by a eunuch general named Bagoas who then tried to rule through a puppet prince named Arses, only to dispatch him two years later when he showed signs of independence. The new ruler, Darius III, wisely began his reign by forcing Bagoas to drink one of his own lethal draughts.

By that time, however, the empire was in terminal decline. The prosperity that had once sustained it had been fatally sapped by inflation. Economic historians pin much of the blame on the kings themselves, whose growing tax demands impoverished their subjects and shrank the money supply, forcing annual interest rates up to unsustainable levels of forty or fifty per cent. Much of the wealth was not recycled but instead ended up hoarded in the royal treasuries. While the kings may have gained, their subjects grew poorer, and economic activity as a whole shrank.

OPPOSITE AND BELOW After the death of Alexander the Great in 323BCE, his generals divided his empire among themselves. Seleucus I took control of the eastern section of Alexander's lands. Although this coin was minted under Seleucus, it depicts Alexander (opposite). By linking his reign with that of his illustrious predecessor, Seleucus attempts to legitimize his position. The reverse of the coin (below) shows the goddess Nike crowning a trophy, which may commemorate a military victory by Seleucus.

The empire Darius III inherited was, then, already in decline when a foreign invader came to give it the *coup de grâce*. The man was none other than Alexander the Great who, having inherited the kingdom of Macedon in northern Greece at the age of nineteen, crossed the Hellespont two years later to defeat the armies of Persia's western satraps in battle at the Granicus River in the spring of 334BCE. The victory gave him all the Persian lands in Asia Minor, and he consolidated it in the following year by invading Syria, where he overcame an army led by Darius himself at the Issus River. In 332 Alexander accepted the crown of Egypt, and one year later again confronted Darius, this time at Gaugamela in Mesopotamia, east of the Tigris. Once more he was victorious, and his triumph opened up Mesopotamia and the Persian heartland itself to his troops. Darius took to flight, only to be murdered by one of his own satraps in central Iran. Alexander's triumph was complete.

The Macedonian conquest brought to an end a whole chapter of Near Eastern history. On Alexander's death in 323BCE, both Persia and Mesopotamia fell under the control of his Greek-speaking successors of the Seleucid dynasty. Mesopotamia, which had already surrendered much of its political importance under Persian rule and had seen its economic prosperity whittled away, now also gave up its cultural pre-eminence; knowledge of cuneiform writing was lost and Greek culture was very much in the ascendant. Persia too became temporarily a backwater, although it would later rise to prominence again under Parthian and Sassanian kings. The Hellenic victory shifted political, cultural, and economic power decisively to the west; only with the Arab conquests of the seventh century CE would the east once more become dominant, and then under a very different, Islamic culture.

THE ENDURANCE OF ARMENIA

The conversion from paganism of King Tiridates III in 294CE led to Armenia becoming the first Christian (Orthodox) nation in the world in 300CE, but over the centuries its ancient monasteries and churches have been pillaged, sacked, or razed and Armenians have had to confront successions of raiders, including Persians, Arabs, Mongols, and Turks. Located between the Taurus mountains in the west and the Caucasus in the east, and bounded by the Mediterranean, Black, and Caspian seas, Armenia's territorial extent has waxed and waned dramatically, but these one-time contemporaries of the Hittites and erstwhile rivals to Rome, Parthia, and Byzantium, have endured by drawing strength from their ancient roots in a region that lies at the crossroads of continents.

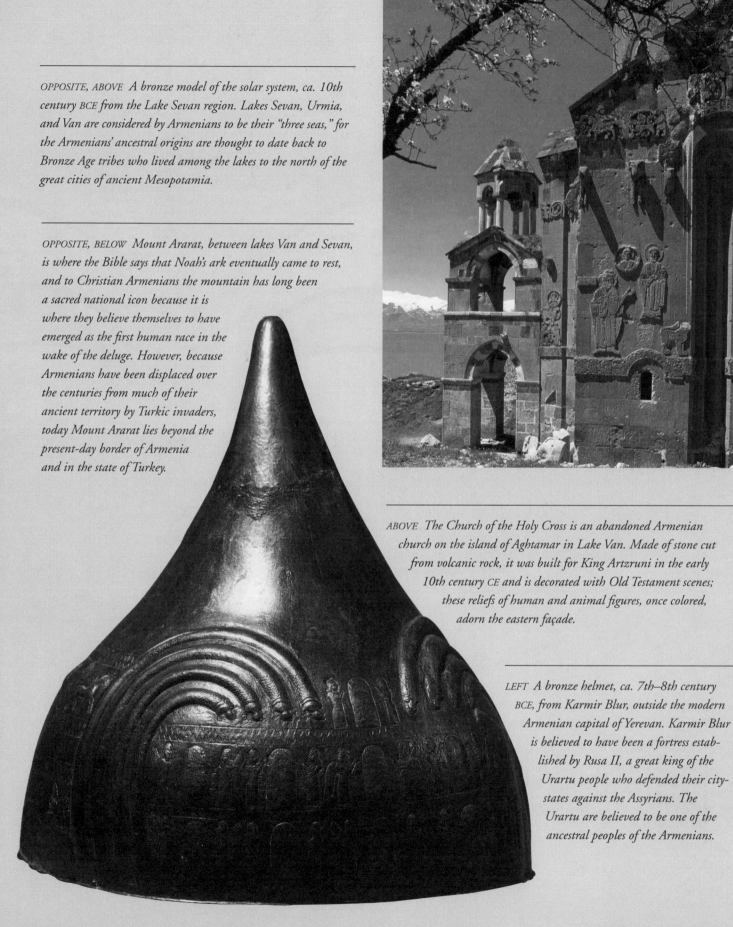

OPPOSITE, ABOVE *A bronze model of the solar system, ca. 10th century* BCE *from the Lake Sevan region. Lakes Sevan, Urmia, and Van are considered by Armenians to be their "three seas," for the Armenians' ancestral origins are thought to date back to Bronze Age tribes who lived among the lakes to the north of the great cities of ancient Mesopotamia.*

OPPOSITE, BELOW *Mount Ararat, between lakes Van and Sevan, is where the Bible says that Noah's ark eventually came to rest, and to Christian Armenians the mountain has long been a sacred national icon because it is where they believe themselves to have emerged as the first human race in the wake of the deluge. However, because Armenians have been displaced over the centuries from much of their ancient territory by Turkic invaders, today Mount Ararat lies beyond the present-day border of Armenia and in the state of Turkey.*

ABOVE *The Church of the Holy Cross is an abandoned Armenian church on the island of Aghtamar in Lake Van. Made of stone cut from volcanic rock, it was built for King Artzruni in the early 10th century* CE *and is decorated with Old Testament scenes; these reliefs of human and animal figures, once colored, adorn the eastern façade.*

LEFT *A bronze helmet, ca. 7th–8th century* BCE*, from Karmir Blur, outside the modern Armenian capital of Yerevan. Karmir Blur is believed to have been a fortress established by Rusa II, a great king of the Urartu people who defended their city-states against the Assyrians. The Urartu are believed to be one of the ancestral peoples of the Armenians.*

CHAPTER ONE

INDIA

The enthralling cultural history of ancient India covers some 3,800 years, from the rise of the country's first great civilization in the valley of the Indus River (ca. 2,600 BCE) to the establishment of Muslim rule in Delhi in the late twelfth century CE. The vast Indian subcontinent enjoyed a degree of geographical protection: to the northeast by towering mountain ranges, to the east by dense jungles, further south and to the west by the blue waters of the Indian Ocean. But through the mountain passes of the northwest came waves of invaders, from the Indo-Iranian Aryans (ca. 1500 BCE) onward. Remarkably, all of these newcomers were absorbed by India's assimilative culture. One key aspect of ancient Indian civilization was a conviction that the multiplicity of the material world was sustained by a unifying divine energy. This belief was married to a perception of time as cyclical. Where Westerners might look to history for clues about their nature and potential, ancient Indians were more likely to turn to myths, which they understood to contain profound insights into human capacities, duties, and the right way to live.

THE SOUL OF INDIA

The peoples of ancient India saw order in the universe. Every part of creation—from the vast planets to the smallest of insects, from unimaginably long spans of time to the briefest flash of thought—reflected and was grounded in this order (in Sanskrit, rita).

Ancient Indians also believed that life was created and sustained by sacrifice (*yajna*), both in the form of rituals performed by priests in the sacred fire pit and as interiorized sacrifice—giving up selfish desires in worship and following one's allotted path in life.

At the core of ancient Indian religious life was a mystical apprehension of unity in multiplicity, of eternal divinity hidden within the time-bound material universe. Some scholars argue that the people of the Indus Valley civilization that thrived in India around 4,000 years ago followed a religious path centered on meditation, and that this approach infused and transformed the ritual religion of the Aryan invaders who followed them. Others argue that the Aryans themselves, while they certainly brought with them a religion based on ritual sacrifice, exhibit in the hymns of their sacred book the *Rig Veda* (see page 150) an awestruck apprehension of divinity in the natural world that is akin to mysticism. Whatever the truth, mysticism certainly fed powerfully into the developing religion of Hinduism.

Ancient Indian temple builders revealed a great affinity with the natural world, never more so than in the case of the 8th-century CE Kailasa temple, hewn from a rocky outcrop at Ellora in western India. Dedicated to Shiva, it was named after the god's mountain home.

• THE CASTE SYSTEM •

The concept of universal order, the vision of divine unity, and the theory of *karma* (the consequences of past deeds) found expression in another key characteristic of ancient India—a commitment to the whole at the expense of the individual, which took concrete form in the caste system.

In this social-layering structure, people were divided into four main groups—*brahmins* (priests), *kshatriyas* (warriors and kings), *vaishyas* (traders and farmers), and *shudras* (laborers and artisans). Most scholars believe that the system probably originated after the Aryan invasion around 1500BCE, when the indigenous population may have been forced into servitude as *shudras* by the invaders, who had brought with them a hierarchical social structure.

The system was set in the form that has survived ever since by about 1000BCE. The word caste, derived from Spanish-Portuguese *casta* ("race"), was first used by the Portuguese in the sixteenth century; Indians used the word *varna*, the Sanskrit for "color," which is suggestive of a racial origin for the system. In myth the caste system was created in the first moments of creation, when the original man Purusha was sacrificed: the *brahmins* came from his mouth, the *kshatriyas* from his arms, the *vaishyas* from his thighs, and the *shudras* from his feet. As the system developed, caste came to determine a person's job, diet, and marital prospects; people from a lower caste, who often performed work that was dirtier and possibly ritually defiling, were forbidden to mix with those of a higher caste. Every individual had a *dharma* ("duty") appropriate to his or her caste, sex, and job. (See also pages 192–193.)

Indian languages do not have a word for "religion" as a separate part of cultural life. The ancient name for the Hindu faith was Sanatana Dharma ("Eternal Law"). Unlike most religious faiths, Sanatana Dharma had no founder: the law was understood always to have existed, from the dawn of time, as were the sacred *Veda*s categorized as *shruti* ("heard") rather then *smirti* ("remembered"). The law was part of the fabric of the universe, an aspect of the divine consciousness underlying and filling the material world. Like the laws of natural science, Sanatana Dharma was a description of the way things were—and applied regardless of whether people were aware of it or believed in it. Knowing and following the eternal law was a means to power. In the sacrificial religion of the early Vedic period, worshippers sought power over natural phenomena and the world outside; in the religion of the Upanishadic sages, knowledge and practice of the eternal law brought power over the world within, over one's own behavior, and the levels of the individual self—ultimately bringing realization of union with the divine reality of the cosmos.

Hinduism's vision of the universe as divine unity was described in the *Upanishad*s and other ancient scriptures (see pages 150–153) and explained in the teaching of the Advaita Vedanta, a philosophy most notably expounded by the mystic-teacher Shankara in the eighth century CE. Vedanta suggested that if all were in truth one, then the multiplicity of the world must in some sense be unreal. According to the concept of *maya* (Sanskrit for "illusion" or "wizardry"), time and material reality were a spell whipped up by the creative power of the godhead; they were real, but beneath them lay a deeper ultimate reality. This ultimate reality, the supreme truth, the divinity enshrouded by *maya* in the phenomenal world, was called *brahman*. The goal of human existence was to become enlightened to this divine reality, to discover *brahman* hidden in the world.

Because unity lay beneath multiplicity, the many were one. This fundamental truth applied not only to the gods and goddesses but also to the whole of creation. According to the *Upanishad*s, each individual had a share in *brahman*: the individual self, or *atman*, was also *brahman*. People who identified themselves

with individual consciousness were simply making a mistake of perception—in Sanskrit, *pragya parad* ("the intellect's error").

Enlightenment was a change of perspective—a new way of seeing in which the individual became aware not only of the parts but also of the whole. This meant that an individual was connected to every other person, to every other part of creation and to the divine creator. The *Bhagavad Gita*, a section of the *Mahabharata* and probably Hinduism's holiest scripture (see pages 152–153), describes a holy and enlightened life: "He lives in wisdom who sees himself in all and all in him … He is forever free who has broken out of the ego cage of 'I' and 'mine' to be united with the lord of love. This is the supreme state." Through self-discipline and sacrifice aspirants were encouraged to control self-will and move away from the narrow ego, to transcend themselves, to be more fully and joyously alive in union with *brahman*.

One important expression of the unity at the core of life was in the union of the sexes. Shiva was sometimes revered as the androgynous Ardhanarishvara. He was also worshipped in the form of the *linga*, which represented the male sexual organs, often in conjunction with the encircling *yoni*, representing the vagina and womb. Together *linga* and *yoni* stood for the divine unity that encompasses all divisions—male and female, matter and spirit, devotee and god.

The many Hindu goddesses—including Lakshmi, Sarasvati, Sati, Parvati, Uma, Kali, and Durga—were understood to be aspects of a single Goddess (see pages 180–181). This great primal deity took many forms as the consort or partner of the major gods—including Sarasvati with Brahma, Lakshmi with Vishnu and (at various times) Sati, Parvati, Uma, Kali, and Durga with Shiva. The goddess-consort was identified as each god's creative energy or force. Without the goddess, the god was lifeless and inert—a concept given memorable form in representations of Durga/Kali dancing on the prone body of Shiva.

Another key aspect of Indian thought was that every action had its consequence. According to the theory of *karma*, each individual carried within him or herself the repercussions of past actions. Moreover, *karma* worked its effects both within an individual lifetime and beyond death, for ancient Indians believed in reincarnation. The process of seeking enlightenment would be carried out through a cycle of births and deaths called *samsara*. To each new incarnation the individual soul would bring the *karma* of his or her previous life. Inequalities of birth in terms of factors such as abilities, personality, social status, and caste were determined by the *karma* of previous lives.

Time, indeed the universe itself, followed a cyclical pattern. In one mythical account, the creator god Brahma experienced days and nights on a vastly extended timescale. He brought the universe into ordered being in the morning and then watched over it for one day, or *kalpa*—equivalent to 4,320 million years on Earth. After this huge period had elapsed, the night of Brahma would fall, and the creator would sleep. When he slept the universe dissolved into chaos. The night of Brahma would last for 4,320 million years, then in the morning he would awake and create the universe anew.

His creation temporarily brought *rita* (order) out of chaos, but contained the seeds of its own eventual dissolution or destruction. The time of ordered being held the two extremes of creation and dissolution in tension. An alternative image was that of Shiva's drum. His playing was the pulse of time: when he paused to find a new rhythm, the universe dissolved and then was drawn back into ordered existence when he began playing once more. The order central to the ancient Indian worldview was temporary, subject to periodic dissolution, but the divine reality behind it was eternal—for Brahma would wake again, and Shiva would begin to play once more on his drum.

In this eastern Indian model of the linga *and* yoni, *the* linga *rises out of the* yoni *and a snake coils around the shaft of the* linga *as a protective guardian. During worship, the* linga *is bathed in milk, yogurt, and honey, and decorated with flowers.*

THE STORY OF INDIA

Humans may have come to the Indian subcontinent as early as 400,000BCE. Settlers from what are now Afghanistan and Tadzhikistan left their mark in the area of modern Pakistan, while in the south of India immigrants by sea from east Africa founded a separate and radically different culture.

For many thousands of years these ancient peoples left few remains of their way of life, until the subcontinent's first great civilization arose in about 2600BCE in the valley of the Indus River in Pakistan. Its people built two great cities, at Harappa on a tributary of the Indus in the Punjab, and at Mohenjo-Daro, alongside the Indus around 190 miles (300km) northeast of present-day Karachi. Each was 2 to 2.5 miles (3–4km) in circumference and probably home to some 30,000 people supported by local agriculture.

Archaeological evidence suggests that the culture—known to scholars as the Indus or Harappan civilization—was highly organized. Harappa and Mohenjo-Daro each had a citadel, communal granaries, and streets of houses laid out in a grid pattern. The people appear to have valued cleanliness and perhaps used bathing as part of religious ritual—most houses had bathrooms served by an elegantly engineered water supply with covered brick sewers for waste, while at Mohenjo-Daro archaeologists uncovered a large bath lined with bitumen in what may have been a temple. The builders used a fired brick—as distinct from the sun-dried mudbrick used, for example, in Mesopotamia—and so were able to repel floodwaters from the mighty Indus despite a lack of natural stone in the area.

The Indus people built a large port at Lothal on the Gulf of Cambay around 400 miles (650km) south of Mohenjo-Daro and traded with Mesopotamia and Egypt. Indus artisans worked in copper, bronze, ivory, and wood. They were the first culture known to have made cotton cloth. Soapstone seals marked with an undeciphered writing and intriguing images suggest they may have worshipped a sacred bull and a horned god that scholars believe could be an early form of the god Shiva. Archaeologists have also found terracotta figurines of women thought to represent a fertility deity. The people buried their dead with grave offerings, suggesting that they believed in an afterlife.

At its height the Indus civilization covered more than 500,000 square miles (1.3 million sq km), an area reaching westward as far as the modern frontier with Iran, north as far as the Himalayan foothills, and eastward to the land between the Ganges and Jumna rivers. The Indus culture thrived for more than 600 years, but began to decline between 2000 and 1750 BCE—perhaps as a result of geological and climate change leading to rising sea levels and the silting up of rivers, which would have damaged trade. Mohenjo-Daro and Harappa were hit several times by major floods of the Indus and also suffered attacks by invaders. Archaeologists' discoveries at Mohenjo-Daro of groups of unburied corpses and clear damage by fire suggest that the city may have been overrun or devastated by a natural disaster.

THE ARYAN INVASION

Perhaps 200 years after the fading of the Indus "empire", its former lands were invaded by groups of warlike nomads whose language, social structures, and

Unlike the ancient Egyptians and Mesopotamians, the people of the Indus Valley civilization left no written records. However, other artifacts, such as this figure of a dancer from Mohenjo-Daro, shed light on their culture.

THE INDIAN WORLD

CHINA

AFGHANISTAN

HINDU KUSH

Jhelum

TIBET

Harappa

MOUNT KAILAS
(MERU)

PAKISTAN

Kurukshetra

HIMALAYAS

IRAN

Mohenjo-Daro

Ganges River

NEPAL

Brahmaputra River

Sarasvati River
(dry bed)

Delhi

Indus River

Mathura

Sarnath

Karachi

Yamuna River

Varanasi

BANGLADESH

Rajagriha

INDIA

Bodh Gaya

VINDHYA RANGE

Sanchi

Dhaka

Bharhut

Tigawa

Dvaraka

Lothal

Ajanta

Elephanta
Island

DECCAN
PLATEAU

Arabian Sea

WESTERN
GHATS

EASTERN
GHATS

Badami

Bay of Bengal

Madras

N

Thanjavur

SCALE

0   500   1,000 km

0   250   500 miles

SRI LANKA

Indian Ocean

religion would be key ingredients of ancient Indian civilization. The Aryans (from *arya*, "noble" in their Sanskrit language), who, in about 1500BCE, crossed the Hindu Kush into northwest India and overran the indigenous peoples, were part of a vast migration that originated from the area between the Black and Caspian seas. From this homeland they traveled far and wide, leaving evidence of their settlement in Iran, Mesopotamia, Greece, Rome, Germany, and Britain.

Most of what we know of the Indian Aryans has been learned from their scriptures, the *Vedas* ("books of knowledge")—a collection of hymns, spells, and descriptions of ritual that were transmitted orally then transcribed in an archaic form of Sanskrit between 1500 and 800 BCE. The *Vedas* give their name to the "Vedic period" of Indian history, in approximately 1500 to 200 BCE. (See also page 150.)

The incomers brought war chariots, iron weapons, a reverence for the cows they herded, and a pantheon of nature deities, such as Indra, god of thunder and storms, and Usha, goddess of the dawn. The Indian Aryans initially lived in clans based on the patriarchal extended family under the rule of a warrior-chieftain (in Sanskrit, *rajac*); group decisions were reached in assemblies.

Priests performed *yajna* (sacrifice) to honor the gods, ensure prosperity, and validate the chieftains' rule. A system of strict social delineation was observed that formed the basis for the enduring caste system (see page 134).

The Aryans gradually became accustomed to a more settled way of life. They turned from cattle herding to wheat farming and established the first Indian states or kingdoms. The warrior-chieftains became kings. Priests continued to perform major public sacrificial ceremonies to demonstrate the status and power of the monarch and his closeness to the gods. In the *asvamedha*, or horse sacrifice, a splendid stallion was set free and permitted to wander in the company of an armed group: any land he walked on without being challenged was claimed by the king as his own; finally the horse was sacrificed with great ceremony. The kings relied upon the priests for their mandate and rewarded them accordingly with rich gifts.

THE BUDDHA AND MAHAVIRA

The second urban civilization of ancient India grew up along the Ganges as trading towns were established on the river's banks in the period 700–500BCE. Craftsmen gathered in guilds and often in mercantile quarters of

• THE NORTH–SOUTH DIVIDE •

From the early period of Indian history and well beyond into the first millennium CE, there was a distinct divide between the north and south of the subcontinent, often said to be marked by the Vindhya hills that cross the country below the northern river plains. While the north saw the rise and fall of the Indus and Ganges civilizations and the Maurya Empire, the south was comparatively undeveloped. Until the first century CE people in the southern tip of the subcontinent continued to build stone circles, probably for the worship of their ancestors. Iron—already used by Aryans to shoe their horses—was not known in the south until around 500CE. The south's isolation is evidenced by the survival there of Dravidian languages such as Tamil and Telugu rather than the Indo-Aryan or Indo-Iranian tongues of Hindi and Urdu spoken further north.

the towns, usually passing on skills from father to son in a hereditary tradition that complemented the caste system. By the late 600s BCE there were sixteen states in northern India. In the following century the kings of Magadha, based at Rajagriha, established themselves as the dominant power in the Ganges Valley.

In the fifth and sixth centuries BCE members of the *kshatriya* caste (warriors) challenged the pre-eminence of the *brahmin*s (priests). Some *kshatriya*s denied the authority of the scriptures and the need for the *brahmins*' elaborate animal sacrifices and claimed to offer a release from the cycle of births and deaths. Foremost were Siddhartha Gautama or the Buddha ("Enlightened One"), founder of Buddhism, and Vardhamana or Mahavira ("Great Hero"), the teacher of Jainism.

Siddhartha Gautama (ca. 566– 486BCE) was a northern Indian *kshatriya*, son of the chief of the Shakya tribe. Abandoning a comfortable existence at the age of twenty-nine, he embarked on the itinerant life of a wandering ascetic or *sramana*, seeking understanding and release from suffering. After six years, the true nature of reality was revealed to him through meditation. His teaching became known as the "Four Noble Truths": that being alive entails suffering and disappointment; that suffering results from selfish desire for pleasure and profit; that to escape suffering one should turn from selfish desire; and that, following an "Eightfold Path," one should aim for right views, right intention, right speech, right action, right way of life, right effort, right awareness, and right concentration. The goal was enlightenment and release from the cycle of births and deaths by achieving *nirvana* ("extinction").

Like the Buddha, Mahavira (ca. 599–527BCE) looked for religious truth through the practice of asceticism. Also a *kshatriya*, Mahavira taught the virtue of *ahimsa* (non-violence) and he recommended five vows of renunciation: of killing, of lying, of greed, of sexual pleasure, and of attachment.

Mahavira's followers tended to become vegetarians and also, since trade could be pursued without violence, they became merchants. The Buddha's basic teaching was developed by his disciples in the centuries following his death. They founded monasteries which became centers of learning. But the Buddha's influence was largely limited to northeast India until the third century BCE when the Maurya king and empire-builder Ashoka became an enthusiastic convert to the new religion and spread its teachings far and wide.

THE MAURYAN EMPIRE

The Maurya kings created the first great empire of Indian history. In 327–326BCE the Macedonian warrior Alexander the Great invaded the Indian subcontinent and defeated King Porus in the Battle of Hydaspes at Jhelum in the Indus Valley. Alexander was intent on proceeding to the Ganges, but his men had heard tales of fierce Indian tribes in that region and refused to go further. General and army headed south until they reached the mouth of the Indus, from where they left India bound for Babylon. Alexander left behind an occupying force in northwest India but also an unstable political situation. The founder of the Maurya dynasty, Chandragupta Maurya, was a ruler of the Magadha kingdom in the Ganges Valley who seized this opportunity to expand his power base, working westward and defeating Alexander's occupying troops, the Greek Seleucids, in the Indus Valley in 305–303BCE.

Chandragupta Maurya (321–297BCE) established control over most of Afghanistan and Baluchistan as well as the Indus Valley. He abdicated, giving way to his son Bindushara, and joined a company of Jain monks, with whom he traveled to southern India, where he died by starving himself to death according to Jain ritual. Bindushara (297–272BCE) extended the Maurya lands to the south; under the third Maurya emperor, Ashoka (272–232BCE), the empire covered the whole subcontinent of India except the far south.

Ashoka attempted a remarkable experiment in government. In 261BCE he embarked on the conquest of the lands on the east coast of India, now covered by the state of Orissa. The carnage he witnessed affected him deeply—as he wrote, "a hundred thousand people deported … and many times that number perished"—and he converted to Buddhism, renouncing war and trying to care for his subjects as if they were his own immediate family. Throughout his vast territories he had pillars and stones erected to promote religious tolerance, mutual respect, and morality (see box, opposite). He greatly improved the lot of travelers, ordering the planting of banyan trees alongside roads for shade and the construction of a network of hostels for shelter. He had medical centers built and healing herbs planted. He sent officials named *dhamma-mahamatta*s throughout the empire to promote and monitor the practical application of his code of conduct, which was based on mutual respect and non-violence.

Ashoka created a strong, centralized government, but after his death the empire quickly fragmented into small rival kingdoms in the face of new waves of invasion—first from Bactria, by descendants of Greeks left there by the army of Alexander the Great, then by Parthians from Iran, then by the Kushanas from the north of the Hindu Kush mountains. Kushana merchants established trading relations with the Roman Empire.

The period after Ashoka's death saw a revival of the power of the *brahmins*' religion. Devotional cults glorifying Shiva and Vishnu became more and more popular. Additions to the great epic poems the *Mahabharata* and the *Ramayana* (see pages 152–153) put growing emphasis on these two gods—the heroes Krishna and Rama were adopted as incarnations of Vishnu, while Shiva's role was expanded in the *Mahabharata*.

The concept of a trinity of Hindu gods—Brahma, Vishnu, and Shiva—developed (see pages 172–175). They were associated with creation, preservation, and destruction and regeneration respectively. Sacrificial ritual of a Vedic type was still performed, but increasingly was reserved for major public events such as a ruler's consecration; religious life began to be centered more on private devotion to a chosen god.

The same era saw the popularization and liberalization of Buddhism—increasingly the Buddha, who had emphasized his humanity, was treated as a god and represented in stone. The first stone Buddhas, probably carved in the first century BCE, showed a strong Greek influence, which had come to India via Alexander's Seleucid successors and the Bactrian invaders, but soon afterward the representations of the Buddha assumed a more Indian style, with closed eyes and serene smile. At a Buddhist council held during the reign of the Kushana monarch Kanishka (78–120CE), delegates ratified the faith's split between the liberalized form, Mahayana Buddhism ("Greater vehicle") and the more orthodox school known as Hinayana ("Lesser vehicle"). The Mahayana Buddhists won many popular converts

FROM THE MAURYAS TO THE GUPTAS

Five centuries of political instability followed the collapse of the Mauryan Empire until the Guptas emerged to forge a new empire in northern India in the fourth century CE. Chandragupta I (ca. 320–330CE) established the dynasty in Magadha, the heartland of the Maurya empire; by the reign of Chandragupta II (380–415CE) the Guptas' lands ran from the Deccan to the Himalayas and from Dhaka to Karachi. Under their rule, northern India enjoyed a "golden age," in which philosophy, literature, sculpture, architecture, and other arts and sciences flowered. The Guptas were Hindus and under their patronage the first stone temples in northern India were built. They especially revered Vishnu and adopted the name Paramabhagavata ("Vishnu's foremost worshipper"). The cult of the Mother Goddess, linked to local fertility deities, became increasingly popular—Durga, consort of Shiva, was an important religious force from the fourth century CE onward.

In the Gupta period the Hindu practice of worshipping images of the gods became established, as did the common pattern of the Hindu temple, with a courtyard and a central shrine, the *garbhagriha* ("womb house"), in which the image of the deity was kept in shadowy

♦ ASHOKA'S IMPERIAL CODE OF CONDUCT ♦

The edicts of the Mauryan king Ashoka, carved on rocks and on polished sandstone pillars, promulgated *dhamma*, a universal law for an extensive empire. At one time, historians tended to believe that Ashoka, who was a committed Buddhist, used his imperial edicts to promote his faith, just as he built Buddhist monuments, such as the Great Stupa at Sanchi (the west gateway to which is shown below), to celebrate the life and word of the Buddha. The inscriptions themselves label his edicts as *dhamma*, the Prakrit translation of the Sanskrit *dharma*, and a term used by Buddhists to refer to the Buddha's teachings. But more recently, scholars have argued that he was primarily trying to create a culture of tolerance and unity in diverse imperial lands that were home to many faiths. This had a religious element but was not narrowly Buddhist—the edicts urged respect for all spiritual practices, including the *brahmin* rituals to which the Buddha had objected. In places where Greek influence was strong, the commandments were carved in Greek, using the term *eusebeia* ("piety") in place of *dhamma*, and did not even mention the Buddha. Ashoka's code urged his subjects to avoid violence, be generous, obedient to one's parents, and respectful to servants.

halflight. The temple tower, representing the gods' home on Mount Meru (see pages 163–164), was pioneered by Gupta architects, who experimented with taller and taller structures. Yet the Guptas were also tolerant of other faiths, notably Buddhism: many fine Buddhas were carved in their reign, while the magnificent rock-cut temple caves and monasteries at Ajanta in western India with their exquisite fresco paintings flourished under Gupta rule.

Gupta power began to decline as trade with Rome fell away and then in the fifth century the Huns and other warmongering nomads swept into the subcontinent, attacking and looting Gupta towns. Northern India split once more into competing kingdoms. But the arts and sciences and the Hindu religion continued to develop. Worship of the Mother Goddess (see pages 180–181) became more and more popular: she was increasingly seen as an aspect of every male deity, his creative force, or *shakti*. The mystic-scholar Shankara expounded the philosophical system known as Advaita Vedanta, which taught that the physical, temporal universe is essentially an illusion, masking a divine reality. The *Purana*s, collections of myths, legends, genealogies, and religious lore, were composed. Temple building continued apace, driven in part by competition between rival Hindu sects. A new form of religious expression, *bhakti*—an intense mystical-devotional faith to a chosen Hindu god—became very popular, especially in the

One of the many local powers that came to prominence following the decline of the Gupta Empire was the Chandella dynasty, which ruled in central India from the 9th to 11th centuries CE. The Chandellas built numerous temples in their capital Khajuraho, including the largest, the Kandariya Mahadeva, which was dedicated to Shiva. This detail from its façade features mithuna *figures (couples) in loving postures.*

south of the subcontinent where it was spread by wandering "saints" devoted to Shiva or Vishnu, who composed stirring hymns in the Tamil language.

TOWARD THE ISLAMIC CONQUEST

Following the decline of the Guptas no major centralizing power established itself until the advent of Muslim rule in India through the Delhi sultanate in the late twelfth century CE. For more than 500 years India saw the rise and fall of local cultures and regional kingdoms. Harsha of Kanauj created a strong kingdom north of Delhi in 606–647 CE: Bana, a writer attached to his court, celebrated the king's reign in the *Harsacarita* ("Deeds of Harsa"), the first major historical biography in Sanskrit. In the Deccan, the Chalukyas were notable rulers in the seventh and eighth centuries. In the south, the Pallava dynasty was at its height in the seventh century: many splendid stone temples were built under its rule. The Cholas were another major southern power in the tenth and eleventh centuries: in their era, magnificent bronze statues were created and large "temple cities" were built, in which the main sanctuary and courtyard were surrounded by a multitude of shrines.

The first Muslim success in India came as early as 711 CE, when Arab forces led by Muhammad ibn Qasim conquered Sind (a region of modern Pakistan across the border from Rajasthan) and local peoples converted to Islam. In the eleventh century the Afghan ruler Mahmud of Ghazni launched more than twenty campaigns across northwest frontier passes into northern India. But these expeditions were little more than looting raids and patterns of cultural and religious life

• MOKSHA •

The aim of every individual soul over several lifetimes was to achieve *moksha* (from the Sanskrit for "release") or liberation from the cycles of incarnations through union of the soul (*atman*) with the sacred force that lives in all things (*brahman*). *Moksha* was a concept in both Hinduism and Jainism, the faith spread by Mahavira. An adherent of Jainism had to pass through fourteen stages, from the first, *mithyatva*, in which he or she is in thrall to falseness, to the eleventh, *kshina-mohata*, the dispelling of all illusion, and the twelfth, *antarayopashanti*, the end of opposition to liberation; a person who attained release became *siddha*, entirely liberated, and left the cycle of incarnations (*samsara*) to reside in the topmost regions of the universe.

In Hinduism there were generally believed to be three paths to *moksha*: through *karma-marga*, or action in performing one's duty; through *jnana-marga*, or knowledge and study; or through *bhakti*, which is self-surrender and devotion to one's deity.

grown from seeds planted far back in the ancient era persisted largely unchanged.

But then came a major shift with the Delhi Sultanate, an era of Muslim occupation that followed the capture of Delhi by the armies of Afghan leader Muhammad of Ghur in 1193. These Muslims had come not to raid, but to live. In Delhi, Muhammad of Ghur's successor, Qutb ud-Din Aibvak, erected a great tower, 240 feet (73m) in height, to celebrate the triumph of Islam in India. In time these invaders, like many before and since, would be absorbed by the assimilative culture of the subcontinent, but the Islamic conquest marked the end of the ancient era in India and the birth of a new period in the cultural history of the country.

THE SCIENCE OF LIFE

The conviction that rita *(order or regularity) prevailed at every level of the universe inspired a scientific search for the hidden rules of existence. Since the whole of creation was a divine unity, these rules would apply everywhere in accordance with* rita—*for multiplicity proceeded from unity in an orderly and regular way.*

Ancient Indians looking for the science of life by studying the natural world and the human body made profound discoveries in the fields of mathematics, medicine, and astronomy. The medical system of Ayurveda ("Knowledge of Life") probably dates back far into the Vedic period. The tradition is based entirely on herbal and other natural remedies, but unlike many folk medical practices it avoids the use of incantations and magic. Its itinerant practitioners were called *vaidya*s. They worked under the protection of Dhanwantari, god of medicine. Ayurveda focuses on eight areas:

surgery; internal medicine; ear, nose, and throat; toxicology; mothers and babies; diseases of the mind; infertility; and longevity. As early as the eighth century BCE Indian doctors were familiar with advanced surgical techniques such as cataract surgery and plastic surgery—in particular, restoring a damaged nose. Several centuries later the medical practitioner Shushruta left a detailed description of these operations in his treatise, the *Shushruta Samahita*. In mathematics, ancient India made breakthroughs that astonished the world. By the start of the Common Era, Indian mathematicians were

familiar with the concepts and use of zero, modern numerals, decimal places, and even forms of algebra. In the fifth century CE the Indian astronomer Aryabhata made use of decimal places in calculating the length of the solar year to 365.3586 days. He also declared that the Earth was a sphere rotating on its axis and moving around the sun—a suggestion that was greeted with grave doubt by his fellows.

But ancient Indians also focused their scientific genius on human behavior and proposed a science of ethics and the right way to live. The theory of *karma*, which explains that our every action and thought has consequences that cannot be escaped, is essentially an application to human behavior of the laws of cause and effect that apply in the physical world. The related theory of *dharma* describes a universal moral and religious law that supports, sustains, and structures life, as inescapable as physical laws like gravity: each individual could only discover satisfaction and honor by finding and following his or her own *dharma*, or path of duty.

The inescapable rules of science also applied in myths and the religious life. The gods and goddesses were bound by them—through meditation and austerities religious men and even *asura*s (demons) could store up *tapas* (heat or power) sufficient to force the gods to grant boons (favors) or to go against their own will.

The theory of cause and effect in human behavior found expression both in the *Upanishad*s and in the teachings of the Buddha—in remarkably similar formulations. Where the *Maitri Upanishad* declared, "One becomes like that which is in one's mind," the Buddha's teachings as collected in the *Dhammapada* scripture reported, "All that we are is the result of what we have thought." Indeed, the Buddha's teaching also set out a

The Buddha, depicted in this 12th-century reclining statue at Gal Viharaya in Polonnaruwa, Sri Lanka, taught that it was possible to escape suffering and disappointment by following systematically an Eightfold Path to happiness.

"science of life," proposing that it was possible to escape suffering and disappointment by setting aside natural desires for pleasure and power and by following a formula for happiness—the Eightfold Path (see page 141).

The sage-teachers of the *Upanishad*s turned the scientific spotlight inward to probe the very tool we use for knowing the world, to produce a science of the mind. By examining different levels of human consciousness such as waking, dreaming, and dreamless sleep, they investigated profound questions of identity and developed the remarkable theory of the *atman* (or "self"), the deepest level of the "I," whose identity with the divine universal consciousness, *brahman*, could, they said, be known and experienced in profound concentration or meditation. These insights were called *brahma-vidya* ("the science of the highest").

The sages distinguished between two types of knowing: *apara* (non-transcendant, intellectual understanding) and *para* (transcendant knowing). According to the *Mundaka Upanishad*, *apara* was a lower form of knowing, encompassing traditional areas of learning such as the arts, knowledge of religious rituals, the study of languages and the scriptures, and the arcane secrets of astronomy; but *para* was the higher form—in the words of the Mundaka, "the knowing [by] which everything is known." To reach the level of transcendant knowing, the sages reported, a man or woman had to go beyond the limits of the mind by seeking unity with *brahman*. In achieving this level of knowledge, the sage would be enlightened—in the words, again, of the Mundaka: "The running river merges with the Sea, the enlightened man becomes one with the Highest." At this level the experiments of the Upanishadic sages moved away from more conventional science, for their goal was not so much knowledge as experience—in this process, the individual became not only the experimenter but also the experiment itelf. The pupil of one of these forest teachers would find that in experimenting with consciousness his consciousness was remade.

SACRED LANGUAGES

From the evidence of 2,500 soapstone seals found among the ruins of the Indus civilization of the third millennium BCE, we know that some inhabitants of Harappa, Mohenjo-Daro, Lothal, and other Indus settlements could read and write. The seals, which were used to close the cotton wrapping on goods when packed for trade, were marked with pictographic symbols.

Scholars have been unable to decipher the Indus language, but believe it to have been a sister to Dravidian languages such as Tamil that survived in the south of India. The symbols were often animals and are thought to have been written and read from right to left.

The language of Sanskrit—in which the earliest Indian scriptures, the hymns of the *Rig Veda*, were composed and later written down—may date to about 1800BCE. Linguistic historians suggest that it may be derived from a dialect of northwestern India; it is one of the group of Indo-European languages spoken by the Aryans and so is a cousin of Greek and Latin. In the mythology of ancient India, Sanskrit was created by Sarasvati, the river goddess, consort of Brahma and patroness of the arts, music, and poetry. She is said to have taken pleasure in playing a stringed instrument called the *vina*, invented by Narada, leader of the *gandharva*s, or heavenly musicians: as Sarasvati played, the root sounds of the language fell to Earth. Her creative energy powered the emergence of the first great works in Sanskrit, the holy *Veda*s, which were said to be the four arms of Brahma—or, in another version, to have emerged directly from Brahma's head.

Vedic India believed Sanskrit to be a sacred language —the *Veda*s had been heard at the dawn of time and the language in which these scriptures were made was the closest humans could come to speaking and hearing the divine sounds that took physical form in the universe. Scholars identify Sarasvati with Vac, the Vedic goddess of speech. She brought the spoken word, which allowed the Sanskrit scriptures to be preserved, through the oral tradition, until they were written down.

◆ KALIDASA ◆

The poet-dramatist Kalidasa is generally lauded as the greatest Sanskrit writer. He is believed to have lived in the fifth or sixth century CE: there is a tradition that he died in Sri Lanka during the rule of King Kumaradasa, who took power in 517. All that is certain is that he lived between the era of the Sunga dynasty king Agnimitra (ca. 170BCE)— who is the hero of one of Kalidasa's plays—and an inscription of 634CE, in which Kalidasa is praised. Kalidasa was probably a *brahmin* who followed Shiva; his name means "Kali's servant" and Kali was one of Shiva's wife-consorts. His most renowned works are a lyric poem *Meghaduta* ("Messenger of Clouds"), two epic poems *Raghuvamsa* ("Raghu's Dynasty") and *Kumarasambhava* ("The War God Is Born"), and three plays including his acclaimed masterpiece *Abhijnanashakuntala* ("Shakuntala's Recognition"). This play's narrative, taken from mythology, depicts the seduction of the nymph Shakuntala by King Dushyanta and her banishment with her son Bharata. The work is notable for its lyrical descriptions of nature's beauty and the pain of lost love. The poem *Kumarasambhava* describes the god Shiva's union with Parvati and the birth of their son Kumara, god of war.

Most of the written scripts used in India—including the Devanagari script subsequently used for Sanskrit—were derived from Brahmi. The Brahmi script, in use by the eighth century BCE, was written from left to right—although archaeologists in Madhya Pradesh have found one fourth-century BCE coin with Brahmi inscribed from right to left.

Scholars distinguish between the script of the Vedic Sanskrit period (ca. 1500–200 BCE) and that from the partly overlapping classical Sanskrit period (ca. 500 BCE–1000 CE). All the great scriptures and epics of ancient India (see pages 150–153) were written in Sanskrit. Great literary and religious figures such as Shankara, Kalidasa, and Jayadeva worked in this sacred tongue. They and the unknown authors of the Indian scriptures achieved poetic effects of great beauty in Sanskrit—indeed, some Indian scholars view the *Upanishad*s as the source of all poetry. In the fifth century BCE Panini helped to standardize the forms of Sanskrit by writing a grammar book, the *Astadhyayi*.

Sanskrit was a learned and élite language. The most widely used spoken languages in the middle of the first millennium BCE were Prakrit, Sauraseni, and Magadhi. The Buddha gave his sermons in Magadhi so that all could understand. Two traditions subsequently emerged among his followers: the Theravada branch recorded his teaching in Pali, a literary language derived from Sauraseni; in the second, Sarvastivaha, his sermons and aphoristic insights were written in Sanskrit. The edicts of the Maurya emperor Ashoka, which he had carved on rocks and pillars throughout his territory in the third century BCE, were written in a form of Prakrit, and in Afghanistan and the trans-Indus region of India also in Greek or Aramaic. In southern India the Tamil language was used from the third century BCE onward.

Similar to a mandala *(see pages 266–268), a* yantra *is an abstract diagram used in Hindu, Jain, and Buddhist ritual or meditation. This* yantra *from northern India is covered in* mantras *written in a form of Sanskrit called Nagari, which is related to Brahmi script.*

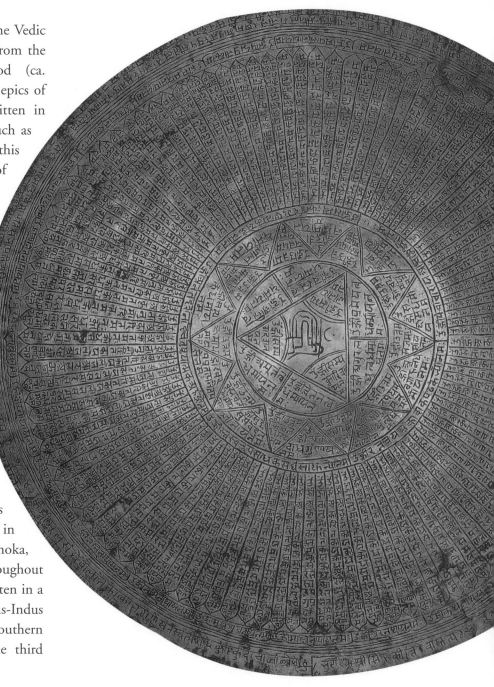

EPICS AND SCRIPTURES

The Vedas *(from the Sanskrit for "knowledge" or "wisdom") are India's earliest sacred books and are made up of: the* Rig Veda, *a collection of hymns; the* Yajur Veda, *a body of sacrificial formulas; the* Sama Veda, *a set of ritual chants; and the* Atharva Veda, *which contains spells and incantations.*

Each of the four *Veda*s is divided into four sections: *Samhita*s, *Brahmana*s, *Aranyaka*s, and *Upanishad*s. The *Samhita*s are the oldest parts, and consist of hymns or *mantra*s (sacred words). *Brahmana*s are collections of prose writings that describe the origin and significance of the sacrificial rites for which the hymns were created—including myths of their origin. While the *Brahmana*s were practical books that would have been an important resource for the *brahmin*s responsible for leading ritual worship, the *Aranyaka*s ("forest manuals," so called because aspirant priests often studied in academies located in the forest) and *Upanishad*s ("private teachings"), focused more on interpreting the meaning of the religious experience.

The *Upanishad*s contain profound speculations about the nature of the universe and the individual soul. Religious concepts essential to ancient Indian religion are first found or clarified in these remarkable documents. The word *brahman* was used in the *Rig Veda* to describe "sacred knowing" or the hymns that expressed this knowledge, but by the time of the *Brihadaranyaka Upanishad* (one of the earliest of the *Upanishad*s) had come to mean the universal soul or divine reality underlying the creation—the meaning described by the philosopher-mystic teacher Shankara and other followers of the Advaita Vedanta school of philosophy. The concept of reincarnation was not found in the *Rig Veda* hymns but both the *Brihadaranyaka* and the *Chandogya Upanishad*s referred to a cycle of births and deaths and contained developments of the later familiar idea that people's actions in one life determined their next birth. The term *samsara* that was later used to describe the cycle of births and deaths did not appear until verse *Upanishad*s such as the *Katha* and the *Shvetashvatara*.

Another key teaching of the *Upanishad*s was the identity of *atman*, the individual soul or the life-force, with *brahman*, the supreme reality or universal soul. *Atman* is perhaps best translated merely as "the self"— an individual's deepest self; certainly in Sanskrit, the word was used simply as the reflexive pronoun. The proposition that *atman* was *brahman*—that at the deepest level each person was united with God—was set out most memorably in the *Chandogya Upanishad* in the phrase *Tat tvam asi*, "You are that." In this work, Uddalaka instructs Shvetaketu, his son, that the divine creator is in all things: "There is nothing that does not come from him." The creator is the truth, the "self supreme"—and also Shvetaketu himself: as Uddalaka tells his son, "You are that, Shvetaketu; you are that."

A great many *Upanishad*s were composed over a long period. Dating of the ancient Indian scriptures is still a matter of scholarly controversy, but the latest thinking suggests that the most ancient hymns were composed around 1500 to 800BCE, the *Brahmana*s and earliest prose *Upanishad*s date from 800 to 500BCE and the later verse *Upanishad*s are from 500 to 200BCE.

Religious tradition made much of the ancient origins of the *Veda*s. In myth they were described as the four arms of the creator god Brahma: they existed from the very dawn of time. They were said to be *shruti* ("heard")—as if dictated by Brahma. By contrast other less venerable scriptures were referred to as *smriti* ("remembered"). But in fact the oldest parts of the *Veda*s, the *Samhita*s, were indeed "remembered"—for after their creation in ancient days they were memorized and passed down for generations before they were ever

---

One of the many artistic treasures bequeathed by the Pallava dynasty of southern India is an enormous 7th-century CE bas-relief (detail shown here) depicting the Mahabharata *tale of Arjuna's penance—a series of privations to which he subjects himself in order to win a gift from Shiva.*

written down. The sacred knowledge was arranged in texts that repeated the words in set patterns to aid recall.

AFTER THE VEDAS

Ancient India's religious-literary heritage also contains two magnificent epic poems that are usually treated with profound reverence as *smirti* scripture. The *Mahabharata*, an examination of *dharma* (duty, the moral law governing life) centering on an account of the struggle between rival cousins the Kauravas and Pandavas, is the world's longest epic poem, running to 100,000 couplets—around seven times longer than the western epics the *Iliad* and the *Odyssey* put together. According to legend, this great work was created by Vsaya, a priest who lived with his disciples on the banks of the Sarasvati River before retiring to a Himalayan cave, where he dictated the poem to the elephant-trunked god Ganesha over a period of two-and-a-half years. Historians report more soberly that the epic was compiled by priests and poets over a period of 700 years between 300BCE and 400CE from a vast range of materials including mythology, philosophy, and hero stories—some of the sources dating from the early Vedic period.

The climax of the Kaurava-Pandava story is a great battle at Kurukshetra (north of modern Delhi) between the rival cousins. Prior to the battle the Pandava warrior Arjuna is unsure whether he should proceed, and is advised on his *dharma* as a warrior by his charioteer, Krishna, who also gives profound teachings about the right way to live and reveals himself as the all-powerful lord of all life. This episode is contained in a separate book the *Bhagavad Gita* ("The Song of the Lord") that was a late addition to the main epic and is revered by many Hindus as the foremost of all their scriptures. Krishna argues that there are three different but comple-

In this artwork inspired by the Ramayana, *the loyal lieutenant to Prince Rama, Hanuman (see page 176), holds an image of the loving couple Rama and Princess Sita close to his heart in a protective gesture.*

mentary ways to achieve release from the cycle of birth and death: firstly, by acting according to one's *dharma* but with detachment from selfish desire; secondly, by pursuing knowledge and withdrawing from the world; and thirdly, through worship on the path of devotion. The emphasis on devotion to a personal god was a new departure that would be of great importance in later ancient Indian religious life.

In addition to the narrative of the cousins' struggle, which takes up only one-fifth of the poem, the *Mahabharata* contains a wealth of mythical material—including the tale of Princess Savitri whose deep love for her dead husband Satyavan persuades Yama, the lord of the dead, to bring Satyavan back to life.

The *Ramayana* tells the tale of Rama, a prince of Ayodhya in about 800BCE, who wins the hand of Princess Sita, is cast into exile then must rescue Sita from the kingdom of Lanka when she is kidnapped by the demon-king Ravana. By tradition, the 24,000-couplet epic was composed by a sage and poet named Valmiki but, like the *Mahabharata*, it was probably compiled over as many as four centuries beginning around 200BCE. The *Ramayana*'s standing as scripture derives from Rama's status as an incarnation of Vishnu.

Between approximately 500CE and 1000CE another important group of religious texts was collected. The *Purana*s were books of instructions, legends, myths, cosmology, and genealogies. This was an era of competition between rival Hindu sects and the *Purana*s are generally grouped by scholars according to whether they primarily celebrate Brahma, Vishnu, or Shiva. Of particular interest is a south Indian example, the *Bhagavata-Purana*, which probably dates from the ninth or tenth century CE. This influential work embraces an intense religious devotionalism, notably in its description of the god Krishna's childhood among the forest cowherds of Vrindavan, his youthful pranks, and his dalliance with the *gopi*s, the cowherds' wives and daughters. By this time Krishna was established as an incarnation of Vishnu; this poem makes much of his mischievousness, beauty, and unpredictability. The lyrical description of the *gopis*' pining for the beautiful young man is a deeply moving image of the human soul's longing for union with God.

The same symbolism was developed in the twelfth-century Sanskrit poem *Gita Govinda*, written by Jayadeva and focusing on Krishna's love for one *gopi*, Radha, while the emotionalism was influenced by the work of devotional poet-saints who wrote in their own vernacular. Particularly celebrated among these saints were the *nayanar*s, Tamil poets who wrote exquisite hymns in honor of Shiva in the seventh and eighth centuries CE—three revered for their devotion were Appar, Nanacampantar, and Cuntaramurtti. They had their counterpart among the worshippers of Vishnu in the itinerant hymning Alvars, who were known to collapse in ecstasy before images of Vishnu.

• BUDDHIST LITERATURE •

Buddhism generated a vast literature, much of it very difficult to place historically. The *Sutta Pitaka* ("Basket of Discourse") in the ancient Indian language of Pali, is among the oldest Buddhist scriptures and contains five collections of discourses said to have been given by the Buddha himself —each is presented as the report of one of the Buddha's disciples and begins with the statement "This I have heard." Part of the *Sutta Pitaka* is the *Dhammapada* (in Pali, "The Truthful Way"), an anthology of ethical teachings as delivered in aphoristic style by the Buddha. In Pali, the book has 423 stanzas in twenty-three chapters; there are also extant and slightly different versions in Sanskrit, Prakrit, and Chinese. The *Sutta Pitaka* also contains an example of the *Jataka*, which developed into a popular genre, retelling accounts of the previous lives of the Buddha.

DIVINITY ALL AROUND

For ancient Indians the sacred lay all around—in the wind, the sun, the rainclouds, the dawn and the night, in mountains and rivers, trees and flowering plants. Nature could be powerful and frightening, but if properly understood was not an enemy. Ritual, when correctly performed, brought power over the secrets of life and made the world safe.

The association between divinity and nature dates from the earliest times: the people of the Indus civilization (see page 138) are believed to have worshipped trees, notably the pipal (*Ficus religiosa*), as well as the bull and other animals.

The hymns of the *Rig Veda* suggest that the Aryans, who moved into the Indus lands in about 1500BCE, also felt an intense connection to the world around them. Their sense of kinship with natural forms was strengthened by the concept of a unified, divinely grounded creation—as revealed in parts of the *Upanishads*. All of nature—from the towering Himalayas to the tiny beetle, not to mention the human observer—was *brahman* (supreme truth) manifesting within the binds of *maya* (illusion; see page 136). In the *Bhagavad Gita*, Krishna revealed himself to Arjuna in all his divine splendor, bright as a thousand suns and emitting the fragrance of exquisite flower-filled forest glades, all the many manifestations of the universe in one dazzling form.

Ancient Indians reserved special reverence for rivers. There were three great sacred rivers in the country: the Sarasvati, the Ganges, and the Yamuna. Each had its associated goddess. Yamuna was the daughter of the sun god Surya and the sister of the lord of the dead, Yama—for this reason, people who bathed in the holy river were said to lose their fear of death. The Yamuna River was also sanctified by Krishna: as a baby he fell into it as he was being carried across by his father Vasudeva, and his touch blessed its waters ever after.

The goddess of the Ganges was Ganga, daughter of the mountain god, Himalaya. Her waters rise in the Himalayas and flow across more than 1,500 miles (2,500km) of northeast India to empty into the Bay of Bengal. According to myth, the holy waters of the Ganges came from Vishnu's toe: they once ran only in the heavenly home of the gods, but by the goodness of Brahma and Shiva they were released to bless the Earth. Concerned that the river would cause great damage if it were allowed to flood out of heaven, Shiva used his matted hair to break the fall of the waters, which ran gently onto the plains of India.

Sarasvati was once one of three wives to the great god Vishnu, but—tired of their incessant quarrelling—he passed Ganga on to Shiva and Sarasvati to Brahma. Later, as Brahma's consort, Sarasvati was honored as patroness of poetry, music, and other arts. The Sarasvati River once rose, like the Ganges, in the Himalayas and flowed westward across northern India; when it dried up in the later Vedic period (ca. 800–500BCE) it was said to have disappeared underground and to feed invisibly into the Ganges.

Across the Indian countryside, worshippers at folk shrines revered trees and stones, representing Mother Earth (see pages 180–181). Fertility spirits, or *yakshis*, were an important part of folk religion and are represented in both Hindu and Buddhist statuary. The banyan tree was held sacred to Shiva, while the coco-de-mer was seen as a symbol of the Goddess. Phallic stones were worshipped as *linga*s in honor of Shiva, and women would make offerings to them in the hope of bearing children. The mighty Himalayas were associated with Shiva, and the ascetic god was said to live there with his consort Parvati on Mount Kailas (see pages 270–271).

A well-developed reverence for the forms of the natural world was reflected in sculpture and poetry; artists in India had a special talent for evoking natural beauty. From the earliest days this gift was apparent: the soapstone carvings of animals made by craftspeople of the Indus civilization reveal a rare capacity for reproducing the forms of nature. This ability was handed down the

◆ THE HOLIEST CITY ON THE GANGES ◆

Kashi ("City of Light") is India's holiest city. Officially renamed Varanasi when India gained independence in 1947, the city lies on the banks of the sacred Ganges in northern India and is one of the world's most venerable continuously inhabited settlements, established in the second millennium BCE by Aryan incomers. By about 650 BCE Kashi was a thriving trading center, renowned for silks and perfumes. The Ganges flowing powerfully through the city represents the force of Shiva, who in some accounts settled here after marrying Parvati. In another version, Shiva manifested in this region as Vishvanath ("Lord of All Creation") long before humans had cleared and settled the land, when jungles grew thickly on the banks of the holy Ganges.

The city is also sacred to Buddhist and Jains. After becoming enlightened to the true nature of existence, the Buddha gave his first sermon close to Kashi at Sarnath. The city was believed to be the birthplace of three of the twenty-four Tirthankaras or "ford builders," the great teachers of the Jain faith.

Half-giant and half-eagle, Garuda, portrayed in this 13th-century CE winged figure from Orissa, is one of the three great animal deities in Hindu myth, along with the elephant-headed Ganesha and Hanuman, the monkey god. He is known for fighting the forces of evil and, above all, for stealing the gods' sacred drink, amrita, *from their celestial home.*

generations in Indian art and sculpture. Carvings of natural beauty—whether foliage, animals, or human figures—adorned Hindu temples from the fifth century CE onward. Human figures were often cut with smooth, flowing lines that evoke plant forms, suggestive of the unity of life; humans were not set apart, but were presented as an integral element in the organic world. In words, too, the ancient Indians' reverent joy in their surroundings is recorded. The beauty of India's rivers, forests, and flowers is celebrated in the *Mahabharata* and *Ramayana* epics, and most notably perhaps in the joyous descriptions of Krishna's idyllic youth in Vrindivan—as celebrated in the *Bhagavata Purana*, the *Gita Govinda*, and elsewhere.

HOLY ANIMALS

Scholars believe that the peoples of the Indus civilization may have worshipped the bull as a symbol of fertility. Carvings on soapstone seals found in Harappa and Mohenjo-Daro depict the animal standing alongside a short post that could be intended to represent a sacrificial altar, or could be a phallic symbol of the kind revered later in Indian history as a symbol of Shiva's power. Other Indus carvings depict a lord of the beasts, shown seated cross-legged as if in meditation.

Rudra, a god of the Aryans, who had originated as cattle-herders, was envisaged as a fierce man mounted on a bull. This powerful deity, whose name means "howler," was lord of cattle and storms, physician to the gods, and keeper of plants used in the healing arts. He was feared for his force and loved as a destroyer of wrongdoers and vanquisher of disease. He was given the epithet Shiva ("auspicious") and later was transformed under that name into a major god of Hinduism.

The cult of Shiva appears to have drawn elements both from the worship of Rudra and from the ancient reverence for the bull and lord of the beasts in the Indus civilization.

The Aryans brought with them a deep reverence for the cow. The animals were a precious resource—

wealth was reckoned by the number owned and battles must have been fought over herds, for the Indian Aryans called war *gavisti* ("looking for cows"). The cow became associated with the earth and fertility—the earth goddess Prithivi, hymned in the *Rig Veda*, was sometimes represented as a cow and the animal was associated with the ancient cult of the universal mother. Her produce—milk, ghee, and yogurt—was honored and used as cleansing agents as well as for nourishment.

Shiva kept his association with the bull and was often represented with a bull, Nandi, as his attendant and mount. In every temple to Shiva a bull is situated facing the main sanctuary, gazing adoringly on the *linga* that symbolizes his lord and master's awesome power. Nandi was white as snow, with red horns. He was sometimes represented as a man with a bull's head; then he was called Nandikeshvara, revered in myth as a teacher of music and dancing.

Other gods and goddesses were also associated with animal attendants or mounts. Brahma was carried on a wild goose. Sarasvati, his consort and sweet-tongued goddess of the arts, was often attended by a peacock; her mount was a white swan. Vishnu and his consort Lakshmi were carried by Garuda, half-giant and half-eagle, renowned for his courage. Garuda was the son of Diti, mother of the giants, and a priest named Kasyapa. To save his mother from a debt to demons, Garuda stole the gods' blessed drink, *amrita*, from heaven. By draining many great rivers he quenched the fire that burned around the drink, then by shrinking his body squeezed between the spokes of a razor-sharp wheel that protected the *amrita* before rubbing dust in the face of two snakes that guarded it. Having seized the drink he flew to Earth. Even Indra could not stop him—his mightiest thunderbolt caused Garuda to drop just a single feather. Garuda was usually gold-colored with eagle's head, human arms, feathered wings, and a powerful round belly.

Rama, seventh of Vishnu's ten *avatar*s or incarnations, was protected and assisted by his monkey attendant Hanuman. Shiva's elder son was the elephant-headed Ganesha, lord of beginnings and guardian of thresholds and the scribe to whom Vyasa dictated the great *Mahabharata* epic. Ganesha's attendant was a tiny mouse. His brother was Karttikeya, god of war, who rode a peacock.

The animals depicted as attendants and mounts gained a detailed symbolism. For example, Brahma's goose mount was believed, when it took flight, to represent the deep and driving desire of the human soul for union with God and release from the round of birth and death, while Karttikeya's peacock mount was reputed to feast on a serpent representing the poison of time. In the temple, worshippers could access the gods through their attendants.

Ancient India also held the snake in awe. Vasuki was king of the *naga*s, serpent inhabitants of the underworld who were sometimes represented as having a human head and torso with slithering serpentine tail. Their mythology developed from fertility cults in which snakes were worshipped. In one important myth the gods and demons used Vasuki as a rope when they churned the cosmic ocean to create the sun and moon and extract *amrita*. In one major creation myth, Vishnu slept on the folds of a hundred-headed cosmic serpent, Shesha, while Brahma arose from the god's navel seated on a lotus to create the universe. In this form Shesha represented eternity.

SACRED SYMBOLS

The *linga*, or sacred phallus, worshipped as an icon of Shiva represented the god's transcendent power. According to a myth told by worshippers of Shiva, the gods Brahma and Vishnu were once debating who was the more important. But their competitive words dried up when Shiva manifested before them as a vast, fiery *linga* that stretched above and below, as far as the eye could see. Brahma took the form of a strong-winged swan and flew powerfully upward, searching for the crown of the *linga*; Vishnu became a rooting boar and dug down far beneath the Earth's surface to find the pillar's root. Both returned to report there was no end to the *linga*: it filled the universe like the divine consciousness underlying creation. Then Shiva emerged from the *linga* and Brahma and Vishnu, humbled, paid homage to him as a god who knows no beginning or end.

The people of the Indus civilization appear to have worshiped phallic posts like the *linga*, perhaps as part of their cult of a lord of the beasts who was an antecedent of Shiva. Scholars believe that Aryan incomers did not approve of phallus-worship, but the *linga* began to be accepted into ritual around 200BCE and was well established by the second century CE. Early *linga*s were naturalistically carved to represent the erect penis, but from the era of the Gupta kings (fourth to fifth century CE), the symbols were given a smooth surface and rounded top like a short column. Some, called *mukhalinga*s, showed the face of Shiva emerging at the side or the top;

others, called *lingodbhavamurti*s, paid homage to the myth in which Shiva humbles Brahma and Vishnu—they depicted Shiva appearing from a burning pillar.

The *linga* was often encircled at its base by the *yoni*, representative of the vagina or life-giving womb as well as of the feminine principle that gave creative force and life to each god. The *yoni* was a symbol of Shiva's consort—who was variously Sati, Uma, Parvati, Kali, and Durga, among others.

The creative union of opposites symbolized by *linga* and *yoni* was also seen in the combination of fire and water, with fire as an upward-reaching male force and water a downward-pouring female power. Vedic poet-priests used the meeting of fire and water as an image for the burst of creativity that brought the many out of the one at the start of creation. Fire was venerated as a symbol of *tapas*. This word referred both to the power generated by sages through meditation and to the concentrated divine desire that manifested itself as creative energy: according to the *Rig Veda*, the *tapas* of the divine creator brought the world into being.

• FIRE AND CREMATION •

The people of the Indus civilization buried their dead. However, their successors, the Aryans, introduced cremation. The sacred fire, honored in Vedic religious ritual, brought its transforming energy to the end of bodily life. Fire gained a new layer of symbolism from its use in cremation: flames that represented the force of creation and transformation marked the departure of the fire of *prana* or life-force from the body in death. As the Vedic priests threw offerings into the fire during ritual, so in the rite of cremation the human body was offered up and transformed. The *Isha Upanishad* contained a prayer that was recited for the dying: "May my life merge in the Immortal when my body is reduced to ashes ... O god of fire, lead us by the good path to eternal joy."

This 11th- or 12th-century stone relief depicts the Vedic sun god Surya. He holds water lilies in each hand—these flowers were commonly used to symbolize the sun which, according to some accounts, rose from the cosmic waters of creation. Surya's elongated fingers may represent the rays of the sun.

Vedic priests also honored fire as the medium of sacrifice—they threw offerings of oil, grain, and clarified butter into the flames to celebrate the gods. The god Agni personified the sacrificial fire. Flames were also associated with the sun, and therefore with the Vedic sun god Surya, and in the *Upanishads* with *prana*—the energy of life, or consciousness. To the sages of the *Upanishads*, *prana* was the life-force that leaves the body at death. As the *Brihadaranyaka Upanishad* stated, a man might lose his ability to see and to move and still have *prana*; but if he lost *prana* instead, eyesight and mobility would be of no use to him—how could he see or move if he were not conscious?

Ancient Indians, who were highly sensitive to the aesthetic appeal of the patterns of nature, celebrated the lotus plant as a symbol of fertility and beauty. The plant takes root at the bottom of a pond and sends a thin white stalk up toward the pond's surface, where it flowers beautifully in the light—just as in a creation myth told by worshippers of Vishnu, the lotus stalk rises waveringly from Vishnu's navel and flowers above, gloriously, in the form of a red flower bearing the creator god Brahma (see page 172). In Sanskrit the lotus is *aravinda* or *padma*: one of Vishnu's many names was Padmanabha ("lotus-navel"); his wife Lakshmi was also called Padma and was often depicted seated on a lotus, while images of Shiva's consort Parvati represented her clutching a lotus bud. The lotus was widely used as a symbol of the Mother Goddess's powers of fertility: an eighth-century stone carving from Sangameshvara in Andhra Pradesh depicted her with a lotus head and displaying her sexual organs.

ACCOUNTS OF CREATION

The Vedas *contained many speculative versions of the world's beginning. One group envisaged creation as a ritual sacrifice similar to that performed by Vedic* brahmins. *The sacrificial victim was an immense primordial man, Purusha, who had 1,000 heads, 1,000 eyes, and 1,000 feet.*

From Purusha's body emerged the gods and wise men, who pinned down the creator father ready for sacrifice. They then carried out a fire sacrifice which resembled the later *brahminic* ritual of casting oil, grain, and clarified butter into the sacred flames (see pages 190–191).

At the beginning of time the offerings of the gods established the movements of the seasons: the butter they threw into the fire was the season of spring, the fuel that flared up in the flames was summer, while the sacrificial act itself was autumn. In the fire pit in which they had performed the ritual they found a large amount of clarified butter, which they used to create

animals, birds, and the sacred hymns, *mantras*, and formulas later used by priests.

Next the gods and sages cut Purusha into myriad pieces, creating the Earth from his feet, the air from his navel and the overarching sky from his head. The sun was his eyes, his breath was the wind god Vayu, and from his wide mouth issued the great thunderer and sky god Indra and Agni, lord of fire. Purusha's soul was the moon. He was also the source of the social divisions of the caste system: the four castes came from different parts of his body (see page 134). Some scholars suggest that Aryans may have performed sacrifices of humans as well as of horses (see page 140), and that this practice lay behind the description of the offering up of Purusha's body.

A myth from the *Taittiriya Brahmana* (ca. 900–700BCE) recast creation as an act of self-sacrifice by the primordial deity. In this version, at first there existed only a universal mind (*manas*), which came into being from non-existence: its concentrated desire to exist produced smoke and flames, which condensed to create a vast and ancient ocean. From these waters emerged Prajapati, the lord of all creatures, initially in the form of a magical formula of the kind used by *brahmins* in their worship. Prajapati tasted the pain of consciousness. He could not understand why he had come into being, and wept: some of his tears fell to become the Earth, others he wiped away upwards and so made the heavens. He created the demons (*asuras*), then sacrificed his own body to make the darkness of night. Coming into existence once more, he created men and women to populate the Earth then took his own body and made the soulful light of the moon; his body emerged a third time and he created the turning seasons before sacrificing himself to make the delicate twilight; his creativity burned once more and he made the gods, then cast aside

• THE HOUSE OF THE UNIVERSE •

Some versions of the creation story present the storm deity Indra as creator (see page 163). In one account in the *Rig Veda* the mighty god built the universe like a simple wooden house. First he measured the available space, then established four corner posts and on these hung the walls of the world. For a roof he used the wide sky. Each morning, the hymn said, Indra opens the east-facing doors of the house to let the sun in, and each dusk he opens the west-facing door and hurls the sun out into the deep enveloping darkness. He was helped in measuring and creation by Savitri, an aspect of the sun god; by Brihispati (lord of invocations), who subsequently was an aspect of Agni, the lord or god of fire; and by Vishnu. A group of divine craftsmen called the Ribhus, sometimes said to be Indra's own sons, also helped him to make the world.

his body in a sacrifice whose fruit was the light of day. In one version Prajapati emerged from the waters floating on a lotus bloom.

The sacrifice-based creation myths were probably formulated in about 1200 to 900BCE when Vedic priests tried to consolidate their social position by claiming that their fire sacrifices re-enacted the primal moment of creation and so sustained the order (*rita*) of the universe. In the Purusha myth, even the gods performed the ritual— life was shown to have come about by sacrifice and was the means by which it could continue. Scholars report that the priests saw the fire pit of their offerings as a microcosm of the universe; in the Gupta era and afterward, temples were also seen as a miniature version of the cosmos and architectural manuals declared that they should be laid out on the plan of a giant Purusha, with the most sacred part of the building, the *garbagriha* (womb-house), which contained the image of the temple deity, established at Purusha's navel (see pages 196–198).

Even in the early Vedic era, priests and worshippers may have understood the ritual as a symbolic representation of the power of sacrifice in a person's interior religious life. The sages of the *Upanishads* spelled out this meaning—sacrifice meant renouncing personal gain and redirecting the force of selfish desire toward seeking union with *brahman*. As the *Isha Upanishad* declared: "The Lord is enshrined in the hearts of all … Rejoice in him through renunciation. Covet nothing. All belongs to the Lord … Thus alone will you work in real freedom." Working in freedom meant not being tied to work: a person who renounced the desire for personal gain and reward could even escape

The god Agni was said to have emerged from the mouth of the cosmic man Purusha. He is often depicted with two heads, as in this wood carving from southern India. In his role as fire deity, Agni was closely associated with sacrifice and he acted as a messenger between worshippers and the gods.

the law of *karma* that would otherwise entangle him or her in the material universe and in *samsara*.

MULTIPLICITY OUT OF UNITY

Many ancient Indian creation myths appear to have derived from mystical experience—the realization through meditation that the many forms of the material and spirit worlds were grounded in unity. In one account, the universe always existed in a mysterious way as the soul or spirit of the universal man Purusha (see pages 160–161), but took form only when he became self-conscious and declared "I am." He had the shape of a man. Looking around, he saw only himself and felt the sensation of being entirely alone. For a moment, he was frightened, just as a person alone in a desert or on a mountain might feel frightened—then he remembered

that there were no other people or creatures to frighten him, and he saw that his fear was groundless.

But he did not find delight in his existence and longed for a partner, a second to go with his one: his desire was so intense that it brought a wife into being. They delighted in their intimacy and from their union the first humans were born. But then Purusha's wife became conscious that their love was not seemly, since her husband was also her father, and she took flight. As she ran, she was transformed into a cow, but Purusha became a strong bull—when they met together in this form the first cattle were made. Purusha's wife fled once more, becoming a horse, but Purusha transformed himself into a swift stallion, caught her and fathered the first horses. Purusha's wife scampered away and was caught several times—creating the first asses, the first goats, the

Indian creation myths itemize in great detail how specific elements of the universe came into being—from the gods to the seasons. Even different times of the day, such as nightfall and dawn, are explained.

sheep and all the many forms of animal life right down to the marching ants. In some accounts the creator god was Prajapati (lord of all creatures) and his daughter-wife was the goddess of the pale dawn.

Purusha knew that he was the whole creation, for he had made it all. Next he created fire, the divine milky liquor *soma* (see box, right), and the gods. This account, from one of the oldest of the *Upanishad*s, the *Brihadaranyaka*, points out that competition between the devotees of various gods was unnecessary—for all the gods came from one source, from a divine unity. The *Brihadaranyaka* proceeds to identify Purusha with *brahman*, the divine consciousness, and also with *atman*, the individual's deepest inner self. The *Upanishad* tells of a sage deep in meditation who realizes that his self (*atman*) is identical to *brahman* (supreme truth). In this moment he discovers his identity and understands the whole of creation, just as Purusha did in his flash of self-realization when he declared "I am."

The hymns of the *Rig Veda* sometimes celebrated the storm god Indra as creator, the bringer of multiplicity out of unity. His birth, as son of Earth goddess Prithivi and the sky god Dyaus, separated sky and Earth for all time, while his heroism in the first hour of his life in defeating the demon Vritra and freeing the stormclouds from the demon's prison brought form and order from chaos (see pages 170–171). In one version, the youthful god not only released the rain waters but also set the sun in the heavens. One hymn said: "Who made firm the shaking Earth ... who measured out the wide atmosphere, who fixed the heaven ... Who slew the dragon and made the seven streams to flow ... Who created the sun, the dawn, and who guides the waters, he, O folk, is Indra."

◆ SOMA: THE DRINK OF THE GODS ◆

The sacred liquid *soma*, celebrated as the drink of the gods and said to have been created by the first man Purusha, was recreated by the ancient Indians and offered in Vedic sacrifices. It was an intoxicating milky drink made from the pressed juice of an unidentified plant, which may have been the hallucinogenic mushroom fly agaric. The plant was pressed between stones and its juice filtered through wool before being mixed with milk and water. The liquid was offered to the gods, and the remainder drunk by priests. When consumed, it appears to have induced visions of divine splendor. Scholars identify it with the drink *haoma*, used for the same purpose among the Indo-Iranian branch of the Indo-European family. *Soma* was personified as the god Soma, who was lord of plants and a great healer. The drink gave Indra his strength and was also associated with the moon god Chandra.

THE MOUNTAIN IN THE CENTER

There are myriad accounts of ancient Indian cosmology. According to one version, the creator Brahma fashioned the Earth in the form of seven circular continents. The innermost continent lay in a salt sea, its land rising majestically to the awe-inspiring peak of Mount Meru, the center of the universe; Bharatavarsa (what is now India) with its snowclad mountains, rich river valleys, yellow deserts and wide plains stretched out to the south.

Seven layers of hell descended below the surface of the Earth, inhabited by serpents and demons, while seven layers of heaven rose above, culminating in the seventh named Brahman, the home of perfected spirits. From the underworld realm of the dead there stretched two paths: one, for those who had achieved *moksha* (liberation from rebirth), following the northern path of the sun to

Brahman, the other taking the sun's southern path to Earth, where souls weighed down with *karma* were reborn.

Buddhism and Jainism developed their own cosmologies, both clearly influenced by the Vedic accounts. According to the Buddhists, the Earth was centered on Mount Meru, which climbed majestically heavenward from an endless plain. Beneath the peak stretched an underground realm of 136 hells, each set aside for the punishment of a particular wrongdoing. From the peak of Mount Meru could be seen the lands of the four great kings, Kubera, Virudhaka, Dhritarashtra, and Virupaksha, rulers of north, south, east, and west respectively. Above them was the heaven of Shakra, Buddhist counterpart to the thunder god Indra of the *Rig Veda*, and forty-four other heavens each with its presiding deity and many varied delights to reward the virtuous. High above these celestial realms was the top of heaven, abode of the spirits who by achieving enlightenment had reached a state known as *nirvana*. There they lived in spiritual peace, in a formless state far removed from material reality, filled with endless compassion for those below.

In the Jain vision, the universe took the form of a man's body—like Purusha in the Vedic account—but without a head, since Jain belief allowed for no omnipotent divinity or directing consciousness behind the manifestations of the universe. The universal man was standing up. In his left leg were seven hells with varied punishments for wrongdoers, while in his right leg lay the realm of the spirits, inhabited by demons and gods arranged in ranks and inhabiting great trees.

The world was in the man's midriff. As with the Buddhist and Vedic versions, the lands of human population spread out from Mount Meru—in the form of eight continents separated by eight oceans. Above rose the man's great torso, containing many levels of heaven: sixteen layers of Kalpa, the lowest heaven, then fourteen levels of Kalpathitha, where compassionate divinities made their home, and topping them the heaven of Indra. Higher still lay the uppermost heaven, Siddha Sila, home to the most advanced and enlightened of spirits—including the great Jain teacher Mahavira. These spirits were not considered to be divine guides or rulers, for they lived in utter peace, far beyond the cycles of birth and death that entrapped mortals.

• HEAVENS OF THE DIVINE ARTISAN •

In some accounts, the divine artisan Tvastr or Vishvakarman built separate heavens for each of the great Vedic gods.

For Indra Tvastr built a movable heaven named Swarga, which took the form of a war chariot. It had many great ceremonial rooms, in which Indra, bedecked with flowers of delicate fragrance, held court. The inhabitants of Swarga burned bright with purity: they included the lesser gods and great sages as well as Indra's servants the Maruts; celestial musicians and dancers entertained Indra and his slender-waisted goddess Indrani.

Tvastr honored Varuna, the god of waters, with a white-walled heaven that floated on the waves of the sea like an island. It was surrounded by trees that were fashioned from the most precious jewels and perpetually bore both blossoms and fruits. Around the celestial palace were beautiful gardens in which rare birds sang sweetly, while within the great white building the rooms resounded with hymns in praise of Varuna.

The divine craftsman built a glowing golden heaven for Yama, god of the dead. In its gardens sweet fruits and exquisitely scented flowers blossomed, while streams of purest water ran both hot and cold and hymns of praise and ripples of joyful laughter filled the blessed air.

Most Hindu, Jain, and Buddhist temples, including the Buddhist Bodnath Stupa in Kathmandu, Nepal (opposite), are topped with a tall tower to represent Mount Meru, the center of the universe.

THE WHEEL OF TIME

A key aspect of ancient Indian cosmology was the understanding that the universe went through many manifestations, that creation would inevitably be followed by disintegration and that both were part of a vast cycle. Brahma the Hindu creator god experienced time on a greatly extended scale: each day, or kalpa, *of his life was equivalent to 8,640 million years on Earth.*

In the morning Brahma created the universe, then in the evening after 4,320 million years of life on Earth, he allowed order to collapse and chaos resumed. By night he rested, and his sleep lasted for another 4,320 million Earth years. Then a new dawn touched the sky and creation began once more with a new *kalpa* (day). Beings who had not achieved *moksha* (liberation from rebirth) were brought into being again according to the merit or demerit accumulated in their previous lives.

The *kalpa* of Brahma was split into 1,000 *mahayuga*s ("great ages"), each of which contained four *yuga*s ("ages"). Age by age the spiritual quality of life gradually declined. The first era was the Kritayuga, a perfect age lasting 1,728,000 years. All people in this epoch were great sages, who had achieved union with *brahman* and were enlightened as to the true nature of reality. There was no work, for people were not entangled by worldly desires, no fearfulness or hatred, no religious rites, no self-regard or disease. Brahma was white in this age and revered as Narayana.

In Hindu belief Shiva appears as Nataraja, the lord of the dance, at the crossing point between two cycles of time. In this way he is associated with both the destruction of the old cycle and the creation of the new one. This 11th- or 12th-century bronze figure of Nataraja from Tamil Nadu in southern India was made under the rule of the Chola kings—a time when Shiva was particularly popular. (See also page 203.)

The Tretayuga lasted 1,296,000 years. Virtue had declined by one-quarter. Humans lost their absolute conviction of union with the universal soul and began to use sacrifices and other rites in religious life. Brahma was red in this age. People began to compete and were sometimes drawn into conflict.

The third age was the Dvaparayuga, in which virtue had declined by one-half. Lasting 864,000 years, this age was marked by increasing human misfortune and the first appearance of disease. People were driven more and more by selfish desire. The holy words of the *Veda*s were split into four parts; while many people still lived honourably, others were dishonest. Brahma was now yellow.

The Kaliyuga, lasting 432,000 years, is the current age of the world, in which virtue has fallen away by three-quarters. Rulers have abandoned their *dharma* and govern by force. People suffer great earthquakes and other natural disasters, and have been driven to live in teeming cities. Brahma has a black aspect.

The mythology of the *yuga*s specified an end to the current age. When its 432,000 years have elapsed then Vishnu himself will appear in his tenth incarnation as Kalki, mounted on a muscular white horse and brandishing a burning sword. His arrival will usher in the destruction of the universe at the end of the Kaliyuga, which marks the close of the current *kalpa*—the destruction is not a punitive act, but a proper expression of the divinely ordained cycle of time.

The extraordinarily long days of Brahma were part of their own even vaster cycle. Three hundred and sixty *kalpa*s amounted to one year in the life of Brahma, and that venerable god was said to live for one hundred years—equivalent to 311,040 billion years on Earth. At the end of his life he would die, and a period of chaos lasting another 311,040 billion years would ensue before a new Brahma was born to create a new universe. Through every creation and dissolution, the divine consciousness, *brahman*, continued to exist, for such an awesome force of life could never be extinguished. There was no end to the cycle of creations, which were like a spinning wheel with *brahman* as the mysterious and majestic force that holds the center of the wheel and creates its movement.

• THE TWO SERPENTS •

In the Jain view, time follows a circular movement—like a giant revolving wheel. In the first half of the circle, a period known as Utsarpini, time moved up toward the top of the wheel. The fortunes of the world improved steadily through six ascending phases supervised by a benevolent serpent, until perfection was reached at the very top of the circle. People lived in truthfulness, avoiding violence, with compassion for all creatures and without greed. But the wheel could not be stilled: it continued turning and the cycle went into a downward movement or Avasarpini, overseen by a wicked serpent. Through six phases of degeneration, the world's fortunes grew worse and worse, until a moment of utter degradation was reached at the very bottom of the circle. Now people lived only for themselves, convinced of their separateness, gathering fearfully in angry groups, inflicting violence on one another and on the landscapes and creatures around them. But just when all appeared lost, the rule of the benevolent serpent began once more and the upward cycle toward perfection was once again initiated.

A MULTITUDE OF GODS

The Western mind often finds itself bewildered by the multiplicity of gods and goddesses in the Indian tradition. The understanding that the many deities were all aspects of a single divine unity provided a solid ground beneath the throng, but it also had the effect of increasing range and variety—because the many were ultimately one, they could be allowed a fluid identity.

Not only were there many deities, but each one could have many forms, often with contrasting natures—Shiva was both a creator and a destroyer, both a fertility god worshipped in the form of the sacred phallus and a mountain ascetic who withdrew into a meditative trance so deep and powerful that it sustained the entire universe. As Nataraja, he was lord of the dance and his steps were both a dance of joy and a frenzy of impending destruction (see page 177).

Different gods might be aspects of one another. Krishna and Rama, for example, were both gods in their own right and incarnations of Vishnu. Brahma was identified with other creative deities such as Prajapati ("lord of all creatures"), and was also sometimes declared to be an aspect of Vishnu. The many and varied goddesses—ranging from peaceful Parvati and benevolent Lakshmi to the bloodthirsty Durga and Kali—were all manifestations of the kindness, fertility, and cleansing anger of the great Mother Goddess.

Shifting identities often reflected priestly rivalries, but also derived from the assimilative nature of ancient Indian religion: progress usually involved absorbing rather than rejecting a competing deity. Rivalry between worshippers of Shiva and Vishnu resulted in the emergence of a syncretic god, Harihara (see box, below); around the fifth century CE, Vedic priests took on the Buddha by identifying him as one of the incarnations of Vishnu. Both the elephant-headed god Ganesha and the monkey god Hanuman were originally local deities who were accepted into the mainstream faith—and the myth of Krishna was partly based on the cult of a non-Aryan south Indian pastoral god.

Perhaps the most multiplicitous of the ancient Indian gods was Vishnu. He was widely believed to have ten incarnations, or avatars, including the gods Rama and Krishna—and even the Buddha. This 18th-century painting from Rajasthan shows Vishnu surrounded by his avatars.

◆ HARIHARA: HALF VISHNU, HALF SHIVA ◆

In the sixth or seventh century CE, the syncretic god Harihara appeared as part of a reaction against earlier sectarian rivalry between worshippers of Shiva and Vishnu. Harihara combined the attributes of Shiva, who was also known as Hara, and Vishnu, who sometimes took the name Hari. Images of Harihara showed Shiva in their right half: the god had a fierce face, as is fitting for a deity associated with destruction, and usually held the trident that was one of his symbols. The left half depicted Vishnu: he had a gentle face, in keeping with his aspect as a preserver of creation. On the right-hand side of the forehead sculptors usually added half of the "third eye" associated with Shiva's meditative powers. The right-hand side of the head was covered in the matted locks through which Shiva allowed the Ganges to fall to Earth from heaven, while the distinctive crown of Vishnu appeared on the left-hand side of the head.

Gods and goddesses were often depicted with four or more arms as a sign of their great power. Durga was regularly represented with ten arms. Some had multiple heads—Brahma and Shiva had four faces to signify their control over all four directions on Earth. Some combined animal and human characteristics—the man-lion Narasimha was one of Vishnu's ten incarnations and Nandikeshvara, a bull-headed human, was a form of Shiva's divine bull vehicle Nandi.

The gods and goddesses had shifting roles and levels of importance at different times. Indra, Varuna, and Agni were prime deities in the early Vedic period (see opposite), but were later sidelined as members of the Dikpalas, a group of minor divinities who presided over the eight directions of the universe. Even within the early Vedic period Varuna suffered a significant decline from his status as a major sky god and personification of cosmic order to that of lord of the sea. Vishnu, one of the three great gods of the *trimurti* (see box, page 172) in the first centuries CE, was a minor god in the early Vedic period, when Shiva was merely a name (meaning "auspicious") applied to the Vedic lord of the beasts, Rudra.

Some deities enjoyed a crossover between the brahmanical religion and Buddhism. Semi-divine fertility beings known as *yaksha* were carved both by Buddhist and brahmanic sculptors. Images of these chthonic

deities from the Maurya period (third century BCE) are among the oldest surviving statues from the Vedic religion. Indra, Sarasvati, and Lakshmi all had important roles in Buddhism and Jainism.

VEDIC GODS

The divine warrior and storm god Indra was the most popular of the gods celebrated in the *Rig Veda*: around one-quarter of the collection's 1,028 hymns honored him. They praised him for his virility and power, his swiftness of action, his muscular golden body, his great belly swilling with the gods' intoxicating drink *soma*. They told how he was born at a time of ecological crisis, when the demon Vritra had rounded up the rain clouds like cattle and imprisoned them. On Earth, farmers and their wives prayed ceaselessly for rain, offering up copious amounts of *soma*—and Indra was born, the son of sky god Dyaus and Earth goddess Prithivi.

In the first moment of his life Indra gulped down the offerings of *soma*: his body swelled with power. Grabbing the thunderbolt weapon that belonged to his father, he leapt into a golden chariot and rode into battle alongside the Maruts, axe-wielding spirits of thunder and tempest. Indra quickly defeated Vritra with his thunderbolt, then sent the Maruts to free the monsoon rains. The clouds broke across the skies like a galloping herd of cattle, sending strong rains down that softened the earth and saved the crops. Next Indra attacked and killed his father Dyaus, flinging his body down to Earth. In the river valleys of northern India the young god's new followers acclaimed him.

Indra's victory represented his rise at the expense of an older god. Dyaus was worshipped by the Aryans before they migrated to India; his cult was carried by

---

Indra's wife and consort, Indrani, is sometimes considered to be a female incarnation of Indra rather than a separate deity. She is depicted on her lion beneath a mango tree in this 8th- or 9th-century CE relief sculpture from the cave temples of Ellora in Maharashtra.

other Indo-Europeans to Greece and survived in the myths of the Greek sky god Zeus. Dyaus was associated with Varuna, another god of the *Rig Veda* era who was honored as the judge of human actions and guardian of universal order, or *rita*. In early Vedic times, it appears, Varuna was the chief of the gods and lord of the sky— his breath was the wind and his eye the sun and he had power over life-giving waters. Varuna's status as a judge and guardian of wisdom associate him with Ahura Mazda ("Wise Lord"), supreme god of the Indo-Iranian faith of Zoroastrianism (see pages 124–125).

Varuna was closely linked to the Vedic god Mitra: some scholars suggest that they were twin manifestations of Dyaus—Mitra was the sky by day, Varuna the sky by night. Mitra was the Vedic Indian incarnation of the Indo-Iranian god Mithra, who in the Roman Empire became the focus of a mystery cult centered on the slaying of a bull. Mitra and Varuna were also worshipped with other gods as the "heavenly deities" or Adityas, who were revered collectively as guardians of *rita*.

The Vedic sun god was Visvasvat at dawn, Surya by day, and Savitri at dusk. Surya boasted golden arms and golden hair and rode the heavens in a chariot pulled by seven great horses or a horse with seven heads. His wife was Usha, goddess of dawn, who was celebrated in beautiful *Rig Veda* hymns.

The fire god Agni was sometimes hailed as Indra's brother—after Indra he was the second most important god of the *Rig Veda*, with upward of 200 hymns sung in his praise. Agni was usually depicted with three legs, seven arms, and two faces—one benevolent and one threatening. His hair stood on end like flames and he often held a flame in his hand. His attendant was a ram. Agni could be seen in the fire of sacrifice and in the flames of the domestic hearth as well as in the celestial fire of lightning. Whereas Indra was the warrior–leader, patron god of the *kshatriya* caste, Agni was associated with priests and sacrifice. He was celebrated as "king of worship" and acted as the messenger between worshippers and the gods.

BRAHMA, VISHNU, AND SHIVA

According to the theory of trimurti *(see box, below), the three gods Brahma, Vishnu, and Shiva were essential aspects of one underlying divine reality. Brahma was celebrated as the creator or initiator, Vishnu the sustainer or preserver, and Shiva the transformer or destroyer.*

Most historians believe that Brahma was never the focus of a cult in his own right. Nevertheless, all temples built to honor Shiva or Vishnu also contained an image of him. Brahma was usually represented with four arms and four faces to symbolise the four *Veda*s, the four castes, and the four ages. In his hands he carried a book of scriptures as well as instruments of sacrifice and prayer beads. He often had yellow skin and wore white clothing and sat either on a lotus or on his vehicle, a wild goose. His wives Sarasvati and Savitri attended him. A myth explained how he came to have four heads: he created a daughter so lovely that he could not stop gazing at her. She was embarrassed by the ardor of his look and tried to escape, but wherever she went—to east, west, north, or south—he sprouted a new head so

that he could see her. When she tried to escape into the sky, he grew a fifth head and followed her: the children of their union were the first men and women. Brahma later lost his fifth head in a quarrel with Shiva over Shiva's fair wife, Sandhya: Brahma transformed himself into a stag to pursue Sandhya, but Shiva shot his head off with a powerfully directed arrow.

In a creation myth told in the *Laws of Manu* (first or second century BCE), the divine consciousness experienced a powerful desire to create living creatures: waters came into being, and on the waters he cast a seed. From the seed came a golden egg that contained Brahma. The egg floated on the waters, glowing with all the brilliance of the sun, for one year until Brahma's divine power split it open: he used the two halves to fashion the sky and the Earth and then went on to create the gods and a multiplicity of plants and creatures to fill the Earth.

In another version of the creation, Brahma emerged not from a golden egg but from a red lotus flower. In this account Vishnu Padmanabha ("Lotus Navel") slept on the vastness of the primordial waters, supported by the 100-headed serpent of eternity, Shesha. Vishnu awoke, just as pink dawn stirred in the overarching sky, to find a lotus emerging from his navel. The delicate plant rose unsteadily toward the sky then gave issue to a glorious red flower, and among its petals was the god Brahma, who created the world.

Like other protagonists in ancient Indian creation myths, Brahma was curious about where he had come from. He looked around him, in all the corners of the creation, then remembered that everything had issued from him. But when he looked within himself, he was able to find the lotus tendril that supported him and by tracing it to its source discovered his connection to Vishnu. In the same way, a devotee might only discover his union with *brahman* by seeking

---

• THE TRIMURTI •

The word *Trimurti* means "with three forms" in Sanskrit. Images of the *trimurti* depict a single god with three faces—representing Brahma, Vishnu, and Shiva. Some scholars suggest that the *trimurti* represented earth, water, and fire: Brahma the creator was earth (associated with the germination of life), Vishnu the preserver was water (which feeds and preserves life) and Shiva the destroyer was fire (which burns life up).

Trimurti doctrine developed in the first centuries CE as a way of reconciling the cults of Shiva and Vishnu with the concept of the divine reality *brahman* presented by the mystic sages of the *Upanishads*. The poet Kalidasa provided a celebrated expression of the idea of the *trimurti* in his Sanskrit epic *Kumarasambhava* ("The War God Is Born").

This statue in Tamil Nadu, southern India, represents the god Brahma with his multiple heads, each one looking in a different direction and from which the Vedas are said to have sprung. Brahma is portrayed rarely in comparison with Vishnu and Shiva.

intently within his consciousness through meditation and religious austerities.

In the *Mahabharata* and *Ramayana* epics, Brahma often appeared as a personalized form of the divine consciousness *brahman*. In this guise he was celebrated as Pitamaha ("Grandfather"), the creator and source of all and the most powerful of the sages. The gods themselves turned to grandfather Brahma for guidance and support. A reworking in the *Mahabharata* of the myth of Indra's slaughter of the dragon Vritra recounted how the gods, downcast by their defeat at the hands of Vritra and a demon army, visited Brahma for help. He told them to ask a great sage named Dadhicha to give up his body in their cause. From Dadhicha's bones the divine artisan Tvastr made the great thunderbolt weapon *vajra* with which Indra then despatched Vritra.

VISHNU AND HIS AVATARS

Vishnu began as a relatively minor deity in the *Rig Veda*, an ally of the great storm god Indra. In the first centuries CE he grew in prominence—worshippers hailed him as the preserver of the universe, who pledged to come to Earth in animal or human form whenever the rule of the universal law *dharma* was threatened by selfishness or greed. By the time of the *trimurti* doctrine and the *Mahabharata* and *Ramayana*, many minor gods and the protagonists of hero tales had been assimilated in his person by means of his *avatar*s, or incarnations.

There were ten principal incarnations. The first was as a fish-man, Matsya, who saved the first human, Manu, from death in a universal flood and killed Hayagriva ("Horseneck"), a demon who had stolen the sacred *Veda*s from a sleeping Brahma. Matsya rescued the scriptures and returned them to the creator god.

Vishnu's second incarnation was as the tortoise Kurma. He played a crucial role in rescuing the gods' drink *amrita* (or *soma*) after it was lost in a great ocean of milk when the universe was dissolved in chaos at the end of a previous creation. The gods and demons used Mount Mandara as a stick to churn the ocean: Kurma willingly swam to the ocean floor to provide a firm base on which the great ones could rest their churning stick. As they churned, using the snake Ananta as a rope to spin the mountain, they brought forth the *amrita*, Chandra the moon god, a magnificent white elephant named Airavata, and the goddess Lakshmi.

Vishnu had to visit the world of men a third time when the demon Hiranyaksha ("Golden Eye") stole the *Veda*s and threw the Earth to the floor of the eternal ocean. The great lord took the form of the boar Varaha

to kill Hiranyaksha, rescue the *Veda*s, and set the Earth back in its rightful place.

Vishnu's fourth incarnation was necessary when Hiranyaksha's brother Hyrankasipu won the promise from Brahma that no animal, god, or man could kill him, inside or outside a building, by day or night. Hyrankasipu set himself up as god on Earth and demanded that all men worship him. He was enraged when his own son, Prahlada, remained loyal to Vishnu, declaring that Vishnu was the true god and could be found all around them. Visiting Prahlada one evening just as gentle dusk fell, Hyrankasipu asked sarcastically whether Vishnu could be found even in the doorpost of the temple in which they stood and kicked at it, declaring he would slaughter Vishnu there and then. In that moment Vishnu incarnated as the man-lion Narasimha and stepped from the doorway to kill Hyrankasipu. He had outsmarted the demon: for he took the form of a man-lion (not a god, man, or animal), emerged from a doorway (neither outside nor inside a building), and killed him at dusk (neither day nor night).

When an earthly monarch named Bali seized the heavenly home of the gods, Vishnu became the dwarf Vamana, a son of the goddess Aditi. Bali granted Vamana as much land as the dwarf could cover in three strides, but then Vamana grew in size and took three great steps that encompassed the entire universe and the heavens save for the underworld. Bali kept his word: Vamana returned the gods' heaven to its rightful owners and gave Bali control of the underworld.

In his sixth incarnation Vishnu was a *brahmin* named Parashurama. He defeated Arjuna, a 100-armed warrior who had threatened *dharma* by tyrannizing the priestly class. In his seventh and eighth incarnations Vishnu was Rama, princely hero of the *Ramayana*, and Krishna, youthful cowherd and spiritual teacher (see right). His ninth *avatar* was Gautama Buddha, founder of Buddhism. The final incarnation would be Kalki, who was to appear in the dying days of the current age to usher in the world's destruction prior to a new creation. In different versions Kalki would be a warrior on a white horse or simply a white horse.

Vishnu was represented in the many shapes of his incarnations. In his own bodily form he was usually shown in the company of his goddesses Bhumidevi and Lakshmi (also known as Shri). He was often depicted reclining on the 100-headed serpent of eternity Shesha, in the position he adopted when the universe had been destroyed prior to a new creation, or seated on a lotus flower. He generally had four hands. One was empty,

standing for generosity. The second held a discus, symbol of the sun, or a wheel, signifying the cycle of death and rebirth. In his third hand he held a conch shell, from which the five elements emerged, while the fourth held a lotus, for creative power, or a club, symbol of time. His skin was usually dark blue, symbolizing infinity, while around his neck he wore the sacred jewel Kaustubha and on his chest was a curl of hair that signified his immortal power. His vehicle was the powerful man-bird Garuda.

RAMA AND KRISHNA

Vishnu came to Earth in the form of his seventh incarnation Rama to defeat Ravana, the ten-headed demon king of Sri Lanka. Rama grew up as a handsome and righteous prince, son of King Dasaratha of Kosala in northern India. He won the hand of Sita, the beautiful princess of Mithila, but was exiled by his father. He lived the simple life of a forest hermit in exile with Sita and his brother Lakshmana, gradually traveling southward. When Ravana kidnapped Sita, Rama and Lakshmana crossed the straits to Sri Lanka and, with the help of his monkey lieutenant Hanuman (see box, page 176), defeated Ravana and freed Sita. They returned to Kosala, and Rama became king.

Rama was generally represented with the trappings of a prince, including a tall cap or *kirita-makuta*. Painted images showed him with blue skin. In temples his statue was accompanied by images of Sita, Lakshmana, and Hanuman. Rama, whose full name was Ramacandra, was revered as the embodiment of courage and virtue, as the perfect husband, warrior, and king. His exploits probably derived from those of a historical prince who lived some time between 1000BCE and 700BCE; the myth took form in the *Mahabharata* and was expanded in the *Ramayana*. Rama was established as an incarnation of Vishnu by the first centuries CE.

The myth of Krishna tells how great Vishnu again took bodily form—this time to defeat wicked Kamsa, king of the Yadavas in northern India. On a night of thunder and heavy rains Krishna was born to Kamsa's sister Devaki: at the moment of birth the rain gave way to a storm of petals that signified the gods' delight. Kamsa wanted to kill the baby, but Devaki smuggled Krishna away to the countryside, where he was raised by the cowherd Nanda and his wife Yashoda. He was a mischievous child, always playing pranks on his mother, often knocking over her milk pails or stealing her butter. But he also had divine strength: as a baby he killed the demon Putana sent by Kamsa to kill him, and as a child he defeated the five-headed snake demon Kaliya.

As a young man in the forest Krishna entranced the *gopi*s, wives of the local cowherds, with his good looks, joyful personality, and exquisite flute playing. His favorite was a *gopi* named Radha. Once he stole the wives' clothes as they were bathing. Another time he enticed them away from their husbands to dance with him in the moonlit forest: by his divine magic he made each woman feel that he danced with her alone, but then he slipped away with Radha for a moment of special intimacy before abandoning her as well. The pining of Radha and her fellow *gopi*s for Krishna, their magical intimacy and sudden abandonment, were understood to be an image of the soul's longing for and intermittent experience of God.

Subsequently Krishna returned to Kamsa's city of Mathura, killed the wicked king, and occupied the throne. He led his people to a new base at Dvaraka on India's western coast (in modern Gujarat). In the *Mahabharata*'s great war between the Pandavas and Kauravas he would not join battle: he offered the two sides a choice between his personal service and the use of his army. He became the attendant of the Pandava prince Arjuna and, as reported in the *Bhagavad Gita*, taught him the way to live a fulfilling spiritual life before revealing himself as an incarnation of Vishnu.

Krishna's story combines tales of a deified princely hero of the northern Indian Yadava people with those of a local or tribal south Indian flute-playing forest god. The main sources for the myth are the *Mahabharata* epic, the *Harivamsa*, and the *Purana*s, especially the *Bhagavata Purana*. The *Harivamsa* is a mythological history of Vishnu, parts of which date from the first or second century CE. It contains the earliest surviving accounts of Krishna's life among the *gopi*s. In these early sections Krishna was essentially a local god but the book was attached to the *Mahabharata* and was augmented continuously up to the eleventh century CE, with many interpolations that emphasized his status as an incarnation of Vishnu.

◆ HANUMAN THE FAITHFUL ◆

Rama's loyal lieutenant, Hanuman, was the son of the Vedic wind god Vayu and a monkey called Anjana. He had a ravening appetite and one day mistook the sun for a golden yellow fruit. Using the powers of flight he had inherited from his father, he climbed to heaven in pursuit of the great sun and came into conflict with Indra, who flung the monkey roughly back to Earth. Vayu retaliated by torturing Indra and the other gods with bodily wind. Then Indra relented and allowed Hanuman to become immortal, a full member of the divine company. Hanuman had many worshippers and in his temples was generally represented as a standing monkey with a red face. His unwavering loyalty to Rama made him the perfect example for a devotee seeking to honor his or her god.

Krishna was often depicted as a mischievous child, in a form known as Balakrishna. He was also represented as a child killing the snake demon Kaliya and as the flute-playing lover of the *gopi*s. Painted images showed him with blue-black skin, a yellow *dhoti*, and a head-dress of peacock feathers, playing his flute.

THE DIVINE CREATOR AND DESTROYER

Shiva—embodiment of opposites, creator and destroyer, lover and ascetic yogi, husband and hermit—was worshipped in many forms. He had five main aspects. The first was as a meditating ascetic, his pale skin smeared with ashes. Seated on Mount Kailasa in the Himalayas, deep in meditation, he generated enough *tapas*, or religious power, to sustain the entire universe. In this aspect he was revered as the greatest of all spiritual teachers, Dakshinamurti.

His second main form was as Nataraja, a divine dancer whose movements were those of life itself—sometimes peaceful, sometimes fervent. The dance was an expression of his divine joy and lordly power; its steps eased the suffering of his devotees. But the movement was also the *tandava* dance of destruction that returned the universe to chaos at the close of each age.

Shiva was also a terrifying foe of demons. He took the form of Bhairava, destroyer of demons; he was also Buteshvara, lord of ghosts, wearing human skulls and writhing garlands of snakes while he danced in cremation grounds—taming any demons that dared to challenge him. His fourth aspect was as a powerful fertility god, worshipped in the form of the *linga* (see pages 157–158), and linked to fertility symbols such as the crescent moon, bulls, and snakes. In his fifth aspect he was a god of medicine, a benevolent protector, lord of

Krishna, the eighth avatar of Vishnu, is shown defeating the serpent Kaliya in this 10th-century Chola dynasty-era bronze from southern India. The serpent's venom was poisoning Krishna's homeland, so the boy trampled Kaliya, and later accepted him as one of his followers.

healing herbs, herder of souls. In his protective aspect he used his hair to break the fall of the Ganges River when it was released from heaven to water the dry earth.

These often contradictory aspects derived from the assimilation of a number of gods in the form of Shiva. For example, from his antecedents in the Indus civilization Shiva apparently took his qualities as a fertility god and as yogic lord of meditation, while from the Vedic god Rudra he received the combined aspect as creator-destroyer and his role as god of medicine. But these features also reflected the ancient Indian capacity to see opposites combined and transformed in one being—as male and female were united in Shiva's androgynous aspect Ardhanarishvara.

Shiva was sometimes depicted as a pale-skinned man, with the matted hair of a *sadhu*, or ascetic. In his hair was often a crescent moon, symbolizing human consciousness as well as fertility. His five faces stood for the four cardinal points and the zenith, representing his all-pervasive presence and power. Around his neck he wore fertility snakes or a necklace of skulls, while in his many powerful hands he carried a trident, symbolizing lightning, together with a sword, a club, and a bow. In one myth he used his bow and arrow to destroy the triple city of the demons. Sometimes he carried a deerskin and a drum, on which he beat out the pulse of time.

In the center of his forehead was a third eye. This appeared one day when Shiva's consort Parvati, lovingly playful, crept up on him and covered his two normal eyes. She did not realize that if he could not see, the universe would be plunged into darkness; in the instant she covered his eyes a third eye sprung into being, sending flames far into the cosmos to ward off chaos. Thereafter he usually focused his third eye inward, where it gave him powerful insight in the realm opened up by meditation and other spiritual disciplines. When necessary, however, he would unleash the flaming power of the third eye to despatch a demon or other opponent.

• SHIVA'S FAMILY •

Shiva and his goddess in her form as Parvati lived together on Mount Kailasa. God and goddess were revered as an embodiment of togetherness. They had two sons: Karttikeya and Ganesha. Shiva and Parvati's firstborn Karttikeya was the god of war and leader of the heavenly army. He was depicted with six heads and twelve arms and rode a peacock named Paravani. His brother Ganesha was a god of beginnings, guardian of thresholds, remover of obstacles, a scribe, and lord of wisdom and good fortune. He had a man's body, with large pot belly, and an elephant's wise head. He gained his head following a family argument. Parvati was tired of Shiva walking in on her when she was in the bath so she fashioned a son out of soap and set him on guard at her bathroom door. When Shiva tried to enter and was stopped, he lost his temper and cut the child's head off. Parvati was grief-stricken, and to console her Shiva said he would restore the boy to life using the head of the next animal to pass by. When a trumpeting elephant arrived, Shiva kept his word; Parvati was delighted with her son's unique appearance.

THE GODDESS

Worship of the Mother Goddess can be traced back to the dawn of civilization in ancient India. The people of Mohenjo-Daro and other Indus settlements in the third millennium BCE made terracotta figurines of wide-hipped women that archaeologists believe were icons used in celebrations of the fertility both of human mothers and of the land, Mother Earth.

The Mother Goddess, or more simply Goddess, was less celebrated in the sacrificial religion of the early Vedic period. Among the deities of the Aryans, goddesses were usually subordinate to their male counterparts. Female divinities were used to personify aspects of ritual worship and of natural phenomena: Ida was the goddess of food offerings while Vac was the goddess of speech who initially presided over the creation of the scriptures—she was "Mother of the *Vedas*"; Usha was lyrically celebrated as goddess of the dawn and Sarasvati, Ganga, and Yamuna personified sacred rivers. However, one of the Vedic goddesses had a more abstract role: Aditi ("infinity") was a benevolent provider who upheld the sky and fed the Earth, sustaining existence itself; she was associated with the sacred cow. Aditi was celebrated as begetter of the Adityas or "heavenly deities" and subsequently she was honored as mother of all the gods.

In the first centuries CE worship of the Goddess returned to prominence. She could take many forms: all the major gods now had wives or consorts, many of whom were formerly the personified goddesses of Vedic religion or assimilated local fertility goddesses. All were forms of the one great Mother Goddess known either as Devi (female form of *deva*, god, and derived from Sanskrit *div* "to shine") or Shakti (Sanskrit for "energy").

Lakshmi or Shri was the consort of Vishnu. She took many forms to be with him through his series of incarnations: when he was the dwarf Vamana, in his fifth incarnation, she manifested from a sacred lotus plant and took the name Padma; when he was Rama, she was Princess Sita; when he took body as Krishna, she was born both as Radha, his beloved *gopi*, and Rukmini, his favorite wife. Lakshmi was generally represented with the full breasts and wide hips of a fertility goddess, standing or seated on a lotus, attended by a white owl and bathed in water poured from the upraised trunks of a pair of devout elephants. Her worshippers praised her as goddess of wealth and prosperity. Brahma's consort Sarasvati, patroness of music, poetry, and scriptures was generally represented with white skin and holding a lyre, standing on a lotus flower or riding a white swan.

Shiva had a number of consorts, all forms of Devi/Shakti. The first was Sati, Brahma's granddaughter through his son Daksha. Shiva and Daksha quarreled and when Daksha excluded Shiva from a major sacrificial ceremony, Sati, determined to prove her love for her husband, threw herself into the sacred fire. Shiva was distraught and taking his beloved's body in his arms, embarked on a tender and mournful dance through the world. Vishnu followed and in his kindness cut away at Sati's body as Shiva danced, so easing Shiva's grief and leaving remnants of the goddess throughout the world.

Shiva's suffering was further relieved when his goddess returned to him in the form of Parvati, daughter of the mountain god Himavan. In her own form, Parvati was represented as a beautiful and full-breasted woman often holding a lotus bud to symbolize her rich fertility. Subsequently she took dual forms as golden-skinned Uma and as fearsome black-skinned Durga (see box, opposite). From Durga's forehead emerged another terrifying incarnation of the Goddess: Kali.

In one myth the Goddess was created when the powerful gazes of the three gods Shiva, Brahma, and Vishnu intersected; in other versions the primal Goddess existed prior to any of the male gods. Toward the end of the era of ancient India, the Goddess in her many forms was widely understood as the creative force of each god and was primarily worshipped under the name Shakti. None of the gods could perform his function—whether creative or destructive—without this energy.

• DURGA AND KALI •

In her aspects as Durga and Kali the Goddess represented the power of goodness to overcome ignorance in the form of demons. Durga was Shiva's spouse in his aspect as Bhairava, destroyer of demons, and she was sometimes celebrated as Bhairavi, the feminine form of that name. Myths recount that Durga (Sanskrit for "unreachable") was born to rid the gods of the man-headed buffalo demon Mahishasura: each of the gods gave her a special weapon for the fight. Durga was usually depicted riding a lion or tiger, with eight or ten arms representing her awesome power, each hand holding one of the particular weapons of the other gods. The seventh-century CE relief sculpture from the Mahishasuramardini cave temple at Mamallapuram in Tamil Nadu (below) depicts Durga's battle with Mahishasura.

Kali (Sanskrit for "black") was renowned for her bloodthirstiness: when she killed the demon Raktavija, she held him up above her head and drank all his lifeblood without spilling a single drop on the ground. Kali was shown with an emaciated black body, open bloodstained mouth, red protruding tongue, a necklace of human skulls, and a belt of human hands. Her four hands usually held a severed head, a noose, a shield, and a sword.

LOVE AND THE LIFE-FORCE

Shiva's complementary roles as yogic ascetic and virile fertility god created an intriguing tension that found expression in the myth of his encounter with Kama, the ancient Indian god of love. In this tale the other gods were suffering at the hands of a demon named Taraka, who had won a boon safeguarding him from all opponents save a future son of Shiva.

S hiva had a beautiful consort in Parvati, daughter of the majestic Himalayas, but the chances of the couple producing any offspring were greatly reduced by Shiva's consuming passion for meditation, which meant that he had no time or inclination for lovemaking. Indra sent Kama to the home of Shiva and Parvati on Mount Kailasa to awaken Shiva's virile power. But when Shiva was disturbed from his meditation, he grew angry: his third eye blazed forth and he reduced Kama to ashes. Shiva subsequently restored the love god to life, but without a body, and sent him out into the world to spread warmth. Then Parvati and Shiva made love and their son Karttikeya was born and went on to defeat Taraka—much to the relief of the other gods, who were able to return to their carefree existences after the hardships inflicted upon them by the powerful demon.

Other elements and versions of this myth emphasize the awesome power of Shiva's virility, recounting how his semen had to be transported by the gods—but it burned so strongly with power that neither the fire god Agni nor the mighty Ganges was able to carry it. Shiva could be both fertility god and ascetic because in ancient Indian religious thought sexual energy was an aspect of divine energy. Whereas in the Judaeo-Christian tradition the physical world is often seen as "fallen" and defiled by sin, in ancient India devotees saw every aspect of creation as a manifestation

These bronze temple images of the divine couple Shiva (left) and Parvati date from the early 11th century CE and originate from the Deccan plateau in central India. Unlike southern-Indian Chola-dynasty bronzes from the same period, which tend to show figures in relaxed, naturalistic poses, these examples are erect and formal.

of the divine consciousness. There was a strong strain of asceticism in ancient India, but this was based on the premise that self-indulgence was a waste of life energy that could better be expressed in worship: in religious austerities and meditation a devotee would seek to learn control of the bodily senses and, thereafter, of the mind. Shiva in his yogic aspect was the perfect role model: he had unimaginable physical power and prowess, but he did not allow his energy to be entangled by his senses, instead pouring the power of his *prana*, or life-force, into meditation.

Some patterns of religious thought proposed harnessing sexual energy in religious worship. From around the seventh century CE, esoteric theories suggested that the union of male and female energies, either within the body or between individuals through controlled sexual activity, could lead to enlightenment. Scholars call these theories Tantrism because they are found in texts called *tantra* (from Sanskrit for "loom"), wide-ranging documents that contain rituals, spells, and symbols as well as teachings on temple building, yogic exercises, and religious worship. The Tantric tradition taught that two types of energy sustained the universe: Shiva (male) and Shakti (female). Through yogic exercises and meditation, the two forces could be brought into a creative union within the body—resulting in experience of divinity (see box, right). Tantric theories also argued that sexual activity could be a form of worship—in particular, that when a man and woman performed prolonged sexual intercourse without the pleasure of physical release, they could achieve a silencing of mental processes that allowed for a mystical experience of the unity of life.

• KUNDALINI RISING •

Tantric theories saw the human body as a microcosm of the universe. Like the wider world, the body relied on the combination of male and female energy.

According to this vision, the spine was the microcosmic equivalent of the awesome Mount Meru, the central pillar of the universe (see pages 164–165). Three main nerve connections on the spine corresponded to the three sacred rivers: the Sarasvati, the Yamuna, and the Ganges. The rhythm of breathing was to the body what the pulse of time was to the universe. There were seven main energy centers or *chakra*s (from Sanskrit *chakrum*, "wheel"), arranged on the line connecting the base of the spine to the top of the skull (see left): each was like a spinning wheel or a flower constantly opening and closing. Female energy, called Shakti or *kundalini*, lay coiled like a great snake at the base of the spine. Rituals and exercises would awaken *kundalini* and encourage her to rise along the spine to the *chakrum* at the top of the head, where she would encounter male energy, or Shiva. In this supreme moment the duality of male and female dissolved to give the devotee a transcendent experience of the unity of life.

DEMIGODS, SPIRITS, AND FABULOUS CREATURES

A rich variety of hybrid creatures, animal spirits, and demigods inhabited the myths and adorned the temples of ancient India. They interacted with and assisted the gods in many different ways: some provided support in battle and others entertainment during less troubled times. On Earth, too, they were believed to play important roles—for example as temple protectors or bringers of fertility.

Dwarf-like spirits called *gana*s were believed to have the power to protect temples against negative spiritual forces and their images were carved on the temple surfaces. The *gana*s were protected by Shiva and commanded by Ganesha, who was known as the lord of the *gana*s. They were originally nature spirits, probably honored alongside Shiva's antecedent, the Indus civilization's lord of beasts. They accompanied Shiva when he visited cremation grounds and battlefields in his aspect as Bhairava, Destroyer of Demons.

*Gana*s were assisted in protecting temples by *vyala*s or *yali*s, often terrifying hybrid creatures combining the powerful body of a lion with the fierce head of an elephant, tiger, or bird. They were depicted with eyes bulging, just at the point of triumphing over an enemy. Some scholars suggest that *vyala*s were symbols of the all-conquering sun.

Other celebrated hybrids were the half-human, half-snake *naga*s, denizens of the underworld kingdom of Nagaloka, guardians of treasure and esoteric writings. Brahma had banished them to the underworld when their numbers had threatened to overwhelm the Earth; he gave them permission to bite those in whose hearts goodness had well nigh disappeared. Their princesses

Yakshis, such as this 1st-century CE example from Sanchi, were commonly carved on the facade of Hindu and Jain temples and Buddhist stupas. In all three faiths, yakshis were portrayed as wide-hipped, voluptuous symbols of fertility. They were believed to be able to cause a tree to bear fruit just by touching it with their foot.

were known for their astonishing beauty, and certain royal houses, including the Pallava dynasty of southern India, claimed their origin in the ancient marriage of a human king and a *naga* queen. *Naga*s were associated with seas, rivers, streams, and wells. At any time they could shift their shape to appear wholly human or wholly serpentine. On temples they were often shown adopting a reverent posture in the presence of the major gods and goddesses.

Other temple protectors included fierce-faced *dvarapala*s carved on the doorposts of shrines, and heavenly beauties named *surasundari*s. *Dvarapala*s usually carried clubs and showed the attributes of the god whose shrine they were defending. *Surasundari*s were often shown with a bird or monkey or performing their ablutions. These maidens—with the wide hips, tiny waist, and swelling breasts of fertility goddesses—were one of many groups of voluptuous spirit-women praised by ancient Indians. Another was the *apsara*s, lithe dancing maidens who added visible beauty to the song of the heavenly musicians the *gandharva*s (see box, below).

In the *Mahabharata*, the *gandharva*s and *apsara*s entertained their divine masters with song and dance in the heavenly halls and gardens laid out by the divine artisan Tvastr (see box, page 164). A narrative in that poem described how the hero Arjuna visited Swarga, the heaven of his father Indra, and was bewitched by the dancing of the *apsara*s, notably one spirit of captivating beauty named Menaka, whose eyes were like the blooms of the lotus. The *Rig Veda* hymns referred to personifications of these two groups in the god Gandharva, celebrated for mixing the gods' intoxicating *soma* drink, and the goddess Apsaras, his consort, maiden of fresh waters. But these two deities are not found in later sources.

*Yakshi*s were female fertility spirits, bringers of abundance, sometimes associated with trees and other natural phenomena. They were probably descendants of the terracotta fertility mothers made by potters of the Indus civilization. Carvings of these spirits survive from the second century BCE. *Yakshi*s had their male counterparts in *yaksha*s and both perhaps were ancestors of the *dvarapala*s and *surasundari*s later carved on stone temples.

♦ THE HEAVENLY SINGERS ♦

The *gandharva*s were celebrated as heavenly singers and instrumentalists, who gave humankind the gift of music. Their melodies eased and dissolved the suffering of men and women. Lonely travelers in the mountains or deep forests might hear the delicate strain of *gandharva*s' songs or encounter a group of the celestial musicians manifesting from the thickening light in a dusky clearing. *Gandharva*s, who lived in the air as well as among trees and on the stony peaks, could work bewitching tricks in the twilight. They were all male and, while soft of voice and lithe of movement, they were renowned for their strength in battle. Often *gandharva*s challenged a traveler to combat: they would carry off any they defeated, but they were bound to share precious secrets of the religious life with those brave men who got the better of them. *Gandharva*s were known for their liking for the sweet smoke of incense and for oils scented with flowers. They lived in numerous tribes and in all were more than 6,000 strong. Their leader, Narada, invented the stringed instrument known as the *vina*; he was also credited with inspiring the composition of the *Ramayana* epic.

ENEMIES OF THE LIGHT

Demons (asuras) were opponents of righteousness, representatives of doubt and ignorance, enemies of the light. They were brothers of the gods, members of an extended divine family who had gone to bad. Although persistent foes of the gods (devas), demons were not irredeemably wicked, for in the ancient Indian understanding there was no pure evil.

The forces of ignorance could take many forms: as giants, serpents, genies, and fierce hybrid beasts. The demoness Vatapi was a foul hag who mistreated the holy men of India until she was finally overcome by the sage Agastya. Demons were particularly known as disrupters of religious rites. Devotees who failed to follow correct ritual or who allowed themselves to become absent-minded were often the victims of asuras. However, when demons performed religious austerities they could build up stores of righteous energy in the form of tapas, and some repented entirely of their ignorance to become great forces for good.

Coming from the same family, ancient Indian demons and gods were ultimately alike. Indeed, in the early Vedic period both asuras and devas were revered as gods. But later the devas were worshipped as gods and the asuras were feared as wicked giants and demons. Devas and asuras were an inheritance from the Aryans' Indo-Iranian past: curiously, in the Zoroastrian religion that developed in Iran the roles were reversed, with devas (or daevas) becoming the forces of evil and asuras (or ahuras) being hailed as the gods (see page 124).

The demons had narrowly missed out on immortality at the time of the churning of the ocean of milk. On Vishnu's instructions, gods and demons shared the labor of churning the great ocean in order to bring forth the divine drink amrita, which made all those who drank it immortal. When the gods' physician Dhanwantari arose from the ocean holding a cup of amrita, the demons seized the precious drink, but before they could consume it Vishnu took it back. Then the gods happily drank down the amrita, and thereafter could never die or be killed. However, the demon Rahu disguised himself as a god and managed to have a taste. The devas tried to slaughter him, but the amrita had made his head and neck immortal: Rahu rose into the sky, where at times of eclipse he gains a measure of revenge against the gods by swallowing the sun and moon. Because they were denied the chance to drink amrita, none of the other asuras could cheat death forever in this way, although from time to time individual demons generated so much tapas through austerities that Brahma was forced to make them invulnerable for a particular time or according to agreed conditions.

However much power the demons accrued, they were ultimately subject to the gods' will. At one time, a trio of demons named Tarakaksa, Kamalaksa, and Vidyunmalin collected sufficient tapas to force Brahma to allow them to construct one magnificent city in each of the three worlds—an iron city ruled by Vidyunmalin on Earth, a silver city ruled by Kamalaksa in the air, and a golden city ruled by Tarakaksa in heaven. There they lived for many years and legions of demons came to reside with them. Then Tarakaksa's son, Hari, performed such great austerities that he won Brahma's approval for the creation of a magical lake with the power to restore slain demon warriors to life. Thereafter the demons ran riot, upsetting *dharma* throughout the universe, so that the gods prevailed upon Brahma to arrange for the destruction of the demon cities. Shiva rode to the cities in a great chariot and, firing a single arrow, vanquished all three. His action reasserted the gods' power and also foretold the cataclysm that will consume the universe when the current age, the Kaliyuga, comes to an end (see pages 166–167).

This detail from a 16th-century Moghul painting depicts the battle between the forces of Rama and those of Ravana, the demon king of Sri Lanka, who had kidnapped Rama's wife Princess Sita (see page 175).

THE COMPASSIONATE
BODHISATTVA

In its earliest form, Buddhism was essentially a practical philosophy of life and had little place for myths about its founder or associated figures, but over the years a mythology of the Buddha and a pantheon of Buddhist deities developed.

The belief that the Buddha's soul must have suffered through many lifetimes in order to achieve enlightenment as Prince Siddhartha Gautama led to the development of an entire genre of myths, the *Jataka*, retelling accounts of his previous incarnations. These often adapted folktales to their purpose. There were more than 500 *Jataka* tales, which described how, over myriad lifetimes, the Buddha took many forms—hare, antelope, deer, vulture, merchant, robber, god. In each incarnation he achieved the fullest degree of perfection possible in that state, and so was reborn in a position higher up the scale of incarnations.

On more than one occasion the Buddha's forebear demonstrated his selflessness and compassion by offering up his own life. In his incarnation as a hare, he was visited by the god Shakra (an alternative form of Indra) and realizing that he had no food to offer his guest tried to make a meal of himself. Shakra stopped him and to commemorate the episode drew the image of a hare on the face of the moon, so creating the markings that in Western culture are described as the "man in the moon." In another life the Buddha was a priest's son who offered himself as a meal to prevent a starving tigress from consuming her young; in still another he was a king who donated his eyes to a beggar and was given new eyes by Shakra.

A fully developed Buddhist pantheon developed over time. Indra was one of many Vedic gods to find a place in Buddhism: as Shakra, he was revered as king of heaven. The goddess Sarasvati was honored by Buddhists as patroness of teaching. Shiva and Parvati were known to Buddhists, but lost their proud position—they were doorkeepers to the Buddha. The earth god Kubera was the Buddha's bodyguard but was renamed Jambhala. The Vedic underworld lord Yama was called Dharmaraja by the Buddhist faithful.

A mythology also grew up about the birth and life of Siddhartha Gautama, weaving a narrative around the bare bones of historical fact. According to these accounts, his mother Princess Mahayama was made pregnant when a great white elephant came to her bedchamber and entered her womb: nine months later a fully grown child emerged from Mahayama's side; a lotus plant sprang from the earth at the point where he first set foot. Disturbed by a prophecy that the boy Siddhartha would abandon his family to seek enlightenment, his father, King Suddhodana, tried to shield him from unhappiness by imprisoning him among palace luxuries, but as a young man Siddhartha left the palace for the first time and was shocked by four sights that opened his eyes to the suffering of life: an old man, a sick man, a corpse, and a begging monk.

Siddhartha was married to the fair princess Yasodhara, but he left her behind to seek enlightenment. After practicing asceticism and the way of knowledge he settled on the middle path between extremes, and through long hours of meditation beneath a tree at Bodh Gaya he achieved enlightenment—despite the best efforts of the demon king Mara to distract him. The Buddha taught for forty-five years, then in a country grove, satisfied that his work was done, lay down and passed into the extinction of *nirvana* (enlightenment).

Followers of the Mahayana ("Greater vehicle") form of Buddhism that arose at the beginning of the common era also built up a significant mythology about *bodhisattva*s, individual souls who had achieved enlightenment but who chose to postpone their entry into *nirvana* in order to help others toward release from rebirth. Like the historical Buddha himself, a *bodhisattva* would suffer through many lives on Earth before achieving this sublime level of enlightenment. A *bodhisattva* was perfect in six areas: patience, wisdom, meditation, morality, generosity, and energy.

The most significant *bodhisattva* was probably Avalokiteshvara ("the Lord who looks in all directions"), celebrated for his infinite compassion for those suffering on Earth. He was revered as the guardian of the Earth in the period between the departure of the historical Buddha and the future incarnation of the Buddha, Maitreya, who would usher in the end of the universe's current phase. Avalokiteshvara was believed to be an earthly form of the eternal Buddha, Amitabha, whose image he wore on his headdress. Maitreya—whose name derived from Sanskrit *maitri* ("friendliness")—would come to Earth when the teachings of the Buddha had fallen entirely away. Avalokiteshvara and Maitreya were particularly worshipped in northern India between the third and seventh centuries of the common era.

A highly complex Jain mythology centered on the cosmological image of the wheel of time and its circular movement through a cycle of decreasing and then increasing sanctity (see page 167). Each of these cycles contained sixty-three spiritual and secular leaders called Shalakapurushas, consisting of twenty-four Tirthankaras ("ford builders"), or spiritual teachers, twelve emperors, and nine triads of heroes. Each triad contained a powerful warrior called Vasudeva, his less powerful older half-brother called Baladeva, and a fierce enemy called Prativasudeva: this pattern was based on the myth of Krishna, his brother Balarama, and their foe Kamsa.

The Buddha attained enlightenment at Bodh Gaya in central India and Buddhist pilgrims have traveled there ever since. In the 6th century CE a large brick temple called the Mahabodhi (right) was built at the sacred site, and the Bodhi tree that stands there today is believed to be a descendant of the one under which the Buddha meditated.

A LIFE OF RITUAL

The sumptuous temples and exquisite votive objects created under the great dynasties such as the Guptas, Pallavas, and Cholas give only a partial impression of ancient Indian worship and ritual. Alongside the often complex sacrificial ceremonies led by the brahmins, *there was an older tradition of honoring trees and animals with simple rituals conducted in the open air.*

The peoples of the Indus civilization left little evidence of formal temple worship. The remains of a large bath at Mohenjo-Daro suggest that the city's inhabitants may have performed ritual bathing as their descendants would on the bathing steps attached to riverbank Hindu temples; images on Indus soapstone seals may depict a bull standing before an altar. But other remains suggest that the Indus people worshipped trees, animals, and the fertile earth in a natural setting.

This tradition persisted throughout the history of ancient India in local cults practiced at village shrines. The Aryans brought with them their sacrificial religion, but this became established as primarily the faith of the upper social classes—the *kshatriyas* (warriors) and *brahmins* (priests). Other social groups gave expression to their religious impulse by worshipping the spirits of trees, stones, snakes, animals, and local protective or fertility deities. Even when Gupta architects began the building of stone Hindu temples in the fourth to sixth centuries CE, folk shrines remained an important part of worship: temples tended to be associated with urban settlements, while local cults continued to thrive in sacred groves and caves throughout the countryside.

The priests of the early Vedic religion did not use temples, but were able to prepare sanctified sacrificial enclosures wherever they chose. Scriptures contained detailed instructions on the necessary preparations: the enclosure or *vedi* included the fire pit and a surrounding area called the *antarvedi*, which was covered in cut grass ritually sprinkled with water. The priest kindled the sacred fire in the pit using fire sticks to ignite a layer of logs. He placed food and other offerings in a sacrificial dish, pressed the *soma* drink with a sanctified stone and used a sacred spoon for throwing substances such as clarified butter, oil, grain, vegetables, flowers, and milk into the fire. There were five main types of sacrifice, held in honor of the supreme reality *brahman* (*brahmayajna*), the gods, or *deva*s (*devayajna*), the ancestors (*pitriyajna*), living people (*purushyayajna*), and other living creatures (*bhutayajna*). This ritual was the *shrauta* rite. A simpler sacrifice called *grihya* could be performed by husband and wife around the domestic fire.

Every element had to be correct for the ritual to be effective. Particular sacrifices were prescribed for different aims—for example, to bring a good harvest or a son. Priests also took part in major public ceremonial sacrifices aimed particularly at consolidating the power and status of the ruler. Examples included the coronation sacrifice (*rajasuya*) and the horse sacrifice (*ashvamedha*).

In the era of the *Upanishad*s (ca. 800–200BCE), sacrifice was increasingly understood as an interiorized event that made public ritual unnecessary. The sages drew out

---

The principal ritual of the Jain faith is the "eightfold puja*," in which eight offerings are made to an image of one of the Tirthankaras ("ford builders") or a related figure. This worshipper is offering light (for enlightenment) to a statue of Bahubali, son of the first Tirthankara.*

• THE MONASTIC COMMUNITY •

The Buddhist and Jain faiths had a monastic element from the very start. In the Buddha's lifetime it was common for wandering holy men to retreat to a forest clearing during the monsoon season when it was difficult to travel. The Buddha himself is said to have followed this custom in a grove near Benares. After the Buddha's departure into *nirvana*, the early Buddhists continued the practice and their first permanent monastic settlements, or *vihara*s, grew up around centers built for these retreats. With contributions from those in secular society the communities became increasingly wealthy.

Groupings of Buddhist and Jain monks were well established by the time of the Maurya emperor Ashoka in the third century BCE. Devotees of the Hindu gods Shiva and Vishnu also subsequently gathered in worshipping communities. The first Hindu monks may have been the Pasupata followers of Shiva, whose community was established by the second century CE.

---

detailed correspondences: the body was the sacrificial enclosure, the head the fire pit, the mind and bodily organs the instruments and containers of sacrifice. The actions of daily living were sanctified as elements of sacrifice: breathing was equivalent to making fire offerings; talking corresponded to chanting sacred hymns and spells; and eating was a form of food offering to the gods.

From around the start of the common era, cults honoring the gods Shiva and Vishnu appear to have been spread by local groups of worshippers. This form of worship was well established by the time of the first Hindu stone temples under the Gupta rulers. The focus of devotions was the viewing (in Sanskrit *darshana*) of an image of the god in question in the central sanctuary of the temple (see page 196).

TO EACH A PLACE

Ancient Indian tradition held that the division of society into castes or varnas *went back to the first of days. In addition to the myth in which the four castes were fashioned from the body of Purusha during the world's creation (see page 134), another story suggested that the system derived from a division of roles within ancient families who were descended from Brahma himself.*

According to this version, which is drawn from a hymn of the *Rig Veda*, the father of the archetypal family was the *brahmin*, safeguarding tradition and acting as teacher and performer of sacrifices, while the eldest brother was the *kshatriya* or armed protector and the other siblings were keepers of the household and tillers of the land. But over generations the divisions were found to function more effectively at a wider social—rather than a family—level.

Some versions of the theory of the four ages or *yugas* (see pages 166–167) also provided an explanation for the social structure: in the first age or Kritayuga, a time of great spiritual purity and peace, all people were of one caste called Hamsa and later known as *brahmins*, then in the second age or Tretayuga, when the first violence was seen, society was divided into *brahmins* and *kshatriyas*; in the third age or Dvaparayuga the *vaishyas* began their work, while the fourth and current age or Kaliyuga has seen the appearance of the *shudras*. The rules governing behavior in and between castes were said to have been laid down by Manu, in legend the first man and the author of the book *Manu-smirti* ("Laws of Manu").

These rules particularly governed cleanliness of body and purity of diet: contact between castes was restricted because the work, customs, and diets of lower castes were potentially polluting or defiling for members of higher castes; people of higher castes even had to avoid touching objects used by lower castes. Men and women were required to marry within their own caste and were excluded from their caste if they broke this rule. A fifth group became established beneath the *shudras*: those who performed the most polluting and menial of work became known as *panchamas* ("fifth grouping") or "outcasts"—and in later times as "untouchables."

Alongside the four *varnas* were thousands of more specific groupings known as *jatis* ("birth group" or "race"). People often settled in *jatis* according to their occupation—as cultivators, stonemasons, goldsmiths,

The principal divisions in ancient Indian society were drawn along lines of caste, but there were also gender divisions. For example, women were not allowed to become "twice-born" (see opposite), nor could they worship Shiva's first son Karttikeya, who is depicted in this 8th- or 9th-century stone figure from eastern India.

and so on. The *jati*-caste system thus promoted the passing on of skills from father to son. Some *jatis* may have been created by people excluded from the traditional castes for breaking rules on marriage or other restrictions. Others probably contained groups of settlers from outside India.

Membership of *varna* and *jati* was determined by birth, which in turn was deemed to be governed by the *karma* of a person's previous life. The men of the *brahmin*, *kshatriya*, and *vaishya* castes were considered to be *dvija* ("twice-born") because they went through a second symbolic birth when they were given a sacred thread to wear on entry into adulthood. The tradition of investing young men with the thread fell into disuse among the *vaishya*s and *kshatriya*s, and was preserved only among the *brahmin*s. Each of the four *varna*s had its associated color: for *brahmin*s white, for *kshatriya*s red, for *vaishya*s yellow, and for *shudra*s black.

The caste system did not apply uniformly. Within Hinduism the *bhakti* devotional movement emphasized the individual's relationship with the deity rather than caste status. In the folk religion practiced in rural areas, elements of the class division applied less strictly, with non-*brahmin*s and women working as priests.

The caste system also drove many people to rival faiths. Resistance to the system's strict social divisions was one of the inspirations behind the religious ferment of the sixth and fifth centuries BCE from which Buddhism and Jainism emerged, and the new faiths won converts among the lower castes. In later years many members of the lower castes were also attracted to Christianity and Islam.

◆ THE FOUR STAGES OF LIFE ◆

Religious tradition structured life according to age as well as social caste. In the sixth and fifth centuries BCE, when the faith of the *kshatriya*s and *brahmin*s was challenged by the emergence of Buddhism and Jainism, teachers of the orthodox brahmanical religion developed the theory of the four stages of life, or *ashrama*s (from the Sanskrit for "living place"). The theory suggested a pattern for an ideal life. This ideal applied only to "twice-born" Indians, and therefore excluded women and *shudra*s (see above).

The first stage was that of the student, or *brahmacari*, who was expected to be celibate, obedient, and show devotion to his teacher. This was followed by the stage of the married householder, or *grihastha*, who could honor his ancestors by having children and please the gods by performing religious sacrifice. The third stage was that of the hermit, or *vanaprastha*, who retired either with his wife or alone to a forest academy or other place of religious instruction, to practice contemplation and spiritual disciplines. The final stage was that of the wandering holy man, or *sannyasi*, who renounced all ties with the secular world, all desires, fears and hopes, duties and responsibilities and whose sole concern was the pursuit of *moksha*.

The associated tradition was that each individual should have four aims in life: to live in accordance with the universal law of *dharma*; to seek wealth (*artha*) and use it according to *dharma*; to enjoy fulfilment of desire (*kama*), including sexual pleasure; to aim for enlightenment or liberation from delusion (*moksha*). But even the most devout were only expected to seek *moksha* during the final two stages of life.

SACRED IN STONE

The most ancient architecture and oldest surviving monuments of ancient India were erected by Buddhists. Under the patronage of the Maurya leader Ashoka (ca. 272–232BCE) and the Shunga kings of the second and first centuries BCE Buddhists built many stone stupas or commemorative shrines and viharas, or monasteries.

The Buddhists built *stupa*s to house bodily remains and other relics associated with the historical Buddha and his early followers: the buildings took the form of a solid stone or brick dome with a top projection known as a *chatra* ("umbrella"). The second-century BCE *stupa* at Sanchi, Madhya Pradesh, was surrounded by a circular railing with four gateways (see page 143), each decorated with carvings of mythological figures, *yaksha* fertility figures grasping spears, and scenes from the Buddha's life. A worshipper would perform the rite of *pradakshina*, walking around the dome in the direction followed by the sun.

The *vihara* consisted of residential rooms for monks around a central courtyard. Originally built as shelters for monks to use during the rainy season, *vihara*s began to be used for worship when the monks set up sacred *stupa*s and Buddha images in the courtyard. Under the Shungas, Buddhists also developed the technique of carving the *vihara* or an excavated semicircular hall known as a *chaitya* from cliffs. The *chaitya* hall was divided in three by lines of columns and housed a small *stupa* at one end.

In this era builders were also erecting large sacred buildings from wood, with many floors, vaulted roofs, and arched windows. Images of these edifices exist in reliefs and murals, but the buildings have rotted away.

The oldest surviving Hindu stone temples, from the time of the Gupta kings in the fourth to sixth centuries CE, derived from the Buddhist tradition. Cave temples cut from the sandstone cliff at Udayagiri, Madhya

Like most of the temples built by the Chandella kings at Khajuraho in central India, the 11th-century CE Kandariya Mahadeva temple features a complex cluster of soaring towers around a central mass.

Pradesh, included a shrine housing a Shiva *linga*, a temple containing reliefs of Vishnu and Durga and another with a fine relief of Vishnu as the dwarf Varaha. They lay behind simple doors cut in the rockface. In the Gupta era the first Hindu temple buildings were erected, initially to a very simple design, with a square sanctuary behind a porch set with columns, then after around 600CE with a more complex sanctuary set on a rectangular platform. An early Gupta Hindu temple at Tigawa, Madhya Pradesh, with a porch and a square shrine is virtually identical to a contemporary Buddhist shrine at Sanchi in the same region.

From the fifth century onward Hindu temple architecture flourished, supported particularly by the Pratihara and Gupta kings in the north of India and by the Chalukya and Pallava monarchs in the south. Increasingly tall towers were raised above the central sanctuary containing the image of the deity honored by the temple. Regional styles developed: in the north towers had a curved profile with *gavaksha* arches in the shape of horseshoes, while in the south towers had many levels gradually shrinking in size to give a pyramid-like profile. The outer parts of the temples contained a wealth of decorative and sacred carving—myriad images of deities, semi-divine figures, and animals in the form of statues in recesses and of carved narrative tableaux depicting scenes of the gods and goddesses from myth. Sacred architects also continued to cut cave temples. Magnificent sixth-century examples were constructed to Shiva at Elephanta Island in Mumbai harbor, Maharashtra, and to Vishnu at Badami in Karnataka.

THE DIVINE WOMB

The form of ancient Indian religious buildings had profound symbolic and ritual significance. The dome of the Buddhist *stupa* was referred to as a *garbha* ("womb") or *anda* ("egg") and was revered as a symbol of the Buddha's enlightened mind and of the moment called *parinirvana* at which he passed from the cycle of birth and death into the release of *nirvana*; its hemispherical

---

◆ TEMPLE CITY: THE BRIHADISHVARA IN TANJORE ◆

The enormous walled temples built under the southern Indian Chola rulers were self-contained cities, containing hundreds of shrines, administrative and residential buildings, sites for ritual bathing, and even bazaars. Larger temples were important educational centers, employers, and artistic patrons. One of the most notable of these temple complexes, housing a vast worshipping community, was the early eleventh-century Brihadishvara temple in the Chola capital Thanjavur (Tanjore).

The temple was built in honor of Shiva between 1003 and 1010CE by Rajaraja I, founder of the Chola dynasty. Two great carved gateways were erected, giving onto a huge courtyard 500 feet by 250 feet (152m by 76m) in area, surrounded by a thick granite wall bearing 1,008 images of Shiva's attendant Nandi. The *garbhagriha* sanctuary contained a large simple Shiva *linga* 12 feet (3.6m) tall. Above the sanctuary a thirteen-story pyramidal tower rose 220 feet (67m), bearing a granite block or *uttamavimana* and a gold-covered copper *kalasha*, or finial, exactly the same height as the *linga*.

Endowed by Rajaraja with a grant of 38,000 *kalanju* (units) of gold that he had collected in his imperial wars, the temple complex was an immense enterprise—employing hundreds of priests, more than fifty musicians, and 400 *devadasi*s, or dancing girls, as well as sculptors, poets, singers, painters, cooks, gardeners, carvers, flower-pickers, and makers of colourful garlands. The king set aside thousands of acres to keep the temple supplied with food. He made good use of his musicians, introducing the daily singing of Sanskrit and Tamil devotional hymns in Shiva's honour. Rajaraja named the temple the Rajarajesvaramudayar, but it was renamed under the Cholas' successors, the Nayakas.

shape was probably copied from that of ancient Indian burial mounds. The dome was also seen as a symbol of the cosmic egg from which, in some accounts, creation sprang. Above the dome rose a pole standing for the world axis, and one or more *chatra*s symbolizing the hierarchy of heavenly beings.

The same concept was applied to the sanctuary of the Hindu temple, which was called the *garbhagriha* or "womb house." The central act of devotion was to see and be seen by the image of the deity in the *garbhagriha*; this sacred encounter was called *darshana* ("viewing" in Sanskrit). Hindu temples were designed to emphasize the approach to the womb house, whether across a simple porch in a small temple or, in a large temple complex, through gateways, across courtyards, along corridors, and through substantial halls.

Devotees would prepare for *darshana* by walking around the *garbhagriha* in a clockwise movement called *pradakshina*—the same word used by Buddhist devotees for a circuit of a *stupa*. Images and statues were posi-

Sculptures of loving couples, called mithunas, *such as this example in the 7th- or 8th-century Durga temple in Aihole, Karnataka, were important symbols of fertility and protective power. They were often positioned at either side of the entrance to the* garbhagriha.

tioned to be seen by worshippers as they made this walk. All these sacred images were perfectly aligned with the position of the deity within the womb house.

The dark and enclosed womb house, in which the deity stood in half-light, was suggestive of a natural cave of the kind in which goddesses and gods would appear in mythical accounts. The temple tower rose directly above the *garbhagriha* and symbolized the sacred peak of Mount Meru—or in temples dedicated to Shiva, the heights of Mount Kailasa on which the god lived with Parvati. The curved profile of the tower in the northern Indian tradition was even called *shikara* ("peak").

Architects made sure that they followed sacred tradition in designing and erecting the temple. From at least

ROYAL TEMPLE PATRONS

In ancient India the king was revered as guardian of *dharma*. Rulers were chief devotees, whose acts of worship benefited the kingdom and its people. Buddhist and Hindu rulers were significant patrons of religious buildings.

Inscriptions at Buddhist shrines record royal patronage. The Maurya king Ashoka (see pages 141–143) raised a celebrated pillar marking his visit to Sarnath, the traditional site of the Buddha's first sermon, where Ashoka built a *stupa*. The great ruler also erected a commemorative pillar and eight *stupa*s at Sanchi. The Gupta kings, while themselves Hindus, oversaw the construction of many Buddhist sites, including rock-cut *chaitya* halls and *vihara* monasteries at Ajanta in western India. In Hindu temples patrons were commemorated by statues or murals of the king and queen. At the Brihadishvara temple, Rajaraja I is depicted in a mural decorating the Shiva-*linga* shrine.

Hindu ruling houses often dedicated themselves to a specific god or goddess. Rulers built shrines to their dynasty's patron deity within the palace and made pilgrimages to existing shrines honoring that goddess or god. Some temples were built to mark military victories: for example, the eighth-century Chalukya king Vikramaditya II had twin temples erected at Pattadakal to celebrate his triumph over the Pallava dynasty at Kanchi.

the eighth century CE manuals called *Vastu Shastra*s laid out requirements for the right kind of site, the ground plan and the position and size of buildings. Temple diagrams were usually laid out on a grid. In some cases the grid was filled with an image of the original cosmic man, Purusha, with his navel at the temple center, and the buildings situated according to the position of his arms, head, and legs within the grid. According to some theories, the center of the grid at Purusha's navel, which was the site of the *garbhagriha*, represented *brahman*. All measurements were strictly in proportion following a scale derived from the size of the sacred image of the deity that was contained in the womb house.

FORMS FOR THE GODS

Ancient Indians did not believe that a statue of Shiva was Shiva himself, but rather a symbol of the mystery of divine consciousness and a vessel into which divine energy might be drawn. Like the Vedic priest laying out the sacred enclosure, or the *brahmin* temple architect drawing up the proportions of a Hindu temple, a sculptor was expected to follow established tradition as closely as possible. Instructions on the making of sacred images in the *Purana*s and elsewhere laid out strict rules, prescribing the correct proportions, posture, gestures, attributes, facial expression, coloring and costume. For this reason sculptures from diverse eras of ancient India have a remarkable uniformity of appearance.

The face of the god or goddess commonly shines with a blissful peace known as *ananda*. Some images, including those of Kali or Durga, exhibit burning anger, but generally deities were radiantly serene even when engaged in an energetic or violent activity—for example, Shiva Nataraja looks down with calm benevolence as he performs the *tandava* dance of destruction. According to the Vedanta school of philosophy, *ananda* (Sanskrit for "bliss") was an essential aspect of *brahman* and could therefore be shared by any individual who came to taste union with *brahman* through meditation and religious devotions. *Ananda* was an attribute of enlightenment.

Artists and devotees also understood a complex symbolic language of *mudra*, hand gestures, and other body positions or shapes. For example, the right hand raised to chest level with palm toward the viewer and all fingers together was a gesture of reassurance, telling the viewer not to be afraid. This was commonly shown on images of Hindu gods and also of the Buddha, who would be shown in this aspect with his left hand extended straight down at his side. The right hand lowered with the palm open facing the viewer signified compassion and the granting of boons or favors. The left hand lowered across the body with the palm down indicated a way out or release—this gesture was often seen in the lower left of the four arms of a Shiva Nataraja, for example, where it indicated release from entrapment in *samsara*. A raised area on top of the Buddha's head, called *ushnisha*, symbolized his expanded consciousness or enlightenment. The long arms on statues of *bodhisattva*s represented generosity.

The oldest known stone statues of divinities in ancient India date to the second and first centuries BCE. Standing male and female figures known as *yaksha*s and *yakshi*s may have been revered as providers of fertility and wealth (see pages 184–185). In the same era the first carved images of the Buddha appeared. Early Buddhists had honored images of a *stupa*, of the Buddha's footprints, of an empty throne, or of the Bodhi tree under which he achieved enlightenment. The first carved Buddhas, exhibiting Greek influence, were derived from images of the god Apollo and made in around the first century BCE. A few images of Vedic gods also survive from this period.

Images of Hindu gods and goddesses were made in abundance following the rise of the *bhakti* devotional movement, beginning in the third and fourth centuries CE, when statues began to be used in worship. The finest examples date from the reigns of the Gupta kings in northern India in the fourth to sixth centuries and the era of the Chola rulers in southern India from the ninth century onward.

◆ A SHARED TRADITION ◆

Buddhist and Hindu religious art and iconography developed side by side in ancient India and show many striking similarities. For example, an image of Lakshmi, the goddess venerated in Hinduism as the wife of Vishnu, was carved on a railing post at the second-century BCE Buddhist *stupa* at Bharhut, Madhya Pradesh. The depiction (recreated below) presents Lakshmi as a lotus goddess of wealth and good fortune, and uses much of the same symbolism found in later Hindu representations: in both she is atop a lotus flower and is bathed by water pouring from the upraised trunks of proud elephants. Other figures familiar from the Hindu tradition appear in Buddhist carvings, including the goddesses Ganga and Yamuna and hooded serpents, or *naga*s, with human torsos.

In myth, the Buddha, sitting in meditation, was sheltered from rain for seven days by the raised hood of the many-headed serpent *naga* Muchalinda and carvings of this scene are markedly similar to images of Vishnu sitting beneath the lifted head of Ananta-Shesha. Another similarity is between images of Vishnu sleeping on Shesha on the cosmic ocean and the Buddha reclining in his moment of *parinirvana* (final enlightenment).

THE ARTIST'S SACRIFICE

In fashioning a statue or an image of a deity, ancient Indian artists did not set out to create what might be perceived in the West to be a "work of art," but to produce an object fit to be used as a divine image—to make a form hallowed by tradition, with proven ritual effectiveness. The same principle applied to exponents of other arts, such as poetry, music, and dance.

If artists failed to follow instructions on proportions, gestures, facial expression, and so on, the statue or image would not be an acceptable vessel for divine energy. Once the image was finished, it was consecrated in a ceremony that summoned up the divine *tapas*, or creative energy, before being installed in the appropriate part of the temple.

From this perspective artists became much less important than their work. No distinction was drawn between artists and craftspeople. Sculptors, painters, musicians, and dancers wanted to prove not that they were brilliant innovators but that they were faithful followers of tradition. For example, the sages who wrote the *Upanishad*s did not seek to leave their mark on history by appending their names to the works: their intention was to provide instruction in sacred and eternal knowledge that had existed before them and so was not of their invention. Their overriding concern was to preserve this lore and to express it as precisely as possible.

Producing a statue, poem, or painting was an act of sacrifice—like the world's creation, like the very processes that sustained life. As in a Vedic *yajna*, if the materials were correctly prepared, the words declaimed and the actions performed in line with sacred teaching, then the gods would be present. Moreover, artists had to sacrifice themselves in dismembering their ego: their aim was not to express themselves but to empty themselves, to become a channel for divine inspiration. Ideally artists prepared for their acts of creation by withdrawing from worldly distractions and focusing all their mental powers on the subject of the work—whether a statue of Vishnu, a painting of Shiva, a poem about Kali, a dance representing the encounter of the *gopis* and Krishna. The *Agni Purana* instructed a sculptor to undergo purification ceremonies on the day before starting work on the carving of a statue, then before sleep to ask the gods to send guidance through dreams on the form the image should take.

The *Vastu Sutra Upanishad*, which also laid down guidance on the conception and creation of statuary, stated that when working on a statue of a god or goddess the sculptor became the divine artisan Tvastr or Vishvarkarman (see page 164). The sculptor was instructed to begin preparations only on a propitious day and to have the stone bathed in the urine of a breed of cow believed to symbolize the creative energy of the great Goddess. After bathing, meditating, and making offerings the sculptor could begin work. As the sculptor labored, the stone chippings would be gathered up and ritually disposed of just as a Vedic priest disposed of the remains of a *yajna* sacrifice.

Ancient Indian statuary, painting, and other art was produced for devotional use—understanding a statue of a god with many limbs, weapons, and other objects, an animal attendant and perhaps a consort required not only knowledge of myth, symbolism, and religious tradition, but also quiet and contemplative attention. The divine archetype presented in the image could lift a devotee to religious experience. The books that provided such detailed guidance for artists also gave instructions for worshippers, prescribing the correct time for devotions, the type and height of seat to use during *darshana*, and so on. In particular they declared that a worshipper should look within through the discipline of meditation before attempting external worship. Some sources indicated that the devotees had to become the god they were worshipping before beginning their outward devotions.

This 12th-century relief from the Hoysaleshvara temple in Karnataka depicts Krishna holding up a mountain to protect his cowherds from the heavy rain sent by Indra. The unnamed artist would have approached the creation of this sculpture as an act of devotion and sacrifice.

• FEELING AND RESPONSE •

Ancient Indian aesthetic theory listed nine main feelings experienced by humans, which corresponded to nine aesthetic tones, known as *rasa*s.

According to tradition, the sage Bharata developed the theory of the nine main feelings in about 500CE. He listed them as: delight, laughter, sorrow, anger, energy, fear, disgust, astonishment, and calmness or tranquillity. The *Vishnudharmottara*, a seventh-century *purana*, provided instruction in the nine corresponding *rasa*s, or feeling tones, in a statue, painting, poem, or other work of art: the erotic, the comic, the pathetic, the furious, the heroic, the frightening, the hateful, the marvelous and the peaceful. *Rasa*, which means "essence" or "taste" but which was also applied to the sap of a plant or tree, referred to the flavor or general tone of a work of art and the blissful response it ideally evoked in the viewer or listener. Without *rasa*, a work of art was lifeless.

THE POWER OF WORDS AND MUSIC

The Aryans, who handed their Vedas *down from generation to generation by oral tradition, developed complex rhythmic and repetitive patterns to ensure that the sacred words were correctly transmitted. These spoken word patterns also formed an integral part of worship.*

In a pattern known as *ghanapatha* ("dense text") the words of the *Veda*s were learned and recited in this repetitive order: one-two, two-one, one-two-three, three-two-one, one-two-three, two-three, three-two, two-three-four, and so on. This ritual practice helped devotees to sense the sacred power contained within each word.

The use of hymns and sacred utterances, known as *mantra*s, was a central part of worship. In Vedic ritual, chanting the gods' names had the power to summon them to the sacrifice. Sacred words conveyed the sacrifice and were intoned throughout the ceremony. Four types of priest were necessary, each a specialist in a form of hymn: the *adhvaryu* priest, who measured and built the sacred enclosure and prepared all the offerings and materials for the fire, chanted the hymns of the *Yajur Veda*; the *hotri* priest, who cast offerings into the fire, declaimed the hymns of the *Rig Veda*; the *udgatri* priest sang the hymns of the *Sama Veda*; and the *brahmin* priest, whose responsibility was to supervise the ceremony and ensure that ritual was correctly followed, chanted the *Atharva Veda* hymns.

In the era of forest academies and the teachings of the *Upanishad*s, those seeking enlightenment used sacred sound as a vehicle to reach the state in which sounds ceased. One form of meditation entailed focusing the attention with all possible concentration on a sacred

As suggested by these sculptures of musicians which adorn the 13th-century Keshava temple in Somnathapur, Mysore, music played an important role in Hindu worship—and still does. Traditional Indian music is divided into two broadly similar schools: the Hindustani school of northern India and the Karnatak school in the south.

name or *mantra*, which with practice could enable the meditator to escape the ceaseless movements of the thinking mind in a state of profound, illuminated peace. In that state, the devotee saw all the forms and sounds of the world as one vast field of energy in which all parts were interconnected. Energy—both in terms of the *tapas* of the divine creator and the *prana* of the individual's life-force—was said to be experienced as a universal sound, the syllable *Om* or *Aum* (pronounced as *a–u–m*), believed to reverberate throughout creation and in some accounts to be the sound of creation itself. Some yogic meditators used *Om* as their *mantra*.

The syllable also represented the all-powerful god. Shaivites (the name given to worshippers of Shiva) declared that *Om* was a form of Shiva. His dancing form, Shiva Nataraja, shown within a circle of flames that represented the syllable *Om* (see illustration, page 166), stood for the patterned movements of divine energy and the periodic destruction that returned order to chaos, the human movement into and out of earthly life, the *samsara* cycle of birth-death-birth.

Early Buddhists chanted verses of their scripture in an attempt to develop fuller awareness of the Buddha's qualities. After the rise of Mahayana Buddhism, Buddhists also began to use *mantra*s in the veneration of *bodhisattva*s. Similarly, Jains chanted *mantra*s and used devotional hymns in the contemplation of images of their Tirthankaras.

In later years devotional music played an important part in Hindu worship. The singing of temple hymns was promoted by the Alvars, the itinerant devotees of Vishnu, and the Nayanars, worshippers of Shiva, who from the seventh century onward traveled throughout southern India promoting their brand of *bhakti* (devotional faith). Around the tenth century, regular singing of hymns was introduced in temple worship. At that time Nandi Ambar Nandi made a celebrated collection of the Nayanars' hymns under the title *Tevaram*.

• THE THOUSAND NAMES OF VISHNU •

The power of the spoken word and of the sacred name is reflected in the devotional use by Vaishnavites (worshippers of Vishnu) of a litany of a thousand of the god's names.

Some Vaishnavites recited the *Sri Vishnu Sahrasra-nama Stotram* ("Thousand Names of Vishnu") in an act of devotion before an image of Vishnu or his incarnation Krishna. The litany was revealed in the *Mahabharata* epic: when Prince Yudhishthira asked the sage Bhishma for the secret of deep and unending joy, Bhishma responded by listing the thousand names of Vishnu and declaring that the repetition of these sacred words deep in the prince's heart would bring him the joy he sought. Some of the names, such as Sri ("beauty"), Kshama ("patience"), and Shanti ("peace"), described qualities. Others looked back to the early Vedic past, including Varuna ("giver of laws"), Sapta-aidhas ("receiver of seven kinds of fuel," a reference to the Vedic sacrifice), and Vashatkara ("he who is honored by the name Vashat"—Vashat was the name intoned at the moment offerings were thrown into the fire). Some made mythical references, such as Govinda ("cowherd youth"—a reference to Vishnu's incarnation as Krishna) or Yama (lord of death). Others referred to the mystical philosophy of the *Upanishad*s—for example, Brahmanya ("the form of *brahman*") or Amurti ("without form").

THE KHMER PRIEST–KINGS

The influence of Vedism or Hinduism traveled beyond India to Southeast Asia, finding arguably its greatest expression in the temple complexes of the Khmer Empire centered at Angkor in what is now Cambodia. A divine caste of all-powerful brahmanic kings presided over a prosperous polity that from the ninth to the thirteenth centuries CE *extended from the Bay of Bengal to Indochina. Khmer architecture reveals the evolution of ideas in the region that led gradually to the ascendancy of Buddhism.*

ABOVE AND LEFT *Angkor Wat was built for King Suryavarman II (reigned 1113–1150) in the 12th century* CE. *Providing a place of perfection for worship—expressed in this Angkor statue (left)—the temple conformed to the Hindu concept of a sacred microcosm. The towers symbolize mountains of the gods and the purification pool the waters that were believed to envelop the world—ideas echoed in Buddhist cosmology and architecture.*

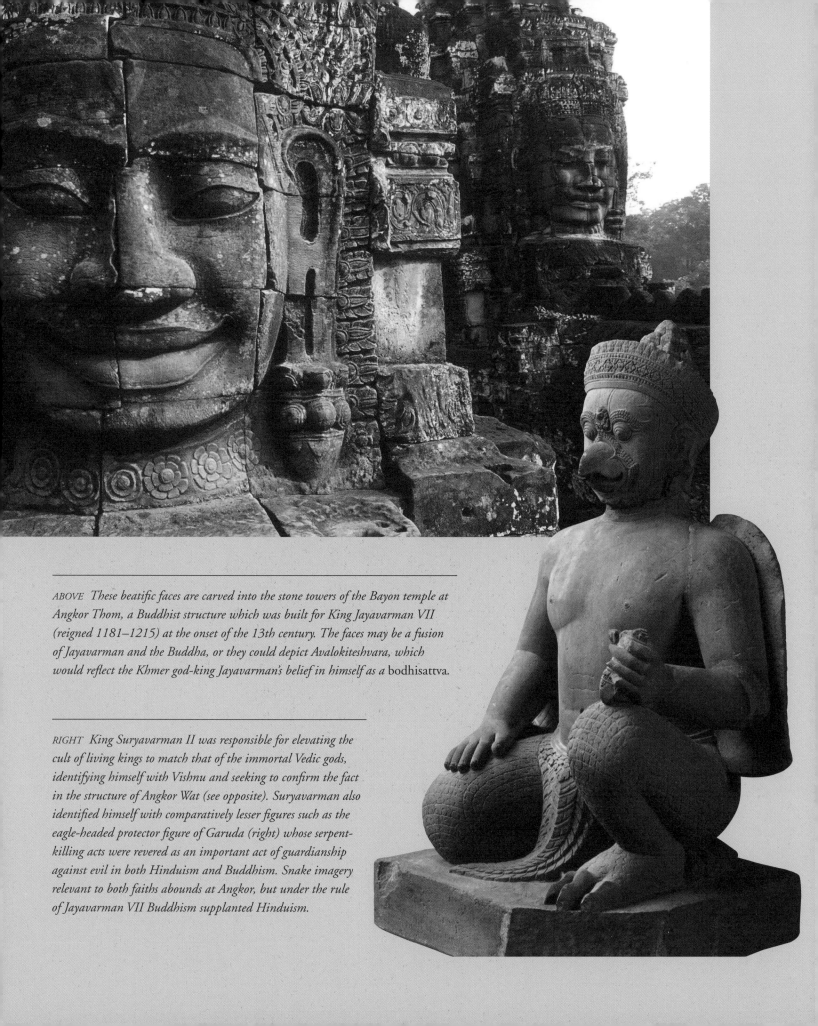

ABOVE *These beatific faces are carved into the stone towers of the Bayon temple at Angkor Thom, a Buddhist structure which was built for King Jayavarman VII (reigned 1181–1215) at the onset of the 13th century. The faces may be a fusion of Jayavarman and the Buddha, or they could depict Avalokiteshvara, which would reflect the Khmer god-king Jayavarman's belief in himself as a* bodhisattva.

RIGHT *King Suryavarman II was responsible for elevating the cult of living kings to match that of the immortal Vedic gods, identifying himself with Vishnu and seeking to confirm the fact in the structure of Angkor Wat (see opposite). Suryavarman also identified himself with comparatively lesser figures such as the eagle-headed protector figure of Garuda (right) whose serpent-killing acts were revered as an important act of guardianship against evil in both Hinduism and Buddhism. Snake imagery relevant to both faiths abounds at Angkor, but under the rule of Jayavarman VII Buddhism supplanted Hinduism.*

CHAPTER TWO

CHINA

Such is the extent of China's vast historical legacy that as early as the time of the great sage Confucius (551–479BCE), people were already looking back on an ancient tradition. Although Confucius changed his country in ways that he himself would never know, he claimed not to be an innovator: "I transmit but do not create. I am faithful to and delight in antiquity." Four hundred years later, Sima Qian (145–ca. 86BCE) compiled his famous Records of the Historian *which narrates Chinese history from the Three August Emperors of mythological times down to the high point of the Han dynasty (Sima Qian's own era). This text was but the first in a series of dynastic histories that traced China's story through to the modern age.*

THE NINE REGIONS

China takes the name by which it is known in the West from the Qin (pronounced like English "chin") dynasty (221–207BCE). According to legend, Yu the Great, founder of the Xia dynasty, divided China into nine regions, each possessing distinct physical and cultural traits, some of which are manifested in their respective cuisines which retain the names endowed long ago by Yu the Great.

China is continental in every respect of the word, encompassing most of the East Asian land mass and including almost every climatic and topographical feature. But while present-day China stretches from the deserts of Central Asia to the grasslands of Mongolia, and from the towering Himalayas to the tropical island of Hainan in the south, the China of antiquity is usually thought to have been cradled in the elbow of the Yellow River (see map, page 211). Beginning in the Kunlun Mountains of Xinjiang and Qinghai provinces, the Yellow River washes through the grainy soil of Ningxia and Mongolia, then turns due south to divide the provinces of Shaanxi and Shanxi before hitting the fastness of the Qinling Mountains, which redirect it eastward to the sea. The area "inside the river," or to the north and east of its great bend, is where the Xia (ca. 2000–1550BCE) and Shang (ca. 1550–1045BCE) dynasties took root, and where the subsequent "Zhong Guo," or Central Kingdoms, were located. This area is in turn cleaved by the Taihang Mountains, which divided the Central Kingdoms into those east of the mountains (Shandong) and those west of them (Shanxi). Throughout much of antiquity, China's primary axis was east–west; thus we have the Western Zhou and Eastern Zhou, Western Han and Eastern Han dynasties, and even as late as the Tang dynasty the two capitals were in the west (at present-day Xi'an) and east (at Luoyang), respectively.

◆ THE HEAVENLY DRAGON ◆

Represented in this Zhou-period bronze musical-instrument stand, the dragon is one of China's most ancient and potent symbols, the embodiment of vigor and strength. Far from a fire-breathing monster, the Chinese dragon is a benevolent creature—the supreme symbol of the emperor—who visits Earth only occasionally in response to the needs of humans. At one time, the rise of the "Dragon" constellation (see page 212) in the east indicated the onset of spring and the beginning of the growing season. The dragon leaped from the subterranean waters in which it had been trapped during the winter and began its ascent into the night sky. By the middle of summer its entire body would be arrayed for all to see.

However, by the time of the Zhou dynasty, if not before, states along China's other great river, the Yangzi, began to provide a counterweight to the civilizations of the north. In time, the long growing seasons of the south would attract more and more people to resettle there, and by the end of antiquity demographic changes had re-oriented Chinese civilization: the divide was no longer between east and west, but north and south.

IMAGINED COMMUNITIES

According to legends, Yu the Great (see pages 216–217) divided China into nine regions, each with certain characteristics. But who exactly were the people inhabiting this territory? Were the subjects of the ancient Xia and Shang dynasties considered Chinese, or did ancient China not begin until the establishment of the Qin dynasty by the First Emperor? Was it even later still amid the glories of the Han dynasty, with which most contemporary Chinese identify their ethnicity, at least superficially, by calling themselves "Men of Han."

A generation or two ago, it was thought that archaeology would provide the answer to this question. The oldest civilizations in China seemed to be the Yangshao and Longshan neolithic cultures located in the Yellow River valley. According to the then prevailing theory of historical development, Chinese civilization radiated out from this one bi-polar source. Today, however, it is commonly accepted that Chinese civilization had multiple origins, with numerous local cultures coexisting, at times in contact with other cultures, at times perhaps isolated; some coming for a while to have predominance over others, some being extinguished, almost without a trace. This theory gained ground during the 1970s due to numerous neolithic cultures discovered throughout southern China. By 1985, when the Sanxingdui culture was unearthed near Chengdu, Sichuan, there could no longer be any doubt that different centers of civilization coexisted. The Sanxingdui created superlative bronze artifacts, but they seem to owe little to the contemporary Shang culture, the heart of which was located far away in the northeast at Anyang. Archaeology reveals a persistent tension between general and local characteristics. In the period known as the Warring States (480–222BCE), some of the most exquisite artifacts have been discovered in what were traditionally regarded as the "barbarian" states of Zhongshan and Chu. Perhaps surprisingly, the élites of these states appear to have subscribed in large measure to the standards of civilization associated with the contemporary Zhou states. And in later periods, too, "barbarians" contributed to what we now know as China.

THE MIRROR OF HISTORY

In China it has long been said that we look into the past as into a mirror, in the hope not only of seeing ourselves clearly reflected, but also of gaining greater control and understanding of the future. As Sima Qian (145–ca. 86BCE), author of China's first comprehensive history, the *Records of the Historian*, explained, "By not forgetting past events, we become masters of future events."

China's historians were able to draw on an extensive tradition: long before Sima Qian's time, various writings from the beginning of the first millennium BCE were compiled into texts that became China's classics. Three in particular, the *Classic of Changes*, the *Classic of Documents*, and the *Classic of Poetry*, were read by all who could do so and quoted by all who could write. By the age of Confucius (551–479BCE), scribes remained in constant attendance upon rulers. Script had developed out of the use of divinatory oracle-bone inscriptions during the Shang dynasty, which means that there is a wealth of inscribed antiquities dating back several thousand years which provide invaluable insights into many fascinating aspects of life in ancient China. Bone progressively gave way to stone, bronze, bamboo slips, and even expensive silk, until paper was invented under the Eastern Han dynasty (25–220CE)—one of ancient China's greatest contributions to world civilization.

By the end of the first millennium CE, when historian Sima Guang (1019–1086) penned the *Comprehensive Mirror for Aid in Government* (a comprehensive history of China from the era of the Warring States [480BCE] until the end of the Tang dynasty [907CE]), China had probably produced more books than all of the world's other civilizations combined. For better and for worse, those books are the inevitable starting point for all that we know about China's antiquity.

THE PROBLEM OF CHRONOLOGIES

The constancy of the sun's rising and setting lulls us into thinking that the passing of time—and the way it is counted—ought to be consistent everywhere. This tendency is reinforced today by the widespread use of the Western calendar—but it was adopted in China only in 1949 and before that, each new dynasty, and even each new ruler, started time over again from year 1. Time was cyclical rather than linear.

In ancient China, it was one of the first responsibilities of a new dynasty to promulgate a new calendar, with not only a new first year, but also a new first month of the year. Already by the Shang dynasty an intercalary "thirteenth" month was added every three years or so. By the Zhou dynasty, intercalation had become routine, with seven months added every nineteen years. Although the Zhou calendar doubtless satisfied the needs of the people of the time, later historians found its chronology confusing. In the early part of the Han dynasty, Sima Qian was able to assign dates only back to a year that corresponds to 842BCE. Before that, historical records were either lacking or contradictory. This did not discourage many subsequent historians from trying to determine the date of at least the Zhou conquest of Shang, the pivotal event of China's early antiquity. Scores of dates were proposed, but none satisfied everyone.

In the mid-1990s, Song Jian, then Minister of Science and Technology, on a visit to Egypt was struck by the exact dates assigned to Egypt's ancient dynasties and pharaohs. Returning to China, he organized an attempt by experts to determine the dates of ancient China's Three Dynasties—the Xia, Shang, and Zhou. Despite being the most expensive historical project of modern China's history, its preliminary results in 2000 were met with almost universal criticism from the scholarly community. China's exact dates prior to 842BCE are still open to question.

OPPOSITE *This map represents China, its provinces (*SHANXI, *in capital letters) and autonomous regions (*QINGHAI, *in italic capital letters), and includes insets to show the territorial extent of three of the historical dynasties.*

LEFT *As well as serving as a cooking pot, the* ding, *or cauldron, was one of the most important ritual vessels in ancestral temples—for example, the ranks of the nobility were denominated by the number of them that they were allowed to display. The king was entitled to nine cauldrons, symbolizing his authority over China's nine regions. This bronze vessel is from the end of the Warring States era (480–222BCE).*

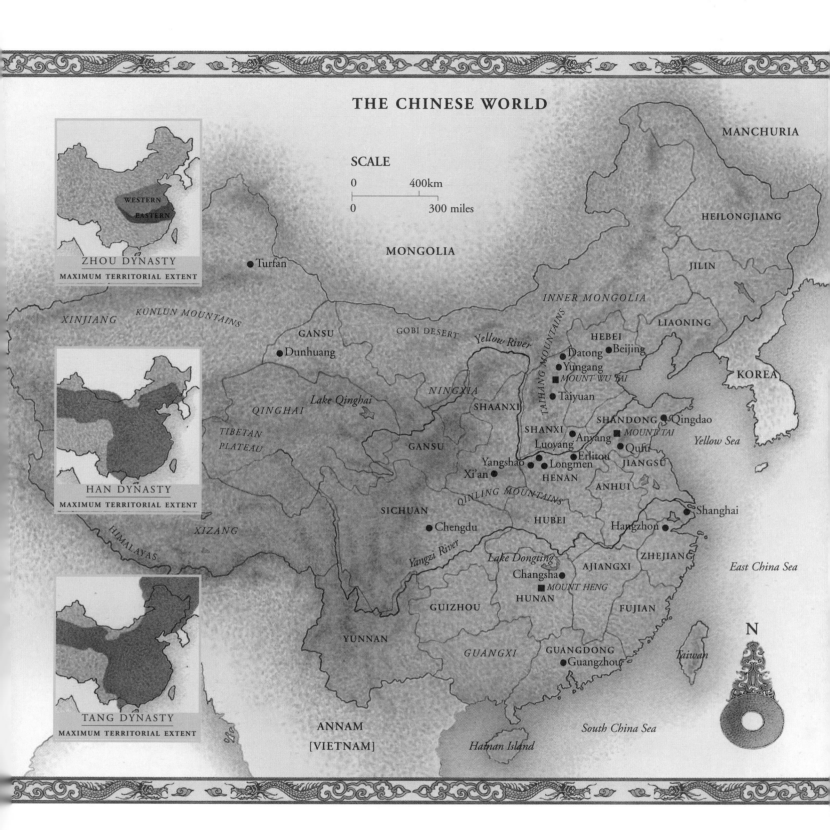

THE CHINESE WORLD

SCALE

0 — 400km

0 — 300 miles

MANCHURIA

HEILONGJIANG

JILIN

MONGOLIA

INNER MONGOLIA

LIAONING

KOREA

HEBEI

Datong ● ● Beijing

Yungang ●

■ MOUNT WU TAI

Taiyuan ●

● Turfan

XINJIANG

KUNLUN MOUNTAINS

GANSU

Dunhuang ●

GOBI DESERT

Yellow River

TAIHANG MOUNTAINS

NINGXIA

SHAANXI

Lake Qinghai

QINGHAI

TIBETAN
PLATEAU

GANSU

SHANXI

Anyang ●

Luoyang ●

Yangshao ●

Xi'an ●

● Longmen

HENAN

Erlitou ●

SHANDONG

■ MOUNT TAI

● Qingdao

Yellow Sea

● Qufu

JIANGSU

ANHUI

QINLING MOUNTAINS

HIMALAYAS

XIZANG

SICHUAN

Chengdu ●

Yangzi River

HUBEI

Lake Dongting

Changsha ●

■ MOUNT HENG

HUNAN

A JIANGXI

ZHEJIANG

Shanghai ●

Hangzhou ●

East China Sea

GUIZHOU

FUJIAN

YUNNAN

GUANGXI

GUANGDONG

Guangzhou ●

Taiwan

ANNAM
[VIETNAM]

Hainan Island

South China Sea

N

ZHOU DYNASTY
MAXIMUM TERRITORIAL EXTENT

WESTERN

EASTERN

HAN DYNASTY
MAXIMUM TERRITORIAL EXTENT

TANG DYNASTY
MAXIMUM TERRITORIAL EXTENT

THE MAKING OF THE WORLD

In China, most myths are preserved in the works of philosophers: humankind's fall from a primordial golden age is narrated in the Daoist text the Zhuangzi. *Such works reveal many important Chinese beliefs, including the idea that the universe is a self-contained entity with no transcendental godhead outside of it and that civilization is a legacy from generations of divine beings and imperial ancestors.*

Classical Chinese philosophical sources describe the origins of the world as a state without differentiations: no light, no dark; no high, no low. Empty yet full, all matter was combined in a moist, dumpling-like sac. According to one source, out of this undifferentiated state, called Tai Yi or Grand Unity, water was born. The mixture of this water with Grand Unity then gave forth heaven, which in turn joined with Grand Unity to produce Earth. Heaven and Earth then united to give birth to the spirits and the luminaries, who gave birth to the *yin* and *yang* (see page 234), which in turn produced the four seasons. From these came hot and cold, which

produced moist and dry, which is to say the year, which is to say time, which is the culmination of evolution.

Humankind is noticeably absent from this account. Mythology provides two different explanations for the creation of humankind—one from a man and one from a woman. The man, apparently, was one Pan Gu, "Coiled Antiquity," the personification of Grand Unity. When nearing death, his body exploded: his breath became the wind, his left eye the sun, his right eye the moon, his four limbs the four quarters of the world, his blood and semen its rivers and seas, and so on. The lice on his skin were touched by the wind, and these became

---

◆ UNLOCKING THE UNIVERSE ◆

The Chinese universe was traditionally believed to contain three realms, those of heaven, Earth, and humankind. During the Han dynasty (202BCE–220CE), philosophers portrayed the king (*wang* 王) as the agent responsible for connecting these three (三) realms and was regarded as the living link between them.

Heaven was the vault of the sky, the field upon which the sun and moon, stars and planets made their movements. The five visible planets (Mercury, Venus, Mars, Jupiter, Saturn) were each believed to have their own personalities, and their effects on persons and events on Earth. The "Grand White," Venus, far from being a goddess of love, was a baleful executioner (white being the color of mourning in China), while Saturn moved slowly like an old man and was associated with the Yellow Emperor of high antiquity. But it was the "Year Star," Jupiter, that was considered the most important of the planets, governing time as it appeared to pass from one constellation to another.

As elsewhere, stars were grouped into constellations: four "spiritual animals" and twenty-eight lunar lodges being the most important. The Dragon was the constellation of the east and spring, and green in color, whereas summer was the time of the Phoenix, red in color and associated with the south. Winter was the time of the black Turtle which lived in the watery abyss of the north. This explains in large part why early Chinese maps were oriented with south at the top; water should of course be at the bottom, with the Phoenix flying above. It also hints at the subsequent notion of the *wu xing* or "Five Motions" or "Five Phases," of which all matter was thought to be composed (see page 224).

people. Another tradition credits a woman, Nü Wa, as the creator of humankind. One telling says that she used the clay of the earth to make people—the noble ones yellow, the meaner ones darker. Another says that she joined with her brother, Fuxi, the only other person alive, and together they made children.

When the progenitors of the world were not having sex, they were busy fighting. Many myths tell of battles between the gods, which seem to have resulted in the differentiation of time. Perhaps best known is the battle between Chi You, a reptilian monster, and Huang Di, the Yellow Emperor. At the beginning of the battle, Chi You, the Yellow Emperor's minister in charge of the waters, caused a great fog to descend, blurring everything. To find his bearings, the Yellow Emperor invented the south-pointing chariot, or the compass. Finally, he sent the daughter of heaven, Ba, or Drought, to dry out the fog, and then he killed Chi You. At this, Chi You transformed into a comet—an inconstant star. In later times, his reappearances foreboded warfare.

Another version of this myth concerns Gong Gong, ruler of a flooded Earth prior to the time of the Yellow Emperor. After being deposed, the enraged Gong Gong butted his head against Buzhou Shan, the Incomplete Mountain, in the western Kunlun mountain range. When this pillar of heaven collapsed, heaven tilted down in the west while Earth tilted up—this is why the stars appear to move across the skies from east to west, and why the rivers of China flow from west to east.

Not all chaos is caused by water—a surfeit of suns can be equally disruptive. In later antiquity, ten suns appeared at once. The people were saved by the archer Yi, who shot nine of them out of the sky. Many other myths are set in the night sky. The feuding brothers Shishen and Yanbo, gods of the Xia and Shang peoples,

A 7th-century CE silk funerary banner depicting Nü Wa and Fuxi—considered by some sources to be the progenitors of the Chinese people—entwined in cosmic harmony. Their wings are a symbol of immortality.

could not stand to be in each other's sight. Their father, the emperor Gao Xin, duly banished them to opposite sides of the sky. They now appear as stars within Orion and the Pleiades, one rises in the east as the other sets in the west. An even better known story is that of the mortal Herdboy and the divine Spinning Girl, the stars Vega and Altair, whose romance offended heavenly authorities. Their punishment was to meet only once a year, the seventh day of the seventh month, when a bridge of magpies forms over the Han River—the Milky Way.

Even Tai Yi or Grand Unity was an astral deity. It referred to the topmost of a group of four stars in an inverted Y-shape located just above the northern Dipper, and seems to have governed military campaigns. By 112BCE, Emperor Wu of Han (reigned 141–87BCE) had established two different altars dedicated to Tai Yi to conduct the state's most important sacrifices. In the *Records of the Historian* of Sima Qian (145–ca. 86BCE), there is the following account of a ritual performed in that same year: "[Emperor Wu] was about to launch an attack on Nan Yue, and offered prayers for success to Grand Unity. A banner painted with the sun, moon, the Northern Dipper, and the Ascending Dragon served as the Grand Unity spear, and was called the Numinous Flag. While performing the prayer for success in battle, the Grand

Scribe raised the flag and pointed it at the country to be attacked." A similar banner to the one described in this ritual was discovered in a tomb dating to 168BCE at Mawangdui, in Changsha, Hunan. It is a painting on silk that is labeled "Diagram for Repelling Weapons."

THE CREATION OF CULTURE

Fuxi, the brother and husband of Nü Wa (see page 213), was responsible for several important cultural inventions. By his union with Nü Wa, he of course invented marriage. The carpenter's square with which he is usually pictured indicates his role in teaching the people to work. And through careful observation of the patterns of the heavens and Earth, he created the hexagrams of the *Yi Jing* or *Classic of Changes*, and these in turn served him as models to make nets for hunting and fishing. His epoch was followed by that of Shen Nong, the Divine Farmer, who invented the plow and also established the first market, so that people could exchange their produce. When Shen Nong died, Huang Di, the Yellow

A large Six Dynasties period (222–589CE) earthenware model of a cart with a bullock and human figures. According to legend, Shen Nong, the Divine Farmer, invented the plow, thus leading the Chinese people away from hunting and fishing toward a more sophisticated agrarian culture. Such mastery of the natural environment of course proved to have a dramatic impact on Chinese life and civilization.

Emperor, succeeded him as the third of the Three August Emperors. He is said to have invented not only armor (to defend himself against the weapons invented by Chi You), medicine, and pottery but also the south-facing chariot—that is, the compass (see page 213).

These Three August Emperors were followed by the Five Emperors of antiquity: Zhuan Xu, Di Ku, Yao, Shun, and Yu, who collectively institutionalized government. The last of the five, Yu (often known as Yu the Great), earned the position of emperor by saving the people from a catastrophic flood that engulfed China. After draining the waters into the sea, he divided the land into nine different regions and established taxes that each region submitted to the central state. He also cast nine bronze cauldrons, each depicting the monsters of the various regions, so that the people living there could recognize them and be protected from

them. The "Nine Regions" has since become a standard name for China, and throughout antiquity the nine cauldrons were thought to symbolize authority over it (see pages 208–210).

THE QUESTION OF XIA
According to tradition, Yu the Great had formerly served as a minister (along with Yi, Gao Yao, and Kui) to the sage emperors Yao and Shun. The emperor Shun named Yu as his successor. On the emperor's death, Yu attempted to turn over power to Shun's son, Shangjun, but the lords of the world would not accept him, and forced him into exile. Thus, Yu became the emperor. When he died, his former colleague Yi was appointed to succeed him. Traditions are divided over what happened next. The earliest sources suggest that Yu's death was followed by a power struggle, with Yu's son, Qi, killing Yi

◆ THE SYMMETRY OF TAOTIE ◆

The *taotie* or animal-mask design was ancient China's most popular motif. It originated on jade pieces, such as this *cong* (a ceremonial item thought to represent the Earth), among the neolithic cultures of eastern China and was common on bronze ritual vessels of the Shang dynasty. In later times the design was associated with an "insatiable monster," but there is no contemporary evidence for this. *Taotie*'s symmetry, focused on the two eyes, was especially well adapted to ancient China's piece-mould method of casting bronze vessels— including the famous cauldrons of Yu the Great (see main text, above). Unlike the lost-wax casting of the West, piece-mould casting allowed the artisan access to the inside of the mould, and so made possible the intricate designs found on the exterior surface of the bronze pieces.

and then taking power for himself. Other sources, which have become orthodox, say that Yi ruled only during the three-year mourning period for Yu, and then voluntarily yielded authority to Qi. Since Qi's kingship marked the establishment of dynastic rule in China, it can be imagined why the earlier story was suppressed.

The *Zhushu Jinian* or *Bamboo Annals* indicates that descendants of Yu ruled as the Xia dynasty for seventeen generations and 471 years. The last king of the dynasty, Jie or Di Gui, is the first of the evil last emperors who have become paradigmatic in Chinese history. Standard sources simply say that he was lacking in virtue, but others describe his sexual debauchery. All suggest that even heaven showed its displeasure: during Jie's reign, the visible planets are said to have criss-crossed (which they indeed seem to have done in 1576 BCE) and some years later, two suns appeared at the same time—apparently symbolizing the rise of a new dynasty, the Shang.

There are no written records from the time of the Xia dynasty—many therefore regard it as legendary. However, archaeologists have isolated an extensive culture with China's earliest bronze vessels and evidence of a large palace that dates to the first half of the second millennium BCE (the time of the Xia dynasty) and extends throughout northwestern Henan and southern Shanxi provinces—the region associated with the Xia dynasty. Many scholars in China regard this culture as proof of the existence of the Xia dynasty. Western scholars have tended to be more skeptical about the identification, demanding contemporary written evidence. The question of Xia has thus become one of the more contentious issues in the study of ancient China.

THE EXPRESSIONS OF HEAVEN

The ancient Chinese were keen observers of the night sky. They saw in the regular and, especially, the irregular movement of the sun and moon, stars and planets, expressions of heaven's will. One of the cornerstones of Chinese political philosophy is that heaven bestows the right to rule only on a worthy recipient (see also page 222). But when that recipient, or his heirs, no longer merits such a mandate, heaven may also take it away. In King Jie's reign, heaven was thought to have demonstrated its displeasure by causing the planets to alter their regular movement and by making two suns appear together (see left). Five hundred years later, in 1059 BCE, there was another celestial omen—a spectacular conjunction of the five visible planets—and this portended that it was the turn of the Shang dynasty to lose its mandate. Its last ruler, King Zhou (not to be confused with the Zhou of the following Zhou dynasty), is usually twinned with King Jie—they have the reputation as the two most evil kings of antiquity. Not only did Zhou follow Jie in debauchery (he is said to have filled ponds with wine and hung meat from trees, under which he made the men and women of his court chase each other naked), but he even surpassed him in cruelty. He instituted the punishment of "roasting"—causing people to walk across a metal beam suspended above a fire until they fell into it; he pickled the lord of one allied state, and then made other lords eat the meat; and he even killed, in a gruesome manner, his paternal uncle, Bi Gan, when he remonstrated against these abuses.

The tales of Jie's and Zhou's debaucheries—told by the subsequent vanquishers of their dynasties, and thus almost certainly much exaggerated—set the tone for later rulers. In a similar vein, King You, the last king of the Western Zhou dynasty (reigned 781–771 BCE) is said to have lost his kingdom trying to please his dour consort Bao Si—a woman who rarely smiled. However, she was once amused when, on seeing that beacon fires were lit (which indicated an enemy attack), allied armies rushed to defend the capital, only to find that there was no attack at all. The king, seeking to make her laugh some more, continued this trick until the allies no longer bothered to respond to the warning beacons. Shortly thereafter, however, the capital came under a real attack, and the king was killed and the dynasty ended. In so many of these legends, women are made to bear the blame for the blunders of men.

POPULAR RELIGION

Three different religions have influenced Chinese civilization. The oldest, Confucianism, traces its roots back to antiquity—Confucius felt he was reviving a golden age of philosophical, ethical, and religious ideas that were in danger of lapsing—but did not become the basis of the state until the Han dynasty. This system of thought largely coexisted with the newer traditions of Daoism and Buddhism.

Confucianism and its body of moral teachings was premised on the notion of a natural hierarchy; it emphasized the interrelatedness of the cosmos and the need to maintain it in a state of harmony. These ideas informed social and family ethics, as well as the rites of ancestor veneration, and its influential teachings were integral to the development of the notion of Chinese statecraft, in which a virtuous ruler dominated.

Much of Chinese society was infused with the orderly principles of Confucianism; the generally more mystical Daoist tradition often offered an escape from such rigidity. However, most Chinese could embrace the tenets of both traditions alongside the ideas and teachings of Buddhism, which reached China from India.

DAOISM

Messianic groups began to appear in China toward the end of the Western Han dynasty (202BCE–9CE). Some of these were led by members of the Li family, which claimed descent from Li Er, more often known as Laozi, author of the *Dao De Jing* or *Classic of the Way and Virtue*. By the second century CE, these groups had coalesced into two or three mass religious movements, all of them inspired by the deified Laozi, and all of them claiming to be the *Dao* or the "Way." In 142, one Zhang Daoling, living in the southwestern province of Sichuan, claimed to have received a revelation from Laozi ordering him to establish a new religion to replace the popular religious practices, which he claimed had degenerated into demonism. Zhang and his descendants created a religious state in Sichuan, largely independent from the Han central government, which was then in decline. The state was organized into parishes, each with its own priest or libationer. The Zhangs ruled atop an intricate hierarchy, taking the title Heavenly Masters (*tianshi*), from which the religion gets its standard name: the Way of the Heavenly Masters.

Just before the final collapse of the Han court, Zhang Lu, grandson of Zhang Daoling, collaborated with Cao Cao (155–220), the warlord of eastern China and future founder of the Wei dynasty; this

A stela from the Northern Wei dynasty, dated 527CE, depicting two major Daoist figures: the deified Laozi—founder of the faith and author of the classic text the Dao De Jing—*and the Jade Emperor (Yu Di), the head of the Daoist pantheon.*

earned the religion official recognition, and brought its hierarchy to the imperial capital at Luoyang. Nevertheless, elsewhere in China other variants of Daoism sprouted. Doubtless the most important developments took place in the southeast, first at Mount Mao (Maoshan), near present-day Nanjing, Jiangsu, where a man named Yang Xi received revelations from gods of the heaven of Highest Purity (Shang Qing). These revelations persisted for six years (between 364 and 370), and Yang transcribed their instructions into a new scriptural religion, known as the Way of Highest Purity. Shortly thereafter, Ge Chaofu, scion of an illustrious southern Daoist family, composed the *Lingbao Jing* or *Classic of the Numinous Treasure*, which gave Daoism a still more elaborate theology.

State support for Daoism was strongest during the Tang dynasty, whose founders, Li Yuan (565–635; reigned as Gaozu, 618–626) and his son Li Shimin (597–649; reigned as Taizong, 626–649), claimed descent from Li Er or Laozi. The Tang emperors were regarded as reincarnations of the historical Laozi.

BUDDHISM

Originally deriving from the teachings of Siddhartha Gautama throughout the Indian subcontinent in the sixth and fifth centuries BCE (see page 141), Buddhism developed over the next several centuries into a sophisticated religion with numerous scriptures, known in Sanskrit as *sutra*s. When Buddhism reached China in the middle of the Han dynasty, it was a time of considerable religious ferment in the country. The earliest missionaries strove to translate the foreign Buddhist concepts into an idiom that would be both linguistically and conceptually familiar to the Chinese people. For

---

• THE QUEEN MOTHER OF THE WEST •

Chinese mythology's antipathy toward women is such that there is no significant mother goddess similar to those found in other civilizations. However, even by the time of the Shang dynasty there is mention of a "western mother," who may well be a goddess figure. By the fourth and third centuries BCE, the Queen Mother of the West had become a standard trope. Living in the Kunlun Mountains of the far west, she presided over a paradise of immortality. She is depicted in various guises, sometimes human, sometimes animal, sometimes a mixture of the two, and sometimes in the form of a woman riding on a tiger—in all cases, she can be identified by her distinctive headdress.

One of the earliest texts describes the travels of King Mu (Zhou dynasty; reigned 956–918BCE) to the Kunlun Mountains. Although the king fell in love with the Queen Mother of the West, and she with him, he had to return alone to the world of men. In later centuries, men from all walks of life sought to join her in the realm of immortality. The "Record of Omens and Portents" of the *Book of Han* records that there was a messianic religious movement devoted to her; the people believed that those who wore her talisman would not die. By the third century, when the Daoist religion coalesced, the Queen Mother of the West was the highest ranking female divinity. Her abode in the Kunlun Mountains became the axis by which to ascend to heaven. By the Tang dynasty, when Daoism had become the state religion, shrines to her occupied central places on both Mount Tai, the sacred mountain of the east, and of course Mount Hua, the sacred mountain of the west, and many of the great poets of the age sang of her glories.

◆ THE YUNGANG BUDDHIST CAVES ◆

The earliest and perhaps most spectacular Buddhist cave-temples in China are those at Yungang (Cloud Ridge), just outside the city of Datong in Shanxi. Called Pingcheng, this was the capital of the Northern Wei dynasty (383–534CE), which ruled much of northern China during the period of north–south division (see pages 230–231). The Wei rulers were Toba people, of mixed Turkic and Mongol ancestry, and were great patrons of Buddhism.

In total, fifty-three out of more than 250 caves at Yungang are said to contain over 51,000 carvings. Work on the caves began in 452CE, the best known of which contain colossal rock-carved statues of the Buddha and *bodhisattva*s ("enlightenment beings"), which are reputed to commemorate earlier Wei rulers. The imposing figure shown here is believed to have been commissioned by Emperor Xiaowen to honor his father.

The walls of many of the caves bear intricate carvings of scenes from Buddhist *sutra*s, the later of the caves showing more and more evidence of native Chinese artistic influence. All the main work on the caves was completed by 490, just before the Wei capital was moved from Pingcheng to the more centrally located Luoyang, in Henan province.

this reason, they borrowed heavily from the language of the Daoist scriptures (in Chinese called *jing*). Over the next two or three centuries, as both Daoism and Buddhism went through numerous developments, it was unclear to many Chinese people precisely what it was that differentiated the two traditions.

Certain aspects of Buddhist theology were quite familiar to the Chinese. The earliest *sutra*s to be translated tended to deal with rules for life and techniques of meditation similar to those that were developing within Daoism, and even the terminology used in the translations tended to borrow from indigenous Daoist terms.

Thus, in 166CE, Emperor Huan of the Han dynasty performed a joint sacrifice to Laozi and to the Buddha. However, as more *sutra*s were translated (according to one count, by the eighth century, as many as 1,124 had been translated into Chinese), and as the translation style became more rigorous, sharp differences between the two faiths came into focus. Perhaps the element that was most foreign to China was the Buddhist insistence

that monks should lead celibate lives—this contradicted the traditional Chinese notion that the first duty of any son was to produce a son of his own so that the ancestral lineage would be perpetuated, and it was often mentioned in nativist criticisms of the religion.

Nevertheless, the Buddhist faith exerted an enormous influence over Chinese civilization. Various dynasties, especially those headed by non-Chinese in north China during the fourth through to the sixth centuries, adopted Buddhism as the state religion and sponsored projects that transformed Chinese art (see box, above); Daoism assimilated much of Buddhism's elaborate description of the other world, and even Confucians accepted Buddhist methods of argumentation and metaphysics; Buddhist monasteries became hubs of commercial activity, contributing, among other things, to the development of paper currency; and the Buddhist community at Dunhuang in northwest China preserved the greatest trove of medieval manuscripts—on many diverse topics and in several different languages.

THE MANDATE OF HEAVEN

China has the longest unbroken history of any of the world's great civilizations, extending from the realm of the undocumented Xia dynasty four thousand years ago, across tens of centuries into the recorded past—each ruler grounding his, or her, legitimacy in the notion of the Mandate of Heaven.

Throughout China's ancient period, dynasties followed each other in irregular succession, some lasting for centuries but others barely outliving their founders. Already by the beginning of the Zhou dynasty (1045–256BCE), the problem of succession had given rise to China's most important governmental principle—the Mandate of Heaven—according to which heaven confers its blessing only on the virtuous. If and when rulers were no longer virtuous, heaven was seen to mandate a new dynasty. From this principle developed a core notion of the dynastic cycle, wherein founding emperors were seen as strong and upright while the last ones were seen as weak and corrupt. Although the material evidence reaches back further, China's written records commence with the Shang dynasty (ca. 1550–1045BCE).

◆ ANCIENT CHINESE COINS ◆

Ancient bronze coins have been unearthed in almost all of the independent states of the Spring and Autumn and Warring States periods (722–222BCE), their widespread distribution providing evidence that commerce thrived in ancient China. The earliest coins were made in the shapes of tools, such as shovels and knives, and denominated in quantities of silk, traditionally the most valuable commodity. Because these tool-coins proved unwieldy, they were later replaced by round coins, which could be strung together through their central hole (see illustration, above).

SHANG: THE FIRST DYNASTY

The Shang or Yin dynasty (ca. 1550–1045BCE) is China's first truly historical dynasty. The *Records of the Historian* of Sima Qian, the orthodox history of China down to about 100BCE, provides a glowing account of Cheng Tang's defeat of King Jie of the preceding Xia dynasty (ca. 2000–1550BCE), and a contrasting glowering account of the reign of King Zhou, the Shang dynasty's last ruler, but there is little of substance about the intervening four hundred and more years.

However, part of this story became clearer just over one hundred years ago, when oracle-bone inscriptions from the period were first recognized. Many of the tens of thousands of pieces of turtle-shell and ox-bone that have been discovered since—and certainly the majority of the most important ones—derive from the reign of King Wu Ding (reigned ca. 1200BCE). Wu Ding appears to have inherited a state in some disarray. His uncle, King Pan Geng (reigned ca. 1250BCE), had moved the capital to present-day Anyang, Henan, north of the Yellow River and just east of the Taihang mountain range, apparently hoping thereby to protect the ruling house. Wu Ding managed in the course of his reign to extend Shang power not only throughout eastern China, but also west of the Taihang. This seems to have opened the Shang state to influences from the west that

Warriors from the famous terracotta army, 210BCE, discovered in Xi'an, Shaanxi, in 1974. The formidable massed ranks of troops represent the armed retinue of unified China's First Emperor, Shi Huangdi (ruled 221–210BCE; see page 228). The 7,000-plus statues that were found near the emperor's tomb were placed there to protect him in the afterlife. Rendered with remarkable realism, each soldier possesses a distinctive hairstyle and facial features designed to distinguish him from the others.

• PHILOSOPHICAL AND MEDICAL TRADITIONS •

All of China's earliest writings portray a universe in which humankind and nature are inextricably linked. This world-view is the foundation for China's correlative cosmology—the notion that actions in the human realm have corresponding effects (but not necessarily reactions) in the natural world, and vice versa. In one influential account of the development of Chinese philosophy, this original union of heaven, Earth, and humans was sundered—probably about the fourth century BCE, in the middle of the period known as the Warring States. This apparently provoked an intellectual crisis that gave rise to the full flowering of Chinese philosophical expression, known as the "Hundred Schools" of thought (see page 226). Confucians, Daoists, Mohists, Legalists, Agriculturalists, Militarists, as well as Logicians, and no doubt countless others whose thoughts have been lost without a trace—all, over the next century or two, debated and wrote about the nature of life and the proper way (in Chinese, *dao*, meaning "road" or "way") to lead it.

Two political and intellectual developments of the third and second centuries BCE would set the terms of most of China's non-Buddhist philosophy throughout the remainder of the ancient period. Part of the triumph of the Qin unification of China was the establishment of a system of correspondences, by which all elements in the world were correlated once again. This system, known as the "Five Motions" or "Five Phases," could be applied to all aspects of philosophical discourse and also governed theories of natural science.

Medicine in China was inextricably bound up with the traditional Chinese worldview. In popular conceptions, the human body was perceived as a microcosm of the universe: the celestial bodies all had their counterparts in the physical organs, as did mountains and waterways, plants and animals. Just as there were sometimes disruptions in the normal functioning of the natural order, such as drought or floods, so too was the body susceptible to malfunction; the purpose of medicine was to restore the natural order.

The development of the notion of the Five Motions was readily adapted to this view of the body. Each of the phases or processes was considered to correspond to an emotional, visceral, or physiological function of the body. Outside the body, the five processes corresponded to different foods and drugs.

At the same time as the system of Five Motions was reaching its mature development, a new, in some ways simpler, conception of the body came to be adopted by élite doctors. They saw the body as being composed of three major constituents: *jing*, or semen, and other concentrated fluids; *qi*, vapor or breath—lighter but more pervasive than *jing*; and *shen*, or spirits. Each of these constituents played a vital role in maintaining a vigorous and healthy body. The desire to preserve and, indeed, to create *jing* led to various techniques designed, on the one hand, to stimulate sexual fluids, but on the other hand, to keep them inside the body. This was especially true for men. *Shen*, which accounts for the psychological aspect of good health, could also be increased.

While *jing* and *shen* might be regarded as the most refined constituents of the body, it was *qi* that was thought to pervade all aspects of it, circulating within it along various specified vessels or channels. The flow of *qi* through these channels gave rise to perhaps the most unique aspect of traditional Chinese medicine—acupuncture—the insertion of needles into specific points on the skin to influence the course that *qi* takes through the body.

transformed many features of life (with, for example, the introduction of the chariot), art, and perhaps even myth (the native religion, centered on Di and the ancestors of the Shang kings, found itself challenged by the more catholic religion of the Zhou that featured a heaven that embraced all peoples). Some of these innovations are apparent from the tomb of Fu Hao, one of Wu Ding's three principal consorts, which was excavated in 1975. Wu Ding's death seems to have brought about a retrenchment in Shang power back behind the natural barrier of the Taihang Mountains.

The last 150 years of the dynasty was a period of relative stagnation. Divinations performed on behalf of the kings became routine, mere expressions of hopes for a happy future; bronze vessels, although still impressive, did not develop greatly from the styles introduced during the time of Wu Ding; and military and political power seems to have become quite limited. But the Shang capital at Anyang remains perhaps the crowning glory of modern Chinese archaeology; it was the first site to be explored by the national Institute of History and Philology, the predecessor to the current Institute of Archaeology, which has established a permanent archaeological station there.

GOLDEN AGE OF THE ZHOU

The fall of the Shang dynasty in 1045BCE ushered in a period that Chinese of all later ages have looked back on as a golden age of government and culture. Shang oracle-bone inscriptions reveal that the Zhou people, located in the Wei River valley of western Shaanxi province, had long been in contact with the Shang, sometimes as allies, sometimes as enemies. Their conquest campaign was planned by King Wen (reigned ca. 1099–1050BCE)—who died before it could be carried out—and successfully concluded by King Wu

A strand of exquisite colored glass beads from the Warring States period (480–222BCE). Glass seems to have been introduced to China at about this time from areas to the west, in Central Asia.

(reigned 1049–1043BCE), who was one of nine sons by King Wen's primary consort. Other sons were deputed to govern colonies and indigenous peoples throughout the eastern territories, establishing a cultural and political network that would develop into the Central Kingdoms—and then, eventually, into the "Central Kingdom," or China.

Many of China's cultural traditions have their roots in the portion of this dynasty known as the Western Zhou (1045–771BCE), including the kinship system and the form of ancestor worship peculiar to it; music and poetry; the worldview that gave rise to correlative philosophy (see box, opposite); tax codes and legal statutes; and, perhaps most important of all, government in which the king and his ministers ruled in an often uneasy tension. Many of these traditions seem to have developed in the middle of the 275-year-long period. Inscribed bronze vessels from this time suggest that the power of the Zhou kings began to wane; as it did so, other types of power developed. Since these other powers were in competition—with each other as well as with royal power—they required codification. In many ways, this provided the foundation for the highly developed bureaucracy of later Chinese history.

In 771BCE, "barbarian" invaders sacked the Zhou capital near present-day Xi'an, Shaanxi, and killed King You (reigned 781–771BCE), the last of the Western Zhou kings. King You's son, King Ping (reigned 770–720BCE), reestablished the dynasty at its eastern capital at present-day Luoyang, Henan, but neither he nor his successors over the next 500 years was able to reassert control over the many states of the east, or to reclaim their traditional homeland in the west.

The Eastern Zhou period (770–256BCE) is usually divided into two separate periods, the Spring and Autumn period (722–481BCE) and the Warring States period (480–222BCE). The latter name is unfortunate in associating what was in fact a dynamic age primarily with death and destruction. There were many positive developments, both technological and intellectual, that transformed the China of high antiquity. Although there was plentiful warfare, it too was influenced by and contributed to many of these developments. For example, the invention of efficient iron plows increased food production, which contributed to a population explosion. This helped to swell the size of the armies put into the field during the era, which led to changed modes of warfare. The chariot battles of antiquity gave way to massed infantry armies, whose soldiers were equipped with the newly introduced and easily mastered crossbow. The greater number of soldiers also made discipline and logistics crucial. To meet this need, professional generals were armed with military manuals, the famous *Art of War of Sunzi* (*Sunzi bing fa*) being just one example of the genre. The administrative skills developed by these generals contributed, in turn, to

---

An extremely rare gilt-bronze sword, dating to the Warring States period (480–222BCE). Swords such as this developed in southeastern China, south of the Yangzi River—an area where many of China's metallurgical developments seem to have arisen.

increasingly sophisticated government administration in several of the independent states, especially Qi in the northeast, Chu in the south, and Qin in the west. Ministers in Qin created a theoretical framework for the art of government that would eventually lead to Qin's absorption of the other major states into a single grand empire, and that formed the basis of most political philosophy throughout China's imperial period.

It is, indeed, philosophy that most people associate with the Eastern Zhou period, and it is clear that it was undoubtedly an age of great intellectual ferment (see box, page 224). It was the time of Confucius (551–479BCE; see below) and Mozi (ca. 478–392BCE), of Laozi (ca. sixth century BCE) and Zhuangzi (ca. 365–285BCE), of Mencius (390–305BCE) and Xunzi (ca. 310–215BCE), and all the other thinkers who would come to be called the "Hundred Schools." It was the time when China's "classics"—particularly the *Classic of Changes*, the *Classic of Documents*, and the *Classic of Poetry*—were first read and studied, and when the first real books were written. Recent discoveries of inscriptions and manuscripts from the period have revealed still more. As in the case of military and government treatises, it is clear that the period saw the rise of much technical literature—works on medicine, divination, farming, and possibly cookery, were written and circulated. This technical literature was also read by the philosophers of the day, who adapted many of its concepts for use in their own work.

Kong Qiu, or Confucius (551–479BCE), is universally acclaimed as China's greatest sage. Although disarmingly simple, his teachings have had a global impact and continue to challenge philosophers today. His core

CHINA'S EQUESTRIAN CULTURE

Although not indigenous to China, the horse came to play an important role in the country's artistic, military, and social history. Horse-drawn chariots were used in Shang-dynasty China from around 1200BCE, but it was not until the Chinese invention of the stirrup in the fifth century CE that man and horse became truly effective partners—in both recreation and war. The horse itself was introduced to China from the west, a product of contact between the Chinese and the horse-riding peoples of Central Asia. By the fourth century BCE, the practice of riding horses had been so sufficiently embraced that it also led to the adoption of the style of dress worn by the horsemen of Central Asia. The horse became a sought after source of power, and in both the Han and Tang dynasties, the procurement of horses, whether from Central Asia or on stud farms in northern and western China, was always a crucial feature of the imperial government's foreign policies. The illustration above is based on the famous Han-dynasty sculpture known as the flying horse of Kansu.

message, based on the concept of *ren* ("humaneness"), was that one should act in recognition of the basic human relationships: those between parent and child, husband and wife, subject and ruler, employer and employee, and so on. Ideally, one should develop the virtue of *ren* and strive to become emotionally centered (*zhong*) but also able to identify with others (*shu*).

THE FIRST EMPEROR OF QIN

Although Chinese historians have traditionally viewed the Qin people as unsophisticated westerners, capable only of warfare and tyrannous governmental administration, recent archaeological discoveries suggest that this is an unfair characterization. Bronze inscriptions from the early seventh century BCE show the Qin rulers to have regarded themselves as the cultural heirs of the founding fathers of the Zhou dynasty, kings Wen and Wu, and bamboo-strip manuscripts from the third century BCE show their administrators to have been conscientious public servants—or relatively so at least. The state would undoubtedly have engaged in aggression and treachery against its rivals throughout the intervening five hundred or so years, but this was standard practice throughout all the states.

Histories of Qin usually focus on King Zheng of Qin, the ruler who succeeded in defeating all the other states and establishing himself as the First Emperor (reigned 221–210BCE; the title Shi Huangdi, which he chose himself, would be better rendered as First August Theocrat, Di being the name for one of ancient China's high gods). Accounts of the era prior to the First Emperor's reign tend to do little more than contribute to the idle gossip and speculation that surrounded his supposed bastardy (his own first prime minister, Lü Buwei [died 238BCE], is believed to have cuckolded his father, King Zhuangxiang [reigned 249–247BCE]). But in the century before the First Emperor's reign, the state of Qin benefited from two very capable rulers: Lord Huiwen (reigned 337–311BCE), who declared Qin to be a kingdom in 324, and King Zhao (reigned 306–251), whose reign set the stage for the eventual Qin conquest.

These rulers were advised by a pair of ministers, Shen Buhai (died ca. 337BCE) and Shang Yang (died 338BCE), who developed a political philosophy, usually referred to as Legalism, that envisioned a governmental apparatus that would be able to function on its own in an objective and unprejudiced manner.

With the final conquest achieved in 221BCE, the First Emperor moved quickly to consolidate Qin rule. He deputed administrators throughout the realm to put in place a rational, centralized government; he instructed that local writing styles be unified and weights and measures be standardized; he had walls dividing the former independent states demolished and the roadways interconnected. Perhaps most famously of all, he ordered the construction of the Great Wall (see illustration, below), marking the northern boundary of the empire. And certainly most infamously, he ordered that all but technical literature should be proscribed; it is also said that he buried alive 400 scholars at court. The First

Emperor proclaimed that his was but the first of 10,000 reigns in the Qin dynasty, but when he died in 210BCE his son's reign was not only short lived—less than three years—but it marked the end of the dynasty.

THE CONSOLIDATION OF HAN

With the collapse of the Qin dynasty in 207BCE, China was thrown into a gruelling five-year civil war between the forces of Xiang Yu (233–202BCE), scion of a leading military family in the southern state of Chu, and Liu Bang (248–195BCE), a local magistrate in eastern China. The forces of Liu Bang were ultimately victorious, and he established the Han dynasty, ruling as its High Ancestor (reigned 202–195BCE).

The first generations of the Han dynasty were almost as turbulent as the years of the civil war. Internally, Liu Bang first divided power among his lieutenants, and then tried to take it back, replacing these confederates with fellow kinsmen of the Liu family. Externally, Liu

Bang was humiliated by the army of the Xiongnu leader (*shanyu*) Maodun, surviving with his life at the battle of Pingcheng only by way of a ruse. When Liu Bang died in 195BCE from an arrow wound suffered in yet another battle, power passed to his consort, the Empress Lü (Lü Zhi, died 180BCE). This caused yet another phase of civil unrest, with the Empress Lü first replacing, in a particularly violent manner, the Liu élite with members of her own Lü family, and then, after her death, with the Lius treating the Lü family in a similarly brutal fashion.

The First Emperor of Qin ordered the construction of a great defensive wall along the empire's northern frontier. The wall was originally made of stamped earth, with watchtowers and barracks along its length, and extended from the Bay of Bohai in the east more than 3,700 miles (6,000km) at its greatest extent to the Jade Gate (Yumen) in the western desert province of Gansu. By no later than the Tang dynasty (618–907CE), the Great Wall had already entered into the national consciousness as the dividing line between China and the outside world.

Still further civil disturbance wracked the country for the next several decades as the court sought to enhance its power vis-à-vis local rulers, even though they were almost all from the same family. Finally, with the lengthy reign of Liu Che (reigned 141–87BCE), more popularly known as Emperor Wu, central power was consolidated and, in addition, a series of military campaigns into Central Asia turned the balance of power against the Xiongnu and in favor of the Han.

Emperor Wu's reign was also notable for other reasons. Not only did he establish an imperial academy with the Confucian classics constituting the sole curriculum, but his age was marked by the convergence of a number of gifted and outstanding individuals, including—among the most illustrious—the philosopher and political theorist Dong Zhongshu (ca. 179–104BCE), the poet Sima Xiangru (179–117BCE), and the historian Sima Qian (145–ca. 86BCE). In 104BCE, the emperor performed rituals on Mount Tai, the sacred peak of the east, to mark the formal establishment of the dynasty.

Historians, beginning with Wu's contemporary Sima Qian, have not been uniformly positive in their assessment of the emperor. It has been suggested that toward the end of his reign he squandered much of the wealth and power that he had accumulated. During the century after his death dynastic fortunes continued to decline, until in 9CE Wang Mang (33BCE–23CE), the Marshall of State, established his own Xin dynasty (9–23CE). Although the Han dynasty was restored in 25CE, and persisted for almost another 200 years (a time of many remarkable intellectual and technological developments, including the rise of Daoism, the introduction of Buddhism, and the invention of paper), imperial power diminished to the extent that the final emperor, Xian (reigned 189–220CE), simply abdicated.

THREE KINGDOMS, SIX DYNASTIES

The demise of the 400-year-long Han dynasty is often seen as a low point in the development of Chinese civilization. Even though the Han imperial insignia were turned over to the Marshall of State Cao Cao (155–220), who installed his son Cao Pi (187–226) as the first emperor of a newly established Wei dynasty (220–264), in fact China was at the time divided into three independent states: Wei, in charge of the former capitals and the northeast; Wu, dominant throughout the south; and Shu, located in the west in present-day Sichuan province. There ensued a sixty-year period of intermittent warfare, known in China as the period of the Three Kingdoms. When Wu was defeated in 280, the victor was neither Wei nor Shu, but another dynasty, the Jin (265–316 and 317–420). Like the Wei dynasty, the Jin was established by a family of warlords who forced the reigning emperor to abdicate. Also like the Wei, the Jin was short-lived: after just three reigns, its capitals were sacked in 311 and 316.

The Jin dynasty reestablished itself as a power in the south of the country, ushering in the age known as the Six Dynasties (also known as the Northern and Southern dynasties). Nobles, the social élite, and commoners alike joined the Jin court there, setting in motion a demographic shift that was to transform China. Establishing a new capital at present-day Nanjing, south of the Yangzi River, the Eastern Jin dynasty (317–420) continued for another century, to be followed by several other even shorter-lived dynasties.

As unhappy as the short century of the Wei and Jin dynasties was as far as political history was concerned, it was one of the most vibrant periods in China in terms of philosophy, religion, and literature. Philosophers such as Wang Bi (226–249) made the period famous for *xuanxue*, "the study of the dark"—in other words, metaphysics; Daoism and Buddhism flourished; Ruan Ji (210–263), Ji Kang (223–262), and the other members of the group known as the "Seven Sages of the Bamboo Grove," helped to establish poetry as the foremost medium for the expression of personal sentiment. Presented with a lush, new intellectual landscape, poets turned more and more to nature, forgetting their political woes. The natural world obviously also inspired artists. No longer mere workmen in the employ of the court, painters such as Gu Kaizhi (345–411) developed landscapes (in Chinese, "mountains and rivers") as the preeminent style of Chinese painting.

Meanwhile, in the north of China, another series of short-lived and more local dynasties succeeded each other, many of them ruled by non-Chinese. The most important of these, the Toba or Tabgatch, in 386 established the capital of their Northern Wei (unrelated to the Wei) dynasty in Pingcheng (present-day Datong), in the far north of Shanxi province. They ruled there for a century, uniting all of north China and redistributing much of the population from the center to the periphery. In 494, they moved their capital to Luoyang, site of the earlier capital of the Han, Wei, and Jin dynasties. It was the rulers of this Northern Wei dynasty who sponsored the Buddhist statues at Yungang (see page 220), just outside of Datong, and at Longmen, near Luoyang. In 534, the dynasty split, yielding in short order to two brief dynasties, Northern Qi and Northern Zhou.

SUI AND TANG REVIVAL

The middle decades of the sixth century saw China not only divided between southern and northern dynasties, but also divided in the north among various generals. Finally, in 581, Yang Jian (541–604), one of the northern generals, succeeded in defeating his northern rivals and founded the Sui dynasty (581–618). Eight years later, he conquered southern China as well, reuniting China for the first time in almost three centuries.

The Sui is frequently compared with the Qin dynasty, the earlier unifier of the warring states. Like the Qin, the Sui is often criticized for the excessive costs of such massive public construction projects as the building of defensive walls and, especially, the Grand Canal, which succeeded in linking the Yangzi and Yellow rivers. Again like the Qin, the Sui was short-lived, its second emperor being overthrown (as the second Qin emperor had also been) in 618 by a peasant uprising. This uprising was led by Li Yuan (565–635), a general from

northern Shanxi province, and his son, Li Shimin (598–649). Together they established the Tang dynasty (618–907), which would prove to be one of the greatest dynasties in Chinese history.

During the first decades of rule, the Tang made every effort to unite the country. Just as the Han dynasty had benefited from the construction projects undertaken during the preceding Qin dynasty, so too did the Tang benefit from the work done in the Sui. The two capitals of Chang'an (present-day Xi'an) and Luoyang, rebuilt on a grand scale by the Sui (the wall around Chang'an was 22 miles [35km] in length), were supplied with the wealth of the south via the Grand Canal and with imported luxury items from central and western Asia via the Silk Road. Chang'an, in particular, became a great cosmopolitan center, with a population of about a million people, including some 50,000 foreign merchants.

The first generations of the dynasty were not without their crises. Li Shimin forced his father to retire in 626. Then, some sixty years later, his one-time concubine, Wu Zhao (better known by her reign name Wu Zetian), declared herself emperor of a new Zhou dynasty (690–705)—the only case in Chinese history of an officially declared female emperor. With the restoration of the Tang emperors, and especially with Emperor Xuanzong (reigned 712–756), the first half of the eighth century became perhaps the high tide of Chinese culture. It was the age of Li Bai (also known as Li Bo, 701–762) and Du Fu (712–770), China's two greatest poets ever; and the time of the monk Xuanzang's pilgrimage to India, which resulted in the translation into Chinese of more than 1,000 scrolls of Indian texts. However, Emperor Xuanzong's long reign ended finally in disaster, with a military revolt led by An Lushan (died 757), a general of mixed Sogdian-Turkic ancestry, and then a subsequent civil war that dragged on for eight years. Although the Tang emperors were restored yet again, and the dynasty persisted for another century and a half, in many respects the An Lushan Rebellion, as it is known, marks the end of China's ancient period.

FAMILY AND SOCIETY

In ancient China, individuals lived within the context of the family. One was not just a child, but rather a son or daughter; not just an adult, but rather a parent; and, if fortunate, not just a senior citizen, but rather a grandparent. It was from the family that one learned society's core values.

Confucian ideas shaped China's social values, which included: the conviction that hierarchies are natural but not static; that social harmony should be placed above personal desires; and that eternal life requires corporate effort. However, there were also significant rites of passage to mark individual lives, from birth and acceptance into the family, through attainment of adulthood and marriage, and to old age.

BIRTH AND CHILDHOOD

As is perhaps fitting, records of birth-giving go back to the very beginning of the Chinese historical tradition. The oracle-bone inscriptions from the Shang-dynasty king Wu Ding (ca. 1200BCE) include divinations concerning at least three pregnancies of his consort Fu

Hao. In one case, which the king predicted would be inauspicious, a post-natal verification confirmed that "it really was inauspicious; it was a girl." In later times, it appears that the role of women was somewhat more highly valued—if only for the fact that they gave birth to the all-important sons. The mother of Mencius (ca. 390–305BCE)—who was, after Confucius himself, the most influential Confucian philosopher in antiquity—is renowned for instructing her son, while still in her womb, on the values of leading an ethical life.

Soon after an infant's entry into the world, he or she became subject to the rituals often associated with Confucianism. The *Record of Rituals* states that on the child's third day of life, divinations were to be performed to determine which male should "raise up" the

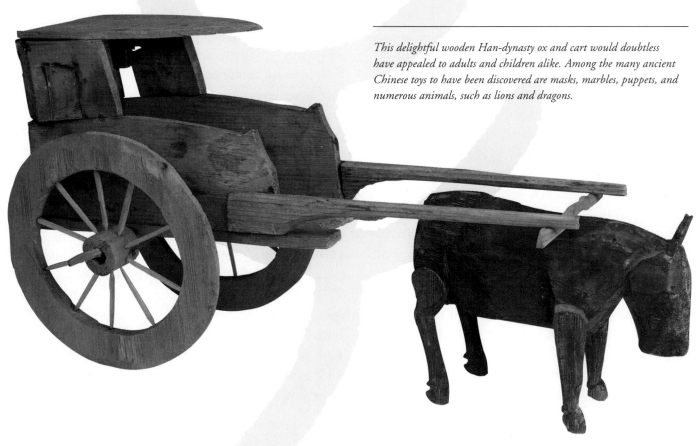

This delightful wooden Han-dynasty ox and cart would doubtless have appealed to adults and children alike. Among the many ancient Chinese toys to have been discovered are masks, marbles, puppets, and numerous animals, such as lions and dragons.

child and carry it outside the birthing chamber. Perhaps inevitably in a traditional society, a number of children—males born with birth defects that would render them incapable of performing ancestral rituals, some girls, and some babies born to parents too poor to care for them—were not raised up, but abandoned. Cruel though this may seem, and there is some evidence to suggest that in the Qin dynasty (221–207BCE) this practice was regarded as a crime, it is grounded in fundamental Chinese notions of human nature, which hold that one's nature (that is, one's life) is a process: one is not born a fully evolved human being, and infancy marks only the initial coalescence of the life forces.

For those youths who were accepted into the family, education seems to have been an overriding concern—at least with respect to the élite families who make up the bulk of the dynastic histories. For example, Ban Gu (32–92CE), who would go on to write the *Book of Han*, is said to have memorized the *Classic of Poetry* by the age of eight, and also to have been proficient in writing his own poetry. Young girls were educated in "female morals" and song and dance, but it was not unheard of that they too should become literate and, in some—admittedly rare—cases achieve renown; thus, Ban Zhao (48–ca. 116CE) completed the *Book of Han* that had been started by her brother Ban Gu.

LINEAGES OF MALES

Men were preeminent in all spheres of life in ancient China: government officials from the emperor to the lowliest clerk were all males, as were intellectuals, artists, artisans, and merchants and those whom we know to have contributed to the development of Buddhism and Daoism. Males were also regarded as uniquely responsible for the perpetuation of the family line—the most important social institution of all. This duty centered on the sacrifices performed in the all-male ancestral temple.

Ancient China's kinship structure was simultaneously simple and complicated. During the Zhou dynasty, when the ancestral system was traditionally deemed to

Affairs of state were very much a male enterprise in ancient China, as suggested in this detail of a grouping of mandarins (left) and Korean envoys, from a Tang-dynasty mural decorating the east wall of the tomb of Prince Zhanghuai in Xi'an. The image is also indicative of the attempts that were made to foster friendly diplomatic relations between China and the outside world during the Tang dynasty.

have been established, there were only about twenty different surnames, but within each family there were numerous lineages and branch lineages, each of which replicated the kinship structure of the family; in time, these lineages would in fact become independent families. The ancestral temple was dedicated in the first place to the historical person considered to be the founder of the family or the lineage. Thus, for the royal Zhou Ji family, the ancestral temple in the capital was dedicated to King Wen (reigned 1099–1051BCE). Subsequent generations of ancestors were arrayed in the temple, in alternating generations, either side of the high ancestor. The name given to this left–right alternation is *zhao–mu*, probably taken from the reign-names of the two Zhou kings when the system was put firmly in place—King Zhao (reigned 977–957BCE) and King Mu (reigned 956–918BCE). It specified that one's place in the temple

• THE UNIFYING ROLE OF FOOD •

Both Confucius and Laozi advised that the state should be governed as one would cook a fish—delicately and with as little fuss as possible. This use of gastronomy as a metaphor for writers was a reflection of the popularity in ancient China of cooking. Indeed, Yu the Great had been mindful of food and regional cuisine when formulating his nine regions.

Collections of recipes were popular. A cookbook found in the tomb of Wu Yang (died 162BCE) contains more than 150 recipes, nearly all of which seem to be elaborate meat preparations. Although part of the text was damaged and the complete version has not yet been published, a recipe for slabs of suckling pig is available. It includes directions for the butchering and preparation of the pig, multiple stages of steaming and boiling, before a final boiling in a fresh sweet beef broth with wine, salt, meat juices, ginger, and magnolia bark. In *Essentials for the Common People* (*Qi min yao shu*), completed in 540CE, Jia Sixie included 280 recipes, ranging from fermentation techniques, to roasts and stews, noodles and breads. There is even a detailed description of how to make cottage cheese. As in all good cookbooks, Jia's recipes record the ingredients, amounts, preparation, and how to present the finished dish.

Although there are similarities between Jia Sixie's cookbook and that of Wu Yang, China's cuisine underwent many changes throughout that long period. The demographic shift southward that had begun in the fourth century CE familiarized China's élites with a host of new crops, including rice. The reunification of China under the Sui dynasty and the construction of the Grand Canal allowed for the transportation of this important staple to the north, transforming the way people ate. In the next centuries, during the Tang dynasty, the introduction of another new southern crop—tea—was to have a profound influence on China's drinking habits, as well as its cultural traditions.

This detail from an anonymous painting of the 10th century CE, entitled Banquet and Concert, *depicts magnificently attired women of the Tang imperial court enjoying music and a fine feast. When not in attendance at entertainments, women at court were generally sequestered in their living quarters, situated at the rear of the palace, where they had charge of the imperial offspring.*

was not beside one's father, but beside one's grandfather. For this reason, it was the eldest grandson who was featured in the ancestor sacrifices, since he was considered to be the personification of his grandfather (for the purposes of the sacrifice, he was referred to as the "corpse"). After a number of generations (seven for the royal family, five for the nobility, and three for the lesser aristocracy), ancestors other than the high ancestor would be displaced from the central temple and grouped together in side chambers. Also after a number of generations (the exact number is not clear, but five seems to have been the norm), younger brothers—who were excluded from the rituals of the ancestral temple—might establish branch lineages and become high ancestors in their own right.

WOMEN'S ROLES

In the Chinese conception of the world, all energy and matter was made up of two natures, *yin* and *yang*. These originally referred to shade and sunshine, but by an early period had been extended to an almost infinite series of oppositions: cold and hot, wet and dry, inner and outer, private and public, and, of course, female and male. Many have contended that this gave rise to an essentially misogynistic conception that was responsible for keeping women hidden and very much out of public view. An alternative view regards *yin* and *yang* as complementary, with both being necessary to complete the circle of life. Both these views are overly simplified.

It is certainly true that on the rare occasions that Chinese women entered into public life—especially political life—it was almost always portrayed as an aberration, usually with unhappy consequences. The falls of

the Shang and Western Zhou dynasties are routinely blamed on the final emperors' infatuation with concubines; and the Han and Tang dynasties were almost cut short when imperial consorts actually usurped power. But there is reason to believe that women were also appreciated. The tombs of some women were lavishly furnished with grave goods, as was the case with the Shang-dynasty tomb of Fu Hao (died ca. 1195BCE) and the Han-dynasty tombs of the ladies Dai (died ca. 165BCE, see pages 242–243) and Dou (died ca. 115BCE), found at Mawangdui and Mancheng. We know too that Fu Hao was an active participant in court life—not only were there divinations about her giving

birth, but there were also some which related to her raising troops and even leading them into battle. It is true that this is an exceptional case, and one, moreover, that was unknown throughout traditional times.

However, the lives of other women were celebrated. Although written by a man (Liu Xiang [ca. 76–8BCE]), one much-read work, *Biographies of Estimable Women*, narrates the lives of 125 notable women who lived from early antiquity down to the time of the book's compilation in 16BCE. For example, the mother of Mencius, the philosopher, was praised for overseeing her son's education. The first work we know of to have been written wholly by a woman, the *Admonitions for Women* by Ban

Zhao (48–ca. 116CE), was conservative in tone, consisting of instructions to women as to their correct conduct in marriage, thereby ensuring they kept to their rightful place. This set the tone for a genre of "women's books," written by both men and women.

MARRIAGE

In ancient China, marriage usually involved far more than just the union of one man and one woman. For ordinary people, evidence suggests that there were communal gatherings of young men and women, sometimes in the spring and sometimes in the autumn, which, after an exchange of songs and love tokens, ended in dances, and often much more. For the élite, however, marriage was viewed as the union of two families. Indeed, during the Zhou period (1045–256BCE), the bride was usually accompanied by her sisters or female cousins, who would serve as secondary wives. In all periods, a man was free to have as many concubines (as distinct from secondary wives) as his family could afford (though the primary wife enjoyed all of the privileges of the marriage).

Marriage relations required the services of an intermediary, or *mei*. Brides-to-be, presented with slippers made of *kudzu* (a vine with various uses related to pregnancy and birth), would perform a dance, reenacting the way in which Jiang Yuan, the progenitress of the Zhou people, was thought to have become pregnant by stepping in god's footprint. Following the dance, arrows would be placed into quivers hanging from the women's girdle sash (the symbolism of which was obvious).

The ritual texts describe a more sedate ceremony. The groom, who was supposed to wait until the age of thirty before marrying, would call on the bride's family. He did so in the evening, in part because the word for evening, *hun*, was homophonous with the word for marriage, and in part because evening was the onset of darkness—according to the ancient Chinese notion of *yin–yang* duality, darkness and women were both *yin*, and so night was the proper time for the bride to come. The groom bore a gift of a wild goose (or, better, a pair of them), because geese were supposed to mate for life. He would confirm that the bride's surname was not the same as his own. This was done so as not to contravene

◆ THE ART OF ADORNMENT ◆

The élite of ancient China were keen to surround themselves with magnificent objects, and especially to wear them. The subtle beauty of materials such as jade and silk was preferred to ostentatious displays of gold and silver. Jade was fashioned into many types of jewelry, such as this glorious Tang-dynasty pendant (left). Glass beads were strung into necklaces, and hair clasps were produced from various media; one surviving example is in bronze, inlaid with gold and turquoise. Silk came in every imaginable color and design. Clothing was intended to be more than just appealing, it was regarded as the outward sign of the wearer's inner virtue and was symbolic of his or her status in life—as indicated by the elegant attire of the women represented in paintings and murals depicting life in the imperial court (see illustration, page 235).

a basic proscription against incest, which in China has long been understood as marriage between persons of the same surname; in ancient times, there were even fewer surnames in China than there are now, which was a limiting factor. After taking the bride back to his own family, the marriage would be consummated, first with a banquet. After three months, the marriage would be regarded as completed and the wife assumed her privileges and responsibilities in her husband's family.

OLD AGE

Bronze inscriptions of the Western Zhou period routinely conclude with a prayer addressed to the deceased grandfather and father of the vessel's patron to bestow on him "august longevity." Later inscriptions, from about the time of Confucius, invoke the longevity of the Duke of Shao, one of the founding fathers of the Zhou dynasty, and there is in fact evidence that he lived a very long life, perhaps more than one hundred years. In an age when life expectancy was probably about forty-five, this must have seemed very old indeed. And although grandfathers were always invoked in prayer, it was probably quite rare to live to see one's own grandchildren.

Those who did live to old age enjoyed not just the respect of their descendants, but also a number of socially sanctioned privileges. The Confucian text *Mencius* states as a matter of objective fact that all elders are owed respect simply because of their age. The same text also indicates that those who reached the age of fifty were to be clothed in silk, and those who reached seventy were to receive meat with their meals; this latter privilege would have been enjoyed by other members of the family only at the feasts following offerings to the ancestors. Outside of the family, the law code of the Qin dynasty, discovered in 1975 in the tomb of a Qin local magistrate, specified that men over the age of sixty were exempt from unpaid labor, and were also to receive pardons from certain forms of punishment.

A Han-dynasty incense burner of the type known as a "Universal Mountain Censer" (Boshan lu). In ancient China mountains were considered to be meeting places of Earth and the heavens, and climbing them was one way for people to ascend to heaven.

WORK AND PLAY

It is perhaps unsurprising that the sense of order and duty ingrained in Chinese society extended to the world of work. Even leisure pursuits could serve the greater good—many, such as archery, chariotry, and board games of strategy, were regarded as important training for warfare.

There were four main categories of workers in ancient Chinese society: farmers, soldiers, artisans, and merchants; they were usually ranked in this order, although soldiers sometimes received the top billing. It is perhaps ironic that virtually all the country's magnificent cultural artifacts were produced by artisans and were paid for, either directly or indirectly, by merchants—in other words, the two least respected classes of workers.

Ranked over these four classes was, of course, the ruling nobility. Such rulers were considered necessary because work, like most aspects of life in ancient China, was almost always a corporate undertaking, and as such required constant administration. According to mythology, Yu the Great single-handedly contained the Yellow River by carving out channels to take its flood waters to the sea, but in reality, armies of workers were mobilized by each succeeding state to keep the river within ever-higher levees. Other projects demanded even greater manpower. The story of the Qin general Meng Tian taking an army of 300,000 soldiers and conscript laborers to the northern frontier to construct the Great Wall is, of course, infamous, but by no means isolated. Even in neolithic times, most cities were furnished with high city walls, all of them constructed by peasants pressed into service when not in their fields. It has been estimated that the wall that was built around the fourteenth-century BCE Shang city at Zhengzhou, Henan—a Shang capital prior to their move to Anyang—required 10,000 laborers to work every day for twelve and a half years. Artisans, too, must often have worked in groups that required considerable coordination. The casting of a bronze vessel, for example, would have required not only potters to shape the model and mould, and smelters to smelt the copper, tin, and lead ore, but also—in the case of a large

vessel, which could reach a weight of several hundred pounds—a great many menial laborers just to pour the molten bronze into the assembly.

But it was in the arena of war that the need for administration was the greatest, and had the greatest repercussions for the state as a whole. There is a romantic notion that in the glory days of the early Zhou dynasty, warfare was an élite affair, undertaken by a handful of charioteers. Although this is almost certainly an underestimation, it is true that by the Warring States period (480–222BCE) warfare had developed into a quite different business: confrontations were now between massed infantry armies, often involving hundreds of thousands of soldiers. The logistics of putting such armies into the field gave rise to both professional generals and to books of administrative science. It was perhaps the mastery of this science, more than any other single factor, that allowed the state of Qin to conquer all the other warring states, and then to lay the foundation for the Chinese imperial bureaucracy.

THE PURSUIT OF LEISURE

Just as Wellington's victory over Napoleon was said to have been won on the playing fields of Eton school, so too was much Chinese play a preparation for the serious game of war. The first games for which we have evidence were archery contests. The Zha Bo *gui*, a Zhou bronze vessel (produced around 1000BCE and discovered in 1993 at Pingdingshan, Henan), was cast to commemorate Zha Bo's victory in one such contest. The inscription states that the king held up a prize and announced that it would go to the winner; Zha Bo then shot ten times, hitting the target each time. Throughout the remainder of early antiquity, archery remained one of the six arts that all educated men were expected to master (the other arts were those of the lute, the chariot, the writing brush, mathematics, and the rites). Some, at least, recognized that it was just a game. Criticized for being an empty-headed philosopher, Confucius asked in jest exactly what his critic would have him master—chariotry or archery. He then answered his own question by announcing that, fine, he would go off and practice his driving.

Other games required still greater athletic prowess. During the Han dynasty, a form of wrestling called *juedi* was enjoyed both at court and in the markets. Since the name means "horns linked" and suggests a face-off between two bulls or two rams, it seems to have been something like the sumo wrestling found in Japan. During the Tang dynasty, polo enjoyed even greater popularity among the élites, and was depicted in murals which adorned the walls of tombs. Another élite pastime also shown in the murals is the grand hunt, involving hundreds of persons on horseback and strikingly reminiscent of the English fox hunt.

There were more cerebral games as well. Both literary references and artifactual evidence suggest that the game of *liubo* (thought to mean "six dice") was one of the most popular entertainments during the late Warring States period and throughout the Han dynasty. It seems to have combined elements of skill and chance, the board on which it was played was conceived as a representation of the universe, which perhaps explains its resemblance to a diviner's board used in determining astrological omens. Another board game (again, a simulation of warfare) was *weiqi*, variants of which are known in the West as "Chinese chess." *Weiqi* seems to have been played throughout China's antiquity, but it reached something of a fever pitch at the time of Emperor Wu of the Liang dynasty (reigned 502–550CE). Emperor Wu himself was a great aficionado of the game, often playing all night with his ministers, and writing various treatises on the game, at least one of which seems to have been preserved. Emperor Wu also once organized a national tournament of *weiqi*. It is a testament to his sense of fair play that even though he participated in the tournament, he did not emerge as the victor.

An impish court jester is represented in this terracotta model from the Eastern Han dynasty. The emperor and his courtiers would often be entertained by such figures who, it is claimed, sometimes attempted to subtly influence the opinions of their rulers by means of their comic performances. Other forms of court entertainment included song-and-dance productions, acrobatics, various tests of strengths, and—especially in the Tang-dynasty period—exhibitions of exotic animals.

DEATH AND ETERNITY

The last passage of life was regarded by many in ancient China as perhaps the most important one, with earthly death providing access to the realm of the spirits and ancestors, to whom the living made offerings until they could join their ranks. As if to symbolize these links, the evidence in the tombs of China's dead has done much to help to construct the detailed picture of China's past.

The popular conception of the human body in ancient China—as opposed to the élite medical conception—was that it is made up of two different types of elements or souls. One, called the *po*, was viscous and material; the other, the *hun*, was vaporous and ethereal. It was thought that the convergence of these two types of souls produced life, and that their separation brought death. The *hun* souls, being lighter and more prone to depart from the body (which they did in deep sleep, their wanderings being the cause of dreams),

were the first to leave at the time of death. Immediately after the apparent death of a person, the son would climb to the roof of the house to "summon" the *hun* souls to return. Only when this ritual failed to revive the person was he or she definitively declared to be "dead."

The deceased was then prepared for the tomb and efforts were made to preserve the body. At the very least, jade, the finest of all stones, was inserted into the mouth to stop the decaying process. In other cases, the corpse was dressed with an entire shroud of jade pieces. In one

• THE TOMB OF EMPRESS WU •

Wu Zhao, better known as Wu Zetian (died 705CE), is one of the most fascinating, even if reviled, figures in Chinese history. She was a consort to both emperors Taizong and Gaozong of the Tang dynasty, becoming Gaozong's empress. When he suffered a stroke in 660, she seized power. After his death in 683, she first put her own son on the throne, but within a few years declared herself emperor of a newly established Zhou dynasty, becoming the only woman in Chinese history to have ruled in her own right. A devout Buddhist, Wu Zetian took advantage of the political, economic, and ideological support of the Buddhist church to secure her power. She made Buddhism the state religion, founded monasteries, and subsidized translation projects and the making of huge quantities of religious art.

The imposing figures shown here (right) are the stone attendants which stand guard outside Wu Zetian's burial mound at Qianling, Shaanxi. The tomb, which she shares with Emperor Gaozong, has a pyramidal tumulus—this may well have been inspired by the pyramids of Egypt. The earliest example in China of such a tumulus, the mausoleum of the rulers of Zhongshan at Pingshan, Hebei province, dates to the end of the fourth century BCE, just a generation later than the celebrated tomb of King Mausolus (reigned 377–353BCE) at Halicarnassus, Bodrum, modern-day Turkey.

notable discovery of 1971, Lady Dai (died ca. 165BCE), the wife of the king of Changsha in the early years of the Han dynasty, was found almost perfectly preserved in her tomb at Mawangdui, apparently the result of a deliberate mummification process. But for most people, it was understood that death entailed the decomposition of the body. This is why tombs were dug into the soil, close to the subterranean Yellow Springs, the abode of the dead. The material substance of the body would be transported there when the viscous *po* souls departed the body and flowed downward through the ground.

One amusing story in the *Zuo zhuan* or *Zuo's Tradition*, a narrative history of the Spring and Autumn period, reveals the nature of the popular belief. Lady Jiang of Shen married Duke Wu of Zheng and gave birth to two sons, the future Duke Zhuang and his younger brother Duan. Lady Jiang always favored Duan, and once even colluded with him in a plot to overthrow Duke Zhuang. Learning of the plot, the duke sent his brother into exile and confined his mother, swearing an oath that he would not again look upon her face until they met in the Yellow Springs. However, after entertaining a commoner who set aside a portion of his dinner so he could share it with his mother, Duke Zhuang came to bitterly regret his decision. But as a ruler, he could not breach his oath. The commoner therefore devised a plan whereby the duke could both keep his word and also meet with his mother. He had pits dug down to the water table by the Yellow Springs, with a perpendicular tunnel connecting them. Duke

Zhuang and his mother each went to the bottom of one of the pits (that is, to the Yellow Springs) and there made peace with each other.

HOMES FOR MORTAL REMAINS

The archaeology of China is overwhelmingly mortuary in nature, probably more so than in any other culture. In a land where almost all buildings were made of wood and most of which has been continuously occupied since neolithic times, few structures above ground have survived the ravages of time and man. Fortunately, despite admonitions in various early texts against great expenditures on burials, many of the tens of thousands of tombs Chinese archaeologists have unearthed in the past century have been lavishly furnished. We owe most of our advances in the understanding of ancient China to the structure and contents of these tombs.

Burial practice underwent considerable change over the course of China's antiquity. During the Shang and Western Zhou periods, tombs were essentially vertical shafts dug into the ground. They varied, of course, according to size and furnishings. All of the tombs of Shang kings at Anyang were plundered in antiquity, probably soon after the Zhou conquest, and the tombs of the Zhou kings have never been found (though latest reports suggest that this may soon change). However, the tomb of Fu Hao (died ca. 1195BCE), one of the consorts of the Shang king Wu Ding, gives some idea of what they may have contained. Although her tomb was modest in size by Shang royal standards, when excavated in 1975 it revealed over 440 bronzes, 590 jade carvings, nearly 7,000 cowrie shells, and evidence of sixteen humans who had been sacrificed to her.

By the early Warring States period, the first signs appear of what would become a complete change in tomb architecture. The tomb of Lord Yi of Zeng (died 433BCE), was still essentially a vertical shaft, even if a very large one; but for the first time, in addition to the coffin chamber, the tomb also included two side chambers furnished with equipment to ensure that he could

continue to enjoy in the afterlife many of the pleasures to which he had become accustomed on Earth.

By the Han dynasty, tombs of élites became veritable microcosms of the universe. Many now included multiple chambers, constructed with brick or stone walls. Some boasted vaulted ceilings, on which were painted the sun and the moon, the stars and planets. The walls were carved with hortatory scenes from history, suggesting the deceased's virtue by association. By the Tang dynasty, these stone carvings gave way to life-sized painted murals depicting the opulence of Tang life and revealing the skill of ancient Chinese painters.

THE AFTERLIFE

Both the oracle-bone inscriptions of the Shang dynasty and the bronze inscriptions of the Zhou dynasty attest to the influence that the dead had over the world of the living. Divinations suggest that reigning Shang kings believed that their recently deceased ancestors regularly caused them trouble—from floods of the Huan River, which flowed through Anyang, to royal toothaches. On the other hand, more distant ancestors were perceived to be beneficent, capable of interceding with the Shang high god Di to provide divine aid with the harvest, city building, and military campaigns, among other state enterprises. The Zhou people seem generally to have regarded all their ancestors as benign spirits, residing in heaven. The Confucian (hence, Chinese) obligation of filial piety that all sons owed their living fathers and mothers developed out of an earlier tradition of making offerings to ancestors (a tradition that never ceased).

Other evidence offers a different perspective on the relationship between the living and dead. A tomb at Fangmatan, in China's western province of Gansu, contained various kinds of texts, including probably the earliest extant ghost story in China. The text describes how a man named Dan was allowed to return to life after it was determined that his death by suicide had been premature. Dan reported on some of the likes and dislikes of the dead: "The dead do not want many clothes. People think that wrapping offerings in white cogon-grass makes them auspicious, but ghosts think offerings are auspicious no matter how they are wrapped. But those who offer sacrifices ought not to spit. If they spit, the ghosts flee in fright."

With the coming of Buddhism in the first centuries of the common era, and especially with the importation of its intricate theories of reincarnation and retribution, indigenous Chinese notions of "hungry ghosts" took on new meaning. Now both Buddhism and Daoism described purgatorial afterlives, complete with judges and jailers, who would punish the dead for sins committed during their lives. One of the most popular tales of the Tang dynasty tells of the quest by Mulian (in Sanskrit, Maudgalyayana), the disciple of the Buddha most adept at supernatural powers, to find his deceased mother. Descending through the gates of the Yellow Springs, Mulian passes through layer after layer of horrific purgatories. He finally finds her in the deepest of all hells, the Avici Hell, where her body is nailed down with forty-nine long metal spikes. The mother, remanded there for sins committed in past lives, is always ravenously hungry, since food cannot pass through her now needle-thin neck. Whenever Mulian offers her food at the ancestral temple, it always bursts into flames upon reaching her mouth. Eventually, Mulian petitions the Buddha, who teaches him to make offerings to hungry monks on the fifteenth day of the seventh month. When Mulian does this, thus inaugurating one of the most important Buddhist feast days in China, his mother is released to live in the highest heaven.

THE ARTS OF CHINA

The ancient Chinese created countless masterpieces of artistic expression, some genres of which—laquer, silk, and jade—constitute a unique contribution to world culture. In addition there is a rich literary, musical and intellectual legacy that is still influential today.

The ceramic tradition in China stretches from the sixth millennium BCE down to modern times. In terms of sheer output, no other medium, artistic or otherwise, can compete with the number of ceramic artifacts made in China over the millennia.

China's earliest pottery can be broadly divided into two types—red painted ware usually termed "Yangshao," and black "Longshan" ware. Yangshao pottery has been found in sites stretching from Gansu in the west to Henan in China's central plain, and from the early fifth millennium through to the late third millennium BCE. Shaped by hand, with flat bottoms, it was fired at around 1,000 degrees centigrade. Many of the pieces were decorated with painted motifs, some were simple whorls, others were more or less realistic depictions of birds and especially fish, with a few examples of human forms.

Longshan pottery, on the other hand, reflects a completely different cultural tradition. It was found mainly in eastern China, first—in the late fourth millennium BCE—in Shandong, and then later also in areas extending west into the central plain. Wheel-thrown with very thin vessel walls (sometimes described as eggshell thin), and with components such as legs and handles, the vessels were subjected to a controlled firing that resulted in their distinctive dense black, uniform surface.

The ceramic creations of almost all of ancient China's historical periods are notable in one way or another. But it is the art of the Tang dynasty that probably constitutes the most important developments in the later history of Chinese ceramics. The *sancai* or "three-color" glazed bowls, and especially figurines, also found in tombs, are surely among the most eye-catching examples of this art. Brown, blue, green, red, and yellow lead glazes were applied to different parts of the figure; the glazes were then allowed to run together naturally in places, producing an almost tie-dyed effect.

Perhaps even more stunning, however, is the Yue ware of the southern Jiangsu and Zhejiang provinces. Drawing on a long tradition of pottery-making in the area, Tang potters there began producing a glorious crackled green celadon that would eventually set the standard for porcelain across all of East Asia. From this time on, the kilns of this region would be at the very heart of a booming ceramics industry.

THE FINEST OF STONES: JADE

China's first dictionary was the late first-century CE *Discussion of Pictographs and Analysis of Characters* (*Shuo wen jie zi*), written by Xu Shen. It included the following entry for jade: "The finest of stones, it embraces the five virtues: clarity is typified by its luster, bright yet warm; rectitude by its translucence, revealing the color and patterns within; wisdom by the purity and penetrating quality of its sound when struck; courage in that it can be broken but not bent; and equity in that it has sharp edges that do not injure." As the Chinese language evolved, the word "jade" was applied to the finest and most mysterious of things, among which were the moon, women, sexual organs, and also, of course, the highest deity in the Daoist religion, the Jade Emperor.

Like ceramics, jade stone had a long history in China. Numerous sites of the Liangzhu culture have been excavated in Zhejiang province. The oldest of the sites date to the late fifth millennium BCE, and contain jades of exquisite workmanship in forms that would undergo little change for the next 4,000 years. Among them are circular disks, or *bi*, and rectangular blocks, *cong*, which are believed to have ritual significance (see illustration, opposite). Very different jades have been found in the far northern provinces of Liaoning and Inner Mongolia. There, in the third millennium BCE, the Hongshan culture produced jade plaques in the

shapes of various birds and animals. These jade-working traditions seem to have influenced artisans of the later Shang dynasty.

BRONZEWORK: THE METAL OF RITUAL

There are many myths regarding the origins of metallurgy in China, but most of them revolve around the figure of Yu the Great, who is supposed to have cast nine bronze cauldrons to represent the nine regions of China (see page 216). Archaeology has presented some evidence for this myth. The earliest bronze ritual vessels found to date come from a site called Yanshi Erlitou, just outside of Luoyang, Henan. The culture associated with this site is more or less coterminous—both in terms of chronology and territory—with the way early texts describe the Xia dynasty (see pages 216–217), the dynasty said to have been founded by Yu.

Although metallurgy surely originated in western Asia—and the notion of smelting ore into a liquid which could then be shaped into a solid metal was probably transmitted from there to China some time in the third millennium BCE—once in China, it developed in a unique way, influenced in large part by the long indigenous pottery tradition. Whereas in the West, bronzes of any complexity were cast using a technique called lost-wax, in China bronze vessels were cast in a sectional ceramic assemblage. This method, known as piece-mould casting, began with the making of a pottery model of the vessel one wished to produce. Around this were placed two or, usually, more pieces of clay. Once the impressions of the model had been registered on the clay moulds, they were taken off and fired. In order to

---

Some of the earliest jade pieces ever discovered include round disks with a hole in the middle, known as bi *disks, which are believed to represent heaven. The jade* bi *shown here is from a later period, the Han dynasty (202BCE–220CE). Also discovered were rectangular blocks with a tubular hole known as* cong, *thought to represent the Earth. The uniqueness of both the* bi *and the* cong, *and the mystery of their precise functions, make it impossible to accurately translate either term.*

dismantle them without losing any part of the model impression, the mould usually had to be symmetrical—this obviously had a great influence on the shapes in which Chinese bronzes could be produced.

Next, the clay of the model had to be scraped away to whatever thickness was desired for the final bronze vessel. The model then became the core of the mould assembly, into which it was replaced; it was held in place by small pieces of scrap bronze of the same thickness as the desired vessel. Finally, molten bronze would be poured into this assemblage. Once it had cooled, the mould and any exposed pieces of the core would be removed. Although this method is far more complex than the lost-wax method of casting, it had the considerable advantage of affording access to the inside of the mould. While any desired intaglio designs could be executed on the model with this method, the bronze caster could also incise directly into the mould, creating relief design on the surface of the bronze. For this reason, it is the ornamentation on Chinese bronzes (the mature expression of which is seen on vessels from the Shang dynasty), rather than their shapes, that is recognized as being so unique in the world.

SCULPTURE

Until relatively recently, it was generally thought that prior to the coming of Buddhism to China in roughly the first century CE, China had no indigenous tradition of sculpture. This perception was dramatically changed by the unearthing of the 7,000 life-size terracotta soldiers, each individually differentiated, in the pit near the tomb of the First Emperor (see illustration, page 223).

The Da Yan Ta or Great Goose Pagoda is the oldest extant multi-tiered brick structure in China. Located in the Temple of Mercy in the Tang capital of Chang'an, it was erected in 652CE to commemorate the return of Xuanzang, the temple's abbot, from his lengthy pilgrimage to India. Within a half century the original structure, comprising five floors, was replaced by a version with six. A seventh was added in the mid-8th century, bringing the pagoda to a height of 196ft (60m).

The years since that great discovery have brought much more evidence of a native tradition of sculpting the human form—from the giant bronze figures found at Sanxingdui (see page 209), to the small jade figurines in the Shang tomb of Fu Hao, to the thousands of statuettes, both male and female, found near the tomb of Emperor Jing of the Han (reigned 157–141BCE). This tradition shows how Chinese artisans transformed Indian Buddhist sculpture when it was introduced into China toward the end of the Han dynasty.

Chinese Buddhist (and Daoist) sculpture is generally characterized by a head-on perspective, with considerable emphasis on the head and little or no suggestion of body movement. Some of the earliest Buddhist sculpture preserved today was created during the Northern Wei dynasty (383–534), whose rulers sponsored the building of massive figures of the Buddha and *bodhisattva*s ("enlightenment beings") in caves, first at Yungang near their first capital at Pingcheng (see pages 220–221), and then, after moving the capital to the more central Luoyang (in Henan), at Longmen.

When China was reunited under the Sui dynasty (581–618), Emperor Wen (reigned 581–605) was also a great patron of Buddhism. It is said that during his reign one and a half million old images of the Buddha were repaired, and 100,000 new ones made. The sculptures of the period are distinctive. They feature the earliest extant free-standing statues, more or less life size. They are considerably less mannered than their predecessors, with a flowing line to the body and a hint of irony in the facial features—a trend that continued into the Tang dynasty.

ARCHITECTURE

Just as, prior to the introduction of Buddhism to China, the human form was not prominently displayed in statuary, so too was there concealment in both residential life and architecture. From the earliest evidence we have through to the end of the ancient period (and well into the modern period, for that matter), Chinese buildings were set, for privacy and protection, behind high walls.

Indeed, urban life in general was hidden from view and conducted within a series of nested walls. Cities were surrounded by walls (the English words "city" and "wall" are often both translated by just one word in Chinese, *cheng*). Within the city, districts might also be divided by walls, within which individual residences were demarcated by yet another wall. And within the exterior walls of the largest residences, and especially of government palaces, there were further recesses, designed to exclude both commoners and enemies: public life was conducted in a forecourt between the exterior gate and a central pavilion, while private life took place around a back court that was situated behind the pavilion (or pavilions). The remains of what Chinese archaeologists believe may have been the royal palace of the Xia dynasty have been excavated at Yanshi Erlitou, just outside Luoyang, Henan; they show these features already in the mid-second millennium BCE. The Forbidden City in Beijing can be seen as the full flowering of this style.

This lacquerware jar dates from the time of the Western Han dynasty (202BCE–9CE). The traditional art of lacquerware is unique to China and has continued, uninterrupted, for thousands of years.

The structure of Chinese buildings in general has tended to be quite conservative. It featured a rectangular foundation of rammed earth which raised the floor of the building above ground level. Into this foundation—and set back from its perimeter—was set a series of wooden pillars to support the roof, also constructed of wooden eaves and holding a superstructure which from early times was covered with ceramic tiles. The nature of the roof required that buildings be wider than they were deep, and that the roof be relatively low. In the mature architecture of the Tang dynasty (618–907), the height of the roof was set at one-sixth of the depth of the building. It was the one feature of the building that might be seen from outside the external wall of the compound, and was therefore often brightly colored and decorated with auspicious animals and symbols.

The one notable exception to this architecture of concealment was the Buddhist pagoda, doubtless the most conspicuous humanmade feature of China's late antiquity. Developing from the *stupa* mounds which were used in India as repositories for relics, the pagoda quickly took on a distinctive look in China. Often built of brick rather than wood, the Chinese pagoda came to be built up in multiple levels. The 196-foot (60m) high Great Goose Pagoda, erected in Xi'an in 652CE (see illustration, page 246), is perhaps the most famous but by no means the tallest of the thousands of pagodas dotting Tang China's countryside.

LACQUERWARE

Lacquerware is almost unique to China (and to the rest of East and Southeast Asia, whence it spread from China), and is thus the artistic medium perhaps least well appreciated in the West. Its name refers to the lac tree (*Rhus vernicifera*), and especially to its sap, and should be distinguished from shellac, which derives from the gummy deposit the *Tachardia lacca* insect leaves on trees. When the sap of the lac tree is exposed to oxygen, it polymerizes—in other words, it forms molecules of much higher weight, and therefore behaves like

Designs on silk (see page 250) came in many different forms, from flowing clouds to continuous geometric shapes to meandering floral motifs, as in this fine Tang-dynasty example (9th to 10th century CE).

a plastic. Impervious to water, and also resistant to heat and acids, it was prized as a protective covering for a range of materials, especially wood and leather, and was used in many different ways—not only, for example, as a coating for all manner of food and wine utensils but also for items such as armor and coffins.

Numerous coats of lacquer were applied usually to a wooden base, although sometimes hemp was used as well, each coat being allowed to dry thoroughly before the next was added. The classical ritual texts state that in the Zhou dynasty when a king first acceded to power, his coffin would be made of the finest wood. Then every year thereafter, a coating of lacquer would be added to it; in the case of a king such as King Ping (reigned 770–720BCE), the first king of the Eastern Zhou period who reigned for fifty years, his coffin must have been very well protected indeed. Coffins from later élite tombs, such as that of Lord Yi of Zeng (died 433BCE),

do feature lacquer coatings that have preserved them almost perfectly, despite the waterlogged environment.

Lacquer itself is clear, but from an early period, Chinese artisans added pigments to it so that it could also be used for decorative purposes. Red and black were the two most common pigments, with a convention for eating and drinking utensils to be black on the outside and red on the inside. However, other colors could also be used, and applied in such a way that lacquer could be said to be the medium for China's earliest paintings. For example, the coffin of Lady Dai (died ca. 165BCE) at Mawangdui features swirling clouds upon which various fantastic demons ride while engaging in battle with each other. Other decorative forms could be carved directly into the lacquer, which when hard could be cut or engraved in the same way as wood or stone.

THE SECRETS OF SILK

Although not ranked as one of China's four great inventions (the compass, gunpowder, paper, and printing), silk was perhaps its greatest contribution to world civilization. Spun from the filaments of cocoons of the domestic silkworm (*Bombyx mori* is the finest), silk is a fiber of extraordinary properties: it has phenomenal tensile strength and is so elastic that it can be stretched by up to twenty per cent of its length before it will tear; and it has the greatest affinity to dye of any natural fiber. Silk clothing keeps one cool in summer but warm in winter. It is no wonder that people throughout the ancient world sought to understand the secret of its production and, failing that, paid great sums to obtain it.

The invention of silk spinning in China is credited to Xiling Shi, wife of the Yellow Emperor, in the third millennium BCE. And indeed, there is artifactual evidence of loom-woven silk from no later than the middle of the second millennium. The cultivation of silkworms and the production of silk were probably not much different then compared with later times. Silk production is a labor intensive and delicate process, which begins with the cultivated mulberry tree and the silkworms. Unlike the wild mulberry tree, which produces many berries but few leaves, the domestic mulberry produces few berries but many leaves. This is essential because it is the leaves that are fed to the silkworms. Over 1 ton (about 1,000kg) of leaves is needed to rear just 1 ounce (28g) or so of newly hatched silkworms, which produce around 6 pounds (2.7kg) of reeled silk. The worms feed for about thirty-five days, for the last few days consuming twenty times their body-weight in leaves. When they reach their mature size of approximately 2 inches (5cm) in length, they spend another five days spinning their cocoon, and then eight to ten days inside it.

Just before the chrysalis is due to exit, the cocoon is immersed in boiling water, killing the chrysalis and dissolving the sericin that binds the filaments; the timing of this step is crucial because if the chrysalis exits the cocoon, it secretes a liquid that ruins the spun filaments. With the cocoon still in the water, the filaments are caught on a comb and reeled with a reeling machine.

By the Han dynasty, when trade along the Silk Road—a chain of oasis towns connecting the imperial capital at Chang'an to Central Asia—first thrived, silk was manufactured on a grand scale. In 110BCE, the office in charge of regulating silk prices had five million rolls of silk in storage. The Han government used silk as a commodity to buy peace among the peoples along its northwestern frontier. In 91CE alone, the silk given to just the southern Xiongnu was valued at 100,900,000 pieces of currency, more than one per cent of the state's gross national product. In addition, silk was a highly desired commodity as far west as the Roman Empire.

PAINTING AND CALLIGRAPHY

If one takes account of the designs and inscriptions on all the ceramics, bronzes, lacquers, and stone carvings in China, then the history of the related arts of painting and calligraphy may be seen as being very old. Even if the definition is restricted to brushwork on silk (and, later, paper), the famous Chu Silk Manuscript from the Warring States period (480–222BCE) would have to count as an early example of both painting and calligraphy. Also found in the same tomb as this manuscript was the earliest known silk funeral banner, a precursor to the more famous example from Mawangdui (see page 242). These attest to what must have been a vigorous tradition of painting. Unfortunately, no actual paintings survive from the period, and no individual artist or calligrapher was mentioned in literary sources.

It is only with the Six Dynasties period (222–589) that we can put names to painting and calligraphy. Wang Xizhi (307–365), known to posterity as the "Sacred Calligrapher," has left not only examples of his penmanship, but also a treatise in which he describes his philosophy of writing—each individual character must reveal the psychology of the scribe. Psychological expression was also paramount to Wang's younger contemporary, Gu Kaizhi (ca. 344–406). Gu rebelled against the tendency of the time to focus on costume and symbolic icons, insisting that the face should be the center of attention. He emphasized the "bone structure" of the painting ("bone" referring to the line of the brush, seeking by way of it to arrive at the inner truth of the subject). He argued that in painting historical pictures, the purpose was not to present a realist scene but rather to display feelings and values.

Landscape painting, the genre most strongly associated with Chinese art, did not really come into its own until the height of the Tang dynasty. Wang Wei (699–759) was an accomplished landscape artist, the first embodiment of the scholar-painter. Even more influential was Wu Daozi (flourished 740–760). Using only black ink, he held that the quickness of the brushwork revealed the clarity of the image in the mind of the artist. On one occasion, it took him only a day to paint a handscroll showing thousands of miles of scenery.

MUSIC AND POETRY

Shortly after the turn of the first millennium BCE, a new type of bronze bell was imported from southern China into the north-China heartland of the Zhou dynasty. This bell, arranged in sets of different sizes (and, thus, timbres) gave rise to the development of a more melodic style of music. Its introduction seems to have had a profound effect on many aspects of Zhou life.

The most direct effect was doubtless on poetry, which was then sung, and sometimes danced, to the accompaniment of music. China's earliest poetry, a collection of 305 poems in the *Classic of Poetry*, includes temple liturgies, court hymns singing of heroes past and present, and "airs" that are variously understood as simple love songs or as political allegories. This poetry, sung to a staccato four-beat line, has had a great influence on all forms of Chinese written expression, both in terms of the symbolism that was derived from it and of the phrasing and formulation of the prose.

Confucius (551–479BCE) is believed to have edited the *Classic of Poetry* and thus to have fixed its form for all time. Ironically, around this period new musical instruments begin to appear—including, prominently, wind and string instruments. These gave rise to a type of chamber music that was probably more lilting and languorous, at least as seen from the poetry that was sung to it. The meter of this new verse became longer, with a breathing caesura built into every line. The length of the line allowed for more description; what we would term adjectives and adverbs became prominent. Although Confucians railed against this "modern" music, and although formal court music continued to make use of the traditional percussion instruments and the shorter meter, the most renowned poets of the next several centuries exploited the free rhythms of the new music.

The collapse of the Han dynasty in the decades before and after the turn of the third century CE saw the rise of a new style of regulated verse that would set the standard for all Chinese poetry thereafter. From the beginning of this period until the high Tang was the age of the great individual lyric poets, from Cao Pi (187–226), who would reign (220–226) as Emperor Wen of the newly established Wei dynasty (220–264); to Ruan Ji (210–263) and Ji Kang (223–262), two of the "Seven Sages of the Bamboo Grove" (see page 230); to Tao Qian (or Tao Yuanming, 365–427) and Xie Lingyun (385–433), who sang of the natural beauty they found in southern China; to the great Li Bai (701–762) and Du Fu (712–770) in the Tang dynasty. It was Du Fu who perhaps penned the epitaph for ancient China. Upon his return to the Tang capital Chang'an after it had been devastated in the course of the An Lushan rebellion from 755 to 763 (see page 231), he wrote a poem entitled *Spring Gaze*, the first line of which reads: "The kingdom is destroyed; the mountains and rivers are here."

CHAPTER THREE

TIBET

"This center of heaven/This core of earth/This heart of the World/

Fenced round by snowy mountains/The headland of all rivers/

Where peaks are high and the land is pure/A country so good/

Where men are born as sages and heroes/And act according to good laws."

This poetic description of Tibet, written in the ninth century CE, gives rapturous

expression to the defining features of Tibetan civilization: the "good laws" of

Buddhism and the high peaks of the Himalayas. Protected by the world's tallest

mountains and drawing only what they needed from the neighboring civilizations

of India and China, the Tibetans developed a unique society, with distinctive

philosophical ideas and forms of art, which has long inspired fascination and respect.

THE SOUL OF TIBET

In order to gain an insight into Tibet, it is essential to understand Buddhism. The fundamental simplicity of the Buddha's teachings may explain their appeal to the Tibetans. With its emphasis on the pursuit of enlightenment, Buddhism has infused all aspects of life in Tibet—from art to government—since its introduction there more than 1,300 years ago.

Although Tibet is a predominantly Buddhist country, the religion was only established there in the seventh century CE—more than one thousand years after the time of the Buddha. Born Siddhartha Gautama in the sixth century BCE, the Buddha was a north Indian prince who renounced the privileges of royal life to seek the truth as a wandering ascetic. The places of his birth (Lumbini), enlightenment (Bodh Gaya), first sermon (Sarnath), and final passing (Kusinagara) became important centers of pilgrimage and were later among the sites visited by Tibetans in search of the Buddha's teachings, known as the *dharma* (see map, page 259).

The fundamental principles of the Buddha's *dharma* are known as the "Four Noble Truths" and their startling simplicity and profundity may account for the appeal of the Buddhist approach to life to Tibetans and others. The Noble Truths are: all beings inevitably endure suffering (*duhkha*); the cause (*samudaya*) of suffering is desire; the cause of desire can be contained (*nirodha*); and to contain the cause of desire one must follow the Buddha's path (*marga*).

The entire philosophical, religious, social, and artistic edifice of the Buddhist civilization of Tibet is built on these four principles. They explain why Buddhism is not simply a school of philosophy, but a practical undertaking that aims to revolutionize human life by putting seekers on the path to enlightenment (*nirvana*, literally "without desire"). Enlightenment is a unique mental state characterized by complete nonattachment to the material world. As Buddhists would say, *nirvana* is neither fullness nor emptiness, being nor nonbeing, substance nor nonsubstance.

Attaining this state of indescribable freedom requires application—the seeker must adopt a lifestyle and environment that are conducive to purity of word, thought, and deed. These requirements led directly to the institution of monasticism, a key feature of Buddhism in Tibet and elsewhere.

Both during and after the Buddha's lifetime, a number of monks attained enlightenment. They were

*This bronze figure shows a fierce Bon deity trampling on two buddhas (rather than the demons often shown under the feet of many Buddhist deities). He holds a figure of Garuda—the eagle-like creature known for his destruction of poisonous snakes—and a thunderbolt (*vajra*), an emblem usually held by Vajra Pani, a protective bodhisattva.*

Avalokiteshvara, the lord of compassion, is represented in this 13th-century CE seated bronze figure. His generosity is shown by his open hand, which symbolizes the granting of wishes. The figure has turquoise inlays, a common feature of Tibetan metalwork.

known as the *arhat*s, or "worthy ones." Little moved by the suffering of others, the *arhat*s had no inclination to teach the *dharma* beyond affirming by example that the Buddha's path provided the way to *nirvana*. For this reason some Buddhist thinkers regarded the *arhat*s as incomplete, in that they lacked the profound compassion that inspired the Buddha to teach the *dharma* for the good of all humankind. For example, the sixth-century sage Asanga gave a famous critique of the Theravada school of Buddhism prevalent in Sri Lanka, Burma, and Thailand (in which *arhat*s are the ideal figures), stating that it focused too narrowly on individual liberation from the cycle of birth, death, and rebirth. This is a key difference between Theravada and the schools of Buddhism found in north India, east Asia, and Tibet, which are known collectively as Mahayana ("Greater vehicle"). While both affirm that liberation, or enlightenment, is the final destination of the human soul, Mahayana emphasizes that an individual's pursuit of liberation must be tempered by a deep sympathy for all other living beings.

This compassion is embodied in the divine figures known as *bodhisattvas*, which means literally "those whose essence is supreme knowledge." In the Mahayana view, the *bodhisattvas* supersede the *arhat*s because they stand on the verge of enlightenment, but delay their final attainment of *nirvana* out of compassion for suffering beings, in order that they may assist others to achieve liberation. Tibetans have always followed the Mahayana traditions and consequently *bodhisattvas* are widely venerated throughout the country. The *bodhisattva* Avalokiteshvara, the supreme lord of compassion, became the patron deity of Tibet—incarnated in the person of the Tibetan priest-king known as the Dalai Lama.

According to the Mahayana view, all individuals are potentially *bodhisattvas*, but this sublime state can be achieved only by the diligent cultivation of virtue over hundreds of lifetimes. In contrast, Vajrayana ("Vehicle of the diamantine thunderbolt") asserts that there is a "rapid path" to enlightenment. The "great adepts" (*mahasiddhas*) followed this path and attained enlightenment immediately by using special techniques and rituals. These powerful practices—developed by the adepts or revealed to them by compassionate deities—are collectively known as Tantra (see page 288).

◆ THE TSANGPO RIVER ◆

The Tsangpo is one of Asia's mightiest rivers—it is more than 1,800 miles (2,900km) long from its source in western Tibet to its confluence with the Ganga River on the great alluvial plains of Bangladesh. The Tsangpo is also known as the Brahmaputra, literally the "Son of Brahma," because its source is traced by some to Lake Manasarovar, a body of water traditionally thought to have been created by the god Brahma for the pilgrims visiting Mount Kailas (see pages 270–271).

Known near its source as the Tachok Tsangpo and the Yarlung Tsangpo further downstream, the river flows eastward across the entire width of central Tibet, drawing water from innumerable mountain streams and tributaries. The Tsangpo is navigable for more than 370 miles (600km) from Lhartse, near Dingri. River journeys and crossings are made in flat-bottomed riverboats.

In ancient times the Tsangpo was an important highway for trade and pilgrimage within Tibet. However, in eastern Tibet, near the border with Assam, the river surges through the world's deepest gorges, plunging more than 9,800 feet (3,000m) in less than 28 miles (45km). This has meant that, although the Tsangpo helps account for the cultural unity of Tibet itself, it has never served as a channel of communication with India.

When the first Buddhist missionaries and masters of Tantra ventured into Tibet, they faced a royal cult strikingly similar to that of ancient India. Violent animal sacrifices, controlled by a priestly élite, were deemed necessary to maintain order in the heavens and to win favor from the gods. Just as the Buddha had effectively challenged the sacrificial culture of India, so the early Buddhists in Tibet were able to displace established priests and rituals, transforming powerful local deities into protectors of the *dharma* (see pages 294–295).

What survived of Tibet's pre-Buddhist cults was reorganized into Bon, a religion which persists to this day. Although distinct from Buddhism—and opposed to many of its tenets—Bon has a monastic organization, textual tradition, and pantheon of deities which are heavily influenced by the Tibetan Buddhist examples.

THE STORY OF TIBET

The history of Tibet is closely linked to the development of Buddhism in the country. The religion was introduced at the time of the unification of Tibet in the seventh century CE. Nearly a thousand years later, political and religious control of the country was consolidated in the person of the Dalai Lama.

Tibet became a unified kingdom in the seventh century CE under King Songtsen Gampo, a dynamic ruler whose forebears came from the Yarlung Valley. Songtsen Gampo was not a practicing Buddhist, but his queens, from Nepal and China, built the first Buddhist temple in Lhasa and furnished it with images. However, Buddhism did not become firmly rooted until the following century, when King Trisong Detsen invited the Indian teacher Shantarakshita to establish Tibet's first Buddhist monastery, which he accomplished with the aid of the charismatic Padmasambhava (see page 265).

The Yarlung Empire disintegrated in the ninth century. Interest in Buddhism remained limited until the tenth century, when Tibetans went to India to study and translate sacred texts. Indian masters also came to Tibet, the most celebrated being Atisha (see pages 290–291), whose arrival in 1042CE traditionally marks the "Second Propagation" of Buddhism in the country. Atisha's followers founded the Kadam-pa religious order, which stressed the importance of applying the ideals of a *bodhisattva* in the practitioner's daily life.

Other orders born at this time included the Sakya-pa, which won powerful allies in the Mongol Empire, notably the emperor Kublai Khan (1215–1294CE). The waning of Mongol power in the mid-fourteenth century weakened the Sakya-pa. A new dynasty, the Pamotrupa, sought to revive the glory of the Yarlung kings, while the discovery of texts "hidden" by Padmasambhava gave fresh impetus to the Nyingma-pa order he had founded.

The most influential scholar and reformer of the time was Tsong Khapa (1357–1419CE). His advocation of monastic discipline motivated his disciples to found the Gelug-pa ("Yellow Hat") religious order. The Gelug-pa at first avoided direct involvement in secular matters, but their piety attracted Mongol attention. In 1578 the Mongol leader Altan Khan gave a prominent Gelug-pa *lama* ("teacher") the title Dalai Lama. Half a century later, with Mongolian assistance, the Dalai Lama became Tibet's sacred and secular leader. This theocratic system of government survived until 1959, when the communist Chinese drove the fourteenth Dalai Lama into exile.

This tall stone slab, known as the Samye Doring, is located beside the main temple at Samye, the oldest Buddhist monastery in Tibet (see page 268). Dating to the 8th century CE, the slab is engraved with a long inscription proclaiming Buddhism as the state religion.

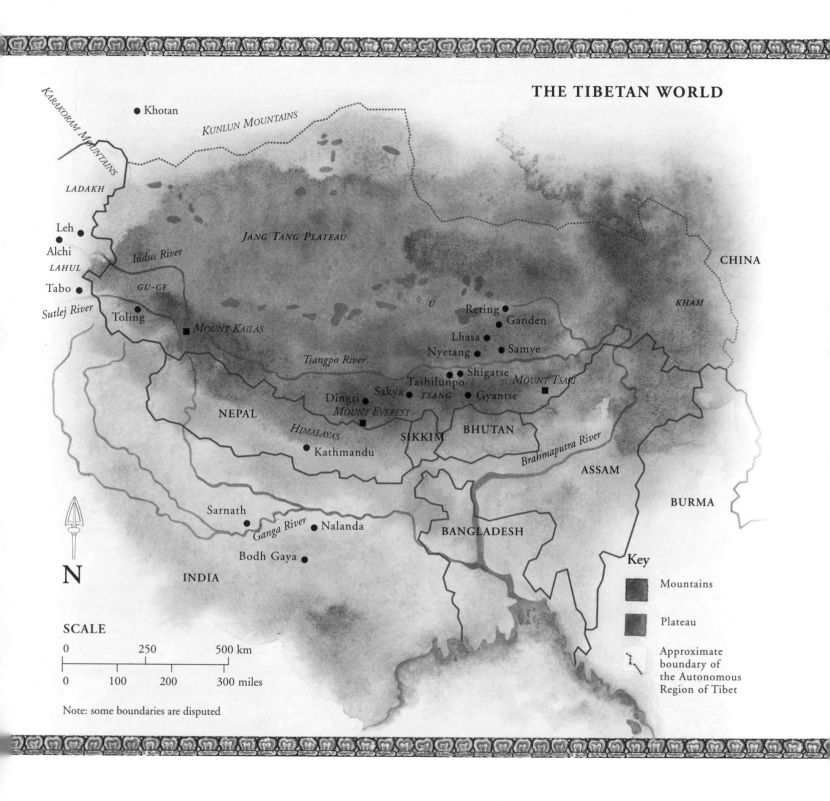

THE TIBETAN WORLD

Khotan

KUNLUN MOUNTAINS

KARAKORAM MOUNTAINS

LADAKH

Leh

Alchi

LAHUL

Tabo

Indus River

GU-GE

Sutlej River

Toling

MOUNT KAILAS

JANG TANG PLATEAU

CHINA

KHAM

Ū

Reting • Ganden

Lhasa • Samye

Nyetang

Tsangpo River

Shigatse

Tashilunpo MOUNT TSARI

Dingri   Sakya • TSANG • Gyantse

MOUNT EVEREST

NEPAL

HIMALAYAS

Kathmandu

SIKKIM

BHUTAN

Brahmaputra River

ASSAM

BURMA

Sarnath

Ganga River • Nalanda

BANGLADESH

Bodh Gaya

N

INDIA

Key

Mountains

Plateau

Approximate
boundary of
the Autonomous
Region of Tibet

SCALE

| 0 | 250 | 500 km |

| 0 | 100 | 200 | 300 miles |

Note: some boundaries are disputed

LHASA: THE HOLY CITY

By the ninth century CE, Lhasa had been designated as the capital of Tibet. Although it lost this status for some centuries following the collapse of the Yarlung Empire and the ensuing fragmentation of political government, the city grew steadily in influence as the religious center of Tibet.

Lhasa is dominated by the Potala, the residence of the Dalai Lamas until 1959 when the communist Chinese forced Tenzin Gyatso, the fourteenth Dalai Lama, into exile. This great building was begun in 1645 shortly after Losang Gyatso, the fifth Dalai Lama—known as the "Great Fifth" on account of his wisdom, tolerance, and effectiveness—came to power. The Potala is named after Mount Potalaka, the celestial abode of Avalokiteshvara, the *bodhisattva* of compassion and patron deity of Tibet. Songtsen Gampo, the king who built the first structure on the site in the seventh century CE, is regarded as an emanation of Avalokiteshvara, as is the "Great Fifth," under whom most of the present palace was constructed in the seventeenth century. Although an architectural project of unprecedented size and ambition, the Potala is built in the typical Tibetan style, with gently sloping walls and flat roofs resting on wooden beams. The palace's curved gables reflect the influence of contemporary Chinese architecture.

The Potala's outer section is known as the "White Palace" and was the seat of government up to 1959. The lower walls of the White Palace are plain and were once used to display giant *thangka* paintings (see page 263) of the buddhas during important festivals. Inside the White Palace are the winter apartments of the Dalai Lamas and a large hall known as the Tsomchen Shar. It was here that the Dalai Lamas were enthroned and where envoys from China were received.

The upper section of the building, known as the "Red Palace," contains a series of temples, images, and shrines, including relics of the Dalai Lamas. This portion of the palace dates to the end of the seventeenth century and is attributed to Desi Sangye Gyatso, the regent who concealed the death of the fifth Dalai Lama so that the building could be completed. The Potala is a physical expression and potent emblem of the way in which Tibet was unified and ruled by the Dalai Lamas and the Gelug-pa order for three centuries.

Not far from the Potala is the Jo Khang, the "cathedral of Lhasa" and the most sacred temple in Tibet (see illustration, pages 264–265). It draws people from many parts of the country, especially at New Year when the passages of the building are crowded with pilgrims. Founded by Bhrikuti, Songsten Gampo's Nepalese queen, the Jo Khang has undergone frequent modification, repair, and restoration since it was first completed in 647CE.

The core of the building, a rectangular court surrounded by cells, follows the plan of Buddhist temples in India. On the eastern side of the court is a large chamber known as the Jowo Shakyamuni Lhakhang, which contains the famous sculpture of the *buddha* known as Jowo Rinpoche. This image has a long history—it is reputed to have been made in India by Vishvakarman, the divine craftsman of the gods (see box, page 164), and presented to China by an early Indian monarch. The details of this story suggest a distant memory of Ashoka, a great Indian king of the third century BCE who did much to further the spread of Buddhism (see pages 141–142). In any event, the statue was brought to Tibet by Weng Cheng, Songtsen Gampo's Chinese queen, and installed in the Jo Khang after the king's death in 650CE. It has remained there ever since and has been the subject of constant devotion and embellishment. The headdress was first added by the scholar Tsong Khapa (see page 258) and the precious outer robe was given by one of the Ming emperors.

Built in the 17th century CE, the Potala Palace towers over the capital city of Lhasa. The Potala served as a monastery and a fortress, as well as being the residence of the Dalai Lamas and the seat of the Tibetan government until 1959.

THE ART OF TIBET

Until recent times, Tibetans viewed every aspect of life from a Buddhist standpoint—education, administration, landholding, and production were controlled or influenced by powerful lamas or monasteries. And the magnificent creations of Tibetan art were almost always religious in purpose.

Tibet was a world in which all boundaries between the temporal and spiritual spheres were erased, a world in which the Dalai Lama was at once the head of state and the supreme authority in spiritual matters. As a consequence, virtually all Tibetan art served a religious and highly symbolic function.

Artists and craftspeople typically worked for monasteries and temples, their finest products finding a treasured place in shrines, chapels, and monastic libraries. Sculptures were carved and cast for worship; precious metals were hammered into lamps and incense burners for temple altars; masks were made for religious processions and ceremonies; and fine fabrics and embroideries—usually imported from India and China—were used to clothe images or to line the scroll paintings that play a key role in Tibetan devotional life. This religious artistic activity continues today, though on a reduced scale in Tibet itself since the depredations of the early period of communist Chinese occupation.

Religious images play a very important role in Buddhism. Sculptures are not simply reminders of cosmic realities or mementos of the Buddha and the great teachers of the past. Rather, each sculpture is a living presence, an actual embodiment of what it represents. In Tibet and elsewhere, objects may be placed inside images in the course of their consecration in order to transform them from mundane raw materials—copper alloy in the case of most Tibetan sculpture—into living realities. Deposits in images vary enormously, but generally they include small scrolls with written or printed prayers and mystic diagrams relating to the deity or person depicted in the sculpture. One crucial element is a shaft or sliver of wood (*sogshing*), a

Dating from the mid-15th century, this thangka *painting shows the Buddha seated on an elaborate throne and flanked by his chief disciples, Sariputra and Maudgalyana. In the vignettes surrounding the main image are figures representing* arhats *(see page 255), auspicious deities, and donors.*

"tree of life" that serves as the living "axis" of the sculpture. Images of historic individuals will also contain a relic relating directly to the deceased—often a small piece of ash collected after his or her cremation.

Once a sculpture has thus been "brought to life," it is treated like a living being. Images, as a result, are usually clothed, placed on a seat, and presented with food, water, and other gifts. Offering-cakes are made of butter and *tsampa* (roasted barley flour), but cakes of painted clay are also offered. A crucial part of worship is the lighting of butter lamps—there may be dozens of such lamps before the most important and popular sacred images.

Like sculptures, Tibetan paintings on cloth scrolls (*thangka*s) are not simply decorative. They depict deities, sacred beings, or saints and are brought to life by dedicatory prayers written on the reverse; sometimes the handprints of the *lama* who performed the dedication were added. *Thangka* paintings are hung inside chapels in accordance with the liturgical and ritual practices of the particular monastery or temple. The images they bear can serve a didactic purpose and the ordinary devotee may well worship them. Some *thangka*s may be viewed only by initiates as part of their mystical training.

◆ THE SPIRIT IN THE SMOKE ◆

The use of incense is an important part of Tibetan ritual life and portable incense burners are often to be found on Buddhist altars. Made of hammered metals such as copper and silver and coming in a wide variety of shapes—from fierce heads with open mouths (right) to rectangular boxes with pierced lids—incense burners are often decorated with the eight auspicious emblems (see page 289). One notable example bears, in addition to the eight auspicious emblems, a "Wheel of *Dharma*" flanked by two deer, symbols of the Buddha's first sermon in the deer park at Sarnath.

THE SACRED COSMOS

The Tibetan people perceive their country as a sacred cosmos, a holy landscape guarded by mighty gods and filled with centers of ritual and mystical power. Within this landscape, every natural feature, every building, and every deed is charged with religious significance.

By marking the landscape with cairns, inscriptions, rock-paintings, banners, and votive offerings, Tibetans perpetually reinvent their world, reaffirming the lives of the ancient saints and sages whose heroic acts infused the universe with potent spiritual meaning. For example, mountains are often the seats of awe-inspiring deities, their caves places for meditation, and their winding trails emblematic of the path to enlightenment.

When Queen Bhrikuti came from Nepal in the seventh century CE to join the court of King Songtsen Gampo, she perceived the form of a great demoness in the landscape of Tibet. To subdue her, Bhrikuti decided that Buddhist temples should be built on the most prominent parts of the demoness's body. The heart—her most vulnerable point—was identified as a small lake in Lhasa. The lake was filled and the Jo Khang, Tibet's holiest temple, was erected on the site (see page 260). Other "extremity-subduing" temples were built on what were believed to be the hips and shoulders of the demoness. The construction of these buildings put an indelible Buddhist stamp on the wider landscape of Tibet, effectively overpowering earlier ideas and beliefs. It was an ancient tactic, used even by the Buddha as a way of spreading his philosophical and social message.

The need to impose a new order on sacred space was faced again in the following century, when the

monk-philosopher Shantarakshita wanted to establish Tibet's first Buddhist monastery at Samye near the Tsangpo River. Local demons are said to have interfered with every aspect of the construction. Unable to continue, Shantarakshita advised King Trisong Detsen to summon the great saint Padmasambhava from India. Padmasambhava came and drew a mystic diagram of the five celestial *buddha*s (see page 286) on the ground. After he had meditated on the diagram for seven days, the demons were powerless to stop the monastery from being constructed.

The severity—and, in Tibetan belief, potential malevolence—of much of the Tibetan environment is nowhere more extreme than on the great northern plateau, the Jang Tang. With an average elevation of 14,800 feet (4,500m), it is a vast high-altitude wilderness. Dotted with brackish lakes, the Jang Tang is known for its severe weather system, which includes biting winds—so ferocious, in fact, that travelers who pass through the region have been known to arrive at their destinations suffering from sunburn on one side of their faces and frostbite on the other.

Other parts of the land are less hostile. In spite of their altitude, Tibet's southern valleys are not inhospitable, and the fertile areas alongside the rivers produce barley, oats, beans, and other basic staples. However, on the mountain slopes above, only seasonal grazing is possible, while the high peaks are completely barren and usually covered in snow year-round.

Tibet, "the Roof of the World," is the highest country on Earth. The Jang Tang plateau, below, is one of its most forbidding and desolate regions, home only to a few wandering herdsmen.

UNFOLDING COSMIC SPACE

The Buddhist cosmos—the outer visible world, the forces that operate within it, and the deities, both great and small, that preside over it—can be mapped in a mandala. *Every element, force, and divinity in the universe corresponds to an aspect of the human personality and physiology, and an awareness of these links between the inner and outer worlds can bring special insight to an adept, or* siddha.

Buddhism's final goal is not simply knowledge and power, but a living and unbreakable awareness of the absolute unity of all existence. Those who have realized this truth enjoy enlightenment—a state of unshakable equanimity, supreme wisdom, and infinite compassion. *Mandala*s are aids in the pursuit of this enlightened state.

In Tibetan Buddhism, the development of an individual's potential is often visualized as the unfolding of a *mandala* in the form of a lotus. Each petal of the lotus is connected with certain deities, colors, and mystic sounds, or *mantra*s. The heart of the lotus represents the Absolute, the supreme being. Complicated esoteric rituals accompany the use of such *mandala*s and devotees undergo long periods of spiritual preparation so that the opening of a *mandala* is accompanied by a parallel "awakening" of the personality and soul. Inadequate preparation can make the whole ritual meaningless or, more catastrophically, unleash cosmic powers that would tear the individual apart.

Tibetan *mandala*s come in many shapes and sizes, from small pieces of paper with printed designs, to elaborate paintings, three-dimensional models, and even entire temples, such as the Kumbum at Gyantse (see opposite). Although paper *mandala*s are made in great numbers, their ephemeral nature has meant that few old specimens are preserved. Murals and painted scrolls are more common. Scrolls, or *thangka*s (see page 263), are often edged with embroidered fabrics and have cloth covers to protect the painted surface.

Certain elements are common to most painted *mandala*s, which generally take the form of a circle within a square. A key feature is the deity (or, in some cases, deities) in the center of the image, whose divine

In the heart of this lotus mandala *is a representation of Chakra Samvara, the esoteric manifestation of the Buddha. He is surrounded by female deities. The exterior of the lotus is engraved with the eight auspicious emblems (see page 289).*

presence the *mandala* is intended to invoke. The central figures are surrounded by emanations and related deities, typically placed on lotus petals. Encompassing these divine beings is a bold square enclosure, which is understood as a wall, with T-shaped gates halfway along each side. Outside the "gates" of the *mandala* there is a series of concentric circles decorated with lotus petals and other patterns—common motifs include waves and

mountains. Beyond this lie rows of small figures, which typically represent protector-deities and saints.

An astonishing variety of *mandala*s resulted from the deft manipulation and elaboration of these basic ingredients. This is because the masters of the Tibetan tradition have had different visions of the path to enlightenment and have consequently developed their own repertoire of *mandala*s and meditation techniques.

CITY OF SHRINES: GYANTSE

Once the third-largest town in Tibet after Lhasa and Shigatse, Gyantse was an important center for trade, mostly in wool, on the ancient road that led from Tibet to Sikkim, Bhutan, Nepal, and eastern India.

A view of Gyantse with the celebrated Kumbum temple in the foreground. In the distance is the hilltop fortress of Gyantse, which was heavily damaged in 1904 by a British military expedition led by Francis Younghusband.

The town grew up alongside a line of curving hills edged with walls and towers, originally part of a fortress attributed to the son of the anti-Buddhist king Langdarma who sought to perpetuate the Yarlung dynasty from here after his father's assassination. Nestled next to the hillside is a self-contained monastic quarter that once housed monasteries belonging chiefly to the Sakya-pa and Gelug-pa traditions (see page 258).

Travelers and monks had passed this way for centuries, but Gyantse's heyday came only in the fifteenth century CE, when it was the capital of a small but prosperous Tibetan kingdom. It was this period that saw the construction of one of Tibet's most extraordinary sacred monuments, the magnificent three-dimensional *mandala* known as the Kumbum (see pages 266–267).

The Kumbum is the best-preserved and most elaborate temple of its type in Tibet. Consecrated in 1436CE, it was built during the reign of Prince Rabtan Kunzang Phags (1412–1442), the chief patron of the Gyantse complex. During this period, famous Tibetan painters and sculptors were attracted to Gyantse to participate in the various construction projects there, apparently assisted by craftspeople brought from Nepal. Inside the Kumbum there are more than seventy separate chapels, each filled with images and murals of Buddhist deities. A dark and narrow passage leads to the small shrine room at the top of the building, containing an image of Vajra Dhara, the cosmic *buddha* (see pages 284–285), which the Gelug-pa tradition regards as supreme and absolute.

The most common form of the Buddhist *mandala*— the idea of capturing the universe in a microcosmic model (see pages 266–267)—is that of a circle within a square. The Kumbum temple consists of a stepped pyramid surmounted by a circular drum and an elaborate spire that serves to represent the Buddhist cosmos. From base to summit, through its nine levels and 108 gates, everything has its proper and ordered place. Through its blend of architecture and its multitude of sacred images, the temple enables the devotee moving through the building to participate in and reaffirm the Buddhist

vision of time, space, and causation. At the Kumbum, the *mandala* attains a wonderful aesthetic elaboration by means of the central circle becoming a tiered finial with an umbrella-like top.

ARCHITECTURE OF ENLIGHTENMENT

Another example of architecture as *mandala* can be seen in the layout of Tibet's oldest monastery, Samye, which was constructed in the eighth century CE in a confidently eclectic and international style under the auspices of Shantarakshita and Padmasambhava. These Indian holy men and their patron, Trisong Detsen, the king of Tibet, sought to create an entirely new place of religious power and spiritual significance. By establishing the institution of monasticism in Tibet, they aimed at a complete reordering of Tibetan society, whereby people would redirect their lives along the Buddha's path to enlightenment and revolutionize their ways of thinking, moving, and being.

Samye's architecture represents nothing less than a fresh vision of the universe: the whole monastic settlement constitutes, in effect, a gigantic Buddhist cosmic diagram. The outer walls are circular in design and the buildings within reflect the Buddhist cosmos. In the center, a large multistoried temple—traditionally said to combine Indian, Chinese, and Tibetan styles—represents Sumeru, the towering mountain at the heart of the Buddhist universe. Flanking it, and representing the four continents, are four *chorten*s, or sanctuaries, in different colors and styles. The entrances are protected by figures of lions and statues of guardian beings, of which the most celebrated is the deity Pehar, who originated in Central Asia.

The Samye monastery complex derives its name from the Tibetan for "unimaginable." It is said that one of its creators, Padmasambhava, used his mystical powers to conjure up an image of the proposed monastery in the palm of his hand, so that its patron King Trisong Detsen could conceive of its splendor.

JOURNEYS OF THE PILGRIMS

Pilgrimage is a form of meditation in Tibet. Holy men make pilgrimages to catch a glimpse of their own souls, or to gain magical powers, while lay pilgrims accumulate merit in this life to win themselves a better rebirth in the next. One of the most powerful destinations is Mount Kailas (also known as Meru or Sumeru), scene of some of the great events in Tibetan history and legend.

Tibet's pilgrimage sites derive their significance from an ancient sense of place, a deep-rooted feeling that the mountains, lakes, and rivers are places of inherent purity and power. Nowhere is more sacred as a place of transcendence and personal renewal than Mount Kailas in the western Himalayas. From near the snow-capped peak of Kailas flow four of Asia's great rivers: the Indus, Sutlej, Tsangpo (Brahmaputra), and Karnali (the latter a tributary of the Ganga). Over the centuries, pilgrims have traced these rivers to their source and invested the region with overlapping and competing religious meanings.

Shiva, the great Hindu god, resides eternally on Kailas and for this reason, it is said, the Buddha chose Kailas as the place to appear as Chakra Samvara (see page 266), and instruct Shiva in the esoteric doctrines of Tantric Buddhism.

The Buddhists also challenged the followers of the Bon faith at Kailas, the mountain becoming a battleground between Naro Bon Chung and Milarepa, his Buddhist opponent. After many displays and counter-displays of mystic power, the two raced to the summit, Milarepa winning the contest by miraculously riding on the rays of the rising sun. Although the Bon lost control of Kailas, out of compassion they were still allowed to circumambulate the mountain in a counterclockwise direction according to their ancient traditions.

In the thirteenth century, the sage Gotsangpa established a trail for pilgrims to circle the mountain. According to legend, the goddess Tara (see page 289) appeared to him near the top of the Drolma-La pass in the form of twenty-one wolves, whose pawprints can still be seen in the rocks. On another occasion, a wild female yak appeared in front of Gotsangpa. He followed it to a cave, where it vanished into solid rock. By meditating Gotsangpa realized that the yak was actually a manifestation of a *dakini* (see page 295) called Senge Dongchan, who fed him during his reveries. Gotsangpa pressed his head into the rock, promising that anyone who bowed into the resulting cavity would escape rebirth into a lower form of life.

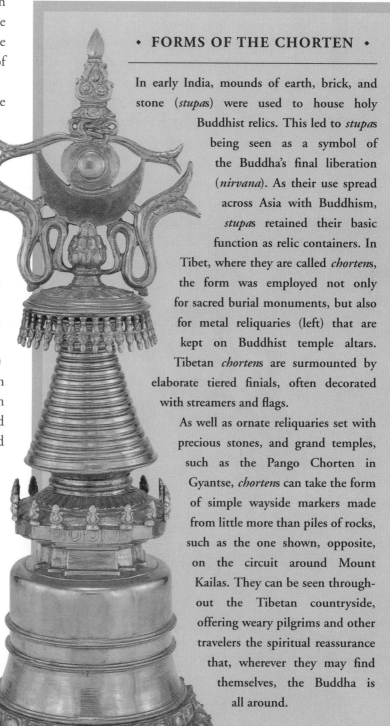

OPPOSITE *The inaccessibility of Kailas is traditionally attributed to the power of the mountain itself, which allows only the pure and spiritually prepared to glimpse its mighty white pinnacle. Like all holy places, respects are paid at Kailas by circumambulation, the circuit around the mountain being an arduous high-altitude trek that can last several days. The route is marked by* chortens *(see box, right), shrines, tablets inscribed with prayers, flagpoles, and caves associated with Milarepa and Padmasambhava.*

◆ FORMS OF THE CHORTEN ◆

In early India, mounds of earth, brick, and stone (*stupa*s) were used to house holy Buddhist relics. This led to *stupa*s being seen as a symbol of the Buddha's final liberation (*nirvana*). As their use spread across Asia with Buddhism, *stupa*s retained their basic function as relic containers. In Tibet, where they are called *chorten*s, the form was employed not only for sacred burial monuments, but also for metal reliquaries (left) that are kept on Buddhist temple altars. Tibetan *chorten*s are surmounted by elaborate tiered finials, often decorated with streamers and flags.

As well as ornate reliquaries set with precious stones, and grand temples, such as the Pango Chorten in Gyantse, *chorten*s can take the form of simple wayside markers made from little more than piles of rocks, such as the one shown, opposite, on the circuit around Mount Kailas. They can be seen throughout the Tibetan countryside, offering weary pilgrims and other travelers the spiritual reassurance that, wherever they may find themselves, the Buddha is all around.

SEEKING SOLITUDE
AND RETREAT

Following the example set by the Buddha himself, the great adepts of Tibetan Buddhism all spent long periods alone, shunning the comforts of ordinary life, in order to perfect their powers and seek liberation. The story of Milarepa, Tibet's most esteemed saint, exemplifies this solitary existence.

The Buddha had only five followers when he first began to spread his teachings, but from this humble beginning the Buddhist community grew into a large and powerful organization. An extensive code of regulations, the *Vinaya*, was soon needed to control all aspects of monastic life and from the Buddha's time to the present most monks have lived in highly organized monasteries. This pattern is especially predominant in Tibet, where monasteries are the main cultural and social institutions in the landscape.

Despite the importance of monasticism, Buddhism has never lost sight of the fact that the Buddha achieved *nirvana* as a solitary seeker and that all who strive for enlightenment must find it by, and within, themselves. Each of the great masters of Tibetan Buddhism has stayed for long periods in lonely places and in isolated caves, pursuing perfection and liberation.

Milarepa, Tibet's most beloved saint, lived an itinerant life. In his youth, he was vengeful by nature and practiced black magic. However, filled with remorse about his evil ways, Milarepa turned to Marpa, a teacher in the south of Tibet who had studied for long periods in the great Buddhist monasteries of eastern India. After undergoing an exceptionally arduous apprenticeship, Milarepa was initiated into the secrets of Buddhist meditation and in particular into the mystical practices of Naropa, Marpa's Indian master. Naropa was a "great adept," or *mahasiddha*—a title bestowed on eighty-four especially holy saints known for their extrasensory insights and superhuman powers. The *mahasiddha*s developed the teachings and texts used by the Kagyu-pa and related Tibetan schools (see page 258).

Milarepa's command of Naropa's teaching gave him astonishing physical strength and enabled him to withstand the bitterly cold Himalayan winters. He left southern Tibet and continued his spiritual quest in the solitude of the mountains. Wandering westward, he

Milarepa is usually shown with one hand raised—a gesture used to indicate that he is reciting one of his celebrated poems or hymns—as in this 18th- or 19th-century bronze figure of the saint.

came to the Namkading cave near Nyalam, where he spent such long periods in meditation that there are said to be impressions in the rock where he sat.

Like all renunciates before and since, Milarepa fled to lonely places in order to pursue the contemplative life. However, retreat from the world meant leaving the secure structure of civilized life and venturing into places that were the haunt of malevolent forces. These forces were both the evils within the human heart and the ancient deities and foes of Buddhism. Milarepa was victorious over his own evil past and vanquished the Bon deities at Mount Kailas (see page 271). Consequently, he is revered by Tibetans—together with Padmasambhava and the Buddha himself—as one of

The peaks and high mountain passes of Tibet are often ornamented with flags and banners, offerings which are believed to distribute blessings across the landscape as they flutter in the wind.

the great trio of enlightened "Conquerors," who used their inner spiritual power to transform hostile gods into protectors of the Buddhist faith.

Milarepa never established a monastery or belonged to one of the religious orders. However, statues of him are found throughout the country, particularly in isolated mountain caves, while his marvelous poems and songs are quoted everywhere.

DISEASE, DANGER, AND DEMONS

From the traditional Tibetan point of view, the world is a place pulsating with forces that directly influence all aspects of life. The heavens, too, are filled with gods, some of them demonic huntsmen who, if angered, can cause sickness and even death.

According to ancient Tibetan belief, all aspects of the natural world, such as rocks, rivers, trees, and the soil, are inhabited by spirits, which need propitiation before a tree is cut, the ground plowed, or the natural order of things otherwise disturbed by human action.

As in India, serpent-kings (*naga-raja*s) are connected with fertility, crops, and water. The association with water, and the potential malevolence of the serpents (*naga*s), is illustrated by the story of the snakes in the lake where Lhasa's Jo Khang temple now stands (see page 260): when the lake was filled in, the snakes were taken and detained in a cave on the sacred mountain of Chakpori at Lhasa. Serpent-kings are the guardians of treasure, generally understood in Buddhist contexts to be relics, the elixir of immortality, and the *chinta-mani* ("radiant thought-gem," see page 283). The great enemy of serpents is the eagle-headed Garuda, who is always depicted with a snake in his beak. He restores the *chinta-mani* to its rightful place in the lotus of Avalokiteshvara; relics to proper worship in *stupa*s; and the elixir to Amitayus, the *buddha* of Infinite Life.

With its ancient emphasis on detachment and renunciation, the high traditions of Buddhism offered few remedies for people who had to deal with a world fraught with real dangers. As a consequence, almost all Buddhist societies, including Tibet, have traditionally possessed various classes of shamans and healers.

Evil influences might be subdued by a type of ritual dagger known as a *phur-bu*, which has also found a place in Buddhist rites. When controlled by a shaman, a *phur-bu* is thought to be able to pin down evil spirits, fly through the air, destroy enemies, and control the weather. Scapegoats and scapegoat ceremonies were also once widespread in Tibet. Individuals, usually of low social rank, were called upon to take on the evils of the community and were chased away in elaborate parades, in which monks wore ferocious masks and colorful costumes. Less dramatic were small wooden "ransom sticks," used to remove or avert the afflictions caused by spirit possession. Most illness was explained as the work of evil spirits which needed to be exorcised if health was to be restored.

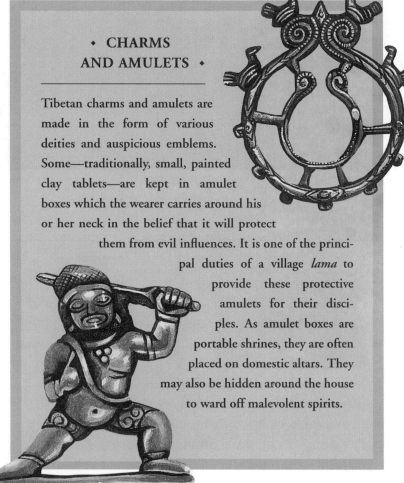

• CHARMS AND AMULETS •

Tibetan charms and amulets are made in the form of various deities and auspicious emblems. Some—traditionally, small, painted clay tablets—are kept in amulet boxes which the wearer carries around his or her neck in the belief that it will protect them from evil influences. It is one of the principal duties of a village *lama* to provide these protective amulets for their disciples. As amulet boxes are portable shrines, they are often placed on domestic altars. They may also be hidden around the house to ward off malevolent spirits.

Tibetans take a pragmatic view of life and acknowledge that just as illness, adversity, and peril cannot be eliminated from human affairs, so demonic and malevolent deities can never be finally destroyed. At best, they can be contained and redirected through prayer, worthy deeds, and the faithful observance of appropriate ritual.

One especially common way of reinforcing and maintaining sanctity, both of holy places and of the devotee, is through talismans and votive offerings. Found throughout the Buddhist world and termed *tsha-tsha* in Tibet, talismans are left in great numbers at sacred places and at pilgrimage spots. They are made of clay and stamped with sacred images, *chorten*s, and holy texts. Clay *tsha-tsha*s may contain sanctifying substances, such as the ashes of an especially holy monk.

These are much prized and worn as protective amulets.

Perhaps the most poignant indication of how the Tibetan tradition has recognized the necessary coexistence of good and evil is the *gon-khang*, a separate chamber found in many Buddhist temples. Such rooms are reserved for ancient fierce and horrible gods, who are now considered to be the custodians of the very sacred places that once belonged to them, but from which they were expelled after the arrival of Buddhism.

Small clay tablets and chorten*s, pressed from moulds, are often left at informal shrines by Tibetan pilgrims. Here, numerous talismanic votive offerings, or* tsha-tsha*, have been deposited at Ganden, a monastic site approximately 25 miles (40km) east of Lhasa.*

THE POTENCY OF SOUND

The sacred world of Tibet is filled with the chanting of Buddhist texts, the recitation of mantras, *the ringing of bells and cymbals, the blowing of trumpets, and the beating of drums. All are essential aspects of Buddhist life and ritual.*

The rich variety of Tibetan Buddhist books and musical instruments—and the care with which they are made, decorated, and consecrated—are testimony to the key role of sacred words and sounds in the Tibetan tradition. The potency of sound goes back to the story of how Sariputra, one of the Buddha's chief disciples, gained enlightenment by simply hearing the words of the Buddhist creed: "The Buddha has explained the cause of all created things and how to contain that cause as well."

For more than 3,000 years the civilizations of south Asia have placed great emphasis on the power of speech. Properly spoken and chanted words are not simple descriptions of the objective world, but holy sounds that are endowed with the very essence of the reality to which they refer. Sound has creative power, an actual capacity to influence objects and generate effects.

Such powerful, transforming words and phrases are called *mantra*s, a technical term that literally means "instruments of thought." There is an enormous variety of *mantra*s in Tibetan Buddhism. Some take the form of an apparently random assortment of sounds and words with no logical meaning. But every *mantra* is intended for a specific purpose in worship or meditation and is designed to have specific effects on the individual and his or her immediate environment.

The knowledge of *mantra*s is usually closely guarded and handed down from teacher to disciple without the details ever being committed to paper. However, some *mantra*s are used by all Tibetan Buddhists as blessings and charms and are thought to be effective in all circumstances. The most popular of these is *Om mani padme hum* ("*Om* the Jewel of the Lotus *hum*"), the six-syllable prayer of Avalokiteshvara, the great *bodhisattva* who is the patron deity of Tibet (see pages 286–287). This *mantra*—in which the first and last syllables have no specific meaning—is found everywhere in Tibet, whether printed on scrolls inside prayer wheels, carved on architectural panels, inscribed on boulders, or cut into the piles of stone that line well-trodden mountain passes (see illustration, opposite). The *mantra* is counted on beads and forever brought to mind in moments of adversity, the invocation appealing again and again to the noble beneficence and compassion of Avalokiteshvara.

THE PATH OF THE MANI

It is not difficult to find written *mantra*s in Tibet, even in places with no obvious spiritual significance. On the

---

• THE ALL-POWERFUL TEN •

The group of letters known as the "All-Powerful Ten" is a *mantra* that is widely used in Tibetan decoration and often appears in low relief on the outside of wooden book covers. This powerful *mantra* is composed of the ten Sanskrit syllables *om ham ksha ma la va ra ya hum phat* and represents the cosmos as described in the *Kalachakra* ("Wheel of Time") *Tantra*, an important Buddhist text in Tibet.

ancient high-road from Kathmandu, the spectacular mountain pass of Langtan marks the border between the lush valleys of Nepal and the dry highlands of the Tibetan plateau. It was through this and similar passes that all the trade goods between Tibet, Nepal, and India were transported. Mules, yaks, and donkeys were the most common beasts of burden for these often difficult trails, carrying furs, hides, yak tails, borax, salt, musk, and medicinal herbs.

The pass is lined with cairns and carefully piled stones and slabs—some carved with *mandala* diagrams

Om mani padme hum—the mantra of Avalokiteshvara—is inscribed on this cliff-face at Lhasa. The talismanic inscription is repeated on rocks and stone tablets throughout Tibet.

(see pages 266–267) and inscriptions, most commonly *Om mani padme hum.* The conspicuous presence of this *mantra* at Langtan thus guards one of the most well-traveled entrances to Tibet with holy invocations of Avalokiteshvara, the patron deity and protector of the Tibetan people.

MUSIC AND RITUAL

Although silent meditation is a prominent aspect of Buddhism, large processions and noisy rituals, accompanied by all manner of music and dance, are also integral to the tradition's religious life. Tibet has its own distinctive ceremonies, in which chanting monks or masked dancers are accompanied by an orchestra of instruments made from materials such as human bone or conch shells.

Music and dance have been a key feature of Buddhist ritual since at least the first century BCE. At Sanchi, in central India, early relief carvings at the great *stupa* depict religious processions with drummers, dancers, and pairs of trumpet blowers. This liturgical tradition was taken to Tibet when Buddhism was first introduced there in the seventh century CE, and almost all Tibetan ceremonies involve chanting and the use of musical instruments. Most ceremonies are monastic services in which only monks participate, but there are also public spectacles involving music and dance, notably, in former times, the scapegoat ritual (see page 274) and the annual mystery play (*lha-'cham*). The play, performed at the year's end by monks in front of their monasteries, involved groups of masked dancers and centered on a human effigy, which was attacked and destroyed so that the New Year could start freshly purged of evil influence.

The most distinctive Tibetan instruments are those made from human bone, which is used as a reminder of the transitory nature of human existence. Trumpets fashioned from thighbones—which are fitted with mouthpieces and decorative metalwork inlaid with semiprecious stones—are traditionally thought to subdue demons and are frequently used in exorcism. They are featured in paintings of fierce deities (see pages 294–295) and are played when these gods are worshipped. The same is true of Tibetan drums made from the tops of human skulls, which are based on the *damaru*, an ancient Indian double-ended drum shaped like an hourglass. In addition to their use in exorcism, these skull drums are played during recitations.

Conch-shell trumpets are unique to India and Tibet. Brought to the Himalayas from the distant Indian coasts, conchs are the instrument par excellence for heralding the gods, and they were once thought to release frighteningly destructive forces in time of battle. In Buddhist Tibet, conchs are employed for the more peaceful purpose of summoning monks to prayer, and in some areas they are also used to avert damage to crops from hailstorms. They are fitted with metal mouthpieces and tubes in order to deepen the sound they produce. Large decorative flanges set with colored stones are also added, as are fabric pendants.

All Tibetan wind instruments are played in pairs: two musicians will play simultaneously, taking turns to breathe so that a continuous sound is produced. Large trumpets, some measuring up to 16 feet (approximately 5m) in length, produce a deep, haunting drone and are often sounded from rooftops to mark the beginning of ceremonies. *Shawm*s (oboe-like instruments) have finger holes and are the only wind instruments that can produce a melody. They are used in almost all Tibetan Buddhist ceremonies, except those connected with exorcism.

Cymbals also enjoy wide usage. Large cymbals, which are generally stored in boxes of lacquered canvas, are used in the worship of both fierce and peaceful deities and to mark the beginning and end of liturgies. Small cymbals, no bigger than the palm of the hand and usually kept in little bags of Chinese silk, are used in private prayers; they make a wonderfully hypnotic sound that draws the mind into a state of calmness and tranquillity.

These monks are taking part in a procession during a prayer festival at the Labrang monastery, Gansu province, China. Their crested hats are unique to the Gelug-pa (or "Yellow Hat") school of Tibetan Buddhism (see page 258).

RECORDING THE *DHARMA*

After the Buddha passed away, a series of councils was held in order to collect his teachings and to codify the rules governing monastic life. This knowledge, collectively called the dharma, *was first passed down by word of mouth, but the use of writing became inevitable as more and more commentaries and philosophical works based upon the* dharma *were composed.*

The earliest Buddhist works are in a language generally referred to as Pali, closely related to Sanskrit and thought to have been spoken by the Buddha. Pali was the language used in the southern Buddhist tradition for writing commentaries and it is still used today in learned circles. However, in north India, Sanskrit—the "classical" language of ancient India—became the dominant literary medium and was used by the Mahayana and Vajrayana schools, the varieties of Buddhism that were carried into Tibet in the seventh century CE. The script used for the Tibetan language was also developed at this time, when King Songtsen Gampo began sending envoys to India to study the art of writing and to create a system for transcribing the language. Tibetan script has changed little since.

Sanskrit learning was especially strong at Nalanda, the celebrated monastic university in eastern India, where many Tibetans went to study. Over several centuries, Sanskrit writings were translated into Tibetan, preserving texts that were subsequently lost in India.

The Buddhist canon was systematically organized into 108 volumes by a Tibetan scholar, Bu-ston (1290–1364). By 1749, this body of literature, known as the *Kagyur*, had been translated into Mongolian—about a century after the Mongols had been converted to the Tibetan form of Buddhism.

THE KAGYUR

The photograph, below, is of the opening pages of the *Prajna Paramita Sutra* ("Text of Transcendent Wisdom"), which is a section of the *Kagyur*, the comprehensive Tibetan anthology of Buddhist scripture. The text is written in gold on dark blue paper and, as with most high-quality Tibetan manuscripts, the opening leaves have silk flaps, which are folded over the face of the writing and miniatures when they are not in use to protect them from wear. The manuscript would once have been stored between wooden book covers. The rectangular format is derived from the earliest Buddhist manuscripts, which were made of strips of palm leaf.

This copy of the *Kagyur* was made and consecrated in the early eighteenth century by monks at the monastery of Shelkar near Dingri in southern Tibet. Built in 1266, the monastery was at first a Kagyu-pa establishment, but had come under the jurisdiction of the Gelug-pa school by the time this manuscript was made.

The opening pages of the Prajna Paramita Sutra, *from a copy of the* Kagyur *produced at Shelkar monastery in the early 18th century.*

PRAYER WHEELS, DRUMS, AND BANNERS

*The prayer wheel (*mani 'khor-lo)* is a uniquely Tibetan spiritual device, employed by both monks and laypeople to repeat the* mantras *which are written on the outside of the wheel or contained inside it on slips of paper. Prayer drums and banners are alternative methods of distributing* mantras.

Handheld prayer wheels have a metal drum which revolves on a pin; inside the drum are tightly rolled slips of paper printed with prayers, the most common being the formula *Om mani padme hum* (see page 276). Prayer wheels are set in motion by a flick of the wrist—with each spin the sacred texts within are understood as being read or chanted once. A prayer wheel can easily contain 40,000 *mantra*s, and so, by Tibetan calculations, a few minutes of spinning will repeat the *mantra*s millions of times. Because the most powerful invocations are those which are repeated mentally or quietly whispered, it follows that the silent turning of a prayer wheel is the most effective way of reciting *mantra*s. It is the act of turning the wheel that brings religious merit and divine blessings—the devotee, the *mantra*, and the deity associated with the *mantra* are just parts of a mechanical ritual which is understood to radiate blessings into the environment.

Large prayer drums, sometimes several feet high and painted with *mantra*s on the outside, are found in most Tibetan temples, where they are arranged in rows in a cloister. Devotees pass along the cloister, rotating each drum as they go. In some cases, prayer drums are turned by the wind or by running water. The perpetual turning of prayers in such drums is believed to fill the world with sacred invocations so that it is ever stable, ever renewed, and ever blessed for those on the path of enlightenment. The Buddha's teaching, the *dharma*, is considered perpetual and universal and is envisioned as a turning wheel, which is one of the eight auspicious emblems of Buddhism (see page 289). Thus, the prayer wheels and prayer drums of Tibet, both in a literal and figurative sense, keep the wheel of the *dharma* rolling.

Prayer flags and banners serve a similar purpose to prayer wheels. They are positioned in prominent places, such as the rooftops of monasteries, and as they flutter in the breeze, the *mantra*s and other blessings written upon them are believed to be freely distributed by the wind across the landscape. Most sets of flags are in five colors to symbolize the five elements of Tibetan tradition: earth, air, fire, water, and space. Some banners bear the eight auspicious emblems or protective animals, such as lions, dragons, and the eagle-headed Garuda (see page 274). Particularly large banners might be displayed during special ceremonies. The size of such banners—they were often so huge it would take dozens of people to unfurl them—endowed the images they bore with enormous spiritual power.

This 9th-century banner from the Buddhist caves at Dunhuang in Central Asia carries an image of the bodhisattva Vajra Pani. *It has long streamers and is closely related in size and function to the banners used in Tibet during formal processions.*

A particularly common device on flags is the *lun-ta* ("horse of the wind"), a trotting steed carrying a precious stone surrounded by flames. This stone, known as the *chinta-mani* ("radiant thought-gem"), is believed to grant victory and all wishes. Prayer flags that depict *lun-ta* are supposed to be especially effective.

Mountain passes are often marked by strings of prayer banners pinned to flagpoles and cairns. Travelers will always pause to add a stone to the cairn and attach a flag, which is sometimes little more than a strip of cloth. The prayers and *mantra*s on prayer flags vary according to the particular deity on whom the devotee normally focuses his or her meditation. Those directed at the goddess Tara (see pages 288–289) are especially commonplace on mountain flags, as she protects travelers from the dangers of the road.

Flags and auspicious banners are used throughout the Buddhist world as votive offerings. In Tibet, they are frequently raised on hilltops and cairns in mountain passes, such as this one between Shigatse and Lhatse on the Friendship Highway that links Lhasa and Nepal.

THE ULTIMATE TRUTH

The religious world of Tibet is inhabited by an elaborate pantheon of gods and goddesses, guardian deities, local spirits, saints, incarnations, teachers, philosophers, and wonder-workers. Most of the gods and goddesses were part of the Indian traditions of Mahayana Buddhism, but new forms were added as a result of the visionary meditations experienced by the great saints and lamas.

Tibetan Buddhism is an outwardly polytheistic religion, with numerous divinities and other supernatural beings. But it is underpinned by an uncompromising belief that all the gods belong to the world of phenomena and are thus—like all things—subject to change, death, and reincarnation. When a deity appeared to a *lama* in a new or variant form, the vision and the means of summoning it were recorded so that it could be passed on in the *lama*'s spiritual tradition. The Tibetan pantheon is thus not rigid and systematic, but an organic view of religious reality which varies according to school and location.

In contrast, the supreme truth is immortal, unchanging, absolute, and eternal. This ultimate truth is known as the Adi Buddha, or "Primordial Buddha." His essence is said to be "pure consciousness," the very same consciousness that lies at the heart of all individuals. For this reason, everyone is thought to have a gateway to Adi Buddha, the ultimate reality, within themselves.

Tibetan Buddhism has a range of religious techniques and rites (*sadhanas*) to guide individuals toward the ultimate truth. The knowledge of these techniques, their application and the way they are to be transmitted to the next generation is controlled by the various Tibetan Buddhist schools and spiritual lineages. During the course of their long histories, these schools have developed differing visions of Adi Buddha. The Nyingma-pa school describes Adi Buddha as Samanta Bhadra ("Entirely Auspicious"); for the Kadam-pa, the supreme reality is Vajra Sattva ("Diamond Being"); while the Gelug-pa view Adi Buddha as Vajra Dhara ("Holder of the Diamond").

◆ ALCHI: TEMPLES OF THE DHARMA ◆

In the steep upper valleys of the Indus River, not far from Leh in northern India, is the Ladakh Buddhist monastery at Alchi. The temples in the monastery are the most important early monuments in the western Himalayas, magnificent reminders of the time of the "Second Propagation" of Buddhism in Tibet (see page 258).

Little is known about the history of Alchi—there are no written records referring to the monastery, except for a few inscriptions attesting that the Sumtsek, the oldest of its temples, was founded by a monk named Tshultrim-O in approximately 1200CE. Alchi is renowned for its wall paintings of the Mahayana pantheon, which have remained virtually unchanged for the last eight centuries. The monastery also features important early woodwork, including ornately carved door frames. One notable example has six receding jambs, each richly carved with a variety of floral motifs and Buddhist figures, including the figure of a Garuda (a protector against malevolent forces). The design is based directly on doors that once graced temples in northern India, but the turbulent history of the Indian plains has meant that only a few stone fragments of these temples have survived.

Although Samanta Bhadra, Vajra Sattva, and Vajra Dhara are conceived as deities, they are not competing gods but rather different aspects of, or approaches to, the supreme being. Both Vajra Sattva and Vajra Dhara are shown holding the diamond *vajra*, or thunderbolt, an emblem of the indestructibility of *sunyata*—the name given by Buddhists to the imperishable "final state" of reality, which is completely separate from existence.

This portable wooden shrine dating to the 19th century contains votive plaques depicting the Buddha surrounded by various deities and lamas. *Below the main Buddha is an image of Yamantaka Vajra Bhairava ("The Destroyer of Death"). The insides of the shrine's doors are decorated with representations of offerings. The Buddhist pantheon is by no means a fixed entity—it varies from one school and region to another.*

SELFLESS HEROES

At the summit of the Tibetan Buddhist pantheon are the Primordial Buddha and the five celestial buddhas *who surround him and who represent his various divine attributes. But it is not only these deities who are venerated, but also the* bodhisattvas, *who selflessly delay their enlightenment in order to help others to be liberated.*

The Adi Buddha is immutable and passive like the celestial *buddha*s who surround him. In Tibetan belief, it is the *bodhisattva*s who are the active creators of the universe. A *bodhisattva* (literally "those whose essence is supreme knowledge") is a perfect being, who heroically delays final liberation or enlightenment in order to help others gain salvation. Five of these *bodhisattva*s, who hold the emblems of the celestial *buddha*s and are understood to be direct emanations of them, are Chakra Pani ("Wheel Bearer"), Vajra Pani ("Thunderbolt Bearer"), Ratna Pani ("Jewel Bearer"), Padma Pani ("Lotus Bearer"), and Vishva Pani ("Double-thunderbolt Bearer").

Among the more commonly worshipped *bodhisattva*s in Tibet are Avalokiteshvara, Manjushri, and Maitreya. The most popular *bodhisattva* of all is Avalokiteshvara, the lord of compassion and the patron deity of Tibet, who is believed to be reincarnated in every Dalai Lama. His name literally means "The Lord who Looks Down," that is, he looks down with compassion on the suffering of the world. In one text, the *Karandavyuha* ("Jewel-box Display"), Avalokiteshvara is described as taking a vow to descend into the realm of Yama, the lord of death. Waters miraculously began to flow from the *bodhisattva*'s fingers to cool the molten iron and flames of hell. Like all *bodhisattva*s, Avalokiteshvara has many forms, but he

Tibetan Buddhists believe that Maitreya, the bodhisattva *of the future, will incarnate himself on Earth and reestablish the truth of the Buddha's doctrine. His emblems are the white campa flower and, more especially, the water pot. Both are shown on lotus stalks beside his shoulders in this 19th-century gilded bronze statuette inlaid with precious stones.*

• AVALOKITESHVARA, THE MANY-ARMED LORD •

Known as Arya Avalokiteshvara, the eleven-headed, multiarmed form of the great *bodhisattva* first appeared in western India in the sixth century CE. Following the traditional definition of space as having ten directions, ten of the heads symbolize Avalokiteshvara's all-seeing dominion over the universe. The eleventh head, at the top, is that of Amitabha, the celestial *buddha* of which Avalokiteshvara is a manifestation. Amithabha is also known as Amitayus, the "*buddha* of Infinite Life" and is usually portrayed holding a pot containing the elixir of immortality.

can often be recognized by a small figure of the *buddha* Amitabha, his spiritual father, which is inserted like a talisman in his hair or crown. The *bodhisattva's* eleven-headed form, Arya Avalokiteshvara, also appears frequently in Tibet (see box, above). The deep attachment of the Tibetan people to this *bodhisattva* is illustrated by legends describing how the very first Tibetans were the children of a fierce mountain goddess and a monkey who was an emanation of Avalokiteshvara.

Manjushri, the personification of transcendent wisdom, is regarded as an offspring of the *buddha* Amitabha or Akshobhaya. He has many forms, but often wields the "sword of discrimination," a weapon with which he is said to cut the roots of ignorance. By worshipping him, devotees enrich their wisdom, develop a more retentive memory, and enhance their eloquence and their ability to master sacred scripture. For this reason, in addition to his sword, Manjushri holds a palm leaf manuscript, traditionally the *Prajna Paramita Sutra* ("Text of Transcendent Wisdom"). Because of this connection with sacred knowledge, Manjushri is often represented on book covers. In the fourteenth century CE, Manjushri is said to have incarnated himself in the person of Tsong Khapa,

Tibet's greatest monk-scholar, whose extraordinary life and work laid the foundation for the influential Gelugpa order (see page 258).

Maitreya ("Loving One") is the name given to the *bodhisattva* who is yet to come. It is believed that he now resides in a paradise called the Tushita heaven and is waiting for the time when he will descend to Earth as the next human *buddha* and reestablish the *dharma* in all its purity.

The celebrated sage Asanga—a sixth-century CE master—is said to have visited Maitreya in the Tushita heaven using the exceptional powers he acquired during a sixteen-year period of intense meditation retreat. Asanga received instruction in philosophical matters and transcribed these points in what are known as "the Five Works of Maitreya."

WISDOM AND COMPASSION

*In Mahayana Buddhism, both wisdom (*prajna *or* sunyata*) and compassion (*upaya *or* karuna*) are essential components of spiritual life. The abstract qualities of* prajna *and* karuna *are considered as female and male respectively, and their union is visualized as a goddess and a god in sexual embrace.*

Wisdom without compassion can achieve nothing because it is inert; compassion uninformed by wisdom is easily overwhelmed by suffering. The ultimate goal of enlightenment entails a combination of these opposites, a goal achieved, in the Mahayana view, by a slow ripening of the necessary "perfections" over many lives and incarnations. The Tantric Buddhist tradition of Vajrayana ("Vehicle of the diamantine thunderbolt") accepts the Mahayana interpretation but asserts that individuals can achieve full enlightenment in just one lifetime. This is believed to be possible through the vigorous application of a variety of powerful techniques, passed down in the master-to-disciple lineages of Tibet. In many cases these techniques are said to have been revealed directly to the great adepts of ancient India by the goddess Vajra Varahi in her mountain retreat at Kailas, where she is the divine consort of Chakra Samvara, the esoteric manifestation of the historical Buddha. The techniques involve the making and

contemplation of *mandala* diagrams, fasting and other penance, and the use of prayers and *mantra*s in meditation and in the performance of rituals. These are collectively designed to unlock the powers hidden within, unfolding the ocean of wisdom and compassion that are believed to lie in the depths of the human heart.

The techniques, deities, and texts of the Vajrayana tradition are often described as Tantra or Tantric, terms popularly associated with orgiastic rites and images of deities in sexual union. The term Tantra is more correctly a description of the comprehensive system of speculative thought which explains how to pursue enlightenment and provides a full range of yogic and meditative techniques to enable the devotee to achieve this end.

GODDESSES OF WISDOM

The great goddess of wisdom manifests herself in twenty-one forms, the most common of which are the

Green Tara and the White Tara. They are traditionally described as being born from the tears shed by the *bodhisattva* Avalokiteshvara, who wept to see the extent of suffering in the world. From his tears sprang lotus flowers from which the Taras were born. As goddesses of divine energy and transcendent wisdom, they gave Avalokiteshvara the courage to continue in his impossible task of delivering all beings from suffering.

The Taras are divine saviors and help deal with everyday dangers. For example, the *Sadhana Mala* ("Garland of Meditative Techniques") states that the worship of Green Tara will deliver one from the "eight great perils,"

which are generally taken to be fire, water, lions, elephants, imprisonment, snakes, thieves, and disease caused by evil spirits. White Tara, in contrast, offers serenity, prosperity, health, and good fortune.

When Buddhism was first introduced into Tibet, the Taras were believed to have incarnated themselves in the wives of King Songtsen Gampo—Green Tara incarnating as the Nepalese queen and White Tara as the Chinese queen. Tara was also the tutelary deity of Atisha, the Buddhist master who came to Tibet from India in 1042 CE, and since that time, the goddess has enjoyed a wide Tibetan following.

• AUSPICIOUS EMBLEMS •

Eight auspicious motifs frequently appear in Tibetan art (below, left to right): the "royal parasol" is emblematic of the Buddha and his heroic pursuit of enlightenment; the eight-spoked wheel represents the Buddha's *dharma*; the endless knot symbolizes the inescapable nature of worldly existence; the "victory banner" stands on Mount Kailas, or Meru, in the center of the Buddhist universe; the two fishes symbolize happiness and utility; the vase represents plenty; the lotus denotes purity; and the conch shell, because it grows in a clockwise direction, is symbolic of turning to the right, that is, turning toward the *dharma*.

TRANSMISSION OF THE *DHARMA*

The special character and strength of Buddhism in Tibet owes much to the devout Tibetans who undertook the long and perilous journey to India in search of holy texts and great religious teachers. And equally important were the revered Indian masters who were persuaded to travel to Tibet.

The Buddha did not appoint a successor but rather ordered that his teachings, the *dharma*, should guide his followers after his passing. This led him to establish a precise system for the ordination of monks and the transmission of the *dharma*. Subsequently, the *mahasiddhas* (great adepts—see pages 256–257) developed spiritual techniques and rituals to enable initiates to acquire superhuman powers and insights, and this necessitated careful procedures of initiation (*sadhanas*). This is because the knowledge of Buddhist scripture, doctrine, and *sadhanas* was considered to be valueless—and indeed dangerous—unless transmitted by a teacher qualified to assess the readiness and spiritual aptitude of potential initiates. The Tibetan word for teacher—*lama*—is a translation of the Sanskrit *guru*.

Spiritual practices received from a *lama* are often described as "esoteric," or "secret," but they are secrets only to the extent that they are disclosed in the right setting at the right time to duly prepared students. A key duty of the *lama* is to select the student's special "meditation deity" (*yi-dam*). The *yi-dam* is a protector and divine guarantor, through whom the initiate attains the spiritual powers which lead to the absolute. The selection of the particular *yi-dam* might be determined by the *lama's* monastery or school, but it may also involve an assessment of the student's personality. A number of deities preside over human vices, which they can transform into appropriate aspects of wisdom and compassion.

In the course of meditation, the deity might appear in different forms to the initiate. Such divine appearances led to an increase in the number of *sadhanas*, each new variation having its source in a particular vision of a deity experienced by a saint. These variants often found their way into temple wall-paintings and *thangkas*.

SAINTS, SAGES, AND ADEPTS

In the late tenth century CE, a leading figure in the effort to establish the *dharma* in Tibet was Rinchen Zangpo, who traveled to India under the patronage of Yeshe-o, king of Gu-ge in western Tibet. After almost twenty years abroad, Rinchen became an active teacher and translator in his homeland at Toling, where he constructed religious buildings from 1014CE.

King Yeshe-o was determined that Buddhism should be properly established in Tibet and repeatedly issued invitations to Atisha, the foremost Indian sage of the day. Atisha was fully conversant with all eighteen philosophical schools of Buddhism and, according to Ratnakara, the abbot of the monastic university of Vikramashila, "held in his hand the keys to all the monasteries of India." Initially reluctant to leave his homeland, Atisha was finally persuaded to make a short visit, arriving in Tibet in 1042 at the age of sixty. After visiting the kingdom of Gu-ge in the west, he traveled to central Tibet and finally settled at Nyetang, around 17 miles (28km) southwest of Lhasa. Atisha died at Nyetang in 1054 and the temple complex there, known as Dolma Lhakhang, contains many personal items, including his bodily relics, begging bowl, books, and some of the sacred images he brought from India.

Atisha was especially devoted to Tara (see pages 288–289). The shrine at Nyetang contains twenty-one Taras, given to the temple in the seventeenth century. Atisha's original sculpture of the goddess is now missing but it is believed to have been a miraculous image endowed with the power of speech. The Nyetang temple also has a *thangka* of Maha Kala, a popular protector deity (see page 294), that is said to have been painted using some of Atisha's blood. Another relic of great sanctity is the skull of Naropa, the great adept with whom Marpa studied (see below).

Atisha's enormous influence owes much to the fact that he learned Tibetan, a language seldom studied by early Buddhist scholars in India. A key feature of Atisha's teaching was his emphasis on the absolute devotion that the disciple must have for their master—only those who had made a complete and uncompromising commitment to their spiritual *lama*s were worthy of receiving the higher truths which could bring them to enlightenment in a single lifetime. Atisha's chief pupil, Dromton, established the Kadam-pa school of Tibetan Buddhism after Atisha died in 1054.

Also in this period, Marpa, who was a farmer from central Tibet, made three journeys to eastern India. He studied with a variety of masters, the most important being Naropa, a Great Adept and the preeminent Buddhist mystic of the eleventh century. On his return, Marpa gained many followers, including Milarepa (see pages 272–273), whose disciples in turn established the Kagyu-pa school.

THE WAY OF A TANTRIC MASTER

When Padmasambhava was summoned to Tibet by King Trisong Detsen to help establish the Buddhist monastery at Samye (see page 268), he first met the ruler near the Tsangpo River at Zurkhardo. A series of *stupa*s was built on the hills there to commemorate this historic meeting of Tantric master and all-powerful king. The *stupa*s are visible for many miles along the Tsangpo, marking the river crossing and traditional pilgrim route to nearby Samye. Zurkhardo recalls the "Invitation Rock" at Mihintale in Sri Lanka where, more than nine centuries before the time of Padmasambhava, the Buddhist elder Mahinda met King Devanampiya Tissa. Just as the early Buddhists had to overcome a local cult of nature spirits (*yakkha*) in Sri Lanka, so Padmasambhava is said to have faced the ancient gods of Tibet at Mount Hepori, a sacred hill overlooking Samye and a seat of power for the Bon deities long worshipped by the old aristocratic families of central Tibet.

REINCARNATION

A striking feature of Tibetan Buddhism is the system by which lamas reincarnate themselves to secure the succession of their schools and monasteries. Tibet's spiritual leader, the Dalai Lama, has been reincarnated thirteen times and will continue to be reborn as long as is necessary for his country's spiritual health. At the death of each Dalai Lama, a search begins for the next one.

The origin of the practice of intentional reincarnation can perhaps be traced to Padmasambhava, who, with his disciples, is said to sometimes take a human form when hidden texts need to be recovered. Although various *lamas* ("teacher" or "master") and schools have made use of reincarnation, it was first deployed over several generations by the Karma-pa school. However, the Sakya-pa hierarchs, who dominated Tibet in the thirteenth century, came to be distinguished instead for their hereditary succession.

The reincarnation system was continued by Gendun Drupa (1391–1474), a disciple of the great scholar and monk Tsong Khapa. Gendun Drupa built up the Gelug-pa order over an exceptionally long and energetic career. Sonam Gyatso (1543–1588), the third head of the Gelug-pa, took the historic step of reestablishing contact with the Mongols, and received the celebrated title Dalai Lama ("Ocean Teacher") when he visited the Mongol leader Altan Khan in 1578 (see page 258). This title was applied retrospectively, so that Gendun Drupa became known as the first Dalai Lama and Sonam Gyatso as the third. The Dalai Lamas are regarded as incarnations of Avalokiteshvara.

Although the Gelug-pa had contacts with Ming China, their powerful position in Tibet was the result of alliances formed with the Mongols. Gushri Khan was deeply impressed by the fifth Dalai Lama (the "Great Fifth"), and with the Khan's military help, the Gelug-pa order established religious and secular hegemony over the whole country, with the Dalai Lama becoming the Tibetan head of state.

THE PRIEST-KING

The death of the thirteenth Dalai Lama in 1933 plunged Tibet into mourning. One of the greatest of the Dalai Lamas, Thubten Gyatso had restored his country's pride and patriotism. It was he who in 1911 had torn Tibet free from Manchu China, which had invaded two years previously. The grief of Tibetans was therefore great, but was tempered nonetheless by the firm belief that their beloved leader, himself a reincarnation of previous Dalai Lamas, would be manifested once again in his successor.

Following ancient practice, the regent, Reting Rinpoche, made a pilgrimage to Lhamo Latso, the "Oracle Lake" in central Tibet. There he had a vision revealing the birthplace of the present Dalai Lama, Tenzin Gyatso, who was born in 1934 to a humble family in the Amdo region of far eastern Tibet. Although only two years old, Tenzin Gyatso revealed his true identity to the monks charged with finding the Dalai Lama by picking out Thubten Gyatso's possessions from others that were unconnected to the former leader. Like other Dalai Lamas, the infant was taken to Lhasa and educated in seclusion at the Potala Palace.

However, world events were soon to disrupt the life of the young sovereign. After the communist revolution in China, the Red Army pushed toward Lhasa in 1950 with the aim of "liberating" the country. In 1959, following a popular uprising, the fourteenth Dalai Lama was forced to flee to India, where he established a Tibetan government-in-exile in Dharamsala.

From the security of his place of exile in the Indian Himalayas, the fourteenth Dalai Lama, Tenzin Gyatso, has been able to continue many of the ancient Buddhist traditions of Tibet, such as festivities and prayers to celebrate the New Year, illustrated opposite. The Dalai Lama and the monks around him are wearing the crested yellow hats that signify membership of the Gelug-pa school.

PROTECTORS
AND WANDERERS

The Buddhist protector deities help initiates to resist the twin hungers of temptation and desire.
Fearsome to behold, they serve as a reminder of the darker shadows that lurk within the human
mind and provide a counterbalance to the deities of compassion.

Many of the gods and goddesses of Tibetan Buddhism appear in a variety of forms, some fierce (*krodha*) and others peaceful (*santa*). This dual form is a reflection of the changeable nature of all created things and the underlying reality that the gods represent the moods and features of human consciousness. While most Tibetan Buddhists are drawn to benevolent aspects of the *bodhisattva*s and Taras, others choose to meditate on more frightening and dangerous forms. Fierce deities preside over the evil aspects of the personality and their propitiation allows aspirants to confront their own greatest fears and weaknesses. In this way fierce gods and goddesses are channels for grace just as much as their benign counterparts. They are often depicted with a third eye in the center of their forehead to represent the special insight that they provide (see illustration of Maha Kala, right).

The stories which surround the life of the Indian saint Padmasambhava (see page 265) describe him as subduing the ancient pre-Buddhist gods of Tibet with his magical powers, compelling them to watch over the Buddhist faith forever as ferocious *dharmapalas* ("protectors of the *dharma*"). Although the protectors have Tibetan aspects, their names suggest that they were originally Indian deities that absorbed local attributes as their cults spread northward into the Himalayas.

Maha Kala, meaning "Great Time," the most popular of the *dharmapalas*, began as a

form of the Hindu god Shiva and was believed to embody time, especially in its role as the inevitable destroyer of all things. In Tibet, Maha Kala is a protector of science and of tents. The latter function received special prominence in the sixteenth century when the

third Dalai Lama made Maha Kala the protector-deity of Mongolia—a land of tent-dwelling nomads.

Yamantaka, whose name means "Destroyer of Death," also holds a unique place among the *dharma palas*. Legends recount that when the god Yama—the lord of death—was ravaging the countryside, the people appealed to Manjushri, the *bodhisattva* of wisdom. He answered their prayers and assumed the form of Yamantaka, a being so ferocious and powerful that Yama was subjugated and made to serve as a *dharma pala* and regent of hell. From the Buddhist perspective, this story represents the abstract truth that eternal wisdom overcomes all ignorance—death being simply an illusion that persists owing to a lack of knowledge about the true nature of things. Yamantaka is the tutelary deity of the Gelug-pa school because its founder, *lama* Tsong Khapa, is regarded as an incarnation of Manjushri.

THE CRUEL WANDERERS

There is an old Tibetan belief that all women who acquire supernatural powers become fierce goddesses known as *dakini*s. This belief is well illustrated by the story of Ghantapa, a great adept (*mahasiddha*) who is much admired in Tibet. He resided at the monastic university of Nalanda during the ninth century CE, and took the daughter of a local courtesan as his partner and ritual consort. However, because monks are bound by vows of celibacy, these actions caused a public scandal. When confronted for his apparent violation of the monastic rules, Ghantapa and his consort rose into the air, transforming themselves into the deities Chakra Samvara and Vajra Dakini.

Known in Tibetan as *khagro-ma* ("ether wanderers"), the fierce *dakini*s are referred to many times in the literature of the Nyingma-pa order, which recounts how they could fly through the air like angels, conveying sages over great distances. As consorts, or "wisdom partners," of the supreme *buddha*s, *dakini*s have an intimate and firsthand knowledge of special *mantra*s,

yoga practices, and esoteric rites. For this reason, the great adepts approached the *dakini*s to learn the secret techniques and rituals which could provide them with superhuman insights and incredible powers. Vajra Dakini, also called Vajra Varahi and Naro Dakini, was considered especially approachable, and was known for her motherly compassion and lack of envy. Vajra Dakini incarnates herself as the abbess of Samding, the most revered female incarnation in Tibet. The ruins of Samding monastery stand on the edge of Lake Yamdrok, east of Gyantse.

• THE GLORIOUS GODDESS •

Emulating the celestial mansion of Avalokiteshvara with its golden roofs and gleaming pinnacles, the labyrinth of shrines at the top of Lhasa's Potala Palace makes a fitting abode for the Dalai Lamas, widely believed to be incarnations of Avalokiteshvara himself. However, long before this magnificent palace was built, the mountain on which it stands was the special haunt of the only female Dharma Pala, Shri Devi, the "Glorious Goddess." Known as Penden Lhamo in Tibet, her powers were contained but not entirely suppressed by Buddhism, as demonstrated by the fact that the "Great Fifth"—the Dalai Lama who made Lhasa the capital of Tibet and constructed the Potala—felt obliged to propitiate her. Since that time, Penden Lhamo has been considered the special protector of the Dalai Lamas.

According to legend, Penden Lhamo killed her son because he was being raised by his father to stamp out Buddhism in the kingdom he was to inherit. She is frequently shown holding a skull cup filled with her son's blood and riding a mule, draped with his flayed skin, across a sea of blood. Penden Lhamo often appears in the retinue of the protector Maha Kala (illustrated opposite).

THE AFTERWORLD

In Buddhism, death is not a final end but merely a gateway to a new reincarnation or—for those who, like the Buddha, are sufficiently prepared—to complete liberation. The period after the death of the physical body is referred to as an "intermediate state" (Tibetan bardo*), and is described in a number of sources, the most famous of which is known in the West as* The Tibetan Book of the Dead.

For Tibetan Buddhists, death and the *bardo* provide an opportunity to rip away the illusions embedded in the physical body and to come face-to-face with reality. This reality is known as the "*buddha*-nature." It is latent in all individuals and manifests itself as the peaceful and wrathful deities that are believed to reside in the mind and heart. In the days after death, as an individual's false universe collapses, these deities appear in a succession of powerful visions. Most people, terrified by what they see arising from within themselves, flee toward the comfortable and familiar—attachments that lead them inevitably to rebirth. The good and virtuous souls may be reborn in heaven and the evil may end up in hell. None of these afterworlds is permanent and reincarnation is regarded as inevitable. The pure and heroic, however, are able to look beyond appearances and, taking refuge in the Buddha, they attain complete liberation from the bonds of conditioned existence.

Vajrayana Buddhism recreated the *bardo* through ritual and mental techniques that mimicked the death experience. This was to prepare individuals for the inevitable and to allow them to reflect on life more clearly.

RITES OF THE CEMETERY

The Tibetans have developed unique ways of disposing of the dead. The most common method is "sky burial," in which the deceased is exposed to the elements, a custom developed in response to the scarcity of wood in most parts of the Tibetan plateau. Following Indian practice, eminent *lamas*—highly respected as spiritual guides—are often cremated and their ashes kept in *chortens* or used in *tsha-tsha* amulets (see page 275). Earth burial, which was used by the ancient kings of the Yarlung dynasty (see page 258), is now reserved for thieves, murderers, and victims of disease.

Although the vital organs may have ceased to function, individuals are not regarded as truly dead until all

---

✦ DANCING LORDS OF DEATH ✦

Frightening skeleton beings known as *chitipati*s—literally, "lords of the funeral pyre"—are one of the unique features of Tibetan art. Attendants of Yama, the god of death, *chitipati*s are usually shown dancing and holding thunderbolt standards. The frequent emphasis on death in Tibetan art is not an indication of a morbid obsession, but rather a reflection of the positive and pragmatic view that the Tibetan people take of life, and their belief in the need to appreciate that all existence is transitory.

This thangka *painting illustrates one of the visions experienced in the afterworld. Although horrific, the vision is presided over by Samanta Bhadra, the cosmic* buddha *shown at the top of the picture in union with his "wisdom partner."*

consciousness has completely departed. This process is assisted by an officiating *lama*, who performs rituals of "transference" (*pho-wa*) and whispers advice about the successive visions that the deceased will encounter in the afterworld. Special prayers and offerings are made which add to the merit of the dead and assure their well-being in the next life.

When these essential religious rites have been performed, the corpse is cut into pieces and taken to a designated charnel ground, usually a hilltop outside the village or town. The remains of the body are left in the open to be eaten by vultures and other animals as a final act of generosity, allowing other beings to be nourished by what has become an otherwise useless residue. Some charnel grounds, including that at Sera in central Tibet, are thought to be especially auspicious; corpses are sometimes brought considerable distances to be disposed of at such sites.

THE DIVERSITY OF BUDDHISM

Across the expanses of Asia, the diffusion of Buddhism over time resulted in a blend of different forms in different places. In the northeastern states such as China and Vietnam, the Mahayana school dominated, whereas in southerly Burma and Thailand the Sinhalese tradition of Theravada held sway, which remained the case in Sri Lanka where it had originated. The islands of Japan developed unique Buddhist practices known as Zen. As well as these distinct schools, there evolved a variety of sculptural and architectural styles.

ABOVE A Sinhalese-style giant Buddha figure at Wat Phra Si San Phet, Ayutthaya, Thailand. It is the site of a former royal temple complex that dates from the 14th-century kingdom of Ayutthaya and the ashes of several kings remain in funerary structures at the complex.

OPPOSITE (INSET) The landscaping at the 14th-century Saihoji Buddhist temple in Kyoto, which belongs to the Rinzai school of Zen, suggests that gardening can be a religious activity. In Japanese Zen belief such places are important as objects of meditation, combining nature, spirituality, and garden aesthetics.

LEFT The spire of the 14th–15th-century Shwedagon Pagoda in Yangon (Rangoon) is covered with plates of gold and crowned with precious stones. The Shwedagon is the holiest shrine in Myanmar (Burma).

BELOW Some of the 72 domed stupas which are set out on the uppermost circular layers of the spectacular, mandala-form Buddhist temple of Borobudur in central Java, Indonesia. Behind the latticework, each perforated stupa contains a statue of a meditating Buddha. The complex was built by the Sailendra dynasty between 750 and 850CE.

CHAPTER ONE

GREECE

The topography of Greece is dominated by two elements which had a profound effect on the development of ancient Greek civilization: the mountains and the sea. On the one hand, these physical boundaries divided Greece into hundreds of autonomous city-states, each free to develop its own form of government. On the other hand, the presence of the sea made the Hellenes great travelers and traders, and enabled them to exchange ideas and goods with peoples all around the Mediterranean—stories from the Near East and Egypt informed the early development of Greek myth, which found expression at first in epic poetry and later in drama and all kinds of representational art. The land of Greece itself was the source of the marble and clay from which were fashioned the temples, sculpture, and pottery that provide our dominant images of Greek culture.

THE SOUL OF THE GREEKS

Each city-state had its own rituals for worshipping a particular selection of gods. However, the fundamental features of religious belief were common throughout Greece—the polytheistic system included not only the major Olympian gods and goddesses but also a host of minor deities, such as nymphs and river gods, and an ill-defined group of semi-divine heroes and heroines.

Unlike the gods of many other ancient civilizations, those of the Greeks were almost all conceived of as being wholly human in form, with just a few exceptions, such as the goat-legged Pan. This tendency toward anthropomorphism can also be seen in the many human figures which personify such abstract ideas as Victory and Peace—it reflects a distinctly human-centered view of the world.

There was no universally accepted religious text or creed among the Greeks. The occasional introduction to a particular city of a "new god"—either a deity imported from another region or a human ideal newly elevated to divine status—suggests that there was flexibility in the system and some openness to new ideas. However, the fact that religion was basically conservative is revealed by the lack of change in many elements of ritual from Homer's time (eighth century BCE) until paganism's demise after Christianity became the official religion of the Roman Empire (312CE).

In both Greek ritual and belief there was a strong emphasis on the here-and-now rather than the afterlife. There was also a firm focus on reciprocity: the most common prayers that were recorded are for success in battle, abundance of crops, and the birth of healthy children, in return for which the deity would usually be reminded of previous offerings made and promised more for the future. One divinity or another presided over every facet of human life, be it agriculture, hospitality, drinking, love, or sleep—even activities which might now seem far removed from the religious sphere, such as drama and athletics, developed as part of the worship of the gods. In daily life the Greeks were surrounded by images of the gods that were painted, carved in stone, or cast in precious metal; they not only stood as individual statues, but were used to decorate everything from temples and public buildings to crockery, jewelry, and clothes.

The few depictions we have of the afterlife reflect a general absence from Greek thought of any opposition between good and evil, since there was no clear correlation between good behavior or religious observance and subsequent reward. Some mystery cults offered a privileged existence in the underworld (see box, opposite), and a few philosophers believed in the transmigration of souls, but generally people do not seem to have had strong expectations of life after death one way or the other: provided their bodily remains had received due burial, it was believed their soul would progress to a shadowy eternal existence in the underworld (see pages 328–330).

This Attic black-figure cup was made ca. 570BCE, not long after the hero Herakles was promoted to divine status in many areas of Greece. Here Herakles is being led by Athene and Hermes before Zeus and Hera on Olympos; the female figure standing between their thrones may be Hebe, "Youth" personified, who will be Herakles's divine consort.

✦ SACRED MYSTERIES ✦

Unlike adherence to the mainstream religion, belonging to one of the mystery cults might have offered the prospect of happiness in the afterlife. The defining feature of a mystery cult was its element of secrecy, with access granted only to those who had undergone initiation.

The best documented cults are the Mysteries of Demeter and her daughter Persephone at Eleusis, which flourished from at least the eighth century BCE to the destruction of the sanctuary there in about 400CE, and attracted initiates from all over the Greek-speaking world. The location of the sanctuary is explained by the myth that Demeter (depicted, right, in a marble statue of ca. 340BCE from the sanctuary) found a welcome there during her search for her abducted daughter (see page 328), as a reward for which she instructed the Eleusinians in her rites. On Persephone's safe return from Hades, Demeter restored fertility to the Earth and gave the Eleusinian prince Triptolemos the task of teaching agriculture to the rest of humankind. The Great Mysteries were celebrated every August in a week-long festival which included purificatory rituals for the initiates and a grand procession from Athens to Eleusis. We do not know exactly what happened during the all-night initiation ceremony, but it seems to have involved drinking a special concoction, handling sacred objects, and watching some kind of torch-lit performance, possibly enacting the birth of a sacred child.

Also of wide repute, particularly in the fourth and third centuries BCE, were the Mysteries of the Great Gods celebrated on the island of Samothrace, in which Herodotus was an initiate. The Samothracian Mysteries were supposed to offer protection from danger, but they may also have had an ethical element, since the initiate was asked to confess his or her gravest sin. Hopes for the afterlife were also offered by the Bacchic mysteries of the god Dionysos, although these were not confined to performance in the context of a sanctuary.

THE STORY OF THE GREEKS

The great sweep of Greek history—from the origins of Greek civilization through the "Dark Age"
to the Archaic, Classical, and Hellenistic periods—begins not on the mainland but with the earliest
phase of Minoan civilization on the island of Crete.

The earliest people on the Greek mainland to leave us with traces of a highly structured society are the Mycenaeans, who began to arrive in Greece toward the end of the third millennium BCE. From around 1600BCE they developed an advanced palace culture along similar lines to that of the Minoans who had flourished on Crete from around 2800BCE (see box, page 309). Excavations at Mycenae itself, Tiryns, Pylos, and other palace sites have all unearthed clay tablets inscribed in so-called Linear B (see page 323), which transcribes an early form of the Greek language.

OPPOSITE *The main map shows the important regions, city-states and places of worship in the Hellenic world, while the smaller map (inset) of the Mediterranean has shaded areas to highlight the major spheres of Greek colonization, notably south Italy, Sicily, and around the coast of the Black Sea.*

Between around 1200 and 1100BCE, for reasons that are still unclear, the Mycenaean palaces appear to have suffered violent initial destruction followed by a period of decline and eventual abandonment. After this collapse of the Mycenaean world, the use of writing disappeared, along with wall-painting and other fine arts, as a result of which the ensuing three centuries are traditionally known as the "Dark Age."

The dawn of the "Archaic Period" is traditionally marked by the foundation of the Olympic Games in 776BCE. The art of writing was reintroduced around 750BCE, using an alphabet borrowed from the Phoenicians. By the end of the eighth century BCE the *polis* ("city-state") had emerged as the principal form of social organization, constituted by an urban center and the surrounding rural territory (see pages 314–315). The appearance of the *polis* was closely tied to the emergence of the hoplite phalanx, a highly efficient fighting unit that required disciplined teamwork. In some states the phalanx provided a power-base for ambitious individuals who sought sole rule, thereby helping to create

LEFT *While the Minoan civilization thrived in Crete, a contemporary culture was flourishing in the Aegean Cyclades ca. 3200–2000BCE. Cycladic civilization is especially well known for the marble figurines found in its rich tombs. The figurines represent violin-shaped females with crossed arms or seated males playing musical instruments, such as this harp-player of ca. 2500BCE.*

MACEDONIA

Pella

Vergina

EPIROS

Dodona

MOUNT OLYMPOS

Corfu

THESSALY

Ionian Sea

AITOLIA

PHOKIS

Ithaca

Delphi

BOIOTIA

Chalkis

EUBOIA

CORINTHIAN GULF

Plataia

Thebes

Kefalonia

Patrai

ACHAIA

Eleusis

Marathon

Brauron

ELIS

Corinth

Piraieus

Athens

Olympia

ARKADIA

ARGOLID

Sounion

Mycenae

Bassae

Argos

Epidauros

Troizen

PELOPONNESE

MESSENIA

LAKONIA

Pylos

Sparta

Mediterranean Sea

Cape Tainaron

Kythereia

Thasos

Samothrace

Lemnos

Troy

IONIA

Lesbos

Aegean Sea

Skyros

Chios

Colophon

Ephesos

Andros

Samos

Kea

Tinos

Ikaria

Miletos

Didyma

Delos

Kythnos

Paros

Naxos

The Cyclades

Kos

Knidos

Melos

Santorini

Rhodes

Karpathos

N

Knossos

MOUNT IDA

CRETE

SCALE

MOUNT DIKTE

125 miles

0   210 km

GAUL

IBERIA

ITALY

BLACK SEA

SICILY

the tyrants who are characteristic of the period. It was this era's political struggles, together with land-hunger, which may have prompted the establishment of Greek colonies all around the shores of the Mediterranean (see inset, page 307).

The Archaic Period ended with the Persian Wars of 490–479BCE, which were fundamental in shaping relations between the leading city-state powers of Athens and Sparta. It took the combined efforts of these two and a number of other Greek states to achieve final victory over Persia at Plataia (479BCE) and usher in the Classical age. Over the following fifty years Athens gained preeminence, until the Peloponnesian War of 431–404BCE, at the end of which Sparta emerged as the foremost power of Greece. Sparta's hegemony was

effectively ended by the disastrous defeat by Thebes at Leuktra in 371BCE. Subsequent small-scale struggles left the southern Greek states open to the rising power of Macedon under King Philip II (359–336BCE), who defeated an alliance of Athenians and Thebans at Chaironeia in 338BCE.

Despite being an era of almost continuous warfare, the "Classical Period" saw all the cultural developments

---

The 1st-century BCE "Alexander Mosaic" from the House of the Faun at Pompeii is thought to be a copy of a late 4th-century BCE Greek painting. It shows a battle, sometimes identified as the Battle of Issos, between Alexander the Great and the Persian king Darius III. In this detail, the young Alexander boldly charges in to the attack.

most associated with Greece's legacy to Western civilization: the dramatic tragedies of Aeschylus, Sophocles, and Euripides; the written histories of Herodotus, Thucydides, and Xenophon; the philosophy expounded by Socrates, who was followed by Plato and later Aristotle; and the rhetoric of famous masters such as Demosthenes and Aeschines.

Once the whole of Greece was under Macedonian control, King Philip II's son, Alexander the Great (336–323 BCE), invaded Persia. His campaigns carried Greek culture to Egypt, Afghanistan, India, and the Persian Gulf. After Alexander's early death, his vast empire fragmented, with several of his former generals vying for power. The "Hellenistic Period" begins with the three victorious "Successors" each establishing a ruling dynasty: the Ptolemies in Egypt, the Seleucids in Asia, and the Antigonids in Macedonia itself. The Antigonids' intermittent control over the whole of mainland Greece was challenged by the rise of various confederacies, of which the most successful was the Achaean League. From the late third century BCE the "clouds gathering in the west," as the historian Polybius dubbed the rise of Roman power, began to impinge on the eastern Mediterranean. A defining moment came in 146 BCE when the Achaean League was smashed and the prosperous Greek city of Corinth was laid waste by the Romans. From then on Greece was administered as the Roman province of Macedonia, with the Peloponnese and southern mainland becoming the separate province of Achaia in 46 BCE.

• KNOSSOS •

The Minoan civilization flourished in Bronze-Age Crete from around 2800 to 1450 BCE. From about 2000 BCE there developed a system of political, economic, and social organization centered on a number of palaces, such as Knossos, Phaistos, Mallia, and Zakros, in which each controlled the surrounding region. In approximately 1450 BCE all the palaces were destroyed with the exception of Knossos, which survived for another seventy-five or so years under Mycenaean occupation, until it was destroyed in its turn.

The Knossos site was excavated between 1900 and 1932 by Sir Arthur Evans, the Englishman who published his finds in the lavish, multi-volume *Palace of Minos*. His work provided the foundations for the study of a culture which had previously only been known through the myths of King Minos, who was said by ancient writers to have ruled a great maritime empire. Many scholars today question Evans's romantic linking of Knossos with the legendary Minos, but there is no doubt that the world the archaeologist uncovered was a rich and sophisticated one. Three thousand clay tablets inscribed in Linear B (see page 323) found by Evans were eventually identified as inventories and accounts, indicative of a complex palace bureaucracy in Knossos's later years. The site today is still dominated by Evans's highly controversial reconstructions, which are more conjectural the higher above ground you go. The grand staircase gave access to various levels of the elaborately decorated royal apartments on the east side of the central courtyard; a few original steps are preserved, but the design of the pillars is reliant on ancient paintings and modern guesswork. Similarly interpretive are the frescoes now on display in Iraklion Museum, and doubts have been raised about the authenticity of the Boston "Snake Goddess" and other ivory figurines.

THE ART OF THE GREEKS

Ancient Greek artists produced art in a wide variety of media and materials—from large-scale sculptures of heroic figures in marble or bronze to the characteristic red- and black-figure pottery, many examples of which still survive today.

After the collapse of Mycenaean culture (ca.1200–1100BCE), art continued to be produced but on a much more modest scale than hitherto. Throughout the Dark Age, pottery was decorated with simple patterns, which developed into the more complex geometric style after about 900BCE (see box, opposite). At the same time, small-scale sculpture of humans and animals flourished in the form of bronze and clay statuettes, which were dedicated to the gods at sanctuaries or buried with the dead as grave goods.

Large figures in carved marble first appeared toward the end of the seventh century BCE. Initially these showed the influence of Egyptian prototypes, but a distinctively Greek style soon emerged. This style included the archaic male figure conventionally known as the *kouros* ("youth"), who is always nude and stands with his hands by his sides, one leg slightly advanced; the archaic female figure, the *kore* ("maiden"), is always fully dressed. Figures of both genders were erected in sanctuaries, where they represented either ideal worshippers or the deity him- or herself, and as grave markers to commemorate the dead. Advanced casting techniques were developed in the late sixth century, from which time bronze became the favored medium. Sadly, few original Greek bronzes have survived, and for the work of the most famous classical sculptors we are dependent on Roman copies (often in marble) and the observations of

ancient writers (see page 370). In the fifth century BCE the sculptor Pheidias was celebrated for his images of the gods, especially the massive chryselephantine (gold and ivory) statues of Athene Parthenos and Olympian Zeus, while his contemporary Polykleitos was better known for his portrayals of mortals. In the fourth century, Praxiteles popularized the female nude with his Aphrodite of Knidos, and Lysippos created the archetypal ruler portrait with his representations of Alexander the Great. Sculpture of the Hellenistic Period (323–31BCE) took realism to new extremes in the representation of individuals real or imaginary.

Stone temples also first appeared in the seventh century BCE, and the idea of adorning them with mythological scenes can already be seen in the painted clay *metopes* (decorated panels) of the temple of Apollo at Thermon (ca. 640BCE). Later buildings would be decorated entirely with relief sculpture,

The "Auxerre kore," from Crete, is a limestone statuette made ca. 640BCE and now named after the town in France where she was first exhibited. Her small size (she stands just 25 inches, or 65cm, high), stiff frontal pose, flatness, and wig-like hair are typical of the "Daedalic" style of mid-7th-century BCE sculpture, a precursor to the more rounded, life-size forms of the 6th century BCE.

which almost always represented scenes from myth. Sometimes these reliefs would have a particular association with the location, but a number of themes are found time and again throughout the Greek world: gods fighting giants, Greek warriors fighting Amazons or centaurs, and the exploits of Herakles. Other relief sculpture was carved on free-standing *stelai* as popular offerings to the gods (known as votive reliefs) or they bore inscriptions that recorded state decisions (decree reliefs). Most common of all are funerary reliefs, which replaced the earlier forms of grave marker toward the end of the sixth century BCE; in the Classical Period these reliefs usually depicted the deceased accompanied by family members.

Large-scale painting, on walls and wooden panels, was also an important feature of public art, but what little we know of it has had to be pieced together from analysis of the few surviving examples found in tombs, comparison with contemporary vase-painting, of which many originals exist, and Roman copies. Ancient

• FORMS OF DECORATION •

The painted decoration on pottery of the Protogeometric (1100–900BCE) and Geometric periods (900–700BCE) at first consisted purely of patterns, from concentric circles to more elaborate motifs, such as the swastika, the *maeander* ("Greek key pattern"), quatrefoil, cross-hatched triangles, lozenge chains, and parallel zigzag patterns (below). Occasional stylized animal and human figures began to appear around 900BCE, but more complex scenes developed from about 770BCE representing such popular themes as battles and shipwrecks. The most striking pieces are the enormous *krater*s and amphoras used as grave markers, which might be as much as 5 feet (1.5m) high. These are decorated all over with geometric motifs, with a panel or an extended frieze depicting mourners gathered around the body at the laying-out or accompanying the funeral procession. Long after the Geometric Period, motifs such as the *maeander* continued to be used for borders on both black- and red-figure painted pottery.

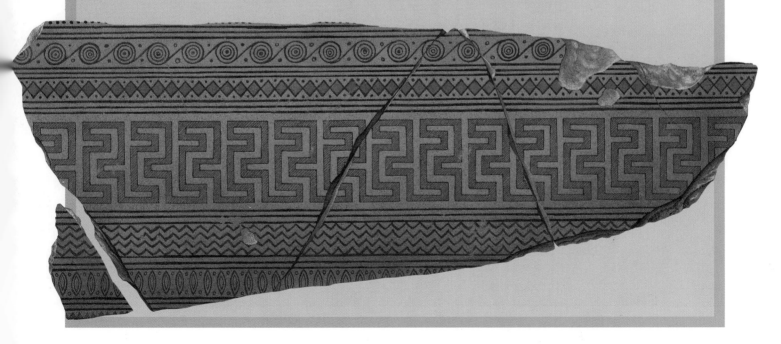

writers' anecdotes concerning fourth-century painters reveal that realism and *trompe l'oeil* effects were admired; the most renowned practitioner of all was Apelles, court painter to Alexander the Great. By 300BCE floors were being decorated with figure scenes made out of pebble mosaics—examples survive from the then Macedonian capital Pella, forerunners of the colorful tesselated mosaics of the Hellenistic and Roman periods.

Its relatively high survival rate means that pottery decorated with figure scenes is now by far the best represented category of Greek art, although its actual status and value in the ancient world is much debated. Such decorated pottery was clearly a step up from the plain ware used by the poorer classes, and less expensive than the gold- and silverware used by the most wealthy, but just how widely it was used is unknown. What is undisputed is the fact that painted vases are the most abundant source of images of Greek myth and daily life. From around 700BCE it became common to decorate pots with mythological scenes, many of which can be firmly identified because of the practice of naming figures with inscriptions.

Throughout the seventh century the main center for the production and export of painted pottery was Corinth—its wares are easily recognizable by the paleness of the clay background and the rosette motifs used as decoration. From about 600BCE the market was dominated by pottery from Attica painted in the black-figure technique, in which the deep-red clay provides a strongly contrasting background to figures painted in

black slip, with incised details and occasionally some added white or purplish-red paint. Around 530BCE the red-figure technique was invented, in which the forms are reserved in the red of the clay against a black background; details here are painted rather than incised, allowing for more subtle effects. Black-figure more or less died out after about 500BCE, but red-figure continued to be used, its imagery moving away from the stylization of the Archaic Period to become ever more naturalistic. Around 400BCE there was a marked decline in Attic production, and throughout the fourth century the red-figure pottery of various regions of southern Italy colonized by the Greeks, notably Apulia, predominated. These goods make use of many of the same mythological themes as Attic ware, but they also reflect a strong local interest in the theater. After about 300BCE, figure scenes disappear entirely to make way for the largely plain wares of the Hellenistic Period.

ARTISTS IN SOCIETY

Artists dealing with material media were generally not as well respected as literary figures. The only artists to be considered worth writing about by ancient authors were sculptors (of free-standing works) and monumental painters—Pliny the Elder devotes a few chapters of his *Natural History* to listing the "masters" and their works, with occasional anecdotes about their lives. A few famous individuals moved in influential circles, such as the sculptor Pheidias, who was rumored to have procured free-born women for Perikles' enjoyment on the Parthenon building-site. Alexander the Great is supposed to have handed over his favorite mistress to Apelles, who had fallen in love with her while working on her nude portrait. Some artists were even able to make large fortunes, like the fourth-century BCE painter Zeuxis, who reputedly showed off his wealth by wearing a cloak with his name embroidered in gold thread.

However, even the greatest artists were liable to the prejudice against working with one's hands: "it does not necessarily follow that, if a work is pleasing because of its beauty, the man who made it is worthy of our serious attention" (Plutarch). As for the creators of relief sculpture, and of pottery and its painted decoration, they are scarcely even mentioned in ancient literature, despite the high skill evident in many surviving works. It would seem that they were regarded in much the same light as cobblers, blacksmiths, and other artisans.

A rare example of classical Greek wall-painting comes from the "Tomb of the Diver," a young man's grave dating from about 480BCE found at the Greek colony of Poseidonia (Paestum) in southern Italy. The inside of the travertine tomb-chamber is decorated with painted stucco; the four walls depict a symposium scene, a detail of which is shown here, while the ceiling shows a diver plunging into the sea.

GREECE AND THE CITY-STATE

Ancient Greece was fragmented into several hundred autonomous, and often warring, city-states.
This division arose in part from the landscape since much of the mainland is riven by mountains—
the population was dispersed over this terrain and throughout the 100 or more inhabited islands.

Two main forms of political organization evolved within this fragmented land, the *ethnos* (people) and the *polis* (city-state). An *ethnos* consisted of a population scattered over an extensive territory in villages loosely bound by political affiliations—this type of tribal organization was common in northern and western Greece (for example, the Thessalians, Epirots, and Aetolians) and in parts of the Peloponnese (Arcadians, Achaeans). A *polis* was an autonomous political community of people living in a territory that included both a rural area with villages and (usually) a more built-up urban center called an *astu* (town). The conventional translation of *polis* as "city-state" is more abstract than the Greek term, which refers as much to the people as to the place—the Greeks always spoke of "the Corinthians" or "the Thebans," rather than "Corinth" or "Thebes." The majority of *poleis* were quite small, with citizen populations in the hundreds rather than the thousands and territories of less than 40 square miles (100 sq km); the vast territories of Athens (1,000 square miles; 2,600 sq km) and Sparta (more than 2,000 square miles; 5,200 sq km) were exceptional.

The work of the philosopher Aristotle (384–322BCE) is an important source of information on the variety of systems by which the *poleis* were governed. In the second half of the fourth century BCE Aristotle's school undertook a huge research project to document the constitutions (*politeiai*) of 158 Greek states, covering the full range of possible systems: traditional monarchy, tyranny, aristocratic oligarchy, and democracy. On the basis of these case-studies, Aristotle's *Politics* sets out to establish what kind of constitution is most effective, both in theory and in practice—he is just as critical of the famed democracy of Athens as he is of other systems, and concludes that in fact the best form of government is one made up of a mixture of democratic and oligarchic elements. In addition to *Politics* itself, we have surviving fragments of the constitutions of more than eighty individual states, and a near-complete account of the *politeia* of the Athenians.

Despite its emblematic status, Athens was not always a democracy. There are mythological accounts of a succession of early kings, ending with Theseus, whom later writers credited with the unlikely act of devolving power to "the people." In the seventh century BCE this power was restricted to a number of aristocratic families, from among whom nine magistrates (archons) were chosen each year to preside over community decision-making, in conjunction with the Areopagus council made up of ex-archons. At the beginning of the sixth century BCE the archonship was opened up to a wider social group and a series of laws was passed, traditionally attributed to Solon, ensuring some basic rights for all citizens. This still oligarchic system was interrupted for much of the second half of the century by the tyranny of Peisistratos and his sons, although they left the archonship intact.

More representative government began to emerge with Kleisthenes's reforms in 508–507BCE, which reorganized the citizen body into ten tribes, each made up of a number of *demes* (villages) which were subdivided into *trittyes* ("thirds"). This broke up the territorial units on which the power of the old aristocratic families had been based, and it provided a new basis for political organization. By the middle of the fifth century BCE all the institutions of democracy proper were in place, crucially the assembly (*ekklesia*) and the council (*boule*). The council comprised 500 members, each of whom held office for one year; fifty members were selected by lot from each tribe. Each tribal group presided in turn for one month of the ten-month civic year. The council prepared measures for discussion and had executive responsibilities, but the ultimate decision-making power lay with the assembly of all citizens (see page 316), *the* characteristic feature of ancient democracy.

After Athens, the state about whose political organization we know most is Sparta—in addition to Aristotle's work, we have a complete *politeia* of the Spartans from the early fourth century BCE, attributed to Xenophon. Unusually, Sparta had a dual kingship, which was hereditary within the Agiad and Eurypontid families, some members of whom exercised a considerable degree of power, especially as military commanders. However, their power was tempered by the authority of the *gerousia*, a council of twenty-eight elders (*gerontes*) whose members had to be aged over sixty but were elected for life. In addition, a board of five magistrates (*ephors*) is supposed to have been instituted at some point in the Archaic Period with the express purpose of curbing the power of the kings; the ephorate was open to all citizens and elected on an annual basis. Finally, there was an assembly (*apella*) which elected people to the ephorate and *gerousia*, and voted on propositions prepared by these two bodies. This unique combination of dual kingship with oligarchic and democratic elements presided over a Sparta whose military supremacy remained unquestioned until 371BCE.

CITIZENS, WOMEN, AND SLAVES

The internal divisions of society provided a set of oppositions by which the Greeks defined themselves: citizen versus non-citizen, male versus female, slave versus free man. Yet, overriding these delineations, there developed a common Greek identity, which was accentuated by contact with non-Greeks.

Even in the most democratic of Greek states, the rule of "the people" was restricted to male citizens, which meant only a small proportion of the actual population. Criteria for citizenship were strict: at Athens, it was necessary to have a citizen father, and from 451 BCE the mother too had to belong to a citizen family. In a democratic state such as classical Athens the citizen's primary right and responsibility was participation in government (see page 315). Citizens also formed the core of any state's fighting force. Athenian full-time military service was compulsory for *ephebes*, citizen youths aged between eighteen and twenty, while for Spartans a strict regime of military training began with boys at the age of seven and extended throughout the citizen's life.

The citizen class of Athens contained a range of groups with differing wealth and social status, but the only socially respectable form of income was that derived from land. In his *Oikonomikos* ("Household Management") Xenophon paints the picture of a wealthy landowner living in Athens and riding out of the city each day to supervise his estate. Smaller-scale farmers would have lived and worked on their properties in

---

This 6th-century BCE terracotta model, found at Thebes in Boiotia, depicts four women kneading dough, their work enlivened by the music of a pipe or aulos *player (left). They could be the slaves of a wealthy household, or workers in a commercial bakery.*

• GREEKS AND BARBARIANS •

Over and above the internal divisions of society there developed a basic distinction between Greeks and non-Greeks. The Greek language was essential to the Greeks' self-definition in opposition to the "barbarians" (*barbaroi*), whose languages were deemed incomprehensible (and mocked for their "ba-ba-ba" sounds). Speaking Greek was a necessary qualification for initiation into the Eleusinian Mysteries and participation in the Olympic Games (see pages 305 and 353). The crucial impetus for the barbarian notion was provided by the Persian Wars of 490 and 480–479 BCE: in the aftermath of the successful repulsion of the Persians by a coalition of Greek states, Athens formed the Delian League, and justified her leadership of it by emphasizing the need for Greek unity against the common enemy.

The defining feature of the barbarian was said to be a lack of *logos*, not just "speech," but the ability to reason, and with it the ability to have political freedom—Aristotle went so far as to state that barbarians were able to endure despotic rule because they were "naturally more slavish in their disposition than the Greeks." All kinds of negative characteristics were said to be typical of the barbarian: a lack of self-control in regards to food, drink, and sex; a penchant for undiluted wine and emotional music; disregard for the rules of hospitality; cowardliness; and effeminacy of clothing, such as patterned fabrics and trousers (as worn by the Persian soldier being overcome by the Greek hoplite in the Attic red-figure cup, ca. 460BCE, shown below). All of these are referred to in Aeschylus's tragedy the *Persians*, performed in 472BCE, which began a long tradition of representing the Persians as barbarians par excellence. Various mythological characters were also recruited to represent barbarity, and sometimes these were explicitly equated with the Persians. The Trojan prince Paris, for example, appears in Persian costume in a vase-painting from the mid-fifth century BCE, underlining the barbarity of his abduction of Helen from his Spartan host Menelaos, and his use of the "coward's weapon," the bow. The ensuing Trojan War was also easy to equate with the Persian Wars, since both conflicts involved the combined of Greek states against an eastern threat. The "Greek-versus-barbarian" theme is strongly represented by the *metope*s in the sculptural program of the Parthenon, which (exceptionally) decorate all four sides of the building. While the gods fighting the giants (east) and the Trojan War (north) illustrate Greek civilization in general pitted against barbarity, the Amazons are overcome by the Athenians in particular, led by their legendary king Theseus (west), who also lends a hand against the centaurs (south).

the Attic countryside; poorer citizens without land could join the navy as oarsmen or practice a craft such as pottery or metalwork. Many commercial activities were in the hands of the *metic*s, free men from other states resident in Athens. *Metic*s were prohibited from owning land and had no political rights, but they were recognized as free men, were protected by the laws, paid taxes, and could be called on to serve in the army.

A number of leisure pursuits were especially associated with the established aristocratic families. Hunting for boar, deer, or hares was part of the education of wealthy Greek youths, as was physical exercise, with the best athletes training for the competitions held as part of local religious festivals or at the Panhellenic sanctuaries (see page 353). Young men exercised naked at the gymnasium (from *gymnos,* meaning "naked"), which led to its association with homosexual romance—the most desirable relationship for the Athenian aristocrat was one between a man in his twenties and a beautiful teenage boy. These partnerships were supposedly educational and conducted largely at the non-physical level, but there are a number of "courting" images, which make the sexual aspect of the pairing abundantly clear. Such relationships are discussed in Plato's *Symposium,* our most extensive account of the kind of highly formalized drinking party enjoyed by upper-class men.

THE ROLE OF WOMEN

The wives and daughters of male citizens were not citizens in their own right, as they had no political role, but they were protected by the law and had a number of religious privileges. In Athens the generally accepted

This Attic lekythos *(oil flask) was produced using the white-ground technique, which flourished in the period 470–400BCE and was especially popular for objects intended for burial with the dead. It presents the image of the ideal citizen wife: a woman seated in a domestic interior, with a basket of wool at her side. The label to the right of the woman's face reads* kale, *meaning "beautiful."*

ideal was for the women of the household to live a sequestered life, only emerging for the occasional religious festival or funeral. However, there is reason to believe that women visited each other in their homes, and women past child-bearing age seem to have had more freedom of movement. Women from poorer families almost certainly had to leave the house to perform daily tasks that in wealthier homes were delegated to slaves, such as fetching water and shopping, and some sold goods in the market. In prosperous households a woman's major role would have been in managing the domestic slaves, but women of all economic classes were expected to devote much of their time to childcare, since the bearing of citizen sons was a wife's most important duty.

A SLAVE'S LIFE

The life of all Greek citizens was predicated on the existence of slavery. The Spartans had a large population of helots, or state-owned serfs, who farmed the land; elsewhere, most slaves belonged to individual households. It is estimated that slaves, obtained through war, piracy, or direct trade with slavers among the barbarian peoples, made up twenty-five to thirty percent of the population of classical Athens. The daily life of many slaves was probably not very different from that of a poor citizen or *metic*—slave craftsmen often worked alongside free artisans, while female domestic slaves shared their mistresses' tasks—although much harsher conditions were endured by agricultural slaves and those who worked in the silver mines at Laurion. Not only slave women but young girls and boys were liable to fall victim to sexual exploitation. A slave's well-being was entirely at the owner's discretion, and legally a slave could only bear witness under torture. However, a more humane master might manumit a slave (to *metic* status) as a reward for good service, and some slaves who worked outside the household, for example as skilled craftsmen, were allowed to keep a proportion of their earnings, with which they might eventually buy their freedom.

THE GREEK DIASPORA

Despite their attitudes toward barbarians, in practice many Greeks found themselves living in close proximity to other cultures as a result of colonization. The settlers established Greek customs and built numerous temples in the colonies, but they were also influenced by the local peoples.

The earliest colony to be established by the Greeks was Pithecussae, on Ischia in the Bay of Naples, founded around 770BCE by settlers from the Euboian city of Chalkis. This was soon followed by further foundations at Cumae and Naples itself, and on Sicily, where some colonies even went on to found satellite colonies of their own—in the mid-eighth century BCE Leontini, for example, was founded by Naxos, itself recently founded by Chalkidians. Southern Italy and Sicily continued to be popular destinations for colonists in the seventh and early sixth centuries BCE, to the extent that the Romans later called the region *Magna Graecia* ("Greater Greece"), and Greek dialects may still be heard in some areas to this day. A few colonists ventured even further west, to Massilia (Marseilles) which was founded in about 600BCE by the people of Phokaia (Asia Minor), who were also responsible for colonies in Italy and Corsica. Others went north, settling in Chalkidiki, along the north coast of the Aegean, all around the Propontis, and the Black Sea. In the southeastern Mediterranean, the foundation of Cyrene is well documented. The settlements at Al Mina in Syria and Naukratis in the Nile Delta did not have the status of independent cities, but were important trading posts

(*emporia*) based on ports, where Greeks from various cities had economic and religious rights through the goodwill of existing local powers.

This dispersion of peoples had important consequences. The Greeks brought with them a "city way of life," but were in their turn influenced by the indigenous societies. The tensions within the relationships are often revealed by a foundation myth that explained how the newcomers came to be there. At Massilia, for instance, a visiting Phokaian is said to have been picked out at a banquet by the daughter of a local king to be her husband. Intermarriage between Greeks and locals must have been quite common, since the original colonizing parties do not usually seem to have included women. This localized two-way cultural influence would have had wider consequences as the colonies opened up trade routes. The new cities also had a capacity for innovation: at Lokri Epizephyri in southern Italy, Zaleukos is reputed to be the author of a written law-code produced in about 650BCE. Megara Hyblaea, on the east coast of Sicily, is one of the earliest examples of Greek town planning, with a regular street grid laid out around a central square (*agora*) in the later seventh century. Other Sicilian cities produced famous men of letters, such as the sixth-century BCE lyric poet Stesichoros from Himera, and the sophist Gorgias (ca. 485–380BCE) from Leontini.

"FROGS AROUND A POND"

By the fourth century BCE there were so many Greek colonies scattered around the Mediterranean that Plato described them as being "like frogs around a pond." The wealth of the early settlements in southern Italy and Sicily can be seen in their monuments, which include

The four-horse chariot and warriors here are a detail from the neck of the massive bronze bowl known as the "Vix Krater." It was made ca. 540BCE at Sparta, but was found in the grave of a Celtic princess in Burgundy, at a key point on the tin route from Britain to Marseilles. The bowl was probably a gift from Greek traders to the local chieftain.

◆ THE WINE-DARK SEA ◆

Many of the Greek city-states and their colonies were divided from one another by the sea, and so ships provided the best means of communication and trade—whoever had control over the sea bolstered their political power. The importance of the sea to the Greeks is reflected in marine motifs, which appear in art of all periods. They range from shells to sea creatures and stylized waves. In Homer the sea is said to be "wine-dark," a traditional description of the waters at dawn or sunset, or under the storm-clouds of a lowering sky.

some of the most impressive in the Greek world. The first temple of Hera at Poseidonia (Paestum), built around 550BCE, is notable for its size (nine columns by eighteen) and a series of forty *metopes* depicting the deeds of Herakles and other heroes. Selinunte (ancient Selinus) in southwestern Sicily boasts no fewer than seven temples, the oldest of which were decorated with striking archaic *metopes*, now in the museum in Palermo, which feature Europa being transported across the sea by Zeus, Perseus beheading Medusa, and Herakles carrying the Kerkopes.

Also in southern Sicily, Agrigento (ancient Akragas, or Latin Agrigentum) likewise has multiple temples, including the Temple of Concord. This was built in approximately 430BCE and owes its good state of preservation to its conversion into a Christian church in the sixth century CE—arches were cut through the inner walls of the temple, but otherwise it was incorporated more or less intact. The attribution of the temple to Concord is a modern one based on a Roman inscription found nearby—it is far more likely to have been dedicated to one of the major Olympian gods (see pages 324–335), as are the neighboring temples of Hera and Herakles.

THE INTELLECTUAL TRADITION

One of the defining features of ancient Greek civilization is its yearning for understanding. Thinkers such as Pythagoras, Socrates, and Archimedes made great strides in philosophy, mathematics, and science, and composers of epic and lyric poetry entertained an increasingly literate public.

The western colonies were associated with some of Greece's greatest thinkers—Akragas was the birthplace of the philosophers Anaxagoras (ca. 500–428BCE) and Empedocles (ca. 492–432BCE). Pythagoras of Samos emigrated to Croton in southern Italy in about 530BCE, where he made important discoveries in mathematics, astronomy, and music, and founded the Pythagorean sect which advocated a belief in the transmigration of souls. Parmenides (ca. 515–450BCE) founded his school at Elea, just south of Poseidonia (Paestum), where Zeno

(born ca. 490BCE) wrote his famous paradoxes. The earliest developments in rational thought, however, were in the Ionian cities of Asia Minor, beginning with the philosophers Thales (ca. 640–550BCE), Anaximander (died ca. 547BCE), and Anaximenes (fl. 546–525BCE) of Miletos, who laid the foundations for Greek geometry, astronomy, and cosmology, and wrote the first prose treaties, "On the Nature of Things," starting a long tradition of Greek natural philosophy. The ideas of the three Milesian philosophers were disseminated to the west via the poetry of Xenophanes of Colophon (ca. 570–475BCE), and later popularized by the itinerant lecturers known as the Sophists.

These philosophers are referred to today as the "Presocratics," reflecting the importance of Socrates (469–399BCE) himself. He never wrote down his ideas, but developed them through dialogues with his pupils at Athens, whom he taught to pursue the truth through rational enquiry. Socrates's philosophy is known to us especially through the writings of Plato (ca. 429–347BCE), who went on to develop his own ideas in such influential works as the *Republic*, and founded the Academy, the first of a number of philosophical schools at Athens. Aristotle of Stageira (384–322BCE) studied there, and later, after several years teaching the future Alexander the Great at the Macedonian court at Pella, established his own school at Athens, the Lyceum. Diogenes of Sinope (ca. 403–324BCE) came to Athens

Portraits of philosophers and other intellectuals were popular in the Hellenistic Period, usually combining a degree of realism with standard features expressive of their role. This portrait of Chrysippos, who was head of the Stoic school of philosophy from 232 until his death in 206BCE, contrasts the external decay of an ageing body with the inner vigor of the mind. This is a Roman-period copy, but the original was probably made in Chrysippos's lifetime.

around 362BCE, where he practiced a way of life which included the rejection of material possessions and all forms of culture. This extreme behavior earned his followers the nickname Cynics ("dog-like"). Zeno of Citium (335–263BCE) came to Athens in 313BCE. He taught in the Agora's Painted Stoa, whence the name Stoic for his school of philosophy. Epicurus of Samos (ca. 341–270BCE) established a secluded community of pupils at Athens around 306BCE, which was known as "the Garden."

Many of the philosophers propounded scientific theories, but only limited use was made of practical experimentation. In the field of medicine, the treatises attributed to Hippokrates of Kos (ca. 460–377BCE) are based on the methodical observation of symptoms, but Herophilos of Chalcedon (ca. 330–260BCE) and Erasistratos of Kios (ca. 315–240BCE) were the first known to have dissected human corpses for the study of anatomy. In the field of engineering, eminently practical experiments were carried out by Archimedes (ca. 287–212/211BCE), whose war-machines were used to defend his native Syracuse when it was besieged by the Romans in 213–211BCE, although the city eventually fell and Archimedes himself died during the siege.

STITCHERS OF SONG

The earliest Greek poetry was oral in form, and was recited directly to an audience, as evoked in Homer's *Odyssey* (ca. 700BCE), in which the *aoidos* (singer–poet) provides after-dinner entertainment in wealthy households. In Hesiod's epics (also ca. 700BCE), autobiographical passages show that the *aoidos* might travel great distances in order to perform at public occasions, and that competition between rival poets was expected. During the sixth century BCE it became common for itinerant *rhapsodes* ("stitchers of song") to compete in the recitation of Homer's poems and other traditional epics at religious festivals all over the Greek world.

Smaller-scale poems collectively known as "lyric" were also popular in the Archaic Period. These might be performed by the poet himself at a private dinner, to the accompaniment of the lyre, or by a chorus in the more public context of a festival. Much lyric was clearly composed to commission, such as Sappho's wedding songs or Pindar's odes for victorious athletes. Poets of the Classical Period continued to compete in public, especially in the media of tragedy and comedy, where both solo speech and choral song were in verse. Poets of the Hellenistic Period made use of traditional forms, such as that used in Apollonius of Rhodes' epic *Argonautica*, but many were now writing for a public who would read, rather than listen to, their work (see below). This is reflected, for example, in the self-conscious academicism of Callimachus, and the rise to popularity of the short, witty epigram.

THE ART OF WRITING

Greek philosophers, scientists, and poets all made use of writing. The art was already known to the Minoans and Mycenaeans, although they seem to have used it primarily for bureacratic rather than literary purposes. The Minoan syllabic script known as Linear A has yet to be decoded, but the Mycenaean Linear B was deciphered in 1952 by Michael Ventris and John Chadwick, who identified it as an early form of Greek. Use of Linear B disappeared with the collapse of the Mycenaean palaces, but the language it recorded continued to be spoken, and writing was re-introduced in the early eighth century BCE using an alphabetic script borrowed from the Phoenicians. At first this script was employed for simple tasks such as marking ownership, but it soon began to be used for recording all kinds of information which had formerly been transmitted orally.

Writing had a profound effect on Greek thought, allowing poetry to be composed and memorized in a completely different way—Homer's epics may have been written down as early as 700BCE—and facilitating the development of prose, which was to become the primary medium for such "rational" disciplines as philosophy and history.

CHILDREN OF CHAOS: TITANS AND OLYMPIANS

The Olympian gods were immortal; each was thought of as coming into existence at a specific point in mythological time. Hesiod's epic poem the Theogony *is a systematic account of the "births of the gods," and of the Greek "Succession Myth," which charts the establishment of the Olympians' rule.*

In the beginning, according to the *Theogony*, was Chaos, followed by Earth (Ge or Gaia), Eros, and Tartaros, the lowest part of the underworld. Earth gave birth to Heaven (Ouranos), to whom she then bore the twelve "Titans," as well as Ocean, the one-eyed Cyclopes, and the Hundred-Handed monsters Kottos, Briareos, and Gyges. Heaven hated his children and hid them away until one day Earth made a flint sickle, which the youngest of the Titans, Kronos ("the crooked-planning"), used to castrate his father; from the resulting blood which fell on Earth were born the giants and the Furies, while the genitals produced Aphrodite (see page 331). Kronos then lay with his Titan sister Rheia, who bore him Hestia, Demeter, Hera, Hades, and Poseidon, but, jealous of his position as king of the gods, Kronos swallowed each child as soon as it was

◆ OLYMPOS, SEAT OF THE GODS ◆

In poetry the home of the gods is consistently referred to as Olympos, but it is not entirely clear how this place was imagined. According to the *Iliad*, the gods have houses there, built by Hephaistos. The site seems to be a mountain, as it has "peaks" and "ridges" and is occasionally even "snowy." On the other hand, the *Odyssey* tells the story of Otos and Ephialtes, giant sons of Poseidon, who threatened to wage war on the gods by piling Mounts Ossa and Pelion on top of Olympos so that they might reach the heavens. This suggests that the gods' abode is somewhere above all these mountains in the sky.

When we look at the real Greece it is easy to see how the idea of the gods living on top of an inaccessibly high mountain might have arisen. A number of actual mountains are called Olympos—the Peloponnese alone has three. However, the best candidate for identification as the home of the gods is the Mount Olympos (seen here) on the border between Thessaly and Macedonia.

born. When a sixth child, Zeus, was due, Rheia sought help from her mother Earth, who hid the baby in a remote cave on Mount Dikte in Crete and gave Kronos instead a stone wrapped in swaddling clothes. Zeus grew up and came out of hiding to overthrow his father, who was induced to vomit up Zeus's five swallowed siblings.

Kronos's Titan brothers went to war against Zeus and his siblings, whose home was Mount Olympos. After ten years of a war known as the Titanomachy ("battle of the Titans"), the Olympians were victorious, and the Titans were for ever imprisoned in Tartaros. Hesiod presents this victory as establishing Zeus's position as king of the gods, although Homer and others refer to a drawing of lots in which Zeus received power over the heavens, Poseidon over the sea, and Hades over the underworld. Zeus's authority was later challenged by the monstrous Typhoeus or Typhon, youngest son of Earth; he too was overcome and consigned to Tartaros. The Olympians were eventually able to multiply in peace for a while, before their supremacy was challenged by the giants; according to some, the gods only won the battle with the help of Herakles. The Gigantomachy (the war against the giants) is not mentioned in epic poetry, but it appears in art from the mid-sixth century BCE onward, and is an especially popular subject for archaic architectural sculpture, where it symbolizes the triumph of Olympian Order over the forces of Chaos.

THE KING AND QUEEN OF HEAVEN

Zeus was the supreme god of Olympos and possessed many admirable attributes. However, his dalliances with other goddesses and mortal women infuriated his consort Hera, who rarely passed up an opportunity to wreak vengeance on his lovers and the children he conceived with them.

A number of standard epithets for Zeus (Roman Jupiter) exist in epic poetry, such as "the far-seeing Olympian;" others reflect his status ("lord," "king"), or his origins as a weather god ("loud-thundering," "rainy"). However, Zeus is most frequently seen in roles reflecting his concern for human justice, hospitality, and fair treatment for the vulnerable. He was widely worshipped as Zeus Xenios, "of strangers," and Hikesios, "of suppliants." As Agoraios ("of the market-place") he oversaw public gatherings and fair commerce, and as Herkeios ("of enclosures") and Ktesios ("of property") he protected individual households. Although he had no major city-center temples, great importance was attached to his main interstate sanctuaries: in the Peloponnese, where the Panhellenic Games were celebrated in his honor at Olympia and Nemea; and the oracular shrine at Dodona in northwestern Greece.

Zeus's position as strongest of the gods was reflected in his sexual potency, a prolific begetting of offspring earning him the title "father of gods and men." After establishing his rule on Olympos, he took a succession of goddesses as his wives: Metis ("Mind;" see page 332); Themis ("Order"), mother of the Seasons and the Fates; the sea-nymph Eurynome, mother of the Graces; his sister Demeter; Mnemosyne ("Memory"), mother of the Muses; and Leto. His sister Hera eventually became his official consort, by whom he had Ares (god of war), Eileithyia (goddess of childbirth), and Hebe ("Youth").

THE VENGEFUL QUEEN

Hera (the Roman Juno) was portrayed from the *Iliad* onward as constantly ready to cause trouble for her husband's lovers and their offspring. Notably, she prompted Semele to request that Zeus appear to her in

At Athens and elsewhere there was a "wedding month," when human marriages were celebrated alongside the "holy wedding" of Zeus and Hera. Here, on the east frieze of the Parthenon, Hera and Zeus face one another, and Hera holds back her veil to symbolize her status as his wife.

all his divine glory, as a consequence of which Semele was burnt to death. Hera also relentlessly persecuted Alkmene's son Herakles. Although Hera did not herself have any extra-marital affairs, according to Hesiod she conceived Hephaistos without Zeus's assistance.

During the Trojan War Hera and Athene sided with the Greeks in revenge against the Trojan prince Paris, who had chosen Aphrodite as the fairest of the goddesses. At one point in the *Iliad*, Hera enlists the help of

The second temple of Hera at Poseidonia (Paestum), a Greek colony in southern Italy, was built ca. 470–460BCE. The interior columns of the inner chamber can be clearly seen here, along with an unusually well-preserved upper colonnade.

Aphrodite and the god Sleep in an elaborate seduction scheme to distract Zeus's attention from the battlefield while the Greeks gain the upper hand. This anti-Trojan bias continued in Hera's persecution of Aeneas during his long voyage to Italy, as related in Virgil's *Aeneid*.

Despite her rather negative portrayal in myth, Hera was widely worshipped alongside Zeus as a patron of marriage, and in her own right she was the dedicant of some of the oldest and most important temples in Greece. The first of several temples at Hera's sanctuary on Samos may have been built as early as ca. 800BCE, while the mid-sixth-century one was reputedly the largest of its day. At Perachora (on the gulf of Corinth) Hera was worshipped from the eighth century onward in two separate temples, as Akraia ("of the headland") and Limenia ("of the harbor"). At Olympia, Hera's late seventh-century temple is considerably older than that of Zeus, and a quadrennial festival was held in her honor, organized by women and with races for girls. The "Argive Heraion," between Argos and Mycenae, was established in the eighth century, but in about 420–410BCE it was equipped with a new temple which housed a magnificent gold-and-ivory cult statue by the famous Argive sculptor Polykleitos.

THE GODS OF OLYMPOS

Zeus and Hera were not the only strong characters in the Greek pantheon. Mighty gods and goddesses such as Poseidon, lord of the seas, and "arrow-pouring" Artemis each had clearly defined attributes and domains, and each was worshipped in their own specially dedicated temples and sanctuaries.

Repeated mention of Poseidon in the Linear B tablets (see page 323) suggests that he was already important in Mycenaean times, and his association with the sea gave him a special significance for the sea-faring Greeks; the Romans identified him with Neptunus, the god of water. Poseidon's official consort was the sea-nymph Amphitrite, by whom he had the merman Triton and other watery offspring, but, like Zeus, Poseidon had many children as a result of amorous affairs. A strikingly high proportion of these are malign, such as the brigands Skiron, Sinis, and Kerkyon who haunted the Saronic Gulf. Odysseus's blinding of his son Polyphemos was punished by years of storm-tossed wanderings at sea, a story which demonstrates Poseidon's dangerous powers. Control over the terrors of the deep is also apparent in the myths of Hesione and Andromeda, both rescued only at the last minute from Poseidon's sea-monsters. Poseidon's power over the sea was matched by an equally terrifying power as god of earthquakes, reflected in his epic epithet Ennosigaios ("Earth-shaker"), and an association with strong land animals. He was sometimes worshipped as Hippios ("of horses"); it was in the form of a horse that he mated with his sister Demeter, begetting the divine horse Areion; he also gave divinely swift horses to his lover Pelops. Poseidon sent a magnificent white bull from the sea as a gift to king Minos, but when Minos failed to sacrifice it, the god drove Minos's queen Pasiphae mad with desire for the animal, as a result of which the minotaur was born.

In Homer the Greeks sacrificed to Poseidon on the seashore, and the god's sanctuaries were often within sight of the sea. The Spartans had a sanctuary of Poseidon at Tainaron (modern Cape Matapan) on the southernmost tip of the Peloponnese, while the Athenians had a sanctuary at Cape Sounion, Attica's most southerly headland (see illustration, page 302). Poseidon was also worshipped in Athens, despite having lost the competition for the city's patronage (see page 333); on the Akropolis part of the Erechtheion was sacred to him, and the name of the month Posidea implies the existence of an ancient festival in his honor. In a contest for the patronage of Corinth he was more successful: under the Hundred-Handed Briareos's arbitration, the sun-god Helios was awarded the citadel of Upper Corinth and Poseidon took possession of the Isthmos. The sanctuary at the Isthmos hosted local worship from an early date, but in about 582BCE the Corinthians founded the biennial Panhellenic festival, which included the Isthmian Games (see page 353).

POWERS OF EARTH AND UNDERWORLD

Zeus's brother Hades ruled over the underworld (also known as Hades) with his consort Persephone (Roman Proserpina). Both Greeks and Romans called him Pluto, "the Wealthy," in reference to the riches within the earth, and this connection is articulated in his major myth. After Hades abducted Persephone to his home, her mother Demeter (Roman Ceres), goddess of grain, searched tirelessly for her, and while she grieved the earth was barren (see page 305). Eventually Zeus ordered Hades to give Persephone back, but Hades managed to achieve a settlement by which she should spend part of the year with him and part with her mother, her time in the underworld coinciding with the winter months.

Images of the underworld are especially popular on South Italian vases, such as this monumental krater *of ca. 330BCE. Various famous inhabitants of Hades' realm are represented, but at the center (shown in this detail) Hades himself is enthroned in his palace with Persephone, who is shown crowned as his queen and holding her trademark torch.*

The geography of the underworld was not precisely defined by ancient writers, but it was always described as a cold and sunless place, with five rivers: the Styx (the Hateful); the Acheron (River of Woe); the Kokytos (River of Wailing); Phlegethon (River of Flame); and Lethe (River of Forgetfulness). The entrance to Hades was guarded by the monstrous dog Kerberos, variously envisaged as having two, three, or even fifty heads. Within the underworld, the Elysian Fields offered a few blessed mortals an afterlife of ease, while a number of famous wrongdoers suffered eternal punishments in the depths of Tartaros, but the majority of the dead led an insubstantial existence in-between.

Three judges of the dead are sometimes mentioned, Aiakos and the brothers Rhadamanthys and Minos, all of whom had a reputation for justice during their lives. Harsh punishments were meted out by the Furies (Erinyes), offspring of Heaven's castration (see page 324) and best known for their pursuit of Orestes. Like Persephone, they are often represented carrying torches.

GUARDIANS OF THE FLAMES

Zeus's eldest sister Hestia plays a minor role in myth and is only rarely depicted in art, owing to her close association with the immovable "hearth" (*hestia*)—no other major deity has such a clearly defined sphere of influence. Poseidon and Apollo once vied for Hestia's love, but she "... swore a great oath, which has indeed been fulfilled, touching the head of aegis-bearing Zeus, that she would remain a maiden all her days, noblest of goddesses. So father Zeus gave to her a fine honor instead of marriage, and she has her seat in the middle of the house, taking the best portion" (*Homeric Hymn to Aphrodite*). Hestia was indeed worshipped in every household, where small offerings of food and drink would be made to her each day. New members of the family were welcomed with rituals such as the *amphidromia*, in which a five-day-old baby would be "run around" the hearth to signify his or her acceptance into the family. Although she never attained the prominence outside the home of her Roman equivalent Vesta, Hestia was honored at the public hearth which each city maintained in a central temple or civic building, such as the Prytaneion in the Athenian Agora.

Also closely associated with fire is Hera's son Hephaistos (the Roman Vulcan). On his birth, Hera, disgusted by his deformed foot, threw him out of Olympos. He was rescued by the sea-nymph Thetis, and later took revenge on his mother

Praxiteles's sculpture of Aphrodite was made for the goddess's sanctuary at Knidos ca. 350BCE, and was the first full-scale female nude in Greek sculpture. We only have Roman copies to judge it by—often incomplete, like this one in the Louvre—but the original prompted ancient writers to lavish praise upon it for its outstanding beauty.

by making her a golden throne with invisible chains. He refused to release her from these fetters until Dionysos made him drunk and brought him up to Olympos on a mule, a scene often depicted in Attic vase-painting. Hephaistos was flung from the heavens a second time by Zeus, for taking Hera's side against him, but rescued by the people of Lemnos; in classical times the island's principal town was called Hephaistia and an ancient fire festival was held there. In the *Iliad* and Hesiod Hephaistos is married to one of the Graces, but in the *Odyssey* he is the unlikely husband of Aphrodite herself. As the archetypal master-craftsman he supplied all the gods' practical needs, and he is present in any story involving craftsmanship: he fashioned the first woman Pandora; assisted at Athene's birth; cast magnificent new armor for Achilles at Thetis's request; and directed the Cyclopes in his forge beneath Mount Etna in Sicily.

Apart from Lemnos, Hephaistos's only major place of worship was Athens, due to the curious myth in which he tried to rape Athene (see page 333–334). Both deities were worshipped at Hephaistos's temple in the Agora, and the Chalkeia ("copper festival") was celebrated in honor of them both. Hephaistos also had a festival of his own, the Hephaisteia, which included a torch race.

THE SEA-BORN GODDESS OF LOVE

Aphrodite (Roman Venus) was the goddess of love and fertility, who wielded irresistible power over all living creatures and even the gods. According to Homer, the goddess was the daughter of Zeus and Dione, who was either a Titan or a sea-nymph and was worshipped alongside Zeus as Dodona. Hesiod's *Theogony*, however, includes the bizarre story of Aphrodite's birth from Heaven's severed genitals: "Kronos cast these from the land into the surging sea, and so they were borne over the main for a long time, and around them arose a white foam from the immortal flesh, and in it grew a maiden." The waves carried Aphrodite to the island of Kythereia and then to Cyprus, where she was greeted by Eros (Love) and Himeros (Desire) and escorted to the assembly of the gods. Aphrodite's name was thought to derive from the foam (*aphros*) in this story—she was also often referred to as Kythereia, Kypris, or Paphia, and her most ancient sanctuaries were on Cyprus.

In the *Odyssey*, Aphrodite is officially married to Hephaistos, but her regular lover is the war god Ares. Hephaistos gained revenge by catching the pair *in flagrante* by means of a magical invisible net, then calling in the rest of the gods to laugh at their humiliation. Aphrodite nonetheless had several children by Ares, including Eros and Harmonia, who became Kadmos's queen at Thebes. By either Poseidon or the Argonaut Boutes, Aphrodite also gave birth to Eryx, who founded her sanctuary in his eponymous city (modern Erice) in western Sicily. The goddess had another affair with the mortal Anchises, whom she seduced when he was away tending his flocks on Mount Ida outside Troy, and she bore him Aeneas. Throughout the Trojan War she supported the Trojan side, for Aeneas's sake and because of Paris's judgment in her favor. Aphrodite's other great passion was for Adonis, the beautiful youth she shared with Persephone until he was gored to death by a boar; later writers make her the mother of the fertility god Priapos by Dionysos, and of the original hermaphrodite (Hermaphroditos) by Hermes.

The public worship of Aphrodite was sometimes connected with city affairs, as in Athens, where she had the cult title Pandemos ("of all the people"). She was often associated with prostitutes, as in Corinth, where her sanctuary was renowned for its "hospitable young ladies, servants of Persuasion" (Pindar), as many as a thousand of whom were dedicated to Aphrodite's work. She was also worshipped throughout the Greek world in connection with marriage, and at an even more private level by individuals, as beautifully evoked in Sappho's *Hymn to Aphrodite*.

ATHENE THE WISE

Like the virgin goddesses Hestia and Artemis (see page 335), Athene (Roman Minerva) was immune to the

power of Aphrodite. Athene's wisdom is explained by her birth story: Zeus married Metis ("Mind") and she duly became pregnant but, on discovering that his wife was destined one day to bear a son greater than his father, Zeus swallowed her. When the child came to term, Hephaistos split open Zeus's head and Athene emerged: "Awe seized all the immortals as they watched; but she sprang from the immortal head and stood before aegis-bearing Zeus, shaking a sharp spear; and great Olympos reeled terribly at the strength of the grey-eyed one; the earth around groaned fearfully; and the sea was moved, stirred up with dark waves ... ." (*Homeric Hymn to Athene*).

This image reflects the Athene of Greek art, the war-goddess recognizable by her helmet, spear, and snake-fringed aegis. However, in addition to her role as a warrior, Athene presided over civilized crafts, especially women's wool-working, but also metalwork and carpentry; she invented the chariot and the bridle, and helped in the building of the first ship and the Trojan Horse. She was patron of various heroes, especially Odysseus, Herakles, and Theseus, and she was a strong supporter of the Greeks in the Trojan War. Her most common epithets were *glaukopis*, "grey" or "flashing-eyed," and Pallas, perhaps referring to her slaying of the giant Pallas during the Gigantomachy. The "little Pallas" (Palladion)

• THE PARTHENON •

Athene's most famous temple—shown, right, dominating the Athenian Akropolis—celebrated her status as a virgin (*parthenos*) in its very name, the Parthenon. After the Persian sack of 480BCE the Akropolis had been left in ruins, but in the 440s' Perikles, the city's foremost general and political leader, instigated a grand program of rebuilding on the Akropolis. The Parthenon, which was constructed between 447 and 438, was the first project to be completed at the site.

The Parthenon was the biggest temple on the Greek mainland, and its purpose was to provide a grand home for Pheidias's new statue of Athene Parthenos. An exceptional quantity of architectural sculpture adorned the building's exterior, all celebrating the goddess in some way. The pediment at the east end, over the entrance, depicted Athene's birth. The west pediment, of which only fragments survive, portrayed her competition with Poseidon.

The frieze that ran around the inside of the colonnade represented a cavalcade of youths on horseback. The riders were accompanying a procession of people on foot, each of whom was shown leading sacrificial animals, carrying water, or playing musical instruments. At the east end of the temple the procession met a gathering of seated gods, in the midst of whom a group of mortals handled a folded cloth. Interpretations vary, but the frieze has traditionally been identified with the Panathenaic procession, culminating in the presentation of the new robe to Athene.

The goddess's civilizing influence can even be seen in the "Greek-versus-barbarian" theme of the *metope*s (see page 317); the Gigantomachy scenes at the east end echo the scenes which were said to be woven into Athene's robe, depicting "her exploits with Zeus against the giants."

was the name of Athene's statue that guaranteed Troy's safety until it was stolen by the Greeks.

Athene was widely worshipped as Polias or Poliouchos ("of the city" or "city-holding"), and the fortified centers of many cities housed a temple to her. On the Spartan akropolis she was Chalkioikos ("of the bronze house"), because her temple was decorated with bronze reliefs, while at Argos she was Oxyderkes ("far-seeing"). But she is especially associated with Athens, the city whose name she shares, and their close relationship is elaborated in two major local myths. In the reign of Athens's first king Kekrops, Athene competed with Poseidon for patronage of the city: he offered salt water, but her gift of the olive was preferred. Ever afterward a "sea" and a sacred olive tree were maintained in the Erechtheion (see page 351), which also housed the ancient wooden statue of Athene Polias, recipient of the robe (*peplos*) presented at the annual Panathenaia festival.

Hephaistos's attempted rape of Athene also occurred in the reign of Kekrops: as Athene fled his embraces, Hephaistos's sperm fell on her thigh, which she wiped off in disgust so that it fell to Earth. In due course Earth produced the baby Erichthonios (sometimes called by the name of his grandson Erechtheus), whom Athene took to raise, and he too later became king of Athens.

Thus the myth makes it possible for Athene to be the mother of the Athenian people while retaining her prized virginity.

APOLLO, LORD OF LIGHT

Like Athene, Apollo was seen as a civilizing power, the god of prophecy and purification, patron of music, and guardian of flocks. As patron of music he was sometimes called "leader of the Muses," and often appears in the company of these goddesses. His most common epithet was Phoibos ("bright, radiant") and from the fifth century BCE he was identified with the sun god Helios. Apollo was also sometimes identified with Paian, god of healing, but in the *Iliad* he is primarily "the far-shooter" and "lord of the silver bow," whose arrows bring plague on the Greeks for dishonoring his priest: "Phoibos Apollo came down along the peaks of Olympos, angered in his heart, carrying the bow and close-covered quiver on his shoulders; the arrows clanged against the shoulders of the angry god as he moved; and he came down like the night."

Apollo's major sanctuary at Delos, at the center of the Cyclades, was closely linked to the story of his birth, as recounted in the *Homeric Hymn to Apollo*. When Leto was pregnant with Apollo and Artemis by Zeus, fear of Hera's wrath meant that no land would give her shelter, until she reached the tiny island of Delos, which was influenced by the offer of the riches which Apollo's sanctuary would bring. Jealous, as ever, of her husband's infidelity, Hera kept the birth-goddess Eileithyia away for nine days, but on the tenth Leto cast her arms around a palm tree and gave birth to Apollo, who was fed on nectar and ambrosia by Themis. As soon as he tasted the divine food, he precociously announced his future roles: "The kithara will be dear to me, and the curved bow, and I shall proclaim to men the unfailing will of Zeus."

♦ ARTEMIS IN THE EAST ♦

Artemis was commonly worshipped in the Greek cities along the Asia Minor coast, but also by their non-Greek neighbors in Lydia and Lykia. The Lydian capital Sardis lay in the Hermos valley (in what is now western Turkey), near the junction of routes from the coastal cities of Smyrna and Ephesos to inland Anatolia. This strategic position led to the later adoption of Sardis as one of the major cities of the Seleucid dynasty (see page 309). Under Seleucid rule, Sardis became fully Hellenized, and in the early third century BCE the temple of Artemis was built. At eight columns wide and twenty long, the construction was on a grand scale. The colossal columns were as much as 6 feet, 6 inches (2m) in diameter and nearly 59 feet (18m) high, and were topped with particularly ornate Ionic capitals.

The Sardis temple was also known as the temple of Kybele, the Asiatic mother-goddess with whom Artemis seems to have been identified at Ephesos, where her cult statue was covered in what have been variously interpreted as breasts, eggs, or even bull's testicles—all denoting fertility. The temple at Sardis may have been designed in emulation of Artemis's temple at Ephesos, which had been rebuilt by a team including the eminent sculptor Skopas after the original burnt down in 356BCE. The original (ca. 560–550BCE), was one of the seven wonders of the ancient world, partly financed by the famously rich Lydian king Croesus. The fourth-century BCE replacement was on an even larger scale, around 230 feet (70m) wide by 440 feet (135m) long and surrounded by more than 100 columns.

The second half of the *Hymn* tells the story of the foundation of Apollo's great oracular sanctuary at Delphi (see pages 354–355). Apollo had no regular consort, but he seduced a number of mortal women, often passing on his skills to their children: Koronis bore him the healing-god Asklepios; Evadne the seer Iamos; and Cyrene a son Aristaios, skilled in healing and prophecy. With other lovers Apollo was less fortunate: Daphne turned into a laurel tree to escape him; the Trojan princess Kassandra accepted his gift of prophecy but then rejected his advances, and so was doomed never to be believed; the youth Hyakinthos was tragically killed by Apollo's own discus.

Worship of Apollo was common in the Greek world. He had a series of oracles along the coast of Asia Minor, notably at Klaros and Didyma; the latter was housed in a small shrine within a spectacularly large temple. In the Peloponnese, Apollo was particularly important to the Spartans, who had an ancient Apollo sanctuary at Amyklai and celebrated two festivals in his honor, the Karneia and the Hyakinthia. In neighboring Arkadia, Apollo was fêted as Epikourios ("protector") in his temple located in the mountains at Bassae. In Athens he was worshipped especially as Patroos ("ancestral") Apollo, and at two important festivals: the Apatouria, during which young men were formally admitted to the citizen body after cutting their hair for Apollo, and the Thargelia, when "scapegoats" were expelled to purify the city and musical competitions were held.

ARTEMIS THE WRATHFUL

Artemis (Roman Diana), the virgin goddess of hunting, was Apollo's twin sister who shared his ability with the bow. Sometimes the two acted in concert, especially in defense of their mother Leto's honor: they shot dead the giant Tityos when he tried to rape her, and when Niobe boasted that she was a more prolific mother, the twins promptly killed all of her twelve (or more) children. This close family connection was mirrored in cult—Artemis and Leto were often worshipped within

Apollo's sanctuaries. Apollo's identification with the sun was mirrored by Artemis's association with the moon (personified as the goddess Selene).

Homer's *Odyssey* provides the definitive portrait of "arrow-pouring Artemis," who "goes across the mountains, over high Taygetos or Erymanthos, delighting in boars and swift-running deer, and with her play the country-haunting nymphs, daughters of aegis-bearing Zeus." Later writers identified Artemis with the Near Eastern mother-goddess Kybele, as well as the huntress goddesses Britomartis of Crete and Aphaia of Aigina. The huntress is also protector of wild things; association with the wild was marked at Patrai in the Peloponnese, where the annual festival of Artemis Laphria included an exceptional sacrifice of wild animals and birds, which were driven onto a massive altar and burned alive.

Young humans as well as animals came under Artemis's protection, and she was connected with rites of passage for both girls and boys. At Sparta she was identified with a local goddess Orthia, from whose altar a group of boys would snatch cheeses while others tried to prevent them by wielding whips; it was said that the ancient cult statue enjoyed watching the blood thus spilt, and that the ritual was a "civilized" alternative to human sacrifice. At Artemis's sanctuary at Brauron, in rural Attica, young girls from select Athenian families "played the bear for Artemis," in a ritual which involved dancing and running races. Within the sanctuary there was also a shrine of the heroine Iphigeneia, where the clothes of women who had died in childbirth were dedicated. Artemis's strong connection with childbirth (she was sometimes even identified with Eileithyia) may in fact be a vestige of her older character as a mother-goddess, but it was explained in antiquity as being due to her anger at loss of virginity. All over Greece girls made placatory sacrifices to Artemis when they were about to leave her sphere for Aphrodite's realm of marriage, and further prayers and offerings were made to dissuade the goddess from inflicting labor pains or even graver dangers during childbirth.

THE HEROIC IDEAL

In addition to the many Olympian gods and goddesses, the Greeks revered a host of heroes, most of whom were believed to have lived in the distant past. Some Greek heroes, such as the Spartan king Leonidas and the Macedonian Alexander the Great, were real historical figures.

In the myth of the "Races of Man" from Hesiod's poem the *Works and Days*, an age of heroes is fitted into an account of humankind's creation and subsequent decline. The tale recounts that in the beginning the gods created humans as a golden race who lived an idyllic life with all their needs met by a fruitful land. After this came a silver race, who were foolish and neglected to worship the gods, so Zeus replaced them with a third race of bronze, who were so warlike that they destroyed themselves. The only race not characterized by a metal is the fourth, "a more righteous and noble one, the godlike race of hero-men who are called demigods, our predecessors on the boundless Earth." After the heroes came the current race of iron.

In fact, not all of Hesiod's race of heroes were "demigods," as he called them (meaning that they were of mixed divine and mortal parentage)—many more were simply born to noble families. All were great warriors, however, and ordinary Greeks aspired to the ideal that the heroes represented of *arete*—literally "manliness," but more broadly, "virtue," "excellence," and "courage."

Homer's *Iliad* played an important part in shaping the image of the warrior-hero, presenting as it does not only the conflict between the leaders of the Greek cities and a worthy enemy in the form of the noble Trojans, but also the great clash of heroic personalities between Agamemnon, nominal leader of the Greeks, and Achilles, "the best of the Achaeans." Achilles is semi-divine, born of the mortal Peleus and the sea-nymph Thetis, but Thetis's attempts to render him immortal have failed and he is fated either to live a long but obscure life at home, or to die young at Troy with everlasting glory (*kleos*). The terrible "wrath of Achilles," which is the *Iliad*'s stated subject, is caused by Agamemnon having taken away the hero's war-prize, Briseis, a great insult to Achilles's honor. Larger-than-life in all things, Achilles steadfastly refuses to rejoin the fighting, despite all offers of compensation, until he is finally roused by the death of his beloved companion Patroklos at Hektor's hands. Stricken with grief, he rampages across the battlefield, slaughtering Trojans "as furious fire rages through the deep valleys of a dry mountain, and the deep forest burns," until he finally avenges Patroklos by killing Hektor.

Other characters in the *Iliad* act as a foil to Achilles's rather excessive brand of heroism. The Trojan leader Hektor is sympathetically portrayed as a family man much loved by his people, although still a formidable warrior, as is his second-in-command Aeneas. Decidedly un-heroic is the Trojan prince Paris, who started the war by breaching all the laws of respect and hospitality when he abducted his host Menelaos's wife Helen from Sparta. Paris is described as beautiful but lacking strength and courage, and his weapon is the coward's bow, with which, ironically, he eventually kills the great Achilles.

WARRIORS OF HISTORY

The Homeric heroes remained the ultimate warrior role models throughout antiquity, and many were actively worshipped in the states in which they were supposedly born—for example, there was a sanctuary of Menelaos at Sparta, and the people of Salamis performed rituals for Ajax—but there were also some historical embodiments of the heroic ideal. The Spartans in general had a reputation for military prowess and courageous refusal to surrender, summed up in the collection of *Spartan Sayings* preserved among the works of Plutarch. These sayings included a Spartan woman's injunction to her son, about to set off to war, to "come back with your shield or on it"—in other words, return either victorious or dead.

The epitome of Spartan bravery, however, was the famous last stand made by King Leonidas and his 300 companions when they defended the pass at Thermopylae against the Persians in 480BCE: "Here they defended themselves with swords, if they happened still to have them, and with their hands and teeth, until the barbarians overwhelmed them ... ." (Herodotus). Some forty years later what were supposedly Leonidas's remains were brought back to Sparta and a cult was instituted in his honor. During the Peloponnesian War, the Spartan general Brasidas was also given heroic honors after his death, not in his home town but at Amphipolis, the city he had "liberated" from Athenian domination.

For the Athenians, the high point of patriotic bravery was marked by the battle of Marathon in 490BCE. It is still possible to visit the enormous tumulus which is the tomb of the 192 Athenians who died at Marathon—all were given the exceptional privilege of being buried on the battlefield in recognition of their courage. Also held in high esteem were the so-called Tyrranicides, Harmodios and Aristogeiton, who assassinated Peisistratos's son Hipparchos in 514BCE. Their act did not, in fact, end the Peisistratid tyranny, and Kleisthenes's reforms (see page 315) were in practice a great deal more significant for the development of democracy, but it was symbolically powerful. The descendants of the Tyrannicides were granted free meals at state expense in perpetuity, and a statue of the pair was erected in the Athenian Agora. When this piece was looted by the Persians in 480–479BCE it was immediately replaced with a new statue, which was much copied by later admirers of the democratic ideal.

In the fourth century BCE, the Macedonian Alexander the Great, a charismatic military leader himself, took a special interest in the heroes of myth. His family claimed descent from Herakles—a hundred years earlier Alexander I had appealed to this lineage in defense of his Greek nationality and consequent right to participate in the Olympic Games. Alexander the Great had himself represented on coins wearing the hero's trademark lionskin, dedicated altars to him, and even gave the name "Herakles" to his illegitimate son by Barsine, daughter of the Persian satrap Artabazos. According to various accounts of his life, Alexander took his annotated copy of the *Iliad* with him on campaign, and when he first crossed into Asia Minor he paid his respects at Troy, where he poured libations to the heroes of the Greek army. He is supposed to have run a race beside the stele which marked the grave of Achilles, and remarked on Achilles's good fortune in having had such a great poet as Homer render his deeds immortal.

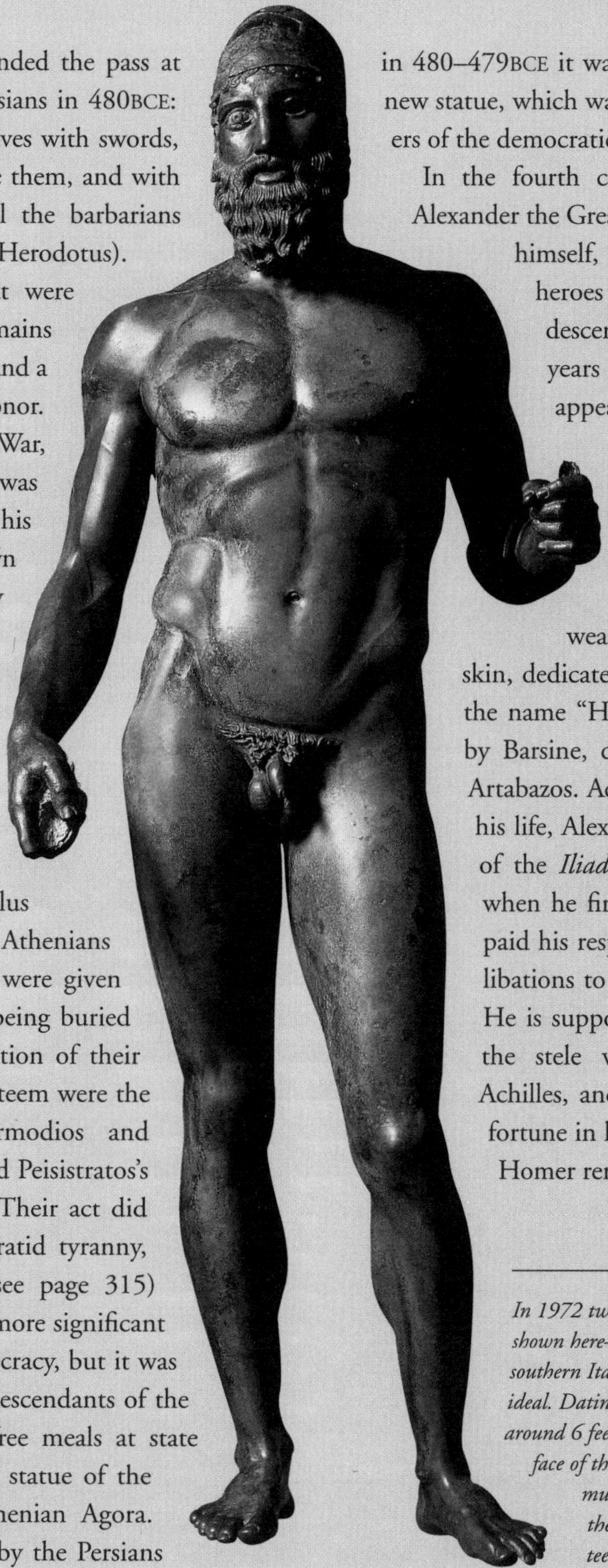

In 1972 two bronze statues—one of which is shown here—were found in the sea near Riace, southern Italy. Both perfectly embody the warrior ideal. Dating from ca. 460–450BCE, each stands around 6 feet, 6 inches (2m) tall. The reflective surface of the bronze shows off the rippling musculature of the statues' heroic nudity; their lips and nipples are copper, their teeth silver, and their eyes are inlaid.

THE TROJAN WAR

The story of the Trojan War extends well beyond the few days recounted in the Iliad. *The reasons for the conflict, the early years of the siege, the actual destruction of Troy, and the Greek heroes' journeys home were recounted in other poems of the "Epic Cycle," and provided much material for Attic tragedy.*

The tale begins when the goddess Eris ("strife" personified) throws into a wedding crowd an apple inscribed "For the fairest," a title hotly contested by Hera, Athene, and Aphrodite. Zeus delegates the task of adjudication to the Trojan prince Paris; Aphrodite then promises him the most beautiful woman in the world—Helen, wife of Menelaos—and thereby wins the contest. When he takes Helen from Sparta, Paris inadvertently activates a vow sworn by all of Helen's suitors, who had agreed to come to the aid of whichever man should win her hand in marriage. In mustering the Greek princes, Menelaos is helped by his brother Agamemnon, who becomes the leader of the expedition against Troy.

The Greeks spend ten years besieging "many-towered Troy," as Homer calls it; the *Iliad* is set in the final year of the siege. After the death of the Trojan leader Hektor, and a brief truce for his burial, war resumes, with a number of allies coming to the Trojans' aid: Achilles slays the Amazon queen Penthesileia and the Ethiopian prince Memnon, son of Eos, but then he himself is killed by Paris and Apollo. The Greeks enlist the help of Achilles's son Neoptolemos, and Philoktetes, who has the mighty bow once owned by Herakles, but Troy falls in the end only because of the trickery involving the wooden horse (see illustration, right). In the course of the sack, Hektor's son Astyanax is flung to his death from the city walls. Just the Trojan hero Aeneas, son of Aphrodite, and one or two companions escape, but the Greeks also suffer heavy losses, and few of them return home unscathed.

THE WANDERINGS OF ODYSSEUS

The longest journey home after the war was that of the "resourceful" Odysseus, as recounted in the *Odyssey*. Having left Troy with twelve ships, Odysseus almost immediately begins to lose men, first at the city of the Kikones, then in the land of the lotus-eaters. In the cave of the cyclopes Polyphemos several men are eaten before Odysseus makes their captor drunk and blinds him with a red-hot stake, announcing his identity as "Nobody;" Polyphemos cries out that "Nobody" is killing him, so no help comes, and the following morning Odysseus and his soldiers escape. As they sail away, Odysseus rashly calls out his real name, bringing the wrath of Polyphemos's father Poseidon upon his head.

The group then visits the island of Aiolos, keeper of the winds, who sends them on their way with the storm winds tied up in a bag. When they are within sight of Ithaca, the hero's home, Odysseus's men open what they think is a bag of treasure, and they are driven back to Aiolos, who again refuses to help. Sailing on they come to the land of the Laistrygonians, savage man-eaters who bombard the ships with rocks and harpoon the men like fish; only Odysseus's own ship escapes.

The party reaches the island of Circe, who customarily turns visitors into animals, but Odysseus counters her magic and spends a year making love to her while his men enjoy unlimited food and wine. Eventually they decide to continue their journey, but first they must visit the underworld to seek advice from the seer Teiresias. After this they safely negotiate the Sirens—monsters whose irresistible singing lures sailors into their murderous clutches—but in steering clear of the whirlpool Charybdis they lose several men to the six-headed sea-monster Scylla. On the island of Thrinakia the remain-

---

This clay pithos *(storage jar) from Mykonos bears one of the few surviving Greek representation of the wooden horse in which the Greeks hid in order to gain entry into Troy. It was crafted around 670BCE, not long after the composition of the* Odyssey. *This detail depicts some of the Greek warriors still inside the wheeled horse, looking out through little windows and handing armor to those who are already outside.*

ing men kill some of the cattle belonging to the sun god Helios, for which sacrilege Zeus sends a violent storm, breaking up the ship. Only Odysseus survives and is duly washed up on the island of Ogygia, where the goddess Calypso keeps him as her lover for seven years, until the gods compel her to release him. Odysseus is once again shipwrecked, but manages to swim to Phaiakia. The Phaiakians deliver Odysseus back to Ithaca, where, disguised as a beggar, he infiltrates his own palace, which has been occupied by the many suitors who hope to marry his wife Penelope and become king. Having proved his identity by stringing the great bow, Odysseus kills the suitors with the help of his son Telemachos and the faithful swineherd Eumaios, before being reunited with the long-suffering Penelope.

IN THE WAKE OF ODYSSEUS

The Ionian island of Ithaca (right), just off the west coast of mainland Greece, has been identified with Odysseus's home since antiquity. Although some scholars have argued in favor of nearby Leukas, Ithaca does seem a fair match for Homer's description of it in the *Odyssey*: "It is rugged and not fit for driving horses, and yet, although narrow, it is not altogether poor. It provides plentiful corn and wine; it always has rain and fresh dew. It has good pasture for goats and cattle; there is wood of every kind, and never-failing watering-places are there." The neighboring island of Kephalonia is sometimes identified with the utopian land of the Phaiakians, Odysseus's last port of call, where he met the princess Nausikaa and the king Alkinoos, and told the story of his wanderings at a feast held in his honor.

This tranquil bay on Ithaca brings to mind Homer's description of the island's coastline: "… there is a bay named Phorkys, after the old man of the sea, where two steep headlands jut out, crouching before the bay, which protect it from the storm-winds' great waves outside; but inside, well-decked ships can ride without mooring when they reach its anchorage."

TALES OF THE HEROES

The Greek heroes most familiar to us are those whose warrior prowess and strange adventures were recounted in epic poetry from Homer and Hesiod onward. Imposing figures such as Herakles, Theseus, Jason, and Perseus stood apart for their courage, determination, and ingenuity in the face of challenges that seemed impossible and monstrous beasts that seemed invincible.

B est known of all Greek heroes is Herakles. Countless monster-slaying exploits were attributed to him, but the idea of the twelve labors has proved the most enduring. These were devised by his cousin Eurystheus, king of Tiryns, usually by way of expiation for Herakles's murder of his own family in a fit of madness.

First Herakles had to kill the Nemean Lion, which he choked to death because its hide was invulnerable; ever afterward he wore this lionskin as both trophy and protection. Next he tackled the Lernaean hydra, a many-headed water-monster which grew two heads for every one chopped off. The next task entailed capturing the golden-horned Kerynian hind, which was sacred to Artemis, and bringing it back to Tiryns alive. Similarly,

All twelve of Herakles's labors are depicted on the metopes *of the temple of Zeus at Olympia, ca. 460BCE. On this one, Herakles has a cushion on his shoulders as he supports the weight of the Heavens, with a little effortless assistance from Athene. He is approached by Atlas, who holds out the apples brought back from the garden of the Hesperides.*

the fierce Erymanthian boar, which had been terrorizing Arkadia, was delivered alive to Eurystheus, who was so scared that he hid in a great bronze jar. Herakles displayed more skill than brute force in the fifth labor, which was to clean out the cattle-stables of Augeias, king of Elis; he achieved this by diverting Olympia's two rivers, the Alpheios and Peneios, to sweep away the

dung. Killing the birds which were infesting the Arkadian lake Stymphalos also involved some cunning—Herakles scared them from their coverts with a rattle before shooting them with his arrows.

The first six tasks were all set in the Peloponnese, but the remaining six took Herakles steadily further afield. He captured the Cretan bull and tamed the man-eating mares of the Thracian king Diomedes by feeding their master to them. He traveled to the Black Sea to fetch the belt of the Amazon queen Hippolyte, and then to the far west to capture the cattle of Geryon, who lived beyond the bounds of Ocean. The garden of the Hesperides was also situated in the distant west, beyond the sunset and near the place where Atlas held up the Heavens; Herakles either fetched the Hesperides's golden apples himself, having slain the guardian serpent Ladon, or sent Atlas to do the task for him. Finally, Herakles descended to the underworld where Hades agreed to let him take Kerberos (see page 330) up to the Earth provided he did so without weapons; having been shown to Eurystheus, the hound was quickly returned.

After many more adventures Herakles eventually died a terrible death, poisoned by the blood of the centaur Nessos, but his sufferings on Earth were rewarded: the gods welcomed him to Olympos (see illustration, page 304), where he feasts among the immortals "untroubled and unageing all his days" (Hesiod).

THESEUS: THE STATESMAN HERO

Unlike the Panhellenic Herakles, Theseus, whose story is told at length by Plutarch, was especially associated with Athens. He was son of Aigeus, an early king of Athens, as a result of a brief liaison Aigeus enjoyed with the princess Aithra at Troizen in the Argolid when he was visiting her father Pittheus on his return from Delphi. Some said, however, that Theseus was the son of Poseidon, who had also slept with Aithra that night. When he was old enough, Theseus immediately proved his worth by lifting a great rock under which Aigeus had left sandals and a sword as tokens by which the boy

might be recognized if he came to Athens. Rather than take the easy sea-crossing from Troizen, Theseus determined to take the land route to Attica around the Saronic Gulf, encountering various villains on his journey. He gave each of these a taste of his own medicine, such as Skiron, who compelled travelers to wash his feet, then kicked them over the cliffs into the sea to be eaten by a monstrous turtle, and Prokrustes, who would offer travelers a bed for the night and then stretch or cut his guests to size.

When Theseus arrived in Athens, Aigeus did not at first recognize him, but the young man proved himself yet again by capturing the Marathonian bull. Shortly afterward the tribute became due for Minos, king of Crete, of seven youths and seven girls who would be fed to the minotaur. Theseus went with them, and succeeded not only in killing the minotaur, but also in finding his way back out of the labyrinth, by means of a ball of thread given to him by Minos's daughter Ariadne. The couple sailed away together, but Theseus soon abandoned Ariadne, either on the gods' orders or because he had fallen in love with another girl. He sailed on to Delos, where he made offerings of thanks to Apollo, before returning to Athens. Theseus had promised his father that he would change the black sail of his ship to white (or scarlet) if he was bearing good news, but he forgot, and the despairing Aigeus jumped off the Akropolis to his death; the Aegean Sea was named after him.

Theseus thus became king of Athens, after which he had various other adventures, but many of the deeds attributed to his mature years are obviously projections of historical political events. He was supposed to have gathered together the Attic villages into a single state of Athens, to have founded the Panathenaia festival and the Isthmian Games, and even to have voluntarily handed over power to the people. This made him the first hero of Athenian democracy, and he was worshipped at Athens with an annual festival and monthly sacrifices.

❖ LEAPING THE BULL ❖

There has been much speculation about the origins of the story of Theseus and the minotaur (see page 343). The myth was obviously popular on Crete in the Roman imperial period, when several coin types from Knossos show a labyrinth, and one even has the bull-headed monster on the reverse. The Minoan palace excavated at Knossos (see box, page 309) is indeed very complex architecturally, and could have appeared "labyrinthine" to a visitor. There are also many bull images among the finds, including a beautiful bull's-head drinking vessel made of serpentine, limestone, rock-crystal, and gold. The wall-paintings of the palace include a scene of bull-leaping (below), in which one figure grasps the bull's horns while another somersaults over its back, and a third stands ready to catch him.

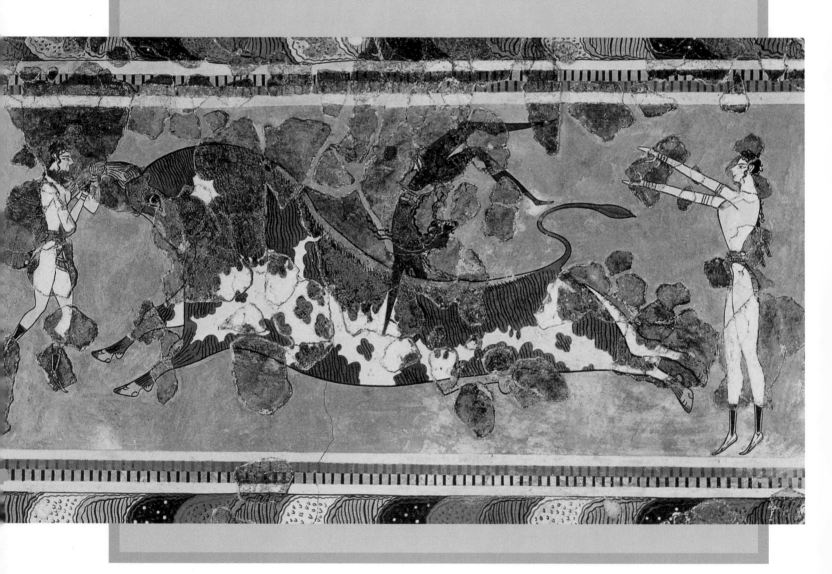

THE QUEST FOR THE GOLDEN FLEECE

Many Greek heroes took part in the voyage led by Jason in search of the golden fleece. The story is alluded to in the *Odyssey*, but it is known to us in detail from Apollonius of Rhodes's Hellenistic epic the *Argonautika*. The golden fleece was that of the miraculous talking, flying ram which had rescued Phrixos and Helle from their wicked stepmother's plots: the girl fell off en route, giving her name to the Hellespont, but Phrixos was carried safely to Aia in Colchis, where he sacrificed the ram to Zeus and gave the fleece to king Aietes, son of Helios. Aietes hung it on an oak tree in a grove sacred to Ares, where it was guarded by a dragon that never slept.

Pelias had usurped the throne of Iolkos in Thessaly, to which his half-brother Jason was the rightful heir, so he set Jason the seemingly impossible task of fetching the fleece. Jason, however, had the support of Hera, whom Pelias had offended; Athene advised on the construction of Jason's ship the *Argo*, and fifty of the bravest heroes in Greece joined the expedition.

The Argonauts had many adventures on their way to Colchis, including their memorable encounter with the women of Lemnos, who had earlier massacred all their menfolk and needed to conceive children to repopulate the island. In Thrace Jason and his followers rescued the blind seer Phineus from the Harpies who kept stealing his food. The Argonauts safely negotiated the Clashing Rocks at the northern end of the Bosphoros, and eventually reached Aia, where Aietes agreed to hand over the fleece if Jason could perform a series of tasks. Hera caused the king's daughter Medea to fall in love with Jason, and with the help of her magic salve of invulnerability he succeeded in yoking the fire-breathing bulls, and killing the army of men sprung from dragon's teeth sewn in the ground. Knowing that Aietes would not keep his word, Medea used her powers to put the dragon to sleep while Jason stole the golden fleece, before escaping with it on the *Argo*.

The return journey, too, was eventful, including encounters with some of the hazards which would later be met by Odysseus, and with Talos, the bronze man who guarded Crete. When they reached Iolkos, Medea tricked Pelias's daughters into killing him: thinking they were rejuvenating him, they cut their father into pieces and boiled him in a pot. He was succeeded by his son Akastos, while Jason and Medea fled to Corinth, where, according to some, Jason was eventually crushed to death by a beam from the *Argo*.

PERSEUS AND THE GORGON'S HEAD

Like Jason, Perseus was initially cheated of his kingdom and sent on an "impossible" quest. His mother Danae had been imprisoned in a bronze chamber by her father Akrisios, king of Argos, after the oracle said he would be killed by a son of hers. She nonetheless became pregnant by Zeus, but when Perseus was born Akrisios shut up mother and baby in a chest and cast it into the sea. They came ashore on Seriphos, where they were taken in by Diktys, brother of the island's king Polydektes, and lived happily until Polydektes decided he wanted to marry Danae. Perseus was sent to fetch the head of the Gorgon Medusa to keep him out of the way.

In his mission Perseus was able to call upon the assistance of both Athene and Hermes, who sent him first to the three Graiai ("Old Women"). Perseus forced them to reveal the whereabouts of certain nymphs, who duly gave him various magical items which add a folk-tale element to the story. Perseus flew on his new winged sandals beyond Ocean to the land of the Gorgons, whom he found asleep. Because anyone who looked at them directly would be turned to stone, he used the reflection in Athene's shield as a guide, and with the *harpe* (curved dagger) supplied by Hermes he cut off Medusa's head. From her severed neck sprang the winged horse Pegasos and the warrior Chrysaor—Medusa's two immortal sisters, Stheno and Euryale, gave chase to Perseus, but he escaped with the help of Hades's cap of darkness.

On his way home Perseus came to the land of the Ethiopians, where the princess Andromeda was about to

be devoured by a sea monster, sent by Poseidon to punish the boasting of her mother Kassiopeia. King Kepheus agreed that Perseus could marry Andromeda if he could kill the monster, which he duly did; Kepheus's brother, who had been betrothed to Andromeda, tried to stop her marrying Perseus, but was soon turned to stone. The same fate befell Polydektes when Perseus reached Seriphos and found that he was persecuting Danae. Having made Diktys king, Perseus gave his magic gifts back to Hermes and handed over Medusa's head to Athene, who ever afterward wore it on her aegis.

Perseus eventually returned to the Greek mainland, where he accidentally killed his grandfather Akrisios with a discus, thus fulfilling the oracle. He was too ashamed to take his rightful place on the throne of Argos, but exchanged Argos for Mycenae (see page 306), where he founded the dynasty which a few generations later would produce Herakles.

BEASTS AND MONSTERS

Heroes such as Herakles, Theseus, Jason, and Perseus demonstrated their physical prowess and cunning by vanquishing monsters, of which a great variety appear in Greek myth. In the *Theogony*, Hesiod describes a whole family of monstrous beings descended from the ancient sea deities Keto and Phorkys, the offspring of Earth and Pontos (Sea). Keto bore the Graiai and the Gorgons (see page 345), then Echidna, who was "half quick-glancing, fair-cheeked nymph, and half again a

This unusual gold fibula (brooch), which was produced in the late 5th century BCE, is decorated with images of a griffin and a sea-horse.

monstrous snake, huge and terrible, writhing and raw-flesh-eating down in the depths of the sacred earth." Echidna's offspring included several of the beasts overcome by Herakles: the multi-headed hounds Kerberos and Geryon's guard-dog Orthos, the Nemean lion, and the Lernaean hydra. The three-headed Geryon was the grandson of Medusa via Chrysaor. Geryon's monstrous form posed a particular challenge to Greek artists who depicted him variously with one or three torsos, up to six arms, and two or six legs.

Fabulous hybrid beasts became popular in Greek art of the Archaic Period under the influence of stories and images from the east. Some of the earliest clay or bronze animal figurines buried with the dead or dedicated at sanctuaries were centaurs (half-man, half-horse) and the griffins that once decorated great bronze tripod-cauldrons. Griffins had an eagle's head and wings but the body of a lion, and were supposed to live at the northern limits of the world, where they guarded hordes of gold against the one-eyed Arimaspians. In the Roman imperial period the griffin becomes associated with the figure of Nemesis ("Retribution"), sharing her relentless pursuit of vengeance. Also part-lion was the Chimaira, another offspring of Echidna, which Apollodoros describes: "it had the foreparts of a lion, the tail of a serpent, and a third head in the middle of a goat, through which it breathed fire ... one creature, it had the power of three beasts." The Corinthian hero Bellerophon was set the task of killing this monster by Iobates, king of Lykia, which he succeeded in doing with the assistance of his winged horse Pegasos, offspring of Medusa.

Many Greek monsters were female in gender, including several which were half-woman in form. Both the

• SNAKES AND DRAGONS •

Creatures of the depths of earth and sea, snakes and water-serpents (Greek *drakones*), had both positive and negative associations for the Greeks. Asklepios, god of healing, and his daughter Health were always accompanied by snakes, which had links with agricultural fertility in the cult of Demeter. A serpent-like dragon guarded the golden fleece (see page 345) and the apples of the Hesperides, and the snakes of Athene's aegis had a similarly protective function. Medusa's hair was often depicted as consisting of snakes (left).

More actively malevolent was the Lernaean hydra killed by Herakles, and the water-serpents which killed the Trojan priest Laokoon and his sons, as portrayed in a famous Hellenistic sculpture.

Sirens (see page 338) and the Harpies (see page 345) were often represented as birds with women's heads, while yet another of Echidna's children was the Sphinx, a winged lion with a woman's head, inspired by the sphinxes of Egypt and the Near East. In myth she is best known for terrorizing the people of Thebes, devouring anyone who gave the wrong answer to her riddle, until Oedipus came up with the solution (see page 349). More generally, though, the image of the Sphinx was carved on tombstones, where it was believed she would guard the dead from disturbance.

FATE, VENGEANCE, AND TRANSGRESSION

Many of the heroes celebrated by Homer and Hesiod had their stories reshaped in fifth-century BCE Athens by playwrights. Audiences were able to watch characters struggle in vain to escape their fate. Other figures from Greek myth endured horrific punishments for having offended the gods.

Aeschylus's *Oresteia* trilogy, produced in 458BCE, elaborates the tale of the return from Troy of Agamemnon, leader of the Greeks, and the bloody events which followed. In the first play, Agamemnon's wife Klytaimnestra murders him in the bath. In the *Libation Bearers*, the royal couple's son Orestes returns from exile and avenges his dead father by slaying both his mother and her lover Aigisthos. The final part of Aeschylus's trilogy is the *Eumenides*, the "Kindly Ones," a euphemism for the Furies who pursue Orestes for having spilt his mother's blood. He seeks purification at Delphi, whence Apollo sends him to Athens to be tried

at the homicide court of the Areopagos; when there is a hung jury Athene gives the casting vote in Orestes's favor. Thus the cycle of vengeance called for by the ancient aristocratic code of honor is finally broken by the intervention of the modern, democratic institution of the law court.

The enlightened city of Athens is also made to offer sanctuary to Oedipus in Sophocles's *Oedipus at Kolonos*, but the main events of the hero's terrible story are related in *Oedipus the King*. The myth is a parable of the inevitability of fate: believing himself to be the child of the king and queen of Corinth, Oedipus flees to avoid

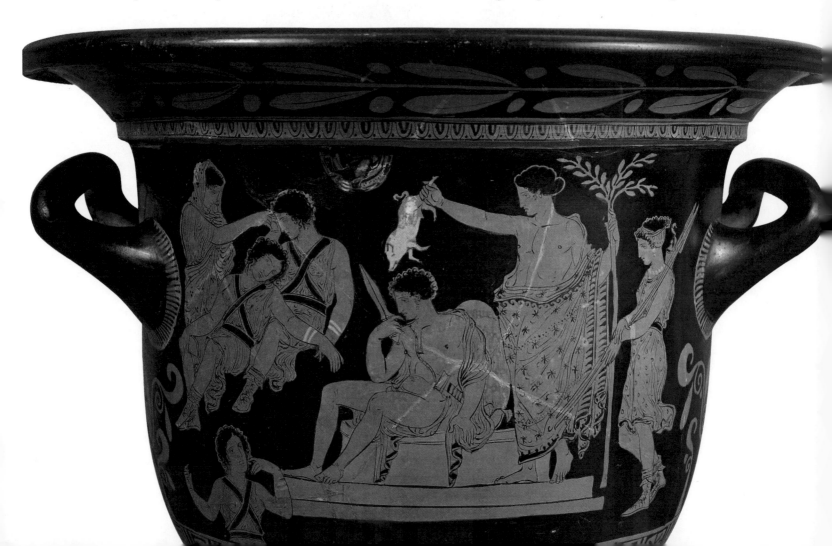

the oracle's prediction that he will kill his father and marry his mother. He travels to Thebes, where he marries the recently bereaved queen Jokasta, unaware that her dead husband Laios was the very man Oedipus had just killed in a roadside brawl. Thus Oedipus fulfills the oracle, because he is really a prince of Thebes, exposed at birth but rescued and removed to Corinth by shepherds.

Sophocles's treatment of the story, however, shifts the focus by starting when Oedipus is already king of Thebes. By this point in his career he has also won great respect for having solved the riddle of the Sphinx: "What goes on four legs in the morning, then two legs, then three?" The answer was "man," who crawls as a baby, walks upright in his prime, and hobbles with a stick in old age. The play centers on Oedipus' determination to root out the cause of the plague which is afflicting his people, which the oracle tells him is the pollution arising from the unpunished murder of Laios. Oedipus relentlessly uncovers the truth, and thus brings about the delayed realization of his own downfall. Oedipus finally asserts his own will by blinding himself and retreating into self-imposed exile.

CAUTIONARY TALES

Alongside the tales of warrior prowess and heroic honor, Greek myth has a number of stories which portray the other end of the spectrum: types of behavior which were liable to divine punishment. A major area of transgression involved offenses against various goddesses' modesty. When Teiresias saw Athene bathing, for example, she struck him blind, but gave him some compensation in the form of prophetic powers (although in another version it was Hera who blinded him, for opposing her in an argument, and Zeus who enabled him to foretell the future). Another frequent kind of transgression was

On this early 4th-century BCE krater, Orestes (center) sits as a suppliant on the altar at Delphi. Apollo stands behind him, and to the left Klytaimnestra's ghost rouses the sleeping Furies.

the challenge to a deity's area of prowess, such as Niobe boasting about her children (see page 335). Arachne presumptuously challenged Athene to a weaving contest, as a result of which she was transformed into a spider. The Thracian bard Thamyris also suffered a terrible fate for challenging the Muses to a singing competition: the goddesses agreed that he could sleep with each of them in turn if he won, but when he lost they struck him blind and took away his musical skills. Worse still was the Phrygian satyr Marsyas's punishment for daring to compete with his pipes against Apollo's lyre-playing: he was hung on a pine tree and flayed alive.

Various other transgressors endured eternal punishments in the underworld. When Ixion attempted to rape Hera, Zeus tricked him into sleeping with a cloud fashioned in Hera's form. The impregnated cloud gave birth to Kentauros, father of the race of centaurs, but Ixion boasted of his conquest, so Zeus tied him to an ever-turning wheel. The site of Ixion's wheel was usually said to be Tartaros, where the giant Tityos, who had tried to rape Leto, could also be found, sprawled over two acres of ground with two vultures tearing at his constantly regenerating liver. In the underworld, Odysseus saw Tantalos, father of Niobe, who had once been a favorite of the gods, but offended them by serving up his own son Pelops in a stew to test their omniscience, or by stealing some of the gods' ambrosia and nectar. His punishment was to stand for ever up to his neck in water, which would drain away every time he bent to drink, and to be surrounded by branches laden with fruit, which blew out of reach whenever he tried to pick them. The *Odyssey* also describes the fate of Sisyphos, who had incurred the gods' anger by a whole series of offenses, including informing on Zeus when he had carried off the river-god Asopos's daughter Aigina, and cheating death by tying up Thanatos, the personification of death, who had come to fetch him. To keep him out of further mischief, Sisyphos was condemned always to push uphill a great rock, which would roll back down again every time he reached the top.

TEMPLES AND SHRINES

The importance that the ancient Greeks attached to religious observance can be surmised from the large number of places of worship that they built. Households had their own shrines, and communities raised imposing temple complexes to demonstrate both their piety and their wealth.

Greek places of worship varied from the small household shrine to the full-scale temple and extended sanctuary complex. Shrines shared by the community usually included an altar, at which animal sacrifices—the central ritual of Greek religion—were performed. For the Olympian gods the altar (*bomos*) was a stone construction raised up from the ground, where the animal was sacrificed with its head pulled back so that the throat was pointing heavenward when cut. If the god had a temple (*naos*), the altar was usually placed in front of it, so that worshippers gathered around the sacrifice would be facing the exterior of the building's east end. The simplest form of temple was a single, roofed chamber, but this developed over the Archaic Period into the more elaborate design with which we are familiar. This consisted of a central chamber with an entrance porch and a rear chamber, the whole surrounded by a colonnade. The central chamber housed a sacred image, a statue which was regarded as especially holy and often closely identified with the deity him-

or herself. Ancient wooden statues were particularly revered and were often dressed in real clothes, such as the statue of Athene Polias on the Athenian Akropolis (see page 333). Nonetheless, communities often spent large sums of money commissioning new statues from the best sculptors of the day, such as the statue of Zeus at Olympia by Pheidias, which became one of the seven wonders of the ancient world. Greek temples combined reverence for the gods with a display of the community's pride and wealth.

A temple might stand alone or form part of a larger sanctuary (*hieron*, or "sacred place"), usually dedicated to one main deity but encompassing temples and altars to other gods and heroes too. The Erechtheion on the Athenian Akropolis (completed ca. 406BCE) incorporated shrines to Athene Polias and Poseidon, as well as to the hero Erechthus himself, and Kekrops and his daughter Pandrosos. In keeping with the taste for lavish decoration, the south porch of the temple features female figures in place of more simple columns.

Shrines to heroes and other chthonic, or earthly, powers usually had a low hearth or pit, where the sacrificial victim's blood could flow directly down into the ground. A hero's shrine might be little more than such a hearth with the sacred area around it enclosed or marked in some way. Some deities who had a particular association with nature were worshipped in natural locations, at springs or in sacred groves; natural caves were often the site of rituals for the pastoral god Pan. Caves were also suitable for the worship of underworld deities, such as the Furies at Athens, who had a sacred cave on the slopes of the Areopagos.

The Doric temple at Segesta in western Sicily was begun in the 420s BCE, but construction work was interrupted when war broke out with Selinus in 416 and the building was never completed. The columns have been left unfluted, and the walls of the inner chamber are missing. Nonetheless, the remains which stand to this day are impressive, with thirty-six columns, entablature, and pediments all intact.

• EPIDAUROS •

Asklepios, god of healing, was often encountered at an individual level. Like Herakles, Asklepios was originally a hero, son of Apollo and of a mortal woman, Koronis. Asklepios learned the arts of medicine from the centaur Cheiron and spent his adult life healing the sick. He was eventually struck down by Zeus's thunderbolt for having presumptuously tried to raise a man from the dead, but despite his death, which should have limited him to heroic cult, Asklepios was paid divine honors from at least 500BCE. From the late fifth century BCE his cult spread throughout the Greek world, with notable sanctuaries on Kos and at Pergamon, and was even exported to Rome in 293BCE.

The most important center of Asklepios's worship, however, was the sanctuary at Epidauros, on the eastern coast of the Argolid in the northeastern Peloponnese. As well as the temple to Asklepios, the complex included a temple to Artemis, a hospital, and sleeping quarters. Epidauros attracted visitors from all over Greece and beyond, who left inscribed records of their miraculous cures. This private invocation of Asklepios by the sick in their hour of need was counterbalanced by the worship of whole communities at regular festivals, such as the Athenian Asklepieia and Epidauria. At Epidauros, the annual festival included athletic events, catered for by a wrestling ground and stadium, the remains of which can still be visited, and dramatic competitions held in the spectacular theater. This was constructed in the mid-fourth century BCE, when the whole sanctuary underwent extensive monumentalization, making use of the natural slope of the hill to support fifty-five rows of seating, for 13,000–14,000 spectators. The theater was found in near perfect condition when it was excavated in the late nineteenth century CE. Today it is used for an annual summer festival of classical drama.

RITES, FESTIVALS, AND GAMES

Ritual expressed the relationship between mortals and the gods. At one end of the scale, individuals prayed and made small offerings to the deities that presided over the household, while, at the other, the whole of the Greek world came together at the major interstate games held in honor of the principal gods such as Zeus, Apollo, and Poseidon.

Images of exercise and athletic competitions were common in Greek art, with runners (as in this artistic interpretation) a popular subject for vase-painting. Sculptures were also commissioned in commemoration of notable victories.

The rites performed at temples and shrines of all kinds varied as much as the holy places themselves. Most rituals were accompanied by prayers, for which there were special formulaic phrases, and which might be spoken privately for individual needs, pronounced before a gathering, or spoken in unison by a crowd following the lead of a herald. There was a formulaic element to hymns, too, which often included reference to the deity's life story and sphere of influence. The simplest form of offering was a libation—a few drops of wine or other liquids poured first into a flat dish and then onto the ground, the remainder being drunk by each of those present in turn. Libations might be performed in the home every morning and evening, or at the beginning of a meal, or just before setting off on a journey. Offerings of hair, clothes, or personal belongings were made at rites of passage, particularly in preparation for marriage and in connection with childbirth. More permanent dedications could be made at a sanctuary in the form of votive reliefs, and even statues, representing either the deity or the worshipper.

The heart of Greek religious ritual, however, lay in sacrifice. A few deities demanded "bloodless sacrifices" in the form of the first fruits of cereal and olive crops, of bread, cakes, cooked vegetables, or even burnt spices, but commonest was the blood sacrifice. The most humble victim would be a dove or cockerel, then a piglet, lamb, or kid, then a full-grown sheep or goat, and at the top end of the scale, the ox. To sacrifice to the Olympians was to "fumigate," because the gods were thought to enjoy the smell of the fatty smoke rising, but to a hero one had to "devote" the victim by burning it whole. An individual or family would probably sacrifice one small animal, but the great city festivals in honor of the gods, which usually lasted several days, entailed the slaughter of dozens of sheep and cattle. A festival procession would be followed by the sacrifice, after which the meat would be prepared for a ritual feast. The cooked meat was divided into portions of equal size but variable quality; its distribution among the assembled worshippers was sometimes decided by lot, sometimes by the recipients' political and social status.

THE BEAUTIFUL CROWN OF ZEUS

Some festivals held at local village or city level included athletic competitions, but the best known are the Panhellenic games at the great interstate sanctuaries. These may have originated in the funeral games held in honor of the dead, such as those for Patroklos described in the *Iliad*, but they developed over time to include more and more events, with subdivisions for different age groups. The oldest were the games in honor of Zeus at Olympia, traditionally founded in 776BCE, followed by the Pythian Games for Apollo at Delphi founded in 586BCE, the Isthmian Games for Poseidon in 580BCE, and the Nemean Games for Zeus

in 573BCE. The Olympic and Pythian Games were held once every four years, the Isthmian and Nemean every two, and between them they made up a "circuit" (*periodos*). Special honors were accorded to "circuit-winners" (*periodonikos*)—individuals who had won victories at all four games. The prizes for the Panhellenic games had no inherent value. Instead the victor in each event was awarded an honorific crown (*stephanos*), made of a plant which had a mythological connection with the sanctuary in question—wild olive at Olympia, laurel at Delphi, pine at the Isthmos, and wild celery at Nemea.

A special feature of the games at Olympia was the Olympic Truce, the terms of which stipulated that all states had to suspend any hostilities for several weeks either side of the festival to allow athletes safe passage to and from the games. The Olympic officials had the power to impose hefty fines on any state which broke the truce and ban its athletes from competing. The earliest games consisted only of the *stadion*, which was a sprint over a distance of a *stade*, or 600 feet (about 180m), but longer foot-races were added over time, the two-*stade diaulos*, the long-distance *dolichos* (ca. 16,000 feet, or nearly 5,000m), and the grueling *hoplites*, run over a distance of two to four *stades* in full hoplite armor weighing around 56 pounds (25kg). There was also wrestling, boxing and the *pankration* (a kind of all-in wrestling), and the *pentathlon*, which consisted of running, jumping, throwing the javelin and discus, and wrestling; two- and four-horse chariot-racing and horse-racing were accommodated in the hippodrome. By 400BCE the games lasted for five days, instead of the original one. All males who were native Greek-speakers and free citizens were entitled to take part in the games, provided they were not ritually impure. Women were not usually allowed among the spectators, although exceptions were made for certain priestesses and virgins, and there was nothing to prevent women from entering teams in the chariot-race, a competition in which the fourth-century BCE Spartan princess Kyniska won several victories.

PROPHETS AND ORACLES

In a world where every aspect of life was governed by the gods, it was clearly important to ascertain their will. This was especially vital when undertaking any hazardous enterprise, such as going on a journey, establishing a colony, or marching into battle.

Divination at the most humble level might involve an individual or family casting lots or looking for meaning in dreams, or in signs, which could be anything even slightly out of the ordinary, from a sudden sneeze to a chance encounter. The interpretation of more complex signs was the realm of professional seers, who might, for example, observe the flight of birds in search of good or bad omens. The entrails of sacrificial victims were also regularly consulted by specialists known as *haruspices*—the liver was of particular interest to a *haruspex*, and unless the organ was of the correct color, markings, and shape the proposed undertaking was proclaimed to be doomed (see also page 407).

On particularly momentous occasions, both individuals and states would take their queries to sanctuaries which specialized in divination: the oracles. Apollo was especially associated with this prophetic power (see pages 334–335), but there were also several oracles of

• DELPHI: CENTER OF THE COSMOS •

Despite its remote location on the slopes of Mount Parnassos, according to tradition Delphi lay at the very center of the world. Zeus once ascertained this by releasing two eagles at the outermost points of the universe, marking the place where they met with the *omphalos*—a curiously carved stone representing the Earth's "navel," a version of which was kept in the inner sanctum of Apollo's temple at Delphi. The *Homeric Hymn to Apollo* tells how Apollo at first chose a site by the spring Telphousa, but was persuaded by its eponymous nymph to settle higher up at Krisa. Here he determined to establish his oracle, and laid the foundations for his own temple, once he had despatched a monstrous serpent, which he left to rot (*putho*); hence Delphi's alternative name "Pytho" and the "Pythian Games" held there.

Historically, Apollo's sanctuary seems to have been established in the tenth century BCE, with the oracle in operation by the eighth century and the games added in the early sixth century BCE. Here we see the lower part of the sanctuary, popularly known as Marmaria ("the marbles"), which was sacred to Athene Pronaia ("Guardian of the Temple") or Pronoia ("Forethought"). Athene had a temple here from the seventh century BCE, and there are remains of two treasuries, one of which was dedicated in the late sixth century BCE by the people of Massilia (see pages 320–321). Although the fourth-century Tholos ("Rotunda"), with three of its twenty Doric columns restored, is one of the most famous sights in Greece, we do not know what it was used for. According to Plutarch, another god, Dionysus (also known as Bacchus), was also worshipped at Delphi. Each winter a group of women, the Thyiades, honored him with ecstatic nocturnal rituals.

Zeus, and others with chthonic connections, such as the oracle of the hero Trophonios at Lebadeia, and of the Dead at Ephyra. The great sanctuary of Zeus Naios at Dodona claimed to be the oldest oracle in Greece, and, while it was occasionally consulted by cities, inscribed lead tablets from the site record many more personal enquiries: "Lysanias asks Zeus Naios and Dione whether the child with which Annyla is pregnant is not by him."

Most famous and authoritative of all were the oracles pronounced at Delphi by Apollo's mouthpiece, the priestess known as the Pythia (see box, below). Recent geological investigations at Delphi suggest that she may

have been put into a trance-like state by inhaling ethylene rising through fissures in the rocks below the temple, but her words were in any case often "translated" into verse by attendant priests. The fifth-century BCE historian Herodotus is a particularly prolific, if not necessarily reliable, source for these verse oracles, which are characterized by their ambiguity and often result in a story with an ironic twist, as in the case of the Lydian king Croesus: on enquiring whether he should fight against Persia, he was told that if he did so he would destroy a mighty empire. Encouraged, Croesus went ahead with his campaign—and his own great empire was duly wiped out.

CHAPTER TWO

ROME

At first sight, the story of Rome seems more the stuff of fantasy or legend

than of history. It tells how the inhabitants of a small town and its hinterland—

a region with few obvious natural or strategic advantages—managed, by military

prowess, to make themselves masters first of Italy and then of the entire

Mediterranean world, including much of Europe, the Middle Eastern area,

and North Africa. Only the Han Chinese (206BCE–220CE), the Romans'

contemporaries far away in the unknown east, could in any way rival their

achievement. Yet there was always more to Rome's progress than simple skill in

arms. The Romans were also builders and law-makers on a heroic scale, and

they left a permanent mark on all the lands that they ruled.

THE SOUL OF THE ROMANS

Anyone seeking to understand the Romans should start with their military background. First and foremost, they were good and valiant soldiers. Initially they fought out of necessity, to ensure the survival of their remote and hilly city. Later, the urge for expansion entered their bloodstream—victory in repeated doses turned out to be a heady drug.

In the days when the Romans were conquering Italy (ca. 500–246BCE), their soldiers were peasant smallholders who, when duty demanded, abandoned their plows and took up the sword. This situation changed from about 100BCE on, when the consul Marius created a professional standing army of long-serving legionaries. Yet well after the citizens' army had faded into history, citizens looked back admiringly to the days of a patriotic yeomanry fighting for hearth and home and continued, above all, to respect such soldierly virtues as duty, hardiness, and courage.

Needless to say, not all Romans exhibited these admirable qualities, and in its later years the empire gained an enduring reputation for decadence and luxury. Even so, moralists regularly harked back to the traditions of earlier, republican times. Meanwhile, the mass of the population retained one essential ingredient of the military spirit: an ingrained respect for authority. Discipline and order were essential parts of the Roman worldview. Such attributes extended beyond a respect for those who wielded political power at any given moment. They also included the concepts of *pietas*, or piety, demanding respectful observance toward the gods and the state, and *gravitas*, seriousness, which implied self-discipline and the need for a sober approach to life.

Notions of order and hierarchy also penetrated the home. The *paterfamilias*, or father of the family, was expected to reign as a benign despot over an obedient household. Mothers were in theory subordinate figures,

An agate cameo bearing the portrait of the emperor Claudius (reigned 41–54CE). Claudius oversaw a significant phase of Roman imperial expansion and was successful in bringing parts of Britain and several North African territories under the Roman Empire's control.

although in practice Roman women had greater legal rights than their counterparts in Greece and could, in private, exert considerable influence.

In time, Roman rule spread so wide that its Romanness—the quality known as *Romanitas*—was inevitably diluted. The empire became a multi-ethnic community whose emperors included Africans, a Syrian, and an Arab; its arts came mainly from Greece and its religions increasingly from the Orient. Yet a kernel of the old traditions always remained. From it came the Romans' most enduring legacy: the practical and intellectual skills that won battles, shaped cities, and developed a legal system that is still influential in many parts of the world today. Such achievements helped bind the Roman Empire together and continued to affect distant peoples long after the demise of the western emperors in 476CE.

OPPOSITE *A Roman stone relief showing the 2nd-century emperor Marcus Aurelius, on horseback, receiving homage from defeated barbarians. A philosopher as well as an able ruler, Marcus Aurelius is perhaps most famous for his philosophical text* Meditations.

THE STORY OF THE ROMANS

The history of ancient Rome extends over a period of about a thousand years and divides into six phases. At first a collection of independent city-states, Rome developed into a single monarchy, and then an empire that covered much of Europe and stretched into North Africa and the Middle East.

The story of the greatest empire of the ancient world begins with shepherds living in wattle-and-daub huts roofed with thatch on the Palatine Hill early in the first millennium BCE. Similar groups set up villages on adjoining hills. At some point, traditionally dated to 753BCE but more likely in the following century, the various settlements coalesced to form the city of Rome.

The remaining thousand years of Roman history can best be summarized in six phases of varying length. The first of these phases was the Etruscan period, lasting through the sixth century BCE. The Etruscans were a people who had settled the region now known as Tuscany immediately to the north of Rome. They grew rich on trade and the profits of mining, and used this wealth to finance a lavish lifestyle in which the arts flourished. Politically, they never coalesced; Etruria remained a world of independent city-states.

When a line of Etruscan kings established themselves as rulers of Rome some time between 625 and 600 BCE, the burgeoning community was effectively incorporated into an expanded Etruria. After more than a century of government by the Etruscans, the last Etruscan king, Tarquin the Proud, was expelled in about

OPPOSITE *The map shows the Roman Empire at its greatest extent during the 2nd century CE under the emperor Trajan. By Trajan's death in 117CE the empire had forty provinces— in total encompassing an area of some 2 million square miles (5 million sq km).*

509BCE and a republic was founded to take the place of the monarchy. Subsequent generations of Romans looked back on the ousting of Tarquin as a liberation.

The next period, covering the years from approximately 500 to 246 BCE, was the time of the conquest of Italy. This era saw Rome's power spread out from its home region of Latium (hence "Latin") over the neighboring Italian peoples, including the city's erstwhile masters, the Etruscans. This was a time that later writers would look back on as the golden age of republican virtue, when honor, courage and a sense of civic duty impelled the nation to greatness.

Last to fall were the sophisticated city-states of southern Italy, settled by Greek colonists many centuries before. The Greeks called for help on Pyrrhos, ruler of Epiros across the Adriatic Sea. The Greek invader inflicted several defeats on the Romans but many of his men were lost in battle—these were the original Pyrrhic victories, bought at an unsustainable cost. When Pyrrhos eventually returned to Greece in 275BCE, he left the path clear for Rome to make itself master of the Italian peninsula south of the Po River. (The Celts, who lived north of the Po in the region known as Cisalpine Gaul, did not succumb until 150BCE.)

RIGHT *A double-edged Roman* gladius *or short sword (27 inches/68cm long), with scabbard. Rome's military supremacy lay in its effectiveness at conducting land warfare, with the short sword being a highly effective stabbing weapon in the close-quarters crush of battle. Other standard fighting equipment of the legionaries included the* pilum, *a spear, and the* scutum, *a long shield.*

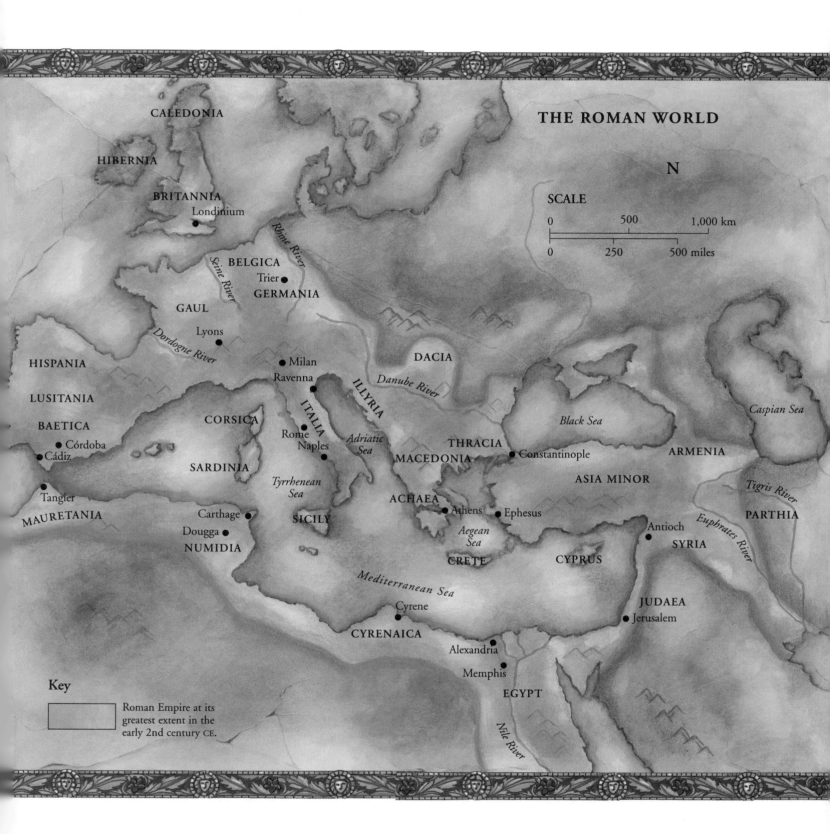

THE ROMAN WORLD

N

SCALE

| 0 | 500 | 1,000 km |
| 0 | 250 | 500 miles |

CALEDONIA

HIBERNIA

BRITANNIA
Londinium

Rhine River

BELGICA
Trier
GERMANIA

Seine River

GAUL

Lyons

Dordogne River

HISPANIA

LUSITANIA

BAETICA
Córdoba
Cádiz

Tangier

MAURETANIA

Milan
Ravenna

ITALIA

Rome
Naples

CORSICA

SARDINIA

Tyrrhenean Sea

Carthage
Dougga
NUMIDIA

SICILY

DACIA

Danube River

ILLYRIA

Adriatic Sea

THRACIA

MACEDONIA

Black Sea

Constantinople

ARMENIA

Caspian Sea

ASIA MINOR

ACHAEA
Athens
Ephesus

Aegean Sea

CRETE

CYPRUS

Tigris River

PARTHIA

Antioch
SYRIA

Euphrates River

Mediterranean Sea

Cyrene

CYRENAICA

JUDAEA
Jerusalem

Alexandria

Memphis

EGYPT

Nile River

Key

Roman Empire at its greatest extent in the early 2nd century CE.

The years from the mid-third to the mid-second century BCE were dominated by the struggle with Carthage, the great trading center set up by Phoenicians many centuries earlier on the North African coast. Three great conflicts—the Punic Wars—set the two rivals at one another's throats. When Rome finally emerged victorious in 146BCE, it precluded the possibility of any further challenge by totally demolishing Carthage and plowing over its ruins, sowing salt in the furrows to ensure that nothing would grow on the site for many years.

The Punic Wars radically changed Rome. First, they turned it into a regional power whose naval strength came to match its military might. Then they made it rich through its domination of the great Mediterranean trade routes. Finally, victory against Carthage, and also against such other enemies of the day as Illyria, Macedonia, and Asia Minor, brought slaves to Italy by the tens of thousands in the form of prisoners of war. From that time on, slaves replaced the hardy farmers of early Rome as the economic foundation of the state.

FROM REPUBLIC TO EMPIRE

The next epoch of Roman history was a transitional one marking the crucial shift from republic to empire. This was a time of high political drama whose leading players—Julius Caesar, Cicero, Pompey, Brutus, Mark Antony—remain familiar to this day. Against a backdrop of social unrest and slave revolts—Spartacus held out with his army of gladiators from 73 to 71 BCE—real power passed from Rome's republican institutions to a succession of military strong men. From this time on the legions became the true arbiters of Roman power.

The culmination of this process came in 27BCE, when Augustus, Rome's first emperor, assumed power. Henceforth, the nation would be ruled by the supreme commander of the army, and the old republican institutions of consuls and the Senate were restricted to a strictly advisory role. The limitations of the imperial model soon became apparent with the appearance of the third emperor, Caligula, who famously made his favorite horse a consul and was almost certainly clinically insane. The instability inherent in a regime based on military approval was also vividly illustrated in 69CE, the "Year of the Four Emperors", when two rulers were murdered and a third committed suicide under pressure from the legions.

Yet for all the confusion of the late republican and early imperial periods, the Roman Empire itself continued to grow. Greece had become a Roman province in 146BCE; Gaul (modern France and Belgium) was conquered by Julius Caesar between 58 and 51 BCE; Egypt was annexed by Augustus; the emperor Claudius oversaw the conquest of what is now England and Wales from 43CE. The last great burst of imperial expansion took place under Trajan, who added Dacia (modern Transylvania), Armenia, and Mesopotamia early in the second century CE. The last two conquests turned out to represent the high water-mark of empire, and were abandoned by Trajan's successor, Hadrian, who introduced a new, enduring policy of preserving what Rome already had rather than reaching out for more.

Trajan and Hadrian, as it happens, feature as the second and third of the "Five Good Emperors"—a succession of able rulers (the first was Nerva, the fourth and fifth Antoninus Pius and the philosopher Marcus Aurelius) who provided the Roman Empire with almost a century of efficient and stable government between 96 and 180 CE. This fifth phase was the imperial heyday when the vast majority of the empire's peoples could go about their business undisturbed beneath the shelter of the *Pax Romana* ("Roman Peace"). Life was comfortable and cosmopolitan, at least for the wealthy; great feats of engineering were achieved, particularly in road-building, and education spread widely.

Yet the empire was always under threat, from the insidious dangers of inflation and corruption within its borders and from the pressure of the foreign enemies the Romans called barbarians without (see page 383). In its final phase, which ended with the collapse of the western Roman Empire, it gradually succumbed. The process was slow—almost three centuries passed between the death of Marcus Aurelius and the abdication of the last western emperor in 476CE—and the decline was by no means unrelieved. These years saw the triumph of Christianity and the establishment of the eastern Roman Empire, which would survive for more than a millennium before its capital, Constantinople, finally fell to the Ottoman Turks in 1453. For the western empire, though, there was no such reprieve. Rome itself was sacked by Goths in 410CE, and under continued barbarian onslaught, the structures of imperial government that had been so lengthily and laboriously constructed were gradually pulled down.

A mosaic (ca. 500CE) from Carthage shows a horseman in Germanic dress. The "barbarian" Germanic peoples who settled in North Africa wished to share in the wealth of Rome and they adopted many of the trappings of Roman life when acquiring control.

LEGENDS OF ROME

Fact and legend became inextricably entwined in Rome's early history. Its most famous names—Aeneas, Horatius, and Romulus and Remus (the children of Mars)—may or may not have existed, but all passed into later Roman chronicles as actual figures who helped shape their people's destiny.

Such well-remembered incidents as the abduction of the Sabine women and the rape of Lucretia may have served to dramatize real events in Rome's infancy. Yet for all their topicality, the legends have more than just local significance. The acts of heroism and violence of which they speak have a universal resonance that has kept them fresh in people's minds around the world to the present day.

THE WANDERINGS OF AENEAS

From early on, the Romans felt that the extraordinary destiny of their race required an exceptional founder. Their real origins stretched back well beyond the written record, leaving the field open to myth. Several different names were offered up, particularly by Greek historians who often chose to portray Rome as one of the many colonies set up in Italy by Greek emigrés in the dark ages after 1000BCE (see pages 320–321). The names that cropped up most often in these sources were Evander and Pallas—this last a youth whose name was later commemorated in Rome's Palatine Hill.

The thought of a Greek origin was less attractive to Romans, particularly after Rome went to war with Greece in the third century BCE. Increasingly, they looked to another venerable figure long associated with the Latium region. This was Aeneas, best known today as the hero of Virgil's great national epic, the *Aeneid*.

The Aeneas legend long predated Virgil, who wrote in the reign of the emperor Augustus. Aeneas is mentioned in Homer's *Iliad*, not as a Greek hero but as a Trojan, second only to Hector in fighting skill. From about 525BCE on, Aeneas also became a familiar figure in Italy, featuring in artworks produced for the Etruscans, often by Greek craftsmen. Rome was under Etruscan rule at the time, so his name must have become well known in the city from that point. The

The great poet Virgil, author of the Aeneid, *which tells the story of the origin of Rome, is portrayed in this mosaic from the 3rd century* CE.

tradition that Aeneas was the founder, not of Rome itself (an honor accorded to his distant successor Romulus) but of the Roman people, was thus well established before Virgil gave it canonical form.

The *Aeneid* describes how Aeneas, son of the mortal Anchises and the goddess Venus, escapes the destruction of Troy carrying his aged father on his back. He also takes with him his household gods, transported in a portable shrine, and his son Ascanius, although his wife Creusa dies during their flight from the burning city. Aeneas then sails off with other survivors in search of a new homeland. The exiles travel first to Thrace, then to the Greek island of Delos, home of a famous oracle of

• ROMULUS AND REMUS •

Of all the Roman myths, few are as rich in folklore as that of Rome's founders, Romulus and Remus. The stories tell how two brothers, Amulius and Numitor, were jointly ruling Alba Longa—a city founded by Aeneas's son Ascanius—when one, Amulius, grew jealous over the succession. Staging a palace coup, he had Numitor imprisoned and forced his daughter, Rhea Silvia, to become a priestess of the goddess Vesta, thereby condemning her to perpetual virginity. But Rhea was subsequently violated, supposedly by the god Mars, and bore twin boys, Romulus and Remus.

Furious, Amulius ordered that the mother should be buried alive and the babies drowned in the Tiber. But the servants charged with the deed took pity on the twins and instead set them afloat in their cradle. The stream carried them ashore, where their crying attracted the attention of a she-wolf. The wolf suckled them with her own milk, sustaining them until human help arrived in the form of a shepherd, who put the boys in his wife's care.

The twins grew up strong and healthy, and on reaching manhood won a reputation for bravery by attacking bandits who were preying on the shepherds. Word of their deeds reached Amulius, and they were summoned before him. At last their true identity was revealed, whereupon Romulus summarily despatched the tyrant who had ordered the death of his mother and restored Numitor to his rightful place on the throne.

the god Apollo. There they are told to seek out "the land of their forefathers"—a place they at first wrongly identify as Crete. After an unsuccessful attempt to settle on the island, however, Aeneas's household gods whisper to him the truth, that the Trojans' ancestors in fact originally came from the Latium region of Italy.

The journey to Latium is cursed by continual hostile interventions by the goddess Juno, sworn enemy of the Trojans. The seafarers have to survive terrifying encounters with legendary monsters of classical mythology—the bird-headed Harpies, gigantic cyclops, the murderous Scylla and Charybdis. They are also frequently diverted from their route, first to Sicily, where Anchises dies, and then to Carthage, where Aeneas is tempted to abandon his quest for the love of the Carthaginian queen Dido. Only divine intervention in the form of a message from Jupiter himself persuades him to abandon his lover in pursuit of his high destiny.

The first part of the *Aeneid*, describing the Trojans' wanderings, recalls Homer's *Odyssey*, which also recounts the tribulations of a hero traveling from the Trojan War (see pages 338–340). The second part, telling of the Trojans' arrival in Italy and the struggle to win a homeland, is closer to the *Iliad* in spirit. The hinge between the two sections is a lengthy description of Aeneas's journey to the underworld in company with the Sibyl of Cumae (see page 407). There Aeneas encounters the spirit of his father Anchises, who prophesies the future glory of the Roman race, culminating in the triumphant reign of Virgil's sponsor, Augustus.

Yet, thanks to the machinations of Juno, the Trojans' arrival in Latium at first brings nothing but strife. Turnus, king of the native Rutulian people, raises an army to resist the newcomers, and bitter warfare follows, culminating when the leaders of the opposing armies meet in single combat. Only by killing his rival is

Legend tells how, following a family feud, Rhea Silvia was condemned by her uncle, Amulius, to a life of perpetual virginity. The plan was thwarted, however, by the appearance of the great god of war, Mars, who impregnated her and for whom she subsequently bore twin boys, Romulus and Remus, who later became the founders of the city of Rome. The stone relief shown here, ca. 100BCE–300CE, was discovered at Aquincum in Hungary and depicts Mars appearing to Rhea Silvia.

Aeneas able at last to fulfill his destiny and provide his people with the promised new home.

The *Aeneid* ends abruptly with the heroes' duel in which Aeneas is successful and secures Rome's future, but references earlier in the poem already imply the subsequent course of events. Inspired by Father Tiber, the spirit of Rome's river, Aeneas sought out an omen, a white sow with thirty piglets, that marked the site where the Trojans were to settle. The place chosen was Lavinium, known today as the small town of Pratica di Mare, some 15 miles (25km) southeast of Rome. There Aeneas duly built a city, and there he finally died, having devoted his last years to merging his Trojans with the local Latin peoples. Subsequently, he won the ultimate accolade his achievements demanded, being worshipped as a god, Jupiter Indiges—the local Jove.

THE BIRTH OF ROME

The legend of Aeneas explained the origins of the Roman people but not of Rome itself. There was a quasi-historical reason for this discrepancy, for by the time that the legends were written down people realized that there was a chronological gap to fill between the two events. Troy was thought to have fallen in the twelfth century BCE, while Rome was not founded until the eighth century—tradition set the date at 753BCE.

To fill the gap, legend provided two separate precursor cities: Aeneas's foundation, Lavinium, and Alba Longa, established by his son Ascanius. A line of fourteen kings was sketched in—they were said to have occupied the Alban throne before the twin grandsons of

the king decided to build a city of their own. But the relationship between Rome's founders, Romulus and Remus (see page 365), turned murderous even before the city was completed. Romulus killed Remus, supposedly in a fit of anger when Remus belittled the town's defenses by jumping over a wall. "So die anyone else who scorns these walls!" he shouted as he delivered the fatal blow.

Even when the walls were complete, the city's future was by no means secure, not least because of a lack of women to bear fresh generations of Romans. So Romulus invited the neighboring Sabine people to attend a festival in the newly completed city, and then set the young men of Rome loose on them. Each youth snatched a girl from the arms of her helpless parents— then over the ensuing months did his best to soothe the outraged feelings of his unwilling bride.

The rape of the Sabine women caused a legacy of bitterness between the two communities that eventually led to war. At first the Sabine forces attacked Rome's defenses. Eventually, however, they found a Roman girl, Tarpeia, who agreed to open a gate for them.

With the enemy inside the gates, war to the death threatened. It was averted, however, by the Sabine women, who had come to care for their husbands as well as for the parents from whom they had been so cruelly separated. They threw themselves between the opposing armies, appealing to both sides for peace. The soldiers recognized the justice of their demand, and a truce was arranged. In time, the pact developed into a lasting alliance that saw Romulus and the Sabine leader Tatius jointly ruling a combined realm. The moral of the tale was clear: Rome had come to stay, and its future lay in friendly alliance with the neighboring peoples.

TYRANTS AND LAWGIVERS

According to legend, Rome had six kings after Romulus: Numa Pompilius, Tullus Hostilius, Ancus Martius, Tarquinius Priscus, Servius Tullius, and Tarquinius Superbus ("Tarquin the Proud"). There was an almost schematic pattern to their tenures of power. The first, third, and fifth—Numa, Ancus, and Servius—were capable leaders and had long, mainly peaceful reigns.

The reigns of the other three kings were marked by upheaval. Numa's successor, Tullus, was a warrior, and under his stewardship Rome was almost constantly at war. This was the time when the city finally conquered its neighbor and predecessor Alba Longa, and one of the most enduring Roman legends grew up around the struggle. It was said that, rather than fight a pitched battle, the two communities agreed to put their fate in the hands of champions. Each army had triplets in its ranks: the Horatii brothers on the Roman side, the Curiatii for the Albans. In the ensuing hand-to-hand encounter, two of the Horatii were quickly killed, but not before wounding their opponents. The third realized that his best chance of survival lay in facing his enemies one at a time rather than together, and so pretended to flee. The Curiatii straggled out in pursuit of him, at which point he turned and killed the foremost. The other two in turn received the same treatment, leaving him and Rome masters of the field.

Tarquinius Priscus, Rome's fourth king, was the first of the city's Etruscan rulers—although, according to the historian Livy, his ethnic background was actually Greek. Nonetheless, Tarquin originally bore the Etruscan name Lucumo, and traveled to Rome with his wife Tanaquil from the Etruscan city of Tarquinia. An ambitious man, he won the trust of the king, Ancus Martius, who made him guardian of his own children. Then, when Ancus died, he sent his wards, the legitimate heirs to the empty throne, on a hunting expedition and in their absence had himself pronounced king.

Despite his deviousness, Tarquin was an effective leader and Rome's borders expanded under his rule. However, Ancus's sons never forgave the usurpation, and many years later they engineered his assassination. Even then the throne did not pass to them, for Tarquin's widow Tanaquil managed to ensure that his adopted heir, Servius, was chosen in their stead. Servius had been favored by Tarquin, partly as a result of a portent: he had been found one day in the palace with a ring of fire around his head. Tanaquil, who had Etruscan powers of divination, immediately foresaw a great future for him and persuaded Tarquin to bring him up as his heir, preferring his claim even to that of their own two sons.

For all his abilities, Servius also came to a violent end—at the hands of one of the heirs he had supplanted. Tarquin the Proud, a son or grandson of the earlier Tarquin, was married to Tullia, a daughter of Servius who was quite as ambitious as he was. In Servius's old age this unfilial child persuaded her husband to stage a coup, in the course of which Servius was killed. Legend then insists that Tullia, who had already had her first husband killed to marry Tarquin, drove her chariot over her father's body as it lay in the street.

Tarquin and Tullia were the Macbeth and Lady Macbeth of Roman history: able, maybe, but vitiated by unscrupulous ambition. Tarquin came to be hated as a ruthless tyrant; he was also resented by later generations of Romans for the period of Etruscan domination that he represented. His downfall was closely linked to the tale of the rape of Lucretia. The story tells that two of the king's sons were boasting one night of the respective merits of their wives while in the company of a young nobleman, Collatinus. Drunkenly, the three decided to ride to the capital to compare the ladies' merits at first hand. They found the two royal brides socializing at parties, while Collatinus's wife, Lucretia, was at home demurely spinning—an appropriate occupation for a Roman matron. One of Tarquin's sons, Sextus, returned to Lucretia's house a few days later and violated her in the middle of the night at swordpoint. Lucretia sent for her father and her husband, who arrived in company with Lucius Junius Brutus, a nephew of Tarquin. She demanded vengeance, then plunged a knife into her breast. Word of the crime spread through Rome, acting as a catalyst for revolt among a people already sorely oppressed by Tarquin's rule. With Brutus at the head of the mob, the monarchy was eventually brought down, and with it the period of Etruscan domination.

CITIZEN HEROES

A whole cycle of legends built up around the first years of the republic, most of them concerned with Tarquin the Proud's attempts to regain the throne—and there were several such. At first he tried conspiracy, plotting with influential Romans to engineer his return. Among the conspirators were two sons of Rome's liberator, Brutus; and, noble Roman that he was, he stoically watched their execution when they were condemned to death for their treason. Next Tarquin allied with the Etruscan cities of

Tarquinia and Veii to win back power by force. Again Brutus frustrated him, this time riding out to confront Tarquin's son, Aruns, in single combat. Both died in the ensuing duel, but the republic was saved.

Tarquin's third attempt was made in conjunction with Lars Porsena of Clusium. This time republican Rome owed its survival to the heroism of Horatius Cocles, who, with two companions, held the wooden bridge across the Tiber River against the invading army while defenders hacked away its supports. When it finally collapsed, he hurled himself fully armed into the stream, successfully swimming through a hail of missiles back to the Roman bank.

Having failed to take the city by assault, Porsena then settled in to besiege it. Again he was confounded by indomitable republican courage. A certain Caius Mucius had himself smuggled into the Etruscan camp, where he attempted to assassinate the Etruscan leader, but mistakenly killed his secretary instead. Taken before Porsena, he was ordered to name his fellow conspirators under threat of torture, but voluntarily thrust his right hand into the fire to show the impossibility of forcing him to speak. Porsena was so impressed by his valor that he withdrew his forces, leaving Tarquin to eke out a lonely old age in the Greek colony of Cumae, his hopes of restoration finally put to rest.

The legendary figures of later republican times were more ambiguous in their heroism than these early champions. The best remembered now is probably Coriolanus, thanks to Shakespeare's play of the same name. Coriolanus won his title of honor by conquering the town of Corioli from the Volscians in the course of a fifth-century BCE war. However, he lost popular support by refusing to distribute corn to the people during a period of famine and was forced into exile. In his anger he offered his services to the very Volscians he had earlier defeated, and in due course led a Volscian army almost to the gates of Rome. There he was met by his wife and his mother, who appealed to his patriotism not to attack his own city. Moved, he called off the attack,

and was later put to death by the Volscians for failing to press home the assault.

Similar clouds hung over the career of Camillus, hero of the ten-year siege of Veii, the last independent Etruscan city, which finally fell to the Romans in 396BCE. For all his services to the nation, he was accused of appropriating booty from the conquered city, and he too went into exile. However, his story had a happy ending. He was recalled to Rome to lead resistance to the Gauls who captured the city in 390BCE, and lived to regain the glory of which he had been unjustly deprived.

IMPERIAL GOSSIP

In imperial times the wilder stories that attached themselves to the emperors smacked more of backstairs gossip than of legend properly so called. In fact, given that the imperial succession sometimes put absolute power in the hands of immature adolescents, many were no doubt true. Suetonius, for example, detailed his subjects' sexual excesses. Caligula, he claimed, slept with all three of his sisters, and forced two of them to share their beds with his boyfriends. Attending the wedding of a leading nobleman, he had the bride carried off for his own enjoyment. When his extravagance left him strapped for cash, he opened a brothel in his palace, stocking it with respectable married women and freeborn boys. In similar vein, Nero is said to have married a boy named Sporus in a wedding ceremony complete with bridal veil and dowry, having previously had him castrated. He liked to dress in animal skins and be penned in a cage, from which he was released to maul the private parts of male and female victims who were bound to stakes in the manner of Christians in the arena.

Such stories contributed hugely to the most enduring of all Roman legends—that of the empire's own decadence. As a corrective, it is important to remember that Caligula and Nero were exceptions—most emperors were hard-working soldiers without whose tireless efforts the Roman imperium would never have survived for almost 500 years.

ART AND ARCHITECTURE

Although initially influenced by Etruscan and Greek styles, the Romans developed their own distinctive brands of art. However, it was in the fields of architecture and engineering that they made the greater impact, with breathtaking basilicas, amphitheaters, and aqueducts that stand to this day.

For those accustomed to thinking in terms of national schools of painting and sculpture, Roman art remains something of an enigma. In truth, it barely existed, if the term is taken to mean work produced by Italian artists in a purely Roman style. Instead, the body of work that goes under that label was always supranational in its inspiration as well as its creative talent. In the early years, it was almost entirely derivative, partly from Etruscan models, but mostly from the Greeks. Later, however, Roman art developed into something altogether more original. It became an international classical style, still taking its inspiration largely from Greece, that extended its influence around the entire Mediterranean world and that traveled wherever the legions carried the standards of Rome.

Like so much else, the taste for Greek art first came to Rome among the spoils of war. The conquest first of the Greek cities of southern Italy and Sicily, then of Greece itself, and finally of Hellenistic Asia Minor in the course of the third and second centuries BCE flooded Rome with pillaged artworks. Greek artists followed, eager to cater for the craze for all things Hellenic that swept through the wealthy classes. The vogue stretched to imitations as well as original pieces, and soon Rome supported a flourishing mini-industry producing painstaking copies of masterworks by great Greek sculptors of earlier times.

Nevertheless, Roman art gradually developed distinctive features with few parallels in the earlier culture. One was a taste for warts-and-all realism, most marked in certain Roman portrait busts and in a series of remarkable sarcophagi (elaborate coffins) sculpted for private clients in imperial times. Although the sculptors were themselves often Greeks living in Italy, the patrons they worked for evidently accepted or even demanded a greater degree of fidelity to nature than their counterparts on the other side of the Adriatic Sea.

Another characteristically Roman artform was the commemorative relief. The earliest examples date from around 100BCE, but the finest and most memorable tend to come from the imperial period. None has stood the test of time

---

RIGHT *In its early days, Rome grew up in the shadow of its wealthier northern neighbors, the city-states of Etruria, and inherited many elements of its civilization from them (see page 360). An enduring part of the heritage was a taste for beautiful things, for at a time when the inhabitants of Rome were still unpolished provincials the Etruscans were already producing impressive works of art, such as this magnificent bronze statuette, ca. 300–280BCE.*

OPPOSITE *The Ephesus Library was built in 135CE in Ephesus (modern-day Turkey) by Julius Aquila in honor of his father, Celsus Polemaeanus of Sardis, a Roman senator and proconsul of the province of Asia. Such initiatives encouraged the spread of literacy throughout the empire and also, crucially, facilitated the promotion of Roman culture and ideology in its far-flung provinces.*

better than the 640-feet-long (200m) frieze that snakes its way up Trajan's Column in Rome.

Painting for the Romans typically meant wall decoration, and art historians now distinguish four separate styles covering the period from roughly 100BCE to 200CE. The first did little more than imitate marble blocks, while the second favored elaborate architectural vistas. In the Augustan age (27BCE–14CE), a third style featuring central panels depicting mythological or pastoral scenes came into vogue, giving way in its turn to a fourth, baroque style that flanked the panels with fantastic perspective effects and fanciful arabesques.

Mural painting fell into decline from the start of the third century CE at a time when many genres of Roman art were in a state of flux. By then classical art in general was giving way to the style now known as Late Antique. Over the next 300 years, the idealized humanism of the Greek tradition would finally fade away, to be replaced by the God-centered priorities of medieval art.

BUILDING THE ETERNAL CITY
Of all the visual arts, architecture best suited the Roman character. Massive construction in stone and brick played to the Romans' talent for organization and to their engineering strengths, and also catered for their rulers' love of display. The remains of many of their great public buildings still stand to this day, mutely testifying to the grandeur that was Rome.

As with much of Rome's artistic inheritance, a considerable amount of the initial impetus came from the Greeks, mediated through Etruscan influences. By historic times, wealthy Romans were living in villas that closely resembled those of Greece or, more precisely, those of the Greek colonists of southern Italy. The town houses preserved at Pompeii and Herculaneum have blank walls giving onto the street in the manner of their equivalents in Sybaris or Syracuse. Inside, rooms radiate off the atrium, a central hall that, unlike its Greek counterpart, was usually covered. However, larger villas often also incorporated an uncovered courtyard in the Greek manner, pleasantly decorated with flowers and artworks and perhaps with a fountain to provide a constant murmur of running water.

Hadrian's Villa at Tivoli in the Sabine Hills, showing part of the Canopus, a colonnaded reflecting pool evoking the canal at Alexandria. Work began in 118CE at the complex, which is spread over some 250 acres (100 hectares) and includes more than thirty buildings. Apart from its luxurious living quarters and an annex to house guests, among the villa's spectacular features were banqueting halls, libraries, pavilions and even a miniature villa set on an artificial island to which Hadrian (reigned 117–138CE) could retreat for peace and solitude.

Most of the more familiar Roman monuments date not from republican but imperial times, when Rome's rulers had the money for major projects. A golden age of Roman architecture extended between the reigns of Nero and Hadrian, from 54 to 138 CE, although there was an earlier surge of construction under Augustus and later revivals under such rulers as Caracalla, Diocletian, and Constantine.

The Romans' greatest technical contribution lay in the development of concrete, which was introduced in the second century BCE. Although marble was also widely used in Roman public building, concrete became the material of choice for large-scale construction by the end of the following century. The finest concrete was made of lime and water mixed with the special soil known as *pozzolana*, so called because the principal deposits were found at Pozzuoli, near Naples. *Pozzolana* was a mix of clay and volcanic cinders that gained great strength when combined with an aggregate of rubble— often the chippings from builders' masonry.

Concrete freed up building techniques when combined with another defining feature of Roman architecture—the semi-circular arch. This innovation came originally from Greece by way of the Etruscans, who

had first realized that a central keystone, held in place by wedge-shaped supporting stones called *voussoirs*, could create a solid framework for construction. When poured into moulds held in place between a skeleton of arches, concrete could be shaped into domes, apses, niches, and vaults, opening up large areas of floor space by reducing the need for pillars and other supports.

Concrete in combination with the arch provided the technological basis for the wave of public building that marked early imperial days. One typical structure of the time was the basilica, usually oblong in shape with a semi-circular apse at the far end, and with twin rows of columns separating the central hallway from parallel side aisles. For the early Romans, the basilica was part law-court, part municipal building. Later it was adopted by Christians as a template for church-building.

Yet it is the bigger, more grandiose structures for which the Romans are best remembered: triumphal arches, victory columns, theaters, and amphitheaters such as the Colosseum in Rome, built to seat around 50,000 spectators (see page 396). Architects may have been brought up to respect order and harmony by writers like Vitruvius, whose handbook of architecture, written in Augustus's reign, was to have huge influence when rediscovered more than a millennium later by the builders of Renaissance Italy. What their patrons sought, however, was splendor and massive grandeur—unmistakable icons of Roman power. To Rome's Dark Age successors, such structures seemed the work of giants, and they still impress by their size and magnificence to the present day.

At the height of its imperial power, Rome was the wonder of the world. A million or more people lived in its crowded streets. The city had been so generously endowed by its rulers that almost half the available space in the central districts was taken up by civic buildings. The most impressive of its monuments were unmatched for grandeur anywhere in the world, and their memory lingers to this day: names like the Capitol, the Colosseum, and the Circus Maximus still resonate. The greatest structures in terms of sheer size were the public bath complexes. The stately architecture was matched by an engineering infrastructure of unparalleled sophistication in which the city's water supply took pride of place.

Splendid though its monuments were, the capital also had a seamy and unhygienic underside. Most citizens lived in multistory tenements the size of city blocks; these were known as *insulae* ("islands") because roads surrounded them. Only the very rich could afford the luxury of villas or of running water in their homes. Life in the *insulae* was crowded and unsanitary. Even though Rome had elaborate public sewers, they did not serve private buildings and much household waste was simply dumped into the street. Fire was an additional hazard. The Great Fire of 64CE left only four of the capital's fourteen districts unscathed.

For all its problems, the city remained a magnet throughout imperial times. Following Constantine's conversion to Christianity, the fourth century CE saw a new wave of construction, this time of churches. And even when the western empire finally collapsed, Rome itself survived, buoyed by the prestige of its bishops, the popes. As the classical period gave way to the medieval era, the city remained an international capital, despite the fact that the source of its authority had moved from the political to the religious sphere.

✦ FEATS OF ENGINEERING ✦

Among the ancient Romans' most impressive achievements was the development of sophisticated engineering techniques that enabled fresh water to be carried into the cities. Although only the very wealthy could afford running water in their homes—most citizens had to fetch their supply from a fountain or buy it from a water-carrier—the new feats of engineering nevertheless transformed people's lives, contributing greatly to their health and comfort.

Through their mastery of the arch as a structural component, engineers and architects were able to combine science and artistry to construct huge monuments such as the magnificent aqueduct Pont du Gard in what is now France, erected around 19BCE to carry water and traffic over the Gard River to Nîmes, 16 miles (26km) away. The upper span of thirty-five small arches is approximately 900 feet (275m) long and 10 feet (3m) wide; it supported a conduit that carried fresh water 161 feet (49m) above the river. Constructed of stone blocks entirely without mortar, the aqueduct formed part of a skilfully engineered system of water channels that ran in all for some 31 miles (50km). Much of its course can still be traced today.

Of equal sophistication was the engineering infrastructure of Rome itself. By late imperial times, eleven aqueducts, covering a total of 270 miles (435km), brought millions of litres of water into the city each day. The water fed into distribution tanks, from which it was carried in lead pipes to public fountains and baths.

SOCIETY AND GOVERNMENT

Roman society was characterized by a number of clear divisions: for example, between classes, between the sexes, and between slaves and freedmen. In response to these divisions, a complex system of government developed, the influence of which can be felt to this day.

The internal politics of early republican Rome were marked by a sharp class divide. On the one side were the patricians, the city's hereditary aristocracy; on the other the plebeians, a heterogenous collection of people, ranging from jobless laborers and debt-ridden peasants to wealthy but non-noble landowners jealous of the patricians' grip on power. Just as the struggle for Italy dominated the first two centuries of the republic's history, so the main theme of the internal politics of the period was the struggle between the two orders.

The origin of patrician power stretched back into the mists of time. As the historian Livy told the story, Romulus created 100 senators, known as "fathers," to help him govern early Rome, and the patricians were their descendants. Early on they established exclusive rights to the chief priestly offices, and they alone were able to take the auspices, which had to be consulted before major decisions were made. They also dominated the Senate.

Even though the patricians were a privileged oligarchy, many were highly public-spirited. Their code of civic duty was summed up in the career of L. Caecilius Metellus, who twice served as consul and saw distinguished service in the First Punic War. At his funeral in 221BCE his son insisted that he had achieved the most noble ambitions a Roman could hope for: "He was a warrior of the first rank, an excellent orator, and a courageous general; under his auspices, deeds of the greatest importance were accomplished; he attained

A bronze relief, 50–75CE, depicting two men, an older and a younger one, of a generic type—solemn-faced magistrates clad in togas and shoes appropriate to members of the patrician class. Even after the plebeians had achieved their political ambitions by gaining access to the Senate, the patricians continued to dominate the very highest public offices.

the highest offices in the state; he was distinguished for his wisdom; he held primacy in the Senate; he won a large fortune by honorable means; he left behind many children; and he was the most famous man in the commonwealth."

The patrician families were linked to certain sections of the plebeians by a complex web of patronage and favors known as *clientela*—clienthood. However, there were also divisions between the orders that were based on classic class-struggle lines. A particular bone of contention was the patrician families' appropriation of public land for their own uses, and the economic burdens that led many small landholders to fall into a form of debt bondage known as *nexum*. Add in the thwarted political ambitions of Rome's incipient middle class, and the scene was set for a prolonged conflict that the plebeians eventually won.

The first plebeian consuls were elected in 366BCE, and soon the Senate started to fill up with "new men," as senators of non-noble birth were called. From 287BCE the decisions of the plebeian Popular Assembly were given the full force of law. Yet the patricians continued to occupy a central position in the state. They played the part of successful ruling classes through the ages, compromising their exclusivity just enough to co-opt their most ambitious rivals into their own ranks, thereby averting the risk of revolution.

SENATORS, CONSULS, AND TRIBUNES

The constitution that Rome inherited from the so-called Struggle of the Orders, pitting patricians against plebeians, was one of intricate checks and balances. The task of putting forward legislation lay with the Senate. In the early days there were 300 senators, chosen by the consuls from patrician ranks. Later the number expanded, to 900 under Julius Caesar, although Augustus then reduced it to 600, and it became customary for ex-magistrates to be chosen, whether patrician or plebeian.

• ROMAN WOMEN •

There was a marked tension between what Roman men expected a woman's role to be and women's own view of the subject, at least among the affluent classes. The traditional and officially accepted male view was of women as homemakers. *Lanam fecit*—"she made wool"—was a eulogy frequently incised on women's tombstones. The emperor Augustus himself insisted on wearing only clothes made from homespun wool, although, needless to say, the actual weaving in the imperial household was done by domestic slaves.

Legally, the position of women was not strong. Daughters were almost entirely in their fathers' power. In early times, husbands exercised similar authority over their wives after marriage, but the wives' rights increased with time, and by the late republican period they could, for the most part, retain control of their own property, even though their financial affairs had to be handled by a male guardian. But women in Rome certainly had greater liberty to get out of the house than their counterparts in ancient Greece and could, for example, go shopping or attend the theater on their own. On such occasions women from wealthy households would wear extravagant jewelry, such as the belt and bracelet (ca. 250–400CE) shown here.

For some high-born women, emancipation went well beyond such modest bounds. One such was Clodia, who has gone down in literary history as the "Lesbia" of Catullus's impassioned love poems. Catullus was, however, very far from being her only lover. The wife of a consul and a member of the high-ranking Claudian family, she became the central figure in a trial that scandalized Rome in 57BCE. She was the accuser, charging a former lover with bribing slaves to poison her. The accused was fortunate to have Cicero, an old acquaintance, as his advocate who succeeded in getting the young man acquitted.

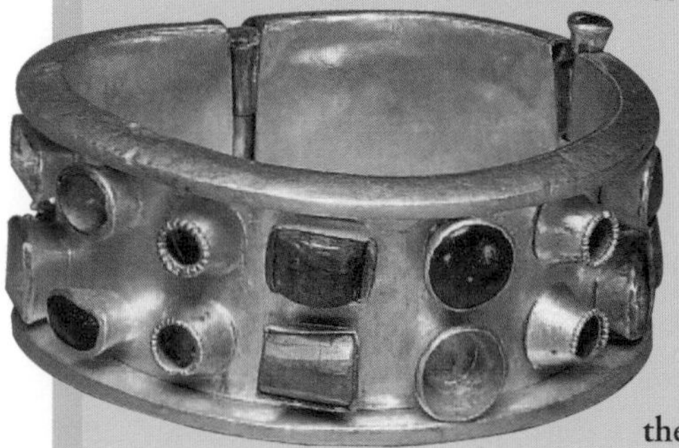

The most unfortunate of Roman women were the slaves, although some fared better than others. One serious problem was that slave girls were regarded as the property of their masters, and so had no legal recourse in cases of sexual harrassment or rape. Even so, their fate was possibly preferable to that of the slaves who worked in the inns and taverns. A law of the early fourth century spelled out that they could not be accused of adultery, because it was taken for granted that they would have sexual relations with the male clientele. Their rights were, quite simply, beneath the law's cognizance.

Besides proposing new laws, which had then to be approved by one of the various popular assemblies, senators had other fingers on the strings of power. They controlled foreign policy, assigned magistrates to govern the provinces and supervised the rituals of the state religion. They could also set up courts of enquiry to investigate wrongdoing. Through much of the republic's life they kept the executive under close supervision—indeed, when they finally lost control, the republic collapsed and Rome was plunged into civil war. Senators gave up sovereign power under the empire, although they continued to play an important role, supervising public finances and controlling some provinces.

The chief executive arms of government under the republic were the two consuls, who had equal power. They were chosen by the *comitia centuriata*, a popular assembly, from the ranks of the senators, and the choice was ratified by the Senate. They held office for only a year, although they could be re-elected. Crucially, they commanded Rome's armies, often serving as generals in the field; in later times they sometimes had their command extended so they could serve as proconsuls governing conquered provinces. At home they were assisted in the task of governing by such other magistrates as the *praetors*, who administered the law, the *aediles* in charge of public works, and the *quaestors* who oversaw state finances.

The tribunes of the people owed their existence to the Struggle of the Orders, when the office was created to represent plebeian interests against the patricians. Tribunes had themselves to be plebeians of free birth, and they were elected annually by the popular assembly. Their powers were considerable, for they could veto any act of any magistrate, and were protected from reprisal by their inviolate status—to harm a tribune merited the death penalty. The tribunes maintained their influence throughout the later centuries of the republic only to lose it under the emperors, who assumed their powers for themselves, claiming to represent the people's interests in their own person.

SLAVES AND FREEDMEN

For much of its history, Rome was a slave society on a massive scale, and servitude did much to corrupt and coarsen Roman life. Although the institution went back to early times, only the very rich could afford to keep slaves in the first centuries of the republic. Everything changed with the wars of conquest of the second century BCE, after which hundreds of thousands of foreign captives were sold into slavery in Italy, 150,000 alone after Rome's victory against the Macedonians at Pydna in 168BCE. To compound the problem, pirates based on Crete and the Turkish coast roamed the eastern Mediterranean snatching victims for the slave market on the Aegean island of Delos, which was said to be able to handle 10,000 transactions a day. Many of these unfortunates also found their way to Italy.

The treatment they met there depended on fate and the disposition of their master. Many ended up working for the state, either as laborers or miners or, if they had an education, as clerks. Some had the good fortune to find themselves in enlightened households where they were treated with humanity and warmth. The obverse, however, could be terrible: they could be tortured to extract confessions if a crime was committed, and if a master was killed, every slave in the household was executed as a possible accomplice in the deed. Until the first century CE, masters could have male slaves castrated or sell them to die in the arena.

In general, the slaves' lot improved with time. Once the mass deportations of the last two centuries BCE came to an end, the price of slaves soared and the value put upon them rose with it. A master could give a slave his liberty at any time by performing a simple ceremony—these slaves became freedmen. They would then take the last name of their former master and they and their immediate heirs continued to be bound to him by some residual ties of duty and obligation; two generations had to pass before their descendants became full Roman citizens. Even so, the descendants of slaves eventually became wholly integrated into the citizen body.

FIRST AMONG EQUALS: THE EMPEROR

For the greatest empire the Western world had known, the Roman imperium had inauspicious origins. Its founder, Octavian, deliberately avoided the title imperator *(emperor), which was not used for the first fifty years of the empire's existence. Instead he chose to be known as* princeps, *a title implying "chief" or "first citizen," and to preserve the Senate and all the symbols of republican government.*

The reasons for Octavian's reticence were not hard to find. He was only too aware of the fate of his adoptive father Julius Caesar, who had been assassinated by men who feared his ambitions. To avoid Caesar's fate, he took care to downplay his intentions. He disbanded much of his army and continued to offer himself annually for re-election to the position of consul, which he had first held in the closing years of the civil war. The Senate responded gratefully by conferring on him the honorary name of Augustus ("revered one"). He

was also given control over the army and assumed the position of tribune of the people, in effect using the mechanisms of republican government to attain absolute power.

Augustus always showed moderation in the use of his considerable powers, but the realities of absolute rule quickly made themselves felt under his successors. His immediate heir Tiberius had been a successful general, but he was an embittered and suspicious man when he eventually became emperor at the age of fifty-six, and his period in office deteriorated into a reign of terror. Caligula, his successor, proved even worse: under his erratic rule autocracy tottered on the verge of insanity. On one occasion, having determined to invade Britain, he lined his army up on Gaul's Channel shore only to set them to gathering seashells, which he described as "tribute from the Ocean." He then returned to Rome.

There would be other emperors scarcely better than Caligula in the empire's long history—among them, Nero, Domitian, and Elegabalus—although the majority of rulers were conscientious and hard-working. A feature common to most of the really incompetent emperors was the hereditary principle, which sometimes raised totally unsuitable candidates simply through accidents of birth. Significantly, the sequence of efficient rulers known to history as the "Five Good Emperors"—Nerva, Trajan, Hadrian, Antoninus Pius, and Marcus Aurelius, who reigned

A sardonyx cameo, 1st century CE, *bearing the profiles of two Roman emperors and their wives: Claudius and his wife Agrippina the Younger (left) and Germanicus and his wife Agrippina the Elder (right).*

between 96 and 180 CE—succeeded each other as adoptive rather than genetic heirs. When Marcus Aurelius reverted to the custom of naming his eldest son as his heir, the result was the reign of Commodus, who renamed Rome Colonia Commodiana ("Commodus's Colony") and came to believe that he was the reincarnation of Hercules. However, when he determined to show off his Herculean skills as a gladiator, his aides arranged for his assassination.

From the third century on, the emperors spent less and less time in Rome as the threat to the empire's frontiers grew. Now a new danger arose as the rulers became increasingly beholden to the army. Emperors were made and unmade by the legions with dizzying rapidity: thirty-one individuals aspired to the title in the fifty years after 235CE, sometimes more than one at a time. Diocletian restored some order in the late third century, but only by recognizing that the task of holding the empire together was more than one man could handle. Instead he set up the tetrarchy, a system that divided the imperial duties between four co-regents, each supervising different regions. This step paved the way for the division of the Roman Empire into eastern and western components. Rome itself ceased even to be an imperial headquarters, although it remained the seat of the Senate.

Diocletian also finally abandoned any remaining notion of simply being first among equals of the Roman people. Instead he chose to rule in oriental splendor, endorsing a tendency that had already been visible in some of his predecessors. Although he elected not to identify himself as a god, he and his fellow emperors were regularly portrayed as companions of gods, Hercules and Jupiter being the preferred models. Ironically, Diocletian decided at the same time to encourage a cult of Rome and the Roman people, even though the city itself was gradually moving to the sidelines of history.

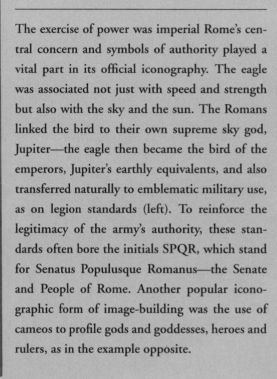

The exercise of power was imperial Rome's central concern and symbols of authority played a vital part in its official iconography. The eagle was associated not just with speed and strength but also with the sky and the sun. The Romans linked the bird to their own supreme sky god, Jupiter—the eagle then became the bird of the emperors, Jupiter's earthly equivalents, and also transferred naturally to emblematic military use, as on legion standards (left). To reinforce the legitimacy of the army's authority, these standards often bore the initials SPQR, which stand for Senatus Populusque Romanus—the Senate and People of Rome. Another popular iconographic form of image-building was the use of cameos to profile gods and goddesses, heroes and rulers, as in the example opposite.

There were great rulers in the last centuries of Roman power who managed to unify the empire under their personal rule; Constantine, who defeated all his rivals to rule single-handedly between 324 and 337 CE, was probably the greatest. Yet the world had changed in the intervening years, and Constantine's rule was very different from the consensual mock-republicanism of Augustus's day. Constantine himself recognized the shifting balance of power by building the new imperial capital of Constantinople near the empire's eastern borders. It was a far-sighted move, for the future was to lie with the Greek-speaking Byzantine world ruled from that city, whose emperors would cling onto power for almost a thousand years after Rome itself had fallen and power in the west had passed to the barbarians.

CONQUEST AND GLORY

No Roman institution could match the army for prestige. The nation owed its success to its martial prowess, which had turned a small Italian city-state into a world power. Unsurprisingly, then, the military virtues of discipline, order, duty, and loyalty were central to the Roman ethos.

For most of its early history Rome made do without professional soldiers. The republican forces that conquered peninsular Italy in the fifth and fourth centuries BCE consisted of ad-hoc levies drawn from the ranks of male, property-owning citizens. Most recruits were peasant farmers, summoned only when required.

The levy system broke down as Rome's military activities widened. Volunteers called upon to serve in the ranks for months or even years at a time could not combine their obligations with the demands of running a farm or advancing a career. So the consul Gaius Marius introduced a radical reform programme at the end of the first century BCE. He abandoned conscription and the property requirement, and instead enlisted volunteers who agreed to sign up for a sixteen-year term.

In effect, Marius created a professional standing army—one that proved a formidable fighting force. However, the weakness of the Marian system was that the full-time soldiers relied on military success for their advancement, and increasingly their loyalties were given not to the state as a whole but to individual commanders. An ambitious general like Julius Caesar could gain the devotion of his men not just by winning battles but also by rewarding them fittingly (he almost doubled their pay). The ultimate loser was Rome itself, which was plunged into the horrors of the civil war.

When Augustus restored peace and order from 29BCE on, he reduced the number of legions from about sixty to twenty-eight, and paid off the redundant soldiery generously with grants of money and land. The new military structure he went on to create formed the basis for Roman might throughout the imperial period.

Each legion of the Roman army was divided into cohorts and centuries. These last were usually made up of about eighty men under the command of a centurion. Total numbers varied, but in early imperial times typically averaged about 5,500 men. The legions were supplemented by auxiliary forces composed of volunteers from outside Italy, serving under Roman commanders. They were paid much less than legionaries and had to serve for twenty-five years. However, they became eligible on retirement for Roman citizenship, which they could pass on to their heirs.

The Roman navy never commanded the esteem afforded to the army. Indeed, for the first two centuries of the republic there was no navy at all. Rome only felt the need for a maritime force when its ambitions spread beyond Italy itself, at the time of the First Punic War in the mid-third century BCE.

Under the emperors the navy guaranteed freedom of trade and ensured that the Mediterranean remained what the Romans called *Mare Nostrum*—"our sea." Sailors were referred to as *milites* (soldiers) like their counterparts on land, and were commanded in the same fashion as legionaries. Even so, most were non-Italians. The Roman genius was for land warfare, and it was by infantrymen that the empire was won and primarily maintained.

◆ ROMANS AND BARBARIANS ◆

After Rome's conquest of Greece in the second century BCE, the concept of barbarism as an antonym for civilization (see page 317) was absorbed by the conquerors along with many other aspects of Hellenistic culture. The Romans applied the term not to all foreigners but only to those who fell beyond the confines of the classical heritage. Romans were often scathing about the Greek people, many of whom they enslaved. They called them weak, effeminate, cowardly, and corrupt—but they never accused them of being barbarians.

The Romans' selective use of the word was by no means arbitrary, for the culture gap that it addressed was a very real one. Roman (and Greek) society was urban and economically developed—different in every way from the tribal agricultural societies that the Romans confronted beyond their borders, at least in Europe and North Africa. The barbarian lands had no equivalent of the high culture of Rome's educated classes, and for the most part lacked writing.

In time, familiarity led certain barbarian peoples to admire and even embrace aspects of Roman culture, just as the conquered peoples of the empire did. Yet those barbarians who found their way to Rome only to die in the arenas or to be worked to death as slaves in mines or on the great agricultural estates can hardly have formed any very high opinion of the general superiority of Roman civilization.

In the long run, the chasm that divided the Roman and barbarian worlds was to prove fatal to the western Roman Empire. In the east, Romans shared many common values with their subject peoples, who became integrated in a way that the inhabitants of the western lands failed to do. Although Roman culture radically altered Gaul and Spain and North Africa and Britain, it remained in comparison a surface veneer that rubbed off easily under the pressure of the great invasions of the fifth century.

A CITIZEN'S LIFE

In truth, one citizen's standard of living might differ greatly from that of another, depending on their wealth and social status. The affluent minority lived in comfortable villas and dined extravagantly, while the rest struggled to make ends meet in crowded tenements.

Wealthy Romans had little doubt that they lived in the greatest city the world had ever seen, and their provincial counterparts also had few reasons to complain. In the empire's prosperous days, Roman citizens enjoyed a standard of living that was almost certainly the highest yet known. However, these fortunates formed only a small minority of the total population. Most people lived in servants' quarters or army barracks, in crowded, noisy tenements or malodorous rural hovels. Daily life in the empire covered a wide spectrum of lifestyles in which one person's creature comforts were often earned by the sweat of another's brow, and where luxury and squalor coexisted in close proximity.

THE ROMAN HOME

The homes in which Romans lived varied greatly according to each individual's wealth and status. At the top of the social pyramid, the wealthy luxuriated in marble villas, their walls bright with frescoes and their floors rich in mosaics. Very affluent individuals might have two or more such residences, one in town and the other in the country, often at the heart of a vast agricultural estate.

By the imperial era the prosperous middle classes could also aspire to comfortable villas. The general plan was one of rooms leading on to an atrium with an open skylight that let in both sunlight and rain (collected in a small pool called the *impluvium*). This provided both a large, central public space and opportunities for privacy. The bigger villas also had a second courtyard, the *peristylum*, which was colonnaded, following the Greek fashion, and often served as a garden. Further sophistications, including central heating, followed in imperial times. Glass sometimes came to supplement wooden shutters in windows, although it remained thick and opaque.

Most inhabitants of Rome itself enjoyed few such luxuries. The mass of the population lived in crowded, rank tenements which were up to five or six floors high—the emperor Augustus limited their height to reduce the ever-present risk of fire. Although there were owner-occupiers, the majority of people rented rooms from wealthy landlords or speculative builders—prices in Rome were about four times higher than those found elsewhere in Italy.

Noise pollution was a major problem for city-dwellers. The poet Martial, who lived in a third-floor flat, complained that, "There's no peace and quiet in the city for a poor man. Early in the morning schoolmasters stop us enjoying any normal life. Before it gets light there are the bakers, then it's the hammering of the coppersmiths all day." Nights were little better, because the use of heavy transport was restricted to after dark to relieve congestion in the daylight hours.

For all the complaints, city apartments were in constant demand; even Martial found that he grew homesick for the bustle of Rome when he retired to a Spanish villa. Tenement-living was made bearable by the fact that much of the day was spent out of the house: in the streets, at the circus, and, above all, at the public baths.

THE DOMESTIC WORLD

"There is nothing more holy, nothing more securely guarded by every religious instinct, than each individual Roman's home," the orator Cicero claimed. And the

---

In ancient Rome, as throughout the modern world, dogs were not only kept as domestic pets but were also often used as guards and protectors to deter thieves or unwanted visitors from private property. The dog on a leash shown here is an example of a late 1st-century CE cave canem ("beware of the dog") mosaic from Pompeii.

chief responsibility for preserving its sanctity rested squarely on the shoulders of the *paterfamilias* or father of the family, who had powers, in theory at least, of life and death over his children. Not only could he order them to be exposed at birth, leaving them to die, he could also hand them over to execution or into slavery, if he so chose—although, needless to say, such behavior was extremely rare.

Wives were expected to conduct themselves with dignity and circumspection. Often they married at fourteen or fifteen, at which tender age they were already expected to take charge of the day-to-day running of the household. In even moderately wealthy families, that meant directing the work of domestic slaves. Well-to-do women left the nursing and sometimes the upbringing of infants to servants.

State policy generally favored large families, and—officially, at least—adultery and extramarital affairs were regarded with horror. In 18BCE Augustus passed a law that allowed a father to kill his daughter and her lover with impunity if they were caught *in flagrante*, and that similarly permitted a husband to kill an adulterous rival, although not his wife; instead, he was expected to divorce her promptly or face punishment. Such a woman could not remarry and lost a third of her property; she also faced banishment to an island. The adulterer, if not killed on the spot, lost half his property and could also expect to be deported to an island, although not the same one as the adultress. Such strictures were no doubt aimed primarily at Rome's fast set, a particular cause of concern to the reforming emperor. A more typical picture of Roman family life comes from tombstones, which sometimes bear touching messages of marital affection that echo down the centuries.

CHILDHOOD AND SCHOOLING

In early republican times, the education of Roman children was left very much in the hands of parents. Cato the Elder, in the second century BCE, refused to entrust his son's upbringing to an educated Greek slave living in his own household. Instead, Plutarch tells us, Cato himself "taught his son reading and writing, the law, physical education, and all sorts of outdoor skills such as throwing the javelin, fighting in armor, riding, boxing, swimming, and how to stand up to heat and cold." Such a man would also expect his boy to follow him in the course of his public duties, whether to the temple for religious observances or to social events, including dinner parties—even to the Senate, if his father were a member.

Later Romans, however, increasingly entrusted their children to teachers, although there was never anything resembling a state school system. Wealthy families might employ a slave, like Cato's educated Greek, to act as a private tutor. Less well-off parents sent their children from about the age of seven, whether boys or girls, to a schoolmaster to learn reading, writing, and arithmetic. These poorly paid individuals held classes in their own homes, or sometimes in rented stalls in the streets. Discipline was harsh, administered with the cane or leather belt. Children learned to write using bone or metal styluses on wax tablets, which could be wiped clean and reused—papyrus rolls were too expensive for school exercises.

Primary schooling came to an end at about age eleven. Following this, the majority of girls were educated at home, learning how to run a household—cooking, spinning, weaving, fetching water, or, if the parents were well-off, giving orders to domestic slaves. Boys, however, might pass on into the hands of a *grammaticus*, Rome's equivalent of a secondary-school teacher, to study Greek and Roman literature. The more ambitious students might then go on to a rhetorician for lessons in oratory in preparation for a career in public life or the law.

Of the two languages of learning, Greek carried the greater prestige, and some fortunate students went to Greece to complete their education. For poorer parents, the choices were much more stark, even to the point of infanticide. A letter sent to his pregnant wife by a

• TOWN AND COUNTRY •

The Romans were urbanizers par excellence. Wherever they went they took the habits of city living with them, even to areas of the empire such as northern Gaul and Britain where towns were novelties. The situation was different in the eastern provinces, which already had a long urban tradition. There too, however, urban communities flourished as never before under the *Pax Romana*, reaching levels of prosperity unmatched in earlier times.

The new foundations tended to follow a fixed pattern. They were built to a grid plan, and were surrounded by defensive walls penetrated by several guarded gateways. At the heart of the town there would be a forum flanked by public buildings—a temple, law courts, municipal edifices. Elsewhere, never too far from the town center, were public baths and an amphitheater—perhaps also a theater and even an *odeum* where musical performances were held. Such towns were focuses for Romanization, spreading Roman culture out into the surrounding countryside.

Yet for all the importance of the towns, it has been estimated that ninety per cent of the empire's population lived in the countryside, earning a living as smallholders or farm laborers. Many were slaves on the big agricultural estates, although the proportion declined over the years as landowners came to appreciate the cost savings involved in employing seasonal labor in their stead. Even as trade grew, the economy of the empire remained primarily agricultural; most people's needs could be satisfied locally, and many practiced subsistence farming, providing all their own food themselves.

Farming and the countryside also, however, exerted a continuing pull on the imagination of towndwellers. Romans constantly harked back to the nation's early tradition of peasant landholding—a time that came to be seen nostalgically as a golden age. Amid the bustle of the capital's crowded streets, they hankered after a quiet rural life, much as modern commuters dream of a place in the country. The strain is often evident in Roman poetry: "Happy is the man who remains far from business and who cultivates the family farm with his own oxen," wrote Horace, himself the proud owner of a small estate in the Sabine Hills. Similarly, pieces of art found in Roman towns demonstrate an appreciation of rural existence—as shown in this detail from a 1st-century CE Pompeiian wall-painting depicting a bird in a garden.

legionary serving in Egypt acts as a reminder of the realities of parenthood for much of the population: "If you give birth to a boy, keep it. If it is a girl, expose it. Try not to worry. I'll send the money as soon as we get paid."

FOOD AND DRINK

Most Romans lived quite frugally. They ate breakfasts consisting of little more than bread and fruit, perhaps with olives and honey. By imperial times it was normal to have a light lunch (*prandium*) shortly before noon. The main meal (*cena*) was taken around sunset, when the day's work was finished.

The poor lived mainly on a porridge of ground wheat mixed with water, known as *puls*; this staple could be rendered more appetizing and nutritious by the addition of some cheese, honey, or an egg, if such ingredients were available. In republican days the elder Cato, an economically minded employer,

A maenad and two satyrs—the carousing attendants of Bacchus, god of wine—are shown in procession in this marble relief, 100CE, from the Villa Quintilli on the Appian Way. Ancient Rome's wine connoisseurs particularly appreciated the product of Falernian vineyards. There was even a legendary vintage, that of 121BCE, whose produce was treasured among the very wealthy well into imperial days. But most Romans never aspired to any such delights, although they may have enjoyed the odd tipple of mulsum—*a sweet dessert wine produced by mixing grape must with honey.*

recommended feeding slaves on bread, windfall olives, oil, salt, cheap wine, and the dregs of fish sauce.

In Rome itself, the poorest free citizens could count on the corn dole to protect them from starvation. Initially introduced as a subsidised food scheme by the consul Gaius Gracchus (ca. 160–121BCE), this project was vastly extended at Julius Caesar's behest as a way of securing support and subsequently became a fixture of life in the capital. Under its terms, a given number of individuals (200,000 under Augustus, although the number varied over the centuries) received handouts of free wheat each month. The cost was borne by the state out of general taxation.

Those Romans who were eligible for the corn dole were happy to receive it, even if their needs were not great. In early imperial times, most citizens could in fact afford to eat well, and a wide range of produce was available. Fish was generally more plentiful than meat, although pork was a firm favorite. There was a good variety of poultry, game birds, and wildfowl. Shellfish were esteemed, including oysters raised in artificial beds. Many different types of bread were produced. Romans ate eggs and cheese in large quantities, but regarded butter as a food for barbarians; their principal fat was olive oil.

Apart from water, the only drink that was consumed in large amounts was wine, which was usually diluted with water. Archaeologists have noted that grape pips that have been discovered only appear in strata under the capital from the last quarter of the seventh century BCE on, so it is possible that the cultivation of vines was not native to Latium and was introduced, like so much else, by the Etruscans. Certainly, a taste for the grape subsequently spread throughout the Roman Empire, and the only provinces that were without vineyards were northern Gaul and Britain, where the climate at the time was not propitious.

While the majority of Romans may have lived relatively abstemiously, the new rich of imperial times became famous for their excesses. As the empire grew wealthier, its people became greedier. In Nero's day, the philosopher Seneca accused his fellow-citizens of "eating till they vomited and of vomiting in order to eat more."

A taste for conspicuous consumption followed the increase in prosperity brought about by the spread of trade. Exotic delicacies became fashionable, and wealthy diners regaled themselves with specialities like roast peacock, mullets' livers, and flamingos' tongues. The gourmet Apicius, to whom the only surviving Roman cookbook is ascribed, provides a menu for boiled ostrich. "Bring pepper, mint, roasted cumin, parsleyseed, dates, honey, vinegar, cooking wine, fish stock, and a little oil to the boil in a saucepan. Thicken the sauce with cornflour. Pour over the pieces of ostrich meat in a serving dish and sprinkle with pepper."

The apotheosis of Roman nouveau-riche dining is Trimalchio's feast, as described in Petronius Arbiter's novel, the *Satyricon*. Petronius was a satirist and given to exaggeration, but even so, the banquet he described would not have raised a smile among his readers unless it had some grounding in reality. The highlight of the meal comes when a huge wild pig is brought into the banqueting room preceded by a pack of hunting dogs; its roasted skin conceals a flock of live thrushes. Other features of the meal include a hare dressed up with wings to resemble the flying horse Pegasus, a goose garnished with small birds sculpted from roast pork, and roast dormice dipped in honey and rolled in poppyseed.

Real life in fact presented fitting role-models for satire. One L. Aelius Verus is said to have provided mules for his dinner guests to carry away the gifts of gold, silver, and crystalware that he offered. Yet for outrageous extravagance, no private citizens could rival the more decadent emperors. Vitellius—one of the short-lived rulers of the disastrous "Year of the Four Emperors" (see page 362)—went down in history as "the Glutton". A banquet given for his arrival in Rome featured 2,000 fish and 7,000 gamebirds; he also concocted a dish whose ingredients—pike livers, peacock and pheasant brains, flamingo tongues, lamprey milt— had to be fetched by warships from all quarters of the empire. Yet even his reputation was eclipsed by Elagabalus, a third-century emperor from Syria who is alleged to have hosted dinners featuring peas served with grains of gold; at one of them, it is said, so many rose petals were released from the ceiling that several guests suffocated. His excesses did not go unpunished— he was assassinated only four years into his reign.

THE WORLD OF COMMERCE

The Roman Empire, in its heyday, was a vast free-trade area encompassing the entire Mediterranean world. A single currency was in use from the Scottish border to Syria. The sea was plied by merchant ships, while on land a first-class road system encouraged the exchange of goods between provinces.

Rome itself was the focus of mercantile activity. "The warehouse of the world," a Greek visitor called it, adding that "whatever is raised or manufactured by every people is always here in superabundance." Goods flowed into Ostia and its near neighbor, the purpose-built harbor of Portus Augusti, for transport up the Tiber by barge to the city itself. The most vital supplies were the grain shipments that fed the city: 400,000 tons were imported annually, mainly from Egypt and Sicily. The trading momentum in Rome and its empire only faltered from the third century on, when high taxes and galloping inflation conspired to sap prosperity, paving the way for the western empire's eventual decline.

In its most affluent years the capital also had an insatiable appetite for luxury goods. Merchants imported silks from China by way of India, ivory from Africa, and

• RICHES OF THE NILE •

Egyptian civilization intrigued the Romans just as it continues to beguile people around the world today. Travelers' tales of Egypt's ancient monuments and bizarre, animal-headed gods had gone the rounds of the classical world since at least Herodotus's day in the fifth century BCE. The scandalous activities of the last pharaoh, Queen Cleopatra, added to its allure—not only did she bear a son to Julius Caesar, but then, by her well-publicized affair with Mark Antony, also helped trigger the civil war that finally put an end to the republic. Thereafter, Egypt became a province of the Roman Empire, and the rich harvests of the Black Lands regularly inundated by the Nile River provided Rome's most important source of grain, vital for feeding the capital's population, as well as exotic animals destined for the Colosseum.

Among the enduring products of the Roman fascination with things Egyptian are several large mosaics depicting fanciful scenes of life on the Nile Valley, such as the example shown here (mid-1st century BCE), which shows hunting scenes against a backdrop of the inundation of the Nile. It originally came from the precincts of the temple of Fortuna at Praeneste (modern Palestrina, where it is now in the archaeological museum).

furs from northern Europe. There was a particularly well-established trade in amber, which found its way from the Baltic region to the north Italian town of Aquileia, where it was transformed into jewelry and ornaments. Aromatic resins and spices—especially pepper—were in demand to satisfy the Roman taste for strongly flavored food, and the demand was met via long-distance trade routes stretching eventually to India and southeast Asia.

For all the excellence of the Roman roads, most goods traveled by boat; horse-drawn vehicles simply could not rival the capacity of ships when it came to bulk transport. Yet seaborne trade itself carried risks that ruined many an entrepreneur, for the Mediterranean was liable to unpredictable storms, particularly between the months of November and March. However, the rewards more than justified the risks—many of the empire's biggest fortunes were first made in shipping.

Goods reached the public through shops that might not seem wholly unfamiliar in Mediterranean cities to this day. The most obvious difference was the lack of shop windows; instead, premises opened directly onto the street, to be closed off at night by wooden shutters. Shopkeepers piled up their wares on the pavement

outside, until the emperor Domitian passed an edict banning the practice. An important difference from modern times was that almost all of the shopkeepers were either slaves or freedmen. Freeborn Romans never overcame a repugnance for trade.

THE ROMAN FORUM

Every Roman town, whatever its size, had a forum where citizens could meet to gossip and do business. Rome itself ended up with several forums bestowed by rulers eager to leave their mark on the city. Over the course of time, the forum of Julius Caesar was followed by the forums of Augustus, Vespasian, Nerva, and Trajan. But the oldest and most venerable was always the Forum Romanum, or Roman Forum, whose origins went back to the city's earliest days.

The space that the Roman Forum occupied started life as a swampy valley in the shadow of the Capitoline Hill. Archaeological investigation has shown that it was used as a burial ground for cremation urns as early as the tenth century BCE. By the late sixth century, a formal square had been laid out. Over time the Forum grew in magnificence as fresh monuments were added.

Initially the Forum served as a market-place as well as a civic center, but in imperial times much of its commercial activity passed to the newer, adjoining centers. Yet the square continued to attract visitors to the capital. They came to see the Tomb of Romulus, the city's legendary founder, the Temple of Castor and Pollux, divine patrons of the city, and the Rostra from which generations of Roman orators had addressed the people. Here too was the golden milestone from which all distances in the empire were measured, for the Forum could truly claim to be the center of the Roman world.

This atmospheric view of the Roman Forum shows the Via Sacra, which runs through the center of the complex. In the middle is the small reconstructed Temple of Vesta with the Arch of Titus visible directly behind in the distance.

PERFORMANCE, SPORT, AND SPECTACLE

One measure of the sophistication of Roman society was the variety of entertainments available to its citizens. At one end of the scale the theater provided an intellectual diversion. Over the centuries, however, the stage gave way to the baser appeal of gladiatorial contests and wild-beast shows.

The chief form of entertainment in Rome other than gladiatorial shows was the theater. The impetus, as with so much of Rome's cultural life, came initially from Greece. The first true plays (as opposed to sketches and burlesques) ever performed in Rome were translations from the Greek, commissioned as part of the victory celebrations that marked the end of the First Punic War in 240BCE. Plays were originally staged in temporary wooden structures put up as part of the *ludi* ("games") that accompanied major religious festivals.

The most popular genre was comedy and, more specifically, the works of the Greek dramatist Menander as adapted by the pre-eminent second-century BCE playwrights Plautus and Terence. Even so, their dramas had to compete with other attractions, not always successfully. In one of his plays, Terence complains of audiences drifting off to watch a tightrope-walker, while the poet Horace bemoaned people interrupting performances to call for boxers or a bear.

More decorous entertainments were offered in the *odeums*—smaller, roofed auditoriums used for musical performances, lectures, and poetry readings. Free entertainment was also available in the law courts, where people flocked to hear celebrity lawyers practicing the rhetorical skills by which Romans set such store.

In the long run, Roman theater lost its audiences to the brutal diversions of the circus and the arena (see pages 396–397). By the third century CE, most theaters were staging mimes, farces, or wild-beast shows rather than dramas. Soon afterward they fell silent altogether, and only the works of Plautus, Terence, and Seneca survived.

THE COMPETITIVE INSTINCT

The satirist Juvenal complained that most Roman citizens cared only about bread and circuses, and the emperors certainly kept them well supplied with both. The circus, for Romans, meant above all the Circus Maximus, the capital's principal racetrack, which could hold at least 150,000 spectators. People flocked there to enjoy chariot racing, the most enduring of all the city's spectator entertainments. Like stage plays, the races formed part of the *ludi* (games) that accompanied public festivals; it has been estimated that in the mid-first century CE there was racing on eighty days each year.

Chariots were usually drawn by four horses. Their drivers raced over seven laps of a track that consisted of two long straights and two 180-degree bends; each lap covered about 5,000 feet (1,500m). The sport was dangerous, as vehicles often collided at the turns. A

ABOVE *A young woman playing ball in the* palaestra, *or gymnasium; detail from a late 3rd- to early 4th-century CE mosaic in the Villa Romana del Casale, Sicily.* OPPOSITE *A Roman theater in Bosra, Syria (ca. 2nd century CE). Like their Greek counterparts, Roman theaters were semi-circular; spectators sat on banked rows of seats and gazed across an open space to the stage. In Rome, that space was occupied by senators and other patricians, sitting on folding chairs; other leading citizens sat on the first rows of banked seats. Most theaters had no roof, but the spectators were protected from the elements by an awning.*

• THE COLOSSEUM •

Known as the Flavian Amphitheater in antiquity, the Colosseum got its present name, after the western Roman Empire's collapse, from a colossal statue of the emperor Nero that stood nearby. The vast stadium was built on the orders of the emperor Vespasian as part of a general embellishment of the capital designed to restore morale after the chaos of the "Year of the Four Emperors" (see page 362).

The building took the form of a gigantic oval more than 320,000 square feet (30,000 sq m) in extent. It was officially inaugurated by Vespasian's successor, Titus, in 80CE with a brutal spectacle which involved the killing of some 5,000 wild animals over several days. The empire's best-known gladiators fought here, and the entire central arena could be flooded for the staging of mock sea battles.

The Colosseum remained in use to the very end of the western Roman Empire, and was even restored by Odoacer, the Germanic general who replaced the last of the emperors. It finally fell into disuse in the sixth century.

funerals to honor the memory of the dead. According to Livy, they were first introduced in the year 264BCE. Under the emperors, the fights came to challenge chariot racing as the capital's favorite entertainment.

Most gladiators were forced into the job as condemned criminals or prisoners of war, or else were sold into it as slaves. There were gladiatorial schools to train recruits in fighting skills; it was from one of these that Spartacus escaped in 73BCE to lead a slave revolt that defied the might of Rome for two years. Different types of gladiator reflected native fighting traditions in their skills: Thracians fought with a round shield and scimitar, while Samnites wore huge, visored helmets and wielded swords and oblong shields. The *murmillo* fought with similar equipment to the Samnite, but with a helmet bearing a metal fish as a crest, while the *retiarius* went into the ring lightly clad with just a trident and a net, relying on agility to take on heavily-armed opponents.

In theory, gladiators fought to the death; in practice, it was not always so. Records of a Pompeiian games show that only three of the nine losers died. A wounded gladiator would raise a hand to ask for mercy from the spectators. They, in turn, would hold up their hands with thumb and forefinger pressed together to signify clemency; if they pointed their thumbs at their breasts, they expected the death blow. It was up to the emperor or some other presiding dignitary to interpret their wishes and give the appropriate command.

Successful gladiators won their freedom, symbolized by the presentation of a wooden sword. They could also become popular heroes and even sex symbols: "Celadus the Thracian makes all the girls sigh," a graffito from Pompeii records. Another Pompeiian inscription speaks of one man winning his fifty-fifth bout, suggesting that successful fighters could have relatively long careers.

However brutal, the gladiatorial contests at least involved real skills. The same could not be said for some of the more ghastly spectactles staged in the arenas. Wild animals were slaughtered in huge numbers. According to Cicero, who attended a particularly

charioteer who lost control risked being crushed under horses' hooves or else being dragged to his death entangled in the reins, unless he could cut them with the small knife that each rider carried for that purpose.

In republican days, chariot teams were privately owned by wealthy individuals, but under the emperors they were managed by contractors identified by their racing colors: red, white, blue, or green. Each color had its band of eager partisans. Passions were further aroused by the heavy betting that accompanied the racing.

The risks that the charioteers ran were as nothing compared with those that faced gladiators. Gladiatorial contests came to Rome from Etruria, where they had their origins in sacrificial displays staged at public

bloody event in Rome, the crowd showed signs of revulsion at the treatment meted out, particularly to the elephants: "There was even an impulse of compassion," he noted, "a feeling that the beasts had something human about them." Such empathy had little longterm effect, for 3,500 elephants were subsequently killed in the arena under the emperor Augustus alone.

Worse still were the public executions that were carried out in the arenas in the guise of sport. Armed criminals were put in the ring unprotected to kill one another, a spectacle that the philosopher Seneca described as "murder pure and simple," or else were left to face wild beasts unarmed. Famously, Christians were among the victims—according to Tacitus, the emperor

Detail from a 4th-century CE mosaic portraying a gladiator fighting a wild beast. In some of the more gruesome shows staged in Roman arenas, lions, tigers, or panthers were released to fight armed men; in other cases, naturally non-aggressive beasts were either goaded into fighting for their lives or were simply massacred.

Nero had some wrapped in wild-animal skins to be hunted down by dogs. Over time, the brutality of the gladiator and wild-beast shows corrupted Roman taste. In pandering to the worst instincts of the mob, the emperors debased their own culture and cast doubt on Rome's claim to moral superiority over the barbarian world beyond its borders.

THE DIVINE SPHERE

Rome's gods present a paradox: they are familiar as names, but are also surprisingly little known. Most schoolchildren have heard of Venus, if not also of Jupiter, Mars, Mercury, and Saturn. Yet the origins of these deities, and what is specifically Roman about them, continue to puzzle scholars.

Romans were avid assimilators of all things Greek, including the Greek gods. Its own divinities were shadowy and insubstantial in comparison with the larger-than-life players in the Olympian soap opera. Accordingly, their native identities quickly became subsumed within the personas of the Hellenic imports. So Jupiter, as we know him from Roman literary sources, is Zeus by another name; Mercury took on the attributes of Hermes, the messenger of Mount Olympos (the home of the gods—see pages 324–325); Neptune, the sea god, became identified with the Greek Poseidon, and Vulcan, the divine blacksmith, with Hephaistos. At least one major Roman deity, Apollo, had no native counterpart, and therefore retained his Greek name.

Tracking down the Roman gods' own identities is difficult as the evidence lies hidden in preliterate times. The earliest surviving sources are annotations found on religious calendars and ritual formulae that were probably enigmatic even to the people who used them. Current knowledge suggests, however, that Jupiter, addressed in later times as *optimus maximus* ("best and greatest"), started life as a typical Indo-European sky god, comparable to the Norse deity Thor or the Hittite god Teshub, and probably arrived in Rome with the Iron Age immigrants who also brought with them the Latin language. Augurs searched the heavens for omens of his pleasure or displeasure, and he was particularly identified with thunderstorms: the Thunderer was one of his epithets. The Etruscans had a similar divinity, Tinia, whom they associated with two goddesses, Uni

Diana, goddess of the hunt, was worshipped extensively in ancient Rome and many temples were erected there in her honor, including one on the Aventine Hill, with others in the provinces. She is portrayed in this 1st-century CE Pompeiian fresco in full hunting regalia.

and Menrva; these three, Romanized as Jupiter, Juno, and Minerva, were the presiding deities of Rome's best-known early temple, founded under the Etruscan kings.

In later times, when Jupiter also became associated with the Greek god Zeus, he took on Zeus's attributes as ruler of the universe. He was portrayed as a divine father figure who epitomized good faith, honor, and justice, and Romans swore their most binding oaths in his name. He was also the protector of Rome and the Roman people, invoked by consuls before any military expedition and always rewarded with a share of the spoils.

The pre-eminent Roman war god, however, was Mars. As befitted the patron of a military people, he occupied a markedly higher place in the pantheon than his Greek equivalent Ares, ranking second only to Jupiter in status. Along with Jupiter, he was one of a trio of gods worshipped above all others in pre-Etruscan days; the third in the trio was Quirinus, a now largely forgotten Sabine deity whose name is commemorated in Rome's Quirinal Hill, where his cult was centered.

Mars started life as a fertility god who presided over the spring equinox; the link lingers linguistically in the month name of March. The main feasts in his honor were held at that time, when a body of priests named the Salians dressed in military uniform to perform a leaping dance intended to encourage new growth—a rite that combined Mars's martial and agricultural aspects. Legend credited him as the father of Romulus and Remus, emphasizing his role as a founder of the Roman state. The Campus Martius ("Field of Mars"), where the oldest altar to Mars was sited, was the Roman army's traditional gathering-place.

If Mars was sacred to farmers and warriors, Mercury was the patron of merchants and tradesmen. His cult always tended to appeal more to ordinary people than to the ruling classes and was centered around his temple which was situated on Rome's Aventine Hill, in the plebeian quarter of the city. The god's Greek equivalent, Hermes, was the messenger of the gods, and Mercury himself took on this role in later Roman tradition. The

adjective "mercurial" is suggestive of the speed with which he carried out his various missions.

One native god who possessed no Greek equivalent was Janus, the two-faced guardian of doors and entrances and the patron of beginnings. Fittingly, his name lives on in the month of January, the first month of the year, when his feast was celebrated. An ancient god, he was reputed to have helped Rome repel an attack on the Capitol, and the gates of his temple in the Forum were ever after left open in time of war. This therefore meant that they were rarely closed over the course of Rome's long and battle-scarred history, although the emperor Augustus made a point of shutting them when in 29BCE he finally restored peace to the empire after decades of bitter civil strife.

One version of Roman myth claimed that Janus had once jointly ruled the world with Saturn, a contradictory deity who became associated with the Greek Chronos. On the one hand, Saturn was a god of wine and revelry, celebrated in the great festival known as the Saturnalia (see page 404); on the other, he was a gloomy melancholic, possessing all the qualities conveyed by the word "saturnine." However, for patriotic Roman mythographers, he and Janus together presided over a golden age that saw the introduction of agriculture and all the arts of civilization. And, unsurprisingly in the light of Roman civic patriotism, they were said to have spread these gifts to humankind not just from Italy, but from the banks of the Tiber River, not far from the spot where the city of Rome itself would one day stand.

THE GREAT GODDESSES

Early Romans seem not to have been overworried by the gender of their deities. The formula *si deus si dea*—"whether god or goddess"—crops up in several dedications, indicating uncertainty as to the sex of some of the lesser divinities. In later times, though, the great goddesses acquired vivid personalities that between them spanned the spectrum of femininity known to the

The open top of the Pantheon, known as the oculus, *allows the sun to shine onto the interior of the dome in a dramatic pool of light. The dome's five levels of coffer represent the five planets known to the Romans.*

Roman world. Thus Jupiter's consort, Juno, represented the idealized Roman matron, full of dignity and authority. Ceres stood for fertility, Venus for sexual desire, while Diana the huntress was a model of tomboyish independence, with even a hint of lesbianism in her character. As for Minerva, she was wisdom and creativity personified, a lofty and remote presence.

As usual in Roman mythology, there were contradictions within the general picture: the vengeful Juno of Virgil's *Aeneid*, mercilessly dogging the hero's path to Italy, was hardly matronly, no doubt because her portrayal there leaned heavily on traditions of her Greek counterpart, Hera. The Roman goddess Juno seems originally to have been a moon deity, but came eventually to be seen as a protector of women, particularly associated with childbirth and with marriage; her festal month of June was regarded as a propitious one for weddings.

The roles assigned to the other goddesses were more specific. Ceres, for example, started life as an ancient Italian grain goddess. The deity presiding over crops and vegetation, she was honored in a springtime festival, the Cerealia, and her name lingers on in the English word "cereal." Minerva seems originally to have been an Etruscan divinity, and was the protectress of several Etruscan city-states. Later, however, she became linked with the Greek Athene, who sprang fully armed from the head of Zeus, and the connection led her sometimes to be regarded as a war goddess. Mostly, though, she was associated with arts and crafts, and as such was the patron of craftsmen and of all who lived by their wits, among them writers, schoolmasters, and doctors.

Venus, the love goddess, had unlikely origins as the presiding spirit of vegetable gardens. Initially she was purely Roman, although in time she became confounded with the Etruscan Turan and the Greek Aphrodite, emerging as the divine beauty familiar in Western culture from the paintings of Botticelli and others. For Romans, however, she had another role as the mother of Aeneas, and was worshipped not only by pimps and prostitutes as the goddess of desire but also more generally among the population at large as Genetrix, the pious begetter of the state.

A SHRINE FOR ALL THE GODS

The emperor Hadrian ordered the construction of the Pantheon early in the second century CE as a sanctuary dedicated to all the gods. The resultant temple's *rotunda* design was an engineering masterpiece, with its revolutionary dome (see illustration, opposite) remaining the world's largest until modern times. The diameter exactly corresponds to the height of the topmost point above the temple's floor, lending the building a sense of harmony that led the poet Shelley, who visited in the early nineteenth century, to speak of "the perfection of its proportions."

Shelley also likened the roof to "the unmeasured dome of Heaven," a comparison that may well have come close to the builders' original intentions. No records survive to name the architect or outline his vision, but scholars believe that statues of gods associated with the sky—Jupiter, Mercury, Mars, Venus—were placed in the niches that ring the building's inner wall. The dome itself, which was coffered (patterned with symmetrical recesses) to reduce its overall weight, probably represented the firmament. Its top was left open to allow light to filter through. This aperture, known as the *oculus*, or eye, symbolized the sun, whose radiance bathed the interior of the building.

The engineers who constructed the Pantheon did their job well. The temple survived the fall of paganism to become a Christian church in 609CE. It remains there to this day, and is often considered the finest intact example of ancient Roman architecture, with its original dome and internal columns still in place.

WORSHIP AND PROPHECY

The Romans were, above all, practical in their beliefs, seeking direct benefits in return for their efforts. Observance started in the home, where the father of the family carried out daily rituals designed to ensure good fortune. Similarly, the state cult sought to win the favor of the gods for Rome as a whole.

Every Roman household, however poor, had its guardian spirits who were honored daily. In return for the attention and respect paid to them, they protected the fortunes of the family and ensured that they had food on the table. These protectors came in several different forms. The *lares* were generally thought of as spirits of departed ancestors. The most important was the *lar familiaris*, who represented the founder of the family; Aeneas and Romulus occupied this position for the Roman state. The *penates* took their name from the *penus*, or pantry, in which food was stored, and their particular duty was to ensure that the family received its daily bread. The first fruits of the harvest were offered up to them, and the salt-cellar placed on the dining table stood there in their honor. The superstitions that linger to this day about spilling salt at table stem from this custom—the *penates*, who might have considered such accidents marks of disrespect, needed to be placated by the offering of a pinch of the spilled salt, traditionally cast over the diner's left shoulder.

The *lares* and *penates* were worshipped at a shrine that had pride of place in most Roman living rooms. It could take the form of a stone altar, typically inscribed with an image of the *genius* (spirit) of the house flanked by two *lares*; or it might be a cupboard containing small statues of the gods made of gold, silver, ivory, or clay, depending on the family's means. The other main focus of family worship was the hearth—the Latin word for it was in fact *focus*. It was sacred to the goddess Vesta, an ancient Italian fire deity. The connection probably went back to early times, when the farmers who first settled on the hills of Rome would gather each evening around the fire in the center of their huts, drawn by the warmth in winter and by the scent of meat roasting. In later times, offerings of food and wine were left on the hearth, as at the family shrine, or were thrown into the fire itself.

There were also public versions of these ubiquitous household deities. *Lares compitales* ("*lares* of the crossroads") were propitiated at shrines marking the boundaries between several farms, in the countryside, or between neighborhoods, in towns. As for Vesta, she was one of Rome's best-known divinities, venerated in a beautiful circular temple in the Forum where her sacred flame was always kept alight. The six Vestal Virgins, chosen from the best families and vowed to chastity for the thirty years they dedicated to the goddess's service, were among the nation's most honored citizens.

GODS OF FEASTS AND FESTIVALS

Public worship in the Roman world centered around the state festivals. The earliest known ritual calendar, ascribed to the reign of Romulus's supposed heir Numa Pompilius (see page 367), already listed forty-five of them. Later, festal inflation set in. The total had risen to sixty-six feast days by the end of the republic, to 135 by the second-century CE reign of Marcus Aurelius (who cut the number back), and to a colossal 175 days near the empire's end in 354CE. The early festivals addressed the needs of an agricultural society, seeking to ensure the goodwill of the gods—Romans called it the *pax deorum* ("peace of the gods"). Over the centuries, however, they lost much of their religious significance and became public holidays pure and simple, celebrated with games in the arenas and with theater shows. Priests continued to perform the timeworn rituals in the temples, but in later years they were often unaware of the true meaning of the formulae that tradition had passed on to them.

Satyrs and bacchantes—followers of Bacchus, the god of wine—are portrayed in various amorous pursuits in this 2nd-century CE Roman mosaic from Numidia (modern-day Tunisia, North Africa).

Many of the more ancient Latin gods had festivals dedicated to them. At the Cerealia, the springtime celebration in honor of Ceres (see page 401), married women gave up drink and sexual intercourse for a week and took part in torchlit nighttime processions. Pales, a deity of flocks and shepherds, was honored in the Parilia, celebrated in late April. A late-summer carousal was dedicated to Consus and Ops, Italian harvest gods. One god invoked less than his reputation might suggest was Bacchus, the wine deity.

No festal god was dearer to Roman hearts than Saturn (see page 399), whose annual celebration, the Saturnalia, took place each December. Originally celebrated on the seventeenth of the month, the festivities later stretched over the better part of a week. In Rome itself the festival began with a sacrifice in Saturn's temple in the Forum, followed by a public feast open to all. Thereafter the festive season was a time of general goodwill in which the usual social norms were overturned. The most solemn senators wore casual tunics in place of formal togas, and there was even some cross-dressing. Slaves were treated as members of the household. Public gambling, normally strictly prohibited, was permitted, and households often appointed a mock king who acted in the spirit of the Lords of Misrule, as known from the medieval period.

Gifts were exchanged and feasting complemented the general merriment. The festival came to occupy such a prominent place in Roman hearts that Christian leaders in the fourth century CE chose to co-opt it for their own purposes rather than to ban it as a relic of paganism. Neither the Bible nor early tradition recorded the date of Christ's birth, but the celebration of Christmas in late December became accepted, partly in order to preserve the festive mood of the Saturnalia in Christian guise.

GODS OF THE PROVINCES

Formulaic and state-oriented as it was, Rome's public religion commanded citizens' patriotism more than their devotion. People had to look elsewhere to find faiths that satisfied their deeper needs. As the nation's military power increased, a growing tide of foreigners reached Italy, whether as merchants or as prisoners of war, bringing with them new gods that better suited these urges. Eastern and Egyptian beliefs helped fill a gap at the heart of Roman life—one that was ultimately to be satisfied by the triumph of Christianity.

At first, Greek and Etruscan deities helped flesh out Rome's own shadowy and insubstantial divinities. From the late third century BCE on, however, more exotic cults made their influence felt. A crucial step was taken in the year 204, when Hannibal's army had been occupying Italy for well over a decade. Following advice from the Delphic oracle and the Sibylline Books (see page 407), the Senate made the momentous decision to bring the cult statue of Cybele from its home in Asia Minor to Rome. The oriental goddess subsequently became known to Romans as the Great Mother (*Magna Mater*). The stone image made the journey in state, accompanied by five *quinqueremes* (galleys with five banks of oars), and was solemnly welcomed to the Temple of Victory on the Palatine Hill. With Cybele, to the Romans' disquiet, came her priests, the *galli*, who performed ecstatic dances and self-flagellation. Worse still, they castrated themselves in honor of Cybele's consort, Attis, who had supposedly emasculated himself in a fit of madness. The Senate looked upon such un-Roman activities with alarm, and Roman citizens were long banned from participating in the rites.

From Egypt came the worship of Isis. For the most part, Romans regarded the various animal-headed Egyptian deities with a mixture of incredulity and scorn, but the Hellenized cult of the goddess and her husband-brother Serapis (as Osiris became known under the Ptolemies) was a different matter. With its stately rituals conducted by shaven-headed priests and its emphasis on loving kindness and female fecundity, the faith appealed strongly to women. In later times, images of Isis cradling the infant Horus in her arms influenced Christian iconography, paving the way for the cult of the Virgin and Child.

In addition to Mithraism, Asia Minor was also the center of the exotic cult devoted to the multi-breasted goddess Artemis (the equivalent of Diana), whose most famous shrine was at Ephesus. This bronze and alabaster statue of the goddess is a 2nd-century CE Roman copy of an eastern original. Under the peace of Rome, Ephesus once again flourished, aided in part by the pilgrim trade focused on Artemis.

Mithraism, which also left its mark on early Christianity, could hardly have been more different. It was aggressively masculine—only men were allowed to attend its services, which were held in small underground sanctuaries. The focus of the faith, which came originally from Persia, was Mithras, a sun god who had sacrificed a bull at the start of time to bring life to the world. Bull sacrifice continued to play a part in the cult, which preached the spiritual equality of all believers and spread initially among slaves brought as prisoners of war from Asia Minor. In time, Mithraism, which stressed comradeship and loyalty and offered various stages of initiation for the faithful, became established among the military and traveled across the empire with the legions. But its appeal, based on what would now be called male bonding, was intrinsically limited—in the long run, it lacked the all-embracing attraction of the Christian message of universal compassion.

TEMPLES AND SHRINES

Temples were the main centers of the state religion in the Roman world, but they were not the only ones. Many ceremonies and festivals took place out of doors, and there were also small shrines, usually placed at crossroads, where the *lares publici*—state or city household gods (see page 402)—could be worshipped.

Roman temples did not function in the same way as churches, synagogues, or mosques do today, in the sense that there was no routine of regular worship attracting congregations. Instead they served as symbolic homes for the gods, who were represented by statues and tended by priests who, in the higher echelons at least, were elected officials chosen from the ranks of the ruling classes. These individuals carried out the formulaic rituals whose regular performance was deemed essential to ensure divine goodwill. Ordinary people might visit the temples, but only as petitioners seeking favors. Typically they would burn incense and then stand with arms upraised to pray for the benevolent intercession of the

effigies were often splendidly carved in marble, painted in bold colors, and adorned with gold, silver, and gems.

The buildings performed other functions besides their religious use. All true temples had been consecrated by augurs (see opposite; the English word "inaugurate" commemorates this custom), and so were considered to be divinely sanctioned for the conduct of

resident deity, perhaps to cure an illness or to help in a business transaction or a love affair.

Early temples were relatively plain though dignified buildings, based on Etruscan models. They were typically raised on platforms and were accessed by steps from the front. Inside, a long room lined by columns would lead the eye to a statue of the god or goddess. In later times, at least in Rome and other major cities, these

important public business; for example, the Senate frequently met there. They also served as museums for works of art looted abroad by the imperial armies.

Oddest of all to modern sensibilities, temples functioned as banks. From early on they were used to house the state treasury, and the custom continued at least into late republican times; after crossing the Rubicon and marching on Rome, Caesar had to threaten to kill the

The city-state of Gerasa in Roman Syria (modern-day Jerash, Jordan) contains extensive free-standing ancient Roman ruins. The city reached its height in the 2nd century CE, flourishing on trade with the Nabaeans. At this point a substantial reconstruction program was undertaken and its large Temple of Artemis was built (dedicated in 150CE), its columns are seen here looming above the ruins of the early Christian church.

augurs, elected for life from the ranks of the ruling class, sought divine guidance by taking the auspices before important decisions were made. The process usually involved scanning the sky for omens in the form of flights of birds—their species, numbers, and direction could all be significant. Alternatively, the augurs studied the feeding patterns of chickens, especially before military ventures. There were several tales told of commanders who had failed to carry out the necessary observances and paid dearly for their temerity.

The Senate, along with many private individuals, also turned for advice to the soothsayers known as *haruspices*, who practiced the skill the Romans called "the Etruscan science." Usually it involved examining the entrails of sacrificial animals, most often sheep or oxen; the shape, size, condition, and markings of the liver and gall bladder were considered particularly significant. The *haruspices* also took note of omens in the form of monstrous births or growths—two-headed calves and the like—and of lightning, seen as a message from the gods. The best remembered of all soothsayers was Spurrina, the Etruscan who famously warned Julius Caesar to beware the Ides of March. According to the historian Suetonius, who tells the story, Caesar chided him minutes before his assassination, saying that the Ides of March had come. "Come, but not yet gone," Spurrina muttered presciently.

Other valuable sources of information about the divine will were the Sibylline Books, preserved in a vault under the Temple of Jupiter on the Capitoline Hill. These venerable documents purportedly contained pronouncements of the Sibyl, a legendary prophetess who had once inhabited a cave at Cumae, near Naples; in the *Aeneid*, Virgil makes her Aeneas's guide for the descent to the underworld. The books, which were said to have been purchased by Tarquinius Superbus, the last Etruscan king, were consulted in times of emergency; it was partly on their advice that the cults of Cybele and of the healing god Aesculapius (Greek Asklepios; see page 351) were brought to Rome from the Orient.

guards of the Capitoline temple before he could gain access to its wealth. Private citizens similarly deposited their valuables in the main state sanctuaries.

DIVINATION AND ORACLES

Convinced as they were that the gods had powers to influence human destiny, the Romans spent much effort working out what their will might be. A college of

THE TRIUMPH
OF CHRISTIANITY

One of the great, abiding mysteries of Roman history is the way in which Christianity, long seen as a bizarre, antisocial, and possibly dangerous cult, rose from persecution to become the official religion of the empire in the course of the fourth century CE. The turnaround was nothing if not sudden.

In 303CE, the emperor Diocletian launched the most direct assault the Christian community had yet faced, seeking to extirpate the faith entirely in favor of a revived paganism. Just ten years later, however, a new emperor, Constantine, issued the Edict of Milan, which granted Christians complete freedom of worship. By the end of the century, the emperor Theodosius I had proscribed paganism, forbidden the veneration of the old classical gods, and pronounced Christianity the official religion of the entire Roman Empire.

Christianity's beginnings hardly seemed to promise any such outcome. Jesus was, of course, crucified at the behest of Pontius Pilate, the Roman governor of Judaea, and the stigma of his execution cast a long shadow over the faith in Roman eyes. The religion nonetheless made its presence felt in Rome as early as the emperor Claudius's reign (41–54CE), to judge from comments made by the historian Suetonius, who made note of the disturbances stirred up in the city's Jewish community "at the instigation of Chrestus [sic]"—presumably a reference to disputes that took place between supporters and opponents of Jesus in the years after the Crucifixion. By the time of Claudius's successor Nero, the Christians were well enough established to be brutally persecuted in the wake of Rome's Great Fire of 64CE, for which they were made the scapegoats.

Persecution continued sporadically for the next 200 years. The Christians' fault was twofold in Roman eyes:

• THE END OF EMPIRE •

The fall of the Roman Empire is traditionally dated to 476CE, yet few people at the time would have guessed that anything epoch-making had happened. The year saw the enforced abdication of Augustulus, the last ruler of the western Roman Empire, and his replacement as king of Italy by the "barbarian" general Odoacer, of Germanic descent. Yet Odoacer himself was thoroughly Romanized in culture, and he continued to use much of the traditional Roman apparatus of government.

Meanwhile, the eastern half of the Roman Empire survived intact, with its own emperor firmly ensconced in his capital of Constantinople on the shore of the Bosphorus, where Europe and Asia meet. The eastern emperors conspired actively to regain the western lands, and in the sixth century they temporarily fulfilled their ambition. A great emperor, Justinian, and a brilliant general, Belisarius, combined to win back first Rome's old North African lands from the Vandals who now held them and then Italy, which had been seized from Odoacer by the Ostrogoths. Their triumph was short-lived: within three years of Justinian's death in 565CE, another Germanic people, the Lombards, were pushing deep into Italy.

they were a clandestine organization—always a cause for suspicion—and they refused to participate in the state cult of the classical gods, including that of the deified emperors. Christian intransigence in this respect led to an upsurge in harassment under the emperor Domitian (81–96CE), who insisted on being recognized as "lord and god," a formula that the faithful could not accept. Meanwhile, the covert nature of their worship led to various accusations among the masses, not least of which was that they practiced cannibalism—probably a misunderstanding of the symbolic consumption of Christ's body and blood in the bread and wine of the Eucharist. Many of the early martyrs met their deaths not at the hands of the imperial authorities, but rather from mobs incensed by rumors or with local scores to settle.

The official attitude for much of this time was one of wary sufferance. When the writer Pliny the Younger was appointed governor of Bithynia on Turkey's Black Sea coast early in the second century CE, he wrote to the emperor Trajan for advice on how to handle the region's Christians. Trajan replied that he should not deliberately seek them out for persecution, and should not pay attention to anonymous denunciations, which were "unworthy of our age" (Pliny had received many such). However, Trajan concluded, if Christians were properly identified and convicted, they should be punished.

Attitudes toward Christianity hardened in the third century when Rome came under renewed pressure from the barbarian peoples beyond its frontiers. Rome's rulers responded with increased demands for imperial unity. At the beginning of the century, Septimius Severus banned Christians from baptizing new converts, and in its middle years Decius launched the first major drive to extirpate the faith. Christianity's darkest years came between Decius's accession in 249 and 311, when Diocletian's measures were rescinded.

The faith nevertheless survived these trials. Yet it was by no means the only foreign religion competing with the pagan gods for the loyalty of the Roman people. All flourished on the inadequacies of the state religion, with its formulaic rites and all-too-human gods. The mystery religions, including Christianity, offered in contrast an outlet for spirituality, the hope of immortality, and a moral urge born of revulsion at the crass materialism of much of Roman life.

Christianity's rivals, however, all had weaknesses that disadvantaged them in the struggle for the empire's soul. The eunuch priests of Cybele were ultimately too alien for Roman tastes, as were the animal-headed Egyptian deities that formed a backdrop to the cult of Isis. Mithraism long provided a serious challenge, but its fatal weakness was that it was limited to men.

The most immediate threat to Christianity came from the cult of Sol Invictus, the "Unconquered Sun," which spread across the empire in the years immediately before its final acceptance under Constantine. This solar faith was compatible with paganism, yet also reflected a monotheistic impulse that paved the way for the worship of a single, all-powerful God. Interestingly, Constantine, Christianity's champion, was said to have been initially won over to the cause by a vision of the cross set over the sun which was accompanied by the words, "Conquer with this." The next stage of his conversion was purportedly a dream that came to him on the eve of the Battle of the Milvian Bridge in 312CE, in which he was instructed to decorate his soldiers' shields with the Christians' Chi-Rho (a monogram of the Greek letters X and P, the first two letters of "Christ" in Greek). His subsequent victory over his chief rival for the imperial throne convinced him to accept the faith and to propagate it, not least by founding Constantinople as a new, Christian capital for the eastern Roman Empire.

The Roman world changed for ever with the triumph of Christianity. Although the western empire still had 150 years to run and the eastern more than a thousand, the old cultural certainties were gone. A new age was dawning, ushered in by such thinkers as St. Augustine of Hippo who, despite being steeped in the classical tradition, rejected many of its tenets. By the fourth century CE, the Middle Ages were already in the making.

EUROPE'S STONE SENTINELS

The now familiar menhirs, dolmen, and megaliths of Europe were placed in their mounds, rows, and circles millennia ago. Silent witnesses to a continent's changing civilizations, the original reasons for the stones' being are now long forgotten, although most appear to have been used in tombs or as tomb markers. However, some groupings conform to celestial alignments, which required skilled observation, measurement, and prediction on the part of early Europeans. Whatever their real function, they represent an extraordinary investment of time and effort.

BELOW *The standing stones of Callanish on the Isle of Lewis in Scotland's Outer Hebrides form a megalithic complex that dates from 2500BCE. Its suffix Tursachen means "stones of mourning," but this local name aside, it is most likely that for its creators the original purpose of the complex was astronomical. Lines can be identified to the moon, the sun, and stars, which means it may have served as a huge lunar calendar.*

RIGHT *Ggantija (Maltese for "giant") temple on the island of Gozo, Malta, dates to ca. 3600BCE and is one of the oldest such sites in the world. Made from limestone blocks, the temple has five apses and a passageway that leads to an innermost section, with altars, carvings, and libation holes.*

OPPOSITE, ABOVE *Thousands of granite stones stand in parallel rows at Carnac in Brittany, France. Longstanding local beliefs associate standing stones with fertility, but the real purpose of the prehistoric arrangements (ca. 3300BCE) remains obscure.*

BELOW *Megalithic circles are the most spectacular type of Neolithic monument, with the majestic, lintel-capped stones of Stonehenge (ca. 2000BCE) on Salisbury Plain, Wiltshire, England, perhaps the most recognizable example of all. Whether it was an open-air temple or ritual enclosure, its power in the surrounding landscape is undeniable.*

CHAPTER THREE

THE CELTS

Thousands of years ago, the Celts emerged in central Europe as a distinctive group of peoples with their own language, mythology, and art. From their heartlands, the Celts migrated in all directions, fighting and trading with the alternative cultures they encountered, and leaving in their wake superbly crafted weaponry, jewelry, and household objects which demonstrated their vigorous and imaginative response to the natural world. Nature provided a symbolic archive: animal and plant forms merge into spectacular patterns on these magnificent artifacts. Today, the objects that have been found allow us not only to follow the movements of the Celts over land, but also to appreciate the artistic brilliance and sophisticated vision of a civilization that, at its height, stretched from Ireland to Turkey.

THE SOUL OF THE CELTS

More than 2,000 years ago, Europe north of the Mediterranean was dominated by the Celts, a collection of peoples with shared traditions of language, art, and culture. Most of what we know about Celtic customs and society comes from contemporary writers in the classical Mediterranean, for whom the people they called Galatae, Keltoi, *or* Celtae *were fearsome but fascinating barbarians.*

Foreign observers were awestruck by the reckless bravery of the Celtic warrior and what they saw as a general fondness for warfare. Even off the battlefield, the Celts clearly possessed an ebullience that left a mark on visitors from the more restrained classical world. "Quarrelsome," "proud," "frank," "insolent," "boastful," and "high-spirited" are among the Greek and Roman descriptions of the Celtic character.

Much of what the classical writers say about Celtic lifestyle resonates with what we know from the later, native Celtic sources of, for example, Ireland. The verbal arts were prized as greatly as all the skills of war, but classical writers rarely mention the incredible inheritance of information through oral art, nor the logic or beauty of Celtic manuscript. Of course, they had no knowledge of Celtic language, so bardic skills were altogether lost on them and manuscripts indecipherable. For the Greeks and Romans, all Celts were intriguing but essentially uncivilized and barbaric—a unified people held together by the common cause of war. But, as with most prejudiced outsiders, the Greeks and Romans generalized, creating a simplistic picture of the Celtic world, which at last modern archaeology has undone. We know now that the Celts formed a complex and varied group of societies rather than a homogeneous whole: social and religious customs differed widely between the Celtic lands, which by about 350BCE stretched from the Atlantic as far east as Turkey. Some Celtic peoples belonged to large and loose confederations, others to small, tight-knit tribal units.

But undermining classical theories does not stop there—the Celts were no more unsophisticated than they were a single set of people who were war mad. They were highly skilled miners, smiths, builders, farmers, and merchants with wide international connections.

Celtic religion expressed beliefs about omens, magic, and transformation through the symbolism of the natural world. Classical artists preferred symmetry and order, but the Celts drew inspiration from the infinitely subtle mutability of nature. In the La Tène style of Celtic art—which began around 500BCE and found its last reverberations in the magnificent metalwork and manuscripts of early medieval Ireland—the merest suggestion of human, animal, or plant form might be achieved through the breathtaking command of curving, swirling lines of marvelous ingenuity and delicacy.

CELTIC MYSTERIES

The ancient Celts have long been associated with mystery—as if the creators of Celtic art and literature had used a secret code that keeps us guessing as to the meaning of their work. These gifted peoples have excited the imagination of countless observers, but our knowledge of them comes mainly from archaeological findings and classical written sources. The only written testimony left by the Celts themselves is found in a few inscriptions in Greek or Latin and medieval literature.

Classical sources claim that the ancient Celts had no written language, but the discovery of such inscriptions has undermined these claims and the implication that the Celts were a primitive people. Certainly, the sophistication of ancient Celtic art presupposes a complex society, which in turn implies the existence of a developed legal and political system.

In the area of Roman influence, Latin was used to spell out Celtic names, especially on coins. Sometimes Celtic languages, such as Gaulish, were rendered in the Greek or Latin alphabet, most notably a bronze tablet of a legal text from Botoritta in Spain; a stone inscription from Gaul (see illustration, opposite); and the "Coligny

Calendar," a bronze plaque listing the days, months, and festivals of the Celtic year in Gaulish (see pages 434–435). Later, between the fifth and seventh centuries CE, a unique Irish script called Ogham was used to inscribe names and places on stone funerary monuments in Ireland and areas of Britain influenced by Irish colonists. The script consists of clusters of strokes along a central line, and its appearance was probably inspired by the Roman numerical system. Most importantly, however, it was easy to carve on stone.

For the most part, though, information and myth were transmitted orally by trained professionals, who

The inscription on this stone slab from Vaucluse, France (2nd–1st centuries BCE), is in Gaulish using Greek letters. The top line in this photograph shows a man's name, Segomaros. The remaining text is part of a dedication from him to a local goddess called Belesama.

used elaborate mnemonic devices to conserve a complex intellectual heritage (see pages 436–437). Lists cataloging tales, laws, and proverbs, usually grouped in threes, and poetry in Irish and Welsh, suggest that the ancient oral transmission continued into medieval times for long enough to be written down.

THE STORY OF THE CELTS

While the influence of the Celts on European prehistory was undoubtedly immense, no single set of cultural characteristics, much less psychological or spiritual ones, can adequately sum up what is meant by "Celtic" civilization.

The earliest cultures that we term Celtic appeared in central Europe in around 800BCE, beginning the first Celtic phase, known as the Hallstatt Period, after an Austrian town near which many spectacular Celtic artifacts have been recovered. The Celtic world at this time stretched from the Balkans and Bohemia to what is now southern Germany. Between about 800BCE and 300BCE, Celtic power expanded to include parts of central Turkey, Italy, Spain, Portugal, and France, and eventually Britain and Ireland. Celtic societies developed in response to a wide range of historical and geographical circumstances. In some areas, the Celts depended primarily on trade, but in others, the main activity was farming or stock breeding. Likewise, some groups were dominated by warrior élites or princely aristocracies, while others formed hybrid cultures with local ethnic groups.

The rich graves discovered at Hallstatt in the mid-nineteenth century and documented by the archaeologist Engels revealed both native and imported goods. Engels's work introduced the world to a sophisticated Iron Age society governed by a princely ruling class whose power lay in the control of nearby salt mines. They built impressive fortifications and were interred in burial mounds, often laid out on funerary carts amid much of their wealth. The later Hallstatt chiefdoms thrived on the international salt trade, exploiting export routes down the Rhône River to the Greek colony of Marseilles, and beyond to the Mediterranean.

Around the fifth century BCE, the focus of Celtic power shifted to a region from which the Celts could better exploit the Alpine trade routes to the increasingly powerful Etruscan centers of Italy. This period was marked by a new style of art named after the Swiss site of La Tène, where artifacts decorated in the new way were first discovered. During the La Tène phase, Celtic civilization reached its farthest extent: beautiful La Tène artwork has been recovered in every area of Celtic influence from the British Isles and the Iberian Peninsula to Asia Minor.

Soon, however, Celtic peoples came into direct conflict with the expanding classical world. In 390BCE, Rome was sacked by Celts whom the Romans called *Galli* or "Gauls." Meanwhile, other Celtic groups moved through the Balkans and into Greece, and are thought to have attacked the great Greek sanctuary of Delphi in 279BCE. The Greeks called these invaders *Keltoi* or *Galatae*, whence the name Galatia in northern-central Turkey (see map, opposite). So appalled were the Greeks at the warring nature of the Celts, that one poet likened them to the mythical Titans, a race of fierce divine giants who fought against the Olympian gods. Nevertheless, the encounter of the Celtic and classical worlds was marked by cultural absorption as much as by conflict, each learning from, as well as fighting with, the other.

By a turn of fate, during the third century BCE, the autonomous Celtic tribes found themselves sandwiched between two expanding cultures: the Romans to the south and the Germanic tribes to the north. In the many battles between the Romans and the Celts, two particularly stand out as marking the end of Celtic power on the European mainland: the Roman victories at Telamon in Italy in 225BCE, and at Alesia in Gaul in 52BCE. From this time onward, the Celtic culture of continental Europe was in retreat, and by about 500CE, it had virtually disappeared altogether. However, in Ireland, the far western outpost of Celtic power, this ancient culture was to enjoy one last, magnificent golden age.

OPPOSITE *The map reveals the extent of Celtic cultural influence throughout Europe: from the Iberian peninsula in the southwest to Britain in the north and Asia Minor in the east.*

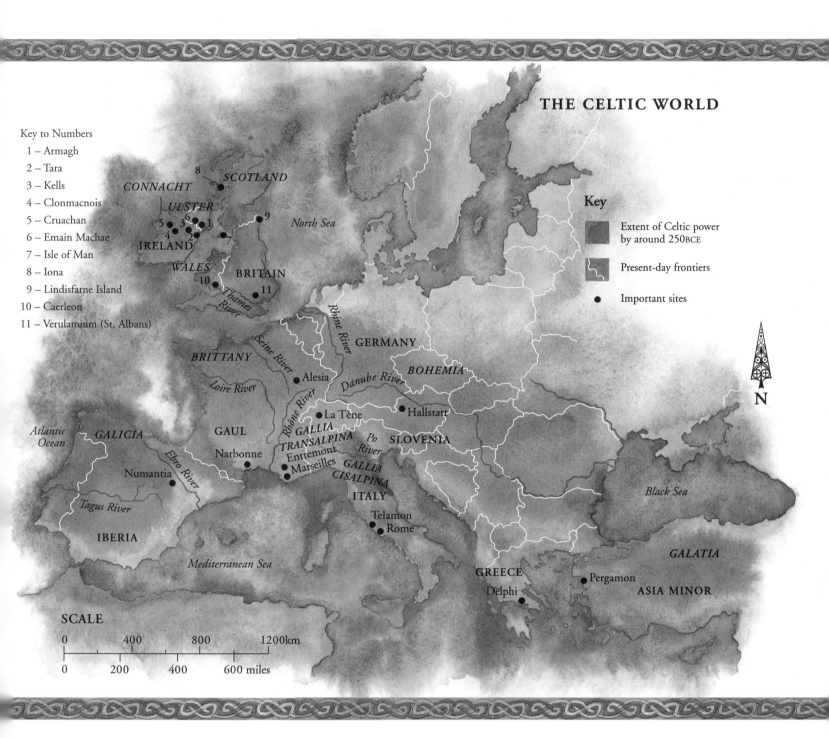

THE CELTIC WORLD

Key to Numbers

1 – Armagh
2 – Tara
3 – Kells
4 – Clonmacnois
5 – Cruachan
6 – Emain Machae
7 – Isle of Man
8 – Iona
9 – Lindisfarne Island
10 – Caerleon
11 – Verulamium (St. Albans)

Key

Extent of Celtic power by around 250BCE

Present-day frontiers

● Important sites

N

SCOTLAND
CONNACHT
ULSTER
IRELAND
WALES
BRITAIN
North Sea
Thames River

GERMANY
BOHEMIA
Rhine River
Seine River
BRITTANY
Loire River
Alesia
Danube River
Rhône River
La Tène
Hallstatt
GALLIA TRANSALPINA
Po River
SLOVENIA
GAUL
GALICIA
Narbonne
Entremont
Marseilles
GALLIA CISALPINA
Atlantic Ocean
Ebro River
ITALY
Numantia
Tagus River
IBERIA
Telamon
Rome
Black Sea
Mediterranean Sea
GALATIA
GREECE
Pergamon
Delphi
ASIA MINOR

SCALE

0   400   800   1200km
0   200   400   600 miles

PROSPERITY AND ELABORATE ARTISTRY

Archaeological discoveries of aristocratic adornments present the Celts as a people who made no secret of their wealth. Princely tombs filled with magnificent jewelry and lavishly decorated ceremonial artifacts abound in all corners of the Celtic world, but especially in the Rhineland and Switzerland.

It is believed that affluent Celtic chieftains commissioned engravers who would produce pieces of ornamented metalware to their precise specifications. Gold and silver-gilt pieces—ranging from cauldrons to brooches, bracelets, and torcs (neck-rings)—display all the principles of stylized, spiral, and curvilinear decoration, as well as patterns and forms taken from nature: leaf shapes, flower designs, and birds and beasts adorn every surface.

Gold and silver also had a practical use, however: taking a lead from the Greeks and Romans, the Celts minted their own coins. Initially based on classical designs, they soon displayed the unmistakable motifs of Celtic decoration. For example, the horses and chariot of Apollo, an image used on the reverse of some Greek coins, gave way to Celtic horse imagery. The obverse ("heads") sides of Celtic coins largely show warrior-aristocratic faces with stiff, lime-washed hairstyles, although some do seem to imitate Roman styles: coins minted in Britain in about 10BCE by Cunobelinos, ruler of the Catuvellauni tribe, romanize the Celtic leader's features and bear a latinized form of his name.

LA TÈNE STYLE

The Celtic pottery and metalwork of the Hallstatt Period (ca. 800BCE–500BCE) were decorated with strik-

Objects associated with ritual drinking were deposited in many early graves, especially during the Hallstatt and La Tène periods. The delicate gold openwork of this design from a 5th-century BCE grave near Schwarzenbach in the Rhineland, Germany, once sheathed a wooden bowl.

ingly simple geometric designs. Artisans copied prestigious foreign imports, such as jars from Attica in Greece, and adapted the motifs to suit indigenous tastes.

However, the most enduring legacy of Celtic art is the beautiful curvilinear form of decoration known as the La Tène style. The interlaced La Tène patterns that adorn early Celtic metalwork survived across centuries of Celtic art, and eventually inspired the spectacular decoration on early medieval Irish manuscripts. We might be surprised to learn, therefore, that these typical Celtic patterns actually represent an enormously cosmopolitan array of sources. For example, swirling Celtic motifs have both classical and Near Eastern precedents. The great achievement of Celtic art lies less in the individual elements of its style than in its original synthesis of those elements, which continued to create a distinct aesthetic that then developed, under its own impetus and momentum, into the many strands of the later La Tène.

The art of the La Tène style, in its early forms, varied from intricate geometric designs, skillfully laid out with compasses, to highly stylized plant and animal motifs. However, by the middle of the fifth century BCE, a characteristic curvilinear style had emerged, which spread via trade and other contacts throughout the rapidly expanding Celtic world. Incised or raised patterns, exhibiting a characteristic tension between symmetry and asymmetry, began to appear on the surfaces of bronze or gold brooches and torcs. Coral and glass inlays added bright color and rich texture to both jewelry and weapons. British smiths crafted mirrors decorated with engraved designs of asymmetrical, but finely balanced, patterns in which the faces of bird-like creatures seem to appear and retreat. After smiths in Britain and Ireland had mastered the technique of enameling, they created even more spectacular patterns, seen on rings, brooches, shields, and scabbards.

Despite the unquestionable beauty and technical brilliance of Celtic art, the precise meanings of its symbols are often difficult to establish. Classical sources note the Celts' love of metaphor and conundrum, and perhaps the intricate asymmetrical and abstract patterns of their art represent a visual equivalent of the type of complex verbal patterns that characterize the later medieval literature of Ireland, Wales, and Brittany.

One possible reason for the lavish adornment found in Celtic art is a close relationship between art and patronage. The elaborate decoration on a variety of prestigious objects suggests the existence of a powerful aristocracy making a dramatic show of its status. Further testimony to this assumption lies in the portability of much La Tène art: small but magnificently crafted pieces of jewelry, flamboyant cloths, and intricately decorated weapons were easy for aristocratic patrons to carry around as traveling symbols of their wealth.

Celtic art is also famous for its fine stone carving, a comparatively late innovation. Stone figurines became widespread during the Romano-Celtic period under

◆ INTRICATE SPIRALS ◆

The swirling, spiraling patterns of La Tène art decorate creations in a vast range of media, from small, gold, sacred objects to massive stone monuments. These curvilinear designs suggest that Celtic artists abhorred a vacuum, filling every space. In producing what, to many, is the most characteristically "Celtic" art, they abandoned strict symmetry for fluid patterns, in which the shapes of humans and beasts emerge and dissolve before our eyes. Palmette and lotus motifs, borrowed from the classical world, display the cosmopolitan nature of Celtic art, while stunning circular forms display its power. This decorative bronze disk (below), from the grave of a fifth- or fourth-century BCE warrior, is adorned with an intricate pattern that would have been laid out using compasses.

the influence of classical culture, while the introduction of Christianity led to the erection of intricately sculpted stone crosses (see page 439) and other monuments.

La Tène design provided inspiration for the Irish style of manuscript decoration. Irish artists created patterns of such splendor, complexity, and delicacy that one observer called them the "work of angels" —the final flowering of a glorious imaginative heritage.

ADORNMENTS AND AMULETS

The ancient Celts clearly so adored finery that they must have presented a bizarre spectacle to their more restrained neighbors in the classical world. Diodorus of Sicily, a Greek historian of the first century BCE, made a point of noting the Celtic fondness for brightly colored clothes adorned with rich embroidered designs, or else woven patterns that were "striped ... with close checks of various colors"—in other words, tartan. In contrast to the short-haired and clean-shaven men of Greece and Rome, who wore simple tunics, Celtic men sported trousers, long hair, and, in the case of the nobility, great drooping moustaches. Some tribes bleached their hair with lime water and wore it spiked. A fierce group of peoples

A bronze crescent-moon fibula (a sprung-pin brooch used to fasten clothes), found in a Hallstatt grave and thought to date from the 6th century BCE. Embossed pendants hang from the boat-like central piece upon which sit two animals, possibly stylized birds (boats and birds were both symbols of the afterlife Otherworld). The body of the "boat" is decorated with circular emblems, thought to represent the sun.

◆ FANTASIES OF LEAF AND FLOWER ◆

Leaf, flower, and plant motifs seem to swirl across every surface of Celtic artifacts of the La Tène era. A great array of objects, especially helmets, brooches, and torcs, was incised with leaf and stem designs. According to the Roman historian Pliny the Elder (23–79CE), oak and mistletoe were used in Celtic ritual, but stylized art forms make specific plants hard to identify. Floral patterns persisted into Irish art from the fifth to twelfth centuries. Enameled and filigree plant forms decorate fine metalwork made for sacred purposes, and elaborate flower and leaf designs frame manuscript texts.

based in Scotland were nicknamed *Picti* (meaning "Painted Ones") by the Romans, probably on account of their tattoos or body-paint.

Striking clothes and hairstyles were complemented by magnificent jewelry of superb handiwork fashioned in bronze, silver, and gold and found all over the former Celtic world. Diodorus was struck by the fashion, among both men and women, for wearing "bracelets on their wrists and arms, heavy gold solid necklaces around their necks, enormous rings, and even golden corselets." Decorated fibulae (sprung pins) and brooches were essential for keeping in place the high-quality woollen clothing.

The heavy "necklace" referred to by Diodorus is the Celtic neck-ring, known today as the torc. Many finely wrought examples have been found in graves, at shrines, and also in buried hoards of treasure (most notably those dating from around the first century BCE), where they would have been placed during times of danger as amulets to invoke the power and protection of the gods.

Torcs were linked to aristocratic or divine status. One magnificent example, thought to date from the sixth century BCE, was found in the lavish grave of a high-ranking woman at Vix in Burgundy, France. Classical authors describe Celtic warriors in battle as naked except for their most valued possessions—their weapons and torcs. The British warrior-queen Boudicca, or Boadicea, who led a revolt against the Romans in eastern England in 60CE, is said to have worn a torc of twisted gold.

As well as being magnificent items of jewelry and symbols of status, torcs were probably worn as amulets to invoke divine power and protection. There are numerous images of Celtic deities depicted wearing these necklaces—symbols of their importance among the Celtic gods and goddesses. The horned god Cernunnos (see pages 426–427) typically has a single torc around his neck and clasps another in his hand. The presence of two neck-rings suggests that he was a highly revered god. A statue of a veiled woman from a healing shrine at Chaumalières, near Dijon in France, who may be a pilgrim, a priestess, or even perhaps the goddess of the shrine herself, is depicted wearing just one torc.

VISIONS OF NATURE

Nature, with its endless permutations of mountains, rivers, lakes, forests, trees, and animals, was sanctified by the Celts and often became the focus of important ritual. The Greeks and Romans, who built elaborate temples, marveled that Celtic deities were worshipped at simple open-air shrines.

It is unlikely that a trans-Celtic religion ever existed, although a range of sun gods, sky gods, and mother goddesses do appear to have been venerated in all parts of the Celtic world. Sun gods are often identified by the attributes of wheels (a symbol of the sun), while sky gods are given hammers (symbolizing thunder) and thunderbolts. Mother goddesses (see page 428) are recognizable from the domestic objects that are often seen accompanying them, such as loaves or linen.

Other important divinities included one that the Roman general Julius Caesar called "Mercury"—giving the deity the name of the Roman god whom the general thought most similar. According to Caesar, this divinity was paramount among the Gauls and was revered as the inventor of the arts and as a patron of commerce. However, the Celtic Mercury was apparently also connected with less peaceful activity, because he was sometimes called by the Gaulish epithets Artaios (which means "bear") and Moccus (which means "pig")—bears and pigs were considered to be sacred animals and were associated with war and hunting.

The actual name of the Celtic Mercury is unknown, but he is often associated with the Celtic god Lugos. It is difficult to identify images on any surviving artifacts with Lugos himself, but modern cities such as Lyons in France and Leiden in Holland recall the ancient place-name Lugdunum ("fortress of the god Lugus"). In the Irish tales, Lugh Samhildénach ("Lugh who possesses all the arts") is an important figure believed to be related to Lugos. But, most strikingly, two similar festivals existed that were associated with Lugos. They were held around the same time of year in both Lyons and Ireland: the August festival of Lugos in Lyons, and the traditional harvest festival of Lughnasa in Ireland on 1 August. However, trans-Celtic deities such as Lugos tend to be the exception. More often, veneration was expressed locally, and about two-thirds of the divine names recorded in ancient inscriptions appear only once.

As Mercury–Lugos exemplifies, Celtic deities were believed to perform a variety of functions. Similarly, the Gallo–Roman god known as "Mars–Lenus," revered by the Treveri tribe in northeastern Gaul, was depicted as a warrior, but worshipped as a healer. Devotees at the Romano–Celtic sanctuary in Trier, the capital of the Treveri, called upon Mars–Lenus to protect children.

Celtic images in metal and stone imply that cults devoted to divine couples were also popular. The goddess in the couple is always a purely Celtic deity, but sometimes the god is Roman or Romano–Celtic. For example, the Celtic goddess Rosmerta is often depicted as the consort of "Mercury." Rosmerta, whose name means "Great Provider," is most commonly represented with symbols of abundance and plenty, such as buckets of wine or honey, while "Mercury" is depicted with a hammer, perhaps in this case implying protection.

The Celts rarely enclosed their places of worship in temples of stone, preferring to use nature's own boundaries, such as trees or the banks of a lake, to divorce sacred space from the secular world. Divinity was perceived to reside in all corners of the natural world—particularly around springs, groves, and lakes. If specially constructed sanctuaries existed at all, they were either open to the sky, such as the wooden platforms near the lake's edge at La Tène, Switzerland, or built of wood and thatch, such as the central structure of Navan Fort in County Armagh, Ireland.

A detail of a head from a cauldron of the 1st century BCE, found in a bog near Rynkeby in Denmark, but made farther south in the Celtic lands. The head was an important motif for the Celts. This figure, with a high-status torc and stylized hair, is believed to represent a goddess.

THE WATERS OF LIFE

The association between water and spiritual power is evident in Europe as early as the Bronze Age, and veneration for water became a hallmark of Celtic religion. Rivers are prominent in Celtic myth, and many have a tutelary goddess, such as Matrona, deity of the French Marne.

For the ancient Celts, there was no clear distinction between the practice of medicine and healing by supernatural means. A great deal of trust was placed in the curative powers of springs, which often became the sites of great sanctuaries. The deity Sequana, for example, who is often depicted standing in a duck-shaped boat, was the eponymous goddess of the Seine River in France, and her sacred healing-place lay among the springs at the headwaters of the river, in Burgundy.

During the Romano–Celtic period, a number of sanctuaries dedicated to other healer-deities were so popular that extensive baths and hostels for pilgrims were constructed at these sites. Among the best known is the sanctuary of the goddess Sulis Minerva at the

ancient springs of Bath, England. The goddess's powers were believed to extend beyond healing to dispensing justice and delivering retribution on behalf of those who worshipped her. Devotees hoping for cures from the god Belenus, the Celtic equivalent of Apollo, the Roman god of medicine, offered figurines of infants and horses at his healing shrine at Sainte-Sabine in Burgundy.

Larger bodies of water, such as lakes, were important sites for ritual activity. The Greek author Strabo mentions a sacred lake near Toulouse in France, said to be filled with treasure that no one dared steal for fear of upsetting the gods. Archaeological investigations have revealed that the "treasure" consists of offerings thrown into the lake, including jewelry, weapons, and body armor. Similarly, ancient Britons deposited high-quality metalwork—much of it deliberately damaged, perhaps to indicate that its function in this world had ended—into Llyn Cerrig Bach on the island of Anglesey, Wales. Although no particular deity is identified with this lake, the votive objects found in its waters are associated with warfare, suggesting that local aristocrats considered the lake's power influential in their battles. Classical sources suggest that Anglesey was home to an important druid stronghold. Other valuable artifacts recovered from British waters include the famous Battersea shield and a bronze horned helmet, which were salvaged in London at different times

Areas such as Snowdonia in Gwynedd, north Wales, are the settings for numerous Celtic folk traditions: the deep, mysterious lakes may lead to Otherworld realms, while mountains represent places of sanctuary or the sites of heroic fights with marauding giants. Gwynedd provides the setting for the entire fourth section of the medieval Welsh set of tales, the Mabinogi, *which centers around the exploits of the brothers Gwydion and Gilfaethwy, nephews of the magician Math.*

• THE SALMON OF WISDOM •

In Irish myth, a particular salmon in the Boyne River was imbued with great wisdom (the salmon represented knowledge). This gift was to be passed on to the first to taste the fish's flesh. The salmon was caught by the bard Finnegas, who gave it to his apprentice Fionn Mac Cumhaill to cook. Fionn touched its flesh and acquired magic powers. Many Celts believed that the sea separated this world from the next, thus aquatic animals (such as the dolphin, left, from the Gundestrup Cauldron) adopted from the Mediterranean world became symbols of connection between the two realms.

from the Thames River. Their quality suggests that they may even have been made specially as votive offerings, rather than practical weaponry to be borne in battle.

High-status possessions such as brooches, shields, and swords were actually thrown from specially constructed wooden platforms into Lake Neuchâtel at La Tène in Switzerland. Such objects were not the only offerings deposited at these lake sites—there is evidence of animal and human sacrifice, indicating that the local water divinities sometimes demanded a higher price for their favor.

Among the items offered to water divinities were cauldrons. These prestigious objects had mythological associations—the "Cauldron of Rebirth," which restored the dead to life in the medieval Welsh *Mabinogi*, is said to have emerged from a lake.

THE SPIRIT OF THE FOREST

According to the Roman poet Lucan (39–65CE), the Celts worshipped bloodthirsty gods in dark woodland sanctuaries. While evidence suggests that this may be a grimly exaggerated description of the truth, the Celts undoubtedly regarded forests and woodlands as sacred places of power and danger.

A widespread Celtic deity that was particularly associated with woods, was the "Horned God," a lord of animals usually depicted with deer-like antlers. Only one representation of this god, dating from the first century CE, gives his Celtic name: Cernunnos, or the "Horned Sacred One." This title, which may have been a local name, is inscribed on a Gallo–Roman altar above a carving of an elderly figure who has both the antlers and ears of a stag and wears two torcs (neck-rings)—one hanging off each horn. The altar comes from a sanctuary of the Parisii, a Gaulish tribe, who gave their name to the French capital Paris.

Much older images of the same, or a very similar, deity have been found in other parts of the Celtic world. For example, a horned figure is depicted on a rock carving of the fourth century BCE from Val Camonica in northern Italy, as well as on the famous Gundestrup Cauldron, which was fashioned about a century later. Cernunnos was linked with prosperity and the abundance of nature, and his close association with the forest-dwelling stag—the god sometimes has hooves as well as deer's ears and antlers—also makes him a symbol of masculine potency. He appears on the Gundestrup Cauldron with the ram-horned snake, a hybrid beast associated with regeneration and fertility. Like the snake, a stag regularly loses and regenerates part of its body: it sheds and regrows its antlers once a year. One recovered statue of Cernunnos has holes for real antlers, which may have been replaced annually by worshippers in a seasonal festival of renewal—perhaps during the spring when new antlers became fully formed. The aristocratic torcs usually worn by Cernunnos indicate his high status, while other attributes, such as food and bags of coins, reinforce his connection with prosperity and well-being.

The sun streaming through the trees of the Black Forest near Stuttgart, Germany, makes it easy to understand why the Celts considered wooded areas to be sacred. At one time almost all of southern Germany, like most of northern Europe, would have been forest. Some classical authors described woodland sanctuaries as dark, frightening places that terrified Celtic devotees, who were loath to enter. Woodland sanctuaries with carved wooden images of heads have been found, but classical authors misjudged the attitude of the Celtic worshippers: many of these sanctuaries were healing shrines to beneficent deities.

Cernunnos was probably revered as a god whose power and favor could influence the success of the chase—as the lord of the forest, he was responsible for a great economic resource that provided food, clothing, and fuel. The attribute of a stag in depictions of numerous other hunter deities from woodland regions testifies to the extent and strength of Celtic belief that these gods held power over hunting success. Equally, they protect the animals of the forest: one image shows a deity resting his hand on the antlers of a stag. The seventh-century BCE Strettweg chariot shows a goddess presiding over a hunting party in pursuit of two stags. A Val Camonica rock carving from the same period also depicts a stag hunt. A recovered stag figurine was dedicated to the British god Silvanus Callirius ("Woodland King") at Colchester, England.

Cernunnos was the most prominent horned deity, but there are others who also display an affinity with the natural world, even if they lack Cernunnos's complex attributes. One such deity is thought to have inspired the medieval Welsh description of a grotesque giant, who summons the animals of the woods by striking a stag so that it bellows. Other gods and goddesses with apparent hunting connections are depicted with hares, another common quarry, or hounds, which were also associated with healing and the afterlife Otherworld.

REALMS OF THE DIVINE

Certain themes and motifs commonly occur in the Celtic imagination. There is a strong tradition of the goddess—female deities often appeared in triple-headed form. The Celts believed in a life after death, which they conceived as an Otherworld full of strange beasts and inexplicable phenomena.

Julius Caesar's list of Gaulish deities mentions only one goddess, whom he calls by the Roman name of Minerva. The Romans also gave this name to Sulis, the British goddess who presided over the famous healing springs at Bath in England (see page 424). However, the role of the Celtic Minerva extended beyond that of a healing goddess, as she was also associated with fertility, good fortune, animal husbandry, hunting, and war. And she certainly was not the only Celtic goddess.

In Celtic belief, the most widely known female deity was the mother goddess, who represented the rich earth, female fertility, and the power of regeneration. Mother goddesses took many forms. For example, the goddess Aveta was one of several deities worshipped at Trier, the capital of the Treveri in northeastern Gaul. Pilgrims to her shrines left small votive images of a maternal goddess holding symbols of prosperity and plenty such as fruit, lapdogs, and babies.

The complex symbolism of mother goddesses was reinforced by the fact that they were often grouped in threes. Several maternal images found in the Rhineland depict two older goddesses flanking a younger one. In Burgundy, one goddess commonly holds a newborn baby, while two others carry objects such as a piece of cloth or washing implements. Some triple-goddess figures are shown with a spindle, linking the mother goddess with the three classical Fates, and thus represent the cycle of life, from birth to old age and death.

◆ ANIMAL SYMBOLISM ◆

Winged beasts and hybrid creatures appear in Celtic art from its very beginnings. For example, the antlered deity on the Gundestrup Cauldron holds a snake with the head of a ram, a curious hybrid popular in the iconography of northern Gaul. A strikingly powerful image, the ram's masculine fertility is combined with the snake's phallic symbolism; and death (because the snake sheds its skin) is combined with regeneration (the skin's renewal). Most menacing of all are the carvings of monsters found in the Celto-Ligurian temples of southern Gaul. In an apparent demonstration of the triumph of death, these creatures, with huge jaws and clawed feet, are shown devouring human heads and limbs.

In the medieval Welsh *Mabinogi*, the birds of the Otherworld woman Rhiannon sing to weary heroes to lull them to sleep. All kinds of birds are connected with Celtic gods and goddesses in similar ways. Peaceful and curative doves are thought to have been intimates of the god Mars–Lenus, a healing deity; a goose (which was known for its aggression and was linked in Celtic symbolism with masculinity and battle) forms the crest of a war goddess from Brittany and was a sacred bird to the Britons; and the crow was identified with Badhbh, a goddess of death. But perhaps the most powerful bird symbol is the eagle: associated with the sun god in pagan Celtic ritual, the eagle was adopted into early Christianity as the symbol of St. John the Evangelist.

Other goddesses were portrayed singly, and their functions can often be surmised from their names and attributes. For example, a small Romano–Celtic bronze figure from Berne, Switzerland, shows a goddess offering a basket of fruit to a bear. The goddess's name is Artio, which itself means "bear." The image suggests either that she protected the bears themselves or that she propitiated the animals on behalf of her devotees, whom she thus protected from attack. A Gaulish goddess, Sirona, carried the attribute of a serpent, but this probably means that she was a healer deity rather than a protector of snakes—the creatures are a widespread symbol of healing in the ancient world. Sirona's role as a curative goddess is confirmed by the fact that many of her sanctuaries were located at springs.

In Irish tradition a female deity called Danu was the mother of the most powerful group of Irish gods, the *Tuatha Dé Danann* (the "Children of the Goddess Danu"). Although she was originally linked with rivers, through her association with the Munster fertility goddess Anu—which may simply be another form of the same goddess's name—Danu came to be regarded as a powerful mother goddess among the Irish Celts, responsible for the fertility of all the land in Ireland. A medieval Irish writer declares of her: "good was the food she gave us." Danu's/Anu's close ties with the land gave rise to the name *De Chich Anann* (the "Paps [breasts] of Anu") for two hills that overlook a valley to the west of Killarney in County Kerry.

Numerous Celtic goddesses presided over war and hunting. The most dramatic visualizations of war goddesses are found in Irish literature and myth. In one famous epic, two grim figures, the Morrigan ("Phantom Queen") and the goddess Badhbh ("Crow"), confront the hero Cú Chulainn at the hour of his death. Cú Chulainn had made an enemy of the Morrigan by refusing her sexual advances. To avenge this humiliation, the Morrigan, who was believed to know the fate of warriors in battle, determined that the hero would die in his next conflict. He was lured into fatal combat by the sorcery of Badhbh, a war goddess, who hovered over battlefields in the form of a crow. The Irish descriptions of these two baleful goddesses echo many of the elements of triplication, transformation, fertility, and aggression that occur in earlier iconography.

THE POWER OF THREE

One of the most important and recurring elements in the art of the western European Celts was the use of triplication, or groups of three, which may be shown symbolically with threefold patterns or designs, or most significantly and importantly as triple divinities. Celtic deities were often venerated in triple-headed and triple-faced forms—such images intensified the already evocative symbol of the head. Stone carvings that show three heads facing in three different directions have been found as far apart as Ireland and Germany, but the motif was especially prominent around Rheims in France, the ancient center of the Remi, a Gaulish tribe. In this area, the faces of what may be a tribal deity are depicted so that they overlap. This stone carving has only two eyes in total, but the clever design means that each head looks in a different direction and none lacks any facial feature. We cannot be completely sure of the meaning of such triple-headed figures, but one theory suggests that because the heads look in three directions at once, they may signify the continuity of time (past, present, and future) or the universe (the Earth, the heavens, and the underworld). One of the most important gods to be associated with trinity symbolism was the horned god Cernunnos, who was sometimes linked with figures such as the three-headed Mercury that appears with the horned god on a first-century CE monument found in Paris. The bull was also a potent symbol, an association that derived from its physical strength. A Celtic image of a bull with three horns is thus particularly evocative. Three-horned bulls were deposited at Gaulish shrines, and one appears on a ceremonial baton which had been buried with other votive objects at Willingham Fen in Cambridgeshire, England.

Medieval literature in Ireland, Wales, and other Celtic regions, continued to use triplication, but as a narrative device rather than as a powerful, visual symbol. For example, goddesses and Otherworld beings are sometimes reported to appear in threes moments before a critical or dramatic event. The ancient British bards of the heroic age may have used similar motifs to enliven their narratives. In the first section of the Welsh *Mabinogi* set of tales, King Matholwch, the king of Ireland, describes the maiden Branwen as one of the three "Matriarchs of this Island." Later, there are three Golden Shoemakers, three Noble Youths, and three Unhappy Blows, to name but a few. Similarly, in Irish myth, a hero is believed to know that his death is imminent when he sees three red-headed warriors riding in front of him.

JOURNEYS TO THE OTHERWORLD

Belief in an afterlife was an important aspect of Celtic religion. Sources suggest that there was no conception of reward or punishment after death, but the recklessness of Celtic fighting men led classical commentators to surmise that the Celts looked forward to being reborn in the afterlife. Although this conclusion can never be verified, the fact that most burials included grave goods does imply that the passage from life to death was viewed as a journey into some sort of new existence for which the dead needed to be prepared. As far as we can glean from later literary sources, the destination of the dead was conceived of as an unearthly, magical region, or Otherworld, which was home also to supernatural beings and monsters. The boundaries of this land were fluid, and all mortals could cross over and enter the

Otherworld—at their own risk. At certain important times of seasonal change, however, this flexible frontier was apt to disappear altogether—for example, on Beltaine (1 May) and Samhain (1 November). At these times, the inhabitants of the Otherworld might stalk the mortal region, emerging from the pre-Celtic barrows and other burial sites (see page 435), which were believed to be entrances to the Otherworld.

In Ireland, the inhabitants of the Otherworld were known as the *Tuatha Dé Danann* ("Children of the Goddess Danu"), who lived in the *Tír na nÓg* ("Land of Youth") or the *Tír na mBeo* ("Land of Women"). As death was not a prerequisite for entry into their realm, some stories tell of mortal women being kidnapped as brides for Otherworld men, or of heroes who entered these strange lands and sometimes never returned.

While storytellers often located these mysterious and beautiful worlds within the ancient burial sites, known in Irish as *sidhe* ("fairy mounds"; see illustration, left), they also envisaged idyllic Otherworld islands beyond great stretches of sea. Examples of these include *Emhain Abhlach* ("Region of Apples") or *Magh Meall* ("Delightful Plain"). Irish tales known as *immrama* describe sea voyages to the Otherworld in which small bands of heroes or holy men visit a series of islands where mysterious and symbolic adventures test their intellect and bravery. Some islands are haunted by strange beasts, such as monster cats; some contain springs pouring forth wine, and ever-fruitful trees filled with exotic birds; others are inhabited by beautiful Otherworld women.

The literature and folklore of Wales also record a strong belief in a mystical Otherworld. The medieval collection of Welsh tales known as the *Mabinogi* relate how the hero Pwyll agrees to change places with Arawn, the king of Annwn, the Otherworld. Pwyll's passage into Annwn is aided by King Arawn, who lets him be guided by magical red-eared dogs. The twelfth-century traveler and historian Gerald of Wales told how he had once met a man who, as a boy, had visited a beautiful sunless realm, the inhabitants of which never lied and ate only saffron and milk. However, the young visitor had violated the sacred rules of this magical Otherworld by stealing a golden cup. His punishment was never to be able to find the entrance to the place again.

MAGIC AND METAMORPHOSIS

Much of the Celtic cultural legacy—whether imagery on ancient artifacts or in medieval literature—suggests that the Celts, in both pagan and Christian times, recognized no clear distinction between the realities of this world and the features of the supernatural.

Metamorphosis, the ability to change shape or form, is a prominent motif in many Celtic tales, and examples are also to be found in Celtic art. The deer-like characteristics of the god Cernunnos—antlers and hooves—certainly suggest that shapeshifting between the animal and human worlds was believed possible, but images of this deity are among the handful of Celtic artifacts that actually attest to this. Other images imply a welding of human and animal essences rather than forms, as in the Gaulish statue of a war god who bears the image of a boar, a symbol of war and hunting, as an attribute (see illustration, opposite).

The interest in magical transformation among the Celts may be rooted in a feeling for the fluidity of the cosmos—the malleability of the boundaries between this world and the next. Movement between the mortal world and the Otherworld was thought to take place at certain special times of year. In Irish myth, the hero Oengus assumed the form of a swan to follow his lover into the Otherworld on the feast of Samhain, when the barriers between the two realms were at their most fluid (see page 435).

Rebirth into a new life through metamorphosis is also touched upon in the tale of Oengus. The hero's brother Midir was unable to resist falling in love with the beautiful maiden Étaín. This brought on the wrath of Midir's first wife, who, in a fit of jealousy, transformed Étaín into a huge red fly. Oengus took pity on the girl and partly undid the magic by allowing her to return to human form each night after dark. But the wife was not satisfied with this, and one day sent a strong wind to blow the fly into the wilderness. After many years, Étaín fell into a cup of wine and was swallowed. This allowed her to be reborn as a beautiful maid. When eventually Midir found her again, Étaín was the wife of the king of Ireland and oblivious to her previous life. By tricking the king into letting him kiss Étaín, Midir reminded the girl of her past life and she fell in love with him again. Both turned into swans and flew away to Midir's home.

As the stories of Oengus, Midir, and Étaín illustrate, birds were frequently the result of human mutation

---

This wide-eyed animal head, probably a bull's, is a bronze mount from a 3rd-century BCE wooden wine flask found at Brno-Malomerice in the Czech Republic. The protagonists of Celtic myth often transformed themselves into animals.

in Celtic belief. Another tale relates how the Children of Lir were magically transformed into swans by their wicked stepmother and sang in the Otherworld. Images of a carrion bird perched on the back of a horse, which appear on Iron Age coins from Brittany, may reflect Celtic tradition known from Ireland in which battle goddesses assume the form of crows and ravens, particularly at the time of a warrior's death. The Irish war goddesses may also appear as beautiful young women or ugly hags—they take on their hideous aspect after they have been wronged in some way.

In some accounts, supernatural beings assume the forms of animals. The set of Irish tales known as the Fenian cycle is rich with examples of transformation. The divine wife of the Irish hero Fionn (see box, page 425) and the mother of his son Oisín, first appears to her husband as a fawn, having been transformed as punishment for failing to fall in love with a druid. Fionn's aunt was briefly turned into a dog, during which time she gave birth to a canine son, who later became one of Fionn's trusted hounds. In the Welsh *Mabinogi* tales, a magical woman who plagues heroes (the wife of Llwyd Cil Coed, the "Gray Man of the Wood"), takes the form of a mouse to conduct her torment.

Welsh legend abounds in accounts of magical shapeshifting. In one story, magicians create a beautiful woman, Blodeuwedd, out of flowers. However, she later proves unfaithful, so the magicians punish her by turning her into an owl, believed to be a creature of the evil forces of darkness. Another tale recounts how Lleu, a Welsh hero, turns into an eagle after being struck with a spear, but recovers his human form through the care of his magician uncle. Culhwch, another hero, must face a

A stone image of a Gaulish god, found at Euffigneix, Haute-Marne, France, and thought to date from the 1st or 2nd century BCE. The presence of the torc around the neck identifies the figure as a deity—probably of nature. The boar impression in its right side indicates that the essences of the god and the animal were believed to be inseparable.

giant boar (a transformed king who would not mend his evil ways) in order to retrieve a comb, scissors, and a razor so that the father of his bride-to-be may groom himself for the wedding.

According to some scholars, these shapeshifting and magical motifs may indicate a Celtic belief in regeneration and the afterlife, which was envisaged as a more perfect version of ordinary life. It is certainly true that many Celtic deities were believed to have a specific regenerative function: divine attributes such as fruit and grain imply fecundity, while animals such as snakes (which shed their skins several times a year to reveal new growth underneath) and deer (which annually shed their antlers and grow new ones) may also imply an association with the cycle of death and rebirth.

Early Christian tradition regarded a variety of creatures as symbols or embodiments of Christ and the evangelists. Given the Celts' own associations between divinity and metamorphosis, the Irish manuscript artists took to this tradition with enthusiasm. For example, the flesh of the peacock was said to be incorruptible, and so the bird came to represent the eternal, resurrected Christ. Similarly, the early Church associated the gospel writers with celestial creatures that appear in the Bible. Matthew was symbolized by a man or an angel, but the other evangelists were all animals: a lion for Mark, an ox for Luke, and an eagle for John.

THE SEASONAL ROUND

The Celts conceived of the year as a wheel and they marked the stages of its turning with a series of festivals which gave them the opportunity to celebrate exuberantly. But there was a darker side to Celtic ritual: bloody sacrifices—of humans as well as animals—were not uncommon.

Early Irish literature records the names of four great seasonal festivals that marked important divisions in the Celtic year. The summer began at Beltaine (thought to mean "Great Fire") on 1 May, and winter began at Samhain ("End of Summer") on 1 November. The two other festivals, closely linked to specific deities, were Lughnasa, the feast of the god Lugh, celebrated on 1 August as a traditional harvest festival; and Imbolg (thought to mean "Sheep's Milk"), which fell on 2 February. Imbolg was under the protection of the goddess

Brighid and, later, her Christian successor, St. Bridget; her festival celebrated the beginning of spring and the birth of lambs and other livestock.

A Gaulish calendar discovered at Coligny, near Lyons, in southern France, at the end of the nineteenth century, and thought to originate from the first century BCE, is a remarkable record of the old Gaulish language as well as of Celtic timekeeping. The calendar covers sixty-two lunar months with two intercalary ("leap") months to keep the lunar calendar in line with the solar

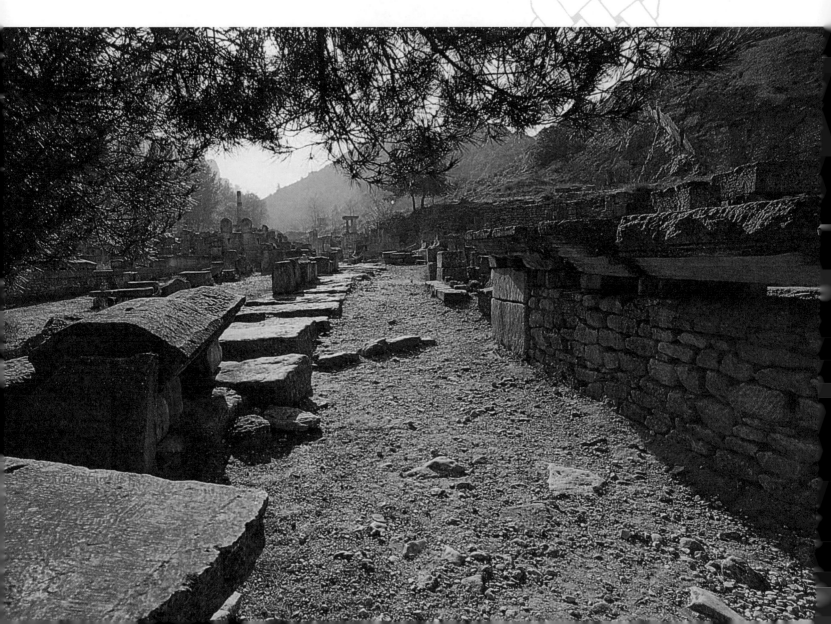

year and ensure that the festivals always fell in the correct season. It specifically names Samhain (spelled Samonios on the calendar itself) as the beginning of the Celtic year. All the Celtic festivals began on the eve of the specific day of celebration.

The four seasonal festivals reflect the pastoral and agricultural cycles of the year, but they were also magical times when the boundaries between the real and supernatural worlds were believed to be at their weakest. In Welsh tradition, the eve of Beltaine (*Calan Mai*, "May Eve") was the night when the magician–poet Taliesin was rescued from the river by his foster father, and the night that Pryderi, a hero of the *Mabinogi* tales, was stolen as a baby from his mother Rhiannon.

The best-known Celtic celebration of all was Samhain (this is the Irish and Gaelic name for the festival—it is *Calan Gaeaf*, "Winter's Eve," in Wales). Many of the key events in Irish mythology, such as the arrival of the mystical *Tuatha Dé Danann* people (see page 431), took place at Samhain, when the boundaries of this world and the supernatural realm were believed to dissolve completely, and the *sidhe* (fairy) mounds, where the people of the Otherworld lived, were open. In one Irish tale, the hero Neara Mac Niadhain ventured out one Samhain night to pursue an army of *sidhe* people who had invaded his country. He knew that, on this night, they would be unable to close the entrances of their fairy-mounds against him.

RITUAL SACRIFICE

Sacrifice played an important role in marking the festivals and served a variety of additional purposes. According to Greek and Roman observers, Celtic sacrificial practices were dramatic and bloody. Celtic priests

---

Imperial Rome usually respected the religion of conquered Celtic peoples, and ceremonies were long allowed to continue at sites such as Glanum, shown here, which was an important Gaulish healing shrine near Saint-Rémy de Provence in southern France.

allegedly stabbed victims and predicted the future from their death throes, or burned captives alive in huge wicker figures. It was said that victims sacrificed to the god Esus were stabbed and hanged in trees until they bled to death. The Roman historian Tacitus claimed that the altars of the druids in a sacred grove on the isle of Anglesey, Wales, were drenched with blood and festooned with entrails. Although such accounts are likely to be colored with classical prejudice and are probably exaggerated, archaeologists have uncovered a number of abnormal burials of individuals who may have been sacrificed. This is certainly true in the case of a man who had been drugged, poleaxed, garrotted, and finally buried in a bog at Lindow Moss in Cumbria, northwestern England.

Animal sacrifice appears to have been particularly associated with funeral rites. One important individual was buried in Yorkshire, England, alongside several of his horses. The bones of some geese—a bird associated with the Celtic Otherworld—have been found in graves in Slovakia.

Modern archaeology provides substantial evidence for Celtic burial rituals. For example, evidence of funeral feasting has been uncovered in several of the Celtic graves at Hochdorf in southwestern Germany. But in terms of major ceremony, the installation of a king was particularly important, because the sacred link between the ruler and the land was evidently central to Celtic kingship and remained so into medieval times. In Ireland, a ritual called the *tarbfheiss* ("bull sleep"), in which a white bull was slaughtered, confirmed the acceptance of the High King and his sovereignty as ruler (see page 437). Writing in the twelfth century, Gerald of Wales describes a ritual in which a white mare was slaughtered and boiled in broth at the inauguration of an Irish High King, who bathed in the broth and feasted on the horseflesh.

Victory in battle, too, was marked with its own ritual sacrifice. The Celtic victors would slaughter captured animals and dedicate them in thanks to the gods.

GUARDIANS OF SACRED LORE

Writing was a relatively late innovation in Celtic society, and so, for centuries, the spoken word was the chief method of maintaining Celtic culture. The principles of law, myth, and religion were upheld by being repeated from one person to another. Those who were responsible for fostering and adding to this body of wisdom were the bards, druids, and seers.

The Greek author Strabo and the Roman general Julius Caesar, among other classical observers, give long accounts of the role of the druids, who commanded the utmost respect among the Celts because they were the supreme guardians of the sacred lore. They were experts in divination and prophecy, as well as in the supervision of religious activities, such as ritual sacrifice at sacred lakes and groves. Celtic metalwork

The importance of music in Celtic society is recorded in statues such as this of a god playing a lyre (from Côtes D'Armor, France; ca. 70BCE). Bards and druids would use music to help them to remember complex poems, legal lists, and matters of religion.

recovered from Llyn Cerrig Bach in Anglesey, Wales, suggests that the site was a druid sanctuary, perhaps even the one referred to by Tacitus as the scene of the druids' last stand against the Roman invaders of Britain. Druids were also required to memorize long and complex law codes and to give judgments on legal cases.

Although all Celtic societies must have had some sort of priestly class, the druids themselves were apparently found only in the British Isles and Gaul. Artifacts believed to be associated with druidic activities include a group of bronze headdresses discovered at a Romano–Celtic temple built in Norfolk, England, during the second century CE; similar objects are known from Ireland. For example, four bronze trumpets, decorated with typical La Tène patterning and perhaps used in druidic ceremonies, were found in a lake near Navan Fort, County Armagh, an important Irish Iron Age stronghold.

After the decline of Roman power in Britain and Gaul, the learned classes were dependent on the patronage of a native aristocracy for their survival. There is evidence for a complex system of poets and patrons in Scotland, Wales, and Brittany, which continued in some areas until the seventeenth century. According to Irish tradition, the bards and *filidh* (poets) took over the role of the druids. As well as these learned orators, Ireland had a special class of lawyers, whose job it was to interpret the intricacies of the ancient Irish legal system.

In ancient times, Celtic keepers of wisdom undoubtedly had to have exceptional powers of recall in order to store all the religious law, mythology, poetry, and songs that they were required to accumulate. According to some classical sources, including Strabo and Caesar, it took a druid up to twenty years to learn everything he or she had to know—all without the aid of writing. Even in later centuries, storytelling from memory was a prized skill. In one medieval Welsh tale, a character called Gwydion vab Don is said to be the best storyteller in the world, but, like a bard or a druid, he is also a great magician and a shapeshifter.

PORTENTS AND PROPHECIES

The druids were intermediaries between the natural and the divine worlds. They were believed to possess supernatural powers that enabled them to peer into the future and to predict the best times for battles, harvests, royal inaugurations, and other events in Celtic life. It was undoubtedly druids who determined which periods of the year were considered "good" (*mat*) or "bad" (*anmat*), as recorded in the first-century CE Gaulish calendar found at Coligny, France (see pages 434–435).

Divination came in various forms. A simple method might be to watch the way that a bird flew through the sky, while on a more complex level divination might take place as part of an elaborate ritual, such as the ancient *tarbhfeiss*, or "bull feast," that inaugurated the reign of the High Kings of Ireland. When a new king was to be chosen, a druid would consume the flesh and blood of a sacrificed bull and then wrap himself in the beast's flayed skin. He then fell into a profound sleep during which he would learn the identity of the next High King.

The Celts associated many Bronze Age burial mounds with the power of prophecy. Anyone brave enough to sleep on such a mound would wake up next morning as either a poet or mad. The twelfth-century historian Gerald of Wales promotes a similar method of inherited prophecy in Welsh lore when he describes seers who gained their insights after lapsing into a trance-like sleep. Coinneach Odhar (died 1577), a celebrated prophet, also called Brahan Seer, is said to have gained his divinatory powers during such a sleep. Similar practices are reported on the remote Western Isles of Scotland as late as the eighteenth century.

This Romano–Celtic pewter mask is thought to represent a priest or a god. The holes along the top of the mask suggest that it is a votive object that was at one time attached to another surface, such as a wall. The mask was discovered near the ancient springs at Bath, England.

TREASURES OF THE LORD

After the defeat of Gaul, Celtic culture vanished almost entirely from mainland Europe, remaining only in the far west—in the magnificent art and learning of the Christian Celts. St. Patrick's mission established Christianity in Ireland in the fifth century CE, and over the next two centuries the Irish sent out their own missionaries: to Iona and Lindisfarne and even to Switzerland and northern Italy.

As the Christian faith became established in Ireland, founding monastic communities, such as those at Kells, Durrow, and Armagh, developed into busy religious, intellectual, and artistic centers. Even during the Viking raids (ca. 795–950CE), monasteries remained steadfast focal points of Irish ecclesiastical culture. From the seventh century CE, contact between the Irish monasteries and those of Britain and mainland Europe produced an elaborate artistic style that represented a remarkable mix of Christian, Celtic, and classical elements. This mingling of influences is referred to as Insular culture. Patronage encouraged the production of a wide range of items: altar vessels and *flabella* (liturgical fans); reliquaries—portable shrines containing the relics of saints; croziers (hooked staffs) for bishops; and, of course, sacred manuscripts—small and comparatively plain volumes for teaching, and large, exuberantly decorated books, such as the Book of Kells (see pages 440–441), for liturgical use. These treasures were usually commissioned by the churches and monasteries themselves, or else by secular patrons who sought ecclesiastical support or divine favor.

OPPOSITE *Boat-shaped oratories, such as the Gallarus Oratory in Dingle, County Kerry (the only remaining one of its kind on the Irish mainland) provided a place for prayer and contemplation for inhabitants of Irish monastic communities.*

Reliquaries containing the bones of holy men and women, or their possessions (such as books or hand bells), were carried throughout the country from one religious establishment to another. Some were actually shaped like the rectangular Irish churches or houses of the period. Perhaps the most famous of these is the so-called "Monymusk" reliquary, thought to be from Scotland and dating from the seventh or eighth century CE. It is made of wood and decorated with silver and silver-gilt. Reliquaries tended to be embellished with biblical scenes as well as interlaced animals, abstract designs, and even figures playing the harp. The precious hand bell said to have belonged to St. Patrick, Ireland's patron, was kept carefully protected in a beautiful shrine that still exists. Carvings on churches and stone crosses depict bishops holding such bells, which would have been rung to indicate the times of prayer. Bishops were also usually shown carrying a crozier, the symbol of their office. Magnificent croziers were adorned with plaques of bronze, silver, and occasionally enamel, which in turn would be decorated with interlaced animals or foliage. Often a small reliquary box was built into the crook.

The beauties of such rich artifacts were not lost on the invading Vikings (see page 450). To the horror of Irish Christians, the pagan marauders would discard the holy relics and tear up the exquisitely illustrated books containing the word of God in order to steal only the valuable casings that protected them. In the wake of these devastating raids, treasured portable shrines were

◆ THE CROSS OF LIFE ◆

Below is the famous Celtic cross, developed from the simple Chi-Rho (a monogram of the Greek letters X and P, the first two letters of Khristos or "Christ" in Greek). The leg of rho became the stick of the cross, while the "x"-shaped chi moved up the leg and became a straight crossbar encircled by the round head of the rho. From the eighth century onward, stone crosses in this form became important in Irish monastic sculpture. Sculptors filled in the main cross with animal interlace and curvilinear decorations. Irish annals sometimes refer to such crosses as *cross an screaptra* ("cross of the scriptures"), presumably because they depicted Bible stories, although the term *cross aird* ("high cross") was more popular. Over time, decoration became more elaborate, culminating in the spectacular crosses of the tenth century with their intricate depictions of gospel stories.

transformed by the Norse raiders into jewelry caskets, and the gilt bronze fittings of religious vessels were removed and turned into brooches for Viking women.

Sacred books were often believed to have talismanic properties—for example, the Book of Durrow was allegedly dipped into sacred water so that any ailing person who later touched it might be cured of their disease—and they were often kept in elaborate covers, known as *cumtach* (book shrines). The stolen cover for the Book of Kells was probably one such book shrine. A *cumtach* was often adorned with an elaborate bronze or silver plaque depicting Christ extending his hand in blessing, the Crucifixion, or the four evangelists.

THE GLORY
OF ILLUMINATION

*The great religious manuscripts, all of which were created during the seventh and eighth centuries CE,
rank among the most outstanding masterpieces of Celtic art. Painstakingly written and illustrated,
they comprise the four New Testament gospels in the Latin of the Bible translation known as Vulgate.*

*An illumination from the gospel of St. Matthew in the Lindisfarne
Gospels (ca. 800CE). The seated figure is Matthew himself, and the
person behind the curtain is believed to be Christ. The gospels were
probably produced by Eadfrith, the Anglo-Saxon Bishop of Lindisfarne.*

In the eleventh century, Irish literary sources record the theft of a manuscript of the gospels of Matthew, Mark, Luke, and John, known as the Gospel of St. Colum Cille (St. Columba). The manuscript, by this time already around 300 years old, was finally recovered. It is known today as the Book of Kells, perhaps the most spectacular of the surviving Insular manuscripts.

The circumstances in which the book was produced are not entirely clear. It may have been fashioned on the

Scottish island of Iona, site of an abbey founded by St. Columba—a mermaid swimming up the center of a genealogy is thought to refer, through a complicated linguistic pun, to Iona and to Columba himself. However, in 795CE, the island was sacked by the Vikings, and in 807CE, the monks fled and settled instead in Kells. We know that the writing of the book began around the time of the escape to Kells, and it may have been completed there.

At least three scribes and five illustrators worked on the manuscript. Elaborate introductions to the gospel accounts follow portraits of the evangelists themselves, while four stunning portrait pages illustrate scenes from the life of Christ: as a baby cradled by the Virgin Mary; the Temptation of Christ in the wilderness; Christ teaching; and Christ's arrest in Gethsemane.

Christ is represented by motifs such as the cross of the Passion, a fish (a Christian symbol of appeal to the Celts, who associated salmon with wisdom, see box page 425), and the two monograms IHS and the Chi-Rho (respectively, the first three letters of "Jesus" and the first two of "Christ" in Greek). Most of these motifs derive from Mediterranean tradition, but the artist in Ireland does add some of his own. Entwined among many initial letters, for example, are two heads, one old, one young, representing God the Father and God the Son.

Large capital letters, used to mark divisions in the text, provided an opportunity for illustrators to show off their talent and display their artistic flourish. Letters may be filled with bright color, form patterns of interlace, or seem to metamorphose into plant, animal, and even human forms. There are more than 2,000 decorated letters in the Book of Kells alone, and each of them is unique. In many manuscripts, scribes left space among clear and uniform script for decorated letters or illustrations which artists put in later.

MORTALS, SAINTS, AND ANGELS

Magical beasts, never-ending spirals, and ornate representations of nature seem to dominate the Celtic gospel manuscripts. Nevertheless, human figures appear frequently: full-page portraits are offset by figures woven into interlace patterns, contorted into letters, and tucked discreetly into corners. The artists show little concern with anatomical accuracy, often stylizing the human form in order to incorporate a figure into their overall decorative scheme. The Book of Kells contains several groups of men drawn in profile as if they are observing the events being described in the text or illustrated on the page. There are also a number of vignettes showing men that seem to have no purpose or relevance other than to adorn. One small drawing shows a soldier standing on a letter, armed with a sword and buckler, and his foot seems to be caught up in the script.

Apart from the Virgin Mary, few mortal women are depicted in any of the Insular manuscripts. One rare example can be found in the Book of Kells close to a reference to the Old Testament story of Lot: a small face worked into one of the letters on the page may represent Lot's wife. There also seems to be a female face among the ornamentation decorating the account of the women who visit the empty tomb of the risen Christ.

Many of the human figures in the Insular manuscripts are no doubt intended to be representations of the four evangelists. For example, the head and feet that appear above and below St. Matthew's name in the Book of Kells are presumably meant to depict the evangelist himself. Similarly, the figure who sits at the top of the opening page of Matthew holding a book is surely the author of the gospel with his work. In the corner of the decorated page that opens St. Mark's gospel in the Book of Kells, a lion, the saint's symbol, appears with a man in his mouth: it seems likely that the man, too, represents the evangelist.

In the Book of Kells, the evangelist portraits that precede each gospel are surrounded by interlaced-border and cross-shaped forms, in keeping with the beautiful decorative style of the entire manuscript. By contrast, the evangelist figures in the Anglo-Celtic Lindisfarne Gospels tend to be more dignified and simple. Even so, they may also be obscure: a mysterious figure, who is thought to be Christ, peers from behind a curtain in the gospel of St. Matthew (see illustration, opposite), and a little head, presumably that of St. John, is incorporated into the first letter of the word *principio* ("beginning") at the opening of this particular saint's gospel.

The style of human figures in the manuscripts is not exclusive to text illumination. A series of statues that now decorate the wall of a romanesque church on White Island, County Fermanagh, Ireland, shows saints and bishops with calm and simplified faces just like those in the manuscript illustrations—they may even have been the inspiration for some of the manuscript art. It is believed that the statues were originally carved onto the wall of a ninth- or tenth-century monastery and there is certainly nothing quite like them anywhere else in the art of the Celtic world.

Illustrations of angels abound in the images that show Christ's birth and resurrection—they reflect the joy at these momentous occasions, and are probably based directly on biblical descriptions of the events. Yellow orpiment, which resembles gilding, was used for the angels' hair and wings. Often these angels carry books, flowering wands, or *flabella* (liturgical fans). On one page, a small angel holds open his hands as if in prayer. He is set in the first letter of *omnia* ("all"), a reminder perhaps that the manuscripts were intended for private meditation and public use.

THE IMMORTAL HERO

A combination of skill and almost supernatural bravery characterized the cult of the hero among Celtic societies. A Celtic delegation to Alexander the Great claimed that they were afraid of nothing except that the sky might fall in. Such boldness held together an empirical Celtic power—in life, the warriors were the political mainstay; after death, their deeds lived on in songs, poetry, and tales.

The Greek historian Strabo (ca. 64BCE–21CE) declared that the Celts were, quite simply, "war mad." They would fight purely for the sake of it, which meant fighting among themselves if no other enemy emerged. While archaeological findings have revealed a complex people who were pastoralists, farmers, and keen traders, the cult of the warrior was undoubtedly central to Celtic society. Three richly furnished tombs, discovered in Germany and dating from 800 to 500 BCE, emphasize the importance of the warrior class. A statue of a warrior with a dagger, and wearing a torc and a conical hat, dominated an aristocratic burial mound unearthed at Hirschlanden near Stuttgart. An apparently important male, also with a dagger, torc, and headgear, was buried in a tomb near Hochdorf in Baden-Württemberg, together with other richly ornamented weapons and elaborately decorated hunting gear. In 1996, a magnificent warrior statue, believed to date from around 500BCE, was discovered near Glauberg, northeast of Frankfurt. The statue—perhaps the best-preserved Celtic sculpture ever found—is thought to show a Celtic prince wearing armor and a carved torc about his neck. The six-foot (2m) statue may once have towered over the prince's grave.

Combat provided an arena where personal, tribal, and family alliances could be tested, strengthened, or destroyed. Military skills might be honed by carrying out cattle-rustling raids on non-allied neighbors, a practice suggested by several Irish tales, notably the *Táin Bó Cuailnge* ("The Cattle Raid of Cooley"). These tales point to a society where courage and fighting skills were paramount. Such values were upheld by a military aristocracy whose structure was maintained through an elaborate system of fosterage: noble children were raised outside their immediate family circle and were trained by fighters experienced in the arts of war.

Great attention has been devoted to the Celts' apparent interest in headhunting, which has given rise to the understanding that, for the Celts, the head was the most important and powerful part of the body, rather than, say, the heart, which was held in the highest esteem by other cultures. Strabo

◆ THE FACE OF THE WARRIOR ◆

The head, as the focal point of the self, was a potent symbol among the Celts. It was not surprising that artists of the time created so many images of faces. The warrior class favored drooping moustaches and heavy torcs worn around the neck. Further insight into warrior appearance comes from classical sources, which describe Celtic warriors as fair-haired, sometimes with hair bleached lighter still with limewater. These men were arrogant and hot-tempered, cultivating war whenever they could.

describes a Celtic custom of decapitating dead enemies and keeping the heads as trophies, but there is no conclusive evidence to suggest that the rites he records were practiced by all Celtic tribes. Nevertheless, the abundance of artifacts in the form of busts, triplicated heads, and skulls, recovered from all over the Celtic world, does attest to the head's trans-Celtic function as an important symbol of power. In the sanctuary at the ancient capital of the Saluvii tribe, Entremont, near Aix-en-Provence, France, human skulls had been placed in niches, and the statuary of the shrine included limestone sculptures of warriors (or gods) sitting cross-legged behind piles of human heads. The discoveries at Entremont, and similar finds at nearby Glanum and Roquepertuse, suggest that this area was home to a distinctive local cult. There are no traces of sacrifice at these shrines, but the prominence given to severed human heads suggests that they may have been dedicated to some aspect of a warrior cult.

The Celts practiced the art of fighting with implements resembling dumbbells. The two figures on this bronze bucket from Slovenia (ca. 5th century BCE) are engaged in such combat. In the Welsh narratives, heroes are said to have fought together every May Day until the end of time for the hand of a beautiful woman.

ACCOUTREMENTS OF WAR

Brave though Celtic warriors undoubtedly were, they were not without assistance. They could call on an impressive armory of swords, shields, and helmets. They often rode into battle, and venerated horses accordingly, and they launched their attacks from spectacular defensive hillforts.

Given the importance of warriors and warfare to ancient Celtic society, it comes as no surprise that Celtic artisans often lavished as much skill on their weapons as they did on jewelry and other luxuries. Smiths who could forge bronze and (from the eighth century BCE) iron into military equipment were no doubt accorded high status. Although they never developed the technology for casting iron, the weapons that the Celts produced by heating and hammering were nonetheless innovative and, above all, deadly.

By the La Tène Period (fifth century BCE), Celtic smiths had perfected a heavy slashing sword with a long flat double-edged blade that could be used by horsemen and footsoldiers alike. Shields were also long—often oval or rectangular in shape. Miniature versions of these shields are commonly found in graves, in which they were placed so that they may protect the soul after death, and have also been discovered at cult sites, where they were offered to the gods in return for strength and protection.

Shields were wielded by a single central handle, with a projecting boss (pommel) on the other side to protect the hand. Sometimes this boss was extended into a narrow spine that ran down the center of the front of the shield, strengthening it and thus affording further protection to the arm and hand. Eventually, Celtic smiths developed the ability to form the boss and handle out of one piece of metal, thus making the whole shield more sturdy. The magnificent bronze shields that have been found in Britain and elsewhere were no doubt for ceremonial or display purposes only—the shields taken into battle were probably made mainly of wood, covered with leather and painted. The ceremonial specimens were highly decorated, the front of the shield filled with scenes of battle, defeated captives, wrestlers, stylized animal forms, and abstract patterns. The pommel, a grip, and a guard were enriched with enameling, and the grip was often hammered into a beautiful stylized figure, to create a perfect fusion of function and design.

Other pieces of armor included helmets and chainmail shirts. Classical writers give detailed descriptions of Celtic bronze helmets with elaborate decoration showing birds and animals. Few examples survive but, like the decorative shields, these helmets were probably for ceremony only and not intended to be worn in combat. However, much simpler bronze and iron headgear, more suited to practical use, have also been discovered. Only the most gifted metalsmiths made the Celts' iron chainmail shirts (literally loops of iron linked together to form a sort of mesh)—and probably only the warrior aristocracy could afford to buy them.

In the middle Danube area, swordsmiths produced spears and daggers that were highly decorated with animals, leaf and flower shapes, and with mystical beasts such as dragons, but again, like the elaborately designed helmets and shields, these weapons were probably used for ceremonial purposes only. More simple designs, dating from around the second and first centuries BCE, have been recovered in significant numbers from sites in Switzerland, but these may reflect the changing artistic styles, which simplified the decoration of weaponry, rather than any more practical use.

Armor aside, the Celts employed some other, highly imaginative forms of protection. The Greek author Diodorus of Sicily records an object known as a *carnyx*. This was an animal-headed war trumpet "of a peculiarly barbaric kind ... which produces a harsh sound to suit the tumult of war." Examples of these instruments with horses' heads are depicted on the third-century BCE Gundestrup Cauldron (see illustration, opposite, far right), while a boar's head, broken off from the top of a *carnyx* and dating from approximately 50CE, was discovered at Deskford in Grampian, Scotland. As we have

seen, war for the Celts afforded warriors the opportunity for personal displays of valor and prestige, and the *carnyx* played an important role in the build-up to battle. Producing a kind of prolonged scream, intended to send shivers of fear through the waiting opponent, the *carnyx* provided a background sound to the riotous clamor of the warriors, who shouted boasting taunts, sang battle songs, and made ritual displays of aggression in a terrifying frenzy before the onset of battle.

DIVINE STEEDS

The horse played a vital role in both Celtic society and religion. Celtic warriors used horses to pull chariots and for cavalry duty; hunters used them to gain speed in the chase; devotees made offerings of horse sculptures to war gods, such as the Gaulish god Rudobius; and Celtic kings stamped their coins with the image of a horse in preference to the eagles, lions, and griffins of other ancient powers. As well as being an emblem of

A procession of warriors, mounted and on foot, feature prominently in this mythic scene depicted on the silver-gilt Gundestrup Cauldron of ca. 3rd century BCE, discovered in Denmark.

royalty and prestige, the animal represented sexual prowess and fertility, and was also associated with the life-giving powers of the sun. In Roman times, horses appeared atop soaring columns as the celestial mount of the Celtic sky god, who trampled the monstrous forces of darkness.

Horses were linked with a number of other gods and goddesses, of whom the most popular was Epona, a mother-goddess figure whose name means simply "horse goddess." Her cult was widespread and deeply rooted among the ancient Celts, and in the Roman period she became the only Celtic deity to be honored with a festival at Rome (18 December). Epona was often depicted riding on a mare, perhaps accompanied by a foal, dispensing the Earth's bounty of bread, grain, or fruit; or she might appear bearing a key and followed by a human figure, an image believed to represent the souls of the dead being taken to the gates of the Otherworld. She protected horses and their riders: one riding master dedicated an altar to her to protect his pupils.

DUN AENGUS

The Celts were skilled in exploiting the natural environment for defensive purposes. The spectacular Irish hillfort of Dun Aengus is dramatically situated on the edge of a vertical cliff overlooking the Atlantic Ocean on the west coast of the island of Inishmore, in Galway Bay. The large enclosure (which would have housed people—including craftsmen and the local chieftain—and animals) is defended by a zone of up to around 70 feet (23m) wide of densely packed limestone pillars. These were rammed into the limestone bedrock either diagonally pointing outward, or upright. We might assume that their function was to slow down the approaching enemy, whether on foot or on horseback, by making access through to the main fortress walls painful and slow. A single, narrow passage leads through this defensive stone forest to the outer and inner walls, each of which today stands at a height of 12 feet (4m)—we can only guess at their height when they were first completed. The innermost of these walls seems impenetrable: accessible only through very narrow gaps in the outer wall, it is as thick as it is high. In Celtic tales, hillforts are often depicted as being populated by fearsome monsters, and the defensive pillars are flaming barriers or rings of stakes topped with human heads.

The waves of the Atlantic Ocean crash on the rocks below the Irish hillfort of Dun Aengus, which dates from the 1st to 5th centuries CE. The sheer cliff face would have been impossible to scale, which meant that invaders would have been limited in the directions from which they could attack the fort, making them easier to repel.

CHAPTER FOUR

THE VIKINGS

In little over 250 years, from the late eighth to the mid-eleventh century CE, *the*

Vikings transformed Europe. Starting as raiders and traders, they became explorers,

conquerors, lawmakers, and founders of nations. In Iceland they created northern

Europe's earliest republic; 2,000 miles (3,200km) to the southeast they laid the

foundations of the Russian state. Norwegian settlers founded Ireland's first cities,

while in far-off Constantinople, Swedes provided the Byzantine emperor with

his personal bodyguard. Above all, though, the Vikings were seafarers. Norse

mariners, carried in longboats, traveled farther north and west than any previous

European peoples, establishing a colony on the west coast of Greenland and beating

Christopher Columbus to America by almost 500 years.

THE SOUL OF THE VIKINGS

The derivation of the term "viking" is usually traced to the Old Norse word vik, *meaning "inlet"*
or "bay"—almost certainly a reference to the steep-sided coastal sounds or fjords of the Atlantic-facing
coastline of western Norway where some of the earliest Viking communities were established.

The deeply indented shore of the North Sea contains littoral twists and turns amounting to some 15,000 miles (25,000 km) although it stretches for less than a tenth of that distance as the crow flies. For mariners traveling the trade route up to the White Sea, known as the North Way (from which Norway possibly took its name), it was a journey during which they remained constantly on the alert for the localized danger posed by the wily, bay-based pirates who lay in wait to pounce on their cargo vessels.

Then, in the year 793CE, news of an unimaginable atrocity spread through Christian Europe. Ship-borne raiders from across the North Sea had descended upon Holy Island (Lindisfarne), off the coast of northern England. The rich treasures of its famous monastery had been plundered, its monks killed or dragged off to slavery. In a savage age, Europe's monastic foundations had long been seen as havens of culture and learning. Now it seemed they were no longer sacrosanct.

The Holy Island cataclysm was one of the first Viking assaults, but it was quickly followed by others. In the ensuing years, similar hit-and-run raids devastated ecclesiastical communities on the coasts not just of England but of Scotland and Ireland too. Before long, towns were also being targeted, and within just sixty years of the first sorties, boat-borne invaders were threatening whole kingdoms.

It is hard to exaggerate the impact that the Viking raids would have had on the rest of Europe. They came at a point when firm government, in the hands of rulers like Offa (died 796CE) in the English kingdom of Mercia, and Charlemagne (ca. 742–814CE) on the Continent, had been restoring order after the troubled centuries following the collapse of the Roman Empire. And they fell upon some of western Christendom's holiest sites, refuges of peace and learning in a strife-torn world.

To their horrified contemporaries the pagan Vikings seemed embodiments of terror and destruction, sent by a righteous God to punish a wicked world. That image was slow to fade, not least because most of the written sources describing their activities were the work of Christian churchmen.

In recent times, though, that negative portrayal has been reappraised. A series of stunning archaeological finds has emphasized the Norsemen's positive achievements as traders, travelers, craftsmen, explorers, settlers, and finally rulers. Increasingly they are now seen not just as a destructive force but as a vitally creative one. Ferocious they undoubtedly were, but their relentless determination and dauntless courage acted as catalysts for change in an otherwise stagnant world. As well as fire and the sword, they brought ambition, enterprise, and boundless energy to peoples whose horizons were for the most part limited, rarely stretching beyond the bounds of the nearest village.

Even though most of the Norse men and women of the Viking age were content to stay at home and work the land like their southern neighbors, the scent of adventure and excitement clings stubbornly to the Viking name. They may have been relatively few, but those youths—many of them younger sons in want of an inheritance—who went out in search of wealth and glory were the agents of historical change. With limitless audacity they set out to take on the world, and in so doing they altered it indelibly.

An elaborately crafted ship's prow symbolizes the Viking tradition of seafaring. The prow bears the image of a serpentine beast and was reconstructed from fragments of the Oseberg ship, excavated in 1904 from a 9th-century burial mound that contained the bodies of two women—probably a queen and her attendant.

THE STORY OF THE VIKINGS

"Viking" started off as a vocation rather than a group name—restless spirits chose to "go viking," which meant raiding. They came from the Norse lands that would one day be known as Denmark, Norway, and Sweden, but at the time their loyalties were tied to a neighborhood or to an individual warchief. The concept of nationhood came later—one of the achievements of the Viking age, in fact.

Although the Norse peoples often fought among themselves, they nonetheless had much in common. They shared both a language (Old Norse) and a religion—the worship of Odin, Thor, and the other northern gods. They came from roughly similar societies, divided broadly among three classes: a warrior nobility; a wide category of freemen, including in its ranks merchants, craftspeople, and especially the *bondi*, or land-owning farmers; and thralls, or slaves. Good agricultural land being a limited resource, there was always, both among the *bondi* and the nobility, a restless subclass of younger sons with no estate to inherit; it was from their ranks above all that the Viking raiders were recruited.

Although the northern lands were little known to other Europeans at the time, the Norsemen themselves inherited a footloose tradition. They were the natural successors of the Germanic peoples who had fanned out across Europe during an age of migrations from the second century CE on, among them the so-called "barbarians" who helped bring down the Roman Empire in the fifth century. The Norsemen also inherited a tradition of trading dating back to the Bronze Age (ca. 2000–500 BCE), when fur and beads of Baltic amber—fossilized conifer resin—were already sought-after luxury goods in much of Europe. Even so, Scandinavia remained something of a backwater until the Viking irruption. Historians still argue over the underlying causes that suddenly drove so many Norsemen far beyond their own shores. Technological improvements in shipbuilding played a part in making the exodus possible, but they could not in themselves provide a motive. Population pressures were undoubtedly a factor, but they seem not to have been dramatically worse than in previous ages; estimates suggest that there were never more than two million people in all the Scandinavian lands throughout the Viking era. Indeed, conditions actually seem to have been improving at the time; a slight but significant warming of the climate caused glaciers to recede, made winters more endurable, and may have lessened infant mortality, creating a greater number of landless younger sons to go adventuring.

The first to venture abroad in significant numbers were the Swedes, whom geography directed eastward. Their main thrust was across the Baltic Sea and into Russia. Taking over the Slav settlement at Novgorod in the late ninth century, they turned it into a key trading post controlling two major routes to the south. One followed the Dnieper River down to Kiev, where a second center was established, and then on to the Black Sea, opening the way to Constantinople. The other took boat-borne travelers almost 2,500 miles (4,000km) down the Volga to the Caspian, beyond which caravan routes led on to Baghdad.

The lure that drew the traders southward was silver, particularly coins from the mines of Arabia. In return they traded furs—sable, squirrel, beaver—and slaves, many of them taken as booty or tribute from the Slavic peoples: the word "slave" derives from "Slav." Trading elided all too easily into raiding, and Viking warriors launched assaults on mighty Constantinople itself, in 860CE and again in 907CE. Although both were repulsed, the second persuaded the Byzantine emperor to offer trading rights to the Norsemen in return for guarantees of peace as well as the provision of bodyguards—the famous Varangian guards—for the emperor's own person.

The Viking impact on Russia was even more marked, for the settlers—known to the Slavs as Rus—played a vital part in setting up the first organized Slavic state. As the *Russian Primary Chronicle* (ca. 1112) tells the tale, the Rus were approached by the leaders of warring

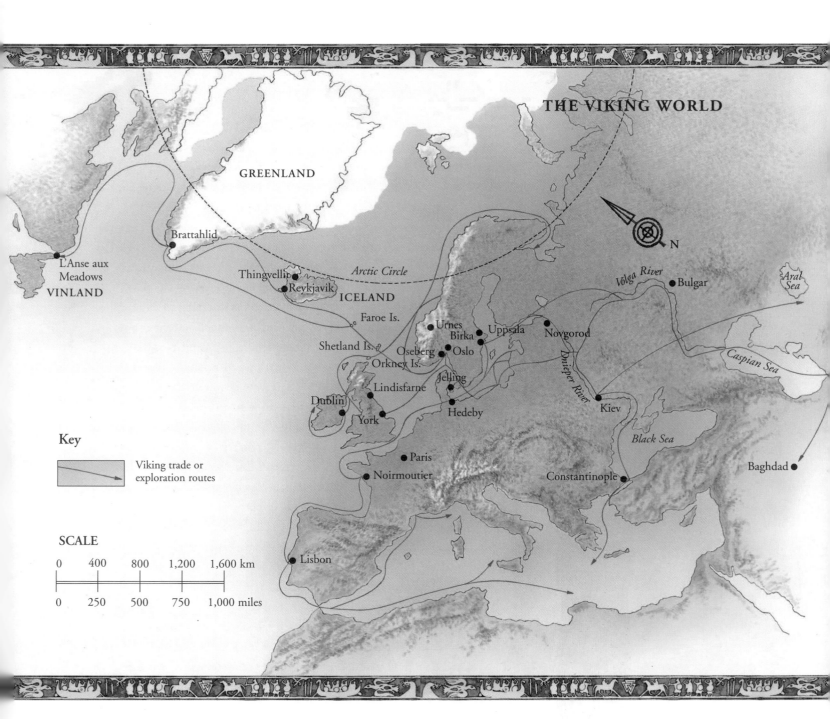

THE VIKING WORLD

GREENLAND

Brattahlid

L'Anse aux
Meadows
VINLAND

Thingvellir
Reykjavik
ICELAND

Arctic Circle

Faroe Is.

Urnes
Birka
Uppsala
Novgorod

Shetland Is.
Oseberg Oslo

Orkney Is.

Dublin
Lindisfarne
Jelling

York
Hedeby

Paris

Noirmoutier

Lisbon

Volga River
Bulgar

Aral
Sea

Caspian Sea

Dnieper River

Kiev

Black Sea

Constantinople

Baghdad

N

Key

Viking trade or
exploration routes

SCALE

| 0 | 400 | 800 | 1,200 | 1,600 km |

| 0 | 250 | 500 | 750 | 1,000 miles |

• THE COMING OF CHRISTIANITY •

More than any political event, the acceptance of Christianity marked the end of the Viking age. By the time the process was complete, at the end of the eleventh century, Scandinavia remained geographically and linguistically distinct, but in other respects was largely integrated into the culture of the continent as a whole.

Christianity's arrival was gradual and piecemeal. As tireless travelers, the Vikings were aware of its presence in other lands long before they accepted it themselves. One Danish king received baptism as early as 826, only to be driven into exile the following year. A missionary named Anskar subsequently built churches in leading market towns—at Birka in Sweden as well as Hedeby and Ribe on the Danish mainland. But the conversion of Denmark as a whole had to wait until 965, when King Harald Bluetooth adopted the new faith.

In Norway, conversion came about because kings seeking to impose their will on the nation's unruly and independent-minded noblemen saw the Church as a buttress of central authority. The process started when King Harald Fairhair (ca. 880–930)—the first to unite the nation—sent his son Hakon to England to be fostered by the Christian king Athelstan. Hakon in fact died an apostate, and the new faith was eventually imposed by two Olafs—Olaf Tryggvason, who set out in 995 to convert the country by the sword, and then the ruler remembered as St. Olaf, who completed the work before his death in battle in 1030. One saga recounts that he offered the pagan earls a stark choice: "Be killed, leave the country, or accept baptism."

At about the same time, Iceland accepted Christianity under pressure from the Norwegian kings, though the decision was made democratically by decree of the Althing. The hold-out was Sweden, where the old religion was slow to die. Although the nation's rulers were Christian from the early eleventh century on, it took almost a century for the Church to gain the ascendant—a period of co-existence predated by the Viking-style Christian symbols on this eighth-century Swedish crozier (left).

For Norse culture the effects of the switch were gradual but profound. Conversion was accompanied by a shift from local hegemony to centralized authority; from an oral culture to one based on writing, above all Holy Scripture; and from a morality of honor and retaliation to one of submission and forgiveness. The new faith was a civilizing force, yet with its coming something of the heroic individualism of the Viking period died. A new age had been born, and the northern world was never to be quite the same again.

tribes, who asked them to reign over them. The Rus set up a joint Swedish–Slav state that came to bear their own name, first at Novgorod and later at Kiev.

While the Swedes looked east, the peoples of Denmark cast their eyes to the south; their influence was most keenly felt in England and in the Frankish Empire of Charlemagne. When in 840 the empire split between three rival heirs, the Norsemen seized the opportunity and on Easter Day in 845 they attacked Paris after sailing 100 miles (160km) up the Seine.

From the 850s on, the Danes stopped staging short, hit-and-run raids and started overwintering in the lands they raided. The next logical step was full-scale occupation, and in 865 the first of many mighty Danish armies arrived in England. At the time the country was divided between a half dozen rival kingdoms, most of which were not strong enough to repel the invaders. East Anglia soon fell, and others quickly followed, until by 880 only the southern realm of Wessex held out. There, an outstanding ruler, Alfred the Great, stemmed the tide, but by that time the Danes had established their hold over more than half of England. In the area under their control, the Danelaw, they left a permanent mark, strengthening the Anglo-Saxon concepts of a written law and of trial by jury, as well as making a lasting contribution to the English language through such everyday words as "take," "die," "sky," "anger," "hell," and "ugly".

The Danelaw in turn provided a base for further raids on France, until in 911 King Charles III offered lands around the mouth of the Seine to the Viking leader Rollo, in return for a promise to fight off rival Vikings. Before many generations had passed, Rollo's Norsemen transmuted into Normans, accepting the language and the Christian religion of their subjects. It was Rollo's sixth-generation successor Duke William of Normandy who in 1066 successfully invaded England.

While the Danes were conquering kingdoms, the Norwegian Vikings were exploring less charted areas. Most of their raiding centered on Scotland and Ireland, where they established settlements: Dublin, Wexford, Waterford, and Limerick are all Norse foundations. They settled islands, including the Isle of Man, the Orkneys, the Shetlands, and the Faroes.

According to tradition, in about 860, two separate crews, one bound for the Hebrides and the other for the Faroes, were blown off course and discovered a previously unknown island. News spread, and within the decade settlers began to arrive to take advantage of the new land's empty acres. Over the next century Iceland developed as an independent realm with the most democratic system of government yet seen in northern Europe. It was dominated by thirty-six local patriarchs, each the spokesman for his district, who met annually in an open-air assembly known as the Althing (see page 481). By the late tenth century the island had 60,000 inhabitants—a quarter of Norway's population at the time.

Once all Iceland's good pasturage had been claimed, adventurous spirits had to look further afield for virgin territory. A late tenth-century outlaw named Eirik the Red sailed 450 miles (725km) to the west in search of a land long rumored to exist. He gave the forbidding landmass that he eventually discovered the more appealing name of Greenland, and by the 980s a colony had been established of several hundred immigrants, living by farming, and hunting whales and walrus.

One would-be settler lost his way en route and came within sight of a shoreline that lay too far to the south to be his destination. When he finally reached Greenland, his story encouraged Eirik's son, Leif Eiriksson, to venture west in search of the mystery land. The result was probably the first European landfall in the Americas, made in 1001, when Leif arrived first at Baffin Island and then at L'Anse aux Meadows near the northernmost tip of Newfoundland. Leif's achievement was a fitting climax to an extraordinary saga of exploration and adventure that within little more than two centuries had seen the Norsemen radiate out from their homeland in Scandinavia to Baghdad and beyond in the east and to the New World in the west, conquering kingdoms and founding states and cities in the lands in between.

THE ART OF THE VIKINGS

The Viking way of life, with many individuals crammed into smoky, earth-floored dwellings, would hardly seem to have encouraged the accumulation of art objects. But in fact, the Norse peoples had a passion for display that encouraged craftspeople to transform everyday utensils into objects of beauty.

Apart from poetry, all Viking creativity was expressed in what would now be called the decorative arts. People used the wealth that flooded into Scandinavia from raiding and trading to buy beautiful yet practical everyday objects, not art for art's sake. The strength of people's craving for such things is reflected in myth in the story of Freyja, goddess of love, and her yearning for the marvelous necklace known as the Brisingamen; its makers, four dwarf master-craftsmen, would only agree to give it to her if she slept with each one of them, an offer she accepted unhesitatingly (see page 469).

The creators themselves were almost always anonymous craftspeople, typically in the employ of kings or chieftains; only at the end of the period did individual artificers add their names to some runestones, and then mostly in a single area of central Sweden. Much of the craftsmen's work must have been done in wood and textiles, but few examples of these survive. Stone carving is also poorly represented, at least for the earlier period; although there was a long-standing tradition of stonework on the Baltic island of Gotland, the taste only developed elsewhere from the mid-tenth century on, perhaps in response to a growing familiarity with Christian monuments from other parts of Europe. There is also little in the way of pottery; Vikings evidently preferred to eat and drink from unbreakable wood or soapstone vessels.

What has survived in the greatest quantities is metalwork, of which there was a longstanding craft tradition in Scandinavia. As early as the second millennium BCE, Norse artisans were among the finest bronzeworkers in Europe, even though they had to import much of the tin and copper needed to make the alloy. Among their masterpieces were the twisting ceremonial horns known

as lurs, which curled up like convolvuluses as far as five feet (1.5m) above the player's lips.

By Viking times, the metalworkers' wares were put to innumerable uses. They included brooches and ornamental pins used to fasten the thick woolen cloaks worn by both men and women; necklaces, armbands, and bracelets; charms and amulets; caskets for storing valuables, sometimes with inset panels of carved walrus ivory; horse collars and harness decorations; windvanes to ornament the prows of longships; and of course splendidly embellished weapons.

Viking taste demanded decoration that was vigorous, striking, and above all intricate, with much interlacing and interweaving. Throughout the period, the principal motifs were taken from nature. The starting point was most often an animal, though the beasts in question were frequently stylized almost to the point of abstraction; plants also started to appear regularly from the mid-tenth century onward. Representations of people were comparatively rare, and when they did appear they were usually (although not always) treated in a semi-naturalistic way that contrasted with the liberties taken with the bodies of birds and beasts.

THE SIX PERIODS

Art historians trace six stages in the development of Viking art, marked by subtle changes in the style of decoration employed; the evolution of taste seems to have been dictated by master-craftspeople responding to

Wood was probably one of the materials most favored by Viking craftsmen, although relatively little of their work has survived. This panel—one of a series illustrating the Sigurd legend—decorated a church doorway at Hylestad in Norway.

This buckle clasp from Åker, in Hedmark, Norway, dates from the 7th century. Made out of gold, silver, and precious stones, it vividly demonstrates the wealth that trade had already brought to the northern lands even before the start of the Viking age proper.

art objects from overseas. The earliest style, exemplified by bridle mounts found in a grave at Broa on Gotland, was the first in Scandinavia to employ a specific motif known as the "gripping beast"—this involved an animal, often placed at the head of the design, whose paws enclose the other elements.

The next two periods, known as the Borre and Jellinge, were largely contemporaneous, both flourishing from the mid-ninth to the late tenth centuries. Both feature so-called "ribbon creatures," whose bodies interlace in serpentine patterns; Borre pieces also sometimes used a ringchain motif that is of a type employed today on metal watchstraps. Good examples of the Borre style come from the celebrated Gokstad ship burial.

In the mid-tenth century, the Jellinge designs developed into the Mammen style, which takes its name from the silver-inlay decorations on an iron axhead found at Mammen in Jutland. The animals are more substantial in these works, though quite as fantastic in the contortions of their writhing bodies; in addition, plant motifs begin to show through in the form of shoots and looping tendrils. Such masterpieces as the Bamberg casket and the serpent-entwined beast on Harald Bluetooth's memorial stone at Jelling fall into this category.

Plant motifs became even more important in the ensuing Ringerike period, which succeeded Mammen at the turn of the eleventh century; by this time foliate patterning had become a regular feature. This tendency reached new heights in the Urnes period, the final phase of Viking art, which takes its name from a church at

Urnes in Norway. The intricate design of interlaced animals, stalks, and tendrils on the eleventh-century wooden paneling on the church's walls (see illustration, page 465) recalls the work of the arts-and-crafts designers of nineteenth-century Britain.

For all the elaborations, it is the consistency of taste through the Viking period that remains most striking. The great change was to come at the end of the era with the adoption of Christianity. By the twelfth century, newly converted Scandinavia had embraced the Romanesque style of the lands to the south and was well on the way to joining the mainstream of European art and design.

JEWELRY AND AMULETS

Living in spartan times, the Viking peoples expressed their love of ostentation through jewelry. Men and women alike wore arm- and neck-rings as well as shoulder brooches that held their outer garments in place; in addition, women wore necklaces, pendants, and occasionally finger-rings. Plain silver neck- and arm-rings were made in standard weights so that they could double up as currency; to settle small amounts they were often cut into fragments known as "hack-silver." Most of the metal used was melted down from Middle Eastern coins brought back to Scandinavia by Rus traders.

One Arab observer left an account of these merchant Vikings, whom he encountered on the Volga trade route. "Each of their women," he wrote, "wears on either breast a drum-shaped brooch of iron, silver, copper, or gold whose value indicates how much her husband is worth. The brooches bear rings to which knives can be attached. The women also wear neck-rings of gold and silver, but their most prized ornaments are green glass beads that they string together as necklaces."

While most jewelry was worn simply for display, some pieces had a deeper significance. From about 400

◆ THE MYSTIC SPIRAL ◆

One distinctive feature of Norse design is a circular disc filled either with whirling black and white curves or else with spiral patterns. In either case the impression given is one of movement—that of a turning wheel. The most memorable representations are found on stones from the Swedish island of Gotland, raised from the early centuries of the first millennium CE up until about the year 1000 to commemorate the dead. There have been various attempts to explain the significance of the patterns, which carry a visual impact similar to that of the 1960s op-art paintings they sometimes call to mind. The discs are generally interpreted as surviving symbols of a Bronze Age sun cult whose influence once stretched across much of southern Scandinavia.

to 600 CE, there was a fashion for small pendants made of gold or silver stamped with images often drawn from Norse mythology. These *bracteates*, as they are now called, were apparently worn for good luck, as were miniature replicas of Thor's Mjollnir (see illustration, page 468) some centuries later.

Jewelry also played a part in myth. The Brisingamen necklace caused strife in Asgard, while the cursed golden ring of the dwarf Andvari set in motion the sequence of greed, murder, and revenge that made up the Sigurd legend. In real life, oaths were taken on arm-rings that had been reddened with sacrificial blood; pagan Danes are said to have made peace with England's King Alfred the Great by "swearing oaths to him on the holy ring."

SECRETS OF THE RUNES

For most literate peoples the power implicit in the written word has been so long taken for granted that it now fails to excite wonder; but for the Vikings the runic alphabet, or futhark, *always retained traces of primeval magic. Its origins are still shrouded in mystery, although it was shared with other Germanic peoples and was in use for many centuries before the Viking age.*

For the Vikings, one of the great advantages of runes was that the letters consisted entirely of straight lines that could easily be chiseled. People who lacked paper and pens could still notch a runic sentence on a stick of wood—probably the normal writing medium. However, most of the 4,000 or more inscriptions that survive are in stone, metal, or bone—many are memorial stones, giving the name and sometimes also personal details of the deceased; some were also used as road markers, or else served to identify the owners of weapons or caskets.

Yet there was also a more magical aspect to runes, little of which now remains as a result of the coming of Christianity and the ensuing destruction of all things pagan. The Viking peoples themselves explained the characters' origins by harking back to myth. Legend told that it was Odin himself who first acquired the mastery of writing, and he did so by undergoing a terrible ordeal in which some mythographers see parallels with Christ's crucifixion. To obtain the secret, Odin voluntarily underwent what might now be termed a near-death experience, hanging on Yggdrasil, the great ash tree linking the three worlds of the Viking cosmos (see box, page 465), and gashing his side with a spear. This enigmatic incident survives only from a single ancient source, a poem called the *Hávamál* ("Words of the High One") preserved in the *Poetic Edda*:

> *I know that I hung/On the windswept tree/*
> *For nine whole nights/Pierced by the spear/*
> *And given to Odin/Myself to myself/*
> *On that tree/ Whose roots/Nobody knows/*
> *They gave me no bread/Nor drink from the horn/*
> *I peered into the depths/I grasped the runes/*
> *Screaming I grasped them/And then fell back.*

The implication would seem to be that runes had originated in the dark domain of Hel, queen of the dead (see page 495), in Niflheim far below the worlds of gods and men, and with the runes Odin also seems to have acquired the mastery of occult wisdom—the very word "rune" derives from the Old Norse *run*, or "mystery."

The medium of the runes, then, brought together religion, language and art in a single, everyday medium, and although few clues now remain it seems likely that they played an essential part in the ritual sacrifices of the Viking era—since they had to be reddened with blood to be effective—and they were also used to cast lots for divination. The role of these inscriptions in the working of charms and spells is better attested. Some Viking amulets bear runic messages that apparently increased their magical potency, while one of a ring of standing stones at Björketorp in Sweden carries an inscription that speaks of "runes of might" and invokes a curse on anyone destroying the megaliths.

There are also clear implications in literature of the magical role that runes played in daily life. In the Icelandic sagas they are used to help in childbirth, to bring health or sickness, to make warriors victorious, to calm storms, and even to make the dead speak. One tale, recounted in the thirteenth-century *Egil's Saga*, describes how the hero traced the cause of a girl's sudden illness to a rune-inscribed whalebone hidden in her bed. Learning that the son of a neighbor had carved the runes, Egil found a mistake in the charm, cut out the runes and burnt them. The young man had meant no harm, but he was a novice at the art. Egil carved new runes and laid them under the girl's pillow, whereupon she awoke weak, but restored to health. He drew the wise conclusion: "Let no man carve runes to cast a spell/Unless he first learns to write them well.

✦ RUNESTONES OF THE KINGS ✦

The two royal runestones that stand side by side at Jelling in central Jutland are more than just magnificent monuments. Between them they mark a turning-point, not only in the history of Scandinavia but also that of Europe.

The smaller of the two runestones was erected by Gorm the Old (died 958), founder of the dynasty that, under Svein Forkbeard and Knut the Great, would one day conquer England and rule a North Sea empire larger than any other of the Viking age. Gorm set up the monument as a memorial to his wife Thyri; after his own death, the couple were buried together in a huge earth mound to the north of the stone.

The second, larger stone was also a memorial, this one to both Gorm and Thyri, and it was the work of their son Harald Bluetooth. Harald himself was a conqueror who temporarily brought parts of Norway under Denmark's sway; but he is now better remembered as the king who converted the Danes to Christianity, a feat commemorated in the stone's inscription. Three sides of Harald's great cenotaph are decorated. One bears a runic inscription commemorating his parents and listing his own achievements; a second bears a stylized image of the Crucifixion that is Denmark's earliest known representation of Christ. The image on the third side (shown here) harks back to traditional Viking iconography; it shows a dragon entwined by a sinuous serpent, a masterpiece of the Mammen style of Viking art. As well as the stone, Harald ordered the construction of a church—one of the first in Denmark.

THE VIKING COSMOS

The Viking world was a multiplicity of realms brought into being by the interactions of the elements, primeval beings, and the gods. These competing domains included Asgard, where there lived two warring races of gods, the Aesir and the Vanir; Midgard, populated by humans, giants, and earth spirits in the form of elves, trolls and dwarfs; and Niflheim, the realm of the dead where Hel resided.

Norse mythology paints an unusually clear picture both of how the world began and of how it will end. Hanging over everything was a dark fatalism, for ultimately the whole world of gods and humans was to be swept away in a final apocalyptic encounter—the confrontation between good and evil—the forces the Vikings called Ragnarok.

The vision of the beginning of things may have been influenced by conditions in Iceland, for it features a very Icelandic combination of ice and fire. The world, as the myths tell it, grew out of a chasm: Ginnungagap, the Yawning Void. Ginnungagap was bordered to the south by Muspell, the abode of fire, where Surt the fire giant stood guard with a flaming sword. To the north lay the freezing land of Niflheim, later to be the land of the dead. Here twelve rivers bubbled up from a cauldron called Hvergelmir, pouring their waters into Ginnungagap. In its unplumbed depths they froze, gradually filling the mighty chasm. As the ice rose, it was touched by the heat of Muspell, and from the meeting came moisture that somehow transmuted into clay.

Eventually the clay took on life in the massive form of Ymir, the primeval frost giant. To provide Ymir with sustenance, another creature also took shape—a huge cow called Audhumla, the Nourisher, whose udder gushed forth milk. To feed herself, Audhumla could only lick the salty rime, and as she did so the outlines of a man began to appear under her probing tongue. This was Buri—the Producer—and he was to be the grandfather of Odin, greatest of the Norse gods.

By now the processes of creation were proliferating, for Ymir himself produced from his own sweat a couple who were to be the first of the giants, the gods' inexorable enemies; as the representatives respectively of good and evil, the two races were fated to irreconcilable conflict. Yet they could also fraternize from time to time—Odin himself was the result of a liaison between Buri's son Bor and a giantess.

Despite his mixed parentage, Odin grew up to be a scourge of the giant race, combining with his two brothers to destroy Ymir, whose blood gushed out in such a flood that it drowned all his gigantic progeny, save for a single couple. These survivors fled to Jotunheim—literally "Giants' Home"—where they begot a new race dedicated to the extirpation of Odin and all his kin.

With this work of destruction done, Odin and his brothers next turned to creation. From Ymir's body they fashioned the world as we now know it: his blood became the seas and rivers, his flesh the land, his bones the mountains, and his skull the sky. Four strong dwarfs, North, South, East, and West, were set to support the corners of the firmament, while the gods scattered sparks from Muspell across it as stars. The sun and moon were placed in chariots to follow each other unceasingly across the sky, pursued by two fearsome wolves, Skoll ("Repulsion") and Hati ("Hatred"), who at the end of time were fated finally to devour the heavenly lights.

Having fashioned the physical world, Odin and his brothers next created beings to inhabit it. First came the dwarfs, who grew from maggots infesting Ymir's rotting corpse; the gods gave them consciousness, and put them underground to search for gold. In some myths these dwarfs seem to be confounded with the Dark Elves, similarly conceived as miners dwelling in darkness; in

---

Steam rises from a vent at Namafjall in Iceland. Norse creation myths imagined life as originating from the joint action of fire and ice—a peculiarly Icelandic combination that may have been suggested by the geysers and volcanoes that dot the island republic.

This "hogback" tomb at Heysham in Lancashire, England, may depict a pair of dwarfs holding up the sky. The tombs take their name from their curved profile, mimicking the bowed shape of large houses of the Viking era. An alternative interpretation is that the design represents Christian figures raising their hands in prayer.

times their respective inhabitants formed alliances, but at other times they plotted and fought against one another. And in this respect too the cosmos reflected the real world the Vikings knew: an uneasy place of shifting allegiances and competing realms, fraught with peril and ruled by an unforgiving fate.

AESIR AND VANIR

The Norse world had not one but two divine families, perhaps originally reflecting different regional traditions, who dwelled in Asgard. The larger and dominant group was the Aesir—the word means "gods"—whose leader was Odin. Other important members of the group included Thor, Baldur, Heimdall, and the war god Tyr, and the goddesses Frigg, Sif, Nanna, and Iduna. In Odin and Thor, it provided two of the three most venerated deities of the old religion.

The third, Freyr, was the best known of the second group, the Vanir, along with his twin sister Freyja and his father Njord. Although the Vanir were worshipped throughout the Norse world, their cult was strongest in Sweden, where they seem to have been associated closely with the Svear people from the central region and came to be seen as the progenitors of the Swedish royal house.

While Thor and Odin were warriors, Freyr and the Vanir were primarily linked with agricultural and

contrast, their radiant counterparts the Light Elves lived in the airy realm of Alfheim, near the gods' own halls.

After the dwarfs the three gods fashioned people—out of flotsam found on the seashore. They assigned to the human race a central region, Midgard, ringed round for protection with a fence made from Ymir's eyebrows. Only after Midgard was made did they build their own home of Asgard, filling it with great halls and palaces. Asgard could only be reached across a bridge guarded by Heimdall, the divine watchman. The bridge was called Bifrost, and to humans it appeared as the rainbow.

The geography of the Norse cosmos was never exact, varying in its details between different myths. Yet it was consistent in reflecting a multiplicity of worlds. Traditionally, there were nine in all, including those of humans, giants, and more than one race of gods; the lowest of all was ruled by Hel, dark goddess of the underworld, who was half living woman and half rotting corpse. The nine worlds coexisted uneasily; some-

sexual fertility. Freyr himself was represented ithyphallically with a prominent male member; Freyja was not only the goddess of love but, according to some myths, was also promiscuous. The Vanir's own fecundity extended to the fruits of the earth; they presided over sunshine, rain, crops, and all growing things, and their special season was spring, when Freyr was honored by ritual feasts and processions.

In the myths, the relationship between the two families was initially hostile. The first war was fought between the Aesir and the Vanir, and it was sparked, for reasons that the myths never make quite clear, by the Aesir's treatment of a giantess named Gullveig—the name means "love of gold." Three times they tried to kill her, by stabbing and burning, but on each occasion

she survived. The Vanir rallied to her defense, and the ensuing hostilities eventually ended in a truce in which both sides exchanged hostages: Njord, Freyr, and Freyja went to live with the Aesir, while Honir and the wise Mimir joined the Vanir.

The most likely explanation of this enigmatic confrontation is that it represented in mythical form the accommodation reached between two rival sets of beliefs. Gullveig's punishment may represent symbolically the distaste felt by followers of the martial Aesir for the emphasis on wealth and prosperity in the Vanir's worship. If so, the aversion was successfully overcome, for subsequently both families coexisted as peacefully in myth as their respective votaries apparently did in the real world for much of the Viking age.

• THE WORLD TREE •

The great ash tree known as Yggdrasil—depicted symbolically in the wooden panels of the church at Urnes, Norway (right)—was the pillar around which all the various Norse worlds revolved. It rose through the middle of Asgard, and the gods regularly assembled around it. It was said to have three main roots. One stretched down to Niflheim and Hvergelmir, the seething cauldron in which life had originated. Another grew in Midgard, where it was nourished by the Well of Knowledge guarded by the wise giant Mimir. The third root sprang in Asgard. As a living entity Yggdrasil was always at risk of decay; four deer fed on the tree, nibbling its leaves, while the serpent Nidhogg gnawed tirelessly at its lowest root. Constantly under threat but endlessly renewed, Yggdrasil was a symbol of life itself, and its influence has endured. Maypoles and Christmas trees both possibly hark back to it, while the notion inherent in it of a global axis survives in the concept of a North and South Pole.

SAGAS OF THE GODS

The Norse peoples passed down stories around fires in farmsteads and great halls. They included tales of all-seeing Odin and mighty Thor, warrior-deities of the Aesir; episodes involving the lusty goddess Freyja; and the often humorous, but ultimately deadly serious, escapades of the trickster Loki.

Odin was not only the supreme Viking deity, he was also the most complex and enigmatic figure in the Norse pantheon. Known as "Allfather" for his part in the creation of humankind, he was also literally the father of several of the Aesir, including Baldur and, according to some, Thor. Where Thor had his hammer, Odin bore the magical spear Gungnir, fashioned by dwarfs to hit its target without fail. He also possessed the finest of horses, the eight-legged Sleipnir, and was accompanied by a pair of ravens, Huginn and Muninn—

literally "Thought" and "Memory"—which scouted the cosmos, reporting back on what they saw. In fact, little escaped Odin, for from his seat high up on the rock of Hlidskjalf he could look out over the nine worlds of creation, observing all that happened in them. In search of more detailed information he would wander through Midgard in disguise, appearing to humans as a tall gray-bearded man in a long cape and broad-brimmed hat.

For all his deep awareness, though, he was a god who was respected and feared by his devotees rather than

loved. For Odin, knowledge was power, and in the myths he went to great lengths to attain it. He was one-eyed, having sacrificed the other to obtain a draft from the Well of Knowledge. The god of poetry, he obtained the mead of poetic inspiration by assuming serpent form to get into the cellar where it was kept hidden by a covetous giant; then, in trickster fashion, he seduced the giant's daughter in order to drain the barrels dry.

Most puzzling of all was the ordeal he endured to obtain the secret of runes (see page 460). As the *Hávamál* tells the story, he hung on Yggdrasil for nine nights, wounded with a spear and "given to Odin, myself to myself," before he was able to snatch his prize. The meaning seems to be that he voluntarily made himself a sacrifice, just as prisoners of war and others were offered up to him in order to obtain a boon, which in this case was the secret of esoteric knowledge. The length of his ordeal may also have been significant, for the number nine seems to have had special significance in Odin's cult. The eleventh-century chronicler Adam of Bremen reported that the principal ceremony at the great temple of Uppsala in Sweden where Odin was worshipped was held once every nine years and lasted for nine days; in its course nine victims of every available species, including humans, were killed.

People apparently accepted such bloodthirsty rites because Odin was thought to bring success, above all in war. If Thor was the archetypal Viking warrior, Odin was nonetheless regarded as the principal god of battle, the "Father of Victories." As such, he was the patron of the aristocratic warrior class as a whole and of the royal houses in Denmark and Norway in particular. He was also the inspiration for the berserkers, followers of Odin who cultivated battle-frenzy as a way of terrorizing opponents; his very name, meaning "raging" or "intoxicated,"

suggests the qualities they sought to display. It was Odin too who owned Valhalla, the Hall of the Slain, to where the fighting dead were taken from the battlefield.

There are indications, mainly derived from place-names, that Odin's cult was a relatively late arrival north of the Baltic, radiating upward from northern Germany and the Jutland peninsula not long before the beginning of the Viking age. It seems to have been particularly weak in southwest Norway, where most of the settlers of the Atlantic islands had their origins. Perhaps for that reason, as well as for its royal connections, the cult appears never to have become firmly established in Iceland, which did not have a royal family; there Odin was invoked as the muse of poetry but does not seem to have been presented with offerings or sacrifices.

Yet even when he was not directly worshipped, the spirit of Odin haunted the Norse world. In the myths he was a pervasive presence, turning up as a *deus ex machina* intervening unexpectedly but decisively in human affairs. He was at best an unreliable ally, who would grant a warrior victory one day only to abandon him the next. Sinister and all-seeing, he was a force that the ambitious courted, for no god had greater power, yet no one could count on his goodwill for long. Changeable in his moods and inscrutable in his actions, he was the embodiment of fate for the anxious human actors in an unpredictable, often violent world.

THE DIVINE THUNDERER

Upholding order against the forces of chaos was Thor, the strongest of the gods, and also the most admired. A huge, red-bearded figure with flaming eyes and a fearsome temper, he seemed the very archetype of the brave Viking warrior. Celebrated for his giant-killing exploits, he was revered as the defender of Asgard and Midgard.

The son of Odin and Jord ("Earth"), he lived with his wife Sif in a 540-room mansion, the biggest ever built. He traveled in a chariot drawn by two goats, Tooth-gnasher and Tooth-gritter, that had magical properties—they could be killed and eaten if food ran short,

A detail from one of the Gotland picture stones shows Odin on Sleipnir, his famous eight-legged horse. The small female figure shown greeting him may be one of his battle-maidens, the Valkyries.

• THE HAMMER OF THOR •

Thor's hammer Mjollnir was one of six treasures made for the gods by dwarfs, the master-craftspeople of the Norse world. The others included Odin's unerring spear Gungnir and his self-reproducing ring Draupnir; and, as gifts for Freyr, a boar with a golden mane and bristles, and a marvelous ship that could sail over both land and sea and could also fold up to the size of a pocket handkerchief. However, the Aesir judged the hammer the greatest of all the gifts for its value as a matchless weapon against their foes—not only did it shatter whatever it struck but it also magically flew back to Thor's hand whenever he threw it. For his human votaries, the hammer became popular in miniaturized form as a good-luck charm. Amulets made in its image seem to have been associated in people's minds with Thor's role as god of storms; in the myths Mjollnir sometimes seems to be confounded with the thunderbolts the god was imagined to throw, while some scholars have traced the name itself back to the Russian word *molnija*, meaning "lightning."

but so long as the bones were left intact they could be restored to life. Thor's other remarkable possessions were his hammer Mjollnir (see box, above) and a belt that had the magical property of increasing his strength by half whenever he wore it.

In the myths Thor features principally as the dedicated enemy of giants; several recount his feats of strength while out looking for trouble in Jotunheim. He killed Geirrod, for example, by catching a lump of molten iron that the giant threw at him and hurling it back with such force that it passed not just through Geirrod but also through a pillar, behind which he was hiding, and then on through the building's outer wall. Yet his relations with the giant race were not always

hostile. He even had two sons by a giantess, Jarnsaxa of the Iron Knife, and it was foretold that they would survive Ragnarok (see pages 472–473) and inherit the hammer Mjollnir in the new age that was to follow.

In the real world, Thor was associated with the elements, and above all with storms; thunder was said to be the noise his chariot made as it careered across the sky. Travelers invoked his protection whenever they set out on journeys, and every time that lightning flashed people remembered his power.

Perhaps as a result of his adoption by travelers, Thor's cult embraced the entire Norse world. On the evidence of place and personal names, he was the most popular of the gods: one in four of the entire population of Iceland in Viking times had names featuring the word "Thor." He presided over the Althing, Iceland's annual assembly, which opened on his day, Thursday. In the temple at Uppsala his statue was said to hold the central position, between Odin and Freyr. Odin may have been the god of the northern aristocracy, but for the bulk of the population—farmers, craftspeople and the like—Thor reigned supreme as a powerful champion, a figure to turn to for help whenever danger threatened.

FREYJA AND LOKI

Freyja was the goddess not just of love but also of birth, death, and fertility—the entire human cycle. One of the Vanir, she went to live with the Aesir as part of the settlement following the war between the two groups (see page 465). She was associated with the love of beautiful things, and was not scrupulous about how she obtained them: for example, she consented to sleep with four dwarfs in order to win the priceless Brisingamen necklace. Yet she was also courageous—she alone was prepared to serve mead to the drunken giant Hrungnir when he threatened to destroy Asgard.

She was renowned for her lascivious nature. She was accused by Loki of having slept with all the gods including her own brother, while the giantess Hyndla charged her with behaving like a nanny-goat in heat. In turn, she incited lust in beings: in one story the giant Thrym stole Thor's hammer, Mjollnir, planning to exchange it for Freyja. Another myth told how the giant who built Asgard's fortifications demanded as payment the sun, the moon, and Freyja—a trinity that has been taken to represent all the forces of light, life, and growth.

Freyja was a popular goddess, and her cult was widespread. Sometimes she was viewed as an emblem not just of passion but also of compassion—she was said to weep drops of gold for the waywardness of her wandering husband Odur, a little-known figure who is sometimes thought to be Odin himself under another name. As the patron of procreation, she was invoked not just by lovers eager to further their cause but also by women in childbirth and in naming ceremonies for newborns.

Yet there was also a harsher side to Freyja's nature. Her anger could be fearful to see and sometimes she haunted battlefields, sharing half of the kill with Odin and welcoming the warriors she chose to her hall of Folkvanger. And, again like Odin, she practiced magic—the powerful witchcraft known as *seid*. "The most renowned of the goddesses," as the *Prose Edda* calls her, she was a figure of power as well as of beauty, passionate by nature and steely minded in the extreme when it came to getting her way.

By contrast, Loki, the master of mischief, and son of a giant was a complex trickster figure, who by the time of the final conflict of Ragnarok (see pages 472–473) had transmuted into a symbol of pure evil. Loki had gained entry to Asgard by winning Odin's friendship (the two became blood-brothers). Quick-witted and handsome, Loki was also malicious and wily; Snorri Sturluson, the major source for the Norse myths, calls him "the slander-bearer of the Aesir, the promoter of deceit."

Some of the Loki tales follow a familiar trickster model in which an individual who is too clever for his own good gets a comeuppance. So, having lost a bet that could have cost him his head, he once ended up with his lips sewn together—a fitting fate for a smooth talker. However, at other times his quick wits saved the day. For example, when the giant had demanded the sun, the moon, and Freyja in payment for building a wall around Asgard, it was Loki who prevented him from completing the task on time and so from claiming his reward.

Loki's stratagem on that occasion was to turn himself into a mare in order to distract the horse that carried the giant's supplies. The incident illustrates his magical powers of shapeshifting—and of changing sex. The story also displays his role in the myths as a begetter of monstrous progeny, for from the union of the stallion and the mare Odin's eight-legged steed Sleipnir was born. Other of Loki's offspring were altogether more fearsome: the giantess Angrboda bore him a brood consisting of Hel, Queen of the Dead, the World Serpent Jormungand, and the ravening wolf Fenrir. The latter two were both fated to play a decisive part in Ragnarok, as was Loki. In this final incarnation, he revealed his true nature once and for all: malice personified, breaking all the bonds of order to bring chaos again.

GIANTS, DWARFS, AND MONSTERS

Humans lived alongside gods, dwarfs, elves, monsters, and giants—and although the giants were defined in myth by their role as the gods' adversaries and eventual destroyers, relations between the two races were not exclusively hostile. There were, in fact, many liaisons between gods and giantesses.

Thor himself was born of the union between Odin and Jord, while Freyr and Freyja were the offspring of the Vanir god Njord and the giantess Skadi. Giants could even on occasion show kindness, as they did to the young prince Agnar, rightful heir to a kingdom that had been usurped by his brother; making his way to Jotunheim, Agnar found shelter and fair treatment of a kind that had eluded him in the human world.

Generally, though, the giants were depicted in the myths as dull and slow-witted—Loki regularly outfoxed them. Giants were fearsome above all for their huge size, for they towered even over the gods—in one comic tale, Thor and Loki mistook a giant's discarded glove for a building, spending the night in one of its fingers.

As creatures of the cold and the dark, giants turned to stone if the sun's rays fell upon them—a characteristic they shared with dwarfs, who lived underground where sunlight never shone. The dwarfs were renowned for their craft skills, responsible for fashioning such marvels as Thor's hammer in their subterranean workshops. The trolls, too, made their homes underground, although in later folk beliefs the mounds in which they lived had tops that could be raised on pillars to let in daylight. Savage and uncouth, the trolls resided in Jotunheim alongside the giants, often acting as their servants.

The elves were altogether more complex in their derivation. They had some ritual significance, for householders offered sacrifices to them at the start of winter, apparently as a fertility rite. Their profile was ambivalent in the extreme; the Light Elves were considered almost as beautiful as the gods, while the Dark Elves were misshapen and hideous. Memories of both traditions survived into the folklore of later ages, respectively in the form of the fairies and the goblins.

Snakes are not common in Scandinavia, so the frequent occurrence of serpents in Norse myths probably owes more to worldwide patterns of storytelling than to everyday familiarity. Although they had their own mythic role, snakes were often confounded with dragons, not least in real life; the longboats of Viking raiders were known as *drakar*—dragon ships—but the mightiest of them all, constructed in the year 998 for King Olaf Tryggvason of Norway, was called the Long Serpent.

By far the most terrifying of all the snakes of Norse myth was Jormungand, the World Serpent. One of three monstrous children born to Loki and the giantess Angrboda, it was cast into the sea by Odin, who foresaw the great harm that the creature would do at Ragnarok (see page 473). There it grew until its body encircled the Earth, biting on its own tail. In one story a giant challenged Thor to lift a cat off the ground, yet try as he might Thor only managed to raise one of its paws. After the event the giant confessed that the cat was in reality none other than Jormungand; seeing its paw move, the giant had panicked, fearing that Thor might indeed raise it from the depths, bringing disaster on the world. In another tale, Thor went fishing for the World Serpent with a different giant, baiting his hook with the head of the giant's prize ox. Again he came close to success, dragging the serpent up to the water's surface. However, before he could kill it with his hammer his companion cut the line, letting the monster sink back into the waves.

The role of dragons was altogether more complex. They inspired fear, as snakes did, but on a much grander scale; their fiery breath could burn up a shield in a twinkling, and their scales were impenetrable to sword thrusts, so that only their soft underbellies were vulnerable to attack. Again like snakes, they lived underground—in their case, in the Bronze Age burial mounds, often the size of small hills, that dotted the northern landscape. Because of their subterranean habits they could only emerge from their lairs after sunset—a poet refers to one as "the old night-flier."

Dragons had a very specific role in Germanic and Scandinavian mythology as the guardians of buried treasure—a reflection of the very real hoards of precious grave-goods that often lay in the tumuli they were imagined to inhabit. Sometimes in literature they seem almost like the lust for gold made incarnate. In the Sigurd saga, for example, Fafnir, having killed his father

to obtain possession of the dwarf Andvari's cursed treasure, physically transmutes into a dragon to watch constantly over it. Yet however repulsive they seemed, dragons were also repositories of esoteric knowledge. Fafnir was reputedly infinitely wise and had advance knowledge of what would happen at Ragnarok, while by accidentally tasting the dragon's blood Sigurd acquired the ability to understand the language of birds.

Sigurd slays the dragon Fafnir in a detail from the carved doorposts of Hylestad church, Norway. The legend tells how the hero hid in a trench so that he could stab upward into the creature's unprotected underbelly.

THE BATTLE AT THE END OF TIME

The dramatic account given of the end of the world in Norse mythology is unique; no other tradition, except perhaps that of the biblical Book of Revelation, has such a detailed vision of how the final catastrophe will occur.

The story is told allusively in two poems, in each case from the perspective of an individual with access to hidden knowledge; in the *Völuspá* (ca. 1000), the longer of the two, the speaker is a female seer described as being cunning in magic.

The story of Ragnarok, the Doom of the Gods, had a profound effect on the Norse worldview, contributing greatly to its characteristic mood of fatalism. It told how, ultimately, the worlds of gods and men would be swept away. Even Odin and Thor, the mightiest of Asgard's defenders, could do no more than delay the onset of the final battle, in which they must inevitably meet their own deaths.

The prelude to Ragnarok is the death of Baldur, son of Odin and Frigg and the best-loved of all the Aesir. Having heard that her son is destined to be killed unwittingly by another of Odin's sons, the blind Hod, Frigg asks all things animate and inanimate to swear not to harm him. However, Loki, who has now become a figure of pure evil, discovers that Frigg had forgotten to ask the mistletoe. He hands a branch to Hod and directs the blind god's aim toward Baldur—the mistletoe pierces Baldur and he dies.

When Frigg goes to the underworld realm of Hel, Queen of the Dead, to request Baldur's resuscitation, it is Loki again who thwarts her mission. In retaliation, Loki is bound with the entrails of his own son Narfi and

---

A fragment from northern Iceland, thought once to have formed part of an 11th-century Doomsday from Hólar cathedral, shows a beast swallowing a human figure. For the island's surviving pagans, the image would no doubt have recalled the wolf Fenrir swallowing Odin in the showdown at Ragnarok.

left pinioned on three sharp rocks to await the day when Ragnarok shall dawn.

As Snorri and the poets tell the story, Ragnarok's coming will be heralded by a time of savage warfare among men—"an ax age, a sword age, a wind age, a wolf age." Then there will be a terrible winter lasting for three whole years. The wolves that have long pursued the sun and the moon will finally catch and devour their prey; the earth itself will quake and trees and crags will be uprooted.

Three cockerels will crow, one on the gallows tree, one in Hel, and one in Valhalla, to signal that the forces of evil have finally been unleashed. The wolf Fenrir will break its fetters, and Jormungand, the World Serpent, will rise up from the sea, scattering venom from its mouth. All the Aesir's enemies will gather for battle. Surt will lead the fire giants from Muspell; as they approach Asgard, the rainbow bridge Bifrost will buckle under their weight. Stirred up by Jormungand, the ocean will flood into Hel, tearing the ship Naglfar from its moorings; this terrible vessel is made of nail-clippings taken from the dead (humans can delay its completion by sending corpses to the grave with their fingers and toes trimmed). Loki will burst free from his bonds to pilot it toward Asgard, accompanied by Hrimir and the frost giants and all the champions of Hel.

Meanwhile in Asgard, Heimdall, the divine watchman, will blow his horn to signal the alarm. The World Tree will tremble, and giants and dwarfs alike will quake in fear. Odin will seek counsel at the Well of Knowledge. The gods, in company with the human heroes gathered over the ages in Valhalla (see pages 494–495), will take up arms and proceed to the battle-field to confront the foe.

In the battle itself, Freyr will be cut down by Surt's flaming sword. Thor will kill Jormungand but will then collapse, poisoned by the serpent's venom. Odin will fall to Fenrir, which will itself be stabbed in the heart by Vidar, the god's son. Tyr will confront Garm, the Hound of Hel, and the two will destroy each other, as

In a detail from one of the picture stones found on the Swedish island of Gotland, of which nearly 400 have survived, a dead human warrior (according to one interpretation of the source) rides to Valhalla, to be welcomed by a Valkyrie offering a cup of mead.

will Heimdall and Loki. Then sparks from Surt's brand will set fire to the earth. The sun will be darkened, the firmament will split open, and the stars will fall from the sky. The ocean will break its bounds and the earth will sink into the sea.

Yet life will continue beyond the final cataclysm. A fresh earth will emerge to replace the lost one, and a new and brighter sun will rise in the sky. Two of Odin's sons will survive, as will two of Thor's; and they will be joined by Hod and Baldur, released from Hel at last. In Midgard too a couple will live through the holocaust, hidden in Hodmimir's Wood—from their children the Earth will be repeopled. And yet, in the *Völuspá*'s vision, the seeds of evil will be present even in this new age of innocence; the seeress's last words before she falls silent tell of a winged dragon risen from the depths, bearing on its pinions the corpses of dead men.

THE RESTLESS SPIRIT

Vikings who set off to seek their fortunes overseas were driven by the same motives that have always inspired adventurers: the desire for land, wealth, and fame. Land hunger was a marked feature of Scandinavian life that continued to drive emigrants abroad up to modern times.

Although it seems to have been less extensive in the Viking era than in the earlier age of migrations, when whole peoples including Goths, Vandals, Lombards, and Burgundians had headed south, land hunger remained an influential force. The typical Viking raider was a younger son, stout and well-nourished on the high-protein meat-and-dairy diet of the north, eager to find himself an inheritance to match the family estate that would be his elder brother's by birthright.

In the course of the Viking age, the demographic pressures were exacerbated by political developments, and in particular by the rise of national monarchies. For example, in Norway, the westward expansion of colonists seeking new lands coincided with King Harald Fairhair's successful campaign around the turn of the ninth and tenth centuries to impose royal control on the independently minded local aristocracy. Many of the original settlers of Iceland and the north Atlantic islands were Norwegians who had fled Harald's heavy hand.

By that stage, a century into the Viking age, the westward routes had already been well charted by earlier generations of pioneers. Yet even the first wave of explorers had been able to draw on a substantial pool of geographical knowledge. Both eastward via the Baltic and westward via the Atlantic, the age of expansion was preceded by a century or more of increasing trade contacts, which had made the Norse peoples more aware than ever before of both the wealth and the accessibility of foreign parts. Even the very first raiders—those who fell upon Holy Island in 793CE—knew where they were going and what they could expect to find. That information could presumably only have come from traveling merchants, the warriors' non-violent precursors.

Yet if the northern peoples—and particularly young, bold, landless males—had the knowledge and the motive to undertake foreign adventures, they also needed the means to fulfill their ambitions. This was provided by the development of fast, maneuverable ocean-going boats. The longship is rightly regarded as the symbol of the Viking age: fully developed by the late eighth century, it gave the Norse peoples the tool they needed to take on the world.

LONGSHIPS OF VALHALLA

Viking longships are among the loveliest boats ever built, yet their beauty was always strictly utilitarian in the eyes of those who sailed in them. Everything that is pleasing to the eye in their design also contributed to making them the most efficient ocean-going craft the world had yet seen.

Longships, built for war and travel, were far from being the only boats of the Viking age. As important were the *knarrs*—cargo ships that were broader in the beam, with a length-to-breadth ratio averaging 4:1 in contrast to the longship's 7:1; the extra width amidships provided room for a central, sunken cargo hold. Unlike the longships, *knarrs* were essentially sailing boats with fixed masts; although there were a few oar-ports on the short stretches of decking at either end of the hold, these would only have been used when the ship was becalmed or maneuvering close to shore. In contrast, the longships had masts that could easily be lowered, whether to reduce wind resistance and improve stability when the craft was being rowed or else to present a low profile for surprise attacks. Sail was the normal method of propulsion on the open sea, but on rivers and in inshore waters the boats were powered by oar.

The combination of sail and oar was the secret of the longship's success. It was only in the period immediately preceding Viking times that northern shipbuilders had mastered the art of providing vessels with tall masts and the concomitant strong keels. The keel was very much the backbone of Viking ships of all kinds; hulls were built outward from it, employing planks of green wood cut radially in thin wedges from the tree trunk (see box, right). Much care was taken to work with the grain of the wood; the keel itself would be cut from a single straight trunk, while the ribs would be shaped from limbs and branches that naturally approximated the curve required. The goal was lightness and pliability; the strakes were shaved thin with axes for maximum flexibility, for the hulls were expected to ride the waves, not to fight against them. A good-sized warship would have required the timber of about a dozen oak trees, which was the preferred type of wood where it was available; in northerly Scandinavia oak does not grow and sturdy pine was the alternative wood of choice.

The end result was a vessel of extraordinary strength and navigability. Experiments with modern replica builds have shown that longships could achieve speeds of more than 10 knots (11.5 miles/18.5km per hour) in good conditions, and over long distances could average 125 miles (200km) or more in 24 hours.

◆ SHIPBUILDING ◆

Viking ships were usually built to a regular pattern. They were constructed from the keel upward through a succession of overlapping ("clinker-built") strakes, nailed together. Fore and aft, curved stems continued the line of the keel, rising up to the prow and sternposts. The mast slotted into a heavy timber known as the keelson that was horizontally attached along the center of the vessel. A single steering oar took the place of a rudder. The oar was fixed to a wooden block as a lever is to a fulcrum, enabling one man to set a vessel's course even in heavy seas. The combination of oar and sail made Viking ships uniquely adaptable, fitting them for raiding far down rivers while opening horizons on a wider maritime world.

Kings and leading noblemen sought to cut a dash by decorating the prows or sternposts of their grandest longships. Some boats bore beautiful bronze weathervanes, elaborately adorned with writhing mythological beasts entwined in serpentine patterns. However, the ornamentation usually took the form of decorated fore- and aft-stems standing proudly at the boat's prow and stern. "Here there were glittering men of solid gold or silver nearly comparable to live ones," wrote one observer rhapsodically, describing an eleventh-century Danish fleet, "there, bulls with necks raised high and legs outstretched, leaping and roaring just as if they were alive." In Iceland, the martial message of such ornaments was regarded as cause for alarm and laws prohibited vessels from approaching land "with gaping heads and yawning jaws, so that the spirits of the land grow frightened at them."

THE WATERY ROAD

In an age when most people never journeyed further than the nearest market town, Viking mariners traversed oceans and crossed continents. Once their shipwrights had mastered the art of building ocean-going vessels, they could cover distances that were unthinkable on muddy, potholed land tracks.

In spite of abundant maritime skills, the majority of Viking sea voyages were land-hugging trips which precluded the need for sophisticated navigation; the helmsman simply followed the shoreline to his destination, keeping a look-out along the way for familiar landmarks that would show how far he had gone. At nightfall he could beach his craft, a relatively easy task thanks to the shallow draft of Viking vessels.

Even journeys across the sea were not necessarily much more complicated. At its shortest, the crossing from Denmark to northern England took no more than thirty-six hours, and from there it was possible to travel on to the furthest parts of Ireland without ever losing sight of land. As the Viking age progressed, the Norse peoples established a network of coastal havens along the most traveled routes, where ships could stop to replenish their supplies; the island of Noirmoutier off France's Atlantic coast was an early example, as were the various Norwegian settlements down the Irish littoral.

However, journeys into the Atlantic to Iceland and Greenland presented different challenges, involving the prospect of several days and nights at sea. By day there was little for most of the crew to do except bale out the water that seeped through the caulking of moss or tarred animal hair that filled the joins in the planking. For food there would be dried fish or meat and unleavened bread; for drink, water from skin bags, or else sour milk or beer. At night, voyagers snatched what sleep they could huddled for warmth under animal-hide blankets.

On these open-sea voyages, navigation was a serious challenge for those setting the vessels' course. In place of rudders, the boats had oars attached to the right-hand side near the stern; the English word "starboard" derives from the Old Norse *styra*, meaning "to steer." Although various ingenious theories have been put forward to explain how Viking pilots could have found their way,

there is little hard archaeological evidence to suggest that they used special instruments; their usual methods were dead reckoning and careful observation of natural phenomena, primarily the position of the sun and the Pole Star. One possible exception is a semi-circular piece of wood with a regular pattern of notches around its rim; found in Greenland in 1948, it might conceivably have been part of a solar compass, used to judge direction from a reading taken on the sun's position at noon.

Mostly, though, navigators relied on land- and seamarks to tell them where they were. A medieval description of the journey from Norway to Greenland suggests the kind of thing they were looking out for. "From Hernar you should sail due west to reach Hvarf in Greenland. The route takes you north of Shetland, which can only be seen if the visibility is very good. You will pass south of the Faroes, where the sea appears halfway up the mountain slopes, and so far south of Iceland that you will only know of its presence from the birds and whales off its shores." Other clues for the experienced sailor included iceblink—the reflected glare of a distant ice field in the sky—and the changing wave formations as the seabed shelved up and land drew near.

Life on long sea journeys was always challenging and sometimes a test of endurance. Yet there were also many consolations for the bold. For all its perils, the sea was a path to riches, offering possibilities of adventure that stay-at-homes would never know in a lifetime of drudgery on the soil. As the gateway to far horizons, the sea haunted the Norse imagination, constantly offering the tempting prospect of a better life beyond the waves.

A mythical beast adorns the top of this elaborately decorated 12th-century weathervane found at Tingelsted in Norway. Such vanes were carried at the stem or masthead, and were highly ornamental.

EAST AND WEST

The hopes of a better life with which courageous Viking mariners set out were amply rewarded by the rich opportunities they found on their travels—unpopulated western territories in which to settle and colonize as well as busy eastern entrepots where lucrative trade could be conducted.

The Vikings who steered east across the Baltic used rather different boats from those who sailed the North Sea. In the east the main trade routes were riverborne, and for this inland traffic lighter vessels were needed that could, when necessary, be portaged overland between headwaters or around rapids. The lure that drew the merchants into Russia was Arab silver. Of the two main routes, the one down the Volga led first to the trading emporium of Bulgar, then on through the empire of the Khazars, a Turkic people who controlled much of the southern steppes, to the Caspian Sea and the heartland of the Abbasid caliphs beyond. From the Caspian's southern shores, Baghdad was a 400-mile (650-km) caravan journey away. This was the capital of

Waves break against Yesnaby Castle off the Orkneys, a group of more than 70 islands off the north of Scotland. Seized by Vikings in the 9th or 10th century, they remained Norse dependencies for more than 600 years until 1472, when they were pawned to the Scottish crown.

the mighty Harun al-Rashid, an *Arabian Nights*-like realm of fabulous wealth, much of it drawn from the silver mines of Transoxiana and Afghanistan.

Norse merchants traded furs, weapons, and slaves for fine Arabian silver coins, which had the double advantage of being precious and easily portable, both essential requirements for traders who traveled light. Back home, the silver transformed the economy: much was melted down, yet even so more than 85,000 surviving coins have been found in hoards, 95 percent of them in Sweden.

Merchants who chose the Dnieper route faced a 1,400-mile (2,250-km) journey to the Black Sea, whose western shores they could then follow to the capital of the Byzantine Empire, Constantinople (see box, right). The hazards awaiting them were memorably described by the emperor Constantine Porphyrogenitus. He reported that traders would gather in Kiev each June, when the winter meltwaters had subsided; they would travel in large groups, seeking safety in numbers. The passage to the Black Sea took at least six weeks, and crossed seven rapids known by evocative names, including Gulper, Yeller, Seether, Courser, and Ever-Noisy. Some of these could only be traversed by carrying the boats overland, at the risk of attack from hostile local peoples, although one could be negotiated on foot, albeit with difficulty, by keeping close to the bank.

It took courage and endurance to make money on the Russian route, and not all who set out returned. A monument to one who did not stands on the Baltic island of Gotland. Raised by four brothers in memory of a fifth, it states simply, "They went far into Ever-Noisy"—and there, in one of the most fearsome of the Dnieper cataracts, the young man presumably died, many miles from home.

A SEAMLESS FLOW

If the taste for plunder first drew Vikings across the North Sea, they soon also showed a desire for land on which they could settle down. On the Scottish islands as well as on the Isle of Man and in the Faroes, they found surroundings that recalled those they had left behind at home. Where the land was vacant and fit for agriculture, they set up farmsteads; where it was occupied, they sometimes took possession by force.

From 795 on, raiders regularly sailed round the northern tip of Scotland to attack targets on the Scottish west coast and in Ireland. They must quickly have grown familiar with the Orkney and Shetland

---

• THE GREAT CITY •

To Norse travelers the "great city" of Constantinople in the east was known as Mikligardr—with half-a-million polyglot inhabitants, it had no parallel in western Europe. Although it lay many months' traveling away, the Byzantine capital acted as a magnet for ambitious Norse merchants, who could trade their wares there for silks, spices, jewelry, and all the luxuries of the Levant. Inevitably, such wealth also attracted Vikings seeking to get rich by less peaceful means. On two occasions, in 860 and 907, raiders sought to breach the city's mighty defenses. Both assaults were repelled, but the defenders were so impressed by the courage and ferocity of their assailants that, once peace had been restored, Norse mercenaries won an honored place in the Byzantine army. Before long they even provided the crack troops that formed the emperor's own bodyguard, known—from the Old Norse word for "pledge"—as the Varangian Guard, among the most famous of whom was Harald Sigurdsson who was to become king of Norway from 1047 to 1066 (see page 492).

---

islands, which lie en route just twenty-four hours' sailing from the Norwegian coast. A hoard of Pictish silver, buried for safekeeping in the Shetlands about the year 800 and excavated in 1958, provides eloquent evidence of the fear the early visitors must have inspired in the local people. Then, at some unspecified moment, possibly as late as the tenth century, raiding turned into occupation, and in time the Orkneys were to become the seat of a powerful dynasty of Viking earls.

Placenames in the Orkneys and Shetlands are now almost entirely Norse in derivation, suggesting that the original Pictish population was totally subjugated. However, down the west coast of Scotland, Norse and Gaelic names both occur, indicating greater mixing of the peoples. Further south, the Isle of Man became the headquarters of an important Viking kingdom that came to include Kintyre and most of Scotland's western islands. Today the Manx people retain many memories of their Viking heritage, including a degree of autonomy and their own parliament, the Tynwald, whose name is an exact linguistic equivalent of the Icelandic *thingvellir*.

Norse colonists left an even more enduring mark on the Faroe Islands, midway between the Shetlands and Iceland, which remain a dependency of Denmark to this day. The Faroes were unoccupied before the first Norwegian settlers arrived, though not entirely uninhabited; from the early eighth century on they had served as a summertime refuge for Irish monks, who quickly took flight when the first Vikings arrived to disturb their solitude. From the monks or other early travelers, the newcomers inherited flocks of wild sheep; the name Faroes means "Island of Sheep." Along with rich fishing-grounds, good pasturage was in fact the islands' main attraction for the immigrants, some of whom may have found their way there by way of Gaelic-speaking areas; the sagas identify the first arrival as one Grim Kamban, a name that combines Norse and Celtic elements.

The occupation of the Faroes established a Norse presence far out in the North Atlantic, more than 400 miles (650km) from the Norwegian coast. In time, though, the islands would prove to be stepping stones, like the Orkneys and Shetlands before them, attracting intrepid adventurers to try their luck on even more distant shores.

THE ISLAND OF FIRE

Proof, if such were needed, that Viking navigation was an approximate art comes from the first voyages to Iceland. The island was actually discovered twice, each time by sailors blown off course while heading for other destinations. A Norwegian Viking named Naddod found his way there around the year 860 when trying to reach the Faroes; having climbed a snow-covered mountain and seen no sign of life, he sailed away again. At roughly the same time, a Swede called Gardar Svavarsson was blown north while en route for the Hebrides. He was sufficiently impressed by what he found to spend a whole year circumnavigating Iceland's heavily indented, 35,000-mile (60,000-km) coastline, overwintering at Husavik on the north coast. Then he returned to inhabited parts to report on what he had found.

In a world where land was in short supply, there was an eager audience for news of virgin territory, however forbidding the surroundings might seem to be. Word of the new land's active volcanoes and fields of lava failed to deter would-be settlers, even though much misinformation subsequently spread about them; one later writer claimed that "the ice on account of its age is so black and dry in appearance that it burns when fire is set to it." Iceland was named by one of its first inhabitants, a Norwegian called Floki Vilgerdarson who, according to the sagas, found his way there by using caged birds as navigation aids. The first he released flew back to the Faroes from where he had set out, while the second merely circled and then landed back on the boat; but the third led him westward to his destination. From this Noah-like stratagem the pioneer won the nickname of Raven Floki. However, Floki's stay was not a happy one:he left before a year was out, having lost all his livestock as a result of failing to put hay aside for winter fodder. The unappealing name he chose for the new land no doubt reflected his own bitter experiences there.

However, others succeeded where Floki had failed. Some sailed from the Western Isles of Scotland, bringing Celts with them as slaves; but most came from Norway, many seeking a place where they could be free of the threat of royal interference. They traveled in *knarrs*, the workhorses of the westward expansion, whose capacious holds provided room to store livestock and provisions. Some traveled the 650 miles (1,050km) from the Norwegian coast directly, setting their course due west; in ideal sailing conditions, the journey could take as little as four days. Others took a more southerly route, making landfalls on the Shetlands and Faroes, which lay about forty-eight hours' sailing across open ocean from Iceland's south-eastern point. Either way the colonists faced a risky crossing, exposed to the perils of Atlantic storms. Those who survived the journey settled on fertile grazing land, building turf-walled farmhouses such as the one reconstructed at Stöng near Thingvellir, the site of the Althing, an assembly of freemen that was Europe's first national representative parliament.

By about the year 930, all the available farming land in Iceland had been claimed, and pioneers seeking fresh horizons had to start looking further afield. One man who had strong personal reasons for doing so was Eirik the Red. Forced to flee Norway for Iceland after the killing of two adversaries in a family feud, Eirik got into trouble in his new home and was banished for three years by order of the Althing. Rather than heading for the Faroes or Ireland, as most people would have done, he set his mind to investigating a story that had been circulating in Iceland for a half century or more. This told how one Gunnbjorn Ulf-Krakason had been blown off course while sailing from Norway to Iceland. Before turning east to regain his destination, he had sighted a huge, rocky landmass in uncharted seas far to the west.

Eirik set out with a boatload of companions in the year 982 to find this land, and after traveling across some 450 miles (750km) of open ocean they duly did so. At first sight the discovery looked unpromising: the coastline that met their eyes offered only sheer cliffs dropping from a gigantic icecap. But the travelers turned south, rounding the tip of the landmass, and on the western coast they found sheltered fjords flanked by rich pasture. There they made their home.

When Eirik's banishment was up, he and his companions returned to Iceland with dazzling stories of the lushness of the new land. With an eye to attracting colonists, Eirik called his discovery Greenland, reckoning shrewdly that "people would be drawn to go there if it had an attractive name." A year later he set out again, this time not as an exile but as a founding father at the head of a fleet of twenty-five ships, fourteen of which survived the Atlantic storms to reach their destination. The 400 men and women aboard formed the foundation of a Viking colony that was to survive not just through the Viking age but also for most of the Middle Ages as well, finally dying out sometime in the fifteenth century after a continuous history of almost 500 years.

• ON VINLAND'S SHORES •

The final stepping stone in the Vikings' expansion across the Atlantic was North America itself. The first sighting of the North American coast came around the year 986 from a mariner named Bjarni Herjofsson who had missed the way to Greenland. Another fifteen years passed before the first landfall was made by Eirik the Red's son Leif Eiriksson, who had bought Bjarni's boat and retraced his route. The region where Leif and his companions overwintered was Vinland, whose name probably derives from the Old Norse "vin," meaning field or meadow. Leif's glowing account on his return to Greenland inspired Thorfinn Karlsefni to launch a full-scale attempt at colonization a few years later, but the hostility of the native peoples—possibly Inuit, but more likely Algonquins—drove the 250 settlers back to Greenland after less than three years. Thereafter Greenlanders continued to make occasional visits in search of timber, which their own land lacked; the last recorded trip was in 1347.

GIFTS FOR THE GODS

In the Viking world religious observances suffused the fabric of everyday life—there do not appear to have been purpose-built places of worship, nor a hierarchy of priests. Gods were honored in humble and impromptu domestic settings or in open air rituals with entire communities present.

Sacrifice was central to Norse religion, and it took many forms. The most structured rituals were conducted at seasonal turning-points. The usual venue was the great hall of the local lord or ruler, around which the blood of a slaughtered animal would be strewn by way of consecration; the sacrifice was the prologue to a feast at which the carcass would be eaten.

The greatest of all such gatherings probably took place at Uppsala in Sweden and at Lejre in Denmark. Both ceremonies are known only from Christian writers who may have distorted the proceedings, yet there are remarkable similarities between the two accounts. Each festival was held every nine years, and both human and animal sacrifices were offered up. The number nine had obvious cultic significance, for at Lejre there were said to be ninety-nine human victims, along with similar numbers of horses, dogs, and cocks, while at Uppsala nine males from eight different animal species, including

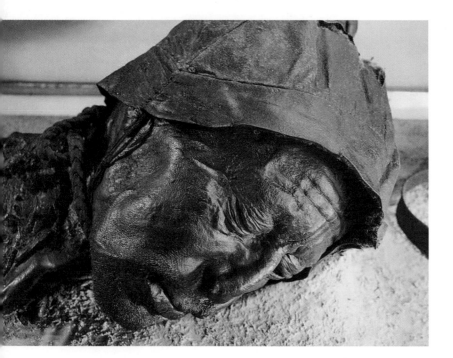

humans, were killed—the corpses were hung in a sacred grove. All of Sweden's provinces were represented, with individuals of note either attending in person or else sending gifts, although Christians, who abhorred the proceedings, were allowed to buy exemptions.

The events at Uppsala and Lejre appear to have been exceptional—most sacrificial rites were on a smaller scale and more personal in their goals. So Rus traders traveling the Volga would set up wooden statues of the gods and sacrifice sheep and cattle to them to solicit good trading. In Scandinavia itself, offerings were made not just to the major deities but also to the spirits thought to inhabit groves, rocks, and waterfalls. One eleventh-century Christian poet described being turned away from a farm where he had sought shelter for the night because the farmer's wife was honoring the local elves.

Individual deities favored certain types of offering. Odin's victims were usually hanged—he was Lord of the Gallows—and killed with a spear, his sacred weapon; stallions and boars were offered up to the fertility god Freyr. Artifacts as well as living beings were acceptable—large caches of ritually damaged weapons have been recovered from lakes, bogs, and other sites. Whatever the offering, the purpose seems to have been the same: to win divine favor in return for something of value.

THE CEREMONIAL FEAST

Feasting was closely related to sacrifice in the Viking world; in all the most significant seasonal ceremonies,

Long before Viking times, people were apparently offered up for sacrifice in the Norse lands. Discovered in a peat bog near Tollund, Denmark, in 1950, this man was naked but for a belt and cap, with the leather rope used to hang or strangle him still in place around his neck. He was sacrificed in about 200BCE.

These trees at Old Uppsala in Sweden may stand on the site of the sacred grove featured in the most celebrated of all the Norse peoples' sacrificial ceremonies. In its course, according to the chronicler Adam of Bremen, the bodies of as many as 72 human and animal victims were strung up, and "each and every tree is considered divine because of the victims' death and putrefaction."

both elements played a part. When circumstances demanded, any location could be chosen. Such was the case of the Danish warriors discovered by Irish monks celebrating their triumph against Norwegian Vikings outside Dublin in 852CE; to the visitors' horror, they had set their cauldrons upon the piled bodies of the Norwegian battle dead.

More typical practice was to celebrate feasts in halls that had been swept clean and decorated festively for the occasion, perhaps with wall-hangings. Large amounts of ale or mead, the principal drinks, would have been prepared in advance and ritually hallowed to the gods. The flesh of the sacrificial animal might be roasted over a spit or stewed, and to accompany it there would be fish, gruel, bread, and vegetables, along with fruit, berries, and nuts. The diners would sit on benches at long tables, carousing by the light of oil lamps, flaming torches, and a fire blazing in a central hearth.

An important part of the proceedings was the drinking of toasts to dead ancestors and to the gods—these would be proposed by the leading figure present. The ale would circulate in great metal-rimmed drinking horns passed from hand to hand among the guests; two such—large examples originating from aurochs (wild ox)—were found in the Sutton Hoo burial site in East Anglia, England. Besides eating and drinking, there would be other entertainments: musicians would play on lyres and flutes; poets would recite verses about the myths; and storytellers would recount the epic deeds of heroes and gods.

Such feasts had a significance that went far beyond mere conviviality. They were an opportunity for host and guests to reaffirm the ties that bound them together. They gave chiefs a chance to reward their retainers not just with their hospitality but also with more tangible gifts, particularly rings and other valuables. Above all they served to celebrate a common culture, as illustrated by a cautionary tale of King Hakon, who sought to bring Christianity to Norway in the tenth century. According to the Icelandic poet and chronicler Snorri Sturluson, writing two centuries later, the ruler deeply offended his pagan subjects by participating only half-heartedly in the important annual Winter Nights' festival. To stave off open revolt he eventually had to compromise his Christian principles to the extent of eating a little of the meat of the stallion sacrificed there in honor of the old gods.

SPECIAL POWERS

Alongside the public and private forms of worship, Norse pagan culture also harbored other, darker traditions—wise women who had prophetic powers of divination (seid), and the existence of potent magic whose practitioners had the ability to shapeshift or effect transmutations.

Magic and transformation both featured strongly in the Norse myths. As in Celtic lore, certain of the gods regularly changed both shape and species in order to conceal their real identity and achieve their goals (see pages 432–433). Odin took on the form of a serpent in pursuit of the Mead of Inspiration. Loki adopted the guise of a falcon to regain the Apples of Youth from the giant who had stolen them, and changed himself into a flea after stealing the priceless Brisingamen necklace from Freyja, who was said to have the power to change into a falcon.

The gods not only had the power to alter their own shapes, but those of others too. On one of their occasional forays into Midgard, Odin, Loki, and Honir tested their magical powers against those of the giant Skrymsli when he came, in ogre fashion, to take and eat the son of their human hosts. First Odin shrank the boy so that he was small enough to hide in an ear of corn, and then Honir transformed him into a feather on a swan's neck, but each time Skrymsli tracked him down. Loki finally saved the boy, first by turning him into a single egg in a fish's roe, and then, when even that failed, by trapping Skrymsli in quicksand in which he drowned.

Other powers exercised by the gods included that of reviving the dead. Thor had the ability to restore his two goats, Tooth-gnasher and Tooth-gritter, after killing and eating them; the twist in the tale was that the bones had to be intact for the magic to work. According to the story, some marrow had been extracted from one of them, causing that particular goat to limp afterwards.

Other beings besides gods also had magical powers. Giants could take on animal form just as the deities could—the storm giant Thiassi became an eagle to pursue Loki in falcon shape as he brought Iduna and the golden apples back to Asgard. So too could certain humans, to judge from the start of the *Volsung* saga. The tragedy of the Sigurd legend was set in motion when Loki killed an otter that was in fact a powerful magician's son, who had assumed that shape to hunt fish.

The shapeshifting in Norse myth inevitably brings to mind the world of the shamans—individuals credited in many cultures with powers that included the ability to transform themselves into animals. Shamanism was common to most of the peoples of northern Eurasia. The most likely channel into the Norse world was through the Saami or Lapps, Arctic neighbors of the Norwegians and Swedes. There are in fact hints in the histories that the remote regions where the Saami lived were regarded with a superstitious awe; the chronicler Snorri Sturluson reported that the beautiful wife of Norway's tenth-century king Eirik Bloodax, who came from the far north, was deeply versed in magic.

Yet the most feared form of magic in the Norse world may well have had other roots. Called *seid*, it was generally malicious in intent, and it was connected in the popular imagination with the Vanir. Its actual origins may be hinted at in one of the most enigmatic of the myths—that concerning the cause of the conflict between the Aesir and the Vanir (see pages 464–465). According to the *Völuspá*, the dispute began when the Aesir tortured a certain Gullveig, piercing her with spears and then burning her without being able to kill her. The Vanir then took up arms in her defense, and the world's first war began.

Gullveig is mentioned nowhere else in the myths and her identity is uncertain. However, the name means "love of gold," an attribute she shared with the principal Vanir goddess Freyja, who was famously fond of golden jewelry and who was said to weep tears of gold. If Freyja and Gullveig were indeed one and the same person, it may be that *seid* was associated from the beginning with her cult and represented a major cause of conflict

Mountains glimmer in the distance on the Lofoten Islands, north of the Norwegian mainland. Viking age inhabitants of more southerly parts of Scandinavia tended to associate the far north with magic, a belief that may have had its origins in the shamanistic practices of the region's Saami peoples.

between the worshippers of the two different sets of deities when their respective cults first came into contact.

Whatever its origins, *seid* continued to be respected and feared in equal measure throughout the Viking age. While female seers could use it to obtain powers of prophecy, male practitioners were condemned: one chronicle reports that Eirik Bloodax, urged by his father King Harald Fairhair of Norway, set fire to his brother's home to punish him for resorting to *seid*—the youth was burned alive together with eighty of his followers.

OMEN AND PROPHECY

Female seers known as *volvas*, who passed from house to house predicting the fortunes of individuals and of entire communities, had special status in the Norse world.

The only detailed account of a *volva* at work comes from the thirteenth-century *Eirik the Red's Saga*. It sets the events in Greenland, though the customs it describes probably reflect earlier Norwegian models. As the saga tells the story, the *volva* journeyed as an honored guest from farmstead to farmstead, offering advice on everything from marriage prospects to the likely outcome of the next harvest. She dressed spectacularly in an outfit fashioned from many different animal skins—reminiscent of the feather cloak that Freyja lent to Loki to give him powers of flight—and carried a brass staff. Sitting on a high seat to deliver her predictions, she started the consultation by consuming a meal made from the hearts of sacrificial animals. Entering a trance while a young girl chanted a spell, she then proceeded to answer questions about the girl's prospects and those of various other interlocutors in her audience. According to the saga, most of her predictions duly came to pass.

It is uncertain from the historical sources how common such figures were in real life, but the *volvas* certainly made their mark in literature and myth. The

poem called the *Völuspá*, our major source for Norse ideas of the beginning and end of the world, is presented in the form of the visions of just such a seeress, who was consulted by Odin. And when the beautiful god Baldur was troubled by premonitions of looming disaster, myth recounts that Odin traveled to the gates of Hel itself to consult a long dead prophetess and had to use the dark art of necromancy to resuscitate her temporarily.

Not all such prophets were women. There are references in the sagas to male seers foretelling the future at sacrificial feasts. Warrior leaders too were expected to have skill in augury, studying the flight of birds in order to interpret dreams and omens and draw lessons about the likely outcome of their actions. In addition, Viking bands practiced sortilege; according to the ninth-century *Life of Anskar*, one group decided to abandon a planned attack on the trading center of Birka when the lots they drew predicted a negative outcome.

IN PURSUIT OF FERTILITY

Fertility in the Norse world was associated with the Vanir, the family of gods dominated by Njord and his twin children Freyr and Freyja. There are also references in the literature to an allied cult of the *disir* or goddesses, tutelary spirits of households and of features of the landscape to whom sacrifices were offered at the time of the Winter Nights' festival. Freyja is sometimes referred to as Vanadis, *dis* (goddess) of the Vanir, and Freyr similarly received offerings at the winter festival, so it is likely that the two forms of worship went hand in hand.

An intriguing glimpse of northern fertility rites in pre-Viking times comes in a famous passage from the Roman historian Tacitus (ca. 56–ca. 120 CE), describing

The volvas—*itinerant prophetesses of the Norse world—carried staffs as symbols of their authority. This birdlike metal figurine dates back to the late Bronze Age, more than a millennium before the Viking era began, but it too was used to top a staff and may have had some ritual significance.*

the religious practices of peoples in Denmark and northern Germany in the first century CE. He refers to the cult of a goddess named Nerthus, the linguistic equivalent of the (male) Vanir god Njord. According to Tacitus, Nerthus's chief shrine was in a sacred grove on an island, probably in the Baltic Sea, where her image was kept under wraps in a wagon. When the presiding priest sensed that the goddess herself was present, the wagon would be hitched to oxen and led out through the surrounding countryside. Warriors would lay down their weapons as she passed, for she was an Earth Mother, a goddess of peace. Yet she also inspired fear, for when the wagon returned to the sacred grove, the slaves who ritually cleansed it were drowned as sacrifices to the goddess in the lake where they carried out the task.

Archaeology has provided corroborative evidence for the cult in the form of two magnificently carved wooden wagons recovered from a Danish peat bog and dated to the period when Tacitus was writing. There are also indications that memories of the cult might have continued into the Viking age. The great Oseberg ship burial bore the corpses of two women, one aged about fifty, the other thirty; to judge from the quality of the grave goods buried with them, at least one of the women must have been of the highest rank. Among the finest of the items that accompanied them into the afterlife was a wheeled wagon with a long yoke, suitable for drawing by horses or oxen. Not only was the vehicle of just the type that must have been used to carry the image of Nerthus, its richly carved body was also designed to be lifted off the vehicle's chassis, possibly for transportation by boat but also conceivably for easy immersion and cleansing.

Restored after 1,000 years in the earth, the Oseberg boat now rests in Oslo's Viking Ship Museum. Although it was seaworthy, its low sides and thin keel suggest it was designed mainly for ceremonial use.

A PEOPLE AT WAR

One point that all contemporaries of the Vikings agreed upon was that they were fearsome fighters. Foreign chroniclers compared them to wild beasts, stinging hornets, and ravening wolves. Their bloodthirsty reputation was further strengthened by the often alarming nicknames that individual warriors won: Eirik Bloodax, Ivar the Boneless, and Thorolf Lousebeard.

Warfare in Viking times was still very much a personal affair. As in Homer's day, warriors rallied to the banner of individuals who had won reputations as military leaders. Success bred success—a commander with victories to his name would attract fresh followers, allowing him in turn to acquire yet more booty and fame. When they first descended on an unwary and unprepared Europe, Norse warbands won a reputation as hit-and-run raiders, and throughout the Viking age mobility was a key to their success. Command of the sea lanes gave them the inestimable advantage of surprise; they could fall seemingly out of the blue on coastal targets, while the shallow draft of their longships also enabled them to launch attacks up rivers inland. When forced to strike far from their boats, they would commandeer horses to reach their objective fast.

Yet for all the emphasis on speed, the Scandinavians were also familiar with more static forms of warfare. The Danes in particular fought lengthy campaigns in England and in the Frankish lands in which discipline and endurance were more important than rapid-strike tactics. And although the Vikings generally avoided siege warfare, they showed that they knew how to raise ramparts and build siege engines when they did undertake it, as at Paris in 885.

Above all, though, Viking armies excelled at hand-to-hand fighting. A typical encounter would begin with the two forces lined up perhaps a few hundred yards apart. The warband leader might take the time to address a few words of encouragement to his men, who would respond by hurling insults at the enemy ranks. To start hostilities, the commander sometimes cast a spear—Odin's weapon—over the heads of the opposing army, shouting "Odin take them all!"; the idea was to offer the foe en masse as a sacrifice to the Norse war god. Then a hail of arrows, stones, and javelins would descend on the enemy's heads as the two sides closed on one another.

In close-contact fighting, the Viking soldiers had a crucial advantage: physical size. Brought up on a high-protein diet of meat and dairy foods, they tended to be bigger than their opponents. Measurement of the skeletons in Viking graves suggests that men of fighting age averaged about five feet eight inches (1.72m) in height at a time when the European mean was closer to five feet five inches (1.65m). In the cut-and-thrust of battle with sword and spear, the Norsemen could count on all the benefits of longer reach that boxers cherish in the ring to this day. One Arab observer wrote of the large Norse

---

◆ THE WARRIOR VISAGE ◆

Norse legend equated the warrior class with the aristocracy and explained its origins through a story of the god Heimdall. Out walking in human guise one day, he stopped at the cottage of a pair of peasants, who let him share their roof and their bed; the result, nine months later, was a son, sturdy but coarse, who was named Thrall—"Slave." Heimdall next stopped at a farmer's house, with the same outcome, only this time the baby was named Karl, or "Freeman." Finally Heimdall came to a nobleman's house, and once more enjoyed the hospitality not just of his host but also of his wife; and this time the end-product of his visit was a strapping lad who grew up skilled in the use of the bow and the spear. His name was Jarl, or "Earl," and his descendants were fighting men.

Excavated in the 1920s in the Vendel district north of Stockholm, this fearsome helmet was no doubt designed to strike terror into the hearts of its wearer's foes. The crest and cap are bronze, but the beardlike face-guard is made of iron. The helmet dates from the 8th century.

warriors he had seen: "I have never known a people so tall; they are as big as palm trees."

The Vikings were also very conscious of the psychological aspect of battle, doing everything they could to seem formidable in the sight of those they confronted. One tactic was to make a fearsome noise; by rattling arrow-quivers and emitting blood-curdling battle-howls they sought to cow the foe into submission. Some individuals also boosted their confidence by resorting to magic: the Eddic poem the *Hávamál* lists various battle spells used to achieve such ends as blunting an enemy's weapons, making comrades impervious to wounds and stopping arrows in mid-air.

One group of warriors carried such stratagems to extremes, working themselves up into a frenzy that apparently made them immune from pain. These were the berserkers, a lifelong fellowship of fighters who took their name from the bearskin outfits that they sometimes wore. They must have looked quite horrifying to their adversaries: they rolled their eyes, foamed at the mouth, bit their own shields, and sometimes even fought stark naked, relying on sheer fury and their fighting prowess to prevail. Some probably fought drunk, but others relied merely on the adrenaline rush of combat

In its day, the fortress of Fyrkat in Jutland was a bustling encampment housing craftspeople as well as soldiers. The fort was one of five, all built in the 980s to an identical plan. Probably commissioned by Denmark's King Harald Bluetooth, it went out of service soon after his reign.

and maybe also on breathing techniques to reach the necessary state of fearless distraction.

At the heart of any action would be the warband's leader surrounded by his bodyguard élite, warriors hand-picked for their fighting skills. One would carry the standard that marked the chief's position, a favorite target for enemy attack. If the leader decided for any reason to call off the fighting, he would do so by raising his shield. More often, though, the battle would continue until the enemy line broke and the remaining soldiers fled.

Seasoned campaigners grew used to these moments of triumph, and to the harvesting of the spoils of war that usually followed. The sheer volume of loot that the Norsemen acquired in the course of their many campaigns is well illustrated by the example of Ireland: in modern times almost as many treasures of eighth-century Irish art have been found in Norway, where the Viking raiders took them, as in Ireland itself where they had been created.

Viking forces were not invincible, but defeats were

extremely rare occurrences. The only people who were able to tame them were women. For Norse fighting men—unlike the colonists who went to the Faroes and Iceland—generally traveled without their womenfolk, with the result that when they did settle down, as in the English Danelaw in the ninth century, they often ended up marrying into the local population.

The results could be dramatic. When Normandy was settled by Duke Rollo and his followers from the year 910 on, acculturation was so rapid that the children of even the first generation of incomers were almost all brought up speaking French. So marked was the culture shift that, one generation on, Rollo's son William Longsword could find no one in his capital of Rouen to teach his own child the Viking language of Old Norse; he had to send to Bayeux 90 miles (150km) away to hire a tutor.

COMMANDERS OF THE BRAVE

The concept of kingship blossomed in Scandinavia in the course of the Viking age; the new wealth and complexity of the times fostered the growth of national monarchies, first in Denmark and then in Norway, with Sweden lagging behind. Yet throughout its course royal power remained personal and insecure in all three countries, resting heavily on the charisma and military success of the individual who held the throne.

Norse kings had to be of royal birth, though strict rules of heredity did not necessarily apply—other candidates beside the ruler's eldest son might contend for the throne, increasing the risk of dynastic strife. Once a king had managed to establish his authority, he could only maintain it by *force majeure*, keeping a wary eye on the ambitions of potential rivals. His chief support came from a committed band of armed retainers, who would serve both as his personal bodyguard and as the core of his army in case of war. The individuals who composed the inner band pledged their loyalty by kneeling before him and laying their hands on his sword hilt. In return for their continued allegiance, the ruler would reward

them with feasts, lodging, and generous gifts. A poet summed up the relationship succinctly: "They are favored with wealth and finest swordblades,/With metal from Hunland and maids from the East./Glad are they when they guess battle's near,/Swift to leap up and lay hands to their oars."

To ensure the continued support of his warriors, the king needed a regular revenue stream, much of which would come from his own estates; other major sources of income included duties levied on trade and fines paid by criminals, along with the spoils of war. Rather than keeping to one residence, rulers were peripatetic, moving constantly around their estates and those of leading nobles. Given the violent ends to many reigns, the mood on the royal progresses must often have been wary and mistrustful—this was a world not very far from that of Shakespeare's *Macbeth*.

There were other parallels too, in that for ruthless ambition, the Viking era produced rulers to rival Macbeth. A tale from the sagas recounted how the eleventh-century king of Norway Olaf Haraldsson once quizzed three young princes, his half-brothers, about their future hopes. One wished for large estates, a second for cattle by the thousand; but the third said he wanted warriors—enough to eat up all his brother's cows. "That boy will be a king," Olaf commented admiringly. The remark proved prophetic: the stripling was the future Harald Hardrada (see page 492), a battle-hardened ruler of Norway who finally met his death in 1066 at Stamford Bridge, near York in northern England, fighting to obtain the throne of England from King Harold of Wessex.

FATE AND GLORY

Viking warriors were brought up in a culture that glorified courage, strength, and loyalty. Children imbibed the message from an early age—these lines were supposedly written by the poet and fighter Egil Skalla-Grimsson at the age of twelve: "My mother once told me/She'd buy me a longship/A handsome-oared ves-

A mounted warrior is depicted on this runestone from the 6th century or earlier from Mojbro in Sweden. For much of the Viking age, Norsemen rarely fought on horseback, but by the 11th century Normans and other groups had turned themselves into accomplished cavalrymen—a fact that was to prove crucial to their eventual, hard-fought, victory over the Saxon forces of King Harold of Wessex at the Battle of Hastings in 1066.

returned home to claim the crown his brother had lost, going on to rule autocratically as Harald Hardrada—Harald the Ruthless.

Even so, such glory had to be bought at a cost. For the Norse warrior, the reverse of the coin of worldly fame was a willingness to confront death fearlessly, even in the face of insurmountable odds. Fighting men were expected to show contempt for the "straw death" of those who died in their beds. To avoid it, the legendary hero Starkad hung all his gold around his neck in his old age with the deliberate intention of attracting the notice of potential assassins. The ploy worked, and he was eventually beheaded by the son of a man he had earlier slain. Even so, his martial spirit lived on, if only briefly; according to one version of the story, his body went on fighting for a time even after his head had been cut off.

Another famous tale told of a celebrated warrior named Ragnar Lodbrok. Captured by King Ella of Northumbria, he was cast into a pit of adders. Far from showing fear, he sang a famous death song: "Gladly shall I drink ale/On high with the Aesir./My life-days are ended./I laugh as I die."

Just as memorable was the revenge taken by his sons when they in turn captured King Ella. They killed him by "carving the blood eagle": breaking his ribs and ripping his lungs from his back, where they continued to expand and contract in a motion that mimicked the flapping of the great bird's wings. Cruelty as well as courage was among the Vikings' hallmarks.

sel/To go sailing with Vikings;/To stand at the sternpost/And steer the fine sea-steed/Then head back for harbor/And hew down some foemen."

A bold and bloodthirsty spirit could lead a man to fame, riches, and, of course, the highest honors. One celebrated example was Harald Sigurdsson, half-brother of a king of Norway, who fled his homeland for the east, where he ended up as commander of the Byzantine emperor's Varangian Guard. Having made both his fortune and his reputation in foreign service, he

• THE ART OF WARFARE •

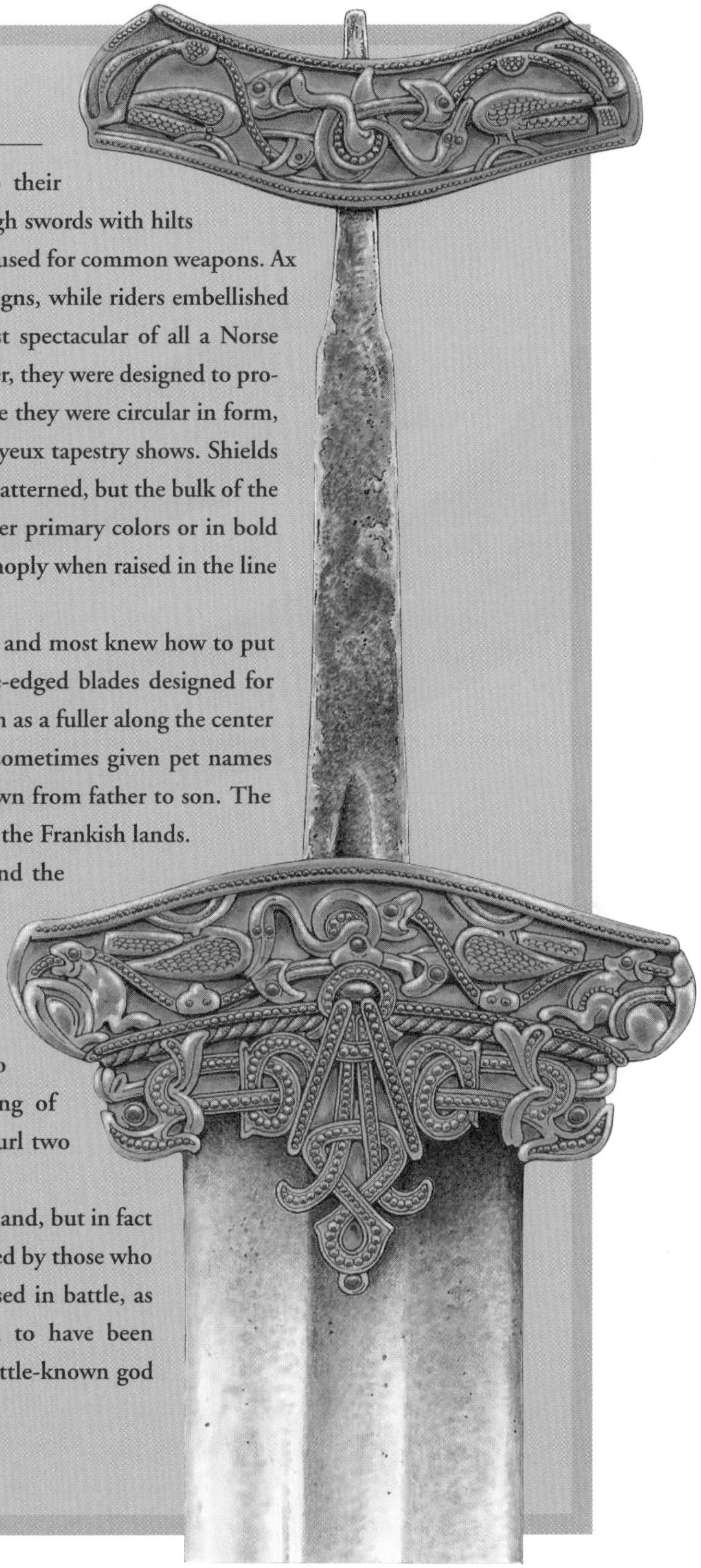

The Vikings' taste for ostentatious ornament extended to their weaponry. Noble warriors would advertise their status through swords with hilts of gold or silver (as depicted here, right) rather than the horn used for common weapons. Ax heads might be decorated with silver inlay in serpentine designs, while riders embellished their horses' bridles with lavish metal mounts. Yet the most spectacular of all a Norse army's accoutrements were its shields. Up to a yard in diameter, they were designed to protect the bearer from chin to knee. For much of the Viking age they were circular in form, although kite shapes became popular in later years, as the Bayeux tapestry shows. Shields had central bosses of metal that were sometimes elaborately patterned, but the bulk of the body was wood. Brilliantly painted in reds, yellows, and other primary colors or in bold abstract patterns, they must have presented a magnificent panoply when raised in the line of battle or stowed for storage along a longship's gunwales.

Every freeborn Norse male was expected to own weapons, and most knew how to put them to good use. The finest were the longswords: double-edged blades designed for hacking rather than thrusting and made with a groove known as a fuller along the center of the blade. Swords were treasured possessions that were sometimes given pet names like "Leg-biter" or "Golden-hilt," and were often passed down from father to son. The best, with increased suppleness and flexibility, were made in the Frankish lands.

Next in status among Viking weaponry were the spear and the javelin, used respectively for thrusting and throwing. These were fearsome implements with blades up to a half yard long, attached to ash shafts four or five times that length. In myth they were particularly associated with Odin, who was known as "Lord of the Spear." In time the weapons also became linked with the memory of Olaf Tryggvason, king of Norway, a formidable warrior who was said to be able to hurl two spears at once, one from each hand.

Legend likes to portray the Viking raider with battleax in hand, but in fact axes were for the most part relatively humble arms chiefly used by those who could not afford swords. Short stabbing knives were also used in battle, as were bows and arrows, although these seem more often to have been employed in hunting; they were particularly linked to the little-known god Ull, perhaps a patron of the hunt.

THE FEASTING-HALL
OF THE DEAD

The Norse peoples had conflicting views about what happened after death. Separate communities held different ideas about the afterlife and what it held in store. The best-known of all their beliefs concerned Valhalla, the feasting-hall in Asgard where Odin played host to dead kings and warriors.

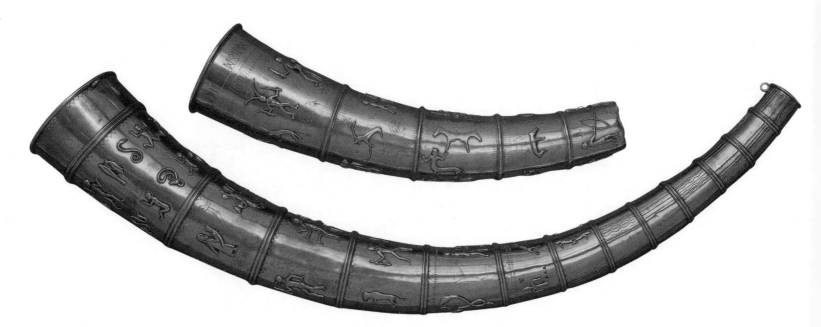

Vikings who gave up their lives on the battlefield were taken to Valhalla by the Valkyries, battle-maidens whose name meant "Choosers of the Slain." The hall itself was impossibly magnificent: it was said to have 540 doors, each of them wide enough to allow the passage of 800 warriors walking abreast. Its walls were made of glittering spears, its roof of precious shields that bathed it in a golden glow. There the chosen feasted on limitless supplies of mead and on the flesh of the boar Saehrimnir, which was made whole again each night.

The warriors made up the ranks of the Einherjar, the army of human heroes who would fight alongside the gods in the final showdown of Ragnarok (see pages 472–473). In the meantime they were expected to keep in training by spending their days fighting one another. However, each evening their wounds healed, permitting them to carouse late into the night amid music and the tales of poets recounting brave deeds of long ago.

Mead and ale were often passed around at feasts in drinking horns. Sourced from domestic cattle, such everyday vessels were simple in form and decoration. However, some more elaborate versions are known to have existed during the later Viking period—these examples are replicas of two celebrated 5th- or 6th-century golden horns from Gallehus in Denmark, the originals of which are now both lost.

There are suggestions that Valhalla was a relatively late addition to the body of Norse myth, and the whole concept has something of a literary ring to it. There is also a degree of confusion in the myths: some indicate that certain dead warriors went instead to Freyja's hall of Folkvanger. Yet the Byzantine historian Leo the Deacon reported that, rather than surrender, Rus warriors would take their own lives in battle. This evidence, together with depictions of what could be Valkyries holding out drinking horns to welcome dead warriors on at least a dozen of the Gotland picture-stones, suggests that the notion of Valhalla did indeed have a real place in the Norse cult of the dead. The fate of those who died the "straw death" at home in bed was far less attractive. They were condemned to a grim afterlife in the shadowy underworld realm of Hel (the origin of "hell"). It was ruled by the sinister goddess of the same name, whose body was half living flesh and half rotting cadaver. From Hel they might pass on to freezing Niflheim, or else be banished to Nastrond, the strand of corpses, where they waded in icy streams of poison before being cast into the cauldron Hvergelmir to feed the monstrous Nidhogg.

Alongside the stories told in the myths folk traditions circulated that apparently told a different story about people's final fate. Loved ones were sometimes laid to rest close to where they had lived in the hope that they would continue to exert a benign influence. In contrast, evil people were buried as far away from habitations as possible for fear that they might rise again as murderous ghouls capable of doing terrible harm to the living. In addition, there even seem to have been skeptics who doubted the existence of any life after death. The *Hávamál*, in its earthy wisdom, noted fatalistically:

"Wealth dies, kinsmen die, a man himself must likewise die: but fame never dies, for him who achieves it well."

However, to judge from the evidence of burials such views must have been limited to a minority. Excavated graves show that individuals were regularly buried with objects they had used in daily life, presumably because they would need them after death. In addition, the prevalence of boat burials—or, in Iceland, of interments incorporating the bones of horses—suggests strongly that people conceived of the passage of the soul as a journey.

One such was described in the myths, when Hermod rode down to Hel in an attempt to ransom the newly dead Baldur from its icy queen. It was a long and bitter voyage of nine nights, through dark valleys leading to the far and frozen North. At its end Odin's messenger had to cross the Gjoll torrent, spanned by a golden-roofed bridge, where Hel's guardian Modgud quizzed him. Then Hermod rode on further north still to Hel gate, which he cleared at a single leap, for he was mounted on the wonderful eight-legged steed Sleipnir. Yet at journey's end all that awaited him was the dark and chill of Hel itself—cold comfort for Hermod and, by implication, for Norse men and women contemplating their own final destiny.

✦ SHIPS OF STONE ✦

Viking men and women were famously buried in ships, but a parallel tradition, dating back in some areas to the Bronze Age, saw the deceased laid to rest in normal graves that were then marked by standing stones erected in the shape of a boat. The best-known examples are at Lindholm Høje, near Ålborg in northern Jutland, where a Viking age cemetery that had been covered with sand sometime around the year 1000 was excavated in the 1950s. Not all the 700 or so graves were boat-shaped—there were also squares, circles, and rectangles—but the characteristic longship pattern seems to have become the most popular from about 800 on. Most of the bodies at the site were cremated, and so could not have been imagined to be physically traveling after death. Even so, the symbolism seems clear: the soul was embarking on a journey, and for Vikings the usual means of transport over distance was a boat.

PART FOUR

•

THE AMERICAS

CHAPTER ONE

THE AZTECS

In 1519, when Hernán Cortés and a band of Spanish soldiers entered the Aztecs' vast capital Tenochtitlán, they were both enchanted and appalled by what they discovered—dazzled by gold and riches, amazed by the vast market in Tenochtitlán's neighboring town, Tlatelolco, but also shocked by the evidence of ritual human sacrifice on the bloodstained steps of the city's temple pyramids. The Spaniards destroyed much of the glory they admired. Claiming the region for the Spanish crown, they imposed Christianity, looted treasures, burned books, and smashed icons which they perceived as wicked. They left little evidence of a thriving culture that was the culmination of almost 3,000 years of civilization in the region since the Olmec people had raised the great cities of La Venta and San Lorenzo in about 1200BCE. But sufficient remains survived to enable us to build up a picture of life in the empire of the Aztecs. Decades of painstaking work by archaeologists and historians have contributed to our ever-growing appreciation of a people who developed prodigious skill in astronomy, mathematics, and computational science, breathtaking metalwork, pottery, and other crafts, and majestic monumental architecture.

THE SOUL OF THE AZTECS

The Aztecs declared themselves the "people of the sun." At the beginning of the current world age, in the sacred city of Teotihuacán, the gods had set the sun and moon in motion in the sky by giving their own hearts and lifeblood as a sacrificial offering. For the Aztecs it was a hallowed duty to continue this tradition, so they made blood offerings to maintain cosmic order and sustain the earth's fertility.

Priests made public offerings of human blood to the gods in large-scale sacrifices on steep temple pyramids that rose powerfully toward the sacred sky. If the gods were not honored with blood, they might decide in their great power to send plagues, famine, and humiliation in battle—or even to bring a sudden and violent end to the world. Long lines of naked war prisoners were paraded up the side of the pyramid to be sacrificed by the priests on a sacrificial stone raised far above the watching crowd. Public sacrifices presented a magnificent spectacle: the temples were decorated with flowers and stained with blood, priests dressed in colorful jeweled and feathered costumes, and bands of musicians played drums, shells, flutes, and bells. The sacrifices both honored the deities and made a spectacular statement of the Aztecs' secular and military power.

The deities whom priests and people feared, the guardians of destiny and of time, were part of the Aztecs' wide-ranging inheritance from the ancient culture of Mesoamerica. Historians use the label "Mesoamerica" to define both a geographical area and a historical time span. Geographically the area runs from the desert region north of the Valley of Mexico southward and eastward through Guatemala and Honduras as far as western Nicaragua and Costa Rica—it therefore includes much of Mexico and parts of some modern Central American countries, but excludes other parts of Central America, such as Panama, entirely. In terms of chronology, Mesoamerican history dates from the influx of the first human settlers in the region in about 21,000BCE to the Spanish conquest of the Aztec Empire in the early sixteenth century CE.

Only one major Aztec god was unique to their people: Huitzilopochtli, the "Humming Bird of the South" and patron deity of the Mexica tribe who founded the Aztec Empire. All their other important deities (see pages 538–545)—including the Plumed Serpent god Quetzalcóatl, the dark lord of fate Tezcatlipoca, the sun god Tonatiuh, the rain god Tlaloc and the god of vegetation Xipe Totec—had close counterparts in the religion of other Mesoamerican groups. The cult of Quetzalcóatl, which was followed with enthusiasm right across the Mesoamerican region, was perhaps of the greatest antiquity. His most venerable surviving image, discovered at Tlatilco, was made in around 800BCE, while a temple pyramid was raised in his honor at Teotihuacán in around the third century CE. The god worshipped by the Aztecs as Quetzalcóatl and by the Maya as Kukulcan may in primeval times have been revered as a dragon sky god, master of wind and rains, of the earth's fertility, and of land-level waters such as floods, rivers, and oceans.

The sky was a sacred arena in which the primeval activities of the gods were played out in the movements of stars and planets. By night the constellation of the Great Bear was identified with Tezcatlipoca in his form as the fearless jaguar—and the dipping of the Great Bear into the ocean re-enacted the moment in one of the prime Aztec creation myths in which Tezcatlipoca lost a foot while fighting Tlatecuhtli, the earth monster. At dawn and dusk the planet Venus, which appears at different parts of its cycle as both Morning and Evening Star, was Quetzalcóatl and his double form Xolotl; the period of the cycle in which the planet is invisible was identified as the time when Quetzalcóatl visited the underworld prior to the creation of the world in the current age. The Aztecs and their Mesoamerican neighbors were prodigiously dedicated and skilful astronomers.

The movements of sun, moon, and planets were in turn played out in a sacred ballgame resonant with

mythological and cosmological meaning. The game was another element of the shared and ancient culture of the Middle American region and was played in various forms by the Mesoamerican Olmecs, Zapotecs, Maya, and Toltecs as well as by the Aztecs. The stone court, which the Aztecs called the *tlachtli*, was shaped like a capital "I," with a long central zone opening out into a wider area at each end. The players sent a small, hard, bouncy rubber ball back and forward across a central line using only their heads, knees, hips, and elbows: they wore protective clothing, including a thick leather belt and helmet. The ball was not allowed to touch the ground, but could be bounced off the walls of the court; players scored points by hitting the ball against

The Aztecs inherited many characteristics from their Mesoamerican predecessors, including a reverence for military achievement. These vast stone warriors at Tollan were built by the mighty Toltecs (ca. 1100CE) and would once have supported the roof of a pyramid-top temple.

decoratively carved markers and stones along the length of the court. High on one side wall was a projecting stone ring with a small aperture, and any player who succeeded in driving the ball through this opening won the game outright. According to Aztec custom, the player who executed this match-winning stroke could seize the jewelry and other possessions of any member of the crowd he chose.

The ballgame was an extremely popular spectator sport. Only members of the Aztec nobility were permitted to play but other classes came to watch and joined enthusiastically in betting on the outcome. However, the contest was also viewed with great reverence. The game could be interpreted as a reenactment of primal struggles between Tezcatlipoca, representing darkness, and Quetzalcóatl, on the side of light. Sometimes a match was played as an act of divination. According to legend, the Aztec emperor Motecuhzoma II played against Nezahualpilli, ruler of Texcoco, to put to the test Nezahualpilli's prophecy that outsiders would take power in mighty Tenochtitlán. The emperor began by winning, but ultimately lost—and shortly afterward the prophecy came true with the arrival of Hernán Cortés. It was customary for the captain of the losing team to be decapitated with an obsidian knife, but this was overlooked in the case of Motecuhzoma.

Divination was more usually performed by priestly diviners consulting a 260-day sacred calendar that the

The sacred ballgame was played by numerous Mesoamerican cultures, including the Zapotecs, who built this ballcourt in their ceremonial center at Monte Albán. As well as being a hugely popular spectator sport, the ballgame was imbued with ritual significance: the court served as a cosmological diagram and the ball represented the sun.

Aztecs used alongside the 365-day solar calendar. They inherited the use of dual calendars from their Mesoamerican forebears: the combined calendar was of great antiquity and may have been developed by the Olmecs in the second millennium BCE. The first day of the two calendars coincided only once every fifty-two years: the Aztecs called this time span the "bundle of years." The transition from one fifty-two-year cycle to the next was a moment of great anxiety, when the Aztecs feared that the gods might well choose to bring the current cycle of creation to an end.

For the Aztecs did not see time as a linear progression. They believed that history was cyclical and that we lived in the fifth age of the world—subject to the pleasure of the gods. Our age was destined to come to a violent end, as had each of its predecessors. Even within a cycle, time could move with all the unpredictability of fate or of the gods themselves. The gods could take many forms, including that of time—every moment was charged with divine unpredictability, with forces for good or evil. Within the 260-day ritual calendar, twenty weeks of thirteen days were each presided over by its own god or goddess. In addition, every one of the days had its controlling deity, as did each of the thirteen hours of the day and the nine hours of night. The divinities in power at the moment of a child's birth were believed to have a fateful bearing on his or her prospects throughout their life. Equally, a farmer deciding when to plant his crop, a soldier preparing for a military campaign, a merchant planning a journey, or an artisan readying himself to start work on a luxurious feathered cloak would need to identify which gods and goddesses would be in control on a particular day or hour, in order to propitiate them. By using the ritual calendar, by examining omens and the movements of stars or planets, priestly diviners could interpret the forces at play in each instant.

◆ MEASURING TIME ◆

An interest in measuring and marking time goes far back into Mesoamerican history. A stone carved by craftsmen of one the Aztecs' major predecessors, the Zapotecs, in about 600BCE depicts a slaughtered prisoner with his lifeblood ebbing from his breast: by his side is carved the date "1 Earthquake"—which may be the day on which he had been born. A calendar dating system was therefore in use by Mesoamericans from at least the middle of the first millennium BCE. The marking of calendar dates may even have been the inspiration for the development of written notation. Some experts declare the Zapotec date carving, which was found at San José Mogote in the Oaxaca Valley, to be the earliest piece of writing in Mesoamerica, although others find evidence of an even older writing system at La Venta, one of the major sites of the Olmec culture, which prevailed from approximately 1500 to 400 BCE. Two other carved dates from around the close of the millennium in about 30BCE have been found in Mexico, one in Veracruz and one in Chiapas.

THE STORY OF THE AZTECS

The Aztecs looked back with reverence at the achievements of their predecessors in Mesoamerica. From their capital of Tenochtitlán, founded in 1325CE, they made pilgrimages to the ancient city of Teotihuacán, erected by unknown builders in the first century BCE. And they felt a deep sense of awe in hearing and retelling tales of the fierce Toltecs, builders of the city of Tollan in the tenth century CE.

The first great Mesoamerican civilization arose in about 1500 to 1200BCE, when the Olmec people built vast ceremonial centers at La Venta and San Lorenzo on Mexico's southern Gulf coast and carved magnificent giant stone heads (see illustration, page 506) in homage to their rulers. The Olmecs developed religious ritual involving human sacrifice and bloodletting, traded vigorously across great distances, built temple pyramids and wide plazas, developed a writing system, and revered the jaguar—all elements that became central to the culture that was inherited and honored by the Aztecs.

The Olmecs' many successors included the Zapotecs, builders in approximately 500BCE of a great settlement and trading center at Monte Albán that flourished for more than 1,000 years, the unknown builders of Teotihuacán, and the Toltecs. From a base at Tollan (near modern Tula) the Toltecs built up an empire in the region of Hidalgo province and the northern part of the valley of Mexico, where the Aztecs would later settle. Like so many Mesoamerican cultures, the Toltecs were keen practitioners of human sacrifice: in front of their temples they carved reclining stone figures called *chacmool*s that carried a receptacle on their stomachs into which priests flung the heart of the ritual victim.

The Aztecs' rise began in the 150 years after the collapse of Toltec power in the mid-to-late twelfth century. In their early days the Aztecs were probably known as Mexica. They came from the barren lands to the north of the fertile Valley of Mexico in the wake of many fierce nomadic groups known collectively as Chichimecs (a derogatory "sons of dogs"). The Mexica settled to the west of Lake Texcoco in the late 1200s under the protection of the Culhua, founders of the city of Culhuacán. They fought for the Culhua against Xochimilco. The

Culhua claimed connection to the revered Toltecs, and the Mexica—keen to gain honor by association—intermarried with their protectors and began to call themselves the Mexica-Culhua. But in 1323 the Culhua, outraged that the Mexica had sacrificed a Culhua princess in a fertility rite, drove the settlers out of their lands and into the marshes of Lake Texcoco. There the Mexica founded their city Tenochtitlán in 1325, and from this base they built a great empire.

The story of the Mexica prior to their settling near the lake is uncertain. The tribe told many tales of their past to account for their use of ritual human sacrifice, to explain the supremacy of their god Huitzilopochtli, and to legitimize their rule. Indeed, the Aztecs and their Mesoamerican forebears were generally happy to combine fact with mythical and religious material: they believed that such mythologized narratives spoke with all the power and authenticity that we ascribe to history.

According to one account, the Mexica/Aztecs once lived at Aztlan ("Place of the Cranes") on an island in a lagoon to the north of the Valley of Mexico. They left this place on the orders of Huitzilopochtli and began a 100-year migration into more fertile lands to the south in search of a place to settle. Another version told that they emerged from Chicomoztoc ("Place of the Seven Caves"; see page 547). Historians have not been able to identify the location of Aztlan: some have suggested Lake Patzcuaro, which lies 150 miles (250km) north of Tenochtitlán, while others even propose sites in New Mexico and Arizona in the southern United States.

During their migration the Mexica sometimes settled for long enough to build temples and ballcourts and lay out fields of crops. But the urging of Huitzilopochtli always drove them on. According to myth, the divine lord had declared that the Mexica would found a city to

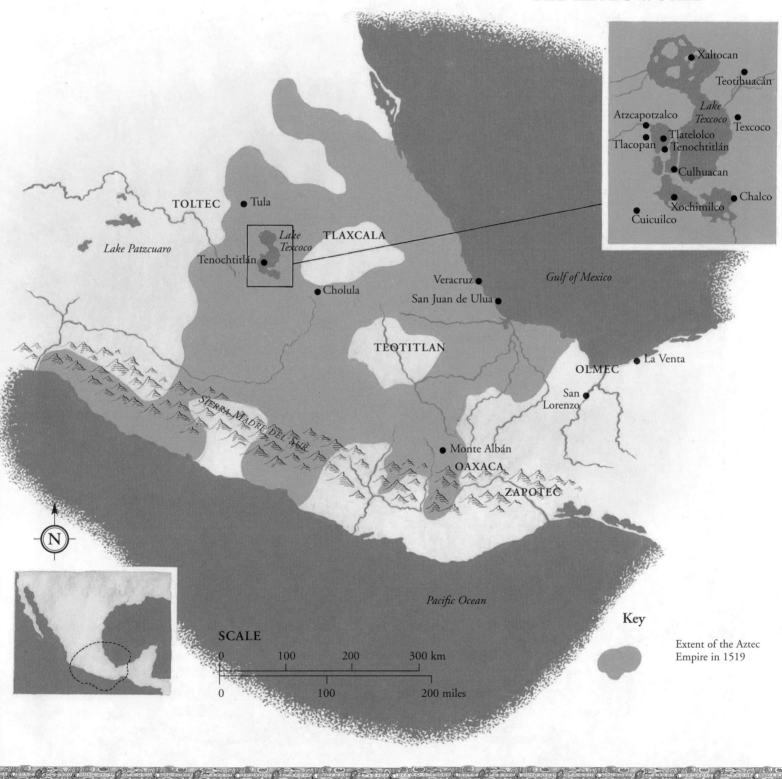

THE AZTEC WORLD

Xaltocan

Teotihuacán

Lake Texcoco

Atzcapotzalco

Texcoco

Tlacopan
Tlatelolco
Tenochtitlán

Culhuacan

Xochimilco
Chalco

Cuicuilco

TOLTEC • Tula

Lake Patzcuaro

Lake Texcoco

TLAXCALA

Tenochtitlán

• Cholula

Veracruz •

Gulf of Mexico

San Juan de Ulua •

TEOTITLAN

OLMEC
• La Venta

San
Lorenzo •

SIERRA MADRE DEL SUR

Monte Albán •

OAXACA

ZAPOTEC

Pacific Ocean

Key

N

SCALE

| 0 | 100 | 200 | 300 km |

| 0 | 100 | 200 miles |

Extent of the Aztec
Empire in 1519

his glory at the place where they saw an eagle on a cactus holding a serpent in his talons. In 1325, driven out by the Culhua, the nomads saw the prophesied vision on an island in Lake Texcoco.

Soon after founding Tenochtitlán, the Mexica built another town, Tlatelolco, on a second island close by. Over the next 100 years, they learned to grow food on artificial islands floating on the waters of the lake, traded with their neighbors, and fought in alliance with the Tepanec ruler Tezozomoc, who was creating an empire based on his city-state of Atzcapotzalco.

Following Tezozomoc's death in 1426, the regional balance of power changed decisively when Tenochtitlán joined with the cities of Texcoco and Tlacopán to defeat Atzcapotzalco. The formation of the Triple Alliance was the birth of the Aztec Empire: Tenochtitlán was the largest and most powerful of the three cities.

Growth was rapid. Coming to power in Tenochtitlán in 1440, Motecuhzoma I launched such a campaign of territorial expansion that after his death in 1469 he was lauded as "father of the empire." His successors largely maintained the progress and by the time Motecuhzoma II became emperor in 1502, the ruler of Tenochtitlán was master of 489 city-states over an area of 58,000 square miles (150,000 sq km). However, he was the last Aztec emperor to enjoy such power. A small force of soldiers from the Spanish colony in Cuba, in alliance with local tribes, imprisoned Motecuhzoma II, captured the imperial capital, plundered its stores of gold, and set in train the sequence of events by which the proud empire was reduced to the status of the colony of New Spain.

Hernán Cortés and 600 Spanish soldiers landed at San Juan de Ulua on the Mexican Gulf Coast in April 1519, lured by reports of an empire with unimaginable riches. Motecuhzoma initially suspected that the newcomers might be returning gods—for they landed at the very spot from which, according to Aztec tradition, the earthly incarnation of the god Quetzalcóatl had departed on a raft at the end of his worldly life, vowing to return. They also came in the Aztec calendar year (One Reed) predicted for his second coming.

The emperor sent envoys bearing magnificent offerings of gold, silver, and ceremonial costumes. The gift included ritually prepared food sprinkled with the blood of a sacrificial victim, which the Spaniards rejected. But the invaders were happy to accept the treasure, which only whetted their appetite for further riches. Cortés and his men marched inland, bound for the imperial capital, and reached Tlaxcala, an independent highland kingdom that had over many years successfully repulsed all Aztec attempts to bring it into the empire. The small Spanish force defeated the Tlaxcalans and then won their support for a campaign against Tenochtitlán.

The Spaniards' rejection of the ritual gifts and their alliance with Tlaxcala made it clear to Motecuhzoma that the new arrivals, far from being gods, were a real threat. He invited Cortés and his men into Tenochtitlán in the hope that Aztec warriors could defeat them there, in surroundings unfamiliar to the invaders. But once inside the city the Spaniards took the emperor prisoner.

Events developed swiftly and badly for the Aztecs: Montecuhzoma died in captivity and his brother, Cuitlahuac, was elected leader; the Spaniards stormed the Great Pyramid and set fire to the temple on its top—a great symbolic victory, for to Mesoamericans the capture of an enemy temple signified total conquest. Fearing major retaliation, the Spaniards retreated by night. After regrouping, they laid siege to Tenochtitlán and on 13 August 1521 they captured Cuitlahuac's successor Cuauhtemoc and seized his capital. Aztec might was at an end. The proud empire was brought to its knees.

SACRIFICE AND THE CYCLE OF ENERGY

The Aztecs believed that the gods had constructed the world, and that they were just as likely to destroy their creation if they were not sufficiently rewarded for their labors. To propitiate their gods the Aztecs conducted all manner of sacrificial rites—from the offering of small animals to bloodletting ceremonies and human sacrifice.

From the sun god Tonatiuh came heat and light, from the clouds sent by the rain god Tlaloc and blown into place by Quetzalcóatl (in his manifestation as the wind god Ehecatl) fell the waters that gave life to the maize crop. The Aztecs knew that they relied on the gods for their survival, that human life was part of a cosmic movement of energy. In the Nahuatl language spoken by the Aztecs, the word for sacrifice—*uemmana*—combined the word *mana* ("to pass on" or "to spread") with *uentli* ("offering"): sacrifice was a way of returning life energy to its source, an act essential to prolong and sustain the cycle of energy.

The Aztecs saw blood as the water of life, the offering that most pleased their gods. They called it *chalchiuatl* ("treasured water"). The most common form of public sacrifice was to tear the victim's heart from his or her chest as they were spreadeagled on a sacrificial stone called the *quauhxicalli* ("eagle stone"). This construction, situated at the top of the pyramid steps before the final approach to the temple, rose to a central point so that a victim held down against it would be forced to arch his back and so present his lower chest to the flint sacrificial knife, or *tecpatl*. The ceremony required six priests: four held the victim down on the sacrificial stone while a fifth seized his or her throat and the sixth and most senior priest sliced the prisoner's chest open. Reaching into the chest, the priest ripped free the victim's heart and held it up to the sun before casting it down before the god's image. The priests then lifted the lifeless body off the *quauhxicalli* and threw it down the steep, blood-slicked steps, and it came eventually to rest at the foot of the staircase. As victim after victim was despatched, the pile of corpses grew.

The Aztecs also made blood offerings in other ways. Aztec priests and worshippers offered up their own blood in rites of "autosacrifice" (see also pages 602–603). To draw blood they used

This early 16th-century handle once formed part of a sacrificial knife. It is made of wood inlaid with a decorative mosaic of turquoise, malachite, mother-of-pearl, and shell. It is not clear who is represented by the figure gripping the handle. In fact, it may not be a depiction of a specific deity, but rather a high-ranking individual from Aztec society.

◆ RITUAL CANNIBALISM ◆

The body of a sacrificial victim would often be consumed in a rite that shocked the Spanish conquistadors. A warrior might house and feed the prisoners he had taken in battle until the time came for their ritual death. After the sacrifice was completed the victim's body was decapitated and the head put on display. The dismembered corpse was removed to be cooked and then eaten with great ceremony by the warrior and his family. The victim's body had been sanctified by its part in the ritual on the temple steps and it now carried the gods' blessing—a reverse transmutation in which human flesh became sacred maize.

pieces of the volcanic glass obsidian and spines of the maguey cactus to cut themselves on the legs, arms, or earlobes, or they drew a cord of thorns across their penis or their tongue. Sometimes they soaked the blood into bark paper before offering it to the gods.

Some victims were sacrificed by burning to honor the fire god Xiuhtecuhtli. To celebrate Xipe Totec ("Our Flayed Lord"), god of vegetation and new shoots, a victim was shot with arrows and allowed to collapse on the ground as his lifeblood flowed out into the earth like the life-giving rains. Once the body had bled dry, it was flayed and the skin worn by a young man in a gruesome rite that represented the emergence of a fresh new plant from the split husk of the old.

Most victims were prisoners of war (indeed some wars were fought with the express purpose of supplying victims; see page 521). Before they met their fate, the prisoners were viewed with reverence. A warrior taking a victim for sacrifice would say "I find here a fine son,"

and he would reply "Here is a respected father." The victims went to their deaths as messengers to the gods. In some ceremonies they were seen as earthly representatives of the deities—they were *ixiptla* ("in the likeness of the gods"). Then the earthly realm was blessed: the gods were visible to the watching crowds as they became one with the victims of the sacrificial knife and reenacted the primal sacrifice at Teotihuacán that had given motion to the sun. To honor Chalchiuhtlicue, goddess of rivers, streams, oceans, and lakes, a young woman regarded as *ixiptla* was put to death during the festival of Huey Tozoztli at a place in Lake Texcoco called Pantitlán. The girl's blood was collected and poured into the water. In the festival of Toxcatl, an earthly representative of Tezcatlipoca was slain.

The Aztecs also made animal sacrifices, killing quails, dogs, turkeys, and jaguars for the pleasure of the gods. A jaguar's bones were interred when the foundations were being dug for the Great Pyramid in Tenochtitlán.

THE AZTEC CALENDAR

The Aztecs, like their Mesoamerican forebears, followed two calendars: one of 260 days and a 365-day count tracking the solar year. Priests used the 260-day cycle, or tonalpohualli ("numbering of the days"), primarily for divining the future, while the 365-day year calendar, or xiuhpohualli ("numbering of the years"), served mainly to mark agricultural seasons and religious festivals.

The *tonalpohualli* consisted of a cycle of twenty day names combined with the numbers one to thirteen. The names were those of animals, elements, and objects of daily life or of sacrificial significance: crocodile, wind, house, lizard, serpent, death's head, deer, rabbit, water, dog, monkey, grass, reed, jaguar, eagle, vulture, motion, flint knife, rain, and flower. The cycle began with One Crocodile, followed by Two Wind, Three House, Four Lizard, and so on. When the calendar reached Thirteen Reed, the numerical cycle began again with the fourteenth name—Thirteen Reed, One Jaguar, Two Eagle, Three Vulture, and so on; and when the sequence reached the end of the twenty names, the name order began again with the next number—Seven Flower, then Eight Crocodile, Nine Wind, and so on. Each time the number cycle returned to one was the beginning of a new thirteen-day "week" within the 260-day year. The Spaniards who recorded the use of the calendar called these "weeks" *trecena*.

Records of the 260-day calendar were kept in long screen-fold books made of bark paper called *tonalamatl* (a combination of the words for the calendar, *tonalpohualli*, and the bark paper, *amatl*). When written down, the numbers were represented by a system of dots and each of the day names was rendered as a small hieroglyphic symbol (see illustration, opposite).

The *xiuhpohualli* consisted of eighteen twenty-day months, plus a period of five ill-omened days called *nemontemi* at year's end. Each month was associated with a particular deity and contained a religious festival, usually connected to the agricultural seasons and honoring that god or goddess. During the *nemontemi*, priests, rulers, and common people tried to refrain from all activity for they felt that any actions would come to no good. They did not leave the house to tend the fields or work the market stalls. They allowed domestic fires to go out, broke their crockery, abstained from eating, and even stopped talking. They looked forward to the new year, but in trepidation.

Using the two calendars together created a longer cycle. A particular day in the year count intersected with a day in the day count only once every 18,980 days—equivalent to once every seventy-three *tonalpohualli* cycles or once in fifty-two *xiuhpohualli* years. Aztec custom was to keep count of the years in a fifty-two-year cycle by making a bundle of sticks. From this practice they took the name "bundle of years" for a fifty-two-year cycle. At the end of each cycle they ceremonially burned the bundle as part of ceremonies to inaugurate the new cycle.

The way in which the two calendars intersected meant that each new year in the *xiuhpohualli* year calendar could begin with one of only four day names from the *tonalpohualli* day calendar: rabbit, reed, flint knife, or house. The name that fell on the first day of the year was celebrated as the "year bearer." There were twenty days in each *xiuhpohualli* month and twenty day names

• THE ORIGINS OF THE 260-DAY CALENDAR •

Use of the *tonalpohualli* can be traced far back into the Mesoamerican past—perhaps as far as the Olmec in the mid-second millennium BCE. There are various theories explaining the origin of the calendar.

Some historians argue that the 260-day interval was originally that between planting and harvest in the Mesoamerican agricultural year. The magical power associated with the period in which plants take life in the earth may have been reinforced by the hallowed cycle of the planet Venus: 260 days corresponds roughly to the time lapse between the first sighting of Venus as the Evening Star and the planet's coming as the Morning Star. But other scholars suggest that 260 days (roughly thirty-seven weeks) may have been the measure used by Mesoamerican midwives to predict the length of a woman's pregnancy when counting forward from her last menstrual period. The Maya also used the 260-day calendar and their descendants in modern Guatemala report that the length of the *tonalpohualli* is based on that of human pregnancy.

in the *tonalpohualli* cycle: therefore the day sign associated with the first day of the year also fell on the first of every month and was celebrated as the "month bearer" as well as the year bearer. Within larger cycles, the years took their name from their year bearer. In the fifty-two-year bundle of years, the year bearers took the numbers one to thirteen in succession: for example, One Rabbit, Two Reed, Three Flint Knife, Four House, Five Rabbit, Six Reed, and so on. The combined calendars could identify any day within a fifty-two-year cycle, but there was no means of distinguishing between one fifty-two-year cycle and the next.

A YEAR OF FESTIVALS

Major Aztec religious festivals were associated with the stages of the agricultural year. Each of the eighteen "months" of the 365-day xiuhpohualli *year calendar (see pages 510–511) was the setting for at least one festival.*

The first month, which corresponded to the period from 14 February to 5 March, shortly before planting of crops, contained the festival of Atlcaualo ("Stopping of Water"), in which children were sacrificed and other offerings made to the maize deities and to the rain god Tlaloc. Planting ceremonies were performed in the *chinampa* floating fields during the festival of Tozoztontli ("Minor Vigil") in the third month (26 March–14 April) and offerings again made to Tlaloc, to the water goddess Chalchiuhtlicue, to the maize god Centeotl, and to the major fertility goddess Cóatlicue.

The close of the dry season was ushered in during the sixth month (23 May–13 June) in the festival of Etzalcualiztli ("Eating of Bean and Maize Stew"), when priests held ceremonial fasts to encourage Tlaloc to send rain, reeds were harvested from the lake to make seating mats and to decorate temples, offerings were made to Chalchiuhtlicue and the Feathered Serpent Quetzalcóatl as well as to Tlaloc, and nobles ate a dish of maize and beans. Harvest was marked in the eleventh month (2–21 September) with the festival of Ochpaniztli ("Sweeping Clean") and offerings to earth goddesses, and in the twelfth month (22 September–11 October) with Teotleco ("Homecoming of the Deities") when all the gods were celebrated and there was general feasting.

Each of the months was held to be sacred to one of the major gods and goddesses of the Aztec pantheon. At the close of the month a sacrificial victim arrayed in the likeness of the deity was put to death with great ceremony. As part of the celebration a new "likeness" was chosen: that person would be kept in luxury for a year then put to death when the festival came round once more a year later (see box, left).

One of the most important religious festivals was Panquetzaliztli ("Lifting of the Banners") held in honor of the Aztecs' patron god Huitzilopochtli during the fifteenth month (21 November–10 December). The festival fell after the harvest, as the Aztecs prepared for a return to military life—either a genuine campaign to restore the rule of Aztec law or another episode in the "flower wars" fought against nearby states to generate a supply of sacrificial victims (see page 521). In Panquetzaliztli, large numbers of victims were sacrificed to Huitzilopochtli—including the "bathed slaves," individuals who had been purchased for slaughter by wealthy merchants who hoped thereby to win the

• DEATH AT TOXCATL •

The fifth month (5–22 May) saw the festival of Toxcatl ("Drought"), in which a youthful impersonator of the god Tezcatlipoca was ceremonially put to death. For a full year the young man was kept in luxury. He was taught the flute and the dance steps of the god and passed by houses at night, playing his instrument as he went: people waited with sick relatives to greet him, believing that he was able to cure illness. In the days before his death, the victim was dressed in sacrificial robes by the emperor himself, and for his pleasure was given four young women, said to be incarnations of major goddesses. For the final five days of the month the emperor went upon a religious retreat and Tezcatlipoca himself was said to be ruling in his stead. On the day of the sacrifice, the young man was led to Tezcatlipoca's shrine in the center of Tenochtitlán and his heart was torn from his chest over the sacrificial stone. Then his body was cooked and eaten by the emperor and leading nobles in a sacred meal.

gods' blessing. The "bathed slaves" were often skilled musicians or dancers, for they were put to work in the weeks before the ceremony entertaining the merchants' guests. Nine days prior to the sacrifice they were washed in the water of a spring blessed by Huitzilopochtli himself. On the day itself the company of slaves was led up the steps of the pyramid to Huitzilopochtli's shrine, where they were despatched one by one on the sacrificial stone. Afterward the merchant and his guests consumed the bodies of the victims, which had been sanctified by their part in the ritual (see also box, page 509).

Some festivals did not fit into the annual calendar. Of these the most important was Toxiuhmolpilia ("Tying of the Years"), held at the transition from one fifty-two-year cycle, or "bundle" (see page 511), to the next—

when emperor, priests, and people feared that the gods might bring the creation to an end. All fires were put out and the people waited in penitence and fearful wonder. A new fire was kindled in the chest of a sacrificial victim in a ceremony on Mount Huixachtlán to the south of Lake Texcoco. Runners waited to carry the new fire from the mountain to temples in Tenochtitlán and across the region.

As well as formal temple ceremonies, Aztec religious observance involved worship in the home. Offerings were made to earth goddesses, who were represented by small pottery figurines. The figures below left and below right depict fertility deities, while the central figure probably represents a male "eagle warrior" (see page 518).

PEOPLE OF THE SUN GOD

Aztec society was divided into two mutually exclusive groups: the pipiltin *(nobles) and the* macehuales *(commoners). No matter how much wealth a commoner might accumulate, it was not possible to join the élite of nobles that surrounded the emperor.*

Many privileges were reserved for nobles: they could take more than one wife, build houses of more than one story, and send their sons to priestly schools to learn the skills of reading and writing, military strategy, and religious lore—including the secrets of divining by the ritual calendar. Nobles were permitted to wear sandals and cotton clothing, while commoners were required to go barefoot and could only wear cactus-fiber garments.

The prestige and wealth of the nobility was boosted by the income they received from landholdings. The most senior nobles were advisers to the emperor: they sat on a noble council and had the right to vote on the question of who should succeed the emperor at the end of his reign. On this decision, they generally followed the emperor's recommendation. Other nobles took senior military posts or positions at the top of the priestly hierarchy. Some were appointed as provincial governors, ambassadors to subject states within the empire, judges, or tax collectors. More junior members of the élite class became teachers and scribes.

Commoners were soldiers or worked as farmers or fishermen. Some men, called *mayeque*, farmed fields belonging to the nobility. Land not owned by nobles

This page from the Codex Magliabechiano, *an original Aztec document with Spanish annotation, shows a member of the noble* pipiltin *class wearing the white cotton robes befitting his rank. He is depicted presiding over an initiation ceremony and offering incense to the god of fire Xiuhtecuhtli.*

was generally held in common by tribal clans, or *capultin*, and most of the farmers worked land or floating fields belonging to their clan. Commoners paid tax to the emperor and, when called, were required to work on major building projects or to serve in the army. A limited form of slavery existed: people could choose to become slaves when they were very poor, but could repurchase their freedom or have it bought on their behalf by members of their tribal clan.

Commoners working as artisans or merchants had the chance to accumulate substantial wealth. Artisans producing ritual costumes, feathered headdresses, splendid jewelry, and ornaments were held in such high regard that they were given a name, *tolteca*, that linked them to the revered Toltecs. Some worked for nobles, but most were their own masters. Merchants also generally worked as free agents. From distant parts of the empire they brought quetzal feathers and precious metals used in Aztec religious spectacle—although these and other rare commodities were also part of the extensive tribute demanded by the Aztec imperial government from subject peoples. Some merchants worked undercover as spies, exploiting their position to gather information on any relevant subject or about allied rulers who might be preparing trouble.

The army provided the best opportunity for social mobility. Lesser soldiers could win significant social privileges, such as the right to wear cotton clothing and sandals, to keep concubines for their pleasure, to drink the alcoholic drink *pulque* in public and to attend feasts in the imperial palace. No commoner could reach the most senior positions in the military hierarchy, which were reserved for nobles. Similarly, while the priesthood

• PRIESTLY HIERARCHY •

The emperor stood at the head of a hierarchy of priests. The Great Pyramid in Tenochtitlán had twin shrines at its summit—one to Huitzilopochtli and one to Tlaloc—and the cults of these two gods each had their own high priest. A third priest, occupying a position immediately beneath these two, was the Mexicatl Teohuatzin, in charge of the priestly school and of religious ritual. Below him, two groups of officials, the Huitznahua Teohuatzin and the Tecpan Teohuatzin, were in charge of all other more junior priests. In particular, the Tecpan Teohuatzin were responsible for land belonging to the Aztec temples and for selecting people to impersonate gods and goddesses at major festivals.

Some priests were members of the army and carried images of the gods and goddesses into battle. Some were writers and painters of codex manuscripts, others were specialists in divination, astrology, and astronomy: these skilled individuals set the dates for religious festivals based on reading the calendar and watching the skies. Some women served as priests, especially in fertility rites in praise of earth and maize goddesses.

took people from all ranks of society, its highest positions were reserved for members of the nobility.

The divisions in Aztec society became blurred as the empire aged, with the growth of a new class of soldiers who had been granted conquered territory as reward for military prowess. They formed a second tier of nobility, beneath members of noble families of long standing. Partly to address this issue, Motecuhzoma II attempted to elevate the standing of the traditional nobility by reinforcing existing rules on what was permitted for members of the two classes and introducing new ceremonies that elevated *pipiltin* further above *macehuales*.

THE DIVINE KING

At his coronation the Aztec emperor was filled with the fire of the gods. His primary roles were as commander-in-chief of the army and chief priest. His people also relied upon him to safeguard the fertility of the land: he was expected to achieve success in battle, thereby providing a plentiful supply of victims for sacrifices that would please the gods who might otherwise send plagues or drought.

The emperor, ruler of Tenochtitlán, was known as *tlatoani* ("he who speaks"). As the chief priest, burning with divine fire, he was lifted above mere mortals and enabled to speak to the gods. As the army's chief warrior he was considered to be an incarnation of the fearsome war god Huitzilopochtli himself. His divine status meant he was set apart: none of his subjects was permitted to look him in the eye or sit with him while he ate—he was expected always to dine alone.

The *tlatoani* led a number of sacrificial rituals himself: they were understood to renew his divine power. He played a leading part in the fertility offering made at a temple high on Mount Tlaloc, near Tenochtitlán, during the dry season in April to May each year. In the company of the rulers of Texcoco, Tlacopán and Xochimilco, the *tlatoani* of Tenochtitlán led a pilgrimage to the mountain temple, which contained a group of rocks laid out to mimic the arrangements of the mountains visible from the peak. The rulers dressed the rocks in ceremonial costumes and made offerings to them of food and a male infant's blood. Then they shared a feast on the open mountainside, beneath the wide sky. The ceremony was intended as an offering to the earth, and in particular to Mount Tlaloc as the bringer of rains.

The divine emperor had a fittingly magnificent appearance. He wore a decorated waistcoat, or *xicolli*, and his body was hung with gold and silver jewelry and stones of jade and crystal. He sported the green quetzal feathers associated both with royal authority and the Plumed Serpent god Quetzalcóatl in his guise as Topiltzin, the wise ruler of Tollan. For religious ceremonial he wore a sacred costume in honor of the gods.

The position of emperor was officially elected rather than hereditary: the *tlatoani* would recommend a successor to his council of nobles, who would then vote on the succession. In practice power often passed to a close blood relation of the ruler: for example, following the triumphant reign of Motecuhzoma I (reigned 1440–1469), three of his grandsons—Axayacatl, Tizoc, and Ahuizotl—came to power one after the other. When the successor was approved he would go through complex coronation rites in the course of which he was blessed by one of the high priests.

After the death of the previous *tlatoani*, the new ruler was presented to the people dressed humbly in a loincloth, then led up the Great Pyramid to the shrine of Huitzilopochtli, where he donned a green robe and devoutly lit incense to the war god. The new ruler then began a four-day retreat within the military quarter or Tlacochcalco in the sacred precinct, ascending to the pyramid-top shrine of Huitzilopochtli every twelve hours to make offerings of his own blood, drawn from his arms, legs, or earlobes.

After the retreat at a palace ceremony the new ruler was dressed in a shining robe, a greenstone crown, and golden jewelry and then seated on a throne covered with eagle feathers and the skins of the royal jaguar. In a splendid litter he was carried to Huitzilopochtli's temple to make further offerings of his blood using jaguar claws to pierce his veins, then returned to the palace for speeches and further ceremonial.

Afterward the new emperor embarked on a military campaign to demonstrate by success in battle that his

---

One of the few to survive, this magnificent headdress was supposed to have belonged to Motecuhzoma II, who ruled Tenochtitlán from 1502 to 1520. Measuring nearly 7 feet (1.75m) in width, the headdress contains 450 quetzal feathers.

rule had the gods' blessing. If this campaign should fail, as in the case of Motecuhzoma's grandson Tizoc (1481–1486), it was considered a very bad prognosis for the new reign. But when the campaign was a success—as in the reign of Tizoc's successor Ahuizotl (1486–1502)—the new ruler returned to Tenochtitlán in triumph bearing tribute, battlefield booty, and hundreds of prisoners destined for the sacrificial knife.

Following the coronation campaign a ceremony called the confirmation took place, which included stately dancing in the palace and culminated in the sacrifice of the war captives at the Great Pyramid.

THE WARRIOR HERO

The Aztecs learned the importance of warfare from early in life—the children of the nobility studied military lore in priestly schools, coming to understand that the best offering they could make to the gods was to fight bravely in battle and harvest enemy troops for sacrifice.

The goal of a young soldier was to become a member of either the eagle or the jaguar warriors, who had the right to wear splendid cloaks, feather head-dresses, jewelry, and helmets. To join one of these élite groups, a soldier had to win great battle honors by performing no fewer than twenty deeds of remarkable bravery. Eagles and jaguars were considered the bravest of creatures: at the beginning of the current world age, when the gods Nanahuatzin and Tecuciztecatl sacrificed themselves by fire to become the sun and moon (see page 529), the eagle and jaguar were the first to follow them into the flames. The two creatures also had royal associations: the decorative paraphernalia of kingship included jaguar pelts and claws and eagle feathers.

In the temple precincts close to the Great Pyramid at the centre of Tenochtitlán, the eagle and jaguar warriors kept meeting houses in which they trained young recruits. Promising youths were allowed to follow their heroes into battle, where the trainees' responsibility was to carry and care for the warriors' military equipment.

Soldiers in battle wore padded cotton clothing made tougher by being given a soaking in brine. The jaguar warriors were permitted to throw a jaguar skin over the top of this simple outfit, while their eagle counterparts could wear a headdress of eagle feathers. Rank-and-file soldiers usually had a simple wrapping around the loins and a maguey-cloth coat and many wore wooden helmets; they sometimes donned body paint to add to their intimidating martial appearance. All soldiers fought at close quarters, using short javelins for stabbing and

The emperor Tizoc (reigned 1481–1486) was relatively ineffective, but he still managed to add 14 towns to the empire. He celebrated these successes with the so-called Stone of Tizoc (opposite), which showed his warriors holding defeated opponents by the hair.

◆ MOTHERS AND SONS REVERED ◆

The Aztecs accorded great honor to women who died while giving birth to male children. Male babies were viewed as warriors from the moment of conception—like their god Huitzilopochtli, who in the instant of his birth seized weapons to attack and kill hundreds of his brothers and his sister the moon goddess Coyolxauhqui. A woman who died in childbirth had been vanquished during labor by the strength of her unborn son. The spirits of women who died in this way, called *cihuateteo*, were transported instantly to the heaven of the sun god in his aspect as Tonatiuh, where they mingled with the undaunted souls of warriors slain in battle. The two groups were also said to share the labor of hauling the sun in his daily passage across the sky. In the morning the sun was pulled from the eastern horizon to the zenith by the spirits of warriors who took the form of hummingbirds for their task; after noon, the *cihuateteo* took over, escorting the sun downward from the top of the sky to his evening position in the west.

wielding clubs fitted with very sharp blades made from the volcanic glass obsidian. The most effective killing tool was probably the *atlatl* dart-thrower, which consisted of a spear into which a dart could be fitted.

A warrior whose main concern was honor had nothing to fear in battle. If he prevailed and took many prisoners he won a proud reputation and military and social benefits. If he was killed, he would be judged to have died an honorable death: his body would be cremated and his spirit would pass to the heaven of Tonatiuichan, reserved for the brave and presided over by the sun god in his aspect as Tonatiuh. If he was captured, he would be treated with respect and was destined for a magnificent ritual death as a victim of the sun god.

THE ART OF WAR

For the Aztecs war was charged with religious significance: it was a reenactment of cosmic struggles fought every day in the sky between the sun, bringing light and warmth, and the forces of cold and darkness. It was fitting that the Aztecs, as people of the sun, should celebrate the star's ancient self-sacrifice at Teotihuacán and his daily triumph in the sky by offering up enemy prisoners. Warfare also brought economic and territorial gains. Clearly, the Aztecs could not have been oblivious to the benefits of their empire, particularly the vast amounts of tribute that poured into Tenochtitlán each year. But empire-building, too, had its religious dimension: when the *tlatoani* (see page 516) and his army embarked on campaigns to

This terracotta representation of an eagle warrior was found in the House of Eagles, near the Great Temple of Tenochtitlán. The building was used for religious rituals such as prayer, penance, and self-sacrifice. Recent studies suggest that this figure may represent the sun at dawn.

consolidate or extend the territory of the Triple Alliance, their endeavor was in part to honor the tribal god Huitzilopochtli and fulfil his prophecy that they would become masters of a great realm.

A major priority was always to generate a supply of sacrificial victims. When no empire-building campaign was under way, a ceremonial war would be launched purely to gather prisoners. These staged conflicts were called *xochiyaotl* ("wars of flowers"), because the magnificently dressed warriors who were taken prisoner were gathered up like a floral garland to please the gods. The earliest known flower war was probably the conflict that pitted the Mexica and Tepanecs against the Chalca, which began in 1376. Over the following century the Triple Alliance cities of Tenochtitlán, Texcoco and Tlacopán fought regular *xochiyaotl* campaigns against Cholula, Tlaxcala, and Huexotcingo.

The brother of Motecuhzoma I, Tlacaélel, was chief military adviser to five successive Aztec emperors— Itzcoatl, Motecuhzoma I, Axayacatl, Tizoc, and Ahuizotl. He made a celebrated summary of the outlook that informed the flower wars, declaring that the Aztecs' god Huitzilopochtli had need of victims just as humans required food, and that through his people he selected victims on the battlefield just as a shopper picks up tortillas in the market. Tlacaélel said that the god preferred the blood of local peoples to that of distant enemies, and so the flower wars should be conducted against neighbors and nearby allies. A flower war should be stopped before the enemy were annihilated, so that conflict could be picked up again in the future when Huitzilopochtli again had need of sustenance.

To the Aztecs, indeed, warfare was generally not a fight to the death: conflict would cease when one side accepted defeat; a warrior's principal aim was to win renown by gathering booty and collecting prisoners. This attitude probably contributed to the Aztecs' downfall at the hands of the Spaniards. On the night of 30 June 1520, when Cortés and his men fled Tenochtitlán, the Aztecs overwhelmed the Spaniards and had them at their mercy—but did not wipe out the invading force entirely. Satisfied that they had won the encounter, the Aztec soldiers returned to Tenochtitlán bearing booty and prisoners, and allowed Cortés to regroup in order to launch the siege of the imperial capital in 1521 that would undo Aztec power.

◆ GLADIATORIAL SLAUGHTER ◆

The Aztecs' liking for ceremonial conflict also found expression in the rite of gladiatorial sacrifice, which took place at Tlacaxipehualiztli ("Feast of the Flaying of Men") held in March, approaching the rainy season. The festival honored Xipe Totec, god of vegetation and generating seeds—and during it priests donned the flayed skins of sacrificed victims and wore them for twenty days. In a separate rite, prisoners of war were placed on a raised platform and tethered to a stone before being pitted against élite warriors. Each prisoner was dressed as Xipe Totec and armed only lightly with a feather-covered club. He was then attacked by up to five Aztecs with sharp, obsidian-bladed clubs—two warriors each from the jaguar and eagle fraternities, together with one from either whose strength resided in his left hand. Although the prisoner was elevated and could inflict fatal blows, he would be disabled gradually by lower-limb wounds, which meant blood flowed into the earth like the farmers' longed-for downpour.

THE POWER OF EMPIRE

Spectators gazing up the steep, blood-stained steps of the Aztecs' Great Pyramid at magnificently attired priests performing a sacrificial ritual against the backdrop of the sun-drenched sky must have felt the stirrings of awe in their hearts. Tenochtitlán's grand buildings and colorful religious ceremonies amounted to an expression of divine, kingly, and state power.

The scale of the towering temple pyramid and the prolonged, time-honored ritual performed by the priests was testament to the eternal force of the gods, to the status of the emperor, and to the wealth and grandeur of the Aztec Empire. Such displays of power were sustained by the flow of tribute from the empire. The Aztecs did not conquer all the territories they governed: many city-states and chiefdoms were required to pay tribute to the Triple Alliance of Tenochtitlán, Texcoco, and Tlacopán but often were otherwise independent. It was policy to allow local rulers to retain power as long as payments were delivered on time.

Each of the three members of the Triple Alliance drew tribute from particular areas of the empire. When the Alliance fought a joint campaign, the prisoners, wealth, and tribute were divided according to agreed terms, with twenty percent for Tlacopán and forty per cent each for Tenochtitlán and Texcoco. The terms of the treaty agreed by defeated opponents specified a timetable for delivery of tribute and the Aztecs usually put a tribute collector in place to see that the treaty was honored; where tribute dried up, the imperial army would be sent to remind backsliders of their obligations.

An enormous variety of tribute was paid, ranging from basic foodstuffs such as maize, beans, and chillies to precious materials such as jade, gold, and jaguar skins. According to Diego Durán's *History of the Indies of New Spain and Islands of Tierra Firme* (1581), tribute

---

◆ THE DEDICATION OF THE GREAT TEMPLE ◆

The emperor Ahuizotl oversaw an awe-inspiring four-day ritual sacrifice to dedicate the Templo Mayor, Tenochtitlán's Great Temple, to the gods. The Mexica had built a small temple, known only from written records, when they settled at Tenochtitlán in 1325 (see page 504), but it was Ahuizotl's grandfather Motecuhzoma I who began the building of the Great Temple, or Great Pyramid. In 1487, some nineteen years after Motecuhzoma's death in 1468, the great building was ready to be sanctified with blood offerings. Ahuizotl had come to power the previous year after the ineffective reign of Tizoc, and spent the first year putting down revolts in imperial provinces. This campaign must have furnished many prisoners of war, for the dedication of the Great Temple is said to have accounted for more than 80,000 lives. Ahuizotl himself despatched the first victim and offered his heart to the new pyramid-top shrine to Huitzilopochtli, which towered high above the city. Ranks of priests stood in attendance, waiting to play their part at the eagle stone with the obsidian-bladed sacrificial knife. For four days seemingly endless lines of prisoners were led through the temple precinct and up the side of the Great Pyramid to a holy death. Blood dried on the steep pyramid steps, then flowed terribly once more. This spectacular slaughter must have cast a terrifying spell over onlookers and made a dreadful impression on the subject peoples of the empire.

---

deliveries included bales of cotton cloth, sacks of cacao beans, rare colored feathers, blankets, cotton clothing and splendid decorated robes, seashells, precious metals, wood, stone, and weapons – including bows, slings and flint arrowheads. Some dependencies paid tribute in birds such as parrots, eagles, kestrels, geese, and goslings; others sent spiders, scorpions, cats, deer, tigers, and even lions; others sent local delicacies such as pineapples, plums, and bananas. Some provided tree bark, chopped wood, or charcoal; others sent flowers, rose bushes, and fine perfumes; still others gave up honeycombs and beehives. Those who had nothing else to offer were required to send their young people—boys and young men to become slaves and construction workers, girls and young women to serve as concubines for the lords of Tenochtitlán.

The supply of tribute was supplemented by commercial trading performed by professional merchants. In the later years of the Aztec Empire the amount of luxury tribute increased when judged as a proportion of the whole. The empire's increasing size meant that there were more provinces able to supply rare goods, while the rising levels of wealth in Tenochtitlán led to a new desire for display among the nobles of the city.

Ceremony and architecture were designed to impress not only the emperor's subjects but also outsiders—enemies or allies. Within the empire some provinces were allied through marriage to Tenochtitlán, and the terms of the alliance often required their youthful nobles and future rulers to live in the imperial capital, where they would witness at first hand the unassailable might of the emperor who presided over the ceremonies, of the army that delivered such vast numbers of sacrificial victims, and of the gods who were worthy of such devotion.

The Aztecs recorded the amounts and types of tribute they were due to receive on codex pages such as the one recreated in this modern artwork. The list of items was long and varied, ranging from simple commodities such as maize to the finest perfumes and precious stones and metals.

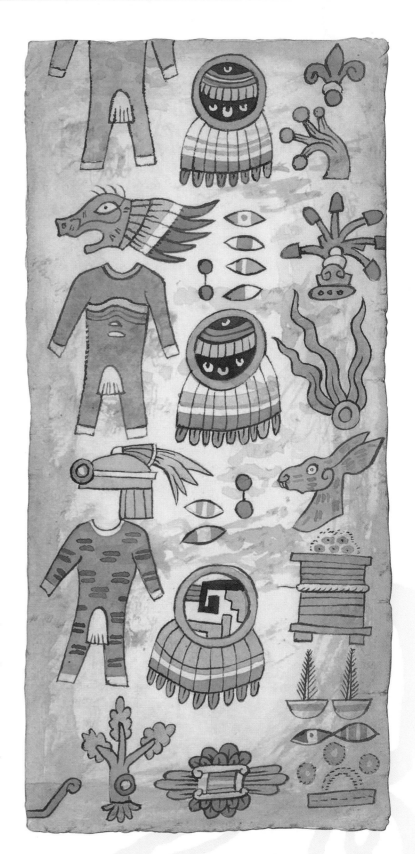

AZTEC WRITING

Key elements of Aztec culture—including instructions for ritual practice, astronomical cycles, details of the sacred calendar, and accounts of cosmology and tribal history—were passed on by oral tradition and recorded in manuscript books called codices.

Documents such as the *tonalamatl* used as reference manuals on the ritual calendar by priests were generally made from strips of deerskin glued together and coated with white lime, then folded over and over in a long screenfold; some were fashioned from *amatl* paper, which derived from the bark of the wild fig tree.

The *Codex Fejérváry-Mayer* (created before 1521) is a rare surviving example of a *tonalamatl* written before the Conquest. It contains details of the 365-day *xiuhpohualli* and the 260-day *tonalpohualli* (see pages 510–511), together with a listing of tribute due to the gods throughout the year. The *Codex Cospi* is another pre-Conquest Mesoamerican book: holding detailed information about the ritual and Venus calendars, it is of the Mixtec culture. The names attached to these manuscripts belong to their later European owners—Gabriel Fejérváry, Joseph Mayer, and Ferdinando Cospi.

Most surviving manuscripts were written after the Spanish Conquest. In the immediate aftermath of the events of 1519–1521, a large number of Aztec books were destroyed by Spanish churchmen driven by a zeal to extinguish native religious beliefs and customs that they saw as idolatrous. Subsequently churchmen made efforts to record and interpret local knowledge, in the belief that information about native rites would be useful when converting Mesoamericans to Christianity. Other post-Conquest manuscripts were written by natives who had been educated in Spanish colonial schools.

In the pre-Conquest era, expert scribes known as *tlacuiloque* combined the skills of writers and illustrators. The iconic script they used combined pictograms (in which a picture represents a word or idea), with phonetic signs and mathematical symbols. To write the word "Tenochtitlán," for example, a scribe would draw a stone (*tena*) with a nopal cactus (*nochtli*) growing from it; the image had added meaning as a pictogram because Tenochtitlán was founded at the place where the Mexica discovered a cactus bearing an eagle holding a snake and

---

• SPANISH INTERPRETERS •

Two compendious accounts of Aztec history, culture, and religious belief were compiled by Spanish churchmen. The *Codex Durán* was written by the missionary-priest Diego Durán (1537–1588) between 1570 and 1581 and collected in three volumes under the title *History of the Indies of New Spain and Islands of Tierra Firme*. Durán's work contains a history of the Aztecs, a survey of deities and festivals, and an account of the calendar and elements of daily life. The *Florentine Codex* was compiled in 1558–1560 by the friar and missionary Bernardino de Sahagún (1499–1590) and collected in three volumes as *General History of the Things of New Spain*. It became known as the *Florentine Codex* because the manuscript ended up in the Italian city of Florence. Sahagún's encyclopaedic survey contains information on Aztec society, history, calendar, religion, and views on the natural world. His work is more sympathetic to the culture it describes than the books of Durán, who declared his conviction that it was necessary to erase from natives' memories "all ceremonies and superstitions and the false worship of the false deities in which they put their faith."

This detail from a page of the Codex Cospi *shows the sun god (top) and the god of darkness (bottom) making offerings. Produced by the Mixtec culture between 1350 and 1500, the* Codex Cospi *is one of the few pre-Hispanic codices not to have been destroyed by the Europeans.*

growing from a rocky island (see pages 504–507). The writing system was largely based on earlier hieroglyphic systems developed by the Olmecs and the Zapotecs.

Several different types of document were produced by the Aztecs: as well as the *tonalamatl* books, there were histories or annals, law books, dream manuals, and tribute lists; some manuscripts combined these different functions. In addition to screenfold books, documents called *tiras* took the form of long rolls of *amatl* paper. Maps were drawn on a single sheet of this paper.

Documents such as tribute lists required a written notation for numbers. The Aztec system of counting was on a base of 20, like those used elsewhere in Mesoamerica. Numbers up to 19 were represented with dots; 20 was symbolised by a feather; 400 (20 times 20) was indicated by a flag glyph; 8,000 (20 times 20 times 20) was a symbol for a bag of incense. A scribe wanting to record "twenty bags of cacao beans," for example, would draw an image of a feather connected to an image of a bag of beans. Historians were able to decipher this numbering system by studying the *Codex Mendoza* (ca. 1541), which contains a list of tribute due to Motecuhzoma II together with Spanish-language annotation alongside the original glyphs.

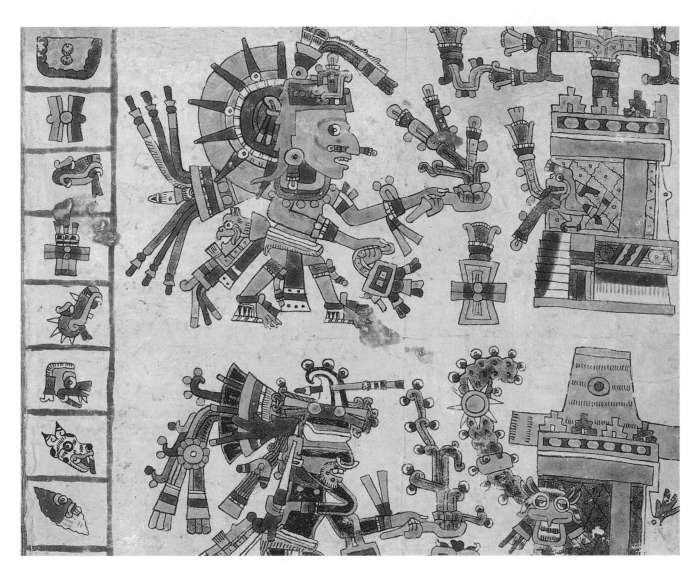

THE FIVE SUNS

The Aztecs believed that the world was periodically destroyed and remade by the gods. We live, they said, in the fifth world age: the current era and each of its four predecessors was under the rule of a particular god, who took the form of the sun in order to govern.

Each world age was named after the day on which it ended: the first world, for example, came to a close on the day Four Jaguar in the year One Reed and so the era was known as the "Jaguar Sun" (Nahui Ocelotl). In the first days Black Tezcatlipoca established himself as

the sun. He was one of the four Tezcatlipocas distinguished by color who, according to one Aztec tradition, were born of the divine primal couple Ometecuhtli and Omecihuatl and charged with creating other gods, the world, and the first people. Black Tezcatlipoca was later worshipped as the god of destiny and darkness Tezcatlipoca. His three counterparts were White Tezcatlipoca, subsequently revered as Quetzalcóatl; Blue Tezcatlipoca, later identified as the Aztec tribal lord Huitzilpochtli; and Red Tezcatlipoca, afterward worshipped as Xipe Totec, the lord of the germinating maize plant.

In the first world age Black Tezcatlipoca began his rule immediately after the creation. In his era, which lasted 676 years and was linked to the element of earth, a race of giants inhabited the lands of Mexico. These huge men were so strong that they could pluck trees from the parched earth and hurl them through the sun-dried air; they lived on a diet of pine nuts. But the first creation was consumed after White Tezcatlipoca, or Quetzalcóatl, grew jealous of his brother's brilliance in the sky and knocked him from the heavens into the seas at the far ends of the earth. Black Tezcatlipoca's anger was great and, turning himself into a ravening jaguar, he killed and ate the giants before rising into the night sky to become the constellation of Ursa Major (the Great Bear).

The second world age was governed by Quetzalcóatl, who rose as the great bright sun in

---

Few representations of Tezcatlipoca survive. This pot in the form of the god's head dates from around 1500. Normally images of Tezcatlipoca can be recognized by their black coloring: in this case the black takes the form of three narrow bands across the god's face.

his form as the wind god Ehecatl. Under his rule, in an age associated with the element of air, the people of Mexico lived on the seeds of the mesquite tree. But the age came to an end when Tezcatlipoca, who himself had an aspect as storm and wind god, sent a powerful hurricane that drove the sun from the sky and swept the Aztecs' predecessors into the thick forest. There they were transformed into a race of monkeys who lived on without the blessing of the sun's light through an age of darkness. The "Wind Sun" (Nahui Ehecatl) lasted 364 years; its final cataclysm occurred on the day Four Wind in the year One Flint.

The third age was linked to the element of fire and endured for 312 years. At its inception the rain god Tlaloc rose into the sky as the sun, and by his light a new people thrived in Mexico: in one account they were agricultural pioneers who lived on an early form of grain, but in another version they were hunter–gatherers who consumed the water lily and other water plants. Quetzalcóatl again destroyed the creation, sending a fiery storm of ash that once more plunged the Earth

According to Aztec belief, the current world age will be brought to an end by earthquakes powerful enough to flatten even the mighty volcano Popocatepetl (see page 528).

into darkness by sweeping the sun from the sky. The firestorm burned up most of the people: a few survivors were transformed into butterflies, dogs, and turkeys. The age was known as the "Rain Sun" (Nahui Quiahuitl) after the rain god and because it came to a close on the day Four Rain in the year One Flint.

The fourth sun, associated with water, was presided over by Chalchiuhtlicue, the goddess of rivers, lakes, and oceans. In this era the people lived on a seed called *acicintli*. Chalchiuhtlicue's era was the first in which the ruling deity brought the age to an end: she swept away creation with a great flood; the Mexicans of this time were transformed into fish. The world of Chalchiuhtlicue, known as "Water Sun" (Nahui Atl), lasted 676 years. It ended on the day Four Water in the year One House.

The current world age was ushered in when the gods, gathered in the sacred city of Teotihuacán, set the sun and moon moving in the sky (see below). Governed by the sun god Tonatiuh, the age saw the full development of agriculture and the cultivation of maize. The era takes its name from the day in the sacred calendar—Four Ollin (Four Earthquake)—on which the creation at Teotihuacán occurred. This sacred day is also one of baleful significance, for according to Aztec tradition the world is destined to be destroyed on a future Four Ollin. Then dark Tezcatlipoca will send powerful earthquakes to rock the foundations of the mightiest mountains, bringing low even the proud peaks of Popocatepetl and Iztaccihuatl. A famine will follow that will wipe out all human life.

CREATION AT TEOTIHUACÁN

The Earth and heavens had to be created anew following the destruction of the Water Sun by the goddess Chalchiuhtlicue. The divine lords Tezcatlipoca and Quetzalcóatl, usually implacable enemies, agreed to work together in the new creation. When they encountered the earth monster Tlatecuhtli swimming the oceans that had engulfed the planet, the two gods took the form of powerful snakes and shot dangerously toward her, their eyes bright and muscles flexing. With a single powerful effort, they raised the monster from the water and tore her in two, casting one half upward to make the sky and laying the other down to form the wide, dry earth.

The other deities now lent their powers to the creation, using the earthly portion of Tlatecuhtli as their raw material. At the divine command springs and sacred

---

The mighty Mesoamerican deity Quetzalcóatl played a varied and significant role in the Earth's five ages of creation. He is depicted here in his guise as Ehecatl, god of wind. It was in this form that he governed the second world age, known as the Wind Sun.

caverns formed from the monster's eyes; rivers flowed from her mouth; trees, edible plants, and sweet-smelling flowers grew from her hair and skin; and mountains and valleys issued from her deep nose.

The new creation was still shrouded in shadow, for the life-giving sun had been swept away at the close of the fourth world age. Then amid the holy buildings at Teotihuacán the gods assembled and their strong voices, powerful with creative desire, were heard in the darkness. They determined that bright bodies should be hung in the heavens to provide light by day and in the long watches of night.

The deities Tecuciztecatl and Nanahuatzin both volunteered to act as the sun, and began austere rites of penitence and self-denial to ready themselves. Tecuciztecatl was proud and wealthy, whereas Nanahuatzin was poor and foully disfigured, with running sores on his face: where the former made magnificent religious offerings of quetzal feathers, gold, coral, incense, and jade, the latter presented simple gifts of reeds and of cactus spines dipped in his own blood.

The other gods lit a huge sacrificial pyre that threw tall, flickering shadows against the sides of the great pyramid temples at Teotihuacán. Tecuciztecatl approached to enter the flames, but at once turned away, fearful of the intense heat. He could not find a pure desire for self-sacrifice in his heart and his will was not sufficient to make the offering of his body to the flames. Three more times he went forward, but three times recoiled from the heat. Afterward Nanahuatzin moved up to the fire. He may have been poor in appearance, but his heart was strong: he stepped without second thought into the blaze, and his body was at once consumed. Then, too late, Tecuciztecatl finally found the courage to enter the fire. As the gods watched, his body disappeared in the flames.

The new sun Nanahuatzin hung bright but motionless at the zenith of the sky. The gods saw that movement was necessary in the heavens so that time could progress. Then Nanahuatzin announced that he would agree to follow a daily path across the sky if his fellow gods consented to honor him with a sacrifice of their lifeblood. At first the assembled divinities were outraged: the Morning Star attacked Nanahuatzin with spear and dart thrower, but was defeated by the mighty sun and despatched to the dim underworld. Then the gods sliced their veins and offered up their warm hearts to facilitate the movement of the sun. In so doing they set the pattern for the many blood sacrifices performed by Olmecs, Zapotecs, Maya, and Aztecs in later years. The Aztec worshippers came to honour the sun as Tonatiuh and Huitzilopochtli, while they revered humble Nanahuatzin as the patron deity of twins.

♦ QUETZALCÓATL AND THE CREATION OF HUMANKIND ♦

According to one tradition, Quetzalcóatl, in his guise as the Plumed Serpent, gathered the raw materials from which the first men and women were fashioned following the creation of the world of the fifth sun. The humans of the fourth world age were transformed into fish and sea creatures when that creation was destroyed. Quetzalcóatl voyaged to the realm of underworld lord Mictlantecuhtli to fetch the bones of these fish-men and women. Mictlanctecuhtli set Quetzalcóatl a seemingly impossible task—to pass four times around the underworld while blowing a tune on a conch shell that had no holes in it. Quetzalcóatl used worms to make tiny holes in the shell and bees to make a droning noise; grim faced, Mictlantecuhtli had no choice but to hand over the bones. Quetzalcóatl took the bones to the heaven of Tamoanchan. Here a mother goddess ground the bones to a powder and mixed them with the blood of the gods to form a magical paste from which she fashioned the first human babies, boy and girl.

AZTEC COSMOLOGY

The Aztecs believed in a multilayered universe, with Earth as a flat expanse, called Tlalticpac, lying beneath thirteen vertical levels of heaven and above nine levels of the underworld. In the Aztec worldview, the same sacred fivefold pattern that structured time was the basis for the arrangement of space on the earthly plain.

Just as history was divided into five successive world ages, so Tlalticpac was split into five areas: the four cardinal directions and the center. Each of these spaces was associated with a god and a color or colors in a pattern matching that of the five suns.

The north was the region of Tezcatlipoca, and of the first world age, the Jaguar Sun. The west was governed by Quetzalcóatl and connected to the second age, the Wind Sun; Tlaloc controlled the south, which was the realm of the third age, the Rain Sun; the east belonged to Chalchiuhtlicue, ruler of the fourth age, the Water Sun. The current world age was that of the center and came under the rule of the Xiuhtecuhtli, god of fire. At the center of the world stood the magnificent Templo Mayor (see page 522) atop the Great Pyramid in the imperial capital Tenochtitlán—as was fitting for an age belonging to the Aztecs. In some versions of this scheme, the south was the realm of Huitzilopochtli rather than Tlaloc and the east belonged to Xipe Totec rather than Chalchiuhtlicue.

The Aztecs compared the world to a flower with four petals, joined at the center and spreading out to the north, east, south, and west. According to another tradition five great trees held the flat Earth in position within the multilayered universe: a great cosmic tree in the center and four outgrowths of this plant, one in each of the four cardinal points. One interpretation of the story of the five world

The Aztec worldview is represented in mosaic on this 15th- or 16th-century ceremonial shield. At the center is the cosmic tree, around which is entwined a serpent outlined in gilded beads. The shield also depicts four gods with raised arms whose role is to hold up the sky.

ages sees it as an image for the establishment of the four quarters of the world and the cosmic tree at the center.

The cosmic tree linked the Earth to the other levels of the multilayered universe. Its roots spread deep below the flat Earth into the underworld realm governed by Mictlantecuhtli and his goddess Mictlancihuatl. The branches of the cosmic tree grew energetically upward into the levels of heaven that rose above the Earth. In the topmost of these levels, Omeyocan, lived the ultimate divine source, the lord of duality Ometeotl, who in creation narratives was the source of the creative energy applied by his male and female forms Ometecuhtli (also known as Tonacatecuhtli) and Omecihuatl (also known as Tonacacihuatl). Other Aztec heavenly realms included Tlalocan, a blissful place ruled by rain god Tlaloc, where water was plentiful and food grew in abundance; Tamoanchan, a fertile, perfumed earthly paradise governed by the beautiful flower goddess Xochiquetzal (see box, right); and Tonatiuhichan, the heaven of the virile sun god Tonatiuh.

The Aztecs did not believe in rebirth in heaven for all people: only certain souls could gain access to these heavens, depending not on how they had conducted their lives on Earth but on the manner of their death. Thus, for example, the souls of babies who died without apparent cause, perhaps in their sleep, were sent to Omeyocan, while those of people who died by drowning or other causes associated with water traveled to Tlalocan. The souls of warriors slain in battle and of women who died in childbirth were given access to Tonatiuhichan (see page 518).

In some versions of Aztec cosmology, Earth was encircled by ocean waters that rose up above the land to form the sky. The gods had it in their power to release these floods from the blue heaven to crash down in a thunderous waterfall that would obliterate life on Earth—and in one account of the Water Sun of Chalchiuhtlicue, the goddess brought the fourth world age to an abrupt end by freeing the sky waters in this way to run down and flood over the land.

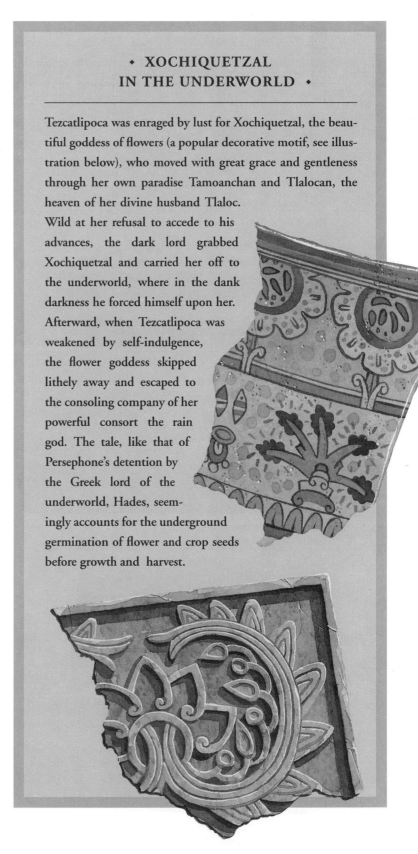

• XOCHIQUETZAL IN THE UNDERWORLD •

Tezcatlipoca was enraged by lust for Xochiquetzal, the beautiful goddess of flowers (a popular decorative motif, see illustration below), who moved with great grace and gentleness through her own paradise Tamoanchan and Tlalocan, the heaven of her divine husband Tlaloc. Wild at her refusal to accede to his advances, the dark lord grabbed Xochiquetzal and carried her off to the underworld, where in the dank darkness he forced himself upon her. Afterward, when Tezcatlipoca was weakened by self-indulgence, the flower goddess skipped lithely away and escaped to the consoling company of her powerful consort the rain god. The tale, like that of Persephone's detention by the Greek lord of the underworld, Hades, seemingly accounts for the underground germination of flower and crop seeds before growth and harvest.

THE SACRED WORLD

The Aztecs saw the sacred all about them—in all the forms of the natural world. Even the humblest plants and shards of rock had their element of divinity. Aztec religion may have had its ultimate source in primeval fertility cults centered on the beauty and abundance of Mother Earth: fertility figurines dating from as early as around 2000BCE have been discovered at Mesoamerican sites.

The sky, the towering mountains, and the lake from which the city of Tenochtitlán majestically rose were viewed with particular reverence. All were sources of life-giving water—according to one tradition the rain god kept his water pots in the mountains, whence his assistants the *tlaloque*s gathered the precious liquid to

make sky-borne rain clouds. Some accounts viewed mountains as hollow, and filled with water. Priests and worshippers addressed Lake Texcoco in annual fertility rites as Tonanueyatl ("Mother Great Water"), celebrating the natural abundance of their setting.

In Aztec cosmology—which pictured the universe as vertically layered, with a flat earth between thirteen planes of heavens above and nine levels of underworld beneath—the Earth layer, realm of human activity, was simultaneously the lowest level of heaven and the uppermost layer of the underworld: all at once terrestrial, celestial, and infernal. Holding the center was the vertical *axis mundi*, which connected heaven, Earth, and the underworld and which was sometimes identified as the force of time. The Earth, its many forms, and the movement of time were all manifestations of divine force, and were charged with divine energy. In some versions five cosmic trees were established, one in each of the four cardinal directions and one in the center—and time, at the gods' decree, flowed in cycles through the trees and over the world. Also passing through these trees under the gods' control were the forces manifesting as cycles of weather, celestial and astronomical patternings, and the movement of life and death.

The world was sacred because the gods were everywhere. In one version of the account of the creation of the sun and moon at Teotihuacán, the many gods—who gave movement to the sun by sacrificing themselves—

This casket, designed to hold offerings to the gods, doubled as a three-dimensional representation of the Aztec concept of the universe. At the bottom of the casket is the center of the universe, embodied by a jade figure of Chalchiuhtlicue, goddess of rivers, lakes, and oceans. On the inside of the lid is a map of the four points of the universe.

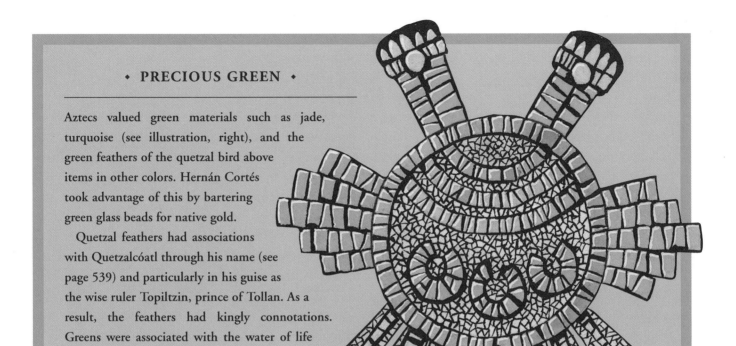

◆ PRECIOUS GREEN ◆

Aztecs valued green materials such as jade, turquoise (see illustration, right), and the green feathers of the quetzal bird above items in other colors. Hernán Cortés took advantage of this by bartering green glass beads for native gold.

Quetzal feathers had associations with Quetzalcóatl through his name (see page 539) and particularly in his guise as the wise ruler Topiltzin, prince of Tollan. As a result, the feathers had kingly connotations. Greens were associated with the water of life and were particularly sacred to rain god Tlaloc and his consort Chalchiuhtlicue, goddess of rivers, lakes, and oceans. Hailed as "Lady of the Jade Skirt," she wore a jade necklace and turquoise ear and nose decorations. When Aztec nobles wore turquoise it was to signify their devout love of the rain god and his green-hued mistress.

subsequently became the myriad creatures of the world. For this reason, every animal had a divine element, but this core had been covered over time by a layer of accretions. The gods had many forms—animal, human, material, or spiritual.

The universe was structured by duality. The primeval god Ometeotl was lord of duality, both male and female. The great eternal battles between Quetzalcóatl and Tezcatlipoca were an expression of the duality of light and darkness. The twin temples atop the Great Pyramid to rain god Tlaloc and sun god Huitzilopochtli represented dualities of water and fire, life and death.

The divine forces everywhere present were at any moment potentially benevolent or malevolent. The rain god had both rain and drought in his power; Chalchiuhtlicue could deliver destructive floods as well as nourishing streams. Even the Plumed Serpent Quetzalcóatl, normally a bringer of good things, could take malevolent form as Venus the Morning Star or Tlahuizcalpantecuhtli, feared for his evil darts and malign influence on human affairs. The sacred universe had to be negotiated carefully, with the help of religious ritual and expert priestly interpretation of the sacred calendar that organized and controlled time.

THE HOLY SERPENT

The snake had profound sacred and symbolic meaning for the Aztecs and played a central role in their religious life. As in many cultures, the serpent was a symbol of fertility, of skill and cunning, and of arcane knowledge.

For both the Aztecs and their Mesoamerican neighbors and forebears, snakes had complex, deep-seated, and powerful associations with celestial fire, physical strength, and the natural world. The creatures suggested the life-giving power of the sun—they also had connotations with rainstorms, rivers and floods, sea water, the earth and plant life, human sexuality and reproduction.

Tracing the distant origins of the great Plumed Serpent Quetzalcóatl as a primeval Mesoamerican fertility and storm deity provides evidence of the serpent's associations with the sky and the sun. Scholars identify the twin-headed serpent represented in Aztec art and jewelry as an image of the wide sky. The snake also represented the burning power and generative force of the sun: the Aztec sun god Tonatiuh followed a fire snake, or *xiuhcóatl*, as he made his way across the sky by day. By night, when he had to endure a series of trials in the underworld, the sun fought off his adversaries using the *xiuhcóatl* as a stick. The solar fire snake became generally associated with physical strength: the Aztecs' tribal god Huitzilopochtli, who was also a sun god, used a *xiuhcóatl* to despatch his brothers and his elder sister the moon goddess Coyolxauhqui when he attacked them with typically martial vigor in the first minutes of his life.

The serpent represented both elements of a significant duality—not only fire but also water: the fire serpent was *xiuhcóatl*, the water serpent Quetzalcóatl. For serpents were also associated with life-giving rains and the most precious liquid of all, sacrificial blood. The rain god Tlaloc typically was depicted with goggles resembling curled snakes around his eyes and a snake on his upper lip; he also carried a serpent scepter; Aztecs saw a storm of driving rain as a mass of water serpents. The reclining *chacmool* figures into which priests flung the heart of the sacrificial victim were representations of Tlaloc, which can be surmised by the serpentine features of their faces. A magnificent statue of the earth deity Coatlicue (see pages 542–543) showed the goddess without a head, but with snakes streaming from her severed neck to represent her lifeblood. A sacrificial stone, discovered on the Gulf of Mexico coast in the nineteenth century, was made in the form of a twin-headed sky snake with an arched back on which the victim was pressed in order to have his heart sliced from his chest.

In creation mythology both heavens and Earth were made at the beginning of the current world age by the gods Quetzalcóatl and Tezcatlipoca from the serpentine body of the earth monster Tlatecuhtli. The serpent also had strong links to the earth. Ancient hunting god Mixcoatl and earth goddess Cihuacóatl both had serpent identities—their names meant "Cloud Serpent" and "Lady Serpent": and in one narrative, they were the parents of Quetzalcóatl. Another earth goddess Coatlicue was said to have petticoats or skirts made of snakes. Moreover in some Aztec accounts the surface of the land was described as an intertangling layer of snakes from which all life including plants, animals, and humans had emerged.

The snake's association with hidden knowledge and arcane rituals is found in its link to visionary religious experience in Mesoamerica. The Aztecs' Maya neighbors believed that individuals who experienced

Among the ruins of the Great Temple of Tenochtitlán slithers this giant stone snake, a representation of Quetzalcóatl in his guise as the Plumed Serpent. The serpent was a profound and wide-ranging symbol for the Aztecs, who associated the creature with fertility, fire and water, skill and strength, and hidden knowledge.

religious ecstasy following rites of blood sacrifice would encounter a vision serpent and could travel along the divine snake's body to meet the gods or enter the world of spirits; one of a celebrated series of lintels carved in the Maya city of Yaxchilán depicts Lady Xoc, the wife of the city's ruler, in ecstatic communion with the vision serpent after making a sacrifice of her own lifeblood to the gods. In Aztec religious carving the wide mouth of a serpent often represents the opening to a holy chamber or sacred cave of the kind found beneath the Pyramid of the Sun at Teotihuacán: the Aztecs believed such caves were an entrance to the underworld or the realm of divine spirits. Monumental serpent heads adorned the steps of their temples. Serpents also carried great Quetzalcóatl away from Mexico. In the sadness of his grief, after his fall from power in Tollan, Topiltzin–Quetzalcóatl journeyed to the seashore and departed eastward on a raft of snakes.

JAGUAR, EAGLE, AND COYOTE

The Aztecs' reverence for the jaguar had ancient roots in Mesoamerica. The Olmec people appear to have worshipped the night predator as a symbol of kingly power and fertility; they made carvings of a sacred figure that blends the features of the jaguar with those of a human infant.

By Aztec times the creature was revered as an animal aspect of Tezcatlipoca, the fierce god of night and fate, and as the form adopted by the sun during the night. The animal's fearsome capacity to hunt by night meant that it was naturally linked to the sun's disappearance: the jaguar's skin was sometimes considered to be a representation of the night sky. The sun, which traveled the sky by day in the form of Tonatiuh, transformed into a jaguar named Tepeyollotl ("Heart of the Rock Mountain") during its passage through the underworld in the hours of darkness.

From the time of the Olmecs onward, the jaguar was also symbolic of the spiritual force of shamans, individuals with a gift for mystical and spiritual exploration

and the power to summon divine powers from the spirit realm. Shamans were believed to transform themselves into jaguars in the course of their dangerous spirit voyages; Tezcatlipoca, who could be seen in the form of the jaguar, was the patron of these spiritual adventurers. At Teotihuacán a carving of a jaguar emerging from an opening adorned with images of starfish and markings representing flashes of light was discovered by archaeologists in a ruined palace near the Pyramid of the Sun in 2001: scholars believe the carving represents a shaman, in jaguar form, returning from a spiritual adventure.

In addition, the jaguar's strength, speed, cunning, and ferocity made it an archetype of martial prowess; the jaguar was the symbol of one of the élite groups of

• ANIMAL FAMILIARS •

The Aztec god Tezcatlipoca could appear as monkey, skunk, coyote, or jaguar (see illustration, left) as well as in human form. The Aztecs believed that divine power could adopt any shape, and many of their divinities had animal aspects. This intense intimacy with animal forms was not restricted to the gods. Each human, too, was believed to have an animal form, a protective familiar called *tonal* in the Aztec's Nahuatl language. The secret science of shifting shape, familiar to shamans but accessible also to others, was called *nahual*.

warriors that graced the Aztec army. Jaguar warriors had the right to wear a jaguar skin over their padded cotton battle clothes. The animal also had regal associations and jaguar pelts were used in the magnificent ceremonial dress of rulers; during the enthronement rites of a new Aztec emperor in Tenochtitlán, the ruler-to-be sacrificed his own blood using jaguar claws to break his skin, before being led to a throne covered in jaguar skins.

The eagle was honored as the animal form of the Aztecs' principal tribal deity Huitzilopochtli, lord of war with many solar attributes. Eagle symbolism played an important role in the rites of human sacrifice. After performing a sacrifice the priest flung the still-warm heart into a vessel called a *quauhxicalli* ("eagle container"); the victim was then called "eagle man" and the heart referred to as "cactus eagle fruit." The Aztecs particularly revered the eagle because of its central role in the foundation of their imperial capital, Tenochtitlán: originally a wandering people, they settled on an island in Lake Texcoco made auspicious by the fulfillment of a prophecy of great Huitzilopochtli himself, that they would see an eagle on a cactus grasping a snake in its talons.

The proud bird was also associated with bravery and military achievement: alongside jaguar warriors, the second élite band in the army of the Triple Alliance was the eagle warriors, who wore an eagle-feather headdress into battle. Soldiers killed on the field of war were declared *quauteca* ("eagle companions") and were carried in the moment of death to the eastern paradise Tonatiuhichán. In some accounts these men then were transformed into hummingbirds and butterflies and became willing laborers in the entourage of great Tonatiuh, serving to haul the sun god up the sky each morning following his daily birth on the eastern horizon. Both the eagle and the hummingbird were understood to be animal manifestations of great Huitzilopochtli himself.

The cunning coyote was also feared and honored as an animal form of a god: dark Tezcatlipoca, god of myriad attributes with powers over fate, magic, shapeshifting, and the darkness of night. The Aztecs thought the animal had particular sexual power and associated it with Tezcatlipoca in his role as patron god of men. Another god, named Huehuecoyotl ("The old, old coyote"), also took the form of the coyote; worshippers made offerings to him in the hope of winning a long life.

As a result of its association with the Aztecs' principal deity Huitzilopochtli, the eagle was often used to represent the power of the king. This eagle figure stands imperiously on a base carved to resemble the wickerwork of the Aztec emperor's throne at Tenochtitlán.

THE CHILDREN
OF OMECIHUATL

The Aztecs paid fearful homage to a bewildering number of gods and goddesses, with wide-ranging forms, abilities, and attributes. These deities were celebrated side by side: individual worshippers did not see the gods as rivals, for the gods and goddesses generally had separate and mutually compatible powers and areas of influence.

In matters of war, honor was paid to Huitzilopochtli or Tezcatlipoca, while to guarantee a good harvest priests made obeisance to Tlaloc, Xipe Totec, or a maize divinity such as Centeotl. Divine powers were sometimes in conflict—Tezcatlipoca and Quetzalcóatl, for example, were opponents in a seemingly eternal struggle between dark and light, deception and wisdom, cunning self-interest and a more compassionate view. But even these two occasionally collaborated with each other, as in the creation of the world from the earth monster at the dawn of the fifth age (see page 528).

The gods were both many and one. All the deities found issue in the one supreme god Ometeotl, who inhabited Omeyocan, the thirteenth and topmost layer of heaven. Lord of duality, Ometeotl took twin forms, male and female, Ometecuhtli and Omecihuatl—alternatively called Tonacatecuhtli and Tonacacihuatl—who were his active, creative force.

In one account all the other gods issued from Omecihuatl. On a day when this primeval goddess was roaming the dry and barren plains of the north, the inhospitable lands that the Aztecs escaped when they ventured south in search of fertile lands, she felt a stirring in her fertile womb that made it imperative for her to squat on her haunches. Adopting the typical position taken by Mesoamerican women when giving birth, she pushed out a sacrificial knife of obsidian that fell swiftly to the plain below. The dark knife crashed among the rocks and sands of that place and marvelously split into 1,600 gods and goddesses of wonderful power. From the first days, therefore, there was the necessity of sacrifice, evidenced by the obsidian knife, and a multiplicity of gods and goddesses existing without conflict.

In another myth Omecihuatl and Ometecuhtli were parents of a group of four gods, initially all known as Tezcatlipoca but subsequently identified with other major deities: Black Tezcatlipoca (later simply Tezcatlipoca), White Tezcatlipoca (later Quetzalcóatl), Blue Tezcatlipoca (later Huitzilopochtli) and Red Tezcatlipoca (later Xipe Totec). These four were told by their parents to perform the work of creating a new world. After an unexplained delay of 600 years, White and Blue Tezcatlipocas began the creation: initially they made fire, then lifted an ancestor of our own sun into the sky before fashioning the first humans Oxomoco and Cipactonal; the Earth they made from a vast primeval crocodile, just as in another account Quetzalcóatl and Tezcatlipoca made the Earth and heaven from the original earth monster. White and Blue Tezcatlipocas also created Mictlantecuhtli and Mictlancihuatl, rulers of the Aztec underworld, devised the 260-day ritual calendar, and gave sweet life to the flower and love goddess Xochiquetzal. Without her beauty, there would have been scant joy in the world.

A third version of the creation suggested that all the gods and all life issued from Ometecuhtli, who blew softly into the all-encompassing darkness that followed the destruction of the fourth world age. His breath condensed to form the great god Quetzalcóatl, who set about creating other gods, the world, and humankind.

THE PLUMED SERPENT

Quetzalcóatl was both god and man—he incarnated as Topiltzin the revered ruler of Tollan who in an elegiac myth abdicated the throne and departed Central America by sea. He was also both man and snake, and was generally depicted in his powerful serpentine shape. He had a twin form, Xolotl, god of monsters and twins, who generally was embodied as a dog and who traveled with Quetzalcóatl to the underworld to fetch the bones of the fish inhabitants of the fourth world age prior to the creation of humans. Quetzalcóatl was also Venus in both its evening and morning forms.

Quetzalcóatl's own name embodies his dual nature. It combines two Nahuatl words, *quetzal* and *cóatl*, and both of these have twin meanings. *Quetzal* means "precious" or refers to the highly prized green feather of the quetzal bird, while *cóatl* means either "twin" or "serpent"; in combination the words can mean either "precious twin" or "quetzal-feathered serpent" (traditionally translated as "plumed serpent").

One account of Quetzalcóatl's birth emphasizes his role as fertility god, with powers over the germinating earth and the winds and rain waters of the sky above. According to this myth, the Plumed Serpent's mother was an earth goddess named Cihuacoatl ("Lady Serpent") who chose to roam mountain and valleys in the form of a deer. In this lithe shape she caught the eye of the ancient hunting god Mixcóatl ("Cloud Serpent"), who gave chase and finally shot her with an expertly directed arrow. But as he watched in wild amazement the strong-haunched deer melted away and was replaced by a young woman of wide hips and great beauty. Once more she fled and Mixcóatl followed. Finally he caught her and made love to her as she laughed with joy—and the blessed fruit of their union was Quetzalcóatl.

Quetzalcóatl embodied the fruitful wind that blew rain clouds into place above the crop fields. In this guise, as Ehecatl, he was often depicted wearing a conical hat. Temples honoring him as wind god were often circular in shape, in reference to the spiralling movements of the wind. A circular temple honoring Quetzalcóatl–Ehecatl stood opposite the Great Pyramid in the sacred precinct of Tenochtitlán. Statues of Quetzalcóatl–Ehecatl also show the god wearing a half-mask like the bill of a duck over his lower face.

◆ AFTER THE CONQUEST ◆

Many of the gods revered in Tenochtitlán were still worshipped by the Aztecs' descendants after the Spaniards had introduced Christianity to Mexico. The Plumed Serpent, Quetzalcóatl, was associated with Jesus Christ himself: the peaceful philosophy and rule of Quetzalcóatl in his guise as Prince Topiltzin resonated with Christ's teachings on loving others while Christ's death by self-sacrifice and his predicted Second Coming were comparable to Quetzalcóatl's departure and promised return from the western seas. Other gods lived on in the guise of Christian saints—for example, the rain god Tlaloc was celebrated as John the Baptist, because of his association with baptismal waters; meanwhile, folk traditions were subsumed by Christian festivals—for example, the annual honoring of ancestors' graves was performed on the Christian festival of All Souls Day.

The ancient earth goddess Tonantzin, revered as "Our Holy Mother" and "Our Lady," found perhaps the most remarkable new role: in 1531 a peasant named Juan Diego experienced an ecstatic vision of a dark-complexioned Virgin Mary close to a temple to Tonantzin, and as the Black Virgin of Guadalupe a hybrid Christian–Mesoamerican goddess became the patron saint of Mexico.

Quetzalcóatl was also said to have brought the maize plant to the Aztecs' ancestors. In ancient days, when the first couple Oxomoco and Cipactonal were alive, ants had hidden the maize plant within a vast mountain. Quetzalcóatl took the form of an ant and followed the creatures' path to their hoard. He carried some maize back to his fellow gods who, after tasting it, decreed that it would make a suitable food for the Mesoamericans. Quetzalcóatl then tried to haul the mountain away from the ants' hoard, but even he was not strong enough to do so. In the end it was left to humble Nanahuatzin, the disfigured god who had become the sun at Teotihuacán (see page 529), to split the mountain with a lightning bolt.

LORD OF THE SMOKING MIRROR

The Aztecs' dark lord, Tezcatlipoca, opposed all that is best in human endeavor. His attributes and powers contrasted starkly with those of his great rival Quetzalcóatl. Where the Plumed Serpent was god of daylight, the sweet winds that usher in the rain clouds, productive thinking, and a peaceable life, Tezcatlipoca controlled the dark hours of night, hurricanes, deception, and conflict. The Spanish chronicler Bernadino de Sahagún compared Tezcatlipoca to the devil of Christianity: like the angel Lucifer, who in the Christian tradition fell from heaven to become Satan, Tezcatlipoca had great and luminous powers but generally chose to put them to wicked ends. He undeniably had a creative aspect—as shown when he combined with Quetzalcóatl to make the new world of the Fifth Sun at the beginning of the current age. But while Quetzalcóatl subsequently introduced people to maize and taught them how to farm, Tezcatlipoca was a bringer of discord and vice.

The untrustworthy Tezcatlipoca was said to wear a mirror of the volcanic glass obsidian in the rear of his skull. This glass gave a dark and smoky reflection

• TOPILTZIN IN TOLLAN •

The great god Quetzalcóatl took human form as Topiltzin, a wise and peace-loving ruler of the Toltecs' revered city of Tollan. But his blessed reign came to an abrupt and tragic end when he abdicated the throne.

Topiltzin's rule was remembered as a golden age of artistic achievement. In some accounts the prince taught his people to turn away from the sacrifice of human victims and to offer their own blood or that of animals to the gods. But he lost the will to govern, according to some versions after he seduced his own sister when drunk on *pulque* liquor provided by his eternal enemy Tezcatlipoca.

Topiltzin–Quetzalcóatl burned the splendid buildings of Tollan and commanded the beautiful birds that had graced its streets to depart and come no more. He made a long penitential pilgrimage to the Gulf of Mexico, where he summoned the snakes of the entire coastal region and bound them into a raft. On this vessel he departed his land, headed for a place named Tlapallan, from which he had originally come. But he vowed to return to Mexico, and to make landfall at the same place.

The enduring strength of this myth is clear: Motecuhzoma II and his people initially believed Hernán Cortés to be the retuning god when he made landfall in Mexico in 1519. In another version of the Topiltzin–Quetzalcóatl myth, the god sacrificed himself on a funeral pyre and his soul rose into the night sky as Venus the Morning Star.

perfectly suited to Tezcatlipoca's ends as an obscurer of truth. He was generally depicted missing one foot, which he lost either when subduing the earth monster during the world's creation or as a punishment for abducting and raping fair Xochiquetzal, the flower goddess. Sometimes he wore a smoking mirror at the end of his shinbone in place of his missing foot.

In his dark mirror Tezcatlipoca could see people's shameful secrets, lustful thoughts, and hidden motives. Fittingly for the god of night hours, he was patron of activities often concealed by darkness—such as adultery and theft. His cult went back at least as far as the Toltecs in the twelfth century. One tale from their mythology told of an obsidian mirror with the power to predict famines: Tezcatlipoca cruelly hid the mirror to prolong the suffering of the people when starvation threatened.

God of violent storms and the infertile, unforgiving northern region, master of the ill-omened color black,

Tezcatlipoca carried a sacrificial knife made of obsidian that symbolized death. Offerings of obsidian knives in Tenochtitlán were often pushed into the mouth or nose of a skull mask to represent the stroke of death stopping the breath of life. In codex representations he was frequently shown with body painted black: in Tenochtitlán his priests painted their bodies black, using a paste ground from tobacco, snakeskin and mushrooms.

The dark lord was often depicted as a warrior, carrying a round shield, or *chimalli*, together with spears and an *atalatl* dart-thrower. In time of war, soldiers encountered him on the battlefield in the fateful guise of Yaotl

---

Quetzalcóatl was revered long before the Aztec era. This carving of the god from the Temple of the Feathered Serpent in Xochicalco, southwest of the Valley of Mexico, dates from before 900CE. The Aztecs made regular visits to the ruined city and worshipped at the temple.

("the foe"), glorying in bloodshed, determining by divine will whether warriors should succeed and capture prisoners or fail and be slain or taken themselves. He carried an image of a skull on his jacket.

By night Tezcatlipoca wandered the countryside, sometimes in the form of his animal double the jaguar, sometimes in human form. Stone benches were built alongside the main roadways as resting places for the god of darkness. When he encountered an unfortunate traveler, he would challenge the fearful individual to a wrestling match; any human who prevailed against him had the right to demand a boon.

When the sun sank beyond the western horizon it entered the underworld realm of Mictlantecuhtli, where it endured many trials in Tezcatlipoca's form, as the jaguar. According to one version of the myth detailing the end of the current world age, darkness was destined to engulf the world when Tezcatlipoca stole and hid the sun. Then there would no longer be a future for the peoples of Mexico. Tezcatlipoca was also "the left-handed one" because his deceptive approaches left humans unprepared. He made fun of human pretensions to importance or permanence and took the credit for any unforeseen disaster that struck individual or nation.

Despite his many unsavory attributes, Tezcatlipoca was also the god of masculinity and in this guise was worshipped in an alternative animal form as a coyote. He had regal qualities and was honored by rulers. In particular the *tlatoani* (the emperor in his role as chief priest—see page 516) made sacrifices to Tezcatlipoca during coronation rites. In one version of the Aztecs' origin myth, Tezcatlipoca is even said to have taken the place of Huitzilopochtli in guiding the tribe as it wandered southward in search of a suitable place to settle.

CULT OF THE SUN KING

Huitzilopochtli, the tribal deity of the Mexica people who founded the Aztec Empire, was an incomparable warrior, god both of war and of the bloodthirsty sun. He set the pattern for Aztec youth by springing into virile martial action in the very first moments of his life. Huitzilopochtli's mother was the serpent-skirted earth goddess Coatlicue, who had already mothered the moon deity Coyolxauhqui and numerous sons, the Centzon Huitznahua ("400 southerners"). Coatlicue was in charge of a mountaintop shrine near the Toltec city of Tollan, and one day as she tended the holy place a ball of eagle feathers landed softly on her bosom; later she discovered that she was pregnant. Suspecting her of promiscuity, her children rallied to attack—but as they approached, Huitzilopochtli sprang from her loins, his skin painted blue and protected by thick body armor, his hand holding a powerful fire-snake of the kind that guided the sun across the sky each day. With this fire-bright divine weapon he killed Coyolxauhqui, as well as her many clamoring brothers, one after another, allowing just a few to escape fearfully toward the south. In this way the infant sun god proved his power and celestial pre-eminence, dismissing both the moon and the "400 southerners," which represent the southern stars of the night sky that are routed each dawn by the rising sun.

The account of Huitzilopochtli's triumph over the moon goddess Coyolxauhqui may be intended in part as an explanation of a solar eclipse, when the moon obscures the sun. Research has revealed that an eclipse occurred in Mesoamerica in 1325, the year of the foundation of Tenochtitlán—when the original structure that developed into the Great Pyramid was built. The very establishment of the city may thus have marked the propitious triumph of the sun god over his celestial rival.

Some scholars suggest that Huitzilopochtli may originally have been an inspirational tribal leader, who led the Mexica in the time of their migrations and was later deified. His people certainly took pains to establish the god's status alongside that of older Mesoamerican deities. The twin temples that stood atop the Great Pyramid in Tenochtitlán to Huitzilopochtli and Tlaloc the rain god symbolically made Huitzilopochtli the equal of Tlaloc. The juxtaposition of shrines to the sun and rain gods was also a celebration of war, the engine of imperial expansion, for Aztecs used the opposition of fire and water as a symbol of warfare.

Huitzilopochtli was thirsty for the blood of sacrificial victims and those slain in battle. Many thousands of sacrificial victims were slain in honor of the god who inspired and led the Mexica's southward migration from the barren north to the fertile environs of Lake Texcoco.

Aztec images of Huitzilopochtli showed him with blue stripes on his muscular legs and arms, and clutching four spears in one hand while his other arm bore a war shield decorated with five tufts of eagle feathers. The eagle was sacred to the youthful war god, who was also associated with hummingbirds. Huitzilopochtli's name means "Hummingbird of the Left;" these birds were linked to blood sacrifice and war. The blood drawn by a priest or worshipper in sacrificial rites was likened to the nectar that a hummingbird extracts from a flower.

LORD OF SKY WATER

In lands never entirely free from the threat of drought, farmers were faithful worshippers of the rain god. So important was the cult of the Aztec lord of rains Tlaloc that one manuscript, the *Codex Borgia*, reproduced a

This Aztec mask, dating from around 1500, is believed to represent Tezcatlipoca. The basis of the mask is a human skull, onto which bands of turquoise mosaic tiles and black lignite have been applied. Codex illustrations suggest that priests would have tied masks such as this one around their waists, using the leather straps attached to the skull.

cosmic map showing the fivefold division of the Earth into four quarters and the center, with an image of Tlaloc in every sacred position. Traditional versions of the map showed a different god in north, south, east, west, and the center, but in the Borgia image each place was occupied by Tlaloc standing on a likeness of the earth goddess, making clear the prime importance of fertility deities in Aztec worship.

All Aztec religious sacrifices were centrally concerned with safeguarding the fertility of the land. By offering the precious liquid of lifeblood to the gods, Aztec priests sought to maintain the flow of life energy that was behind the rising of the sun, the appearance of rain clouds, the germination of seed in the earth, and the growth of maize and other crops. To Mesoamericans the rain god was among the most senior of a large number of fertility gods and goddesses.

The rain god's cult dates back at least as far as the Olmec civilization. The lord of the rains was worshipped under different names by various peoples of the region: the Zapotecs knew him as Cocijo, the Maya as Chac, and the Totonacs as Tajin. The Aztec name Tlaloc derives from the Nahuatl *tlalli*, meaning "the Earth" and *–oc* meaning "on top of"—the rain god occupied the space above the Earth's thirsty surface and had to be persuaded to release his precious cargo of water.

Tlaloc was honored with copious sacrifices in the form of blood and other offerings. Rain god Tlaloc and war god Huitzilopochtli shared sacred space atop the Great Pyramid at the center of the Aztec world, but scholars suggest that in the fields and provinces—and especially, perhaps, among people not descended from the Mexica, whose tribal deity was Huitzilopochtli—the ancient cult of the rain god was probably more popular than the more recent devotion to the war god.

Like many other Mesoamerican deities, Tlaloc had both good and bad in his gift: he sent both the gentle rains for which the crops thirsted and torrential storms that crushed and spoiled the harvest. He sometimes unleashed disease to blight the maize plants; he also had

power over droughts and frosts. According to his Aztec worshippers, Tlaloc stored rainwater in four huge jars, which he kept in the north, south, east, and west. From the eastern jar he sent lifegiving rains, and from the others unwelcome storms or punishing droughts. The Aztecs also told that Tlaloc kept rainwater in the mountains visible from the Valley of Mexico and that he sent his fleet-winged helpers, the *tlaloque*s, to draw waters from these stores. Blowing hard, wind god Ehecatl–Quetzalcóatl gave strength to the *tlaloque*s to climb to the top of the sky, where they unloaded their water into the rainclouds. But the clouds might not be welcome: the *tlaloque*s had power over five types of rain, including gentle and nourishing precipitation, but also diseased fungus rain, stormy wind rain, hard flint rain, such as hail, and "fire rain," which probably referred to lightning storms or drought. Tlaloc was usually depicted wearing a many-pointed hat that was meant to resemble the mountains in which he stored his supplies of water.

Chalchiuhtlicue, known from ancient times as wife or sometimes sister of Tlaloc, was represented as a beautiful young woman. Known as "Lady of the Jade Skirt," she wore green or blueish clothes; in her hair she had a regal headdress of blue reeds and she wore a jade necklace with turquoise ear decorations and a turquoise nose ring. She had power over streams, rivers, lakes, and the sea and was protector of water-carriers and fishermen. Her sacred spaces were on the banks of rivers and lakes and at Pantitlan, a place marked by banners in the middle of Lake Texcoco, where a young female impersonator of the goddess was slain during the festival of Huey Tozoztli in the fourth month (15 April–4 May) of the Aztec year: the victim's blood was sprinkled on the waters of the vast lake in a rite of renewal.

This image of Tlaloc the Aztec rain god forms part of the crenellations of the Temple of Tlaloc in Teotihuacán. Most representations of the god share certain features, such as large, prominent eyes, animal fangs, and a headdress symbolizing the mountains where he stored his water.

EARTH MOTHER, SEED LORD

The Aztecs deified and worshipped the fertile earth as Tonantzin ("Our Holy Mother"), celebrating the land as the progenitor of the people themselves. Another name for the goddess was Teteoinnan-Toci ("Our Mother's Mother" or "Mother of the Gods").

The Aztecs generally represented Teteoinnan-Toci wearing a plaited cotton headdress and with a serene expression on her face. Tonantzin, by contrast, they associated with the moon. Following the Spanish Conquest the cult of the earth goddess intermingled with that of Roman Catholicism's Blessed Virgin Mary and subsequently with worship of Mexico's patron saint, the Black Virgin of Guadalupe (see page 539). Her shrine, the Basilica de Guadalupe, was built on a spot once occupied by a temple dedicated to Tonantzin.

A third incarnation of the earth goddess was known as Coatlicue ("snake-skirted"), who was celebrated as the mother of the moon goddess Coyolxauhqui, as well as of the great sun and war god Huitzilopochtli himself (see pages 542–543). Each morning Coatlicue was believed to give birth to the sun anew on the eastern horizon. As indicated by her name, the fertility goddess wore a petticoat of writhing snakes.

Within the earth the germinating seeds and first shoots of the crops were controlled by Xipe Totec. In his honor during the festival of Tlacaxipehualiztli priests skinned sacrificial victims and wore their flayed skins over their own (see page 521): many surviving carvings and images show the god or one of his priests wearing a flayed skin in this way, with the hands of the living emerging at the wrists of the suit of skin, and holes cut in the eyes and nose to allow the wearer to see and breathe. Images of Xipe Totec have been found at Monte Albán (ca. 500BCE), and he was also revered at Teotihuacán in the first centuries of the Common Era. In Aztec creation narratives he was identified with Red Tezcatlipoca, one of the four sons of the primal divine couple Ometecuhtli and Omecihuatl at the very dawn of time (see page 526). His quarter lay in the east, region of the rising sun, and he was associated with the color red. He was depicted carrying a *chicahuaztli*, a hollow staff full of seeds that represented the falling shafts of sunlight that awakened the seeds in the earth.

The flower princess Xochiquetzal and her husband or brother Xochipilli were protectors and providers of sweet-smelling flowers. Both were also associated with love, beauty, and lovemaking (see page 550)—indeed, according to myth, the very flowers with which Xochiquetzal delighted humankind were made from her sexual organs. In this account, Xochiquetzal was married to the Plumed Serpent Quetzalcóatl: one day as he was washing himself, his hand moved over his penis and his seed spilled forth. From these divine seeds, the other gods made the first bat. They sent the bat to visit Xochiquetzal: it bit the goddess's sexual organs and bore a piece of her flesh back to heaven, where the divinities made roses from the gift. But these flowers did not have a pleasing scent, so the bat flew to the flower goddess a second time. Now he carried a piece of her intimate flesh down to Mictlantecuhtli, the underworld lord: from this the gods made the sweetest and most delicately colored flowers. They decreed that they should be scattered in the lands of Mesoamerica to give sensual pleasure to the hardworking people.

Xochiquetzal was represented as a young woman of ravishing beauty and voluptuous figure. Her many happy and light-footed followers took the form of beautiful butterflies and birds in order to attend upon her. In myth one of the first women was made from her hair to be wife to the son of Oxomoco and Cipactonal, the primal human couple.

Xochipilli shared with his flower goddess control of dance and song. A statue of Xochipilli discovered at Tlamanalco on the lower slopes of the Iztaccihuatl volcano depicted the prince sitting on a flower-throne with four blooms emerging, one in each of the cardinal directions (see illustration, opposite). In this position he

represented the god of the center elsewhere identified as fire god Xiuhtecuhtli or the lord of duality Ometeotl, the force of life in the fifth or current world age.

One version of the origins of the Mexica tribe from which the Aztecs derived told that they emerged from Chicomoztoc ("Place of the Seven Caves"). In some versions they found the seven caves during their travels (see pages 504–507) and may have undergone a rite of renewal there: the story of coming forth from seven caves was a common element in the mythology of many Mesoamerican peoples as an expression of their connection to the sacred earth. The people came from, belonged to, and were bound in an eternal relationship with, the earth. From ancient days, caves were a hallowed place for Mesoamericans. The Pyramid of the Sun at Teotihuacán appears to have been built atop a natural cave with seven chambers that could well have been an ancient site of pilgrimage and may even have been the "seven caves" referred to in the origin myth.

SACRED PLANTS

Centeotl was principal among the gods of the Aztecs' staple food, maize. He was celebrated with the maize goddesses Chicomecoatl and Xilonen in the important festival of Huey Tozoztli ("Large Vigil"), when corn seed was blessed and children were sacrificed in fertility rites on Mount Tlaloc and at Pantitlan on Lake Texcoco. One myth detailed how Centeotl was the source of the maize plant for the Aztecs' hungry ancestors. In this account, he was born the grandson of the first human couple, Oxomoco and Cipactonal, after their son Piltzintecuhtli had taken a fair maiden created from the hair of the

---

Xochipilli the god of flowers is depicted in this statue discovered by the Mexican dramatist and historian Alfredo Chavero near Tlamanalco on the slopes of Mount Iztaccihuatl. On each side of Xochipilli's throne is a butterfly drinking nectar from a flower in full bloom—an image of the flowering of the universe.

flower goddess Xochiquetzal as his bride. The young Centeotl grew up a strong and healthy youth, with earthy skin and the good looks of his mother, brimming with the rugged vitality of the Mexican landscape. But then inexplicably he weakened and died—as the cold of winter seizes the air, so the chill of grief took hold of his young parents: weeping loudly, they buried him and tended his simple grave. Then the gods descended to Earth and brought forth plants from Centeotl's strong body—maize came from his nails, cotton grew from his hair, and the sweet potato issued from his fingers. Centeotl was usually shown as a strong young man dressed mainly in yellow, with maize in his headgear.

Centeotl was lord of the ripe maize, while Xilonen was particularly the goddess of the first tender young maize to appear each year and Chicomecóatl was goddess of seed corn. At the harvest-season festival of Ochpaniztli ("Sweeping Clean"), held in September, Xilonen and Chicomecóatl were celebrated in a violent rite mirroring the ceremony used to honor Xipe Totec earlier in the year: a priestess of the maize goddesses beheaded a young woman victim, then skinned the corpse and wore her skin as a ceremonial suit. The Chicomecóatl priestess and a representative of the earth mother Toci flung handfuls of seed corn into the crowd. The seeds were kept for the following year's planting.

The Aztecs held certain plants to be sacred, most notably maize, which provided their staple food. They also revered the maguey cactus, shown here growing in the Oaxaca Valley, from which they made the alcoholic drink pulque, *known as the "divine intoxicant."* Pulque *was drunk to celebrate notable military victories and special religious days.*

A statue of Xilonen discovered at Teloluapan (in the Guerrero province of modern Mexico) depicts the goddess as a youthful woman wearing a cotton headdress and grasping two corn cobs in each hand. In Tenochtitlán, Chicomecóatl's temple contained a statue representing the goddess as an adolescent girl holding her arms open wide; scholars report that she was once dressed in a fine red dress decorated with goldwork and feathers and her cheeks were painted red. Codex images often show Chicomecóatl wearing a large rectangular headdress called an *amacalli* ("paper dwelling") and holding a seed-filled *chicahuaztli* staff of the kind associated with Xipe Totec. Priestly impersonators of the goddess shook the staff, which represented the power of the sun to germinate seeds, during festival celebrations.

The Aztecs honored other plants in addition to maize. The maguey cactus, used to make the alcoholic drink *pulque*, came under the protection of the goddess Mayahuel. Although there were strict laws against public drunkenness, *pulque* was revered as the "divine intoxicant"—according to myth, the drink was the gift of the great god and culture hero Quetzalcóatl. In this account Quetzalcóatl fell in love with a goddess named Mayahuel, granddaughter of one of the night demons, or *tzitzimime*. The divine couple traveled to Earth, where they celebrated their love by taking the form of a two-forked tree in a desert oasis. But Mayahuel's grandmother was far from happy about the goddess's choice and followed her with a contingent of demon followers, eager as ever to spread sickness and woe among humankind. High above the desert they unleashed a furious storm that split the great tree in half, separating Mayahuel from her dear husband; then they

• HOLY SMOKE: THE SACRED TOBACCO PLANT •

The Aztecs believed that the tobacco plant was holy, originally created in the thirteen heavens for the pleasure of the gods. To the Aztecs, tobacco—which they called *yetl* in their Nahuatl language—had magical properties. Along with the fermented drink *pulque* and certain hallucinogenic mushrooms such as *Psilocybe aztecorum*, tobacco was used in religious ritual to induce visions and trances. But people also smoked the leaves in normal circumstances, either by grinding them up and packing them in clay pipes or rolling them in cylinders and lighting them like one would a cigar. Archaeologists at Aztec sites have found a large number of clay pipes, many of which were shaped into animal heads. Experts believe that priests may have used these pipes to summon the god whose *nahual*, or animal double, was represented by the pipe. For example, a pipe carved into the likeness of a dog's head would be used in rites honoring Xolotl, the aspect of Quetzalcóatl who was believed principally to take a dog's form.

swept down and attacked her furiously, tearing her limb from limb. Afterward, in silent grief, Quetzalcóatl gathered the remains of Mayahuel and buried them in the desert; he allowed his divine tears to soften the hard ground. Subsequently the maguey cactus grew from that spot, and many years afterward the Aztecs' ingenious ancestors discovered how to make *pulque* from the plant. A variant myth told how a rabbit discovered the secret of making *pulque* when its curiosity drove it to bite into the maguey cactus one day. The Aztecs associated rabbits with drunkenness; a god called by the date name Two Rabbit was one of the alternative patron deities of *pulque*.

LOVE AND BEAUTY

Love and beauty, sexuality and childbirth were principally the province of the Earth Mother and of Xochipilli and Xochiquetzal. As goddess of flowers, Xochiquetzal was linked to sensual pursuits, such as the fine arts and dancing, and also lovemaking.

Xochiquetzal was said to have performed the first sexual act and to have been the first mother to give birth to twins. She was patron of prostitutes—both of the *ahuianime*, or city prostitutes, and the *maqui*, the temple priestesses who looked after the sexual needs of young warriors and marched with the army into battle.

In some accounts Xochiquetzal was married to Tlaloc, after whose downpours the flowers appeared or revived in the fields. In one myth she was ravished by dark Tezcatlipoca and carried off to the underworld (see page 531), while in another she was expelled from the heaven of Tamoanchan when her curiosity overcame her and she broke an interdiction of Ometeotl against touching the blossom of a flowering tree. Then she was condemned to wander the Earth; her beautiful floral creations, which catch at the hearts of men and women, were thereafter condemned to be subject to decay. In this guise she was known as Ixnextli ("Eyes of Ash").

Tlazolteotl, a powerful mother figure and widely revered fertility goddess, was a dual deity—goddess both of excrement and of childbirth, of sexual indulgence and also of purification—with unsettling consequences. In her name young Aztec women were forced into prostitution in the army barracks, then were later ceremonially killed and buried in the marshes of Lake Texcoco. She delivered punishment for self-indulgence in the form of sexually transmitted diseases. In some myths she was identified as the mother of beautiful Xochiquetzal and of the maize god Centeotl.

Tlazolteotl was the form of the mother goddess particularly worshipped by the Huastecs, subjects of the Aztec Empire from the Gulf of Mexico region. The Huastecs lived largely by cultivating cotton, and paid imperial tribute in the form of cloth and clothing: codex images of Tlazolteotl show her with spindles and unspun cotton in her headdress. A celebrated carving of the goddess shows her squatting with an ecstatic grimace of pain on her face and a baby emerging from between her legs. The expression of extreme emotion is not common in Aztec sculpture.

One myth, which accounted for the creation of the first scorpions, cast Tlazolteotl as a seductress. When a pious man dedicated himself to religious observance, abandoning his family to live in self-denial on a desert rock, the gods determined to test his self-control to the limit. They sent Yaotl (meaning "the enemy"), a cruel incarnation of Tezcatlipoca, who paraded before the man a collection of the most beautiful women. They called up to him from the desert floor, some singing sweetly, others laughing raucously, but he would not be distracted by any approach. However, when Yaotl presented the man with Tlazolteotl his resolve crumbled and he fell into her embrace—then the cruel gods laughed and Yaotl appeared on the rock. He transformed the man into a scorpion, summoned the man's wife and revealed the full story of his shameful fall before turning her, too, into a scorpion.

Another deity linked with childbirth and infants was the river and ocean goddess Chalchiuhtlicue. She was patron goddess of newborn babies and was honored as the protector of faithful lovers and married couples. In a folk tradition likened by Spanish chroniclers to the Christian rite of baptism, parents carried their new babies to the priestess of Chalchiuhtlicue: the priestess sprinkled a few drops of spring water on the infant and dedicated him or her to the cult of the goddess.

This Huastec statue depicts Tlazolteotl, a goddess associated, among other things, with carnal behaviour. The Aztecs absorbed Tlazolteotl into their pantheon following their conquest of the Huastecs in the 15th century during the reign of Motecuhzoma I.

DEATH AND THE UNDERWORLD

The Aztecs did not promise many joys in the afterlife. A few souls, lucky or exceptionally brave in their manner of death, rose to the nine levels of heaven: pleasurable experiences awaited warriors slain in battle and those killed by drowning or in childbirth, among others. But most people were doomed to traverse the nine gloomy levels of the underworld, a place of endless terror.

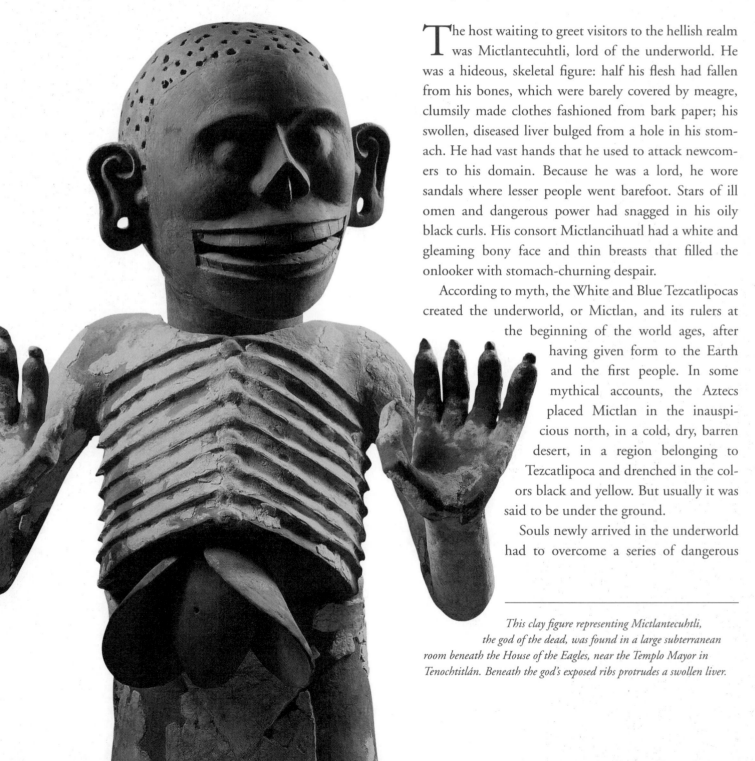

The host waiting to greet visitors to the hellish realm was Mictlantecuhtli, lord of the underworld. He was a hideous, skeletal figure: half his flesh had fallen from his bones, which were barely covered by meagre, clumsily made clothes fashioned from bark paper; his swollen, diseased liver bulged from a hole in his stomach. He had vast hands that he used to attack newcomers to his domain. Because he was a lord, he wore sandals where lesser people went barefoot. Stars of ill omen and dangerous power had snagged in his oily black curls. His consort Mictlancihuatl had a white and gleaming bony face and thin breasts that filled the onlooker with stomach-churning despair.

According to myth, the White and Blue Tezcatlipocas created the underworld, or Mictlan, and its rulers at the beginning of the world ages, after having given form to the Earth and the first people. In some mythical accounts, the Aztecs placed Mictlan in the inauspicious north, in a cold, dry, barren desert, in a region belonging to Tezcatlipoca and drenched in the colors black and yellow. But usually it was said to be under the ground.

Souls newly arrived in the underworld had to overcome a series of dangerous

This clay figure representing Mictlantecuhtli, the god of the dead, was found in a large subterranean room beneath the House of the Eagles, near the Templo Mayor in Tenochtitlán. Beneath the god's exposed ribs protrudes a swollen liver.

challenges. First they were required to cross a raging river, then find a way between two clashing mountains. They had to climb a mountain of the volcanic glass obsidian, the material sacred to dark Tezcatlipoca, before facing an icy wind so cold it could peel the flesh from a person's face. They had to defeat a snake, overcome an alligator, survive the crossing of eight deserts, then reach the top of eight towering mountains. They came then into the teeth of a wind of obsidian knives and faced two demon foes. At last they discovered Mictlantecuhtli and Mictlancihuatl. Now the new arrivals might try to curry favor by offering insincere praises or gifts laboriously carried from their tombs, but their efforts would be in vain: for the underworld lord was impatiently waiting for the moment at which he could rip the new arrivals into many pieces.

Some accounts reported that the souls of the dead thereafter found the peace of extinction, but others suggested that every one was doomed to live on eternally in the terrible darkness and among the dank smells of that place. Their only respite came once a year, on the Day of the Dead, when the deceased could visit their relatives in the lands of the living, who would lay out earthly foods in welcome.

An alternative vision of the Aztec underworld was provided in a codex depiction of Quetzalcóatl's voyage there at the beginning of the current world age. Quetzalcóatl went down into the underworld by passing through the body of the earth goddess Coatlicue, then in the east of the subterranean domain he cremated himself on a pyre—and his body was remade in the form of birds. He traveled on to the south of that dark land, where he faced death by beheading or dismemberment, but managed to pass on without injury by moving through the body of the goddess Tlazolteotl. In the west he found two temples, one to the souls of women who had died in childbirth and

• BURIAL AND CREMATION •

Most Aztecs were cremated. Usually a corpse was dressed in good clothes, bound in a squatting position and encased in cloth before being burned. Rulers and members of the nobility were buried in a stone vault— sometimes a noble's wife or servants were killed in order to be buried with him at his death.

Often a man was entombed or burned with his living dog: the creature was expected to be useful as a guide to the deceased on his underworld travels and, moreover, the dog was a propitious reminder of the triumphant voyage made to the underworld by the Plumed Serpent Quetzalcóatl and his dog-double Xolotl. People were generally buried or burned with equipment intended to help them through their underworld trials: food, water, blankets, a jade bead to act as a heart, paper clothes, even presents to win the favor of Mictlantecuhtli and Mictlancihuatl.

one to the spirits of warriors killed in battle: he passed safely on, through the body of the earth monster Tlatelcuhtli, and split into two forms, Red Quetzalcóatl and Black Quetzalcóatl. He came at last to the north: here he made a sacrifice of his red self and then threw himself onto a sacrificial pyre. His undaunted spirit rose powerfully from the underworld into the heavens and reigns there as Venus the Morning Star.

THE SUN AND THE MOON

In ancient times the gods had sacrificed their blood to persuade the sun to travel across the sky. The Aztecs, who in turn offered their blood to the gods, approached each dawn with the fear that their sacrifices had been insufficient and that the sun would not rise again. The sun's appearance was a divine birth: from the loins of Coatlicue emerged the mighty sun god to scale the eastern sky.

The sun god took different forms through the hours of day and night. In the morning hours he was Tonatiuh, an ancient Mesoamerican deity envisaged as a virile youth, his body drenched in red and his face painted yellow and ochre. He followed a fiery serpent, the *xiuhcoatl*, across the expanse of the morning sky. In some accounts the souls of warriors who had died in battle had been transformed into hummingbirds, which lent their strength to the sun god by hauling his chariot through the steep ascent to the top of the heavens.

At its zenith, the sun in full glory became the Mexica's tribal lord, brave Huitzilopochtli. Darkness fled, for with the sun rampant in the noon sky there was scarcely a shadow to be seen on the ground: the light beat down with martial vigor. Through the long afternoon Huitzilopochtli was pulled toward the western horizon by the *cihuateteo*, the souls of women who had died in childbirth (see page 518).

The setting of the sun at dusk was a divine death: the sun god, weakened by his long voyage, was consumed among the mountains of the west by the earth monster Tlatecuhtli. After dark the sun had to travel through the underworld and many trials before—if the sacrifices had been sufficient—he would be born once more in the

• THE RABBIT IN THE MOON •

In the folk tradition of Mesoamerica—and indeed in many other diverse cultures—the markings referred to as the "Man in the Moon" are instead likened to the shape of a rabbit. The Aztecs told that gods in Teotihuacán decreed that the moon (shown here above the Avenue of the Dead in Teotihuacán) should be marked in this way.

When the moon and sun first rose at Teotihuacán the moon was too bright—it seemed to outshine the sun. This probably derived from the belief that the sun had originally been the unappealing but brave god, Nanahuatzin, whereas the moon had been the handsome but cowardly Tecuciztecatl (see page 529). The moon also subverted the natural order by appearing in the heavens before the sun. One of the assembled deities decided to punish the overbearing pride of the moon by throwing an ancestor of the rabbit up at its face, leaving the distinctive mark. In an alternative tradition, the gods decided to place the mark on the moon's face as an eternal record of Tecuciztecatl's cowardice in three times refusing to enter the sacrificial flames at Teotihuacán, whereas Nanahuatzin's bravery in entering the flames meant that he was permitted to shine so brightly that humans cannot safely look upon him.

new morning. By night the sun took the form of Tepeyollotl, a fearless jaguar whose angry roars were caught in the depths of the mountains that swallowed him at night. His voice could be heard in volcanic eruptions and the rumble of an avalanche. Tepeyollotl took the *xiuhcóatl* fire snake with him to fight the foes of darkness in the underworld. It was a common Mesoamerican tradition that the sun became a jaguar by night and spent the hours of darkness fighting in the underworld. The Maya sun god Kinich Ahau became a supernatural jaguar by night (see page 598).

In the hours of darkness the power of the *tzitimime* demons was at its height. These female spirits spread disease and ill fortune wherever they went. They were feared most particularly at times of solar eclipse, when Tonatiuh was believed to be weakened. Then the Aztecs made sacrifices of fair-skinned captives in the hope of strengthening Tonatiuh sufficiently to enable him to overcome the unnaturally encroaching darkness.

The conflict between darkness and light was played out in the history of the struggles between dark Tezcatlipoca and bright Quetzalcóatl that were re-enacted in the ballgame played with such enthusiasm by the Aztecs and their Mesoamerican forebears and neighbors (see pages 500–502). In the sky each day, the brightness of the sun vanquishes the moon. Both the major Aztec accounts of the sun's clash with the moon end with the sun's triumph. In the tale of the first rising of the sun and moon at Teotihuacán, the gods decreed that Nanahuatzin should travel ahead of his rival Tecuciztecatl and shine the more brightly. In the tale of Huitzilopochtli's violent birth, the youthful sun god despatched his sister the moon in the first moments of his life.

ASTRONOMY AND DIVINATION

The Aztecs—like their Mesoamerican neighbors and forebears, especially the Maya—were dedicated astronomers. They made detailed observations and kept meticulous records of celestial phenomena such as the orbits and phases of Venus and the other known planets.

According to Aztec belief, astronomical patterns were charged with divine energy. They were understood to replay sacred episodes such as Quetzalcóatl's sojourn in the underworld and to be a manifestation of universal forces that had daily impact upon human activities: they were pregnant with cryptic information about current and future events that could be spelled out by diviners and priestly interpreters.

Astronomers and priests used observation of the skies as one way of keeping a precise record of the cycles of time. It was the priests' responsibility to set religious festivals at exactly the right time: if the calendar was not followed properly, then the gods might be angered, with disastrous consequences; the calendar also provided a sanctified timetable for essential stages of agricultural life such as sowing and harvesting. Priests regularly consulted their *tonalamatl* screenfold books, which contained detailed information on the movements of the planets and stars and their possible meanings; they also kept meticulous records of the sun's movement to the north and south during the year—religious festivals were set according to the precise position of the sunrise on the eastern horizon each day.

The astronomers were additionally expected to keep watch for bad omens or propitious celestial movements. The emperor and his military advisers consulted with astronomers before setting the date for a military campaign, for example. Indeed, the emperor himself took regular notice of heavenly movements—it was one of his duties as *tlatoani* to inspect the skies, no doubt with expert astronomers at his side, three times every night: at sunset, midnight, and sunrise. Motecuhzoma II witnessed the comet that burned over Tenochtitlán ten years before the arrival of Hernán Cortés's Spanish

◆ THE PROPHETIC BEAN GAME ◆

Spanish chroniclers reported that the Aztecs were inveterate gamblers. Foremost among their games was *patolli*, the "game of the mat," a game of great antiquity, having been played by Mesoamericans since the time of Teotihuacán. Used as a means of divination, as well as simply for money or leisure, it was played on a cross-shaped board with blue and red pieces and using five kidney beans for dice—indeed, it took its name from the word for fava or kidney bean in Nahuatl. Scholars are unclear exactly how the game worked; Diego Durán described how players would throw incense into a bowl of fire before commencing and would invoke the patron god of gambling, Macuilxochitl, each time they threw the beans. Both the wealthy and the poor played for money—the nobles betting great riches in jewels and gold.

It appears that the game also had a religious dimension: diviners interpreted the way the beans fell, but exactly how the future was consulted remains unclear. However, it is probably significant that the number of squares on the board, fifty-two, equated to the total number of years in a cosmic cycle (see page 511).

expedition: his experts and Nezahualpilli, the *tlatoani* of Texcoco who was a celebrated diviner, informed him that this was a terrible omen, portending deep misfortunes for the Aztecs.

The movements of Venus were of particular importance in this celestial patterning. The planet follows a near-circular 225-day orbit around the sun: in Mesoamerican latitudes, it shines brilliantly and is clearly visible to the naked eye at some stages of its cycle. Mesoamerican astronomers plotted four phases in the planet's appearances, totalling 584 days. In the first phase, they reported, Venus appears before sunrise and is visible in the morning sky for 236 days as "the morning star." Next it is outshone by the sun's light: for ninety days it cannot be seen. In its third phase, lasting 250 days, the planet is visible around sunset as "the evening star." Finally it becomes invisible once more for eight days before rising once more as the Morning Star.

In the final eight-day phase Quetzalcóatl was understood to descend to the underworld to confront Mictlantecuhtli and bring back the raw materials for the creation of the human race: after this adventure he rose to the sky in the form of Venus the Morning Star. The appearance of Venus in the morning sky must therefore have been symbolic of Quetzalcóatl's supremacy, a celebration of the god of light's victory over the dark lords of death. Yet the Morning Star did not have a positive role in Mesoamerican religious lore: the planet was seen as an enemy of the sun, and a malign influence on human activity; the Morning Star was Quetzalcóatl in vengeful form as Tlahuizcalpantecuhtli, whose anger was widely feared. Those who came under his influence faced disaster. He sent drought when his ever-burning rage turned against and dried up the rains.

The mysterious pre-Toltec Cotzumalhuapa people from the Pacific coast of Guatemala produced more than 200 stone stelae, including this one which shows a priest offering a heart to Quetzalcóatl, here identified with Venus. The circles above the priest denote dates.

ART AND ARCHITECTURE

The Aztecs constructed large religious ceremonial areas containing temple pyramids. These sacred arenas replicated elements of the natural world—particularly the mountains that the Aztecs held to be holy and which they associated with key scenes from the histories of the gods.

The Great Pyramid in the heart of Tenochtitlán, which bore twin shrines to Tlaloc and to Huitzilopochtli, was intended as a recreation in stone of mountains sacred to these two gods. The holy mountains were Tonacatepetl, the "food mountain" in which Quetzalcóatl had discovered the first grains of maize, and Coatepec, the place of Huitzilopochtli's birth. The stepped pyramid rose to a peak from a base platform some 270 feet (82m) square. The identification with Mount Coatepec was reinforced by the placing of a carved image of the moon goddess Coyolxauhqui on the platform, at the foot of the stairs to the shrine of her brother Huitzilopochtli, recalling how Huitzilopochtli decapitated his sister and flung her body down to the plain beneath Mount Coatepec.

The architecture of cities and their pyramid temples also mirrored the structure of the cosmos. Aztec cosmology (see pages 530–531) proposed that the universe was divided into the thirteen layers of heaven above, nine layers of the underworld beneath—and in between, the flat terrestrial plain split into four quarters and the center. In the Templo Mayor the base platform that contained the carving of Coyolxauhqui represented the terrestrial level and the temple itself was the center, with the four quarters spreading out to north, east, south, and west across the ceremonial area and the city. Archaeologists report that the great majority of offerings to the gods have been found on the base platform or in the foundations of the pyramid—a lower level that may have represented the underworld, to which most souls were destined to voyage after death. The rising levels of the pyramid itself probably represented the layers of heaven: the top platform would then have stood for the highest layer of heaven, where the gods lived. The sacred pyramid was a magical point of access both upward to the heavens and downward to the underworld.

Mesoamerican architects commonly built temples with twin shrines. A fourth-century BCE example of this kind of sacred building has been discovered at Cuicuilco, Mexico, but the identities of the gods celebrated there are as yet unknown. In Tenochtitlán the erection of shrines to both Tlaloc (associated with water, food, and life) and Huitzilopochtli (associated with war and sacrifice) made the Great Pyramid a place of duality,

---

◆ A WEALTH OF VOTIVE OFFERINGS ◆

Archaeologists have recovered around 6,000 objects left as gifts to the gods in caches on the base platform level and in the foundations of Tenochtitlán's Great Pyramid, the Templo Mayor. The offerings included articles from all corners of the Aztec Empire, and masks created by great Mesoamerican cultures such as the Olmec and the builders of Teotihuacán, which suggested that the Aztecs were in awe of a deeply heroic past. The bones of a jaguar may have been intended to represent the power of the king or of Huitzilopochtli; the animal had a greenstone ball in its mouth that perhaps stood for the spirit of a deceased noble honored by burial (see page 553). The skeleton of a crocodile may have been a reference to the creature from which the White and Blue Tezcatlipocas made the Earth. Many offerings celebrated the life-giving waters controlled by Tlaloc and his consort Chalchiuhtlicue. These included pots in the image of these deities, seashells, the bones of fish and water-birds, and pieces of coral. Mother of pearl and jade were delicately carved to represent canoes and sea creatures. Jade was sacred to Chalchiuhtlicue ("Lady of the Jade Skirt."

an expression of death-in-life and life-in-death. The twin shrines may also have symbolized alternative heavens: on Huitzilopochtli's side, the heaven of the sun god, place of reward for brave warriors slain in battle or those killed by sacrifice; on Tlaloc's side, the watery heaven Tlalocan, lush and fertile place of refuge for those killed by lightning storms, drowning, waterborne disease, or other watery cause.

Tenochtitlán's twin city of Tlatelolco also contained a large central ceremonial area with a stepped pyramid sacred to these two gods. Alongside it was a circular building dedicated to Ehecatl–Quetzalcóatl and a construction now called the Temple of Numbers, the walls of which were covered in notation of sacred numbers and the days of the ritual calendar.

THE DECORATIVE ARTS
The Aztecs held their artists and craftspeople in high regard. Their stunning achievements in metalwork,

The Pyramid of the Niches in El Tajín on the Gulf of Mexico is believed to date to ca. 600CE. The structure contains 365 niches, reputedly designed to accommodate an idol for each day of the year.

sculpture, featherwork, pottery, monumental architecture, and other areas were in large part a tribute to and celebration of their inheritance from the glorious past of Mesoamerica. The Aztecs revered the cultural and artistic achievements of the Toltecs in Tollan, and their language reflects this sense of admiration: in Nahuatl the word for artist was *tolteca* and the term for artistic capacity or gift, *toltecayotl*. In the legends the Mexica told of their own wanderings prior to founding Tenochtitlán, they cast themselves as a primitive northern people who learned and developed artistic capacities during a spell staying in the ruins of Tollan. They regarded great Quetzalcóatl–Topiltzin (see page 540), the semi-mythical ruler of Tollan, as the source of the arts and of artistic skill.

According to Friar Bernardino de Sahagún, the Aztecs classified a range of creative workers as *tolteca*. They included featherworkers, artists working with turquoise, jade, and other stones, the scribes who produced codices, gold- and silversmiths, potters, spinners and weavers, painters, carpenters, and bricklayers.

Stoneworkers and potters paid homage to the art of Teotihuacán and of Tollan. The stone figure of the earth and fertility goddess Coatlicue found in 1780 in Mexico City stands more than 8 feet (2.5m) tall and was in the idiom of the great stone warrior figures discovered at Tollan (modern-day Tula). Potters producing water pots, incense-burners, and other wares for use in the temple followed styles used in Teotihuacán and Classic Period Maya cities.

Artists lived in specialized neighborhoods within the city. Some were employed by individual nobles, but others created work for the wealthy to buy on the open market. The Spaniards were astounded by the range of colorful and exquisitely worked ornaments, jewelry, pottery, and other artistic wares available in the market in Tlatelolco. Certain types of work were the speciality of different peoples under Aztec rule—for example, Mixtec artists were renowned for producing exquisite mosaics and metalwork.

Sculptors cut stone records of military triumphs in honor of the sun and tribal god Huitzilopochtli, who delivered battle glory. The *tlatoani* was under a sacred duty to commission these monuments, known as *temalácatl-cuauhxicalli*. Motecuhzoma I and his son Tizoc both left celebrated examples bearing a symbol of

• RHYTHM AND HARMONY •

In temple ritual, public ceremony, and domestic celebrations the Aztecs used a wide range of musical instruments. Two main types of drum were vertical-standing *huehuetl* or horizontal *teponaxtli*. They were intricately carved and sometimes covered with jaguar skin. A magnificent wooden *huehuetl* of ca. 1500, three feet (1m) tall and carved with images of eagle and jaguar warriors and the symbol for holy conflict (*teoatl-tlachinolli*, "fired water"), was found in Malinalco, southwest of Mexico City in the nineteenth century. The horizontal drums were slit along the top to make two "tongues" that were played with rubber sticks. The Aztecs and their predecessors viewed this type of drum with particular reverence. Trumpets, flutes, and whistles were molded from clay or made from seashells. An unusual instrument played at feasts and other celebrations was made from human bone or an animal's horn and when scraped with a shell made a rasping sound.

the victorious sun and images of battle victories cut around the side (see the illustration of the Stone of Tizoc, page 519); another, the sun stone, was probably cut during the rule of Tizoc's brother Axayacatl.

Stoneworkers also achieved magnificent effects in cutting the precious volcanic glass obsidian associated with the god of darkness Tezcatlipoca and semiprecious stones such as turquoise, jade, and mother of pearl. They overcame the brittleness of obsidian to produce vessels, polished mirrors, thin earspools, scepters, and even a remarkable face-mask. Artistic work in mosaic was seen at its most beautiful in the inlaid masks probably worn by the *tlatoani* and by priests or impersonators of the gods during religious festivals.

Artist–artisans in Tenochtitlán also excelled in basketwork and reedwork, making a wide range of baskets used for storing food or clothes and also reed seats and mats. In both wealthy and humble homes reed mats were an essential item, for the Aztecs had little use for furniture beyond simple low tables. Most people sat on the floor—the only chairs were thrones, which were covered with jaguar skins and reserved for the ruler.

Specialist weavers called *amanteca* practiced the ancient Mesoamerican art of featherwork: during weaving they tied the stems of brightly colored feathers into the material to make featherwork cloaks, mantles and loincloths for the use of the nobility and by priests or senior officials in public or religious ceremony. The feathers were supplied by professional hunters, who tracked birds for their plumage in tropical rainforests. The *amanteca* also produced decorated shields and military wear for ceremonial use by the highest-ranking Aztec warriors.

Colorful plates such as this one, often standing on three elaborate feet, would have been used to serve food to the nobility and to hold offerings to the gods. This refined style of decoration originated in the Mixtec settlement of Cholula, 80 miles (130km) southeast of Tenochtitlán.

THE CENTER OF THE WORLD

When the Spanish conquistadors came upon Tenochtitlán in November 1519, the Aztec capital was close to the zenith of its power—the vast water-metropolis was home to around 250,000 people, more than twice the size of Europe's largest city at the time.

The invaders took in Tenochtitlán's magnificent setting, its towering white temple-pyramids framed by snow-topped peaks, the city surrounded by the fertile green of floating fields and linked to the mainland by causeways across glittering blue water dotted with canoes. They were struck by the elegant layout of four quarters with a sacred arena at the center, the network of crisscrossing canals, the white residential buildings interspersed with captivating gardens in which fountains played and tropical flowers created a riot of color, the menageries in which nobles kept birds and animals.

They were astounded by the wealth and size of the market in the neighboring city of Tlatelolco, which could hold 60,000 people. One of the conquistadors, Bernal Diaz del Castillo, declared the imperial capital to be like an enchanted vision or a dream.

The Aztecs had built this great water-metropolis from an unpromising beginning. The Mexica came late to the Valley of Mexico, when most of the best land had already been claimed by other groups. The twin islands in Lake Texcoco on which they founded Tenochtitlán, and shortly afterward Tlatelolco, had not attracted the attention of any of the region's great powers—Culhuacan, Atzcapotzalco, or Texcoco. On the instructions of Huitzilopochtli, the Mexica laid out their city in four equal quarters. The twenty tribal clans were each assigned their own zone and held land in common. They each had their own temple: several sacred buildings built on truncated pyramids were erected in the different quarters of the city. But there were just two large open spaces—the ceremonial plazas of Tenochtitlán and Tlatelolco. Three great causeways connected the city to the mainland: according to Hernán Cortés, these were each 12 feet (3.5m) in width.

The Aztecs reclaimed land by building *chinampa* floating fields. In shallow parts of the lake, these were built up from the lakebed with levels of earth and plants and fixed in place with tall poles, whereas in deeper areas reed beds filled with earth were anchored to the bed. The fields were divided by narrow canals used by farmers as a source of water and to move produce by canoe. Each *chinampa*, which might measure anything from 1,000 to 9,000 square feet (90–840 sq m), would be farmed by clan groups of up to fifteen people.

The city's location had two major drawbacks. Firstly, it was naturally vulnerable to flooding: a great flood in 1500 during the reign of Ahuizotl caused severe damage and was interpreted as a sign of the gods' displeasure. Secondly, it could easily be surrounded by an enemy. This weakness was exploited by Hernán Cortés who obstructed the city's three causeways and imposed a blockade of barges as part of a three-month siege in 1521 that led to the final defeat of the Aztecs and the end of their Empire.

Yet the lake setting also had advantages: birds, fish, and other marine life were abundant; there was plenty of room to expand once the Mexica/Aztecs had mastered the science of building such fields; transport was quick and easy by canoe—in contrast to the difficulty of moving heavy items on land for a people who did not have the advantage of using beasts of burden. Moreover, the islands on which Tenochtitlán and Tlatelolco developed were at the center of a triangle made up of the lake's existing powers—Culhuacan to the south, Atzcapotzalco to the west and Texcoco to the east. This was of crucial importance when the great marketplace became established in Tlatelolco.

Tenochtitlán's island setting also had major religious and cultural significance for the Mexica/Aztecs, because it reminded them of Aztlan, the mythical original homeland of the Mexica that was said to be dry land in the midst of a northern lagoon. Its situation also made Tenochtitlán an image of the Earth itself, which the Aztecs believed was a flat expanse encircled by ocean; they sometimes called their capital Cemanahuac ("place encircled by water").

The city was also celebrated as a recreation of a sacred mountain—just as the Great Pyramid at its heart was also a homage to the mountains of the gods (see page 558). The word for city in Nahuatl was *atl tepetl* ("water mountain"). The Aztecs saw mountains as the places where water was stored before Tlaloc and Chalchiuhtlicue released it as rain. The city was entirely dependent on the water that Tlaloc and Chalchiuhtlicue sent from the heights and its people celebrated the sacred peaks. Mountains close to Lake Texcoco—including Tlaloc, Iztaccihuatl and Popocatepetl—were worshipped as sources of rain.

THE RITUAL PRECINCT

Archaeologists and historians have reconstructed the sacred precincts in the center of Tenochtitlán. The vast square contained four temples, a ballcourt, and other buildings in addition to the great stepped pyramid sacred to Tlaloc and Huitzilopochtli and called the Templo Mayor by the Spaniards. The vast Templo

Mayor rose 150 feet (45m) on the eastern side of the square, with vertiginous twin staircases running down its western face, which gave onto the ceremonial area. At the top of these staircases on the pyramid's flat top, facing westward toward the square, stood the twin temples: one, on the northern half of the platform, to Tlaloc, with a *chacmool* sacrificial figure recumbent in front of it; the other, on the southern half of the platform, honoring Huitzilopochtli, with a bloodstained sacrificial stone standing before it. The Tlaloc temple was decorated in blue and white, colors associated with the god because of his influence over water, while the Huitzilopochtli shrine was painted in red and white,

colors connected to war as well as blood sacrifice. At the foot of the staircases was a second platform, where the stone carving of moon goddess Coyolxauhqui lay directly before the steps up to Huitzilopochtli's shrine (see page 558). Beyond this lower platform, another shorter staircase led down to ground level: this second staircase was decorated with painted stucco images of the Plumed Serpent Quetzalcóatl and of frogs, which were sacred to Tlaloc.

Assembled on the ground before these steps crowds would have gazed up toward the twin shrines, watched as priests ripped the heart from a victim's body, and then witnessed the body tumbling down the steep staircase to land on the stone of Coyolxauhqui. On ground level looking north and south on either side of the Templo Mayor the crowd would have seen further temples. Archaeologists have not yet identified the temple to the north of the pyramid; the one to the south was sacred to Tezcatlipoca. Behind the crowd, directly to the west of the steps of the Templo Mayor, was a circular temple to the wind god Ehecatl–Quetzalcóatl and behind that on the western edge of the square was a ritual ballcourt. To the south of the ballcourt and the Ehecatl–Quetzalcóatl temple was a rack on which the skulls of slain sacrificial victims were displayed. Two other buildings lay within the precinct: to the north of the ballcourt was a building set aside for the priests, while to the south lay a temple dedicated to Xipe Totec.

Archaeologists have discovered that the pyramid of the Templo Mayor, in common with many other Mesoamerican sacred pyramids, was constructed in several stages over a long period, with each new level built over and

This monumental stone disk depicting the dismemberment of the moon goddess Coyolxauhqui by her brother Huitzilopochtli was located at the bottom of the steps up to Huitzilopochtli's shrine on the Templo Mayor. Its chance discovery in 1978 gave fresh impetus to Aztec studies.

encompassing the one that went before. The first structure was built at around the time of the establishment of Tenochtitlán in 1325. According to codex accounts, when the Mexica founded the city they erected a base platform and a temple to Huitzilopochtli from mud and reeds at the place where they had seen an eagle clutching a snake on a cactus—so fulfilling their god's prophecy (see pages 504–507). No archaeological evidence of this base-level construction has yet been uncovered. A second stage was built on top of this rudimentary platform in around 1390, bringing the structure to a height of around 50 feet (15m). Twin shrines to Tlaloc and Huitzilopochtli had been established on the temple platform by this point.

In around 1431—three years after the establishment of the Triple Alliance of Tenochtitlán, Tlaxcala, and Texcoco—the sacred building was greatly enlarged, suggesting that the city was already wealthy enough to divert substantial numbers of agricultural and military personnel to the project; alternatively, labor may have been provided by conquered or allied territories, who were required to send workers to Tenochtitlán. Significant and extravagant improvements were then made in around 1454 in the reign of Motecuhzoma I (1440–1469), when the empire of the Triple Alliance was already generating great wealth for the people of Tenochtitlán. At this time a grand staircase was added on top of the original on the pyramid's western face and a carved greenstone image of Coyolxauhqui laid at the foot of the staircase. This was a forerunner of the celebrated image of the goddess, which dates to around 1469—the first year of the reign of Axayacatl; braziers and decorative serpent heads, along with an image of the *pulque* goddess Mayahuel

and pots celebrating the goddess of food Chicomecoatl were also deposited at this stage. This phase of expansion involved the extending of the platform at the foot of the main west-facing staircase.

Further improvements and additions were made in about 1482 in the reign of Tizoc, in 1486 under Ahuizotl and in 1502 under Motecuhzoma II. Hernán Cortés's Spanish troops and their local allies razed the Templo Mayor to the level of the lowest of its platforms in August 1521. Major excavations of the site were begun after an electricity company worker discovered the celebrated stone image of Coyolxauhqui (see illustration, opposite) while digging in central Mexico City in 1978.

Among the many offerings (see page 558) left on the base platform of the Templo Mayor was this pot decorated with a mask of Tlaloc the rain god. Made during the reign of Motecuhzoma I (1440–1469), the vessel was found in a stone box pointing toward the shrine of Tlaloc.

CITY OF THE GODS

Teotihuacán was a revered place of pilgrimage for the Aztecs. The magnificent ancient metropolis was constructed by unknown architects in the centuries after about 100BCE. At its height in 500CE, the city covered 8 square miles (20 sq km) and was home to between 125,000 and 200,000 people.

Teotihuacán was built on a sacred site used for offerings since time immemorial off the main Valley of Mexico, 30 miles (50km) northeast of Tenochtitlán. By the time of the Aztecs, Teotihuacán lay in ruins. But although its once great pyramids and temples were probably no more than vast, overgrown mounds in the fourteenth century, their setting in an ancient sacred site and their awe-inspiring scale were sufficient to make the Aztecs imagine that these were the creation of the gods or of an ancient race of giants. The Aztecs made regular journeys to the ruined city, to make sacrifices and offerings and to remove artifacts for ritual use back in Tenochtitlán. Such was the impression this city made on

them that its buildings were used as the backdrop to the Aztec creation narrative in which Nanahuatzin and Tecuciztecatl passed through sacrificial fire to become the sun and moon (see page 529). The ruins gained added resonance because the Aztecs also associated them with the revered culture of the Toltecs.

Teotihuacán was laid out on a grid pattern around its main artery, a ceremonial way 1.5 miles (2.4km) long and 130 feet (40m) wide that links the city's principal pyramid-temples. On the eastern side of the roadway lies the Pyramid of the Sun, erected in about 150CE and rising to a height of 216 feet (66m). In 1971 archaeologists discovered a cave beneath the pyramid containing

offerings from an early period BCE, indicating that the city's location was long established as a holy place. At the northern end of the ceremonial way was the smaller Pyramid of the Moon, 140 feet (43m) in height. The roadway was lined on both sides with low buildings, probably used as royal residences; the Aztecs believed the buildings to be tombs and named the road the "Avenue of the Dead." Directly behind the Pyramid of the Moon was the extinct volcano of Cerro Gordo.

To the east of the southern end of the Avenue of the Dead was a large sunken courtyard which contained a pyramid-temple with seven tiers or steps honoring the Plumed Serpent Quetzalcóatl and the rain god Tlaloc and containing scores of sculptural representations of these two gods. On this site the Aztecs built their own temple, perhaps because the ruined Quetzalcóatl–Tlaloc pyramid was buried and they did not know it was there or perhaps because they felt reverence not so much for the ancient buildings as for the sacred setting close to the cave beneath the Pyramid of the Sun and on the plain before the holy Cerro Gordo and wanted to build their own sacred structure in that place.

Viewed from the steps of the Pyramid of the Moon, the Avenue of the Dead stretches southward. To the left of the roadway is the tallest building in Teotihuacán, the Pyramid of the Sun, which rises to a height of 216 feet (66m). In the distance, at the southern end of the Avenue of the Dead is the Temple of Quetzalcóatl.

◆ THE RISE AND FALL OF A GREAT METROPOLIS ◆

Teotihuacán was first settled in about 400BCE but did not expand significantly until around 100BCE, when a volcanic eruption devastated a settlement at Cuicuilco, in the southwestern part of the Valley of Mexico, and sent many refugees heading northeast to Teotihuacán. The city thrived: it was close to supplies of the highly prized volcanic glass obsidian and on the trade route between the Gulf of Mexico and the Valley of Mexico. It also lay on the San Juan Teotihuacán River, which provided water for agricultural irrigation.

At its zenith in approximately 500CE Teotihuacán was one of the world's largest cities, containing thousands of residential buildings and 600 temples, as well as a thriving mercantile and crafts center with 500 workshops where skilled craftspeople worked in obsidian and made pots. But the great city's golden age did not last beyond 650CE. In the seventh century, fierce nomads swept southward from inhospitable regions to the north of the Valley of Mexico and destroyed the grandeur of Teotihuacán. They smashed the staircase of the Pyramid of the Moon and put to the torch the palaces lining the Avenue of the Dead.

NORTH AMERICA'S "ANCIENT ONES"

Those native peoples encountered from the sixteenth century onward by Europeans in what is now the United States and Canada were comparatively unsophisticated societies in terms of their patterns of urban settlement or adoption of monumental architecture. Yet there was evidence across the continent of the presence of advanced earlier peoples—perhaps influenced by Mesoamerican cultures further to the south—such as the Mississippians and Anasazi who had created noteworthy structures but had declined and disappeared.

ABOVE AND RIGHT The Cliff Palace, Mesa Verde (above), resembles an apartment block. Built ca. 1200CE by the Anasazi ("Ancient Ones") people, the site was abandoned soon after and the inhabitants mysteriously vanished. Pottery and rare artifacts such as this ceremonial headdress (right) have been found, but otherwise there are few clues.

LEFT The Mississippian "Mound" builders of the river valleys of the eastern woodlands of North America left behind many ceremonial and burial mounds, which have been interpreted as evidence of a belief in earthly divinities. Some were built to resemble animals: one of the most spectacular examples is the Serpent Mound in Ohio's Mississippi Valley. Such mounds are thought to have been constructed ca. 650CE–1100CE by the descendants of the Adena and Hopewell cultures.

BELOW A circular, subterranean room at Pueblo Bonito, Chaco Canyon (ca. 1100CE), which is thought to have been used for ceremonial ritual purposes by male Anasazi. The Pueblo Indians who live in the region today still use such kivas, as these underground chambers are known.

CHAPTER TWO

THE MAYA

Maya civilization was the longest lived and one of the most widely spread of all the great cultures of ancient America. Monumental architecture and vivid imagery are testament to the complexity and sophistication of a sometimes ferocious people whose history has been—and is continuing to be—revealed to us through the translation of their intricate hieroglyphic texts. The tremendous artistic legacy of the Maya continues to inspire awe and fascination—it is most spectacularly seen at the great temple complexes but is equally magnificent to behold on a lesser scale in works of art in paint, jade, stone, and pottery. The world depicted was one in which Maya kings ruled with absolute authority over their people, seeking guidance from the heavens to enable them to plan for the future. Their fascination with the stars enabled the Maya astronomer-priests to chart the movements of the stars and planets, to accurately measure and record time, and to formulate a sophisticated calendar system. The more macabre practices of sacrifice and bloodletting reflected belief in a cosmic cycle of time, which the continuation of which and the need to appease the deities in order for the world to continue.

THE SOUL OF THE MAYA

The ancient Maya were a formidable people whose cities were built on a monumental scale. Society was stratified—the majority of the population lived in thatched huts, but the nobles were housed in lavish stone palaces and, after death, their bodies were often entombed beneath vast pyramid temples.

The Maya's sophisticated, and in many ways unified, culture developed despite the fact that they never established a single empire, but remained divided into small city-states that were frequently at war with one another. Some of the common themes that draw the Maya people together, and enable their civilization to be viewed as an entity, are their myths and creation stories; their understanding of the cosmos; and their religious beliefs and conception of the afterlife.

Maya mythology tells how divinities from a previous world age created the Earth, and then formed the first people from maize—the staple food of the region. The same deities taught humans how to make sacrifices in order to repay them for their beneficent act of creation. Thus, the Maya believed that their very existence was dependent on the continued goodwill of the divinities. Elaborate rituals, during which participants dressed up in costumes of iridescent quetzal feathers, formed one essential means of sustaining this relationship. Surviving Maya books show tables that were drawn up to suggest how the deities should be appeased through offerings.

In a society so completely governed by the divine and the regal, it is no surprise that both feature prominently in Maya works of art. The ruler's image dominated monumental sculpture—he commanded a particular respect and position of power because he was considered to be an intermediary between humankind and the omnipotent divinities.

The late 8th-century CE murals from three rooms of the temple at Bonampak are perhaps the finest to survive from the Maya world and they reveal to scholars much detail about court life. This detail—the vivid colors only now made apparent by computer-aided reconstruction—from the second room shows a scene with prisoners of war before King Chan Muan, the supreme lord of Bonampak.

◆ APPEASING THE DEITIES ◆

The Maya gods and goddesses demanded constant propitiation, and kings led slave-raids to supply their priests with victims for human sacrifice. One such raid is depicted at Bonampak (opposite): in the center, a vanquished warrior tumbles amid the bodies of his comrades, the broken spear signifying defeat. The triumphant lords of Bonampak are led by King Chan-Muan, who wears the pelt and head of a jaguar, symbols of royal power and authority. The king seizes his adversary by the hair—in Maya iconography, this represents the moment of conquest. The warrior to his left, who firmly grips another victim in similar fashion, may be the ruler of Lacanhá, a city mentioned in the accompanying glyphs as Bonampak's ally in the conflict. Like Chan-Muan, this Maya chieftain wears a decorated human head around his neck, perhaps a trophy from another military victory. Chan-Muan's efforts to ensure that the gods looked with favor on his reign proved fruitless. These murals were never completed, and Bonampak was itself abandoned shortly after they were painted.

THE STORY OF THE MAYA

The ancient Maya occupied a widely varied territory that included Chiapas and the Yucatán peninsula in Mexico, all of present-day Guatemala and Belize, and the western parts of Honduras and El Salvador. In the south of their land was an area of volcanic mountains whose temperate valleys provided ideal conditions for agriculture.

The central area of the Maya domains—the lowlands of the Petén region of modern-day Guatemala and the adjacent states—was covered in dense tropical rainforest where animals, birds, and insects abounded. The powerful jaguar, which plays a prominent part in Maya artistic imagery (see page 598), inhabited these forests. It was in this inhospitable terrain that some of the largest and most successful cities, such as Tikal and Yaxchilán, were built.

In the north, stretching toward the Caribbean, lies the Yucatán peninsula—a plateau of limestone, covered in low, scrubby vegetation. The Yucatán has no surface rivers owing to the nature of the rock, but subterranean streams create caves and, when their roofs collapse, holes in the ground are formed called *cenotes*. These were very important to the local Maya: not only did they provide the only water source, but they were also believed to be entrances to the dreaded underworld.

It is generally accepted that peoples entered the Americas from Asia at least 12,000 years ago during the last Ice Age, when there was a land bridge across the Bering Strait. Research suggests that this occurred not just in one wave but several, and that there may have been entry points other than the land bridge, perhaps along the Pacific coast. For several thousand years humans existed as nomadic hunter–gatherers, penetrating to the tip of the continent. Stone tools and arrowheads from this "Archaic Period" suggest a continuous occupation of what was to become the Maya homeland. The emergence of settled Maya villages began in the first, or possibly the second, millennium BCE. By approximately 500BCE, major centers had been established in the central lowlands at sites such as Nakbé and El Mirador. Settlements had also been founded in the southern highlands and in the northern parts of Yucatán.

These developments took place in an era that archaeologists have labeled the "Preclassic." During the first half of the twentieth century, scholars divided Maya civilization into three periods. The Preclassic, which was perceived as a time of relatively small, primitive village settlements, began around 2000BCE and ended in 250CE. The era that followed, the "Classic Period" (ca. 250–900CE), was thought of as the golden age of the Maya during which the civilization reached its zenith, with great advances in the arts and sciences. A grand building such as the three-tiered palace at Sayil offers a fitting testament to this age, dating from about 750CE to 1000CE, but then inexplicably abandoned. The final era was the "Postclassic Period" (ca. 900CE–early 1500s), believed to be a period of cultural decline following the collapse of most major urban centers in the lowlands.

However, it is now recognized that many achievements attributed to the Classic Period actually occurred during the Preclassic era, and that large Maya settlements existed centuries earlier than had previously been estimated. The traditional view of the collapse of Maya civilization has also been revised. It had been thought that most Maya cities were abandoned at the end of the ninth century CE as a result of internal rebellion, invasion, famine, or disease. More recent scholarship has revealed that the Maya Empire was not unified, as originally thought, but made up of city-states that were constantly waging wars against each other or forming alliances. Toward the end of the Classic Period, population and warfare increased dramatically, while land depletion and disease apparently reached a high point. These factors may have led to the Maya collapse in the lowlands, but in the southern highlands and Yucatán peninsula the Maya continued to flourish until the arrival of the Spanish in the sixteenth century.

THE MAYA WORLD

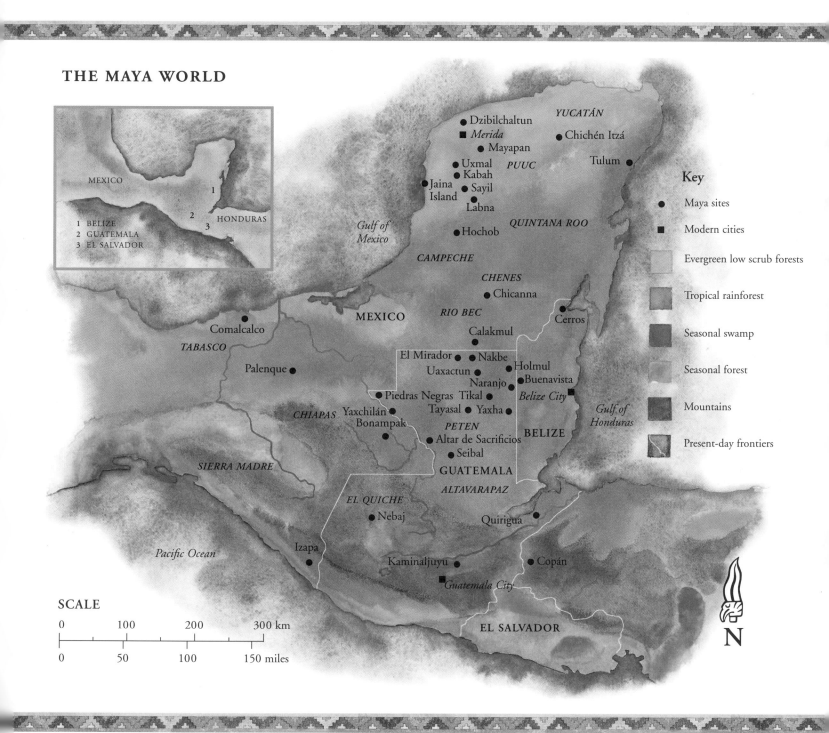

MEXICO

1 BELIZE
2 GUATEMALA
3 EL SALVADOR

HONDURAS

YUCATÁN

Dzibilchaltun

■ *Merida*

Mayapan

Chichén Itzá

Tulum

PUUC

Uxmal
Kabah
Jaina
Island
Sayil
Labna

*Gulf of
Mexico*

QUINTANA ROO

Hochob

CAMPECHE

CHENES

Chicanna

RIO BEC

Cerros

MEXICO

Calakmul

Comalcalco

TABASCO

El Mirador
Nakbe

Holmul

Uaxactun

Buenavista

Palenque

Naranjo

Belize City

Piedras Negras
Tikal

BELIZE

Yaxchilán
Tayasal
Yaxha

*Gulf of
Honduras*

CHIAPAS

Bonampak

PETEN

Altar de Sacrificios

Seibal

GUATEMALA

ALTAVARAPAZ

SIERRA MADRE

EL QUICHE

Nebaj

Quirigua

Pacific Ocean

Izapa

Kaminaljuyu

Copán

■ *Guatemala City*

EL SALVADOR

N

Key

● Maya sites

■ Modern cities

Evergreen low scrub forests

Tropical rainforest

Seasonal swamp

Seasonal forest

Mountains

Present-day frontiers

SCALE

0   100   200   300 km

0   50   100   150 miles

THE ART OF THE MAYA

The Maya produced some of the world's most beautiful art, in a wide variety of media that included stone, wood, plaster, paint, ceramic, jade, and shell. The interiors of Maya buildings—despite their often drab appearance today—would originally have been the setting of many spectacular and brightly colored murals which, unfortunately, have largely disintegrated owing to the humid atmosphere.

Those rare instances in which Maya murals have survived, such as at Bonampak (see illustration, page 573) and Tulum, indicate that Maya towns would once have been places of vibrant color, since the exteriors of many buildings would also have been painted.

The subject matter of Maya art ranges from earthly rulers and nobles to the activities of the divinities, and graphic depictions of the underworld. Members of the nobility, particularly the rulers of Maya city-states, were commonly celebrated in the form of the stela (plural stelae)—an upright standing stone usually around three

feet (1m) high, although some were as much as ten times that height. The largest stela discovered so far is at the site of Quirigua in southeastern Guatemala. This monument, erected in 771CE and dedicated to King Cauac Sky, towers nearly thirty feet (10m) above the plaza. Stelae often bear hieroglyphic texts which give details such as the dates of the ruler's birth, accession to the throne, marriage, and important victories in battle. Erected in the great plazas of each Maya city—several good examples erected by King 18 Rabbit still stand in the main plaza at Copán in Honduras—stelae served

Classic Period techniques of stone carving from the Puuc region are displayed in this detail of the Palace of the Masks at Kabah, one of the driest areas of Maya territory, in the Yucatán peninsula. A plain facade was built first, and a veneer of cut stones was then applied, creating an intricate frieze of portraits or symbols. A stylized image of the rain deity Chac, one of 260 identical examples, is believed to be shown here.

both as monuments to the king and as public statements of his right to rule. They were, in effect, giant pieces of political propaganda set in stone.

Maya artwork varied in size from these colossal stelae and monumental architectural sculpture, such as the portrayals of the rain god Chac adorning the Palace of the Masks at Kabah (see illustration, left), to tiny carved shell ornaments less than one inch (2.5cm) long. Whatever the genre or context of an artwork, however, every line, symbol, and motif was intended to convey meaning: the concept of purely decorative art was lacking in Maya thought (see box, right).

On the smaller scale, Maya artists produced exquisite works in jade, shell, and flint. Jade was their most valued material—unlike the Aztecs or the Inca, they had minimal access to gold, and then only during the Postclassic era. Rulers were commonly depicted in jade, almost always in profile in order to display the long sloping forehead that the Maya considered desirable. The notion of beauty in Maya culture would today seem alien to most Westerners. For example, the Maya so greatly admired a sloping brow that they would strap pieces of wood to the front of a baby's head so that the skull would be molded into the required shape. This process does not seem to have harmed the brain.

Some of the most expressive objects of Maya art are painted ceramics, particularly plates and cylindrical vases. These often show scenes of courtly life, such as processions, dancing, or rituals, and are sometimes painted with deities from the Maya pantheon. However, they also depict the more sinister lords of Xibalba, the underworld (see page 597), perhaps because many of

◆ ABSTRACTION IN MAYA ART ◆

Much Maya art is concerned with naturalistic portrayal, but artists did sometimes employ patterns whose purpose seems solely to be decorative. This impression is deceptive, however, because the notion of pure decoration was alien to the Maya. Thus, while their designs can certainly be appreciated on an exclusively artistic level, they always contain a message. Some motifs and designs are far easier to decipher than others—a few, simply shaped astrological symbols, for example, are more straightforward to interpret than motifs that are repeated and intertwined to form dynamic patterns of complex, multi-layered symbolism (such as that depicted here, below).

these ceramics were placed in tombs to accompany the deceased on their journey through the nether regions.

The Maya artist, unlike those of many other ancient cultures, did not always remain anonymous. Several stone carvings bear the name of their sculptor, and Maya ceramics are often "signed." It has recently been discovered that many artists were members of royal families—often younger brothers of the king. In order to draw attention to their regal connections, these élite artists frequently positioned their names on their work alongside a depiction of the ruler.

RECORDING THE MYSTERIES

In the late 1560s Fray Diego de Landa wrote of how Maya books, or codices, of "ancient matters and sciences" had been burned because they contained "superstition". A mere four codices survived, only one of which, the Grolier Codex, *has remained in the Americas.*

Maya codices are not books in the sense of having many leaves bound together along one edge. Instead, they consist of long strips of paper made from the bark of the fig tree, and are several feet long. Codices are folded in concertina fashion, much like a modern map, allowing as much of the book to be viewed at any one time as required. The paper was prepared with a layer of limewash on which the scribe painted.

Judging by those few that have survived, it seems that the codices were used predominantly by priests for prognostication and divination. They contain tables devised for regulating the times of rituals and agricultural tasks, and for keeping track of astronomical cycles. The reasons why Landa, bishop of Yucatán, was so keen to destroy these texts are complex, but he would probably have been most offended by the many images depicting Maya deities, including the voluptuous, bare-breasted, young moon goddess (see box, page 599).

Each codex displays a variety of pictures, hieroglyphs, and numbers. Every page is made up of individual tables, or "chapters," and is read from left to right; each chapter is specific to a particular topic, such as war or marriage. If a priest wanted to predict, say, the best days on which to plant crops, he would first look up the appropriate chapter for this subject. Stretching down the left-hand side of the table was a column of day-signs from the sacred 260-day calendar, and horizontal rows of numbers were arranged across the page (see pages 589–590). The priest would use these tables to make detailed calculations by which he would arrive at a selection of day-signs. The auguries for each day are indicated by the picture and text associated with it. The image shows which deity has an influence on that day, and the hieroglyphs tell if the day is auspicious.

Other activities regulated by the codices included beekeeping, traveling, hunting, the times at which to

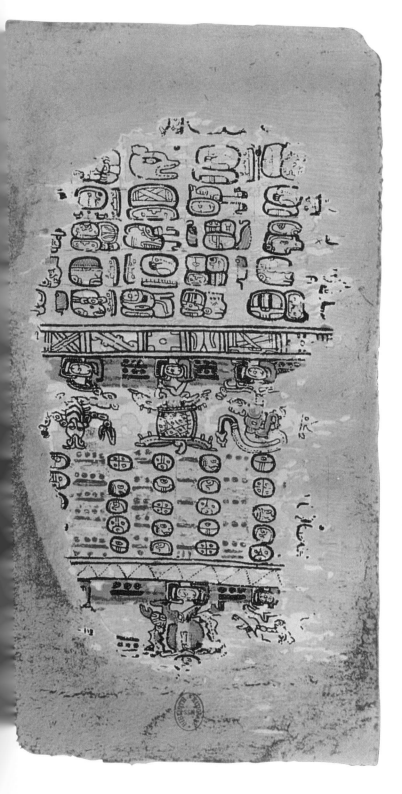

make offerings to the deities, and when rainmaking ceremonies should take place. There are also tables for monitoring seasonal changes and, most importantly, for predicting the appearances of Venus (see page 590) and eclipses of the sun and moon. (Eclipses were viewed with foreboding because celestial objects appeared to be swallowed up by an invisible force.) The codices demonstrate the Maya belief that all things have their preordained place in time, and that the divinities retain ultimate control of destiny.

GLYPH AND SYMBOL

Maya hieroglyphic writing has only recently become understood. It was thought that the script was a combination of rebus, or pictorial representation, and logograms, symbols representing a single word or concept. It was recognized in the nineteenth century that many Maya texts included information about the calendar and astronomy, leading scholars to believe that the Maya were a peaceful nation of astronomer–priests. The inability to read the Maya glyphs correctly meant that this misconception persisted for decades, despite the evidence of warfare and sacrifice in much Maya art.

It is now generally recognized, thanks to the theory of Yuri Knorosov, that the hieroglyphs were largely a phonetic writing system (there were some logograms) and that the different signs stood for individual sounds, whole words or concepts, numbers, days, and months. The shape of the glyphs demonstrates a fascination with the interplay between naturalism and abstraction, drawing upon a variety of animate and inanimate forms.

Two rows of animals can be deciphered hanging from horizontal bands in these badly damaged pages from the Postclassic Paris Codex. These are the animals of the Maya zodiac. The upper band is a skyband, composed of symbols thought to represent constellations. A series of bar-and-dot numbers and signs from the 260-day calendar suggests that these tables were used to predict the movements of the constellations. However, the calculations made by astronomer–priests remain a mystery.

FOREST, EARTH, AND STONE

The Maya were sensitive to the spiritual dimensions of their environment. Through stone architecture and sculpture, they symbolically re-created both the patterns of the cosmos and the earthly world. The towering pyramid temples replicate mountains, the dwelling places of the ancestors; the plazas can be envisaged as lakes or seas; and standing stones are arranged in imitation of the forests.

Yaxchilán lies deep in the rainforest of Chiapas on a site that is bordered by a horseshoe bend of the great Usumacinta River. Today its ruins lie scattered among the trees; difficult to reach, it exudes an air of mystery. However, during the Classic Period, Yaxchilán lay at the heart of one of the most populous Maya regions. As with most ancient Maya cities, we do not know exactly what it was called by its inhabitants; it was named "Yaxchilán" by an Austrian explorer during the nineteenth century, but hieroglyphs at the site suggest that it may have been called something like "The Place of the Split Sky."

Surrounded on three sides by the river, Yaxchilán occupied a good defensive position. The city stretched upward into the hills—huge terraces were built against the steep slopes, and many of the most important temples were situated on the highest hilltops. It has been suggested that some of these constructions may have been used as astronomical observatories. On the morning of the summer solstice, a viewer in such a temple would have been able to watch the sun rising out of a cleft between two high mountains on the eastern horizon. According to Maya belief, this spectacle represented the jaguar-sun (see page 598) emerging from the underworld.

Discovered at El Pasadita—a city in Guatemala that was under the rule of King Bird Jaguar of Yaxchilán—this lintel depicts the king performing a ritual to celebrate the completion of a 10-year period, or half katun. Bird Jaguar (left) stands opposite an administrator from the city, and is wearing an elaborate costume, befitting his superior status. He has just engaged in an act of great religious devotion in the form of bloodletting from his penis (see page 603). The dotted streams flowing from his hands represent his royal blood. (Equally gory was auto-sacrifice by means of tongue laceration.)

A distinctive architectural feature of Yaxchilán is the large vertical roofcomb. Such masonry structures raised the height of the temples considerably and were thought to transform them into the mountain homes of the Maya ancestors. In the plazas between the stone "mountains," a large number of carved standing stones, or stelae, were placed (see illustration, page 608). The Maya name for such monuments was *te tun*, or "tree stone." Not only did these stelae record important events, but in unison they also replicated the forest that surrounded Yaxchilán. Thus, in effect, the city was a re-creation in stone of the natural environment in which the Maya lived.

A large number of the surviving stone monuments at Yaxchilán bear inscriptions that describe the city's history. These buildings often had carved stone lintels, some of which are considered today to be among the finest works of Maya art, including dramatic depictions of scenes of bloodletting and its aftermath. The inscriptions record a series of kings dating back to Yaxchilán's founder, Jaguar Penis, who came to the throne in 320CE. Yaxchilán attained its greatest prosperity under two kings, Shield Jaguar II and his son Bird Jaguar III, who between them ruled from 681 to the 760s CE. However, the success that Yaxchilán enjoyed during their reigns did not continue—only a few years after Bird Jaguar's death, the city was abandoned, by the Maya and the artificial forest of "tree stones" was reclaimed by natural woodland, until the city's rediscovery more than 1,000 years later.

SACRED MOUNTAINS

One of the most impressive aspects of any ruined Maya city in the lowland rainforests of Guatemala and the

◆ PYRAMIDS OF THE MAYA ◆

The shape of pyramids in the Maya region varied widely. At Tikal, in the Petén rainforest, the pyramids are tall, with relatively narrow sides, and extremely steep stairways—some reaching an incline of seventy degrees. At Chichén Itzá, however, the main pyramid has a square base and is squat; its dramatic serpent (left) was a reminder that pyramid temples provided access to other cosmic realms (see pages 602–603). Despite their differences, most Maya pyramids had two fundamental functions: they were temples—each incorporated a sanctuary for worship, usually at its summit—and they were funerary monuments, often housing elaborate royal crypts.

The 8th-century CE Temple II at Tikal, in the heart of the dense Petén jungle, stands in the Great Plaza—the locus of the site—opposite Temple I (from where this photograph was taken). Behind Temple II, the roofcombs of Temples III and IV rise above the forest like mountain peaks. More than 30 rulers from the 3rd to 9th centuries CE have been identified from evidence at Tikal, but it is not known why Tikal was abandoned after centuries of settlement. It is believed that Temple II was built around 700CE by the then ruler Hasaw (whose tomb is in Temple I) as a monument for his wife Lady Twelve Macaw.

---

surrounding regions is the sight of pyramid temples towering above the forest canopy and soaring into the sky. The Maya word for such pyramids was *witz*, a term also used to mean "mountain." According to Maya belief—one still held today by the Maya of Chiapas—mountains housed the souls of their ancestors.

For the lowland Maya, the nearest high peaks lay hundreds of miles away. Consequently, it was necessary for them to construct artificial mountains, in the form of great stone pyramids, at the hearts of their cities. Although all pyramids served as dwelling places for the souls of honored predecessors, many also contained the actual tombs of great Maya kings and nobles—such as Palenque's Temple of the Inscriptions (see box and illustration, pages 584–585), buried deep within which was the sarcophagus of King Pacal.

At the top of the pyramids stood temples where the deities were worshipped and propitiated. A great procession up the side of the pyramid formed the climax to many Maya ceremonies, though ascending the steep stairs with their narrow treads was no easy matter—in fact, the necessity of placing the feet sideways may even have been part of the ritual, making the climb more difficult and thus ultimately more rewarding.

Pyramids frequently employ number symbolism to remind the viewer of their cosmic significance. Temples at both Tikal and Palenque are constructed with nine levels, representing the nine layers of the underworld through which the king was believed to pass during a long and arduous journey after death. However, Temple II at Tikal was built in three layers (see illustration, opposite). These allude to the three hearthstones of Maya creation mythology, and also recall the promise of resurrection suggested by the maize god's miraculous return to life (see page 594).

THE GLORY OF LORD PACAL

The dramatic ruined city of Palenque in northern Chiapas is set in an idyllic location—it nestles at the bottom of forest-covered hills facing out on to low plains (see illustration, pages 584–585). In appearance it is quite different from other Maya central lowland sites in that its architecture is much lighter and more delicate in style. Intricate plaster reliefs, often brightly painted and depicting the rulers and their families, once adorned its buildings. Only a few such reliefs remain today. Dominating the center of Palenque is the palace, which has a three-storied square tower that is unique in the Maya region. Scholars disagree as to whether this structure was intended as a watchtower or as an astronomical observatory.

Much of the architecture that has survived in Palenque was built on the orders of Lord Pacal (603–683CE), perhaps the best known Maya king, and his son Chan-Bahlum. Under Lord Pacal's rule, Palenque enjoyed a golden age, during which art and architecture were carefully nurtured. The potential of art as a means of manipulating history was pushed to its limits, particularly in order to legitimate Pacal's problematic succession.

Chan-Bahlum continued his father's architectural program by ordering the construction of a group of three pyramid temples: the Temple of the Cross, the Temple of the Foliated Cross, and the Temple of the Sun. These structures are elegantly arranged to face inward across a lower plaza, and during Chan-Bahlum's reign they marked the most sacred space in Palenque. The temples stand atop pyramidal bases, and were designed to echo the shapes of the distant mountains. Inside each is a small inner sanctum called a *pib na* ("underground house"). On their rear walls, carved stone panels display images flanked by long hieroglyphic texts relating the Maya story of creation, and the birth of the first deities. On one such panel, Pacal and Chan-Bahlum are portrayed standing on either side of the World Tree—thus locating both men, and Palenque itself, firmly at the center of the Maya cosmos. In another panel, the World Tree has been replaced by a giant maize plant but, in place of the maize cobs, human heads are depicted. This reflects the creation story recounted in the *Popol Vuh* ("Record of the Community"), in which the first people are formed out of maize flour (see page 595). A third panel, in the Temple of the Sun, shows Pacal and his son on either side of a war shield that is decorated with the head of the jaguar-sun and a pair of crossed spears.

◆ THE SECRETS OF PALENQUE ◆

This view of Palenque shows the center of the city, looking toward the distant Usumacinta River delta. On the left, the monumental Temple of the Inscriptions stands nearly 100 feet (30.5m) high. In 1952, the Mexican archaeologist Alberto Ruz Lhuillier noticed that one of the stone slabs making up the floor of this temple had rows of holes along its edge, suggesting that it was a doorway. Lifting it up, he discovered a steep stairway filled with rubble. Over the next four years, this passage was cleared to reveal a tomb buried inside the pyramid—the final resting place of Lord Pacal, who had ruled Palenque for sixty-eight years until his death in 683CE. Outside the crypt lay the skeletons of five sacrificial victims; inside was the sarcophagus holding Pacal's body. His face was covered in an exquisite jade mask, and jade figures were found near his body.

Facing the Temple of the Inscriptions is the great palace which covers an area of about 54,000 square feet (5,000 sq m) and was built during the seventh and eighth centuries CE. The building is made up of long rooms surrounding internal courtyards. Around its perimeter there are numerous galleries, many still intact, that were open to the exterior. Originally, much of the city would have been decorated with intricate and vibrantly colored stucco.

These masterpieces of Maya sculpture may be read on many different levels, and they tell us an enormous amount about how the Maya perceived their world. The hieroglyphic texts relate the creation and lineage of Pacal's family, and the images reveal three qualities that the Maya believed their kings should possess: the World Tree signifies the king's ability to move beyond the earthly realm in order to communicate with the deities and ancestors; the maize plant suggests that the king will ensure that his people continue to enjoy good harvests; and the shield and spears are a reference to prowess in battle.

Toward the end of his life, King Pacal ordered the construction of his own funerary monument—the Temple of the Inscriptions, which was located at the foot of a sacred mountain. When the great king died

in 683CE, he was laid to rest inside the temple, in a sarcophagus with a magnificent carved-stone lid on which the king was depicted at the moment of his death, wearing a turtle necklace that represented his rebirth as the mighty maize god.

CHICHÉN ITZÁ: TEMPLES OF THE WARRIORS

Chichén Itzá, in the north of the Yucatán peninsula, was one of the last great Maya cities. It rose to prominence during the ninth century CE, at a time when the previously powerful sites of the central lowland rainforest were declining. The name translates as the "Opening of the Wells of the Itzá," and refers to two sinkholes, or *cenote*s, which not only provided water, but were also believed to be divine. Many offerings of gold and jade have been recovered from the larger of the two, the Sacred Cenote.

"El Castillo", the vast central pyramid of Chichén Itzá, has an unusual feature. At the base of one of the stairways, the balustrades terminate in open-mouthed

OPPOSITE *Although its roof and much of its facade have gone, Chichén Itzá's Temple of the Warriors remains an impressive sight. The columns are in the form of serpents, and dominating the entrance is a* chacmool *or reclining figure with a bowl on its stomach to serve as a receptacle for sacrificial human hearts.*

The view from the Temple of the Warriors toward El Castillo—also known as the Temple of Kukulcan, the local term for Quetzalcóatl—reveals just how large this Postclassic plaza is in comparison with those of the Classic era. It was planned during the 9th century CE, when the city was at the height of its power, and cities in the lowlands to the south were in terminal decline. Chichén Itzá itself was conquered by neighbors from Mayapan in the early 13th century CE.

serpent heads (see box illustration, page 581). At sunset on the spring and autumn equinoxes, the shadow cast by the edge of the pyramid creates an undulating pattern running down the staircase—thus forming the body of the serpent. This is just one example of how a fascination with celestial bodies has influenced the construction of Maya buildings. (Another is the famous "Caracol," used for astronomical observation.) El Castillo has nine layers, evoking the nine levels of the underworld, and the stairways on each of its four sides have a sum of 364 steps which, with the addition of an upper platform, is equal to the number of days in the year. Although this dramatic pyramid displays characteristically Maya features, it also reveals the influence of a new architectural style that was brought to the city by the Itzá, a group of Maya originating from Tabasco (the area between the Maya realm and central Mexico). Composed mainly of fierce warrior-merchants, the Itzá pushed north into the Yucatán, seizing the opportunity offered by the collapse of the Classic Period cities. Their influence has resulted in the presence of two distinct styles in Chichén Itzá: the southern part of the site is built in traditional Maya style; in the north, Mexican architectural features prevail.

The largest ballcourt in Mesoamerica lies to the west of the main buildings at Chichén Itzá. Its walls are lined with carvings depicting the sacrifices performed at the conclusion of the game. An extraordinary stone platform, decorated with several hundred carved skulls, stands next to the ballcourt. This structure would originally have been surmounted by a wooden rack that was filled with the real skulls of defeated ballplayers—these were used as sacrifices to the deities. Prominent skull imagery, alien to the Maya, was another Mexican characteristic introduced by the Itzá.

The eastern side of the Main Plaza is occupied by the Temple of the Warriors. At its entrance is a *chacmool*, a reclining figure holding a sacrificial bowl on his chest (see illustration, opposite). The doorway was originally formed by columns in the shape of Quetzalcóatl, the Feathered Serpent, a great central Mexican deity. The heads of these creatures rest on the ground, and their tails would have supported lintels spanning the entrance. At the base of the temple are a multitude of columns, each carved with reliefs of armed soldiers. They form part of a now roofless structure, the Mansion of the Warriors, which was probably used for militaristic rituals.

TIME, FATE, AND PROPHECY

The Maya were fascinated by time and the heavens, and it inspired them to develop one of the most accurate calendar systems in existence before the modern period. The stars and planets were meticulously charted in order to produce tables that could then be used to predict their movements.

Most of the ancient peoples of Mesoamerica were intrigued by the movements of the stars and planets, but it was the Maya, during the Classic Period (ca. 250–900CE), who developed regional knowledge of astronomy to its greatest extent. Through careful accumulated observation, Maya astronomer–priests recorded such events as the rising and setting of Venus (considered to be a highly significant celestial body), eclipses of the sun and moon, and the passage of the constellations of their zodiac through the seasons. This information, documented in their codices (see pages 578–579), was vital. For the Maya, not only did it explain the past and guide them in the present, it was also the key to predicting the future. Used in conjunction with the complex calendar the priests could make methodical forecasts, by which people could regulate their daily lives, and plan ahead.

In order to calculate the movements of the stars and planets, and indeed for many other uses, the Maya needed a mathematical system that could deal with large numbers. This they achieved through the development of a "vigesimal" count (based on the number twenty). The numbers one through four are represented by the appropriate number of single dots (so • = one, and ••• = three); five is a bar (—); and six through nineteen are comprised of one or more bars and dots as necessary. The Maya also developed place notation and the use of zero (represented by a shell-shaped symbol). Numbers were written in columns (see above, right). The bottom line is for units (one through nineteen); the next line up is for lots of twenty; the next for lots of 400 (20 times 20); then lots of 8,000 (20 times 20 times 20); and so on. Thus, the Maya could calculate into the millions.

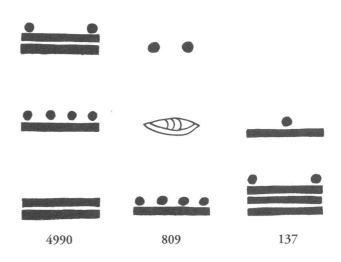

4990   809   137

CYCLES OF TIME

The Maya were in fact masters of recording time, and their calendars were more accurate than those used in Europe during the same period. As with their number system, the Maya calendars were based on units of twenty—each cycle of twenty years was called a *katun*. The Maya employed not one calendar, but several, which interlocked to give information on the ritual year, the solar year, the lunar cycle, and the count of days since the beginning of the current world age—a cycle of some 5,200 years, which is due to end on 23 December, 2012.

The first calendar was one of 260 days which was used by Maya priests, or "daykeepers," for making

---

This detail from a painted vase made in the 8th century CE depicts the outcome of a battle conducted in accordance with the position of the planet Venus. A naked captive is being marched back to the home city of the winners. Behind him is the leader of the victorious army, probably the ruler of the city, who is dressed in a jaguar pelt with the head hanging at his waist. In one hand he holds a bloodstained club, and in the other, a shield and spear.

• ANIMALS OF THE ZODIAC •

The Maya had a zodiac of constellations conceived mainly of animals. However, the only creature that can be found in both the Maya and the familiar zodiac of Western astrology is the scorpion. Other animals that feature in the Maya zodiac include the turtle, which corresponds to part of Orion; the peccary (a hog-like animal) and the turkey, both of which may have represented Gemini; the jaguar; the bat; and a mythical fish.

Many of these animals also figure prominently in Maya mythology and art, particularly the turtle, which plays a significant role in the creation story—it was often depicted bearing the three hearthstones of the Maya creation myth on its back (see illustration, page 593) and in a double-headed version is said to crack open for the rebirth of the important maize god.

Star signs depicted on images of the animals often indicate celestial associations. A carved stone zodiac survives at Chichén Itzá, and zodiac animals, including the turtle, are portrayed at Bonampak. The scorpion is illustrated in the *Paris Codex*.

predictions and organizing rituals. Various explanations have been put forward as to the origin of the number 260: some theories are based on astronomy, while others relate the period to the approximate length of human pregnancy. Each day of the calendar has a unique name that combines one of twenty day-signs with a number from one through thirteen.

The 365-day solar calendar is simpler. It contains eighteen months of twenty days, and one of five days which was known as Uayeb and considered to be a very unlucky period. The third calendar is known as the Long Count, and consists of a continuous count of days beginning from the start of the current world age on 13 August, 3114BCE. Dates in this calendar are usually expressed by five numbers. In the date 8.12.7.0.9, for example, nine represents the number of single days; zero is the number of months; there are seven years (each of 360 days); twelve lots of twenty years; and eight lots of 400 years.

VENUS, PLANET OF DESTINY

For the Maya, the most important heavenly body after the sun and the moon was Venus. As a deity, Venus was far from the benign goddess of love and fertility familiar to Europeans from the traditions of ancient Greece, Rome, and the Near East. The Maya version of Venus was masculine and baleful, and the planet's appearance in the morning or evening sky heralded the onset of malign influences. At such times, the priests and the people had to prepare themselves spiritually and physically for hunger, drought, or war. Many Maya even believed that the planet gave off harmful rays, and kept their windows shuttered when it was visible.

With no astronomer's tools beyond the naked eye and an extraordinary patience that spanned many generations, Maya priests were able to predict the comings and goings of this planet with great accuracy. In the Yucatán city of Chichén Itzá, the Maya built the circular structure known as the Caracol—Spanish for "snail" and derived from its internal spiral passageways—as an observatory to chart the movements of Venus. Three passages or apertures leading into the Caracol align directly with points on the western horizon where Venus appears as the Evening Star during the planet's 584-day cycle, including the most southerly and northerly places at which it sets.

This achievement was not as straightforward as it seems. From our viewpoint, the sun, the Earth, and Venus take on average 584 days to return to the same alignment but, in practice, the Venusian cycle can be anything between 580 and 587 days long. In the course of its cycle, the planet is visible from the Earth before dawn for about 260 days as the Morning Star, and for another 260 days after sunset as the Evening Star. Between these two periods it is invisible, because it is either behind or in front of the sun, or so close to it that it cannot be seen with the naked eye.

The Maya determined that the Morning Star and Evening Star were the same heavenly body—in itself no mean achievement. They then learned to predict the exact times at which Venus would appear in the pre-dawn or post-sunset sky to within 0.08 days in 481 years, or one day in every 6,000 years. No other ancient civilization—on either side of the Atlantic—surpassed this astonishing feat. Maya astronomer-kings would observe and record appearances of the star, and the times at which it coincided with the rising of other planets, and plan their battles to correspond with these dates. Venus continued to be of great relevance after death—many important events that occurred during the journey to the underworld were related to the times at which Venus rose.

At a temple built by King Yax Pac at Copán (see box, opposite), the entrances to the inner sanctum are covered with texts linking earthly events of the ruler's life to cosmic movements, such as the cycles of Venus and the number of eclipses they expected Venus to undergo in a million years. Yax Pac employed his knowledge of Venus to assert his status as ruler, and to emphasize the role of the king in maintaining cosmic order.

◆ COPÁN: CITY AT THE EDGE OF THE COSMOS ◆

Copán lies in Honduras, on the fertile banks of the Copán River, and is the most eastern of the large Maya city-states. Hence, it was considered by the Maya to be on the very fringes of their universe. The city has a long history, with evidence of occupation stretching back into the first millennium BCE, and it has a particularly large number of hieroglyphic inscriptions on stelae, altars and architectural stones. For many years, Copán intrigued Mayanists, who believed that the site was of special cosmic importance to the whole of Maya civilization.

Much of this supposed significance was based upon the interpretation of Altar Q, a square structure erected by Yax Pac, the sixteenth king of the dynasty that ruled Copán in the prosperous Classic Period. The altar depicts sixteen individuals who were long believed by Maya scholars to represent a conference of astronomers from all over the Maya region, who had gathered at Copán in order to agree on a standard calendar. Recent advances in the understanding of Maya hieroglyphs, however, have revealed that Altar Q actually depicts King Yax Pac and his fifteen predecessors. But despite this discovery, the influence of the cosmos remains apparent in several aspects of the city.

King 18 Rabbit, one of Copán's most famous leaders, was responsible for many of the site's extant buildings, including the dramatic ballcourt dedicated in 738CE (see below). The architecture constructed during King 18 Rabbit's reign displays a striking interest in cosmic patterning, with designs that frequently symbolize the celestial motions. Many of the giant stelae erected in the Great Plaza, in the north of Copán, depict 18 Rabbit in the guise of various characters from the Maya creation myths—as gods, such as the maize god, and even as embodiments of the World Tree. The positioning of the stelae relates to the movements of the planets and constellations.

Cosmic concerns shaped Copán's structure as a whole, but they also dictated much of the intricate relief work and sculpture. The inner entrance to Temple 22, for example, is framed by a double-headed serpent that represents the sky or, more precisely, the Milky Way—the symbolic axis of the Maya cosmos. The ornate markings of this creature include many astronomical references, and the scrolls comprising its body are thought to represent clouds—used by the Maya to depict the heavens.

King 18 Rabbit was destined to meet a gruesome death. A short distance from Copán lay the smaller city of Quirigua, which for many years had been controlled by its larger neighbor. In 734CE, a new king ascended the throne of Quirigua, with the name of Cauac Sky. Four years later, Quirigua successfully rose up against its masters and 18 Rabbit was captured and sacrificed.

Copán's main ballcourt is located between the acropolis and the Great Plaza, its central position at the heart of the city confirmation of the importance of the ballgame to the Maya. The ballcourt was thought to be an entrance to the underworld, and inscribed stone roundels set into the playing area depict the king of Copán playing the ball-game against an underworld god. The ballcourt was rebuilt several times during Copán's history, and markers (delimiting the zone of the court) shaped as macaw heads have survived from earlier eras. These birds may represent a mythical character, Seven Macaw, who believed that he was the sun and suffered a terrible fate as a consequence of his vanity (see page 598).

VISIONS OF CREATION

The Maya constructed an elaborate mythology to explain the creation of the world and the emergence of the first people, who were made by the goddess Xmucane out of maize flour. The cosmos itself had three planes—the celestial realm, the Earth, and underworld—linked by a cosmic tree, and it was in the celestial plane that the tales were symbolically played out each night in the movements of the stars.

According to the sixteenth-century CE *Popol Vuh*, in the beginning nothing existed except the sky and a vast primordial ocean. The sky deities met with those of the oceans and agreed that they needed worshippers. Firstly, however, they had to create somewhere for these beings to live. This was easily achieved—the divine creators merely uttered the word "Earth" and immediately, "it arose, just like a cloud, like a mist, now forming, unfolding." The creation was expressed as "the fourfold siding, fourfold cornering, measuring, fourfold staking, halving the cord, stretching the cord in the sky, on the Earth, the four sides, the four corners." This description resembles the process by which Maya farmers measured out their fields, or *milpa*s, before they planted their crops—thus, the mythological creation of the Earth reflected an everyday agricultural procedure.

The earthly realm was believed to be square and bounded above and below by two supernatural arenas. Above the Earth was the celestial realm in which the many deities resided; below lay the dreaded underworld known as Xibalba (see page 597), inhabited by the unsavory Xibalban lords. According to some accounts, the sky consisted of thirteen layers, each with its own deity, and the underworld had nine layers. At the center of the cosmos stood the World Tree. Four other trees, one standing at each corner of the Earth, were thought to support the sky.

Hieroglyphic inscriptions from various sites add further details to the creation story. Many of these give the date of creation as 13.0.0.0.0 4 *Ahau* 8

LEFT *The rebirth of the maize god is shown on this late Classic Period plate. He is depicted rising from a cracked turtle shell with the aid of his sons, the Hero Twins: Xbalanque (right) and Hunahpu (left). The turtle's head emerges from one end of the shell, but its tail has been replaced by the head of a deity.*

OPPOSITE *In this detail of a page from the Postclassic Period Madrid Codex, the turtle constellation is depicted (bottom left) suspended by cords from a skyband. The turtle bears the three hearthstones of the Maya creation myth on its back. The two elements attached to the turtle symbolize solar eclipses which were thought of as omens of great danger—perhaps reflecting the uncertainty felt by the Maya regarding the creation process.*

Cumku (using a combination of the 260-day and the 365-day calendars; see pages 589–590), which translates as 13 August, 3114BCE. On this date, according to myth, the "Three Stones of Creation" were put in place. Because the traditional Maya cooking hearth is made up of three stones, this stage can be interpreted as the setting up of the first fireplace.

The noble who requested the first hearth to be laid out was Hun Hunahpu, the maize god and father of the Hero Twins (see pages 600–601). According to the *Popol Vuh*, he was killed in the underworld, but Classic Period Maya texts tell us that he was reborn with the help of his sons, an event which was sometimes represented by his emergence from a cracked turtle shell (see illustration, page 593).

The turtle plays an important role in Maya creation accounts, some of which describe the Earth resting on a great turtle that floated in a vast primordial ocean. The constellation of Orion was conceived of by the Maya as a turtle, and three stars of Orion (Alnitak, Saiph, and Rigel) are intimately linked with the "Three Stones of Creation." (In the Bonampak murals, a turtle has been

depicted with the three stars of Orion's belt embedded in its shell, while in the *Madrid Codex*, it carries the three hearthstones on its back—see illustration, page 593.) The association between Orion and the primal hearth is preserved in modern Maya myth. Each year, on the night of 13 August, the anniversary of the date of creation, Orion rises in the sky near to the point at which the Milky Way crosses the ecliptic. Just before dawn, it reaches its highest point in the sky, and it is here that the maize god is said to be reborn and the cosmic hearthstones are believed to come into being.

THE FIRST PEOPLE

Once the deities had formed the Earth, they set about creating their worshippers. First, they made the animals, but the only praise that they received were squawks and howls. They then attempted to fashion a human from mud but, although it was able to speak, its words made no sense, and it rapidly dissolved back into a shapeless mass. Next, the divinities tried to create people out of wood. These wooden beings looked human, possessed human speech, and even began to procreate, but they had no souls, and therefore did not recognize their creators. The deities decided that the wooden people must be destroyed and, to achieve this, they produced a variety of dangers, including a great flood and attacks by fearsome jaguars. The gods even turned the domestic animals and cooking utensils against the wooden beings—their pots burned them and their grinding stones damaged their faces. Most of the wooden people were eventually eliminated; the few that survived were transformed into monkeys, which inhabit the forests to this day.

The frustrated divinities made one last attempt to create humans. They gathered together some maize kernels (the staple food of the Maya), and an old goddess called Xmucane ground the kernels nine times. She added some water and thus, miraculously, she successfully formed the first four people who quickly learned how to worship and make appropriate sacrifices to their creators.

THE COSMIC TREE

The Maya perceived the world as essentially square and flat. Each side was oriented toward one of the cardinal directions—east, west, north, south—and the entire cosmos was focused around a central vertical axis. Each direction had a special color associated with it: east was red, the color of the rising sun; west was black, the color of death; south was yellow; and north was white. The center was associated with green, the color of new vegetal growth and life itself.

The central axis took the form of the World Tree, known to the Maya as *wakah-chan*, or "Raised-up-

This clay monkey, found in Guatemala, has articulated limbs and head, suggesting that it was a toy. In Maya creation myth, monkeys are the result of the deities' failed attempt to form humans. But in other stories, monkeys were prestigious beings—there was a monkey-scribe who was a half-brother of the Hero Twins and a patron god of the arts.

Sky"—a name referring to Maya creation myths that tell of the gods raising the sky at the beginning of the current world age, and supporting it with a supernatural tree. However, the World Tree was more than a mere prop for the heavens; it also acted as a cosmic channel along which the souls of the dead could travel. Its roots lay deep in the underworld, its trunk was in the earthly world, and its branches penetrated the celestial realm.

One of the finest representations of the World Tree is to be found on the huge (12-feet/3.8-m long) stone slab that covered the sarcophagus of King Pacal of Palenque. This intricate carving, rich in symbolism, depicts Pacal poised on the point of death within the jaws of Xibalba (the underworld). The World Tree rises out of these

◆ THE BRINGER OF GROWTH ◆

Hun Hunahpu, the maize god, was perhaps the most important deity for the Maya because he was believed not only to have brought about the creation of the present world age, but also to preside over maize, their single most essential crop. He appears as a young man, often with maize foliage sprouting from his head, and his status is demonstrated by the fact that he was represented throughout both the Classic and Postclassic eras. Some magnificent portrayals of this god have survived, and the illustration here is based on painted figures from a vase found in the tomb of a young lord, buried during the early eighth century CE, at the site of Buenavista in Belize. On his back is an elaborate "rack," which is actually a mythical creature in a miniature "temple" formed of elements representing the three layers of the cosmos: the floor of the temple is the head of a monster, and denotes the underworld; the back wall is a "woven mat" emblem representing the earthly realm; and the roof is a skyband with a bird perched on it, symbolizing the celestial level. The position of the maize god's arms and hands indicate that he is engaged in a dance. In fact, he is dancing out of the dark underworld from which he was released by his sons, the Hero Twins, after their defeat of the Xibalbans (see main text, opposite).

jaws and, although Pacal is sliding down the trunk into the land of the dead, the celestial bird perched on the top of the tree expresses the hope that he will eventually rise out of the underworld and be reborn into the heavenly realm.

XIBALBA: THE PLACE OF FRIGHT

The Maya underworld was known as Xibalba, or "The Place of Fright," and its inhabitants were indeed frightful characters. Often depicted as diseased creatures with distended bellies and foul breath, the Xibalbans emitted streams of excrement and flatulence (the modern Maya word for the devil is *cizin*, literally "the flatulent one"), and are frequently shown wearing necklaces of plucked-out eyeballs. The two principal lords of the underworld were known as One Death and Seven Death, and they were accompanied by lesser nobles with names such as Scab Stripper, Blood Gatherer, Demon of Pus, Demon of Jaundice, Bone Scepter, and Skull Scepter. It was into this evil realm that the Hero Twins descended to avenge the death of their father (see pages 600–601).

Round markers in Maya ballcourts often depicted the twins playing the ballgame in Xibalba. However, it was not only mythical characters who were forced to confront the terrors of Xibalba—the Maya believed that mortals also descended into the underworld to do battle with One Death and his fellows. The great Maya kings were thought to be faced with particularly ferocious challenges.

Not all depictions of Xibalba are repellent. One of the masterpieces of Maya art, the so-called "Princeton Vase," portrays a very different picture, with a lord of Xibalba shown in a luxurious palace, waited on by beautiful women. The only indication that the setting is the underworld is the presence of the Hero Twins performing a sacrifice. Xibalba was generally represented by artists as being underground, but it was also envisaged as underwater, with its surface marked by images such as water lilies, shells, or crocodiles. Nobles were sometimes depicted traveling to Xibalba by canoe—the Maya believed that if the canoe sank its passengers would be plunged into the watery underworld.

This Classic Period vase depicts three Xibalbans. The figure visible here is skeletal, and his intestines are bursting out from his rib cage. His necklace consists of plucked-out eyeballs, complete with optic nerves. The intimidating representations of the lords of Xibablba emphasized the dread nature of the lords to ordinary human beings.

FACES OF THE DIVINE

The Maya had a vast pantheon of divinities—some were associated with the elements and the cycles of agriculture, and others were embodiments of celestial phenomena. From the evidence of Maya art, it seems that masks were used during celebrations and rituals to impersonate the most powerful gods and goddesses. Divinity was claimed by human rulers of Maya cities to legitimate their earthly power.

The sun was a crucial celestial feature in the life of the Maya. Providing the light and heat vital for life, it was envisioned as a male deity known as Kinich Ahau, or "Sun-faced Lord." This god was believed to be young when he rose at dawn, but by sunset, after he had completed his journey across the sky to the western horizon, he was thought to have become old and bearded.

Representations of Kinich Ahau show an apparently fierce being with a single front tooth, and barbels emanating from the corners of his mouth. These refer to the appendages of the part-catfish creatures that the Hero Twins become after being sacrificed in the *Popol Vuh* myth (see illustration, pages 600–601). After defeating the lords of Xibalba, the twins ascend into the sky as the sun and the moon.

The hieroglyph for *kin*, a symbol with four petals meaning "sun" or "day", is often found on the forehead of Kinich Ahau. Some depictions show him with jaguar characteristics since the sun was thought to be transformed into a supernatural jaguar during the night (see main text, right). The Maya also believed that there had been a time before the sun existed. One of their myths relates that in this dark era there was a Seven Macaw, who vaingloriously decided that he could be the sun because of his brilliant white teeth and shining, bejeweled eyes. Every day this impostor, also known as "the false sun," would visit the nance tree to eat its fruit, and there the Hero Twins lay in wait to destroy him. First they aimed a shot with their blowguns that hit him on the jaw and dislocated it, and loosened his teeth. He fled home, but then, disguised as healers, they tricked him into replacing his bright teeth with ground corn—whereupon his face collapsed and he died.

JAGUAR, LORD OF THE FOREST

The jaguar was the most fearsome beast to inhabit the dense forests surrounding ancient Maya cities. This powerful feline was revered for its solar and divine associations, and its supposed supernatural powers. Jaguars are predominantly nocturnal in their habits and, because they were identified with night and darkness, they were also linked intimately with Xibalba, the gloomy Maya underworld.

According to Maya belief, the sun, on setting, traveled into the underworld, where it was transformed into a supernatural jaguar. In this guise, it was forced to do battle with the Xibalban lords of death. Several painted vases depict the jaguar-sun on this perilous passage—some show the jaguar with the Maya glyph for the sun (*kin*) impressed on its belly; others are decorated with stylized jaguar markings that have the sun glyph at their centers. A sculpture from Izapa, on the southeastern Maya frontier, shows the jaguar-sun suspended over a fire, as a captive of the underworld lords. Luckily for humankind, the deity always escapes from the clutches of his evil captors to rise again as the sun every morning.

Like the lion in the Old World, the largest cat of the Americas was a potent emblem of kingship. Maya rulers wore the jaguar's pelt as part of their regalia, and offered it to the deities as a sacrifice. Several Maya kings went as far as to incorporate the word for jaguar in their names as a mark of their high status.

MASTER OF RAIN AND THUNDER

Chac, the Maya god of rain, thunder, and lightning, was both adored and feared. The rain he brought was needed for the growth of crops, but if it fell too heavily it could also destroy them, and his storms and bolts of lightning often spelled death and disaster.

One of the longest-lived deities of the Maya pantheon, Chac is often shown in Maya books painted blue (symbolizing rain), with a curving pendulous nose, hair tied up on top of his head, and barbels projecting from the corners of his mouth. Sometimes these barbels are in the form of snakes, which were often associated with lightning. Chac holds a hatchet with which, as he strides through the celestial realm, he occasionally hits a hard object. The resulting sparks are transformed into shafts of lightning which come down to strike the Earth. The sound of the blade's impact rolls around the sky as thunder.

Carvings on second-century-BCE stelae at Izapa in Chiapas, make his dual roles apparent. On one stela he is depicted in a beneficent aspect providing rain and gathering fish from a river; on another stela, however, he is presented as the aggressive ax-wielding warrior.

Chac is still worshipped by the Maya today. In the Yucatán, toward the end of the dry season, shrines are prepared and small boys, tied to the corners of the altars, croak like frogs to urge Chac to bring on the rains.

EXPLOITS OF THE HERO TWINS

The two most famous characters in Maya mythology are the Hero Twins, Hunahpu and Xbalanque, whose story is recounted in the Popol Vuh, *a work by the Quiché Maya of Guatemala. The twins were miraculously conceived in Xibalba, the underworld, where their father, Hun Hunahpu, the maize god, had been summoned for disturbing the Xibalban lords with a noisy ballgame on Earth.*

The lords punished Hun Hunahpu by decapitating him and hanging his head in a tree. When an underworld girl named Blood Moon went to the tree, the head spat into her hand, causing her to become pregnant. She fled to the upper world to escape her father's wrath, and there she gave birth to the twins. Their father already had one set of twin sons, who disliked the new arrivals and harassed them. In response, Hunahpu and Xbalanque changed their half-brothers into monkeys who, famous for their creative skills, eventually became deities of the arts.

The twins were keen ballgame players, and the noise of their games again provoked the Xibalbans. Hunahpu and Xbalanque were commanded to travel to the underworld, across rivers of blood and pus, and forced to take part in a series of trials. On the first night they were each given a burning torch and a lit cigar and told that they must return these items in the morning exactly as they had received them. The twins put them out and substituted red macaw feathers for the torch flames and fireflies for the glow of the cigars, thus fooling the Xibalbans. Next, they endured nights in houses of knives, jaguars, extreme cold, and fire. Finally, they were shut in the house of Zotz, the killer bat. To escape this murderous creature they used their magic powers to create blowpipes which they then hid inside. Just

before dawn, Xbalanque asked his brother if it was safe to emerge but, as Hunahpu looked out Zotz swooped down and snatched off his head. The cruel Xibalbans then forced Xbalanque to play using Hunahpu's head as a ball, but Xbalanque cunningly managed to divert their

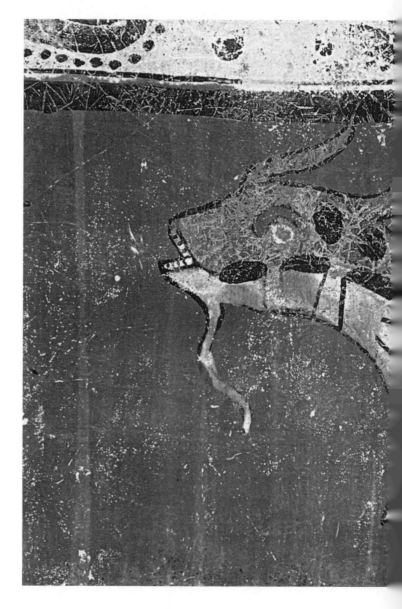

This late Classic Period vase painting depicts two fish which, despite their simple appearance, are images that contain significant symbolic meaning. After the Hero Twins had allowed themselves to be sacrificed in Xibalba, their bones were ground up and thrown into a river from which they later emerged as catfish people. The barbels hanging from the jaws of these two painted creatures identify them as catfish, suggesting that they may be representations of the twins.

attention for long enough to join the head back on to his brother's body (see pages 604–605).

The twins then devised a plan to avenge the death of their father. They allowed themselves to be sacrificed by jumping into a fiery pit but, five days after the Xibalbans had scattered their remains in a river, they emerged from the water as half-human, half-catfish beings (see illustration, below). Assuming the role of itinerant entertainers, they soon became renowned for their magic tricks and dances. Hearing of their miraculous deeds, the two prin-cipal Xibalban lords summoned the disguised twins to perform at their palace. The brothers were ordered to sacrifice themselves. This they did, yet revived instantly. Suitably impressed, the Xibalbans commanded the twins to use the same magic on them. They did so but, in this trick, they did not bring the Xibalbans back to life. Thus the underworld was finally vanquished—through trick-ery rather than violence. In triumph, Hunahpu and Xbalanque ascended to the heavens, where they became the sun and the moon.

THE BLOOD OF SACRIFICE

Maya belief dictated that humankind must continuously appease the deities to ensure the survival of the world. The ceremonial sacrifice of captives taken in battle was the most common way to achieve this throughout the year. However, at times kings needed to appeal to or consult with the gods and ancestors directly—this was effected by rituals involving the painful shedding of their own blood.

Once considered to be a race of peaceful astronomer–priests, the Maya are now recognized as having been as ferocious and warlike as any of their Mesoamerican neighbors. Their leaders engaged in warfare to gain territory, as well as to acquire captives for the ceremonial rounds of human sacrifice—a process that was often horrendously tortuous. They also performed ritual bloodletting ceremonies on themselves.

Relief carvings from Yaxchilán show just how gruesome and bizarre these occasions must have been. On one panel, Lady Xoc, the richly attired wife of a king of Yaxchilán, is depicted pulling a rope threaded with thorns through a hole pierced in her tongue. This act of auto-sacrifice must have taken place in the dark interior of a temple, because her husband, Shield Jaguar, is shown holding a flaming torch above her. Another carved lintel from the same building portrays the next stage of the ceremony. The blood shed by Lady Xoc has dripped on to bark paper in a bowl placed beneath her. This paper is then set alight and coils of smoke rise up

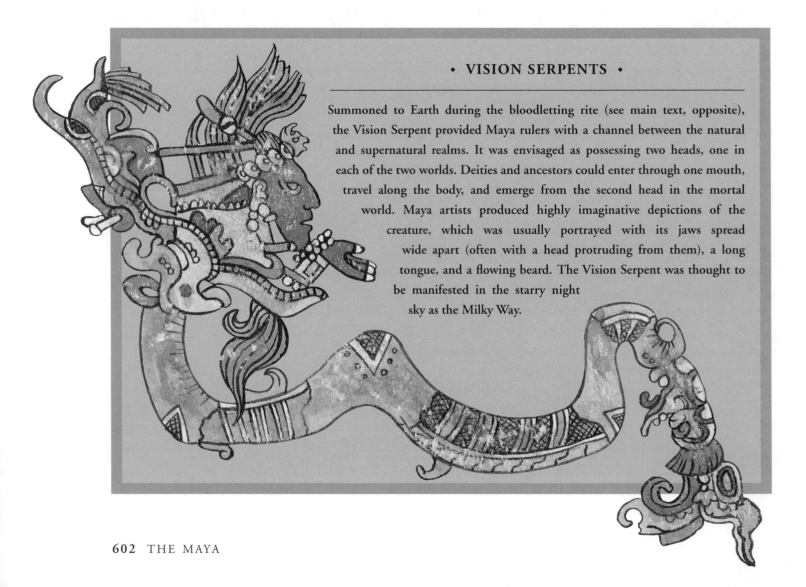

• VISION SERPENTS •

Summoned to Earth during the bloodletting rite (see main text, opposite), the Vision Serpent provided Maya rulers with a channel between the natural and supernatural realms. It was envisaged as possessing two heads, one in each of the two worlds. Deities and ancestors could enter through one mouth, travel along the body, and emerge from the second head in the mortal world. Maya artists produced highly imaginative depictions of the creature, which was usually portrayed with its jaws spread wide apart (often with a head protruding from them), a long tongue, and a flowing beard. The Vision Serpent was thought to be manifested in the starry night sky as the Milky Way.

into the interior of the temple. Lady Xoc, who may have fasted for days in preparation for the event and may also have taken hallucinogenic drugs from a natural source, sees in the swirling smoke a manifestation of a creature called the Vision Serpent—a scaly beast with two heads. From the open jaws of one head emerges the skeletal features of the war god; from the jaws of the other, the founder of the Yaxchilán dynasty, Yat Balam, or Jaguar Penis, appears. He is wearing the same warrior head-dress as the war god, and bears a lance and a shield.

One purpose of this bloodletting was to enable Lady Xoc to enter an ecstatic state in which, it was believed, she could break through the barrier between the natural and supernatural realms. By doing so, she was able to communicate with the deities or ancestors in order to ask their advice, or to request their help. The Vision Serpent (see box, opposite) represents the threshold between the two realms; the open jaws of the beast act as a portal through which divinities and ancestors can enter the earthly sphere. In this case, Lady Xoc is asking for the help of the war god and of an ancestor, Yat Balam, in a battle that her husband is about to undertake. The bloodletting also commemorated the accession of Shield Jaguar to the throne of Yaxchilán, and the birth of the royal couple's son, Bird Jaguar. From accompanying inscriptions we know that these events took place in around 724–726CE.

The act of bloodletting was no less painful for men. Several small clay figurines (see illustration, right) depict nobles sitting cross-legged, holding sharp obsidian knives or stingray spines poised to lacerate their own penises. To modern eyes, these practices may seem bizarre, but to the ancient Maya they were an essential way in which to communicate with the supernatural world. Such rites were most frequently observed by Maya rulers and nobles (and indeed were regarded as a privilege). In the codices, there are depictions of the gods themselves performing similar acts of auto-sacrifice on behalf of the Maya. Bloodletting thus symbolized a reciprocal obligation.

This clay figurine, from late in the Classic era, shows a man cutting open his penis to provide blood for the deities. To the Maya this was considered an act of intense piety. The figure is dressed as a captive, with a rope around his neck, but he may actually be a king or noble who is wearing these garments in order to symbolize his humility.

A GAME OF SOULS

The Maya shared with all their neighbors an enduring addiction to "the ballgame," a sport with many regional variations but the same basic form everywhere, and thought to date from the second millennium BCE. The game took place on a court shaped like a capital letter "I," which consisted of a narrow central playing alley with vertical or sloping sides and wider end zones.

The first European eyewitnesses report that the ballgame was played for popular entertainment, with spectators gambling costly fabrics on the outcome. But matches played in the shadow of the temples were not intended as ordinary spectacles for the mere amusement of mortals. These games were macabre rituals played for stakes that were, quite literally, a matter of life and death—players on the losing side were sacrificed in honor of the deities.

Often the losers were captives who had been deliberately weakened through starvation or injury in order to guarantee the outcome of the game. The sacrifice of the losers might be followed by another game in which a victim's head was encased in latex and used as the ball. Evocative figurines that have survived reveal important details about the game. The ball could be bigger than a modern soccer ball or as small as a baseball; it was thought to have been made from wood, leather, or rubber. Irrespective of its size, the ball could cause injury as a result of its hardness and the speed it attained.

The precise rules of the ballgame remain something of a mystery. But the evidence of art and archaeology tallies closely with early European accounts. Teams had between one and four or more players, and while the

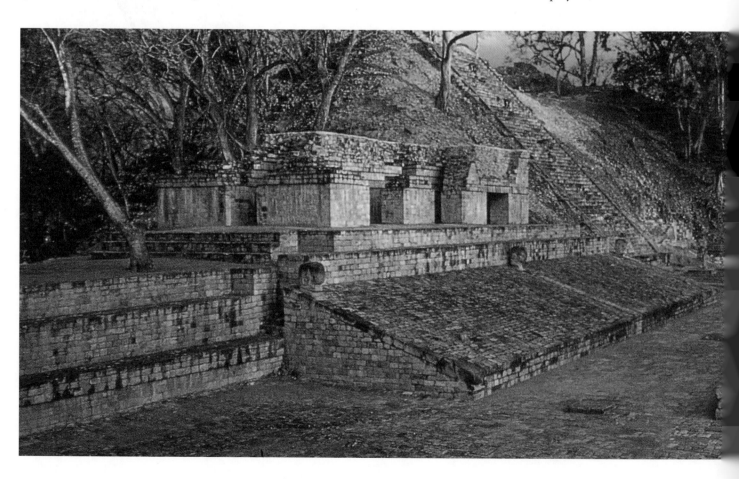

ball was in play competitors were not allowed to touch it with their hands or feet. The ball was struck mainly with the shoulders, torso, thighs and hips, and players wore thick padding and elaborate girdles, or yokes, to protect themselves on one shin, one forearm, and around their waists.

In one ninth-century CE depiction of the game, a contestant with a scarred face is shown wearing the minimum of protective clothing. The reason for this could be the diminutive size of the ball. But there is another explanation: his mutilated face suggests he has undergone bloodletting rites and has been marked out as a human sacrifice. This will therefore be his last game—the infliction of a few bruises in the face of death would be an irrelevance.

A player apparently scored by hitting the ball into a designated area of the court, or by striking a stone hoop set high into the wall and perpendicular to the ground. The ultimate aim, however, was to get the ball through this hoop, a task of such extreme difficulty—the hoop was barely wider than the ball—that its achievement must have been a high point of any game. The center of the ballcourt was sometimes marked by a carved stone roundel, an example of which was found set into the dramatic ballcourt at Copán; it is decorated with a relief of the Hero Twins playing the ballgame in the underworld. The ballcourt itself was actually considered to be a portal to Xibalba.

Two-a-side was most usual in the Maya ritual ballgame, which commemorated the creation myth in the epic *Popol Vuh*. This describes how the Hero Twins (see pages 600–601), Hunahpu and Xbalanque, were obliged by the gods of the underworld to compete in a ballgame tournament. At one point during their game, Xbalanque is forced to play with his brother's head as a ball. Cunningly, he obtains a large squash and carves it into a likeness of Hunahpu. He continues playing with the real head but, after a few minutes, he kicks it out of the court. At this moment, a rabbit, which has been hiding nearby, scampers off through the undergrowth. While the Xibalbans are busy chasing the rabbit, believing it to be the ball, Xbalanque recovers his brother's head and joins it back onto Hunahpu's body, reviving him. Xbalanque then produces the squash, and shouts to the Xibalbans that he has found the ball. Play continues until the squash splits open and the Xibalbans realize that they have been tricked. When the Maya played the ritual ballgame, they were reenacting this mythical underworld contest in their own cities.

Maya ballcourts fall into two distinct types: one has straight vertical walls, such as the great ballcourt at Chichén Itzá; the other has shallow sloping sides, such as the ballcourt at Copán shown here. Participants may have used the sloping surface as part of the playing area, giving an extra dimension to the game. Copán is thought to have been one of the first ballcourts to include rooms built on top of the structure, where the players bathed, steamed, and took part in other ritual activities.

CELEBRATIONS FOR LIFE

Music and dance played an important role in the lives of the ancient Maya. Not only were they part of everyday entertainment, but they were also a crucial ingredient of sacred ritual. Lavish festivities would have accompanied significant events, such as the accession of a ruler or the dedication of a temple, during which richly attired lords would dance to the music of trumpets, whistles, rattles, and drums.

The nobility's costumes would have been made from brightly colored feathers and jaguar skins, and participants would have been adorned with jewelry crafted out of jade and shell. These ceremonies were frequently recorded in Maya art—the finest examples being the mural paintings at Bonampak that celebrated King Chan-Muan's presentation of his young heir to the nobles of the city in December 790CE (see illustration, opposite).

As with much Maya ceremonial, the dances performed on such occasions were reenactments of episodes in mythology. For example, when the Hero Twins (see pages 600–601) descended into the underworld, they disguised themselves as dancers and entertainers. The underworld lords were amazed by their skill, particularly the dances of the Armadillo, the Weasel, and a bird called the Poorwill. Maya ceramics from the Classic Period furnish several excellent examples of scenes portraying sacred dancers and musicians in animal costume or wearing animal masks—in some cases supernatural creatures also take part. Early Spanish accounts describe ceremonies in which the story of the Hero Twins is reenacted by costumed dancers. One such text explains how the actors playing the twins appear to throw themselves on to a bonfire, but later emerge from a hidden trapdoor in the ground as the triumphant conquerors of Xibalba. In traditional Maya communities these festivals still take place—in the modern version, however, representations of Spanish conquistadors take their place alongside the evil lords of the underworld.

• CEREMONIAL ADORNMENT •

Maya rulers and élite classes are usually portrayed wearing bulky and elaborate costumes which, despite their incredibly complex appearance, are probably accurate representations. The headdresses and backracks were made using a wooden framework, which was covered with feathers, beads of various materials, textiles, shells, and sculpted jade. Costumes were not designed solely for visual drama, but also had symbolic meaning. The headdress and adornments for the chest and waist generally included images of one or more deities. The king donned this attire to proclaim himself as the embodiment of the divinities on Earth, thus justifying his right to rule.

OPPOSITE *The spectacular murals at Bonampak were commissioned by King Chan-Muan to celebrate his designation of an heir. A grand ceremonial procession, shown in this detail from one of the murals, was organized for the dedication of a temple. The date of the event, 15 November, 791CE, had special significance because it was the day on which Venus appeared as the Evening Star. Bizarrely dressed dancers perform to the music of trumpets, rattles, and drums. One participant wears a crayfish mask and huge crab claws; other costumes include that of a giant caiman. The dancers, whose headdresses are adorned with water lilies, are impersonating the deities of the watery underworld in order to obtain their blessings for King Chan-Muan's heir.*

HONORING THE DEAD

Tikal was one of the most powerful Maya kingdoms of the Classic Period. Set in the dense lowland rainforest of the Petén region of Guatemala, this huge ruined city continues to fascinate travelers. At its peak, in the eighth century CE, it was a bustling metropolis with a population estimated at somewhere between 80,000 and 100,000 people.

The name Tikal derives from the Mayan *ti ak'al*, which means "at the waterhole," an indicator that the site had been occupied for centuries before a major settlement developed. That process had begun around 600BCE and, by the second and third centuries CE, the kingdom of Tikal had become a regional force (the earliest stela so far dated is from the late third century CE).

Today, tourists stand in the central plaza and marvel at the pyramid temples rising above them. Some visitors, however, may not realize that they are standing within one of the most important burial complexes in the Maya region. Archaeological investigation has shown that, although Tikal was a vast living urban centre, some of its most impressive architecture was actually

built to honor the dead. The North Acropolis contains the tombs of many early Tikal kings. What remains today is the final stage of a construction process that lasted many centuries. Initially, there would only have been a small platform supporting a pyramid shrine, the first of which was constructed in about 200BCE. As successive rulers died, their tombs were built over earlier ones, resulting in superimposed burials and temples. Excavation has revealed that many of the early pyramids had huge plaster masks placed on either side of the central stairway, possibly representing the sun god.

The offerings that were placed in tombs to accompany the dead on their journey through the underworld are some of the finest discovered in the Maya area. Painted or incised pots show rulers as they would have appeared in life—enthroned and surrounded by attendants. The tomb was not thought of as the final resting place of the king. Originally the pots would have been filled with food or drink to sustain the deceased after death; drinks made from cacao were especially valued. A set of carved bones found in one tomb depicts the maize god traveling to the underworld in a canoe, accompanied by supernatural creatures. According to Classic-era belief, after a period in the underworld, the maize god was resurrected as the creator of the Earth. The bones from the Tikal tomb suggest that Maya kings were also thought to undergo a similar journey, culminating in triumphant reincarnation.

The finest pyramid in the central plaza, Temple I, is the resting place of one of the most successful kings of Tikal, Ah Cacau, who ruled from 682CE to about

723CE. He began to situate burial chambers in an area surrounding the North Acropolis, some of which may still await discovery.

ISLE OF GRAVES

Another major burial site during the late Classic era was Jaina Island, situated off the coast of Campeche and west of Uxmal and Kabah, which contains many thousands of graves. Its location, to the west of the Yucatán peninsula, was significant because, viewed from the mainland, the island lay in the path of the setting sun. Because the Maya believed that the sun descended into the underworld at night, Jaina was an appropriate place for the dead, whose souls could accompany the sun on its nocturnal journey. In ancient times, the island may have been reached by a wooden bridge. This was significant because the Maya underworld was thought to lie below the surface of a primordial ocean which had existed before the creation of the Earth. By crossing water, therefore, the body made a symbolic transition between this world and the next. The name Jaina was introduced by the Spanish; to the Maya, the ceremonial center was known as Hanal, or "house of water."

The graves contained a vast array of ritual offerings, but the objects most commonly found are small clay figurines or statuettes. Most of these were made using molds, and were originally painted in bright colors. Some contained clay pellets and were also rattles, others were hollow or had holes bored in them so they could be used as whistles. However, the finest were solid, handcrafted pieces, which must have been made for highclass burials. They portray men and women of various ages and rank, and may represent the people buried on the island. Many depict warriors—the island may have been a final resting place for those who had excelled in battle. The Maya divinities are also depicted, most frequently the sun and moon deities, who were believed to have survived the perils of Xibalba. These items may have been symbols of encouragement and guidance for the souls of the deceased.

Tikal's North Acropolis is a complicated structure of temples and tombs. During the late Preclassic Period, it consisted only of a small number of burial shrines, but over the centuries it became the most significant resting place for Tikal kings. A variety of architectural styles may be discerned in the layers of construction, including the influence of the huge central Mexican site of Teotihuacán (dating from the early Classic Period). This suggests that Tikal had contact with other peoples far beyond the realm of the Maya.

CHAPTER THREE

THE INCAS

"Where have men ever seen the things they have seen here?" marveled Pedro de Cieza de León, a sixteenth-century Spanish visitor to Peru. He arrived in the high Andes just a few years after the invasion of Francisco Pizarro's conquistadors, and could scarcely believe the splendors that he saw. Despite the depredations of his countrymen, the sacking of the cities and the stripping of the shrines, evidence of the awesome Inca achievement was all around. "And to think," he wondered, "that God should have permitted something so great to remain hidden from the world for so long in history, unknown to men … !" When we think of the Incas today, we have the same sense of a civilization set apart, an empire come from nowhere, as mysterious as it was magnificent. But while much remains to be learned, we now have a far better understanding of where the Incas came from culturally, and how they fit into the history of their region as a whole.

CHILDREN OF THE ANDES

The cultural achievements of the Incas stand comparison with those of any of the other great civilizations of the world. Each was shaped by a particular environment, yet even the mightiest of Inca monuments seem to meld inseparably with their breathtaking mountainous setting.

Although now in ruins, the citadel of Sacsahuaman at Cuzco inspires awe: its massive masonry takes the breath away. Its walls enormous boulders, but sculpted to minute precision for a perfect fit, it seems more the work of giants than of human builders. No wonder that the conquistadors who first came upon the Inca capital in 1532 should have compared it to the greatest monuments of the Old World. "Neither the bridge of Segovia nor other constructions of Hercules or the Romans are as magnificent as this," reported Pedro Sancho de la Hoz. It is revealing, though, that the conquistador felt called upon to mention a legendary hero together with the real achievements of Roman engineers. In its seeming aspiration to equal the magnificence of the natural environment, there was something about this stronghold that sent the European imagination straining beyond the historical record and into the realm of myth. Sancho de la Hoz's remark that the stones of Sacsahuaman were "as big as pieces of mountains or crags" suggests not only the astonishing scale of the Inca construction but the way it seemed to partake in the majesty of its setting.

Architectural masterpiece the defensive wall may have been, but the mountains of the Andes provided their own topographical splendour that made it difficult for any human construction to upstage. Part of the

The land from which the Incas carved out a civilization was one of dramatic contrasts, with the dizzying peaks and valleys of the Andes separated from the Pacific Ocean by only a thin strip of desert.

"Western Cordillera" which runs down the whole length of the Americas, from Alaska to Tierra del Fuego, the Andes are the product of colossal geotectonic forces. Expanding inch by inch over millennia as magma seeped up through fractures in the seabed, the Pacific plate pushed inexorably eastward against the American continent. Its deep-formed rocks comparatively dense, the oceanic plate drove downward when it met the landmass, forcing up a mighty mountain range to a height of almost 23,000 feet (7,000m). Such "subduction" was not accomplished smoothly: rather, it proceeded in a series of jolts and judders, as geological strata strained to resist unimaginable forces then finally broke or buckled. Even now, the geotectonic torture of the Cordillera is marked by seismic anarchy, with volcanic eruptions and devastating earthquakes.

In terms of physical relief, the Andean region can be seen as a gigantic shockwave frozen in stone; its jagged heights and plunging slopes the graphic trauma recorded on an electronic monitor. Life here can be as harsh as such imagery would suggest, but there are positive aspects, too. In few places in the world are so many different environmental zones crammed so closely together. Beside an ocean rich in fish, on account of the microlife-laden waters of the Peru Current, lies one of the driest deserts in the world. Thanks to the rivers which race across it carrying rain and snowmelt from the Andes, it is cultivable in parts. Maize, squash, and other crops can be grown in the desert under irrigation. Above the coastal plain the zone known as *yungas* rises to a height of around 10,000 feet (3,000m); a wide variety of tropical fruits and other crops can be raised here. Next comes the *quechua*, rich ground for the cultivation of maize, beans, and tubers, including potatoes—although the

• THE MISCHIEVOUS CHILD •

Every December, in the southern summer, a minor change in temperature in the mid-Pacific has far-reaching climatic and ecological consequences for adjacent coastal waters. The normally frigid Peru Current, rich in nutrients, is suppressed for a time as warm water spills eastward. Approximately every seven years, for reasons that are still not fully understood, the effects of this local warming are greatly amplified. In extreme cases, fish stocks collapse, causing grave problems both for animal and human fishers, while wind and rainfall patterns ashore are thrown into confusion. Torrential downpours and flashfloods on the one hand, catastrophic droughts on the other: there's no knowing quite what the results will be. Called El Niño—"the child"—because signs of it occur around Christmas, the nativity of Jesus, the phenomenon has attracted great attention in recent years because it has been found to have an impact indirectly all around the world. But the inhabitants of the Andean region have been living at close quarters with this wayward child for many centuries.

latter grow better at one level higher in the *suni* zone. A damp, chilly wasteland, the *puna* is largely reserved for herding camelids (llamas, alpacas) and for hunting their wild ancestor, the guanaco. The highest zone, the snow-covered *janca*, is unsuitable for farming, but its mineral resources have been exploited since early times. There are variations on these broad themes: a deep valley will have its own microclimate, while in Peru itself a high, broad plateau or *altiplano* extends between the two main ranges forming the Cordillera. On its eastward side the mountains slope away into Amazonia, from where ancient Andean peoples obtained products ranging from wood and gold to ornamental feathers.

BEFORE THE INCAS

Although the civilization of the Incas appears quite distinct, they only acquired a dominant position in the fifteenth century CE. Historical evidence has revealed the extent to which the Incas were the inheritors of a rich tradition of civilization which had been many centuries in the making.

The roots of the Andean lineage can be traced back many centuries: what archaeologists refer to as the "Initial Period" in Andean history began around the start of the second millennium BCE. This preliminary stage saw nomadic hunter–gatherers settle down to an existence of sedentary farming; there are signs that primitive pottery was made, and that cotton and camelid wool were woven into textiles. The basic building-blocks of civilization were in place, then, but it would not be for another thousand years that anything we would recognize as a developed culture had appeared.

CHAVÍN DE HUANTAR

The first major civilization to emerge in Peru, around 900BCE, is named for the cult center discovered at Chavín de Huantar in the Andean foothills of the Pukcha Valley. It remains in many respects mysterious: though in some ways a quintessentially upland culture, it appears to have borrowed cultural influences both from coastal and from inland jungle areas. The latter are more striking: the stone sculpture to be seen in Chavín shrines features jaguars, caymans, snakes, and other forest creatures which must always have seemed exotic in the highland context. Sometimes these images of alien fauna stand alone; at other times they occur in fantastical combination with anthropomorphic forms, the whole often incorporated into apparently abstract patterns of baroque complexity. The same aesthetic finds more colorful expression in the brightly painted patterning which adorns the fine ceramics created by Chavín hands. Altogether, this extravagant imagery suggest the sort of shamanistic culture to be found among other Amerindian peoples, in which priests spoke to ancestral spirits embodied by totemic animal species. Shamanism seems to have been brought to the Americas by the first Eurasian peoples who came across the land-bridge of Beringia anything up to 20,000 years ago. The shaman typically went into a trance to talk with the spirits of the dead, and was assisted in entering that state by the use of intoxicant drugs—coca, very likely, in the Andes. Objects in the Chavín style have been found throughout the Andean region, testifying to an extensive trade network and far-reaching cultural influence.

THE PARACAS PEOPLE

In one of the languages of Peru's indigenous peoples, Quechua, the word *paracas* means "sand falling like rain," an appropriate enough name for the Paracas Peninsula. Across this barren promontory high winds whip up a semipermanent sandstorm through much of the year—it would be hard to imagine a less promising site for human settlement. But intermittent supplies of river water were enough to allow agricultural development, while offshore fishing provided a rich source of food. The sea also offered edible shellfish, as well as the spondylus shell, prized throughout the region for ornamental use. Endowed with such resources, the people of Paracas not only survived but prospered, building a successful civilization some 2,500 years ago. Although they left no ruins of any note (they seem to have lived in simple, reed-covered pit-dwellings), the necropolises in which their dead were housed reveal something more spectacular. The ancestors were left seated upright in circles, as though in eternal conversation, effectively mummified by the aridity of the desert air. Simple shaft-tombs were eventually superseded by elaborate underground burial complexes with courtyards and corridors, but whatever their surroundings the dead were dressed luxuriously. Wealthy individuals were wrapped in up to a hundred layers of sumptuous textiles and accompanied by jewelry and other precious items. From the evidence of such burials, it has been calculated that

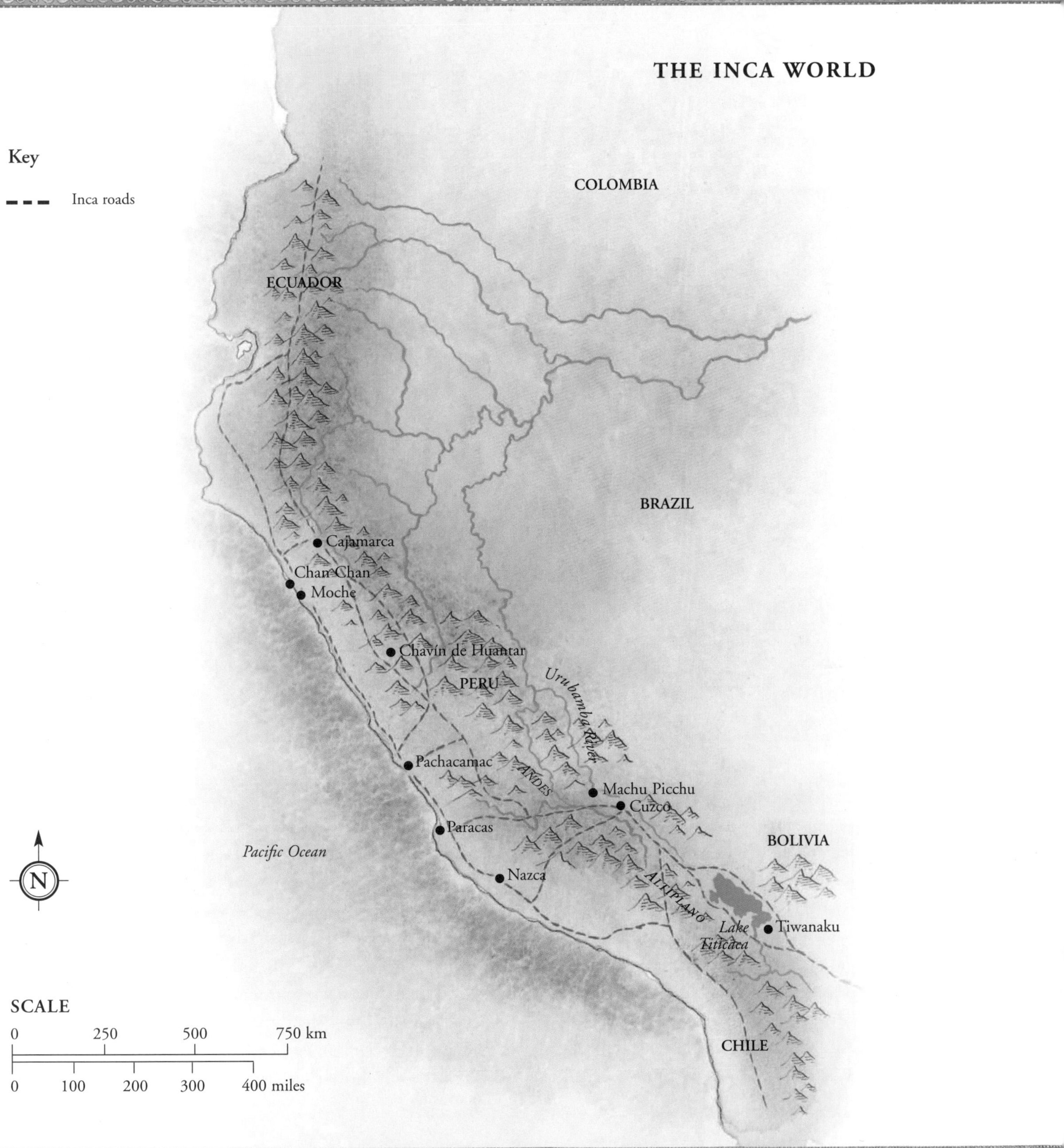

THE INCA WORLD

- - - Inca roads

COLOMBIA

ECUADOR

BRAZIL

● Cajamarca

Chan Chan
● Moche

● Chavín de Huantar

PERU

Urubamba River

ANDES

● Pachacamac

● Machu Picchu
● Cuzco

● Paracas

BOLIVIA

Pacific Ocean

● Nazca

ALTIPLANO

Lake Titicaca ● Tiwanaku

CHILE

SCALE

0	250	500	750 km

0	100	200	300	400 miles

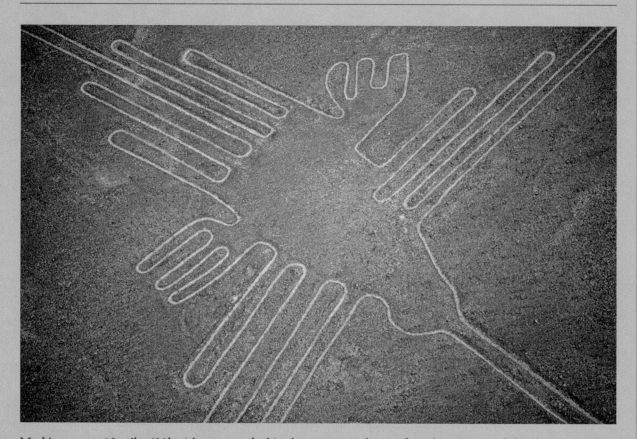

Markings up to 13 miles (20km) long are etched in the *pampas* or desert of southern Peru and they have been there since Nazca times. They consist of gigantic geometrical shapes—zigzags, spirals, and trapezoids—and spectacular geoglyphs or "earth-drawings" in the form of enormous renderings of animals and plants: everything from hummingbirds (as in the example, above) and lizards to monkeys, orcas (killer whales) and flowers. The origins and purpose of these mysterious figures has spawned some sensationalist explanations, but the evidence points to local inhabitants as having been the creators. However, some pieces are too large to be seen in their entirety from the ground or surrounding hills, which has caused some to wonder why the Nazca would have produced images which no mortal was ever likely to see (the lines only became visible to archaeologists in the age of aviation). Archaeologist Rebecca Stone-Miller has pointed out that the cross shape made by the intersection of nave and transept in Europe's medieval cathedrals could not be seen by the worshippers inside, but they knew it was there and felt protected by its symbolic power. And just as medieval worshippers also used labyrinths in medieval churches for meditative purposes, some scholars have argued that the Nazca lines may have been ritual pathways.

up to 29,000 hours of skilled labor would have gone into making the textiles and jewelry some of the dead carried with them to the grave. While cotton was cultivated under irrigation by the Paracas people themselves, camelid wool was obtained from mountain communities in exchange for dried fishmeal and spondylus shell. So too were the Amazonian birds' feathers which were miraculously incorporated into some of the more spectacular fabrics. In all, 190 different shades have been identified in Paracas textiles, based on a wide and ingenious palette of dyes created from minerals, plants, barks, insects, and shellfish. Every skill known to modern textile workers had been mastered, from brocade and lace to tapestry, and their embroidery has never been rivaled, still less surpassed. Filled with dynamism and color, their designs range from flying shamans (see illustration, page 625) to weapon-wielding warriors, as well as a strange goggle-eyed figure who may have been a sun god, but is known to archaeology only as "the oculate being."

THE NAZCA

A little way down the coast from Paracas another civilization gradually emerged from the shadow of its northerly neighbor. By the middle of the first millennium CE the people known as Nazca had built a sophisticated culture of their own. The continuing controversy over their geoglyphs (see box, opposite) overshadows the extraordinary achievements of the Nazca in other spheres. It can reasonably be claimed, for example, that they did for ceramics what Paracas had done for textiles, producing decorative pottery of breathtaking beauty and skill. They were also masters of irrigation, building a complicated network of underground canals which brought water across considerable distances from remote aquifers. One of the most curious aspects of Nazca culture seems to have been their construction of an uninhabited capital city at Cahuachi, a site on the Nazca River some 30 miles (50km) inland. Here the remains of a ruined temple and smaller shrines have been found, but this ceremonial center seems to have lain empty for

much of the year. Their communities scattered by necessity (even under irrigation, sites suitable for cultivation were few and far between), the Nazca came together regularly for communal rituals and festivities.

EARLY ANDEAN STATES

Too much emphasis on accomplishment in arts and crafts may give a misleading impression of the early Andean civilizations as having been dedicated entirely to peaceful pursuits. On the contrary, military power played an important role and it would eventually be crucial to the rise of the Inca Empire. Militarism's first major manifestation was in the culture of the Moche, as it took shape in the middle centuries of the first millennium BCE. This fascinating people created fine pottery and exquisite ornamental metalwork, but their key contribution to history was their establishment of the region's first fully-fledged state in the northern part of Peru.

A little to the south of Lake Titicaca, in what is now Bolivia, the ancient city of Tiwanaku stands on the *altiplano* at approximately 13,000 feet (4,000m) above sea-level. First settled around 1500BCE, it reached its height toward the middle of the first millennium CE. Tiwanaku was a fascinating civilization, but most of its accomplishments have been obscured and are known to us partly because they influenced Inca culture. Upon seeing the huge stone statues of Tiwanaku, the Incas thought they represented an earlier race of men and women turned into stone by an angry creator and they incorporated the idea into their cosmology (see page 619).

The Incas were also in awe of the material and monumental splendor of the Sicán and Chimú civilizations which flourished from around 700CE along the northern coast of Peru. The first of these was conquered by the second, before both were absorbed by the expanding Inca Empire. Captured by the Inca in the 1460s, the Chimú capital, Chan Chan, appears to have served as an inspiration to its Inca conquerors who found here a spectacular model of what might successfully be accomplished by a well-organized Andean state.

THE MULTIPLE CREATIONS OF WIRAQOCHA

In a people as proud as the Incas, and in a region of the world so comparatively isolated, a certain solipsism might be expected. Sure enough, in their dramatic conception of the creation of the universe, the Incas placed themselves at center stage.

The Incas' account of their origins is often confusing and exasperatingly inconsistent, reflecting perhaps the fact that for all the overarching power of what would eventually become an imperial state the people we now refer to as "the Incas" were actually an agglomeration of local tribes with their own traditions. Each had ideas of their own about how the world had come into being: the seventeenth-century Spanish Jesuit chronicler Bernabé Cobo complained that he had been told "a thousand absurd stories." Each community, he said, "claims for itself the honor of having been the first people and says that everyone else came from them."

Broadly speaking, though, there was agreement that the world had taken shape around the Andes, and that the source of all life had been the watery depths of sacred Lake Titicaca.

A WORLD IN DARKNESS

From the waters of Lake Titicaca, it was explained, Wiraqocha (or Viracocha) Pachyachachic, "Creator of All Things," had emerged into an empty world of darkness. He decided to people it, and set to work fashioning the first men and women from solid stone. To begin with he made giant figures, sculpted into shape out of

◆ THE SACRED LAKE ◆

Lake Titicaca (see illustration, opposite) is a remarkable stretch of water: at 12,500 feet (3,800m) above sea-level it is the highest navigable lake anywhere on Earth. Sandwiched between what are now the southeastern part of Peru and the western region of Bolivia, it is 110 miles (177km) long and on average 35 miles (56km) wide. But such statistics cannot possibly do justice to the bleak beauty of its setting, or the mystic thrill the visitor feels simply by standing on its windswept shore.

Titicaca retains a sense of primal emptiness; it is no surprise to find that the Incas identified this as the scene of the Earth's creation. And, it now appears, many other Andean peoples before them held the lake to be sacred: researches by archaeologist Brian Bauer on the Islands of the Sun and Moon on Titicaca's southern side suggest that the islands were places of pilgrimage a good millennium before the emergence of the Incas. The Wiraqocha myth can be interpreted as a means of asserting an Inca cultural hold over a place whose sanctity had been established long before.

vast boulders, but these were much too large, he quickly saw. Next he created a new humanity, in the same proportions as we have now, and ordered it to live together peacefully without quarrelling. For a time they followed this prescription, but before too long the vices of pride and covetousness started to show themselves, and soon the world was made miserable by greed and conflict. Enraged at what he saw, Wiraqocha often turned on the men and women he had made: he turned some to stone, and had some swallowed up by the earth or ocean. He then sent sixty days and nights of rain: the resulting flood washed away almost all traces of his first accursed creation; just two were saved (in some accounts his sons) to be the founders of a new humanity.

The first, ill-fated creation had existed not merely in moral but in literal darkness, for it was only now that Wiraqocha decided to create the gift of light. He went onto an island in Lake Titicaca, and called forth the sun and moon from the waters and set them in the sky, bidding them to take turns in illuminating the Earth. To begin with, the moon shone the brighter—so much so that the sun was seized with envy and flung ashes in her face; ever since, the moon has beamed that bit more wanly. Wiraqocha returned to the lakeshore and walked inland a little way, taking with him the men he had saved from the Earth's first age as his servants. When they got to Tiwanaku, he stopped, for it was here that he would set about creating the world a second time. Again he fashioned from stone the statues and images of the peoples he intended to bring forth; he painted on them the distinctive colors and costumes each community would wear. He then had his assistants memorize the names of all these different peoples and those of their countries and the landmarks among which they would live. It was then simply a matter of bringing his creation to life and endowing everything with its

name. Wiraqocha sent one servant westward toward the ocean, the other eastward into Amazonia, while he allocated to himself the high mountain heartland, calling forth its peoples and naming every peak, every crag, every cave, every lake, and every stream. Eventually his journey took him as far as the Pacific coast: here the creator turned and addressed his peoples. He was leaving now, he told them, but his messengers would return one day—they should, however, beware of interlopers. Then, his servants at his side, he set out across the ocean, walking on the waves until he had disappeared over the far horizon.

The same basic story of Wiraqocha's two creations circulated in many different local versions: for example,

the number of people saved as helpers from the first creation varied. There was also disagreement as to the precise point on land from where the creator had departed to walk over the ocean. Some accounts claimed that he left from Pachacamac, on the central coast of Peru, a site which would become an important shrine. Others named a site much farther north in Ecuador—and there seem to have been several other candidates. This particular inconsistency may actually originate in the progressive revision of the basic creation myth to reflect the expanding borders of the Inca Empire and the extending horizons of the Inca world. Their sense of where the world ended was changing from one year to the next. Yet whatever their potential for territorial expansion, it is strikingly clear from the legend that the Incas felt no

• THE MONKEY MEN •

The idea that creation proceeded in cycles seems to have been common to the various Andean civilizations, as shown by stories told by the Chimú in the centuries before the Inca conquest. They speak of the floods which washed an earlier world away and of the devastating drought (both quite possibly based on actual El Niño events; see page 613) by which the creator Con punished an ungrateful humankind. Eventually taking pity on them, he restored the rains again, only to find his own reign as deity threatened by his brother Pachacamac. The siblings fought—Con was vanquished and driven from the world, while his usurper stood and contemplated his creation. Dissatisfied with what he saw, he turned Con's men and women into chattering monkeys which he sent off to the forest; in their place he created the human species which endures today.

temptation to subjugate the landscape they inhabited: the mythical account represents the creation of humanity as an act of physical fashioning, but the creation of the Earth as one of identification and of naming. The rocks and mountains of the Earth predated these creations: they were an eternal, and non-negotiable, presence in the life of humanity. Where other peoples inhabited their landscapes, there is a sense in which the Andean environment inhabited the Incas: their consciousness was constructed by their relationship with their Andean setting. Not only geography but human history were embodied in the physical features around them, and little distinction was made between the works of gods and men. Hence the incorporation into Inca mythology of the monolithic statues at Tiwanaku as the remains of the first race of giants petrified in Wiraqocha's rage, alongside naturally formed outcrops and standing stones.

CYCLES OF DESTRUCTION

Another Andean tradition illustrated by the story of Wiraqocha's two creations is the idea that existence proceeds in endless cycles of cataclysm and re-creation. Every thousand years, it was said, the world would be destroyed in a moment of *pachakuti*, at which everything would come to an end and then start all over again. Wiraqocha's wrathful destruction of his first creation was an example of this—though so too was his second creation: literally a "turning over of time and space," the notion of *pachakuti* offered hope as well as fear. According to Felipe Guamán Poma de Ayala (ca. 1536–1616), a chronicler of mixed Spanish and Inca ancestry, the Earth had already experienced five ages by the time of the conquistadors' invasion (another moment of *pachakuti*). Although punctuated by death and disaster, the overall process brought a steady improvement in the human condition, from the darkness and savagery of Wiraqocha's first creation. Men and women in that age, reports Guamán Poma de Ayala, "did not know how to do anything": they could not

A detail of an Inca tunic woven out of camelid fibre and in a design style known as "checkerboard". The cloth may be qompi, *the finest of Inca materials. According to Andean tradition, it was during the third age of creation that wool was spun and woven for the first time.*

make clothes, but simply draped themselves in leaves; they did not know how to build houses, merely throwing up rude shacks for shelter. In the second age or "sun," he says, humanity had learned to cover themselves in animal skins; they had also learned the basics of agriculture. The third age saw the onset of more systematic agriculture, as well as the spinning, dying, and weaving of camelid wool. The knowledge and skills of mining and metalworking were mastered at this time, which can thus be seen as a time of technological revolution, with all the advantages that brought—but it was also a time of intercommunal rivalry. The fourth age was that of the Auca Runa, the "warlike people"—it was indeed an age of conflict, marked by suspicion, enmity and, for much of the time, outright war. It was in this period that tribal divisions were formed which would have a continuing influence through the fifth era, a golden age in which the Incas brought order and stability to the world.

A MIGHTY PANTHEON

Wiraqocha, revered as the creator of the cosmos (see pages 618–621), seems to have played little part in the everyday running of the Inca universe. This task was shared out among a pantheon of gods and goddesses, with Wiraqocha's son Inti the most prominent of them.

Having established everything under its rightful name and in its rightful place, Wiraqocha, also referred to as "Instructor of the World," seems effectively to have retired. The Incas, for their part, honored their maker but do not appear actively to have worshipped him: no significant ceremony seems to have been held in his name. For all intents and purposes, the ruler in Inca heaven was not Wiraqocha but his son Inti, god of the sun. Inti's splendor lit up the day and made life possible, warming the Earth and enabling the crops to grow. Earlier Andean civilizations—much as others worldwide—had worshipped the sun for these reasons, but for the Incas, Inti had a special status. They believed that the son of Wiraqocha was a father in his turn—successive royal rulers, who were known as the Inca, regarded themselves as Inti's sons. His cult was thus at the center not only of religious life but of state ideology: his power underwrote the authority of the Inca Empire. Made, appropriately enough, of gold, Inti's idol has not been seen for centuries: it is believed to have been

hidden at the time of the conquistadors' invasion. Some reports suggest that it was later seized and tossed into the furnace to be melted down with the rest of the Incas' gold, but its fate seems destined to remain obscure. The chroniclers agree, however, that Punchao ("Day"), as this figure was called, was the statue of a little boy in a seated position. Gold spools adorned his ears; a sunburst radiated out around his head and shoulders; and lion and serpent figures lay around his body. His hollow stomach was the receptacle in which the internal organs of dead kings were burned and stored, underlining the identification between Inti and the ruling family. The cult of the sun also played as crucial a part in the Inca economy: in addition to richly endowed temples in every urban center, vast areas of cultivable land in the countryside were consecrated to Inti, who also had his own storehouses, workshops, mines, and metal foundries in which many thousands must have found employment.

Inti was married to Mama-Quilla, the goddess of the moon, whose waxing–waning rhythms formed the basis for the Inca calendar. As in many other cultures, the moon was seen as essentially gentle and feminine, in contrast to the fiery ferocity of the masculine sun. She had her own temple complex in Cuzco and was served by her own designated priestesses. Just as the Inca king was believed to be the son of Inti, so his queen was deemed to be the daughter of Mama-Quilla.

HEAVEN, EARTH, AND SEA

A more intimidating presence in the heavens was that of the thunder god Inti-Ilapa, imagined as a fearsome warrior in the sky. He held a terrifying club in one hand and in the other swung a sling whose whipcrack was believed to be the cause of the rolling thunder. The flash of lightning was said to be the glittering of his garments as he soared across the sky; where bolts struck the Earth it was believed that a stone from his sling had landed. Yet he had his more benign side: it was Inti-Ilapa who drew water for the rain from the Milky Way, a starlit river, and whose iridescent costume created the colors of the rainbow. The name of the goddess Pachamama translates literally as "Earth Mother," and she stood for those same values of fertility and nurture that the name would suggest today. She was particularly associated with agriculture, and sacrifices were offered to her for a successful harvest. Another goddess, Mamacocha, was identified with lakes and the sea: as would be expected, she was especially revered by coastal communities.

The Incas believed that the giant statues left by their antecedents the Tiwanaku, including the Ponce Monolith (viewed here from the Kalasasaya Observatory), were people turned to stone by Wiraqocha, the creator of the cosmos (see page 619).

THE ANCESTORS
AND THE KINSHIP *AYLLU*

Inca society contained complex groups of kinship collectives known as ayllu, *which cut across what we would understand today as cultural or socio-economic "class" boundaries, and ancestral spirits played a continuing part in the everyday existence of the living.*

Spanish missionaries in the seventeenth century made determined efforts to root out "idolatry," believing it necessary in order to save the souls of their Inca subjects. The missionaries discerned this in many forms, but none was quite so repulsive to them as the Incas' relationship with the dead. Had it been the overvaluation of memories of the deceased it would have been bad enough—their sights should have been set above earthly ties of family and on the world beyond. But the Incas actually preserved their dead as mummies and, worse still in the eyes of the Spanish, paraded them in public and regarded them with reverence, as though the dead were respected elders. The practice was a general one, by no means confined to kings: between 1656 and 1658

appalled Catholic priests conducted a macabre "census of the dead" in the caves around San Pedro de Hacas. In one they found 214 mummies; in another 471; in still another 402 bodies were preserved. One cave, at Ayllu Carampa, was home to 738 mummified corpses, yet they were treated as though they still belonged among the living. At certain times of year they were dressed in new clothes, and regular offerings of food and drink were brought to them—thanks for the good luck they supposedly conferred at planting and harvest times.

The modern nuclear family—husband, wife, and children—is a novelty, an aberration, some would say: in most cultures in history individuals have taken their places in extended families. In shamanistic societies, however, those families extend not just outward to embrace cousins, aunts, and uncles but chronologically to include previous generations. Not all such societies have gone to the lengths of literally living around the preserved bodies of their forebears—apart from anything else, in most climates this simply would not have been practical. But men and women in many Old World cultures would have seen nothing strange in the idea that the ancestors were an enduring presence in the midst of the living, to whom they could offer advice and assistance of many kinds.

The institution of the *ayllu*, or kinship group, seems to have been unique, if not to the Incas, then at least to the Andes: tribe, clan, economic self-help cooperative—all these labels are applicable but none is quite accurate. The *ayllu* derived its identity from the claim that all its members were descended from a common ancestor, but its function was as much economic as familial. Typically, the *ayllu* included a number of nuclear families of varying size and status, generally dispersed across the whole

◆ THE DRINK OF ECSTASY ◆

Spanish priests were horrified not only by the Incas' idolatry but also by their consumption of alcohol. Brewed from fermented maize-mash, *chicha* was consumed in great quantities at communal festivities—drunkenness was seen as a way of leaving behind the humdrum here and now for a more ecstatic spiritual plane. But it was also poured onto the ground as an offering to ancestral spirits: they too were invited to the party. To make *chicha*, the maize was first chewed up into a sticky pulp; this was then boiled in water and left for a few days until it frothed up and was ready to drink. In more moderate amounts it was taken every day with meals: drinking water was regarded as a hardship.

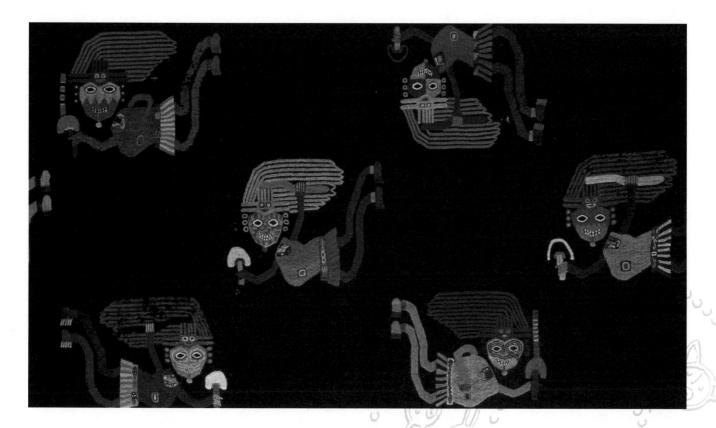

This detail of a Paracas textile features a pattern made up of flying shamans—a common motif in Paracas embroidery. The shaman acted as both a healer and an intermediary between the living and the dead, making perilous spirit journeys to consult the ancestors.

range of climatic zones in which different sorts of live-stock were kept and a variety of crops were grown. This geographical spread helped make the group as a whole more or less self-sufficient, with access to essential resources of all kinds. Produce was passed back and forth freely between the member-families: fish from the coasts; corn and squash from the lowlands; potatoes and wool from the higher ground. And while richer house-holds might assist their poorer kinsfolk financially when occasion demanded it, they knew that their help would be willingly reciprocated with whatever food or labor might be needed. The loyalties of the *ayllu* were invalu-able in oiling the wheels of a highly centralized state which conscripted large numbers for military service or work on state farms. The young man called up for serv-ice of this kind could set out in the confidence that his family would be protected and his fields maintained by other *ayllu* members: without such cover, the imperial economy as a whole would have broken down.

The *ayllu* in its turn depended on the authority of the ancestors: it was respect for them that assured the coherence of the kinship group. Despite the mutual benefits it brought, the institution of the *ayllu* would clearly have been vulnerable had the relatively strong and wealthy decided that their interests lay in going it alone. But such individualistic attitudes were alien to the Incas: they deferred unquestioningly to the dead, and the idea of neglecting traditional responsibilities did not occur. Their commitment to the *ayllu* and its principles was renewed each time they honored the mummies of their ancestors, whose disapproval was feared above all things.

THE ORIGINS OF THE INCAS

The "history" of the Incas is every bit as hard for us to grasp as their cosmology. Whereas Western notions of history are rooted in the desire for impartial assessments and a search for the truth, official Inca annals are more fanciful and seem to have been unabashedly revised and reinterpreted for reasons of ideological convenience as kings succeeded kings, circumstances changed, and the empire grew.

The Jesuit Bernabé Cobo was withering about the inconsistency of the Incas' accounts of their past, and of the self-aggrandizement inherent in their "history." Of course, all empires have freely reinterpreted the events of the past to their own advantage: the Spanish conquerors of the New World were themselves no exception. Cobo's caution is reasonable enough, though: Inca history clearly set the past to work on behalf of the present state. But if it is hard to separate the historical fact from the fanciful myth in the Incas' accounts of the lives and conquests of their later kings, there is no such problem with their—quite clearly mythical—explanation of the origins of the royal line.

THE INN OF DAWN

Out on the *altiplano* some 20 miles (33km) south of Cuzco, at a place named Pacariqtambo, the "Inn of Dawn," there was once a cave with three entrances, called Tampu T'oqo, the "House of Windows" (see box, opposite). Through the "windows" on either side, the Maras T'oqo and Sutiq T'oqo, emerged the Maras and Sutiq (Tambo) peoples, who were to prove longstanding allies of the Incas. But the central entrance was the Qhapaqh T'oqo ("Rich Window"), and it was through this aperture in the earth that Wiraqocha summoned forth the four brothers and four sisters he intended to be the progenitors of a mighty race. The first to emerge, and thus the senior, was Manqo Qhapaqh (or Manco Capac; "First Rich Ancestor"), who bears the title as first Inca king; he took in marriage his sister Mama Oqllu ("Plump Mother"). With them came Ayar Awka and his consort Mama Waqo, along with Ayar Kachi and his wife Mama Kura. Ayar Uchu ("Ancestor Chili Pepper") and Mama Rawa brought up the rear: from these eight siblings the entire Inca nation would be descended.

The name Ayar comes from the root *aya*, which literally means "corpse" but was given to these ancestors in their moment of creation. The identification of the dead body and the living presence was thus made explicit at the outset: it would hold not only for these originating couples but for all the Inca dead. (Intriguingly, the name *ayar* is also given to the crop *quinoa*, a staple food for the Incas through many centuries.) For the moment, though, the four founding couples were very much alive. Despite Manqo Qhapaqh's preeminence as king, it seems to have been Mama Waqo who seized the initiative. "We are born strong and wise," she told the others in a rousing speech, "and with the people who will here join us we shall be powerful. We will go forth from this place to seek fertile lands and when we find them we will subjugate the people and take the lands, making war on all those who do not receive us as their lords." Mama Waqo was "fierce and cruel," notes the sixteenth-century Spanish chronicler Pedro Sarmiento de Gaboa disapprovingly, but she knew what she wanted for her people—and her prophecy seems to have been borne out by later history. The details may be sketchy in the extreme, but the Incas were indeed destined to carve out an empire for themselves as conquerors.

IN SEARCH OF A HOMELAND

Because Inca achievements were collective ones, to which thousands contributed, the modern perspective ascribes to them the idea of being a people, but such highly modern notions of "nation," or even "race," may easily mislead. The term "Inca" should, strictly speaking, be confined to that line of kings brought out of the earth by Wiraqocha to lead the other peoples of the Andes. Mama Waqo makes the distinction when, in her address to her brothers and sisters at Pacariqtambo, she

• THE TRUE TAMPU T'OQO? •

The site at which the eight ancestors originally appeared out of the ground has traditionally been held to be a cave outside the town of Pacariqtambo. The town exists, as indeed does an unexceptional-looking cave, whose main entrance adjoins a patch of scrubby undergrowth. More recently, however, it has been suggested that another cave, at Puma Orqo, near the "old city" of Maukallaqta, is the site from which the creator-siblings emerged. In this cave's favor is the fact that it was clearly the center of an important shrine and palace complex in the earliest Inca times: rich jewelry reminiscent of the gold-and-silver nose ornament (left) and dress pin (right), illustrated below, has been found here amid the ruined walls of more than 200 buildings. The rock of the outcrop beneath which the cave opens has been carved with puma forms, appropriate for the place where the Inca dynasty first appeared. But there is absolutely no proof, of course: the actual location of Tampu T'oqo must, for the time being at least, remain a matter of speculation.

speaks of "the people who will here join us." The first act of the ancestors, according to the chronicles, was the organization of those living in the vicinity of the Inn of Dawn into the ten *ayllu* (see pages 624–625) that would form the basis of the Inca order ever after. In the words of Sarmiento, they "began to stir up the people who lived in that part of the mountain, setting as the prize that they would make the people rich and that they would give them lands and estates which they conquered." From those who were inspired to join them were formed the ten *ayllu*.

The entire company then set out in search of lands in which they could realize their destiny as wealthy rulers—yet their quest was to prove a discouraging one. Time and again they rounded an outcrop or crested a rise to look out over some new expanse of territory, only to see wastelands extending to the horizon. To add to their troubles, one of their number, Ayar Kachi, repeatedly provoked and picked fights with the peoples they met along the way. Events moved on regardless, though: at Tamboquiro Mama Oqllu gave birth—Zinchi Roq'a was to be the second Inca king. They pushed on to a place called Palluta, say the chronicles, where they settled for a few years and attempted to coax a living from the soil. Here too, however, the land proved unproductive and before long they were on the move again. They stopped once more at Haysquisro: here the siblings decided that the quarrelsome Ayar Kachi had become too much of a liability and hatched a plan to rid themselves of him. Telling him that they had forgotten something at the Tampu T'oqo cave, they tricked him into returning into the ground then rolled a boulder across the door and sealed him up inside.

THE HEIGHTS OF HUANACAURI

Yet again the ancestors and their allies struck camp and continued northward: now they found themselves at a place called Quirirmanta, from where they scrambled up the rugged slopes of the now-famous mountain called Huanacauri. This name literally means "rainbow" —and that is just what they saw before them, spanning the sky, as they looked out in awe over a wide and fertile valley. The rainbow was a sign that this land would not be swept away by floods as previous creations had been. So said Manqo Qhapaqh to his companions. Taking one of the two gold rods the expedition had been carrying, Mama Waqo hurled it far out across the valley: all watched with bated breath as it fell to earth. There was consternation when, hitting the ground at Matagua, it bounced—this was not the fertile soil they had been seeking. But Mama Waqo seized the second rod, and this too she flung into the air; it landed farther down the valley at Wanaypata. It sank straight into the earth, so deep it could no longer be seen—a further indication that this was indeed the promised land.

One final sign was needed that this valley was their destined homeland. It came through the offices of Ayar Uchu. He had wings, it is reported, and now he spread them and soared high into the sky above, flying straight toward the searing fire of the sun. After a time, he returned: he had spoken to Inti, he said, and the sun god had indeed confirmed that the Incas were to make this valley their eternal home. Manqo Qhapaqh was their rightful king, said the sun god, and he and his descendants should establish their capital where a man named Alcavicça had his settlement. There they would find a rocky outcrop, a perfect site for a citadel, with fine farmland stretching away across the *altiplano* below. His message delivered, Ayar Uchu's work was done and he turned to stone on the spot: the resulting rocky pillar would be revered as one of the Incas' holiest monuments.

Another popular version of the myth sees Ayar Uchu simply turning to stone atop the mountain. In this account it is Ayar Awka who takes to the air and flies across the valley. He is sent by Manqo Qhapaqh to take possession of the territory on behalf of the Incas: when he lands on a heap of rocks in the middle of the valley he too turns to stone. A heap of clods or rocks was once known in the ancient Andes as a *cozco*—hence the name which was thenceforth given to the capital, Cuzco.

A rainbow stretches across an Andean valley—a scene reminiscent of the one that greeted the wandering founders of the Inca order when they first set eyes on the fertile Cuzco Valley, which was to become their homeland (see main text, opposite).

In this account, Alcavicça's people were the original inhabitants of the Cuzco Valley region. Other sources name the Indian groups known as Ayarmaca or Huaya, and their reported reaction to the new arrivals varies too. In some versions of the legend they welcomed the wanderers who came bearing a message from the sun. In others the incumbent peoples had to be violently suppressed by the newcomers and driven out by force. In these accounts Mama Waqo features prominently, fighting every bit as ferociously as might have been expected. She seized one enemy warrior, it is said, and, tearing his body open with her bare hands, blew up his lungs like a balloon as she stormed into the mass of his terrified comrades.

The Incas also had to take possession of their new homeland in a more peaceful sense by making its soil submit to cultivation. They had brought the seeds of maize with them all the way from Pacariqtambo, precisely for this purpose. Some accounts claim it was Manqo Qhapaqh in his capacity as king who broke the surface of the soil and planted the first seeds here; in other accounts this part is played by Mama Waqo.

A pivotal mythic moment, this episode represents the symbolic "domestication" of the earth, the moment at which humankind began to bend the earth to its will and make it productive. From a more historical point of view, of course, it really is one of the "thousand absurd stories" of which Bernabé Cobo would complain: corn had been cultivated in the Cuzco Valley for many centuries before the Incas came along. But it is in keeping with the self-universalizing tendency of the Incas that they should award themselves this particular honor. Many civilizations have seen their capitals as the center of the Earth, but most have had a wider geographical and historical perspective than the Incas. It was a mark of their comparative isolation that the Incas so readily took their own experiences for the whole of history, that they assumed their empire was the entire world.

CHRONICLES OF THE KINGS

The part fact, part fiction nature of the annals which detail the early Inca rulers means that they can only be categorized as somewhere between the realms of history and myth. Although scholars may still puzzle over the truth, the stories about the lives and conquests of these kings are undeniably exciting.

In several accounts of the Inca story as described by the chroniclers and dutifully set out in their turn by modern scholars, the original inhabitants of the Cuzco Valley are named as the Ayarmaca Indians. It was their defeat in battle that allowed the Incas to establish themselves in what would become their heartland. The historian María Rostworowski de Diez Canseco has questioned the nature of this achievement by pointing out that there may be more to the Ayarmaca than meets the eye. The name Ayarmaca is obtained by putting together two major staples of the Inca diet: *ayar*, or *quinoa*, is a grain which flourishes at high altitudes, while *maca* is an edible tuber. When the name is dissected, the Inca-constructed edifice of history begins to crack. While it is not of course inconceivable that there could have been a people called the Ayarmaca, it seems far more probable that they were an allegorical enemy. It suddenly makes more sense to see the victory in "battle" as having been a symbolic one, representing the moment at which the knowledge and skills of agriculture were mastered. History is one of the ways in which a culture makes sense of itself and explains how it got to where it is at. But whereas modern academic history in Western culture seeks to distinguish itself from propaganda presented as fact, certain caveats need to be kept in mind when assessing the annals of ancient societies such as the accounts of the early Inca kings. These may often lend greater weight to the drama of narrative and be far more concerned with symbolic explanations for events.

A SYMBOLIC SUCCESSION

The reign of the second king Zinchi Roq'a was said to have been characterized by peaceful relations with neighboring peoples. He was wise and benevolent, more interested in forming alliances than in fighting wars. He married Mama Kuka, who came from the city of Saño,

---

• GARCILASO DE LA VEGA: A CULTURAL GO-BETWEEN •

"El Inca" Garcilaso de la Vega (1539–1616) was born in Cuzco, the son of a prominent conquistador, Sebastian Garcilaso de la Vega y Vargas, and his concubine, an Inca princess, Isabel Suarez Chimpu Ocllo. In 1560, at his father's behest, he moved to Andalusia in Spain, where he received a European education, but he retained pride in his Inca roots. By 1563 he had assumed his father's name, despite it having been tarnished by accusations of treason. Repression in the wake of a native rebellion made it inadvisable to go home, so he settled near Cordóba and became a humanist scholar who wrote sympathetically on Inca life, culture and empire, his most famous works being the *Royal Commentaries of the Incas* (1609) and *A General History of Peru* (1617). Eloquently, he stresses that the disastrous effects of conquest were due to a cultural misunderstanding and that the Incas had deserved respect.

to the east of Cuzco. This could all be strictly factual, of course, but we have no way of knowing for certain, and it seems as likely that this ruler's reign was used symbolically to establish the principle that good government and diplomacy were as important as military conquest. Zinchi Roq'a is credited with the introduction of the potato to the valley: again, this makes more symbolic than historical sense. His successor, Lloq'e Yupanki (meaning "left-handed," or tricksy), stands as an example of how cunning strategy can succeed more readily than war—again, we have no way of knowing his true character. His marriage to the beautiful Mama Kawa produced a son and heir, Mayta Qhapaqh, who was a role model of another sort—a brave and belligerent warrior, he made the Incas feared throughout the Andes, and put down rebellions among the subject peoples.

Mayta Qhapaqh's successor is believed to have been Qhapaqh Yupanki, another warrior-king, under whom the realm of the Incas grew in both glory and extent. But the chronicles become confused here, the normal inconsistencies becoming compounded by the fact that several kings seem to have had the same names as their predecessors. Qhapaqh Yupanki's queen, Mama Qori Willpay ("Jewel of Gold") is said to have given birth to a son, Inca Roq'a, who was perhaps the greatest conqueror so far. In turn, Inca Roq'a's son was kidnapped by one of the king's enemies; his abductor fully intended to murder him but stayed his hand when by some miracle the boy began weeping tears of blood. In honor of this, when the boy eventually came to take his own place as king, he reigned under the title of Yawar Waqaq ("he who weeps blood"). He would weep no tears of pity: he turned out to be a ruthless ruler, although he increased the dominance of the Inca kings in the Cuzco Valley. The eighth king, Wiraqocha Inca, having adopted the name of the creator, was the first of the kings to claim divine status for his dynasty and himself. In doing so, however, he was inaugurating an important tradition which would gather momentum in the generations which followed (see page 633).

Although presented in this 18th-century engraving by an unknown European artist as if they were real historical rulers, the early lords of Cuzco may well have been legendary figures. The Incas recounted their royal line, starting with Manqo Qhapaqh (see pages 626–629), to the Spanish chroniclers, who recorded it at face value.

THE EMPIRE BUILDERS

By the early fifteenth century, the Incas were the dominant power in the altiplano *and were soon establishing a presence beyond, extending their empire and pushing back the boundaries of their known world. However, the extent of the confusion that exists concerning the early history of the Incas becomes apparent when we attempt to assess the scale of their conquests in this period.*

An empire as glorious as that of the Incas required an epic history, or so it was believed by the Incas themselves who appear to have regarded their annals not as a simple record but as an assertion of destiny. Differing sources imply that the Incas occupied vast areas, while others are far more cautious about such claims. Scholars today suspect that for several generations the Incas were a local power, and that it was only with difficulty that they made themselves masters of the Cuzco Basin. Although signs of earlier settlement abound, archaeologists are sceptical as to whether any significant state existed here much before the beginning of the fifteenth century.

The precise moment at which the fight for survival transformed into what might be termed a campaign of imperial expansion cannot be identified, but it is generally held to have come toward the end of the reign of Wiraqocha Inca and during that of his son and successor Yupanki, who ruled as Inca Pachakuti. His name—renderings of which include "He Who Re-makes the World," "Earthshaker" and "Re-former of the World"—suggests a fresh start, a re-creation, and just like his predecessors on the throne, he seems as much a symbolic as a literal figure. The symbolism makes sense, though, for history certainly seems to show that, at some point, the Incas reinvented themselves as empire builders.

As ever, the chroniclers disagree wildly, but there does seem to be a degree of consensus that the Incas' expansionist policy was actually defensive in its origins. Wiraqocha Inca's realm was subjected to an escalating series of attacks by the Chanka tribes, whose heartland lay some way to the west of Cuzco. Finally, it is said, the Chankas threatened the stronghold of Cuzco itself with a huge army: Wiraqocha Inca was actually put to flight in one version of the story. But Inti, the sun god,

appeared to the king's son in a vision and bade him not to be afraid. Accordingly, Yupanki marched out to meet the invaders completely undaunted, despite his own force being overwhelmingly outnumbered. The advantage shifted dramatically when hundreds of well-armed warriors appeared out of nowhere to fight on the Inca side, enabling Yupanki's army to carry the day. His mystic reinforcements had apparently taken shape from the rocks and boulders that littered the *altiplano*, and once the battle was won they resumed their original form.

It is no easy task to tease out fact from such a tangle of myth and history, but Inca expansion undoubtedly took place. Although the detail in the Inca chronicles may be far-fetched—Bernabé Cobo described them as "absurd"—the broader picture they painted was accurate. Yupanki quarrelled with his father, who feared the mounting influence of his heir apparent and took the unprecedented step of establishing his other son, Urqon, as king in his own lifetime. After years of bitter dispute, Yupanki made his father a prisoner. His father abjectly apologized and awarded Yupanki his new title of Pachakuti, describing him as Intip Churin, "Son of the Sun." Once again, symbolism seems to permeate this story: Yupanki's assertion of authority over his own father clearly represents the moment at which the influence, in religious terms, of Wiraqocha the Creator was surpassed by that of Inti, god of the sun. Certainly as the Inca Empire expanded the preeminence of Inti grew. If Wiraqocha Inca had claimed divine status for the Inca monarchy, the accession of Pachakuti would represent a shift in allegiance from the creator of the Earth to the glory of the blazing sun.

It was with the accession of Pachakuti to the throne, in around 1438 in conventional chronology, that ritual and social order increasingly became organized around the life and death of the king, creating the institution known as the Sapa Inca ("Unique King"), or emperor. His worship, in association with the sun, became central to the spiritual life of the nation, and religious observance was extended to embrace just about every aspect of ordinary life. Since the royal priesthood presided over the economic existence of the state, from production to distribution, the seal of the ruler's patronage was all-encompassing. Every sustaining mouthful, each bale of wool and benefit of life was, in short, deemed to be the fruit of his generosity. In return, his people served him—with their honor and their offerings, with their willing labor and even with their lives in time of war: the whole life of the nation revolved around the emperor.

The Sapa Inca took responsibility for the aggrandizement of his state. He was expected to prove himself in youth as a fearless and resourceful warrior. Pachakuti had no problems here: throughout his reign the territorial gains came thick and fast. The conquered Chankas were now recruited as allies and Pachakuti's forces moved south into the Titicaca Basin, where the hitherto dominant Qolla people were defeated. To the north,

• THE INCAS AT WAR •

Inca warfare contained highly ritualized elements. Warriors wore their finest jewelry over ponchos or tunics in the distinctive colors and patterning of their *ayllu* (see pages 624–625), and the king might even be carried into battle on a litter. Combat was preceded by a great deal of dancing and chanting, with boisterously issued threats, but it was by no means all posturing—these were real wars with genuine casualties, as the conquered subjects of the Incas could have testified.

Plates of gold, silver, or copper offered combatants some rudimentary protection to the chest and back, but quilted clothing was probably as effective in muffling blows. Helmets made out of cane afforded some protection to the head, but only agility on the wearer's part could help against the hails of slingshot-stones that filled the air in a typical engagement. Those who occupied the high ground had a clear advantage in the Andean context: they could roll boulders down at the ranks of an advancing army.

At close quarters, Andean soldiers fought with heavy clubs of bronze or stone, their handles made of wood—about 3 feet (1m) long. Bows and arrows were introduced by troops hailing from the Amazonian territories; wooden javelins were also thrown. Tactics appear to have been relatively sophisticated and included ambushes, flanking manoeuvres, feints, and counterattacks. The numbers involved in such battles were almost certainly exaggerated by the chroniclers: armies of a quarter of a million have been reported. However, modern scholars suggest that most campaigns were fought by armies of only a few thousand strong, even though forces of up to 100,000 may have been fielded on occasion.

meanwhile, his armies pushed their way over the high Andes and down to the coast where they annexed the empire of the Chimú kings. This conquest more than any other is believed to have been crucial in setting the tone for the future: the Chimú had built themselves what was by any standards an impressive state. Its wealth, its power, and the majesty of its capital, Chan Chan, must surely have given the Incas an exhilarating foretaste of what their own empire might become.

Whether under the leadership of Pachakuti himself or that of his son and successor Thupa Inca Yupanki (reigned 1471–1493), Inca armies occupied new territories on the coastal plain, as well as thrusting further north into Ecuador. There were campaigns in the eastern lowlands, too, in the jungles of what is now Bolivia, although, unsurprisingly, Inca forces found it hard going fighting in the rainforest. The Incas' hold over their Amazonian territories was never absolutely secure:

they were always vulnerable to guerrilla tactics in the jungle. Similar environmental problems arose in the marshy coastal regions of Ecuador, where intermittent rebellions became a feature of Inca rule. There were also uprisings in the *altiplano*: people had competing focuses for their loyalties, some local and others relating to their *ayllu*. Although the Incas could be ruthless, particularly with manifestations of "disloyalty," they preferred to expand their empire not by open warfare but by a

diplomatic combination of alliances and negotiated agreements. The Incas presented their civilization as a model from which peoples could benefit. It was possible for subject communities to obtain degrees of autonomy merely by maintaining good relations and adhering to Inca requirements. Most communities were prepared to comply without recourse to rebellion.

Particular factors worked in the Incas' favor. For one thing, they literally controlled the commanding heights. Scattered far and wide among the valleys and plateaux of the Cordillera, enemies of the Incas found it hard to organize any concerted resistance: the mountainous terrain imposed division among them and enabled the Incas to assume control. Skilful diplomacy, which maintained this disunity, was reinforced by a policy of transplantation: whole communities were uprooted and ordered to move to new colonies in unfamiliar territories. Not only did this strategy break up tribal groupings at a local level, it also allowed more effective exploitation of important agricultural and mineral resources.

Division within the ruling house was, of course, less desirable, yet seemingly endemic. While Wayna Qhapaqh's bloody accession to power as Thupa Inca Yupanki's successor in 1493 ultimately produced stability and a stronger empire, the same cannot be said for the dynastic struggles of Waskhar and Atawallpa after their father's death in 1525. The king's two sons had been born to different mothers and their rivalry sparked a civil war which went on for years and very nearly brought down the empire altogether. Atawallpa, the eventual victor, was only able to ensure his security by the wholesale murder of Waskhar's relations and friends, a formula for perpetuating enmity and suspicion.

Chan Chan, the capital of the Chimú Empire, was the largest city in the Andes, with a population of 30,000 at its peak. Its center was made up of distinct compounds surrounded by thick adobe walls. Some scholars believe that each compound housed a particular king and that after the king's death it would be sealed up and serve as his mausoleum.

MYSTIC GEOGRAPHY

The Incas' physical landscape was as highly mythologized as their history: every peak had its own deity or apu; *every fold, every cleft in the rocks, every boulder, every stream was invested with symbolic value and had its own story to account for its place in the Inca scheme of things.*

For the Incas, the landscape resonated with significance. The story of Pacariqtambo and of the emergence of the ancestors from the mouth of a cave (see pages 626–627) is the most obvious example of how the real and spirit worlds interpenetrated. Long after the time of Thupa Inca Yupanki, people made offerings to the fifteen stones which were believed to have come to life as warriors to defend Cuzco against the Chankas (see page 632). There were hundreds of human-made features too: little cairns known as *apachita*s were piled up on mountaintops as homes for the deities, or beside pathways and mountain passes. While these cairns clearly played a practical role in marking out major routes, they were nevertheless also invested with considerable spiritual significance. There were hundreds of sacred places, known as *huaca* or *wak'a*, in the landscape where sacred power was believed to be pervasive and they came in every conceivable form, from springs and standing stones to ruined pre-Inca remains. At some of these sites objects or acts were attributed to the Inca gods: a distinctive boulder consecrated to Wiraqocha, the great creator; a field where Mama Waqo was said to have planted the first maize; and a spring discovered by Zinchi Roq'a. Assigned great ritual importance in Inca religious beliefs and practices, collectively these sanctuaries constituted a form of sacred geography.

One notable site was located around 20,700 feet (6,300m) above sea level, on a snowswept peak at Nevado Ampato, Peru. It was here that archaeologists found the frozen remains of a teenage girl to whom they gave the name "Juanita." She was richly dressed, and her bright red-and-white shawl was held in place by silver pins. From the black alpaca thread which tied her long black pigtail to her waistband hung a little box, two tiny drinking cups, and a dog or fox, all intricately carved in wood. Beside her had been placed some female figurines dressed rather as she was herself, as well as offerings of coca leaves and maize. She had lain here peacefully for centuries despite the violence of her death—she had been felled by a heavy blow to the back of the head. Two other children (believed to be a boy and a girl) were found further down the mountainside, placed like mortal milestones by the path to the summit. They too had been left with decorative human and animal figures: the former statuettes dressed Inca-style and adorned with beautiful spondylus shell necklaces; the latter several little llamas carved in silver.

Similar shrines have been found on several other Andean summits: the same sorts of combinations of offerings tend to recur. The presence of both male and female victims and statues is thought to imply honor to

• THE SAYHUITE STONE •

A little way to the west of Cuzco stands the Sayhuite Stone, which from a distance appears to be a large but otherwise unremarkable boulder. But on closer inspection one can see that its upper surface has been richly carved with myriad animal, vegetable, and human forms, from pumas, monkeys, and lizards to maize-stalks and men and women holding drinking cups. There are architectural features too: buildings, patios, a staircase, doorways, and what appear to be canals. Many archaeologists believe that the Sayhuite Stone represents a comprehensive symbolic map of the idealized Inca cosmos and that the sculpted stone may have been a focus for rituals during which liquid offerings were poured in order to run along the incised miniature canals.

both the male sun and the female moon, a pairing reinforced by the presence of gold and silver items. Spondylus items are thought to be there in deference to Mamacocha, Mother Sea. Mountaintops were especially sacred sites, and not only because, for the Incas as for so many other ancient cultures, they seemed to represent meeting places between heaven and Earth. Viewed from below, mountaintops marked points on the skyline by which the Incas oriented themselves both physically and spiritually. They were also awesome in their sheer scale, of course: to a people for whom a rock could resonate with the presence of a venerated ancestor, a mighty peak exuded far greater spiritual power.

Despite the best efforts of archaeologists and other scholars, the Inca sense of spatial relations remains difficult to fathom, but it is quite clear that it was extraordinarily highly developed. The idea of the division of space, the construction of creative opposition or *tinkuy*, seems to have run deep in the Inca psyche. The Inca appear to have seen reality in terms of a dynamic asymmetric dualism, in which differently sized members of a pair were intimately bound to and dependent on each other. The principle is seen in everything, from the facing figures in textile patterning to the reverence accorded to river confluences and road junctions. Their word for their empire was Tawantinsuyu ("The Land of the Four Quarters"), the four provinces of which reflected a notion of unequal-sized parts that were indispensable to a greater whole. The culture's complex sanctification of space is nowhere better illustrated than in the astonishing capital city the Incas built at Cuzco.

PLACE OF THE PUMA

Cuzco was much more than a majestic city: it was the embodiment of a theology, the expression of a worldview. Some of the spiritual associations of the Inca capital's layout have been unraveled by modern scholars, but much remains obscure and the mystique of Cuzco still haunts the visitor today.

According to tradition, Cuzco was founded by Manqo Qhapaqh, but the Inca metropolis in its full glory was the vision of the great king Pachakuti. He razed the existing settlement, it is said, and set in motion an ambitious plan which was brought to completion by his son Thupa Inca Yupanki. The new city was the religious as well as the political capital of the Inca Empire. Its temples and shrines were every bit as important as its royal palaces and plazas, and its setting as significant as its actual structures.

Cuzco's highly elevated location, ringed by mountain peaks, made perfect sense from a defensive point of view. But this was the very least of its attraction to the Incas: for them the site was deemed propitious because it was a place of meetings—mountain ranges faced one another across this valley, in which three rivers (the Watanay, Tullumayo and Chuchul) had their confluence. Four main overland routes converged here too: again, the Incas reaped the benefits this brought in terms of communications, but they also valued the location in terms of *tinkuy* (the reconciliation of opposites). Cuzco has been referred to as the navel or center around which both the Inca Empire and the world itself were ordered (see page 641). The conquistadors were sensually overpowered by Cuzco; they gasped literally,

because of its extreme altitude, and metaphorically, due to the city's magnificence of architecture and well-ordered public spaces. The Incas' characteristic genius for administration and engineering reveal a gift for practical problem-solving, but it was also intimately related to a perspective rooted in religious mysticism.

THE LION IN THE MOUNTAINS

The "lion city," as the chroniclers called it, was conceived in the form of a puma or mountain lion, symbol of the strength of the Incas and their ferocity in war. The shape of this totemic animal was actually built into the city. As Sarmiento tells the story, it was Thupa Inca Yupanki who, returning to the city following his first triumphant tour after becoming king, remembered that his father Pachakuti had called Cuzco the "lion city." He said that the tail was the meeting point of the two rivers which flow through it, that the body was the great plaza and the houses round it, but that the head was wanting. The king discussed this question with his counsellors, who said that the best way to make a head would be to build a fortress on a high plateau to the north of the city.

The Sapa Inca then issued an instruction to the provinces for the local chiefs to supply a large workforce for construction of the fortress. On arrival, the workmen were divided into parties, each with its own duties and officers: some brought stones, others worked them, others placed them. The diligence was such that in a few years the great fortress of rough stone was built: sumptuous and exceedingly strong. The buildings within it were of small worked stone that gave them an appearance of beauty.

The remains of the city's symbolic "head" can still be seen today above modern Cuzco on the heights where the massive citadel of Sacsahuaman stands. Lower down, the point in the valley where the two rivers were

Looking eastward across the valley toward Sacsahuaman from an outcrop just outside Cuzco is the "throne" from which the Inca king is supposed to have surveyed his capital. Gigantic steps are cut into the rock here, although the overall contours of the hillside have been respected in a typically Inca marriage of the human-made and the natural. The rising sun illuminates this position before it is seen from the city below, which has led some archaeologists to speculate that it actually served as an altar rather than a throne. The comings and goings of the sun in both its daily and its seasonal cycles were central to the ceremonial life of the Inca state.

• DINING WITH THE DEAD •

The presentation of the mummified ancestors of the *ayllu* (see pages 624–625) was one of the most important rituals of Inca life throughout the empire, but nowhere was it more crucial than in Cuzco, the imperial capital. The closest advisers of the Inca king were the mummies of his ancestors and they formed an audience for the everyday ceremonies of state. These human remains were also given food and drink, a spectacle witnessed with astonishment by the conquistadors, one of whom, Pedro Pizarro, described the scene in *Relation of the Discovery and Conquest of the Kingdoms of Peru* (1571):

"Most of the people served the dead … who they daily brought out to the main square, setting them down in a ring, each one according to his age, and there the male and female attendants ate and drank. The attendants made fires for each of the dead in front of them … and … burned everything they had put before them, so that the dead should eat of everything that the living ate."

The mummies must have been an extraordinary sight: *"Their bodies were so perfect that they lacked not hair, eyebrows, or eyelashes,"* recalled Garcilaso de la Vega (see page 630):

"They were in clothes such as they had worn when alive … They were seated in the way Indian men and women usually sit, with their arms crossed over their chests, the right over the left, and their eyes cast down … I remember touching a finger of the hand of Wayna Qhapaqh. It was hard and rigid, like that of a wooden statue. The bodies weighed so little that any Indian could carry them from house to house in his arms or on his shoulders [a scene illustrated in this sixteenth-century drawing by the chronicler Felipe Guamán Poma de Ayala]. *They carried them wrapped in white sheets through the streets and squares, the Indians falling to the ground and making reverences with groans and tears, and many Spaniards doffing their caps."*

canalized to come together as one is still known as the Pumachupan, the "puma's tail."

A vast plaza of two sections—a larger Awkaypata and a smaller Kusipata (sometimes spelled Huacapayta and Cusipayta)—formed the space beneath the big cat's belly and were used respectively for religious processions and military parades. The first represented Hanan (Upper) Cuzco and the second Hurin (Lower) Cuzco, the principal division of the city. Around 7.5 acres (3 hectares) in area, the Awkaypata was covered with about an inch of sand from the Pacific coast, in which gold and silver figures and vessels and other sacred items had been buried. This gave the sea-goddess Mamacocha a hallowed place at the inland heart of the Inca Empire. The imperial ancestors were presented here at festival times and plied with offerings of food and drink. Beside a gilded stone was a hole into which libations were poured: it was drained by an ingeniously constructed underground channel. The royal palace complexes and temples seem to have adjoined the Awkaypata plaza, judging by the impressive dimensions and rich decoration of some of the remains uncovered by archaeologists, and there are encouraging indications that many traces of the Inca capital may yet remain.

Hanan Cuzco, the puma's head and forequarters, became the seat of temporal power, while religious authority held sway in Hurin Cuzco, a demarcation that was said to have been introduced by Inca Roq'a. But many archaeologists believe that the division predated the Inca age and reflects an existing tradition incorporated by the Incas. Whatever its origins, the opposition between upper and lower city was taken very seriously and may be an indicator that at one time each was ruled by different kings. The sections were then further divided, with the upper city having two distinct districts in Chinchaysuyu and Antisuyu (in the northwest and northeast), and the lower having two in Kollasuyu and Cuntisuyu (in the southeast and southwest). The names of these quarters, and their distribution around the city, corresponded precisely with those of the four provinces of the Inca Empire as a whole, each of which was named for the major cultural group of its region. Cuzco thus replicated the fourfold plan of the Inca world: it was Tawantinsuyu in miniature (see page 637).

THE CENTER OF THE WORLD

As Delphi was for the Greeks, Cuzco for the Incas was the *omphalos* of the world (see page 354). From the main plaza radiated the four main roads and axes of the empire, which lay along the intercardinal points. Within the city the Qorikancha ("Golden Enclosure"), the splendid Temple of the Sun, was revered as the spiritual center of the Incas' world. It was also the nodal point from which forty-one invisible *ceque* (or *zek'e*) lines radiated in all directions, embracing the entirety of creation and extending to infinity. Sightlines were made by the city's streets and the walls of buildings, as well as by a total of 328 *huaca* shrines and natural features in the surrounding countryside: every feature seems to have had its place in this astonishing scheme, which linked terrestrial landmarks and celestial phenomena. The *ceque*s system was fantastically complicated—according to Bernabé Cobo a thousand priests were required to keep track of all its sacred sites and associated rituals.

It is difficult today to interpret the lines' astronomical or calendrical significance, although much research continues into the detailed organization and operation of the *ceque*s. It does seem that they were not necessarily straight lines, but could be crooked, and that they may have contributed to the apportioning of territories or water resources. However, we understand enough about this extraordinary system to see that it embodies the complicated and sophisticated nature of the Inca worldview. We also know that these ideas were ever-present in Inca daily life, being reinforced at rituals conducted throughout the year at the numerous sites that formed part of the system. Indeed, the process may have been calendrical and through the *ceque*s the Incas may have had a cosmological system which unified history, religion, the landscape, sky, time, and space.

WORKING WITH THE MOUNTAINS

As intimate as the Incas' relationship was, in both thought and practice, with the natural beauty of their environment, to an outsider the harmony of such a partnership is manifested most strongly in the settings and workmanship of Inca architecture, particularly their virtuoso masonry work.

The presence within the Inca Empire of hundreds of *huaca*s (see pages 636–637 and page 641) is certainly evidence of the importance of the environment to the Inca system of thought, but investing nature with spirituality is also true of countless other cultures, as far apart as Celtic Europe (see pages 422–427) and Tibet (see pages 264–265). What is perhaps more remarkable about the Incas is the way in which, in a difficult, high-altitude location, they sought to impose their idea of order on a natural world and more often than not achieved it in such a harmonious way that the construction is almost seamless. To look at an Inca site is to marvel at the way in which naturally occurring forms, particular stone, meld with humanmade ones, or the manner in which the Incas have reconfigured the landscape without undermining its beauty. For example, the inadequate supply of cultivable land was overcome by fashioning spectacular, contour-hugging terraces (see illustration, opposite). These plunging hillsides seem at once to sculpt and to celebrate every wriggle and fold of the landscape's interlocking valleys, spurs, and ridges. Such measures provided more land area in which a wide range of crops could be grown, watered by carefully directed water channels. In fact, the Andes actually take their name from the Spanish word *andén*, which means "platform" or "terrace"—a reference to the astonishing stepped fields that the conquistadors encountered, rising up sheer mountainsides in valley after valley.

In places, the terraces served not a practical but an aesthetic function. The Spanish reported that some contained colorful flowers and appeared to be pleasure gardens. At Moray, not far from Cuzco, the Incas created concentric terraces within the precipitous sides of natural sinkholes that drop deep into the earth, and in the absence of a regular water supply it is unclear whether these modifications were anything other than an Inca-inspired regularization of the land.

Upon careful inspection, many other parts of the Andean terrain reveal subtle Inca manipulations. The "throne" of the Inca king (see illustration, page 639) that overlooks Cuzco at Rodadero Hill is an interplay of human sculpture and natural stone that acquires an additional dimension by means of its sculpted edges, which results in displays of light and shadow when exposed to the sun's unremitting gaze at high altitude. With the rituals performed there and at other similar outdoor settings it makes perfect sense to discover that the Incas identified strongly with stone itself—in many Inca stories humans and stones are interchangeable (see page 645)—which they invested with great spiritual power. It seems they may have fashioned their finest stonework not for the admiring eyes of humans, but for the approving ones of the gods.

THE MOUNTAINS AND MACHU PICCHU

The most famous Inca site of all, the remote "lost city" of Machu Picchu (rediscovered only in 1911) appears inseparable from its mountain setting. Perched upon a saddle between two peaks, it stands around 1,300 feet (400m) above the Urubamba River as it twists and turns its way through a rocky gorge. Terraces line the slopes between, shading up into the lower edge of a settlement

---

The steepness of much of the Inca domain necessitated the creation of agricultural terraces on the hillsides, such as this one leading up to the magnificent "lost city" of Machu Picchu. By such means the Incas could maximize the amount of fertile land available for growing crops.

This stone from a wall of the palace of the archbishop of Cuzco—the one-time palace of Inca Roq'a—shows one of the most famous pieces of Inca masonry, known as the "stone of the twelve angles." Such is the skill and sophistication of the stonework, that blocks such as this required no mortar because they fit so precisely.

with some 200 buildings, whose walls and streets cluster along the contours of the ground. At times the city's structures seem to "rhyme" with nearby outcrops and peaks, their forms replicating the skyline behind. (A similar effect can be seen in the zigzagging battlements of Cuzco's Sacsahuaman citadel, whose angles echo the spurs and indentations of the surrounding valley walls.) Seen up-close, the interrelation of city and setting, and of organic and geometric forms, is consummately done: the rounded wall of the Torreón, or "observatory," emerges seamlessly from a rocky outcrop, beneath which a natural cleft has been subtly enlarged and built around to create a room. Machu Picchu in its entirety—both in setting and execution—is among the acknowledged wonders of the world, a truly impressive surviving ancient monument that can take its place alongside such magnificent constructions as the Great Pyramid at Giza, the Palace of Persepolis, and the Colosseum of Rome.

THE SPIRITUALITY OF STONE

A stroll around Sacsahuaman, or through the streets of Cuzco below it, is to encounter stonework without peer. Some of the largest stones in the citadel walls are more than 25 feet (7.5m) high, and would weigh in at several hundred tons. Yet, incredibly, Inca stonemasons were able to cut every individual stone with such exactitude that it nestled comfortably into place without the need to use mortar. So perfect is the fit that often it is not possible to insert the blade of a knife between adjacent stones. The famous Hatun Rumiyoc or "great stone" in the wall of the Cuzco street that now bears this name has been shaped with no fewer than twelve angles on each side (see illustration, opposite). Although not quite so flamboyantly polygonal, perhaps, other stones have the same tendency toward the irregular: a pillowy, even slightly oval shape is preferred over a regular rectangle or square. One advantage of such construction is that stones are held together by pressure from several sides, making them hard to dislodge—a valuable asset in the earthquake-prone Andes.

The chronicler Pedro Sarmiento de Gamboa noted the handicaps faced by Inca masons: "What makes it still more worthy of admiration is that they did not possess tools to work the stone, but could only work with other stones." It seems unlikely, in fact, that the Incas considered themselves at any disadvantage when it came to working in stone. Their chosen techniques suited their purpose and their skills. Their stone tools would have made it extremely difficult for them to produce European-standard rectangular blocks, but nothing could have been further from their intention. From a practical point of view, squared slabs would have collapsed ignominiously at the first significant tremor; they would also have displeased the Incas on both aesthetic and spiritual grounds. The evidence is abundant that the Incas had a taste for the irregular, the curved, the sort of oval form which naturally occurring boulders possess. Their building slabs resemble this shape, not only minimizing work but allowing the mason the satisfying sense that he was going "with the grain" of his material. Pounded (rather than cut) to approximate shape at the quarry, the stones would then have been hauled with ropes to the required site. Each stone would

have been raised on an earth ramp and held just above its destined place on a wooden scaffold, while its base—and the upper surface of the stone below, earmarked to receive it—was further pounded to ensure a perfect fit.

Artists and craftspeople often feel as if the media in which they work are more responsive—more "alive" even—than inert materials. The Inca stonemason would no doubt have felt this too, but his relationship with the stone he worked would have been stronger still. Stone was particularly revered by the Incas: people had been turned into stone after Wiraqocha's first creation; the rocky pillar at Huanacauri, above Cuzco, was held to be the petrified form of Ayar Uchu, "Ancestor Chili Pepper" (see page 628); and the Inca kings even had stone statues of themselves to serve as stand-ins for ceremonial duties. The "seated puma" stone at Qenqo was almost as sacred as the pillar at Huanacauri: it is thought to have marked the death house in which the mummy of Pachakuti was kept. Finally, every Inca knew the story of how stones had come to life as warriors to help the army of Yupanki to save their city (see page 632). Stone had its own sanctity, its own inner life and energy. The stonemason's task was to help it fulfil its destiny.

• THE "TIRED STONE" •

On a hillside above Sacsahuaman stands a giant stone, partially carved. It is known by the name of Collaconcho, the "Tired Stone." Although actually a natural formation, originating where it can be seen, legend has it that it was quarried for use in the construction of the great citadel, but that the journey there exhausted it, and it stopped dead in its tracks, weeping tears of blood. It has stood there ever since: far from being angry, the Incas took pity on its sufferings, and it became one of their most venerated *huaca* shrines.

AN EARTHLY EMPIRE

Tawantinsuyu ("The Land of the Four Quarters"), at its height, extended over more than 2,200 miles (3,500km), from Ecuador to northern Chile and Argentina. From east to west, it was about 500 miles (800km) across at its widest point. Administering these immense territories was as much a challenge as conquering them had been, and constituted one of the more remarkable Inca achievements.

Each of the four quarter sections, or *suyus*, of the Inca Empire had its high officials, both in Cuzco and on the ground. The four quarters were then further divided and the empire had more than eighty provinces in all, which imperial officials ran with the help of local élites. Inca authority was exacting: men were conscripted into military service; families were also required to contribute labor to construction and roadbuilding projects and state-run mines and farms. The ability to command such manpower was a great boon to the Incas, of course, but co-ordinating it must have presented a bureaucratic challenge. Hence the division of the population by heads of household into units of ten, fifty, 100, 500, 1,000, 5,000, and (in the most populous provinces) of 10,000, each organized by a corresponding hierarchy of officials. Even the Romans did not regiment their empire strictly as this, but the system was not as inflexible as it sounds. In sparsely populated,

isolated areas it would have been absurd to enforce control too rigidly, and in practice there was probably a great degree of autonomy. One factor enabling the administration to remain "invisible" was that the state system meshed so closely with Andean society's traditional *ayllu* structure (see pages 624–625).

The smooth functioning of the empire relied on its impressive infrastructure, central to which was a network of some 25,000 miles (40,000km) of well-made roads. These were the arteries of empire: communications were entrusted to special messengers or *chaski* stationed every few miles—urgent messages could be carried up to 150 miles (240km) a day in relays. Goods were transported on the backs of porters, or by strings of llamas (see box, below); troops could be moved easily from one front to another; officials could supervise provincial administration. State-run waystations known as *tampu* offered accommodation and also housed garrisons to

---

◆ RELUCTANT HAULIER OF THE ANDES ◆

Inca technology, advanced as it was, did not extend as far as the wheel (which, in any case, would not have been overly useful over much of the difficult Andean terrain). In the absence of the horse or heavy ox, the llama was the main beast of burden in the Andes, although it was not ideally suited to the task, either physically or by temperament. Typically, the llama can carry a modest 70 pounds (32kg) at the leisurely speed of around 10 miles (16km) a day, but it requires frequent rests and a great deal of care and attention. Even when well looked after, it is liable to sicken and die without apparent reason; when weary, it will refuse any inducement to proceed. The animal was more productive as a source of wool (that said, its camelid relations the vicuña and alpaca provide more luxurious fibers); for the higher echelons of Inca society it also yielded meat for feasting. Whatever its shortcomings, the llama was highly prized as a sacrifice to the sun, and images of it recur constantly in the artwork of the Incas.

ensure the security of travelers. At a time when roads in Europe were abominable, and bandits made cross-country travel extremely hazardous, the Inca system came as a revelation to the Spanish. "In human memory," wrote Pedro Cieza de León, "I believe that there is no account of a road as great as this, running through deep valleys, high mountains, banks of snow, torrents of water, living rock, and wild rivers … In all places it was clean and swept free of refuse, with lodgings, storehouses, sun temples, and posts along the route. Oh! Can anything similar be claimed for Alexander or any of the powerful kings who ruled the world … ?"

The Inca Royal Highway, as the road network was called, had two major north–south strands, one tracing a path through the highlands from a point outside Quito in what is now Ecuador to Mendoza in modern Argentina. A second road followed the coast, but skirted the most hostile desert sections, finding an easier way along the Andean foothills further inland. A series of east–west routes tackled the mountain heights head-on, reaching altitudes of more than 3,000 feet (4,800m) above sea-level in some of the most spectacular scenery in the world. Deep river gorges were crossed over swaying suspension bridges made with braided-grass ropes and wooden floors. Lower-lying wetlands were negotiated by means of rubble causeways or reed pontoons. In difficult terrain, a road might be no more than 3 feet (1m) wide, but with no wheeled vehicles this would not have been a problem. Some stretches were paved with cobbles, in others hard-packed dirt was considered adequate: drainage was vital if roads were not to be washed away, and countless streams were diverted into channels alongside roads or under them through culverts. They were so well made that many remain in use today.

The Inca Empire, with a population estimated at anywhere between 4 million and 16 million, would have been impossible to govern without its extensive network of roads, which overcame all manner of hostile terrain, such as this steep mountain face near Machu Picchu.

MNEMONICS, MEASURES, AND MEDICINES

Inca medicine was broadly similar to our own, but their understanding of and approach to mathematics and measurements was markedly different, revealing flexible solutions that made sense for their environment.

Extraordinarily, for so sophisticated a civilization, the Incas had no written script, but they did have their own way of keeping records by means of knots or *khipu*. Use of this ingenious system of mnemonics allowed them to collect and communicate facts and figures— and probably also narratives such as history and myth. The system is by no means fully understood: at its simplest the sequence in which successive strings were tied on to the main cotton cord seems to have been significant—standing for hundreds, tens, and units, for example. But there were other variables: not only the number and position but the forms of the knots—and their colors, from a palette of several hundred shades. The possible combinations are endless, and the system has not so far been decoded by scholars, although researchers are finding some intriguing parallels in the binary coding systems used in modern computer science.

THE MEASURE OF MAN

The Incas displayed extraordinary problem-solving skills, but so far as we can tell showed little interest in the universal or the abstract. They were more concerned with the concrete world as they experienced it. Hence, short measurements were based on the spans of the outstretched hand, from the tip of the thumb to the end of the index finger, or from thumb to little finger for slightly longer stretches. Greater distances along the ground were measured in paces (although they counted

The khipu *was a system for recording and communicating administrative data, such as population figures, by means of tying knots on different-colored cords. As well as numerical information, the Incas may have used the device to preserve epic poems and legends.*

a step with each foot, producing a "pace" of some 4 feet 3 inches (1.3m). The unit of measurement for journeys, the *tupu*, seems to have varied according to the type of terrain involved; the likely time on the road was factored into the figure. A *tupu* on easy ground might have been as much as 6 miles (9.7km), it is thought; on more rugged terrain it might have been only 4 miles (6.4km). It is a mark of the flexibility of the *tupu* that it was also used in calculations of land area: again, it could vary wildly in extent. Basically, the *tupu* seems to have been the area of land needed to support a single household for a year. Since land varied in productiveness, the *tupu* naturally varied in size. The logic cannot be faulted, and made perfect sense in the Andean context—even if the measurement is meaningless in modern terms.

It is in keeping with this attitude that the Incas seem to have restricted themselves to a barter economy, rather than using currency for exchange. They did have other options: although coinage as such had never existed, some coastal communities had used seashells as a currency, while others had exchanged what the Spanish called *hacha*s, stylized axheads of copper. For the most part, Inca communities were happy enough to trade commodities; however, there is evidence that sought-after goods such as salt or coca may have been used for exchange. Wealth could be accumulated in such valuables, in precious metals and minerals or manufactured luxuries—fine textiles or ceramics, for example.

MEDICINE

Inca medicine was administered in the course of shamanistic ritual, with cures being prescribed by the ancestors through the medium of the priest or *curandero*. When the ceremonial is stripped away, however, we find a resourceful use of herbs and other natural medicines: Inca medicine was probably as effective as any of its time. The San Pedro cactus was widely used by Andean shamans on account of its hallucinogenic properties, but its medicinal benefits are also well attested. Like the *peyote* of North America and Mesoamerica, this

◆ COCA: "OUR MOTHER'S FRAGRANCE" ◆

Coca leaves are still chewed today by Andean peasants, partly for the mild pleasure they provide, but mainly for their ability to relieve the effects of fatigue and hunger. In pre-Columbian times, coca was offered to the ancestors and the gods in reverent sacrifice, and prized as the narcotic vehicle of the shaman's trance. Stories abound of its origins: it is considered to be quintessentially feminine—in some cultures it is spoken of as "our mother's fragrance." One tale tells how it first grew up out of the body of a faithless woman, killed for her crimes: it helped to ease the sufferings of the men she had wronged. A more sympathetic story says that its properties were first discovered by a woman wandering, crazed with grief for the loss of her child: she chewed the leaves and found they soothed her broken heart.

cactus contains quantities of mescaline which, in addition to producing visions, helped reduce pain and high body temperatures. Recent research has found intriguing evidence of antibiotic properties too. Quinine, obtained from *chinchona* bark, was also good for controlling fevers, and the *curandero* could call upon several other powerful painkillers, including *molle*, a boiled-up bark, *chillca*, a kind of curative leaf, sarsaparilla—and, of course, coca. This last in particular will have been used by Inca surgeons who are known to have carried out difficult trepanning operations—removing sections of the skull to ease pressure on the brain. Practitioners presumably explained these procedures in terms of the opening up of the head to expel evil spirits, rather than in the language of modern neurological science. But the fact remains that there is clear archaeological evidence that these operations were widely conducted, and that in many cases they prolonged the patients' lives.

CHARTING THE HEAVENS

The sky and its stars were as much a part of the Inca scheme of things as the terrestrial landscape, their rhythms every bit as vital to the cosmic order. The Incas carefully recorded the movements of the stars and planets, and developed their own stories to explain the patterns observable in the night sky.

The highly visible star clusters of Pleiades and Orion intrigued the Inca imagination, as was the case in other parts of the world. In the European astronomical tradition the Pleiades were named for the seven daughters of Pleione and Atlas in Greek mythology. These handmaidens of Artemis, the goddess of hunting and chastity, had fled through the woods to escape the attentions of Orion, mighty hunter and sexual predator. The gods took pity on the maidens' plight, transformed them into stars and set them in the heavens, but even here they are perpetually pursued by Orion, who is present in his own distinctive cluster. For the Incas, the Pleiades were also unmistakably female, although they associated the cluster with fecundity rather than with barren chastity. They knew it by three different names—one, *qatachillay*, means "what glitters," but the other two help explain the enormous significance that

the star cluster had in the celestial scheme. The first of these was *uquy*, a term applied to the cycle of womanly fertility from menstruation through pregnancy to childbirth; the second was *qollqa*, or "granary." Pleiades was thus associated not only with the cycle of human reproduction, but with the agricultural cycle which, by producing the annual bounty of the harvest, guaranteed the continuing life of the community. The Incas sang hymns to the Pleiades, and offered sacrifices to it each year, to ensure that it went on protecting the most fundamental rhythms of their existence.

The seventeenth-century Spanish writer Juan Polo de Ondegardo attributed to the Incas the view that every animal and bird species on Earth had its corresponding constellation in the sky. This heavenly creature presided over the fortunes of its terrestrial equivalent, particularly its fertility. His claim cannot be verified, but does not seem improbable. There is good evidence that the Incas worshipped three specific stars (although it is uncertain which ones) as a ewe, a lamb, and a llama—they pleaded to these stars to afford protection to the corresponding livestock on Earth. Other stars (again, specifics are not known) were revered for their ability to protect people from attack by jaguar, puma, snake, bear, and other dangerous beasts. Interestingly, for the Incas the absence of stars was significant too: in the night skies of the southern hemisphere there are several areas that appear profoundly dark and without apparent stars. As well as images picked out "positively" in the way that we normally identify constellations, the Incas also saw animal forms "negatively" in these areas of deep blackness.

The sun, of course, appears to us on Earth as the greatest star in the sky, and it was the central object of Inca worship—its splendor a fitting symbol of the Inca state. But the sun was not revered for its majesty alone: it was venerated in the mystery of its annual comings

◆ DREADFUL PORTENTS ◆

The Incas had learned to predict the more regular routines of the universe; but there were significant gaps in their knowledge, nonetheless. Comets invariably came as a shock to them, and were held to portend grave events—one crossed the sky during the conquistadors' invasion, for example. Eclipses were viewed with deep apprehension: solar eclipses were thought to signify the sun mourning the imminent passing of some important person. Lunar eclipses were believed to be caused by a snake or puma eating the moon and when they took place a huge cacophony would be raised to scare the beast away.

The star cluster known to Europeans as the Pleiades was of great significance to the Incas. They associated it with fertility, both of women and of the land, and based the timing of the planting and harvesting of crops on its movements. Inca astronomers are believed to have recorded their observations by means of khipus (see page 648).

and goings, which were tracked by the Inca priests. Observations are said to have been taken from four stone pillars set in the ground at strategic points on the horizon around the Cuzco Valley, but their locations have not been satisfactorily identified. The assumption has been that the Incas' main "astronomical" interest in the sun related to its solstices, but there may also have been a particular point in its progress that signaled the start of the auspicious moment for August sowing. At the highest point in Machu Picchu there stands the Intihuatana Stone, the "Hitching Post of the Sun." For just a brief moment in its cycle, the rising sun seemed to hang there, as though tethered to the Earth, its power at the service of the Incas. Elsewhere at Machu Picchu, observations of both the sun and the Pleiades seem to have been taken from the Torreón temple.

Just as they followed the natural lie of the land and the sit of the stone, so the Incas adapted to the eternal rhythms of the heavens—and when they realized that the sun and moon gave them two incompatible calendars, their answer was to use both: they took the solar round for their everyday chronology, and used the lunar months as the foundation for their ritual year. Rather than allow the two to drift further and further apart, the Incas seem pragmatically to have adjusted the schema slightly at regular intervals, adding a day each month, perhaps, or a short intercalary month for the moon each year, so that the two calendars were more or less comfortably reconciled.

THE RITUAL YEAR

The Inca year was played out in an elaborate ceremonial cycle which reaffirmed the relationship between the people and their universe. The festive rites ranged from the spectacular Inti Raymi, attended by thousands, to the secretive Qhapaqh Raymi from which outsiders were excluded.

In 1535, with Cuzco under occupation by the conquistadors, the Incas' culture and their way of life was under grave threat. For a while an uneasy calm prevailed. The incomers might have sacked the treasuries and assassinated the king, replacing him with a puppet, Manqo Inca, but they had left the structures of the state more or less intact for the time being. The Spanish did not have anything like the numbers required to establish colonial rule in any depth, or to attempt the wholesale suppression of the Incas' "idolatrous" religion. Thus it was that, one day in June that year, the priest Bartolomé de Segovia found himself an observer out on the *altiplano* in the early morning, when it was still chilly and dark. He was there to see one of the last full-scale celebrations of Inti Raymi ("Festival of the Sun"). He was impressed despite himself: the entire Inca state seemed to be there—the king, his nobles, his priests and priestesses, all resplendent in their ceremonial costume. Not to mention the royal ancestors, of course:

"They brought out all of the effigies from Cuzco's temples on to a plain at the edge of Cuzco, toward the area where the sun dawned. The effigies with the greatest prestige were placed beneath rich, finely worked feather canopies ... The space [between] formed an avenue more than thirty paces wide, and all the lords and other principal figures of Cuzco stood in it."

There were some 600 living dignitaries lined up there, the priest believed, watched by the mummies (see box, page 640) and a crowd of commoners several thousand strong. When the first light of daybreak came, the king initiated a solemn chant—more a murmur at first, but an inexorable crescendo came to a climax as the sun reached its zenith in the sky at noon. Priestesses passed to and fro bringing sacrificial offerings for the ancestors and gods, placing llama meat and coca in a blazing fire and pouring libations of *chicha* into the ground. Along with the pomp and circumstance, there were lighter

◆ HUMAN SACRIFICE ◆

The Incas did not offer human sacrifices to their gods on anything like the scale of the Mexican Aztecs, who routinely slaughtered enemy captives in their thousands (see pages 508–509). But a human life was considered the highest offering which could be presented to the sun god Inti, and such sacrifices were indeed made on particularly significant occasions. Eclipses and natural disasters such as earthquakes terrified the Incas, who slew youths and maidens selected for their beauty at a special Itu ceremony intended to appease the sun god's wrath. The Qhapaqh Ucha ceremony was held to commemorate the beginning of a new reign, and can be seen as representing a ritual rededication of the Inca Empire's *huaca* shrines and a redrawing of its boundaries. Those bodies of boys and girls which have been found in recent years at mountaintop shrines in the high Andes (see pages 636–637) provide mute, yet still eloquent, testimony to such ceremonies.

moments: a herd of llamas was set loose in the square and the commoners shrieked with delight as they ran to catch the stampeding animals. As the day wore on, though, the tone changed almost imperceptibly: the chanting faded as the sun sank slowly in the sky. By evening there was histrionic mourning for the passing of the day, and the symbolic death of the people's protector, the setting sun. The canopies were taken down, and the mummies returned to their resting places, only to be brought out again for a repeat of the festivities the following day. According to Segovia, the festival lasted eight or nine days in all and concluded with Manqo Inca's ceremonial breaking of the ground, which was a sign that the tilling season could begin.

The festival of the Sun was not in fact the most important ritual of the Inca year: that position was occupied by Qhapaqh Raymi (the "Magnificent Festival"), which was the inaugurating feast of the ceremonial year, held at the time of the December solstice. It seems to have been a secretive affair: all outsiders were banished from Cuzco for its duration. This exclusivity was increasingly difficult to enforce under Spanish rule, so we have hints from chroniclers of what was involved.

As the opening ceremony of the Inca year, Qhapaqh Raymi was seen as a new beginning. It was also the moment when the coming-of-age of noble boys was celebrated. Cakes of maize and llama blood were eaten, which were regarded as the food of the sun. Like the Inti Raymi, the occasion brought together solemn ritual and raucous revelry.

The Qoya Raymi or Situa ("Queen's Festival") involved ceremonies of purification. It was held in March, at the height of the rainy season, a time when-

showers would have suggested the washing away of sin but also when dampness and chills would have been associated with sickness and disease. As described by Bernabé Cobo, people struck each other ceremonially with torches to drive out evil spirits, and shook out their clothing outside their homes to divest themselves of impurities. Other accounts explain that nobles handed sacrificial ashes to inferior relations, who then passed them down through the social strata of the *ayllu* to the very humblest, who would carry these "burdens" from the city. These people then bathed in rivers, well beyond the urban outskirts, to ritually cleanse themselves and thereby purify the *ayllu* as a whole.

To the Incas the llama was more than just a beast of burden—it also played a key role in their rites and festivities. Not only was the animal sacrificed in its own right, but gold llama figures have been found placed with human sacrificial victims in mountaintop shrines.

BIRTH, CHILDHOOD, ADULTHOOD, AND MARRIAGE

Every stage of Inca life had its own appointed rituals and allotted tasks. Men and women had different responsibilities, but each individual was expected to make a full contribution—indeed his or her position within society was related to how well they performed the duties ascribed to them.

The Incas were supremely pragmatic in their solutions to problems experienced on a day to day basis. Hence the concept of the elastic unit of measurement, the *tupu*, that grows or shrinks according to the terrain (see page 649). Similarly flexible was the way in which they estimated age, not in terms of years but according to the individual's place in the family and the economic contribution made. There is some evidence that the Incas also conceived the stages of human life in a way that is more familiar to us. A collection of golden statues representing a child, an adult, and an old man—the human lifespan—have been found in the Coricancha temple in Cuzco, which have been interpreted as symbolically representing the respective life-cycle stages of the sun as it passes from dawn to high noon to dusk.

THE "ROADS OF LIFE"

Felipe Guamán Poma de Ayala, the half-Inca historian and chronicler, set out the "roads," or stages of life. They were listed not in chronological order, but according to the perceived importance of the part they played in the social scheme. Thus, for men, the sequence started with the warrior, followed by the mature working man—the elderly and crippled ranked below these in

Childbirth is rarely represented in ancient American art, but this stirrup-spout vessel from the pre-Inca Moche people shows a woman giving birth. Although the Moche woman shown here is attended by midwives, most Inca women gave birth unassisted.

654 THE INCAS

Particularly attractive girls from good families were taken from home at the age of about ten and brought up as *aqllakuna* or "chosen women." Special settlements were set aside for the training of such girls in advanced weaving and catering skills and their induction into the official religion and ideology of the Inca state. These communities produced prestigious textiles for clothing the king and his officials, or for burning as offerings in important rituals. They also brewed the best *chicha*, which was poured in sacrifice or drunk in festive revelry. But perhaps their most important function was as Inca "finishing schools," turning out attractive and educated wives for dignitaries.

contribution and therefore dignity. Boys could be helpers (see page 656), but infants obviously contributed little to the general economic good. A woman's most prestigious role was as a warrior's wife, although that did not imply a merely ornamental function. A drawing by Guamán Poma de Ayala shows a woman in her prime as an expert weaver—all but the oldest women could make a contribution in this manner. Younger girls could help with various associated tasks, such as spinning, or domestic chores such as bringing water for the household. The youngest were again listed last for patent reasons.

INFANCY AND CHILDHOOD

The Incas' approach to childbirth might be understood to have been businesslike, their attitude to infants austere, although this is not to suggest that they did not love and cherish their children. Women carried on with their work in the fields or the home right up to the moment that they went into labor, after which both parents-to-be fasted until their child was born. A midwife was not required: the Inca mother was expected to see her own baby into the world, then wash both herself and her child in a nearby stream. (Like other Native American peoples, some groups bound the baby's head with bands of cloth to cause distinctive deformities which were regarded as aesthetically attractive marks of tribal identity in adulthood.) At four days old, the Inca infant was wrapped in restrictive swaddling clothes and tied into a rigid cradle of wood which could be strapped on to the mother's back for transportation. "Every morning," wrote Garcilaso de la Vega, "the baby was washed in cold water, and often exposed to the night air and dew … . The mothers never took the babies into their arms or on their laps either when giving suck or at any other time. They said it made them crybabies … ."

But many children must have died without ever making it out of infancy. A high mortality rate perhaps helps to explain the mothers' apparent reluctance to bond with their babies in Garcilaso's account, and the fact that children were not even named until the age of about two. This took place at a special *rutuchicoy* ceremony, a joyous occasion with dancing and revelry, at which friends and relations took turns to cut off fingernails and tufts of hair from the child. The taking of such bits and pieces of the body bestowed great responsibility, for if they fell into the wrong hands they could be used to cast harmful spells upon the individual.

Few children received anything resembling a formal education—although the sons of the nobility were taken to special schools in Cuzco to be brought up as high officials and upholders of Inca culture. This practice was as much a matter of philosophy as of social élitism. There was no place for learning in the abstract: children acquired the skills they would need as adults by helping their parents in their own work. Boys helped out as messengers, hunters, herdsmen, and agricultural laborers; they also learned crafts as informal apprentices to their fathers if they did such work. Girls learned to cook and clean and were initiated into the skills of weaving and needlework by their mothers; they also undertook manual and domestic work when required.

A period known as "adolescence" is a recent concept even in the developed world. There was once no time of

heedless freedom for "teenagers," troubled only by the demands of academia. In common with most of their European contemporaries, Inca children were inducted early into the disciplines of work. The idea of adolescence as an extended developmental period, and one of work-exemption, did not exist—this moment of life was no more than one of transition to adulthood. As exciting as this was in the lives of boys and girls alike, it was also a time of great significance for their parents.

THE ADVENT OF WOMANHOOD

Menarche generally occurred around a girl's thirteenth or fourteenth year: her first period was marked by both solemnity and joy. The attendant ceremonies were known collectively as *quiquchiquy*, and started with a three-day spell of complete seclusion. Throughout this time, the girl would purify her body by fasting. Not until the last day was she allowed anything to eat at all, and then it would be no more than a small quantity of raw maize. On the fourth day it was deemed that the ritual transition had been made: she was washed down by her mother and kitted out in a new costume. It was always as rich and splendid as the household could manage, and specially made with this ceremony in mind. A party was given, at which the girl, acting as hostess, brought food and drink to all her relatives. Her highest-born uncle made an improving speech, urging her to be a dutiful daughter, before conferring on her the name she would take with her into adulthood. Such names

Ear ornaments were a recognizable social marker among many Andean peoples. This example, depicting a deity warrior, is a spool from the Moche people—the mosaic is made of semi-precious stones, gold, and shell. Inca boys of noble birth had their ears pierced at the age of around fourteen to enable them to wear ornamental ear spools.

tended to be associated with precious value, purity, or feminine fertility: popular choices included Ocllo ("Pure"), Qori ("Gold"), Cuyllor ("Star"), Rontu ("Egg"), or Koka ("Coca").

BECOMING A MAN

A boy's attainment of physical maturity is, of course, not quite so clearly signaled as a girl's. A boy's transition to manhood was marked by a collective ceremony known as *waracikoy*, which was held once a year as part of the Qhapaqh Raymi festival. All the boys in a given community who had reached the age of around fourteen would be given loincloths woven specially by their mothers. Like their female counterparts, they were given adult names as part of this ceremony. As might be expected, these tended to denote strength and ferocity and included such names as Waman ("Hawk"), Amaru ("Snake") and Kuntur ("Condor").

The higher up the the social scale the family was, the more elaborate the ceremony: the upper echelons of Inca society placed the utmost emphasis on this rite of passage. The preparations could take weeks, starting with a sacred pilgrimage to the *huaca* at Huanacauri to seek divine approval for the festivities to proceed. The boys had then to make slings for themselves, and chew the corn kernels to be used in the *chicha*, which would be drunk by both the living and the mummified ancestors in the coming revelry. A second procession to Huanacauri set the festival proper in motion: a full month of dancing and feasting, with sacrifices and other ceremonies held in the heart of the capital, Cuzco. In between the two processions, the boys made further pilgrimages to other *huaca* around the city, where they themselves would offer more sacrifices, especially of llamas and bales of wool.

There were trials of endurance too, with adult patrons whipping the candidates savagely about the legs as an essential test of their strength and courage in the face of pain. Urged on by the girls of their caste, who waited at the finish with gifts of *chicha*, the young men ran a terrifying hour-long race down a precipitous mountainside. This headlong descent routinely resulted in serious injuries—fatalities were by no means unknown—and those who survived could legitimately claim to have been tested to the limit. The festival ended with gifts and, again, wise words of counsel from

---

• GUAMÁN POMO DE AYALA •

Felipe Guamán Poma de Ayala was born in Huamanga in 1536, the son of a conquistador and a high-born Inca woman, much like Garcilaso de la Vega (see box, page 630). As a young man, he took his father's lead, becoming a faithful servant of the colonial authorities, but he found himself increasingly torn in his sympathies as time went on. In 1613 he published what amounted to an enormous "open letter" to King Charles V of Spain—an attempt to explain the Incas, their history, and their culture, to the conquering nation. He illustrated his text with almost 400 of his own drawings which depict aspects of Inca life—invaluable historical resources in their own right. Guamán Poma de Ayala's role as intermediary between two cultures was not a comfortable one; there are tensions, even confusions, at the heart of his work. However, his writing constitutes an importance historical source, one in which scholars have increasingly found the contradictions insightful.

eminent elders. One final stroke of the whip, and then the ritual was rounded off by the piercing of the ears (itself a painful ordeal) which readied them to wear the spool earrings which were the mark of the nobility (see illustration, page 656). In recognition of this characteristic, the conquistadors used the term *orejones*, "big ears," to distinguish the nobility from the masses.

ADULTHOOD

For all the ceremonial surrounding it, adolescence was not seen as conferring full adulthood. This status was brought only by marriage. In addition to the ritual recognition that was accorded to a young wedded couple, the graduation to manhood and womanhood was marked in concrete terms by the conferring of land. Each couple was given its own *tupu* by the *ayllu*, with additional grants offered for any children born; from the first, the family was an economic unit.

The Inca attitude to marriage could hardly have been more brisk and businesslike. In principle, the state had authority over such things, and there are indeed stories of provincial governors acting as matchmakers by lining up the communities' youths and maidens then summarily deciding their destinies on the spot. It seems more likely, however, that officials were generally content to remain in the background, even though their sanction was required for a marriage to take place (in some circumstances it could be withheld).

Men of the élite were allowed to marry more than one woman, and with marriage bringing property rights this meant that they could accrue more land, wealth, and status. However, the prevalence of rivalries in human affairs enables us to infer that some in authority would wish to arrest the over-rapid rise of a local magnate or his dynasty by preventing him from adding further to a collection of wives. Ordinary people, who were no threat to the state, would have had more freedom, at least as far as matrimonial choices were concerned.

The Incas adorned the ceramic vessels they used to store food and drink with geometric designs as well as images of their staple foods, such as beans, chilis, and corn. The modern artworks below show some common forms of adornment.

However, there were limits to that freedom. Although marriage with close relations was taboo, there was pressure to keep property within the wider *ayllu*. For precisely this reason, the *ayllu* was divided—like Cuzco and the Inca state itself—into "upper" and "lower" sections, the *hanan* and *hurin*: marriage partners were chosen across this dividing line. Both sexes needed parental permission, but their marriages do not seem to have been "arranged" as such. By and large, it was a partnership freely entered into, and most couples seem to have been content in their cooperative venture. Ultimately authority lay with the male, but in practice women seem to have enjoyed a fair degree of influence. As individuals within the all-powerful Inca state, neither sex, of course, had much freedom of action, but such autonomy as households had seems to have been shared within it by husband and wife, with the exception of the domestic workload.

The actual wedding ceremony was appropriately informal, although traditions varied regionally and from *ayllu* to *ayllu*. In some cases, states Bernabé Cobo, the young man took his prospective mother-in-law a little bag of coca as a gift: if she accepted it, the match was made—no further rites were needed. In other instances, the relations of both partners assembled at the house of the bride to watch the young man place a sandal on her foot. All then went to the bridegroom's home, where the young woman produced a set of gifts she had hidden in her clothing, including a woollen tunic and a headband. By putting these items on, her husband ratified the marriage, and the raucous wedding party could begin.

DOMESTIC LIFE

Despite the nominal seniority of her husband, a woman seems to have been the mistress in her own home, although her authority was accompanied by hard work. Two main meals a day had to be prepared: the first was served around nine o'clock in the morning and the second an hour or so before sunset. Many hours were spent on preparation—grinding up maize, tubers, and

---

• A MYSTIC UNION •

The balance between male and female ran through the entire Inca order from the heavens to the home, however down-to-earth the day-to-day existence of the average dutiful couple. Some snatches of verse that were written down by Guamán Poma de Ayala make it clear that romantic love was also present:

What barriers keep us apart, princess?
You are a chinchiroma *flower, my love:*
You haunt my heart, you rule my thoughts,
You are like the sparkling water…

---

other foodstuffs, and gathering llama dung for fuel—before the cooking proper could actually start. Stone tools were used for cutting and grinding, but Inca women had ceramic vessels for storing and serving food, which would have been cooked over an open fire. Fresh meat was the rarest of treats for all but the highest born; fish, cooked in stews, was more readily available. Little cakes of maize were made—popcorn was also prepared—although only for the nobility was maize a major feature in the Inca diet. Men of more humble rank got maize in the form of the *chicha* that was doled out to them as part of the *ayllu*'s patronage system. Women and children relied on freeze-dried potatoes and other tubers for their main staple; herbs and chillies—traded across huge distances—added savor. One of the great virtues of the *ayllu* system was that it facilitated the exchange of produce across the different agricultural zones, giving families access to a good variety of foodstuffs. Inca homes had neither tables nor chairs: the family sat on the ground to eat, the élite spreading a cloth before them on the floor.

WORLDS OF WORK

The vast majority of the Incas' subjects knew that they had been born to work—both for the survival of their families and in the service of the state. In order to meet these two responsibilities, the typical family could expect to labor extremely hard.

Work was by no means the exclusive responsibility of adulthood: children of both sexes were expected to make themselves useful (see page 656). The majority of labor on the land was done by grown-ups, though: both men and women were involved, although they followed a ritualized strict division of labor. Men broke up the soil—symbolically a phallic function, anthropologists have pointed out; by the same logic it was the women who worked the seeds. Agriculture was laborious: only the most rudimentary technology was available—stone-bladed knives and digging-sticks, for example. But many hands made light work: children helped as best they could, and *ayllu* members gave one another mutual support. Work itself was made into a ritual: it was invariably accompanied by chanting, which gave everyone a rhythm and a sense of participation. That spirit, building through the days of toil, would culminate in the outbreak of communal rejoicing which characterized the *aymoray*, or "harvest home."

WORKING FOR THE STATE

People worked not only for their own subsistence but as a form of taxation to the state, which demanded military service in addition to set amounts of civilian labor. In addition to the royal family's own extensive holdings, thousands of hectares up and down the Inca Empire were worked in the name of the state, and similar areas were designated as belonging to the sun. The wealth that the sun's estates produced was

---

This sixteenth-century drawing by the half-Inca chronicler Felipe Guamán Poma de Ayala shows Inca men and women harvesting potatoes. The man uses a digging-stick to unearth the potatoes—only men were allowed to till the soil.

channeled into the maintenance of the cult of Inti, with its hundreds of temples and thousands of priests. Officials at local level allocated tasks, which could be on construction or roadbuilding projects or in an extensive network of sun- or state-owned farms and mines. In some places vast estates were created, to which large workforces were sent for extended stints on a rota basis; in others little plots could be cultivated by local families during odd hours here and there. This allowed a considerable degree of flexibility, but required ingenious organization on the part of officials. A large, and highly efficient, bureaucracy was in any case required for the smooth running of a system which had to be sensitive to local needs and available skills. It made no sense to set skilled dyers or experienced fish-salters to break stones, for example, or ask accomplished sandal-makers to herd llamas when they could be contributing far more in their customary line of work. In addition, those organizing things had to consider what they wanted to accomplish in terms of infrastructure development, for which priorities over time were more variable: major new temples, fortresses, and roads all needed to be built, for example. The more responsive the system was going to be to such subtleties, the greater the challenge of coordinating it all, and the more manpower that was needed for its organization.

Whereas military conscription affected adult males only, labor service was exacted from the entire household. Women participated fully, even in heavy, dirty, and dangerous work, and the more children a family had the less onerous the burden. In addition to many thousands of conscripted human, the state had enormous herds of llamas (perhaps over a million) in its service. These were used primarily for military transport, but each year the animals were shorn and their wool dumped on subject's households with the expectation that it be spun and woven into coarse cloth. Herding this livestock between campaigns was another chore for conscripted labor—adults were chosen to do this rather than children, who often did it at community level.

• A MANAGED ECONOMY •

On a hillside above Huánuco Pampa, a provincial city north of the metropolis of Cuzco, rows of ruined *qollqa* or storehouses can still be seen: their total capacity has been estimated at more than 1.25 million cubic feet (35,500 cubic metres). An impressive installation, but dwarfed—if the chroniclers are to be believed—by the facilities at Cotapachi, in what is now Bolivia. This was the depot which housed the produce of the nearby state farms of Cochabamba—said to have been the biggest in the Inca Empire. There were 2,400 storehouses at Cotapachi, where maize, tubers, and other foods were stockpiled prior to their distribution wherever they were needed. Remains of a complex on an equivalent scale have been found by archaeologists working on a site in the Peruvian highlands, in the Mantaro Valley: such massive undertakings seem to have been an accepted part of the Inca way of life and constitute achievements as remarkable as any temple or citadel.

The insistent centralizing zeal of the Inca regime is one of its most distinctive traits. Ultimately, the scale and complexity of the economic system as a whole was as impressive in its way as its storage installations were gargantuan. The evidence suggests there were up to 2,000 of these depots, strategically sited next to the thousands of miles of state highways that ran the length and breadth of Tawantinsuyu. This awesome network required the mobilization of tens of thousands of people to enable it to function—much of the Inca worldview may have been mystical, but there was nothing vague or impractical about the way they managed the economy, built and maintained its transportation routes, put millions of hectares into production, efficiently stored the fruits of their labors and then moved foodstuffs over vast distances to meet everyday requirements or offset shortages.

SWEAT OF THE SUN, TEARS OF THE MOON

The fabled wealth of the Incas meant less to them in material terms than it did as a symbol of their place in the wider cosmos. Acquiring these riches was no easy task, however: mining for gold and silver was a dangerous activity, undertaken only by the strongest and bravest.

When Pizarro and his conquistadors seized Cuzco, they took the Inca king Atawallpa prisoner: vastly outnumbered, it made sense for them to have a royal hostage. The king attempted to negotiate: taking them to a room around 20 feet (6m) long by 16 feet (5m) wide, and about 16 feet (5m) high, he offered to fill it to half its height with treasures of gold. Not only that, he told his dumbstruck captors, but over the next two months he would fill the whole room twice over with silver objects. The conquistadors' indiscriminate greed for gold had shocked the Incas: if the idea of a room piled high with precious metal staggered the Spanish, it must have seemed faintly ridiculous to the Incas. In the Andean scheme of things, gold and silver were not capital to be accumulated, but precious substances, resonant with religious associations. Gold, they said, was the sweat of the sun and silver the tears of the moon. Beautiful items made from these metals helped cement the bond between the Incas and their cosmos; they represented the divine presence in the everyday.

Not that such sought-after substances did not have enormous economic significance. The Incas had a major mining industry and one mine in what is now Bolivia is reported to have been worked by a thousand miners, with a 5,000-strong community providing ancillary support. Some mines were owned by the state, others by wealthy *cacique*s or local lords (although much of their production then found its way to the Inca kings by way of tribute). It was seasonal work, not only because the agricultural economy had to be kept going, but because conditions in the mines were so extreme. Only comparatively short bouts of work could be endured. Most mines were at high-altitude sites, beset by buffeting winds and searing cold, while conditions underground were even worse. Miners had to twist and wriggle through winding passages to reach narrow, often intermittent veins of ore; solid rock had to be chipped

Many of the finest metalworkers in the Inca Empire originally came from the Lambayeque Valley in northern Peru. Transported from their homeland by the Moche, then moved on by the Chimú, the Incas in turn took the Lambayeque smiths from Chan Chan to Cuzco where they made distinctively exquisite works such as this gold pectoral.

away from cramped corners with only the most primitive of tools. The atmosphere was suffocating, the lighting woefully inadequate; rockfalls were a (frequently fatal) fact of life. Gold, silver, and copper were all mined in this way, although some of the richest copper deposits were at lower altitude, on the coastal plain of what is now northern Chile. Less dangerous conditions prevailed where it was possible to get gold by panning or sluicing from the gravel beds of rivers, but this was still backbreaking work.

The metalsmiths worked miracles with these minerals. In one house, noted Pedro de Cieza de León, "there was an image of the sun, of great size, made of gold, beautifully wrought and set with many precious stones … . There was a garden in which the earth was lumps of fine gold, and it was cunningly planted with stalks of corn that were of gold—stalk, leaves, and ears."

Cieza de León's countrymen, unfortunately, melted down just about all the precious objects they could obtain, but enough has been found subsequently to justify his rapture. Exquisite ornaments were made, stunning jewelry, beautiful votive figurines—a wide range of techniques, from stamping to soldering, were used. Gold was rolled to paper thinness, then wrapped tightly around a carved-wood core to make wonderfully characterful, and often witty, "effigy beakers."

Other precious substances were used in combination with gold. Spondylus shell was highly prized and brought from Ecuador to Cuzco in large quantities. It was valued not only for its translucent quality and breathtakingly ethereal beauty but also for its association with Mamacocha, Mother Sea. The Incas recognized precious stones: the mines they established at Muzo and Chivor, in what is now Colombia, are still famous for the quality of their emeralds. Amber—fossilized resin—was imported from the forest regions of Central America; obsidian, a kind of hard volcanic glass, made fine ornamental blades. Lapis lazuli, turquoise, and chrysocolla—a form of copper silicate—were all used by Inca craftspeople to magnificent effect.

• CERAMIC SPLENDORS •

Pottery was not as valued by the Incas as it was by other Andean peoples, but that did not mean that it was not of a high standard. Some people created their own, others bartered for mass-produced pots of indifferent quality, and there were also state factories making prestigious vessels. Geometric stiffness in their polychrome patterning (as illustrated below) tends to be offset by the flowing elegance of their forms, and the lustrousness of their well-fired finish.

A WEALTH OF TEXTILES

The Incas produced textiles of great beauty. These served as a currency, but they were also of great symbolic significance, encoding a range of social and spiritual meanings. As well as dressing people to withstand the bitter climate, cloth was a means of identifying different sectors of the populace.

Like their predecessors in the Andean region, the Incas created magnificent textiles, investing enormous amounts of imagination, time, and skill in their manufacture (see box, below) and ascribing to them the greatest of value. The "ethnic" fabrics on sale to tourists today, attractive as they often are, can give no sense of the full range and sophistication of production in Inca times. An elaborate social and tribal hierarchy was woven into the fabrics men and women wore, marking their lineage and their status within the Inca Empire. Colors, type and grade of wool or cotton and the precise patterning which was used all helped to give a clear impression not only of the identity of the wearer but also of their rank and origins. The rich variety of patternings may have represented rather more than a taste for experimentation, or the survival of indigenous traditions. There is evidence that, in its quest for centralization and control, the state may have ordained the use of particular patterns in different places and on different ranks, as a sort of bureaucratic coding of the populace. "The men and women of each nation and province," noted Bernabé Cobo, "had their insignia and emblems by which they could be identified, and they could not go around without this identification or exchange their insignias for those of another nation, or they would be severely punished. They had this insignia on their clothes, with different stripes and colors …"

Given the directed movement of workers and settlers around the empire in large numbers—as well as the bureaucratic desire to manage and control, and the Incas' penchant for demographic engineering on a large scale—it was rational to have a system that made it instantly clear who was who and who belonged where.

CLOTH FOR WEARING

Textile designs may have been decorative, but clothes were cut for practicality in the often harsh environment of the Andes. In the highlands and *altiplano* men and women both wore wool; cotton suited the hotter conditions of the coastal plain. Garments were untailored and simple in design: typically, a woman wound a long rectangular piece of cloth around her body, under her

---

◆ THE CRAFT SETTLEMENT OF MILLIRAYA ◆

To the northeast of Lake Titicaca lay the settlement of Milliraya, a community established specifically as a center for ceramic and textile crafts. Its weavers were especially famous: more than a thousand were brought here and set to work making some of the finest feathered-cloth and tapestry the Inca world had ever seen. The settlement had its own governor, reporting directly to the Inca capital at Cuzco rather than to local lords—its location here is believed to have been an attempt to check perceived restiveness among the nobility of the district. Officials were also stationed at Milliraya to represent the different *ayllu* of the workers who had been brought from cities and villages throughout the empire.

arms, and then pinned it at each shoulder; a long sash encircled her waist two or three times before being loosely tied. She also wore a mantle, pinned at the front, which provided extra warmth but also doubled as a multipurpose carrying-cloth. Men wore the loincloth made for their *waracikoy* ceremony (see pages 657–658). On top of this they wore a simple tunic: a rectangular cloth, folded over and sewn at the sides with spaces left for the arms, and with a hole cut in the fold to allow the head through. For extra warmth a heavy cloak could be worn. Sandals with soles of leather or plaited plant fiber, tied over the instep with cords of wool or cotton, completed the typical outfit for men and women.

This basic style did not vary much according to social status; it was the type of fabric worn which denoted that. The king and his concubines wore matching costumes in textiles reserved for the very highest ranks; warriors were literally "decorated" for bravery in battle, the king awarding them the right to wear finer fabrics. Headdresses were another indicator of ethnic affiliation and social rank, most obviously in the case of the red woollen fringe which the king wore across his forehead. The mummified ancestors were wrapped up in death in the same sort of clothes they would have worn in life. Textiles lasted almost indefinitely in the arid air of the mountains, so these costumes remained an indication of status long after the body within had withered away.

CLOTH AS CURRENCY

Clothing was not the only—or even, perhaps, the primary—use of textiles: prestigious fabrics were a form of wealth. They could be hoarded as capital, given as gifts and tribute to kings or noble patrons, or burned in sacrifice to ancestors and gods. Their value rested in the first place in the sheer quantities of labor and skill that their creation embodied: a large and complex cloth could represent hundreds of man- or woman-hours. But often, too, they incorporated substances of great intrinsic value, from imported hummingbird feathers and spondylus shell to fine threads of silver and gold.

For the Incas, textiles were not important just as a form of clothing (although, of course, in the harsh climate of the Andes, protection against the elements was vital), they also served as a mark of status and perhaps even ethnic origin. This 16th-century poncho from the south coast of Peru probably belonged to a person of high rank.

THE FINAL PACHAKUTI

The arrival of Pizarro's conquistadors in the Inca kingdom was the culmination of what had been an epic journey in its own right, across Colombia, down the coast of Ecuador and up into the mountainous Andes. On 15 November 1532 the Spanish found themselves in the regional center of Cajamarca, blinking in bewilderment at the grandeur—and the strangeness—of the alien city.

In overpowering the Incas the achievement of Francisco Pizarro (ca. 1475–1541), shown in this early 19th-century portrait by the French artist Amable-Paul Coutan, was remarkable by any standards. Despite being outnumbered by 80,000 to 128, he managed to seize the Inca king Atawallpa and, soon after, his entire empire.

The incomprehension of the Spaniards was shot through with a measure of anxiety which was, in the circumstances, entirely understandable: they were aware that the king, Atawallpa, was not far away with an army of 80,000 men. Pizarro's party—only 128 strong—had been drawn deeper into the Inca realm and allowed to pass unhindered because the Incas were otherwise occupied by an important religious fast. Posterity has been censorious about the conquistadors' behavior in the Inca kingdom—and not without reason—but theirs was by any standards an extraordinary accomplishment. Their horses, entirely unfamiliar in South America, would probably have intimidated the Incas, and the interlopers were equipped with Old World armor and weaponry, including a few cannon and fuse-fired muskets—although the effect of these has almost certainly been exaggerated, creating more impression through their noise, smoke, and smell than any actual penetrating power. Even so, this bold few were a long way from home (or even from the main Central American and Mexican colonies), deep into "enemy" territory, and overwhelmingly outnumbered. And yet Pizarro prevailed, thanks in part to luck, in part to cool composure and presence of mind. He seems to have followed impulse rather than any clearly worked-out plan. In retrospect, however, it is difficult to see how Pizarro could have managed events more effectively than he did.

When Atawallpa came to confront him, he left the bulk of his army outside the city, bringing a smaller detachment with him into Cajamarca. A priest with the conquistadors went out to meet the king; through interpreters the party had brought with them from up the coast, he explained that they had come to bring them the rightful word of God. Atawallpa listened a while, but quickly grew impatient, and brushed the man aside.

In response to this affront to piety Pizarro's men fired off a cannon and flung themselves at Atawallpa's astonished bodyguard: in the next few hours they killed some 7,000, with no casualties of their own. Completely unimpressed by his divinity, they took the king of the Incas prisoner: the very idea of which was almost inconceivable to his subjects. Its ruler captured, a god held hostage, the Inca Empire was effectively decapitated.

The king's offer of a ransom resulted in the looting of the empire by royal decree, with the Incas forced to assist in the pillaging of their own cities. Sacred and ceremonial items of every sort, from beakers and breastplates to bangles and vases—even the gold-plated façades from Inti's temples. About a dozen tons of silver, and half as much again in gold, are believed to have been cast into the furnaces. Although some of the conquistadors' memoirs remark on the skills of the goldsmiths, no account seems to have been taken of any artistic value added by these craftspeople. The Europeans were adventurers rather than art aesthetes, and it was far easier to carry gold and silver as bullion than keeping it in its original form, however beautiful.

THE INCA AFTERMATH

By April 1533, Pizarro's partner Diego de Almagro had arrived with reinforcements and the conquistadors began to feel more confident. On 26 July, Atawallpa was tried for treason and garotted: Pizarro had decided to have his life as well as his ransom. Although stronger now, the Spanish were still massively outnumbered and it made sense to try to rule the empire through a native puppet. They sought to do this by promoting Tupa Wallpa, a son of Atawallpa's old adversary, Waskhar, but he fell sick and died a few weeks later. Another prince, Manqo Qhapaqh, was then enthroned as Manqo Inca.

His "reign" set the tone for the centuries of history to come, in which the incompleteness of the conquest was always clear. Starting out as a grateful ally of the Spanish, he quickly grew disillusioned as the true powerlessness of his position came home to him. He escaped Cuzco and fled into the countryside, where he established himself as a leader of the Inca resistance. In 1536, he attacked the city with up to 400,000 men. Despite being in desperate straits, the conquistadors managed to withstand the siege. Their victory underlined the paradoxical position they were in: they could hold the empire, but could not change its people. This did not necessarily matter to men more interested in enriching themselves than in winning favor, but it explains much about the region's culture as it developed into modern times.

There would be further rebellions: most famously the rising of Tupac Amaru in 1572; this too was savagely

---

• PIZARRO: THE CONQUEROR OF THE INCAS •

Francisco Pizarro was born around 1475, in Trujillo, a town in Spain's Extremadura province—an impoverished region which produced a number of conquistadors. He went to the Americas in 1510, joining Vasco de Balboa's expedition to the Pacific in 1513, and settling in Panama on his return. A few years later he went into partnership with Diego de Almagro: they struck south and west across the Isthmus in two campaigns of conquest (1524–1526 and 1526–1528). It was in his explorations along the western coast of Colombia and Ecuador that Pizarro first heard about the wealth and power of the Incas and became convinced that this would be the greatest prize of all.

suppressed by the conquistadors. The adoption of Tupac Amaru's name by a series of twentieth-century guerrilla groups in Peru and beyond was obviously opportunistic, but the revolutionaries attempted to invoke the authority of a claimant to the Inca throne because they recognized the romantic glamor of the royal line.

Ultimately, though, that glamor seems shallow alongside far deeper-running currents of indigenous tradition, still clearly to be traced in the cultural and religious life of Peru and the other Inca areas. This seems to have happened with the tacit acceptance, if not perhaps the approval, of the Spanish colonial authorities, who early abandoned plans to extirpate the old religious ways. Efforts were made to stamp out "idolatry," and

This engraving by the 16th-century Flemish printmaker Theodore de Bry shows Pizarro and some of his men meeting the Inca army. One of the factors in the conquistadors' favor was their use of horses—creatures unknown to the Incas that may have struck fear into them.

various *huaca*s were destroyed—when the people could be persuaded to reveal where they were. But it was soon found more effective to reach a cultural compromise and (consciously or not) co-opt native beliefs to Christian faith. As elsewhere in the Americas, a degree of "syncretism" (the combination of different religious traditions) developed, with aspects of older deities being grafted on to Christian figures (see box, opposite).

• A MELDING OF FAITHS •

No figure is more closely associated with Roman Catholicism worldwide than Our Lady, the Blessed Virgin Mary, mother of Christ. In the Andes, though, she is revered with a particular intensity, on account of her identification with Pachamama, the Earth Mother of Inca times (see page 623). In mid-July, in the depths of winter, the four-day fiesta of the Virgin of Carmen is held at Paucartambo, east of Cuzco. Participants wearing magnificently colorful handmade masks and headdresses form the vibrant carnival processions; there is beer in abundance, song and dance and general good cheer. The dead join in the fun, the merrymakers visiting the town cemetery to include them, taking food and drink so they can party beside their graves. But the highlight of the fiesta comes when the figure of the Virgin (see illustration, right) is taken from the church and carried around the town center amid great rejoicing. Her intercession, it is believed, will ensure that the winter comes to its end and the life of the Earth be renewed for another year.

In 1780, it is said, a young boy, Mariano Mayta, who was out herding the family livestock in the mountains, met a snow-white apparition of the Christ Child. The local boy played with his new friend until the men of his family came and tried to seize the dazzling vision. It immediately turned into a crucifix and Mariano fell dead on the spot; a church built on the site became a place of pilgrimage. Every year in December, the faithful flock in their thousands through the snow and ice of the high Andes to honor the image of Señor de Qollur Rit'i ("Our Lord of the 'Snow Star'"). After three days of dancing and prayer, they descend the mountainside carrying heavy crosses and ice, in time for the winter solstice on 21 June. The festivities are in fact a Christianized version of an ancient devotion to the Qollqa, or "granary" constellation, the Pleiades (see pages 650–651), believed to assure the earth's fertile rebirth in the spring.

The old beliefs live on, then, although semi-submerged in a current of Catholic tradition, which is sincerely held, however unorthodox it appears in some regards. For many people the ancestors are still regarded as a living presence and the "holy souls" of mainstream Catholic doctrine find physical embodiment in mummified remains. The human sacrifices of former times have found symbolic replacement on many mountain heights in crucifixes that commemorate the sacrifice made by Christ, the Savior of the World. These are brought down to the valleys each year at the festival of Cruz Velacuy, when they are decorated and blessed by the village priest before being returned to their mountaintop shrines. There, ostensibly consecrated to the Christian God, they are considered by local people still to be charged with the spirit of the *apu* of old and they help to keep alive the inheritance of the Incas.

THE FORESTS OF AMAZONIA

Although the peoples from the depths of the Amazonian rainforest to the east of the Andes were seemingly far removed from Andean highland civilization, the two disparate worlds—those of the hunter–gatherers and the urbanized cultivators—were in fact linked by trade networks. The Incas feared the fiercely independent, and sometimes warlike, forest-dwellers, known as Antis because the imperial province of Antisuyu bordered the world's greatest jungle where, among other things, feathers from tropical birds, such as the parrot and the macaw, were sourced to supply the extensive Andean market.

LEFT A figurine of an Amazonian female, ca. 900–1600CE. The woman is elaborately adorned with geometric designs and wears a headband with stone charms or amulets known as muiraquita*. It seems likely that the presentation of the bowl—to hold maize or* manioc *beer—marks a special stage-of-life occasion, perhaps a marriage or birth.*

OPPOSITE *The rainforest's many rivers—not least the mighty Amazon itself (shown here)—provided fish as a source of food. Fish were caught using hooks made from plant spines, wood, or bone.*

RIGHT *The Amazonian world is rich with the souls of dead ancestors and supernatural animals. People communed with this realm through trance-inducing rituals and dreams or visions, and shamans could even be transformed into the spirits by using masked representations such as this one.*

BELOW *A funeral urn (ca. 900CE) from Marajó Island, at the mouth of the Amazon, in which people kept the bones of their dead ancestors as a way of maintaining contact with their spirits. The imagery represents death and rebirth. This example shows a human figure on each side, with eyes, navel, and hands. One is male, the other female, apparently pregnant, so that the design seems to represent a human life cycle that continues after death.*

FURTHER READING

GENERAL

Bechert, Heinz, and Gombrich, Richard (eds.). *The World of Buddhism: Buddhist Monks and Nuns in Society and Culture*. Thames & Hudson: London, 1984.

Boardman, J. (ed.). *The Oxford Illustrated History of Classical Art*. Oxford University Press: Oxford and New York, 2001.

Braudel, Fernand (trans. Richard Mayne). *A History of Civilizations*. Penguin: Harmondsworth, 2004.

Cotterell, Arthur. *Penguin Encyclopedia of Ancient Civilizations*. Penguin: Harmondsworth, 1989.

Fernandez-Armesto, Felipe. *Civilizations*. Pan: London, 2001.

Joseph, George Gheverghese. *The Crest of the Peacock: Non-European Roots of Mathematics*. I.B. Tauris: London, 1992.

Lowenstein, Tom. *The Vision of the Buddha*. Duncan Baird Publishers and Little, Brown: London and New York, 1996.

Stearns, Peter. *World Civilizations*. Pearson: London, 2000.

Trainor, Kevin (ed.). *Buddhism*. Duncan Baird Publishers and OxfordUniversity Press: London and New York, 2004.

EGYPT

Aldred, Cyril. *Egyptian Art*. Thames & Hudson: London, 1980.

Baines, John, and Malék, Jaromír. *Atlas of Ancient Egypt*. Phaidon: Oxford, 1984.

Hart, G. *A Dictionary of Egyptian Gods and Goddesses*. Routledge & Kegan Paul: London, 1986.

Hart, G. *Egyptian Myths*. British Museum Press: London, 1990.

Kemp, Barry J. *Ancient Egypt: Anatomy of a Civilization*. Routledge: London, 1989.

Lichtheim, M. *Ancient Egyptian Literature*, 3 vols. University of California Press: Berkeley, 1980.

Murnane, William J. *The Penguin Guide to Ancient Egypt*. Penguin: Harmondsworth, 1983.

Quirke, Stephen. *Ancient Egyptian Religion*. British Museum Press: London, 1992.

Shaw, Ian, and Nicholson, Paul. *The British Museum Dictionary of Ancient Egypt*. British Museum Press: London, 1995.

Silverman, David P. (ed.). *Ancient Egypt*. Duncan Baird Publishers: London, 1997; Oxford University Press: New York, 1997.

Smith, W. Stevenson. *The Art and Architecture of Ancient Egypt*. Pelican: Harmondsworth, 1981.

Strouhal, Eugen. *Life in Ancient Egypt*. Cambridge University Press: Cambridge, and University of Oklahoma Press: Norman, 1992.

MESOPOTAMIA AND PERSIA

Baigent, Michael. *From the Omens of Babylon: Astrology and Ancient Mesopotamia*. Penguin: New York, 1995.

Black, Jeremy, and Green, Anthony. *Gods, Demons and Symbols of Ancient Mesopotamia*. University of Texas Press: Austin, Texas, 1992.

Collon, Dominique. *Ancient Near Eastern Art*. British Museum Press: London, 1995.

Contenau, Georges. *Everyday Life in Babylon and Assyria*. Edward Arnold: London, 1959.

Dalley, Stephanie (ed.). *Myths from Mesopotamia*. Oxford University Press: Oxford, 1991.

Huart, Clément (trans. M.R. Dobie). *Ancient Persia and Iranian Civilization*. Kegan Paul & Co.: London, 1927.

Kramer, S.N. *History Begins at Sumer*. Thames & Hudson: London, 1961.

Oppenheim, A. Leo. *Ancient Mesopotamia*. University of Chicago Press: Chicago, 1977.

Postgate, Nicholas. *Early Mesopotamia: Society and Economy at the Dawn of History*. Routledge: London and New York, 1992.

Reade, Julian. *Mesopotamia*. British Museum Press: London, 1991.

Roaf, Michael. *Cultural Atlas of Mesopotamia and the Ancient Near East*. Facts on File: New York, 1990.

Roux, Georges. *Ancient Iraq*. Penguin: Harmondsworth, 1966.

Saggs, H.W.F. *The Babylonians*. British Museum Press: London, 1995.

Sandars, N.K. (trans.). *The Epic of Gilgamesh*. Penguin: Harmondsworth, 1972.

Wellard, James. *By the Waters of Babylon*. Hutchinson: London, 1972.

INDIA

Baker, Sophie. *Caste: At Home in Hindu India*. Jonathan Cape: London, 1990.

Cooper, I. and Gillow, J. *Arts and Crafts of India*. Thames & Hudson: London, 1996.

Easwaran, Eknath. *The Mantram Handbook*. Nilgiri Press: Tomales, California, 1977.

Easwaran, Eknath. *The Bhagavad Gita*. Nilgiri Press: Tomales, California, 1985.

Easwaran, Eknath. *The Constant Companion*. Nilgiri Press: Tomales, California, 1987.

Easwaran, Eknath. *The Upanishads*. Nilgiri Press: Tomales, California, 1987.

Goodall, Dominic. *Hindu Scriptures*. J.M. Dent: London, 1996.

Johnson, Gordon. *Cultural Atlas of India*. Facts on File: New York, 1996.

Mackenzie, Donald. *Myths and Legends of India*. Gresham Publishing Co.: London, 1913.

Michell, George. *Hindu Art & Architecture*. Thames & Hudson: London, 2000.

Shearer, Alistair. *The Hindu Vision*. Thames & Hudson: London, 1993.

Stein, B. *The New Cambridge History of India*. Cambridge University Press: Cambridge, 1990.

Zaehner, R. *Hinduism*. Oxford University Press: Oxford, 1962.

CHINA

Granet, Marcel. *La pensée chinoise*. 1934. (Reprinted Albin Michel: Paris, 1968.)

Legge, James. *The Chinese Classics*. 5 Vols. London, 1865–1872; Oxford, 1893–1894. (Reprinted Hong Kong University Press: Hong Kong, 1960.)

Lewis, Mark Edward. *Writing and Authority in Early China*. SUNY Press: Albany, 1999.

Loewe, Michael, and Shaughnessy, Edward L. (eds.). *The Cambridge History of Ancient China: From the Beginnings of Civilization to 221BC*. Cambridge University Press: New York, 1998.

Needham, Joseph. *Science and Civilization in China*, 8 vols. Cambridge University Press: Cambridge, 1955–.

Rawson, Jessica (ed.). *Mysteries of Ancient China: New Discoveries from the Early Dynasties*. British Museum Press: London, 1996.

Scarpari, Maurizio. *Splendours of Ancient China*. Thames & Hudson: London, 2000.

Shaughnessy, Edward L. (ed.). *China: Land of the Heavenly Dragon*. Duncan Baird Publishers and Oxford University Press: London and New York, 2000.

Tsien, Tsuen-hsuin. *Written on Bamboo and Silk: The Beginnings of Chinese Books and Inscriptions*, 2nd rev. ed. University of Chicago Press: Chicago, 2004.

Twitchett, Denis (ed.). *The Cambridge History of China*. Vol. 3, Part 1: *Sui and T'ang China, 589–906*. Cambridge University Press: Cambridge, 1979.

Twitchett, Denis, and Loewe, Michael (eds.). *The Cambridge History of China*. Vol. 1: *The Ch'in and Han Empires (221BC–AD220)*. Cambridge University Press: Cambridge, 1986.

Watson, William. *The Arts of China to AD900*. Yale University Press: New Haven, 1995.

Yang, Xiaoneng (ed.). *The Golden Age of Chinese Archaeology: Celebrated Discoveries from the People's Republic of China*. Yale University Press: New Haven, 1999.

TIBET

Dowman, Keith. *The Power Places of Central Tibet: A Pilgrim's Guide*. Routledge & Kegan Paul: London, 1988.

Goepper, Roger. *Alchi: Ladakh's Hidden Sanctuary, The Sumtsek*. Serindia: London, 1996.

Heruka, Gtsansmyon. *The Life of Marpa the Translator*. Shambala: Boston, 1986.

Jackson, David. *A History of Tibetan Painting*. Österreichische Akademie der Wissenschaften: Vienna, 1996.

Ricca, Franco, and Lo Bue, Eberto. *The Great Stupa of Gyantse*. Serindia: London, 1993.

Richardson, Hugh. *Tibet and its History*. Oxford University Press: London, 1962.

Snellgrove, David, and Richardson, Hugh. *A Cultural History of Tibet*. Weidenfeld & Nicolson: London, 1968.

Snellgrove, David. *Indo-Tibetan Buddhism: Indian Buddhists and their Tibetan Successors*, 2 vols. Shambala: Boston, 1987.

Thurman, Robert A.F. (trans.). *The Tibetan Book of the Dead*. Aquarian: London, 1994.

Tucci, Giuseppe. (trans. G. Samuel). *The Religions of Tibet*. University of California: Berkeley, 1980.

Zwalf, W. *Heritage of Tibet*. British Museum: London, 1981.

GREECE

Beard, M. *The Parthenon*. Profile Books: London 2002.

Boardman, J., Griffin, J., and Murray, O. (eds.). *Oxford History of Greece and the Hellenistic World*. Oxford University Press: Oxford, 2001.

Blundell, S. *Women in Ancient Greece*. Harvard University Press: Cambridge, Massachusetts, 1996.

Carey, Christopher. *Democracy in Classical Athens*. Bristol Classical Press: Bristol, 2000.

Graf, Fritz. *Greek Mythology: an introduction*. John Hopkins University Press: Baltimore, 1993.

Lapatin, Kenneth. *Mysteries of the Snake Goddess: Art, Desire and the Forging of History*. Houghton Mifflin Company: Boston and New York, 2002.

Melas, E. *Temples and Sanctuaries of Ancient Greece*. Thames & Hudson: London, 1993.

Osborne, Robin. *Archaic and Classical Greek Art*. Oxford University Press: Oxford and New York, 1998.

Price, S. *Religions of the Ancient Greeks*. Cambridge University Press: Cambridge, 1999.

Sparkes, Brian. A. (ed.). *Greek Civilization: An Introduction*. Blackwell: Oxford, 1998.

Woodford, Susan. *Images of Myths in Classical Antiquity*. Cambridge University Press: Cambridge, 2003.

ROME

Beard, M., North, J., and Price, S. *Religions of Rome*. Cambridge University Press: Cambridge, 1998.

Boardman, J., Griffin, J., and Murray, O. (eds.). *The Roman World (The Oxford History of the Classical World)*. Oxford University Press: Oxford and New York, 1988.

Brilliant, Richard. *Roman Art*. Phaidon: London, 1974.

Flower, H.I. (ed.). *Cambridge Companion to the Roman Republic*. Cambridge University Press: Cambridge, 2004.

Gibbon, Edward. (ed. J.B. Bury). *The History of the Decline and Fall of the Roman Empire*, 7 vols. [Orig. 6 vols. 1776–1788.] Methuen: London, 1896–1900.

Goldsworthy, Adrian. *In the Name of Rome: The Men Who Won the Roman Empire*. Weidenfeld & Nicolson: London, 2004.

Grant, Michael. *Roman Myths*. Penguin: Harmondsworth, 1973.

Holland, Tom. *Rubicon: The Triumph and Tragedy of the Roman Republic*. Little, Brown: New York, 2003.

Jones, Peter V., and Sidwell, Keith C. *The World of Rome: An Introduction to Roman Culture*. Cambridge University Press: Cambridge, 1997.

Ogilvie, Robert M. *Roman Literature and Society*. Penguin: Harmondsworth, 1980.

Scarre, Chris. *The Penguin Historical Atlas of Ancient Rome*. Penguin: Harmondsworth, 1995.

Woolf, Greg (ed.). *Cambridge Illustrated History of the Roman World*. Cambridge University Press: Cambridge, 2003.

THE CELTS

Cunliffe, Barry. *The Ancient Celts*. Oxford University Press: New York and London, 1997.

Gantz, Jeffrey. *Early Irish Myths and Sagas*. Penguin: New York and London, 1981.

Gantz, Jeffrey (trans.). *Mabinogion*. Penguin: New York and London, 1976.

Green, Miranda. *The Celtic World*. Routledge: New York and London, 1995.

Jackson, K.H. *A Celtic Miscellany*. Penguin: Harmondsworth, 1971.

Jacobs, Joseph. *Celtic Fairy Tales*. Bracken: London, 1991.

Joyce, P.W. *Old Celtic Romances*. Talbot Press: Dublin, 1961.

Kinsella, Thomas. *The Taín*. Oxford University Press: New York and London, 1970.

MacCana, Proinsias. *Celtic Mythology*. Chancellor Press: London, 1983.

Megaw, Ruth, and Megaw, Vincent. *Celtic Art from its Beginnings to the Book of Kells*. Thames & Hudson: New York and London, 1989.

Piggott, Stewart. *The Druids*. Thames & Hudson: New York and London, 1985.

Ross, Anne. *Pagan Celtic Britain: Studies in Iconography and Tradition*. Constable: London, 1992.

THE VIKINGS

Crossley-Holland, Kevin. *The Penguin Book of Norse Myths*. Penguin: Harmondsworth, 1980.

Davidson, Hilda Ellis. *Gods and Myths of Northern Europe*. Penguin: Harmondsworth, 1964.

Graham-Campbell, James. (ed.). *The Viking World*. Frances Lincoln: London, 1980.

Graham-Campbell, James. (ed.). *Cultural Atlas of the Viking World*. Time-Life Books: Amsterdam, 1994.

Haywood, John. *The Penguin Historical Atlas of the Vikings*. Penguin: Harmondsworth, 1995.

Jones, Gwyn. *A History of the Vikings*, revised ed. Oxford University Press: Oxford, 1984.

Logan, F. Donald. *The Vikings in History*. Routledge: London and New York, 1991.

Page, R.I. *Norse Myths*. British Museum Press: London, 1993.

Roesdahl, Else. *The Vikings*, revised ed. Penguin: Harmondsworth, 1998.

Sawyer, Peter. (ed.). *The Oxford Illustrated History of the Vikings*. Oxford University Press: Oxford, 1997.

Simek, R. *Dictionary of Northern Mythology*. Boydell and Brewer: Woodbridge, England, 1993.

Taylor, Paul B., and Auden, W.H. *The Elder Edda: A Selection*. Faber & Faber: London, 1969.

THE AMERICAS (GENERAL)

Bierhorst, John. *The Mythology of Mexico and Central America*. Oxford University Press: Oxford, 2002.

Carrasco, David (ed.). *The Oxford Encyclopedia of Mesoamerican Cultures*. Oxford University Press: Oxford, 2001.

Coe, Michael D., Snow, Dean, and Benson, Elizabeth. *Atlas of Ancient America* (repr. 2000). Facts on File: New York, 1980.

Coe, Michael D. *Mexico: From the Olmecs to the Aztecs*. Thames & Hudson: London, 1996.

Longhena, Maria. *Splendours of Ancient Mexico*. Thames & Hudson: London, 1998.

Lothrop, S.K. *Treasures of Ancient America: Pre-Columbian Art from Mexico to Peru*. Skira: Geneva, 1964 (republished Macmillan: London, 1979).

Miller, Mary E. *The Art of Mesoamerica, from Olmec to Aztec*. Thames & Hudson: London, 1996.

Olguín, Felipe Solís, and Leyenaar, Ted (eds.). *Art Treasures from Ancient Mexico: Journey to the Land of the Gods*. Exhibition catalogue from Nieuwe Kirk: Amsterdam, 2002.

Pasztory, Esther. *Pre-Columbian Art*. Cambridge University Press: Cambridge, 1998.

Spence, Lewis. *The Myths of Mexico and Peru*. Harrap: London, 1913.

Taube, Karl A. *Aztec and Maya Myths*. British Museum Press: London, 1993.

Von Hagen, Wolfgang. *The Ancient Sun Kingdoms of the Americas*. Thames & Hudson: London, 1962.

THE AZTECS

Boone, Elizabeth Hill. *The Aztec World*. Smithsonian Institute: Washington D.C., 1982.

Fagan, Brian. *Kingdoms of Gold, Kingdoms of Jade*. Thames & Hudson: London, 1991.

Gruzinski, Serge. *The Aztecs: Rise and Fall of an Empire*. Thames & Hudson: London, 1992.

Leon-Portilla, Miguel (ed.). *The Broken Spears: The Aztec Account of the Conquest of Mexico*. Beacon Press: Boston, 1992.

Olguín, Felipe Solís, and Moctezuma, Eduardo Matos (eds.). *Aztecs*. Exhibition catalogue from the Royal Academy of the Arts: London, 2002.

Townsend, Richard F. *The Aztecs*. Thames & Hudson: London, 1992.

Vaillant, George C. *Aztecs of Mexico*. Penguin: Harmondsworth, 1950.

THE MAYA

Coe, Michael D. *The Maya*. Thames & Hudson: London, 1987.

Coe, Michael D., and Kerr, J. *The Art of the Maya Scribe*. Thames & Hudson: London, 1997.

Culbert, T. Patrick (ed.). *Classic Maya Political History: Hieroglyphic and Archaeological Evidence*. Cambridge University Press: Cambridge, 1991.

Fash, William L. *Scribes, Warriors, and Kings: The City of Copán and the Ancient Maya*. Thames & Hudson: London, 1991.

Freidel, David, Schele, Linda, and Parker, Joy. *Maya Cosmos: Three Thousand Years on the Shaman's Path*. William Morrow & Co.: New York, 1993.

Miller, Mary E. *Maya Art and Architecture*. Thames & Hudson: London, 1999.

Schele, Linda, and Freidel, David. *A Forest of Kings*. William Morrow & Co.: New York, 1990.

Schele, Linda, and Miller, Mary E. *The Blood of Kings: Dynasty and Ritual in Maya Art*. Kimbell Art Museum: Fort Worth, Texas, 1986.

Sharer, Robert J. *The Ancient Maya*. Stanford University Press: Stanford, California, 1994.

Tedlock, Denis. *Popol Vuh*. Simon & Schuster: New York, 1996.

THE INCAS

Bankes, George. *Peru Before Pizarro*. Phaidon: Oxford, 1977.

Brukoff, Barry, et al. *Machu Picchu*. Little, Brown: Boston, 2001.

Burland, C.A. *Peru Under the Incas*. Evans Brothers: London, 1967.

D'Altroy, Terence N. *The Incas*. Blackwell: Oxford, 2002.

Davies, Nigel. *The Ancient Kingdoms of Peru*. Penguin: Harmondsworth, 1997.

Guaitoli, Maria Teresa, and Rambaldi, Simone (eds.). *Lost Cities from the Ancient World*. White Star: Vercelli, Italy, 2002.

Hemming, John. *The Conquest of the Incas*. Harcourt Brace and Papermac: New York and London, 1970.

King, Heidi, et al. *Rain of the Moon: Silver in Ancient Peru*. Metropolitan Museum of Art: New York, 2001.

Milligan, Max. *Realm of the Incas*. HarperCollins: London, 2001.

Morris, Craig, and Thompson, Donald E. *Huánuco Pampa: An Inca City and its Hinterland*. Thames & Hudson: London, 1985.

Moseley, Michael E. *The Incas and their Ancestors: The Archaeology of Peru*. Thames & Hudson: London, 1992.

Quilter, Jeffrey. *Treasures of the Andes*. Duncan Baird Publishers: London, 2005.

Stone-Miller, Rebecca. *Art of the Andes, from Chavín to Inca*. Thames & Hudson: London, 1995.

Urton, Gary. *Inca Myths*. British Museum Press: London, 1999.

Urton, Gary. *Signs of the Inka Khipu*. University of Texas Press: Austin, Texas, 2003.

Yogerst, Joe, and Mellin, Maribeth. *Traveler's Peru Companion*. Kümmerly and Frey: Zollikofen, Switzerland, 1999.

INDEX

Page references in *italics* refer to captions.

chacmool figures *587*, 587
chaitya halls 194
Chakra Pani 286
Chakra Samvara *266*, 271, 288, 295
chakras (energy centers) 183
chalchiuatl (blood) 508
Chalchiuhtlicue 509, 512, 527, 530, 531, *532*, 533, 544, 550, 558, 563
Chaldeans 96
Chalkeia festival 331
Chalkidiki 320
Chalukya dynasty 145, 195, 196
Champollion, Jean-François 17
Chan Chan 617, 634, *635*
Chan-Bahlum, King 583, 584
Chandella dynasty *145*, *194*
Chandogya Upanishad 150
Chandra 163, 174
Chandragupta I and II 142
Chang'an 231
Chan-Muan, King 572, *572*, 606, *606*
Chaos 324, 325
chariots 227, 238, 353, 394–395, 445
Charlemagne, King 450, 455
Charles III, King of France 455
charms 45, 274, 460
Charybdis 338, 365
Chavín de Huantar 614
Cheiron 351
Cheng Tang 222
Chi You 213
Chiapas 574, 583
chicha drink 624, 652, 655, 659
Chichén Itzá 581, 586–587, 589, 590
Chichimecs 504
Chicomecoatl 547, 548, 549, 565
Chicomoztoc 504, 547
childbirth 232, 335, 460, 518, 531, 550, 554, *654*, 655
Children of Lir 433
Chimaira 347
Chimú civilization 617, 634
China
    arts 244–251; bureaucracy 225, 238; Classics 209; cosmology 212–217, 224; dynasties 222–231; family life 232–237; gods 213–215; invasion of Tibet 258, 260, 262, 292; inventions 216, 230; literature 219, 226, 228; medicine 224; music 225, *234*, 251; neolithic cultures 209; Nine Regions 208–211; People's Republic 211, 258; philosophy 224, 230; poetry 225, 230, 231, 251; religion 218–221; writing, early 209–210
chinampa floating fields 562, *563*, 563
chinta-mani ("radiant thought-gem") 274, 283
Chi-Rho 439, 440
Chiti Patis 296
Chola dynasty 145, *166*, 195, 198
Cholula 521
chortens (sanctuaries) 268, 271, *271*, 296
Christianity 14, 17, *32*, 97, 128–129, 193, 304, 428
    Celtic 433, 438–439, 440–441; Roman era 363, 374, 375, 397, 401, 404, 405, 408–409; Spanish American 499, 524, 539, 540, 546, 550, 668–669; Viking era 450, 454, 459, 461
Christmas 404
Chrysaor 345, 347
Chrysippos *322*
Chu Silk Manuscript 250
Chung, Naro Bon 271
Cicero 363, 378, 384, 396
Cieza de Léon, Pedro de 611, 647, 663
Cihuacoatl 534, 539

cihuateteo souls 518, 554
Cipactonal 538, 540, 546, 547
Circe 338
Circus Maximus, Rome 375, 394
cities
    Athens 308, 314–315, *315*, 316–319, 328, 331, 333, 335, 337, 343, 348; China 238, 248; city-states 76–79, 96, 303, 306, 314–315, 360, 572, 574; Cuzco 638–641; Harappan civilization 138; Mesopotamia 58, 60, 63, 66–67, 68–69; Rome 372–375; Teotihuacán 566–567; Tenochtitlán 558–559, 562–565; town planning 321
Classic of Changes (*Yi Jing*) 215, 226
Classic of Documents 226
Classic of Poetry 226, 233, 251
Classic of the Numinous Treasure (*Lingbao Jing*) 219
Claudius, Emperor *358*, 362, *380*, 408
clay 66
    clay cones 99; clay tablets *82*, 83
Cleopatra VII 30, 41, 42, 390
clientela (clienthood) 377
Cliff Palace, Mesa Verde *568*
Clodia 378
clothing
    Celtic 420–421; Chinese 236, 237; Egyptian 41; Inca 633, 664–665; Maya 606; Sumerian 69
Coatepec, Mount 558
Coatlicue 512, 534, 542, 546, 553, 554, 560
Cobo, Bernabé 618, 626, 629, 632, 641, 653, 664
coca 649, 652
Codex Borgia 543–544
Codex Cospi 524, *524*
Codex Durán 524
Codex Fejérváry-Mayer 524
Codex Mendoza 525
codices
    Aztec *511*, *523*, 524–525, 560; Maya 578–579, 588, 603
coffins *92*
coinage 115, 222, 418
Coligny calendar 414–415, 437
Collaconcho Stone, Sacsahuaman 645
Colosseum, Rome 374, 375, 396
Columba, St. 440
Columbus, Christopher 449
comets 100, 650
Commodus, Emperor 381
compasses (navigation) 216, 476
Con 620
concrete 373–374
Confucius (Kong Qiu) 207, 226–227, 234, 236, 239, 251
Confucianism 218, 221, 224, 232, 243
cong jade pieces 216, 244, *245*
Constantine, Emperor 373, 375, 381, 408, 409
Constantinople 363, 381, 408, 409, 449, 452, 479
constellations 55, 100, 212, 215, 650, 651, *651*, 669
consuls 377–379
cookery 226, 234, 389, 659
Copán 576, 590, 591, 605, *605*
copper 663
Coptic writing 17, *32*
Coricancha temple, Cuzco 654
Corinth 309, 312, 328, 331
Coriolanus 369
corn dole 388–389
Cortés, Hernán 499, 502, 507, 521, 533, 540, 556, 563, 565
cosmic tree 530–531, *532*
cosmology 100–101, 163–164, 166, 167, 212–217, 224, 3324–325, 530–531, 532, 558
Cotapachi 661

cotton 617, 664
Cotzumalhuapa people *557*
Coyolxauhqui 518, 534, 542, 546, 558, 564, *564*, 565
crafts
    Aztec 515, 559–561; Chinese 238; Egyptian 20; Inca 644–645, 663, 664–665; Indian 138, 200; Sumerian 67, 69
creation myths
    Aztec 526–529, 534, 538; Egyptian 22–24, *24*, 26, 54; Inca 618–621; Indian 137, 160–164, 166–167, 172; Maya 572, 584, 589, 591, 592–597; Mesopotamian 62, 86; Viking 462–465
cremation 158, 553
Crete 306, 309, *310*, 335, 343, 344, 365
Croesus, King 115, 334, 355
Cruz Velacuy festival 669
Cú Chulainn 429
Cuauhtemoc 507
Cuicuilco, Mexico 558, 567
Cuitlahuac 507
Culhua people 504, 507
Culhuacán 504, 563
Cumae, Italy 320, 365, 369, 407
cumtach (book shrines) 439
cuneiform script 64, 71, 116, 127
curandero priests 649
Cuzco 623, 629, 638–641, 652
Cuzco Valley *629*, 630, 632
Cyaxares 113
Cybele 334, 335, 404, 407, 409
Cycladic civilization *306*
Cyclopes 324, 331, 365
cylinder seals 70, 99
cymbals 276, 278
Cynic philosophy 323
Cyrus, King 97, 102, 113, 114–115, 116, 118, *120*

D

Dadhicha 173
daevas (sky-gods) 122–123, 124
Dai, Lady 235, 241, *243*, 250
Dakinis 271, 295
Daksha 180
Dakshinamurti 177
Dalai Lamas 256, 258, 260, 262, 286, 292, 295
Danae 345, 346
dancing
    Egyptian 16; Maya 606; Shiva 177
Danelaw 455, 491
Daniel 102, 124
Danu 429
Dao ("Way") 218, 224
Dao De Jing (*Classic of the Way*) 218
Daoism 212, 218–219, 220, 221, 224, 230, 233, 243
Darius I 64, 116, *117*, 118, 120, 124, 126
Darius II 116, 126
Darius III 126, 127, *308*
darshana ("viewing") 196
death
    Aztecs 552–553; China 240–243; Egypt *44*, 50–55; Sumer 92–95; Tibet 296–297
Decius, Emperor 409
Deir el-Bahari, Egypt 36, 43, 53
Delhi sultanate 133, 145
Delos 334, 364–365, 379
Delian League 317
Delphi 354, 355, 416
Delphic Oracle 404
Demeter 305, 324, 326, 328, 347
democracy 315, 337, 343
Dendera, Egypt 22, 30, *31*, 32
Dendera Zodiac 22, 55

ACKNOWLEDGMENTS AND PICTURE CREDITS

Commissioned Artworks

Neil Gower (The Organisation): pages 19, 20–21, 27, 61, 73, 83, 84–85, 99, 113, 139, 347, 505, 523, 531, 533, 536, 553, 577, 596, 598–599, 602, 615; Celia Hart: 259, 417, 575; Iona McGlashan: 421, 439, 442; Robert Nelmes (The Organisation): 15; Sally Taylor (artistpartners ltd): 152, 158, 174, 183, 199, 263, 274, 287, 288–289, 291, 294, 296, 361, 381, 627, 633, 658, 663, 669; Peter Visscher: 211, 216, 222, 227, 307, 311, 352, 453, 459, 468, 475, 493. All decorative borders by Iona McGlashan, except for those in China, Greece, and The Vikings (by Peter Visscher) and those in Rome (by Sally Taylor).

Writers

Joann Fletcher (Egypt); Tony Allan (Mesopotamia and Persia); Charles Phillips (India); Edward L. Shaughnessy (China); Michael Willis (Tibet); Emma J. Stafford (Greece); Tony Allan (Rome); Juliette Wood (The Celts); Tony Allan (The Vikings); Charles Phillips (The Aztecs); Timothy Laughton (The Maya); Michael Kerrigan (The Incas).

Picture Researchers

Julia Ruxton (Egypt, China, and Tibet); Susannah Stone (Mesopotamia and Persia, India, The Aztecs, and The Incas); Julia Brown (Greece and Rome); Cecilia Weston-Baker (The Celts, The Vikings, and The Maya).

Picture Credits

The publisher would like to thank the following people, museums, and photographic libraries for permission to reproduce their material. Every care has been taken to trace copyright holders. However, if we have omitted anyone we apologize and will, if informed, make corrections to any future edition. All material from Jules Selmes was photographed from fascimile copies of the Maya codices, courtesy of the library at the University of Essex, Colchester.

KEY
t top; **b** bottom; **l** left; **r** right

AA	The Art Archive, London	**Getty Museum**	The J. Paul Getty Museum, Malibu, California
AKG	AKG Images, London	**NGS**	National Geographic Society, Washington D.C.
BAL	The Bridgeman Art Library, London	**RAA**	Royal Academy of Arts, London
BL	The British Library, London	**RHPL**	Robert Harding Picture Library, London
BM	The British Museum, London	**SAP**	South American Pictures, Suffolk
Christie's	Christie's Images, London	**WFA**	Werner Forman Archive, London

8–9 K.M. Westerman/Corbis; **10** Jeremy Horner/Getty Images; **12–13** Graham Harrison, Oxon; **17** Cairo Museum/Jürgen Liepe, Berlin; **18** BM; **21** Louvre, Paris/AKG; **23** Louvre, Paris/BAL; **24** Kunsthistorisches Museum, Vienna/Erich Lessing/AKG; **26** Louvre, Paris/BAL; **28** Ary Diesendruck/Getty Images; **31** Chris Caldicott, London; **32** Schimmel Collection, New York/WFA; **33** Henri Stierlin, Geneva; **34** Powerstock Zefa; **37** WFA; **40** Erich Lessing/AKG; **41** Staatliche Museum zu Berlin Ägyptisches Museum/WFA; **42** BAL; **44** Staatliche Museum zu Berlin Ägyptisches Museum; **45** BM/AA; **47** Louvre/WFA; **48–49** Richard Passmore/Getty Images; **50–51** BM; **52** BM/AKG; **55** BM; **56** Paul Almasy/Corbis, London; **58** Desmond Harney/RHPL; **59** Archivo Iconografico/Corbis; **62** Ed Kashi/Network Photographers, London; **63** Adam Woolfitt/RHPL; **65** BM; **66** Nick Wheeler/Corbis; **68** Erich Lessing/AKG; **69** BM; **70–71** BM; **72** Erich Lessing/AKG; **75** Erich Lessing/AKG; **76** Eileen Tweedy/BM/AA; **77** Erich Lessing/AKG; **78–79** BM; **80** Charles & Josette Lenars/Corbis; **82** BM; **87** BM; **89** BM; **90** BM; **92** BM; **93** BM; **94** BM; **95** BM; **97** Paul Almasy/Corbis; **98** Erich Lessing/AKG; **103** BM; **104;** BM; **105** BM; **107** Dagli Orti/Corbis; **108** Erich Lessing/AKG; **111** Nick Wheeler/Corbis; **112** BM; **113** BM; **114** Brian A. Vikander/Corbis; **117** Dave Bartruff/Corbis; **118** Charles & Josette Lenars/Corbis; **119** Paul Almasy/Corbis; **120** Charles & Josette Lenars/Corbis; **121** Dagli Orti/Corbis; **122** Dagli Orti/AA; **125** Roger Wood/Corbis; **126** BM; **127** BM; **128b** David Keaton/Corbis; **128l** Historical Museum of Armenia, Erevan/Dagli Orti/AA; **129t** Adam Woolfitt/Corbis; **129b** Historical Museum of Armenia, Erevan/Dagli Orti/AA; **132** Charles & Josette Lenars/Corbis; **135** Lindsay Hebberd/Corbis; **137** BM; **138** Archivo Iconografico/Corbis; **143** Lindsay Hebberd/Corbis; **144** Charles & Josette Lenars/Corbis; **146** Pierre Vauthey/Corbis/Sygma; **149** BM; **151** Dinodia Picture Agency, Bombay/BAL; **155** Stone/Getty Images; **156** BM; **159** Burstein Collection/Corbis; **161** Musee Guimet/Dagli Orti/AA; **162** Ian Berry/Magnum Photos, London; **165** Wild Country/Corbis; **166** BM; **169** Victoria & Albert Museum, London/BAL; **170** Linday Hebberd/Corbis; **173** Lindsay Hebberd/Corbis; **177** Angelo Hornak/Corbis; **178** Chris Lisle/Corbis; **181** Michael Freeman/Corbis; **182** BM; **184** BM; **186** National Museum of India, Bombay/BAL; **189** Sheldan Collins/Corbis; **190** Chris Lisle/Corbis; **192** BM; **194** Lindsay Hebberd/Corbis; **197** Gian Berto Vanni/Corbis; **200** Gian Berto Vanni/Corbis; **202** Lindsay Hebberd/Corbis; **204l** Luca I. Tettoni/Corbis; **204r** Glen Allison/Getty Images; **205t** Getty Images/Image Bank; **205b** Luca I. Tettoni/Corbis; **206** Keren Su/Getty Images; **210** Christie's; **213** BM; **214** Keren Su/Getty Images; **215** BM; **218** National Museum of Chinese History, Beijing; **220–221** WFA; **223** Mausoleum of Emperor Qin, Xian, Lingtong County, Shaanxi/Keren Su/Corbis; **225** Christie's; **226–227** Christie's; **228–229** Keren Su/Corbis; **232** Christie's; **233** Robin Hanbury-Tenison/RHPL; **235** National Palace Museum, Taipei/WFA; **237** Christie's Images, London; **239** Cultural Relics Bureau, Xindu County, Sichuan/Ray Main/Mainstream; **240–241** Lowell Georgia/Corbis; **242** Institute of Cultural Relics, Beijing; **245** Christie's; **246** Veronica Birley/Tropix, Surrey; **248** Asian Art and Archaeology, Inc./Corbis; **249** BM; **252** Ian Cumming/Tibet Images, London; **254** BM; **255** BM; **256–257** David Tockeley/RHPL; **258** Julia Hegewald, Cambridge; **261** Ian Cumming/Tibet Images; **262** BM; **264–265** Jim Holmes/Axiom, London; **266** BM; **267** Ian Cumming/Tibet Images; **269** Ian Cumming/Tibet Images; **270** Mani Lama/Tibet Images; **272** BM; **273** Ian Cumming/Tibet Images; **275** Julia Hegewald; **277** Gavin Hellier/RHPL;

279 Ian Cumming/Tibet Images; 280–281 BL; 282 BM; 283 Ian Cumming/Tibet Images; 285 BM; 286 BM; 291 John Eskenazi Ltd, London; 293 Raghu Rai/Magnum Photos; 297 BM; 298l BuddyMays/Corbis; 298r Bruno Barbey/Magnum Photos; 299t David Cumming/Eye Ubiquitous/Corbis; 299b Michael Freeman/Corbis; 300 Museo Nazionale Terme, Rome/Dagli Orti/AA; 302 Scala, Florence; 304 BM; 305 BM/BAL; 306 Getty Museum; 308 Museo Archeologico Nazionale, Naples/BAL; 310 Louvre/BAL; 312 Paestum/Erich Lessing/AKG; 314 BAL; 316 Louvre/BAL; 317 National Museum of Scotland/BAL; 318 BM/BAL; 320 Musée Archéologique, Châtillon-sur-Seine/BAL; 322 Louvre/BAL; 324–325 Dagli Orti/AA; 326 Michael Holford, Essex; 327 AA; 329 Staatliche Antikensammlungen, Munich/Erich Lessing/AKG; 330 Louvre/BAL; 332–333 BAL; 337 Museo Nazionale, Reggio Calabria/AKG; 339 Mykonos Museum/AKG; 340–341 Corbis; 342 Olympia Museum/AKG; 344 Heraklion Archaeological Museum/AKG; 346 Birmingham Museum and Art Gallery/BAL; 348 Louvre/BAL; 350 BAL; 454–455 Michael Holford; 156 Angelo Hornak, London; 358 Kunsthistorisches Museum/BAL; 359 Museo Capitolino, Rome/Dagli Orti/AA; 361 Provinciaal Museum G.M. Kam te Nijmegen/Dagli Orti/AA; 363 BM/Michael Holford; 364 Museo della Civiltà Romana, Rome/BAL; 366 Magyar Nemzeti Galeria, Budapest/BAL; 370 Ellen Rosenbery/Getty Museum; 371 Corbis; 372–373 BAL; 374 Michael Holford; 376 Ellen Rosenbery/Getty Musem; 377 Ellen Rosenbery/Getty Musem; 378t Ellen Rosenbery/Getty Museum; 378b Ellen Rosenbery/Getty Museum; 380 Kunsthistorisches Museum/BAL; 382 Leslie Garland Photography, Northumberland; 385 Museo Archeologico Nazionale, Naples/BAL; 387 Accademia Italiana, London/BAL; 388 BM/Michael Holford; 390–391 Museo Archeologico Prenestino, Palestrina/Dagli Orti/AA; 392–393 Erich Lessing/AKG; 394 Dagli Orti/AA; 395 BAL; 397 Galeria Borghese, Rome/Dagli Orti/AA; 398 Museo Archeologico Nazionale, Naples/BAL; 400 Angelo Hornak; 403 Archeological Museum, Sousse/Dagli Orti/AA; 405 Museo Archeologico Nazionale, Naples/BAL; 406–407 Corbis; 410t Joe Cornish/Getty Images; 410b Hubert Stadler/Corbis; 411t Erich Lessing/AKG; 411b Michael Brusselle/Corbis; 412 Paul Wakefield/Getty Images; 416 Dagli Orti/AA; 418 BM/BAL; 419 Private Collection/DBP Archive; 420 Naturhistorisches Museum, Vienna/AKG; 423 Musée des Antiquités, St Germain en Laye/Dagli Orti/AA; 424 Jean Williamson/Mike Sharp; 425 National Museet, Copenhagen/AKG; 426–427 Connie Coleman/Getty Images; 430–431 Paul Harris/Getty Images; 432 Moravska Museum, Czech Republic/AKG; 433 Musée des Antiquités, St Germain en Laye/Dagli Orti/AA; 434 Scope, Paris; 436 Conseil Général, Saint Brieuc/Dagli Orti/AA; 437 The Roman Baths Musem, Bath; 438 Mick Sharp Photography, Caernarfon; 440 BL/BAL; 443 National Museum, Ljubljana/AKG; 445 National Museet, Copenhagen; 446–447 Imagefile Island, Dublin; 448 RHPL; 451 RHPL; 454 WFA; 457 Oldsammlung, Oslo/Dagli Orti/AA; 458 Historiska Museet, Oslo/Dagli Orti/AA; 461 Dagli Orti/AA; 463 Joe Cornish/Woodfall Wild Images, Denbigh; 464 WFA; 465 WFA; 466 Statens Historiska Museet, Stockholm/Dagli Orti/AA; 471 Oldsammlung, Oslo/Dagli Orti/AA; 472 Thjodminijasafn, Reykjavik/WFA; 473 Historiska Museet, Stockholm/Dagli Orti/AA; 477 Historiska Museet, Oslo/Dagli Orti/AA; 478 Jon Sparks/Corbis; 482 WFA; 483 WFA; 485 Val Corbett/Woodfall Wild Images; 486 WFA; 487 WFA; 489 Upplandsmuseet, Sweden/WFA; 490 Ted Spiegel/Corbis; 492 Statens Historiska Museet, Stockholm/Dagli Orti/AA; 494 National Museet, Copenhagen; 498 Dagli Orti/AA; 501 Chris Sharp/SAP; 502 Danny Lehman/Corbis; 506 Chris Sharp/SAP; 508 WFA; 509 Archivo Nacional, Mexico/Mireille Vautier/AA; 510 AA; 513 BM; 514 Archivo Nacional, Mexico/Mireille Vautier/AA; 517 Dagli Orti/Museum für Völkerkunde, Vienna/AA; 519 Dagli Orti/Museo Nacional de Antropologia, Mexico/AA; 520 Michel Zabé/RAA; 525 WFA; 526 Michel Zabé/RAA; 527 Corbis; 528 Michel Zabé/RAA; 530 BM; 532 Michel Zabé/RAA; 535 Tony Morrison/SAP; 537 Michel Zabé/RAA; 541 Iain Pearson/SAP; 543 BM; 545 Archivo Iconografico/Corbis; 547 Richard A. Cooke/Corbis; 548 Tony Morrison/SAP; 551 BM; 552 Michel Zabé/RAA; 554–555 Randy Farris/Corbis; 557 WFA; 559 Danny Lehman/Corbis; 561 Michel Zabé/RAA; 562 Nicholas Sapieha/Museo de la Ciudad de Mexico/AA; 564 Dagli Orti/Museo del Templo Mayor, Mexico/AA; 565 Dagli Orti/Museo del Templo Mayor, Mexico/AA; 566–567 Stone/Getty Images; 568t George H.H. Huey/Corbis; 568–569b Dewitt Jones/Corbis; 569t Richard A. Cooke/Corbis; 569b David Muench/Corbis; 570 Paul Hams/Royal Geographical Society, London; 573 Doug Stern/NGS; 576 Justin Kerr, New York; 578–579 Jules Selmes; 580 Rijksmuseum voor Volkenkunde, Leiden/Justin Kerr; 581 Grant Taylor/Getty Images; 582 Olaf Soot/Getty Images; 584–585 Robert Frerck/Getty Images; 586 Cosmo Condina/Getty Images; 587 David Hiser/Getty Images; 588 Kimbell Art Museum, Ft Worth/Justin Kerr; 592 Museum of Fine Arts, Boston/Justin Kerr; 593 Jules Selmes; 594 Museum of Fine Arts, Boston/Justin Kerr; 595 Private Collection, New York/Justin Kerr; 597 New Orleans Museum of Art/Justin Kerr; 600–601 Princeton Art Musem/Justin Kerr; 603 American Museum of Natural History, New York/Justin Kerr; 604–605 Richard A. Cooke III/NGS; 606 Kimbell Art Museum/Justin Kerr; 607 Doug Stern/NGS; 608 Justin Kerr; 610 Brian A. Vikander/Corbis; 612 William James Warren/Corbis; 616 Yann Arthus-Bertrand/Corbis; 618–619 Marion Morrison/SAP; 620 Nathan Benn/Corbis; 621 Museo Nacional de Arqueologia, Antropologia e Historia del Perú, Lima/Mireille Vautier; 622–623 Chris Lisle/Corbis; 625 Dagli Orti/Corbis 629 Jim Zuckerman/Corbis; 633 Bettmann/Corbis; 636 Pablo Corral Vega/Corbis 638 Maria Stenzel/National Geographic Images; 641 Tony Morrison/SAP; 642 Nick Saunders/WFA; 645 Mireille Vautier; 646 Charles & Josette Lenars/Corbis; 649 Roman Soumar/Corbis; 650 WFA; 653 Roger Ressmeyer/Corbis; 655 Museo Nacional de Arqueologia, Antropologia e Historia del Perú, Lima/Mireille Vautier; 656 Staatliches Museum für Völkerkunde, Berlin; 658 J.C. Kenny/Corbis/Sygma; 662 Pedro Martinez/SAP; 664 C.J. Kenny/Corbis/Sygma; 667 Staatliches Museum für Völkerkunde, Berlin/WFA; 669 Musée du Château de Versailles/Dagli Orti/AA; 670 Biblioteca Nazionale Marciana, Venice/Dagli Orti/AA; 672t Layne Kennedy/Corbis; 672b Fernando Chaves; 673l Fernando Chaves; 673r The Board of Trustees of the Royal Botanic Gardens, Kew.

Captions for Chapter Opener Illustrations

pages 8–9: temple ruins, Persepolis, Iran; 10: pyramids of Giza, near Cairo, Egypt; 56: frieze depicting Persian dignitaries, Persepolis, Iran; 130–131: summit of the Kumbum temple, Gyantse, Tibet; 132: statue of Shiva dancing, temple of Channa, Keshava, India; 206: dawn in Yangshuo, China; 252: chorten at dusk above Ganden monastery, southern Tibet; 300–301: detail of the Ludovisi sarcophagus, now preserved in the Palazzo Altemps, Rome; 302: the temple of Poseidon at Sounion, Greece; 356: the Via di Mercurio, Pompeii, looking north toward Mount Vesuvius; 412: the Burren, County Clare, Ireland; 448: detail from a wooden cart found with the Oseberg ship near Oslo Fjord, Norway; 496–497: Maya pyramid known as El Castillo ("the castle"), Chichén Itzá, Mexico; 498: detail of the temple of Quetzalcóatl, Tenochtitlán, Mexico, with the Pyramid of the Sun in the background; 570: the Pyramid of the Magician at Uxmal, northwest Yucatán, Mexico; 610: the Inca royal settlement of Machu Picchu, Peru.